Criminal Courts

Fourth Edition

Craig Hemmens dedicates this book to Rolando Del Carmen, who taught him how to write about the law without sounding (too much) like a lawyer, and to Mary and Emily, for giving him something he loves even more than his work.

David Brody dedicates this book to Jim Acker and Nick Lovrich for their past and continued mentorship.

Cassia Spohn dedicates this book to her children, Josh and Jessica, and to all the students whose inquiring minds and insightful questions have helped shape her thinking about prosecution, sentencing, and other court processes.

Sara Miller McCune founded SAGE Publishing in 1965 to support the dissemination of usable knowledge and educate a global community. SAGE publishes more than 1000 journals and over 800 new books each year, spanning a wide range of subject areas. Our growing selection of library products includes archives, data, case studies and video. SAGE remains majority owned by our founder and after her lifetime will become owned by a charitable trust that secures the company's continued independence.

Los Angeles | London | New Delhi | Singapore | Washington DC | Melbourne

Criminal Courts
A Contemporary Perspective
Fourth Edition

Craig Hemmens
Washington State University

David C. Brody
Washington State University

Cassia Spohn
Arizona State University

Los Angeles | London | New Delhi
Singapore | Washington DC | Melbourne

FOR INFORMATION:

SAGE Publications, Inc.
2455 Teller Road
Thousand Oaks, California 91320
E-mail: order@sagepub.com

SAGE Publications Ltd.
1 Oliver's Yard
55 City Road
London, EC1Y 1SP
United Kingdom

SAGE Publications India Pvt. Ltd.
B 1/I 1 Mohan Cooperative Industrial Area
Mathura Road, New Delhi 110 044
India

SAGE Publications Asia-Pacific Pte. Ltd.
18 Cross Street #10–10/11/12
China Square Central
Singapore 048423

Acquisitions Editor: Jessica Miller
Content Development Editor: Adeline Wilson
Editorial Assistant: Sarah Manheim
Marketing Manager: Jillian Ragusa
Production Editor: Veronica Stapleton Hooper
Copy Editor: Colleen Brennan
Typesetter: Hurix Digital
Proofreader: Theresa Kay
Indexer: Beth Nauman-Montana
Cover Designer: Candice Harman

Printed in Canada

Library of Congress Cataloging-in-Publication Data

Names: Hemmens, Craig, author. | Brody, David C., author. | Spohn, Cassia, author.

Title: Criminal courts : a contemporary perspective / Craig Hemmens, Washington State University; David C. Brody, Washington State University; Cassia Spohn, Arizona State University.

Description: Fourth edition. | Thousand Oaks, California : SAGE Publications, Inc., [2020] | Includes bibliographical references and index.

Identifiers: LCCN 2018044897 | ISBN 9781544338941 (pbk. : alk. paper)

Subjects: LCSH: Criminal justice, Administration of—United States. | Law enforcement—United States. | Criminal courts—United States.

Classification: LCC KF9223 .H46 2020 | DDC 345.73/01—dc23
LC record available at https://lccn.loc.gov/2018044897

This book is printed on acid-free paper.

MIX
Paper from
responsible sources
FSC® C004071

19 20 21 22 23 10 9 8 7 6 5 4 3 2

BRIEF CONTENTS

DETAILED CONTENTS

SECTION II • COURTROOM ACTORS AND THE COURTROOM WORKGROUP

SECTION III • COURT PROCESSES

PREFACE

This is a textbook for an undergraduate criminal justice/criminology course on courts. The book is comprehensive in its treatment of courts, covering all the areas that are generally covered in courts textbooks intended for criminal justice courses, such as court structure, courtroom actors, and the trial and appeal process. In addition, it covers related areas often not covered in courts textbooks. These include judicial decision making, specialized courts, and comparative court systems. This comprehensive approach allows instructors to cover all the "standard" material and also add selections that they consider interesting and relevant to their particular course.

In this textbook, we cover several areas: (a) criminal court processes; (b) the courtroom actors and their different roles; (c) court structures and operation, in both the federal and state systems and from trial through appeal; and (d) the nature of legal and judicial reasoning.

OUR APPROACH IN THIS BOOK

In the first section of the book (Chapters 1–4), we provide a discussion of the judicial function, the role and purpose of law, sources of law, the different types of law, and the structure of the American court system. These topics are essential building blocks for the detailed discussion of the criminal courts system and its participants that follows. We first explain why it is important to study courts and the decisions that court actors make as they process criminal cases. We discuss the origins of the modern court system, which can be traced back hundreds of years to early Roman law and to English common law. We also explain how the traditional view of courts, in which courts and court actors simply apply the law, is inadequate; because laws are often vague and ambiguous, courts also make law. We then discuss two competing views of the criminal justice system—the crime control model and the due process model—and explain how these models can be used to examine and analyze the criminal court system. We then provide an overview of the historical development of the court system, and we discuss the structure and organization of federal and state courts today. This is followed by an introduction to each of the courtroom actors and the roles they play as well as a discussion of the path that the typical criminal case follows as it is processed through the court system.

In the second section of the book (Chapters 5–9), we provide an in-depth discussion of the various participants in the criminal court system—prosecutors, defense attorneys, judges, criminal defendants, crime victims, and the jury. While this book is intended to cover the criminal court *system,* a complete understanding of the system is impossible without an understanding of its major *actors.* We explain that the judge plays an important but limited role in the criminal process; the power of judges is constrained by rules that require them to be fair and unbiased, by procedures to disqualify or remove them if they are not impartial, and by appellate court rulings on questions of law and procedure. We also discuss the methods of selecting judges, the effects of recruiting more women and racial minorities to the bench, and the consequences of using nonlawyer judges. We discuss the inadequacies of the traditional adversarial model and explain that criminal case processing is characterized more by cooperation and consensus than by conflict. Our discussion of prosecuting attorneys focuses on their highly discretionary and largely invisible charging decisions and the factors that affect these decisions. We also discuss legal and practical constraints on prosecutorial discretion. Our discussion of defense attorneys includes an examination of the right to counsel and of Supreme Court decisions interpreting that right as well as an examination of research comparing the effectiveness of private attorneys and public defenders. Our discussion of jurors focuses on the jury selection process, with an emphasis on the issue of racial discrimination in the selection of jurors. We also examine the role of jury consultants, the factors that jurors take into consideration during deliberations, and the practice of jury nullification.

In the third section of the book (Chapters 10–14), we discuss the pretrial, trial, and posttrial processes. We cover a diverse range of court-related topics, including the courtroom workgroup, courtroom legal culture, and plea bargaining. We next discuss the goals of sentencing, focusing on retributive and utilitarian justifications for punishment. We also examine the judge's options at sentencing and summarize the results of research analyzing the factors that judges take into account as they attempt to fashion sentences that fit offenders and their crimes. We discuss the rules that guide the appellate process and explain how the writ of habeas corpus has evolved over time. We conclude with a chapter on specialized, or problem-solving, courts. We explain that these courts—drug courts, domestic violence courts, and juvenile courts—take a broader and more comprehensive approach to delinquency and criminality; they also attempt to address the underlying social and economic factors that contributed to the defendant's involvement in crime.

PEDAGOGY INCLUDED IN THIS BOOK

In this book, we use several pedagogical tools designed to help the undergraduate student gain a fuller understanding of the criminal court system. These include the following:

1. *The criminal court system as seen through the eyes of a participant.* Several chapters feature a "View From the Field" concerning a topic covered in the text written from the perspective of a participant in the process. This provides students with an enhanced understanding of the rules and processes covered in the text, while explaining the nuances of the court process and the interinstitutional aspect of the criminal justice and court systems.

2. *Examination of current controversies.* Several chapters feature a "Current Controversy" related to the chapter's topic. This will serve both to foster thought and discussion and to increase the student's interest in the subject matter. The

discussion is presented in a neutral manner with equal coverage to the various theoretical, political, or ideological positions raised by the issue.

3. *Comparative courts feature.* Several chapters feature a "Comparative Courts" item related to the chapter's topic. This feature includes a discussion of how a foreign court system deals with the topic. This feature provides students with some context for their study of the American court system and allows instructors to engage students in a compare/contrast pedagogical exercise.

4. *Discussion of relevant social science research.* Several chapters include a discussion of "Current Research" related to the chapter's subject matter. These discussions are written with the undergraduate reader in mind and focus on how research can help policy makers and court system workers evaluate and implement processes and programs.

5. *Movies and the courts.* Several chapters feature a "Movies and the Courts" discussion of famous movies depicting the court system and how these movies correctly and incorrectly portray the court system.

In addition to these highlighted pedagogical features, each chapter includes the following pedagogy:

1. Tables and figures in each chapter

2. Chapter-opening photographs that set the stage for the chapter to come

3. Key terms at the end of each chapter

4. Chapter summaries at the end of each chapter

5. Discussion questions at the end of each chapter

6. Lists of relevant Internet sites at the end of each chapter

Additional items included in the book include a glossary, references and suggested readings, case index, and general index.

INSTRUCTOR TEACHING SITE

A password-protected site, available at **edge.sagepub.com/hemmens4e,** features an extensive test bank, PowerPoint presentations, lecture notes, access to selected SAGE journal articles as well as video and web resources.

STUDENT STUDY SITE

An open-access student study site, available at **edge.sagepub.com/hemmens4e,** provides access to several study tools, including eFlashcards, web quizzes, selected SAGE journal articles as well as video and web resources.

NEW TO THIS EDITION

- A new feature examines Key Cases that have impacted the courts, such as *Manuel v. City of Joliet, Illinois, et al.* (2017) regarding Fourth Amendment rights and *Rippo v. Baker* (2017) related to the importance of judicial impartiality.

- Many new Current Controversies are examined, such as the changing laws on marijuana usage, the recent addition of Neil Gorsuch to the U.S. Supreme Court, prosecutorial discretion, and the balance between victim's rights and defendant's rights

- Updated discussion of the death penalty, court-administered bail, domestic violence courts, race and waiver to adult court, and new research on habeas corpus and the effect of attorney type on bail decisions offer coverage of important topics affecting the court system.

- The latest cases, data, and research have been updated throughout to provide students with a view of the court system today.

- As recommended by reviewers, the chapter on Specialized Courts has been moved to the end of the book and is now Chapter 14.

- Chapter 8 now includes an example of a Victim Impact Statement.

- The chapter material has been streamlined and the number of boxed features has been reduced to enhance students' reading experience.

ACKNOWLEDGMENTS

We would first of all like to thank SAGE executive editor Jessica Miller. Jessica's faith in and commitment to the project helped make this book a reality. We also would like to thank Jessica's editorial assistant, Rebecca Lee, who helped shepherd the book through the review process and whose gentle prodding ensured that deadlines would be met. Our copy editor, Colleen Brennan, made sure that there were no errant commas, misspelled words, or missing references and also smoothed out our occasionally tangled prose. Thank you one and all.

We are also very grateful to the reviewers who took the time to review early drafts of our work and who provided us with helpful suggestions for improving the text. Their comments undoubtedly made the book better than it otherwise would have been.

Heartfelt thanks to the following experts who reviewed the first edition:

Gad J. Bensinger
Loyola University Chicago

Alton Braddock
University of Louisiana at Monroe

Don Bradel
Bemidji State University

Jack E. Call
Radford University

Lisa Decker
Indiana State University

Eugene J. Evans Jr.
Camden County College

George Guay
Salem State University

Lori Guevara
Fayetteville State University

Peter Haynes
Arizona State University

Richard Hill
University of Houston Downtown

Jennifer L. Lanterman
Rutgers University

Nancy Merritt
California State University Los Angeles

Steven Philbrick
Northwest Vista College

Eric W. Rise
University of Delaware

Joe Sanborn
University of Central Florida

David Spencer
Texas State University San Marcos

Sheryl Van Horne
Penn State Altoona

Keith Wilmot
Florida Atlantic University

Thanks also to the following experts who reviewed the second edition:

Rossie D. Alston
George Mason University

Elizabeth P. Biebe
Morehead State University

Catherine L. Bonventre
University at Albany, SUNY

Thomas Dreffein
Triton College

Melissa Garmo
Saginaw Valley State University

Tony Gaskew
University of Pittsburgh–Bradford

Jacinta Gau
University of Central Florida

Doug Henderson
University of South Florida

Gale Iles
University of Tennessee–Chattanooga

Sara Jane Phillips
University of Texas, Arlington

Thanks also to the following experts who reviewed the third edition:

Rossie D. Alston Jr., Judge
Court of Appeals of Virginia

Sylvia Blake-Larson
Tarrant County College

Steven Briggs
North Dakota State University

Emil Moldovan, MPA
Radford University

Dr. Mai E. Naito
University of West Georgia

Elizabeth Perkins, PhD
Morehead State University

Danielle M. Romain
University of Wisconsin–Milwaukee

And lastly, thanks to the following experts who reviewed the fourth edition:

Ross Allen
Rutgers University–Camden

Raymond L. Hasselman, JD, PhD
Northeastern State University

Barbara B. Koehler, JD
Metropolitan State University of Denver

Elizabeth B. Perkins, PhD
Morehead State University

Danielle M. Romain
University of Wisconsin–Milwaukee

Mercedes Valadez, PhD
California State University, Sacramento

ABOUT THE AUTHORS

Craig Hemmens is a professor in the Department of Criminal Justice and Criminology at Washington State University. He holds a JD from North Carolina Central University School of Law and a PhD in criminal justice from Sam Houston State University. Professor Hemmens has published 20 books and more than 200 articles, many dealing with legal issues in criminal justice. He currently serves as editor of the *Criminal Law Bulletin* and previously served as the editor of the *Journal of Criminal Justice Education* and as president of the Academy of Criminal Justice Sciences. His current research interests include criminal law and procedure.

David C. Brody is a professor in the Department of Criminal Justice and Criminology at Washington State University. He received a JD from the University of Arizona College of Law and a PhD in criminal justice from the State University of New York at Albany. He is the author of casebooks on criminal law and criminal procedure, as well as scholarly articles that have been published in such journals as the *American Criminal Law Review, Crime and Delinquency, Justice System Journal,* and *Judicature.* His current research focuses on the selection and evaluation of judges, jury reform, and the interaction between law, politics, and criminal justice policy.

Cassia Spohn is School Director and Foundation Professor of Criminal Justice at Arizona State University. She is the author of several books, including *The Color of Justice: Race, Ethnicity, and Crime in America* (with Sam Walker and Miriam DeLone) and *How Do Judges Decide? The Search for Fairness and Equity in Sentencing.* She has published a number of articles examining prosecutors' charging decisions in sexual assault cases and exploring the effect of race/ethnicity on charging and sentencing decisions. Her current research interests include the effect of race and gender on court processing decisions, victim characteristics and case outcomes in sexual assault cases, judicial decision making, sentencing of drug offenders, and the deterrent effect of imprisonment. In 1999, she was awarded the University of Nebraska Outstanding Research and Creative Activity Award.

THE PURPOSE AND STRUCTURE OF AMERICAN COURTS

SECTION I

CHAPTERS

© Comstock/Stockbyte/Thinkstock Images

1

INTRODUCTION

Law and the Judicial Function

$$SAGE\ edge^{™}$$

Master the content at **edge.sagepub.com/hemmens4e**

WHY STUDY COURTS?

A glance at the headlines of any major newspaper reveals that crime is a pressing national concern. Stories about crime, especially violent crime, figure prominently, as do the crime-fighting strategies proposed by legislators, county attorneys, and other government officials. Decisions by prosecutors and judges—particularly in high-profile cases involving heinous crimes or well-known victims or defendants—also get front-page billing, along with appellate court decisions that strike down or affirm criminal convictions and Supreme Court decisions that affect the operation of the criminal court system. Clearly, the editors of these newspapers believe that the public has a voracious appetite for news about crime and the handling of crime by our nation's courts.

This degree of media attention to courts and their outcomes is not really surprising. Every day, in cities throughout the United States, court officials make decisions that affect the lives of ordinary Americans and determine how private businesses and governmental institutions will operate. Some of these decisions—such as a judge's ruling that a woman ticketed for speeding must pay a small fine—are relatively trivial and have little impact on persons other than the speeder herself. Other decisions—for example, a prosecutor's decision to seek the death penalty or a jury's decision to acquit a defendant charged with a serious crime—are weightier and have greater impact. Decisions of appellate courts, especially those handed down by the U.S. Supreme Court, have a farther reaching impact. Consider, for example, the Supreme Court's 1963 decision that all persons charged with felonies in state courts have the right to an attorney (*Gideon v. Wainwright*, 1963) or its decision in 2005 that U.S. district court judges are not required to follow the federal sentencing guidelines (*United States v. Booker*, 2005).

Courts provide several functions. First, courts settle disputes by providing a forum for obtaining justice and resolving disputes through the application of legal rules and principles. It is in court that injured parties may seek compensation and the state may seek to punish wrongdoers. Private parties may seek redress in civil court, and the state may seek to punish violators of the criminal law in criminal court. Although the courtroom is obviously not the only place that people may go to settle disputes, Americans traditionally have turned to the courts for redress. Other cultures, such as the Japanese, use the courts much less frequently.

Second, courts make public policy decisions. Policy making involves the allocation of limited resources (such as money and property) to competing interests. America has a long tradition of settling difficult policy questions in the courtroom rather than in the legislature. This is because politicians often avoid settling complex or difficult problems for fear of alienating their constituents or because the competing interests are unable to compromise. In addition, the rights of minorities are often unprotected by the legislature, which, by its very nature, represents primarily the interests of the majority, so courts are forced to step into the breach. Finally, there is a tradition of using litigation as a tool for social change.

Third, courts serve to clarify the law through interpretation of statutes and the application of general principles to specific fact patterns. Courts are different from the other branches of government in many ways, but perhaps the most significant difference is that courts are reactive; that is, courts do not initiate cases but rather serve to settle controversies brought to them by others—plaintiffs and defendants, in legal parlance. This frequently involves the interpretation of statutes written by the legislature.

WHAT IS LAW?

Laws are created by the legislature, provide rules to guide conduct, and are a means of resolving disputes and maintaining order through the medium of the courts. Courts are forums for dispute resolution. This dispute may be between two private parties, such as a dispute between a landlord and a tenant or between a buyer and a seller of property. Or the dispute may be between the state and an individual, as when a defendant is charged with violating some provision of the criminal code.

The court system has a complex set of rules and procedures. Evidence law governs what information the jury can see and hear and how this evidence may be presented to them. There are seemingly innumerable rules governing how parties to a lawsuit may proceed and what motions they can make, either prior to or during trial (and even after the verdict is entered!). The court system has a number of important roles. These include the prosecutor, defense attorney, judge, witnesses, and the defendant.

Courts are charged with settling legal disputes. But what is a legal dispute? For our purposes, a legal dispute is a disagreement about a law—what it means, how it is implemented, or, in the case of criminal law, whether a person has violated the law. The next question, then, is what exactly is "law"? Our definition is this: **Law** is a written body of rules of conduct applicable to all members of a defined community, society, or culture that emanate from a governing authority and are enforced by its agents by the imposition of penalties for their violation.

This definition is appropriate for all modern systems of law, but it would not completely fit preliterate societies because, by definition, such societies do not possess writing, nor do they typically employ agents to enforce rules of conduct. However, law as a system of proscribed and prescribed behavior is certainly not unique to highly developed societies with written statutes and a formal system of law enforcement. All people living together in organized groups have had at least some type of rudimentary rules for governing conduct. They would not last very long as organized groups if they did not, for law is at the center of all organized social life. Indeed, the word *law* itself has come to us from a variety of Latin and Nordic words meaning "to bind" (people together). People who are "bound together" share a common culture, and all cultures share certain core elements. Our first task is to see how these common elements are related to law.

THE CODE OF HAMMURABI

The first legal codes showed that there were well-advanced societies that exhibited signs of mature civilizations many centuries ago. The **Code of Hammurabi** (Hammurabi was a king of Babylonia who lived from 2123 to 2081 BC) was long acknowledged as the oldest known written code of law. We now know, however, that other documents of this type existed in the area of the Middle East called Mesopotamia, but no other was so broad in its scope. The code was discovered inscribed on a round pillar 7 feet, 4 inches high.

On the top of the pillar was Shamash, the Sun god, handing the legal code to Hammurabi. On the back and front of the lower portion of the obelisk was the legal code of King Hammurabi. It was not law in the sense that law is understood today—that is, a set of abstract principles applicable to all. Rather, it was a set of judgments originally pronounced to solve a particular case. Nor was it an attempt to cover all possible situations as modern codes do, and as far as we know, it was never copied and distributed to those officials charged with the day-to-day administration of Hammurabi's vast kingdom. Nevertheless, the system of justice contained in the code showed signs of mature development, although it was obviously quite different from what we would recognize as such today.

Hammurabi's Code governed relationships in the society related to sexual behavior, property rights, theft, and acts of violence. The law forbade retaliatory actions and deadly blood feuds among the people, leaving punishments to be dispensed by the king's agents. The "eye for an eye, tooth for a tooth" (*lex talionis*) concept of justice is clearly stated in the code, predating the Old Testament passage familiar to Jews, Christians, and Muslims. The law introduced specified standards of conduct and amelioration by an independent third party to settle disputes. Cruelty and inhuman behavior to those accused of wrongdoing were restricted by the legal code. A written code, theoretically impartial in its application, represented a tremendous advance for society in general and the administration of justice in particular.

TWO OPPOSING PERSPECTIVES: CONSENSUS AND CONFLICT

Sociologists who study the law as a social institution and its function as a social control mechanism tend to view it in terms of one of two broad perspectives. Which perspective a scholar favors tends to depend on his or her more fundamental perspective on society. Some scholars view society as basically good, just, and more or less providing equal opportunity for all individuals within it. These people hold what is called the consensus view of society. Others view society as basically unjust, unequal, and discriminatory. These people hold what is called the conflict view. **Consensus theorists** emphasize how society is structured to maintain its stability and view it as an integrated network of institutions (the family, church, school, economy, government) that function to maintain social order and the system as a whole. Social stability is also achieved in this view through cooperation, shared values, and the cohesion and solidarity that people feel by being part of a shared culture. Consensus theorists are aware that conflicts often arise in social life but stress that such conflicts are temporary and can be and are solved within the framework of shared fundamental values, as exemplified by a neutral legal system.

Conflict theorists consider society to be composed of individuals and groups with sharply different interests and to be characterized by conflict and dissension. People and groups everywhere, they maintain, seek to maximize their interests. Because resources are limited, conflict between different individuals and groups is inevitable and continuous. The stability and order that consensus theorists see is only temporary and maintained by coercion rather than consensus—that is, the ability of more powerful people and groups to impose their will on the less powerful. The social institutions so lauded by consensus theorists function to maintain the privilege of the few and to keep the many subservient to them.

Which view is correct? The simple answer is that it is impossible to say without specifying what society we are talking about. All societies are characterized by both consensus and conflict; it is almost impossible to imagine any society not being so. We have to remember that these two competing models are examples of what sociologists call *ideal types*. Ideal types are abstract conceptual tools that accentuate the phenomenon being studied purely for analytical purposes; they lay no claims to mirror the day-to-day reality of any concrete example of that phenomenon. Let us examine law in the context of these two ideal-type models of society.

The Consensus Perspective

The consensus perspective views law as basically a neutral framework for patching up conflicts between individuals and groups who primarily share the same set of fundamental values. Law is viewed in a manner analogous to the immune system of the body in that it identifies and neutralizes potential dangers to the social body before they can do too much damage. Thus, law is a just and necessary mechanism for controlling behavior detrimental to peace, order, predictability, and stability and for maintaining social integration. Specific legal codes are assumed to express compromises between various interest groups regarding issues that have been contentious in the past, not the victories of some groups over others. Law is also seen as reflecting the community's deeply held values and as defining the rights and responsibilities of all those within it, and it is a legitimate expression of morality and custom. If coercion is sometimes needed to bolster conscience, it is because the individual, not the law, is flawed. The law is obeyed by the vast majority of people not out of fear but out of respect, and it is willingly supported by all good people.

The Conflict Perspective

Underlying the conflict perspective of the law is a view of human nature that sees human beings as basically exploitive and duplicitous creatures (although conflict theorists believe we have become that way because of the greed and egoism instilled in us by living in a capitalist society, not because we are born that way). It also avers that law functions to preserve the power and privilege of the most exploitive and duplicitous among us, not to protect the weak and helpless. The conflict perspective of law rests on the assumptions of conflict sociology, which asserts that social behavior is best understood in terms of struggles and conflicts between groups and individuals over scarce resources. As we have seen, although thinking of social processes in terms of conflict between rival factions (usually between social classes) goes back as far as Plato, the more formal treatment of conflict as a concept traces its origin to the thought of 19th-century German philosopher Karl Marx.

Marxist legal scholars certainly agree with scholars from other perspectives that law exists to settle conflicts and restore social peace but insist that conflicts are always settled in favor of the ruling class in any society. The ruling class always wins out because it is this class that makes the rules governing social interaction. For Marxist legal scholars, society is divided into two classes: the rulers and the ruled. The ruling class—by which

Marx meant the owners of the means of production (i.e., factory owners and entrepreneurs)—controls the "ruling material force of society." Because these individuals control the means of production, they are able to buy politicians, the media, the church, and all other social institutions that mold social values and attitudes, and thus law.

Why do the exploited not recognize their exploitation and the ways in which the law supports it? Marx and Engels explained this puzzle with reference to the idea of **false consciousness**. By false consciousness, Marx and Engels meant that the working classes have accepted an ideological worldview that is contrary to their best interests. Workers have been duped into accepting the legitimacy of the law by the ruling classes and are not aware that the law does not serve them. They blindly and docilely obey the law, believing that they are behaving morally by doing so. The ruling class is able to generate the false consciousness of the workers by virtue of its control over key institutions such as education, religion, the media, and, of course, the law itself. These institutions define what is right and wrong, and they control the flow of information so that it conforms to the worldview of the ruling class.

Because both consensus and conflict are ubiquitous and integral facts of social life, we have to address both processes in this book while attempting to remain agnostic with respect to which process "really" characterizes social life in a general sense. It is hoped that it will become plain to the reader that the consensus perspective is most suitable for explaining certain sets of facts and that the conflict perspective is better suited to explaining other sets of facts. We hope that it will also become plain that conflict is as necessary as consensus to maintain the viability of a free society.

WHAT IS THE RELATIONSHIP OF LAW TO JUSTICE?

When most people think of justice, they probably think of law, but law and justice are not identical. Law *can* be in accordance with justice, but it can also be the farthest thing from it. Law is in accordance with justice when it respects, cultivates, and protects the dignity of even the lowliest person living under it; it violates justice when it does not. Believers in natural law maintain that it should be the goal of positive law to bring itself into conformity with what is just. We have to be confident that we can find justice and that we can harness it and put it to practical use for the benefit of humankind, just as scientists seek to harness the laws of nature and put them to practical use. When all is said and done, it is only through law that justice can be achieved.

Equity is a term derived from the Latin word for "just" and refers to remedies for wrongs that were not recognized (neither the remedies nor the wrongs) under English common law. Equity principles are heavily used in family and contract law since they allow judges to fashion necessary remedies not readily apparent from a reading of legal statutes.

The idea of equity in law in medieval England evolved on parallel tracks with the evolution of the role of the king's chancellor, who was essentially the king's most important minister (his "prime minister"). One of the chancellor's responsibilities was to handle petitions from the king's subjects seeking relief from rulings in the courts. This relief was sorely needed because by the 13th century, the court system had become very inflexible. Judges frequently applied the same abstract principles and procedural rules rigidly to every case regardless of the issues involved. Judges also failed to realize that ever-changing social circumstances and mores require a dynamic "living" system of law. As a result of the rigidity of common-law practice, many people felt unjustly treated by the courts and turned to the king (through his chancellor and his staff) to seek justice. This does not mean that the common law of the time was inherently unfair. The law was more incomplete and inflexible than purposely unfair, and equity was conceived of as a corrective for the rigidity and impersonal nature of law.

With an increasing number of petitions being filed, an entirely independent court system with its own distinct set of principles and procedures was eventually implemented, known as the Court of Chancery. The first mention of such a court was in 1280, during the reign of Edward I (1239–1307). Judges presiding in these courts were directed to view each case as unique, to be flexible and empathetic, and to think in terms of principles of fairness rather than rules of law. Because it was a corrective, many equity decisions were contrary to the principles of the common law as a rational and predictable legal system (Reichel, 2005). It is important to note that equity supplemented, not replaced, common law: Equity "begins where the law ends; it supplies justice in circumstances not covered by the law" (McDowell, 1982, p. 23). In other words, if justice was to be served in England, the cold formality of common law alone would not suffice. Courts of Chancery were a necessary "add-on" because of the equity defects apparent in the rigid common law at the time.

Over the centuries, common law and equity engaged in dynamic cross-pollination to the benefit of both. The common law became fairer and more flexible, and the judges of the chancery courts began relying on rational legal principles and precedent to make equity more predicable. They eventually became so alike that formal distinctions between the two courts were removed in 1875, although there are still provisions for separate courts of law and equity in England. Some states in the United States (notably, Delaware) have chancery courts, but most U.S. judges are empowered to hear cases of both law and equity.

What kinds of legal decisions violate equity, and what exactly is an equity decision? Civil law (i.e., noncriminal law) in the United States throughout most of the 19th century was very much oriented toward protecting the legality of contracts between individuals. As long as no specific contract was violated, the defrauding, maiming, and killing of innocent consumers and workers by defective products and dangerous working conditions was not cause for legal action. Victims of defective and/or dangerous products could not sue the manufacturers because the guiding legal principle was *caveat emptor* (let the buyer beware). Companies had no legal duty to be concerned with the welfare of those to whom they sold their products; it was incumbent on buyers to be concerned with their own welfare. Similarly, unhealthy and dangerous working conditions in mines, mills, and factories were excused under the Contract Clause of the Constitution. American law in this period was as rigid as 12th-century English law as judges mechanistically applied legal rules without concern for standards of equity. Equity became more and more a consideration of American courts in the late 19th and early 20th centuries, however, as laws were passed making companies liable for defective products and protecting workers from unsafe working conditions.

THE RULE OF LAW

The only way we can be reasonably assured of integrating important aspects of justice with a legal system is to ensure strict adherence to what is called the rule of law. This idea of the rule of law, not of men, evolved in the English-speaking world from the time of the Magna Carta (1215) through the English civil wars (1642–1646 and 1648–1649) and the Glorious Revolution (1688–1689) of the 17th century. These struggles of the English people were efforts to gain the freedom from arbitrary government power and oppressive sovereigns. The struggles for freedom and liberty continued with the American Revolution and Civil War and are still going on today around the world.

Although the rule of law can be violated, the fact that it exists serves as a rallying point and source of legitimacy for those who would oppose individuals and governments who violate it. According to Philip Reichel (2005), the rule of law contains three irreducible elements:

1. It requires a nation to recognize the supremacy of certain fundamental values and principles.

2. These values and principles must be committed to writing.

3. A system of procedures that holds the government to these principles and values must be in place.

The first element is relatively unproblematic; it is difficult to imagine a modern organized society not recognizing a set of fundamental values that they hold supreme. These ultimate principles may be secular or religious. The second element is also relatively unproblematic. Any culture possessing a written language would be expected to put such important guiding principles into writing so that all may refer to them. Documents containing these principles may be the culture's holy books or a nation's constitution. The third element is much more problematic because it determines whether a country honors its fundamental values in practice as well as in theory.

At its core, law is a set of lifeless statements; it has no life apart from human actors. If the law is to be consistent with justice, it can be so only if the procedures followed by the servants of the law are perceived as fair and equal.

The system of procedures to hold the government to its principles is best articulated by the concept of **due process**. When we speak about something that is due to us, we are usually referring to something that we feel we are rightly entitled to. Due process is procedural justice that is due to all persons whenever they are threatened with the loss of life, liberty, or property at the hands of the state. Due process is essentially a set of instructions informing agents of the state how they must proceed in their investigation, arrest, questioning, prosecution, and punishment of individuals who are suspected of committing crimes. Due process rules are thus rules that attempt to ensure that people are treated justly by the state. Unlike distributive justice, due process is not something a person earns by his or her actions; it is something that is due (hence the term) to everyone without exception simply because of their humanity.

To understand what due process means today and how far we have come in implementing it, let us examine what people went through in times when the idea of due process would have been foreign to most people. Imagine you are in France 300 years ago. Soldiers come to your house in the dead of night, batter your door down, arrest you, and lodge you in a filthy dungeon. Further imagine that you genuinely do not know why this is happening to you. You try to find out for years while rotting in that dungeon, but no one you ask has the slightest idea. All you and they know is that you are the victim of one of the infamous *lettres de cachet* ("sealed letters"). These letters were issued by the king, his ministers, or some other high-ranking aristocrat, ordering authorities to seize and imprison anyone who had in any way offended them. When (or if) you were finally released, there is nothing you could do about what had happened because it was all perfectly legal under the Code Louis of 1670, which governed France until the implementation of the Code Napoleon in 1804. The Code Louis is a perfect example of a system of positivist law being at odds with justice.

JUSTICE, THE LAW, AND PACKER'S MODELS OF CRIMINAL JUSTICE

Every matter of controversy in criminal justice has as its core at least two competing sets of ideas. With regard to courts, every decision a judge makes, at either the trial or appellate level, tends to pit two contradictory sets of values against each other. Consider a criminal trial. The prosecutor presents a case that represents the interests of the state, one that is designed to prove that the defendant is guilty and should be held accountable for the crime with which he or she is charged. In contrast, the defense attorney presents a case in the interest of his or her client. The defense attorney attempts to raise doubt about the defendant's guilt and insists that the legal procedures designed to protect the defendant's rights be followed. The competing sets of values that each of these actors brings to the table—and that are found at all other stages of the criminal justice process as well—have been described by Herbert Packer (1968) as the crime control and due process perspectives.

Packer's (1968) models of the criminal process are just that—models, and not depictions of reality. He sees them as polarities—as the two ends of a continuum along which the actual operation of the criminal justice system will fall. He also cautions against depicting one model as the way things work and the other as the way things ought to work. In his words, the two models "represent an attempt to abstract two separate value systems that compete for priority in the operation of the criminal process" (Packer, 1968, p. 153). The value systems that "compete for priority" are regulating criminal conduct and preventing crime, which the crime control model views as the most important function of the criminal process, and protecting the rights of individuals, which the **due process model** emphasizes.

In the sections that follow, we describe the crime control and due process models in detail, focusing on their differences. These differences are summarized in Table 1.1.

TABLE 1.1 ■ Packer's Crime Control and Due Process Models

	Crime Control Model	Due Process Model
Views criminal justice system as an	Assembly line	Obstacle course
Goal of criminal justice system	Controlling crime	Protecting rights of defendants
Values emphasized	Efficiency, speed, finality	Reliability
Process of adjudication	Informal screening by police and prosecutor	Formal, adversarial procedures
Focus on	Factual guilt	Legal guilt

TWO MODELS OF CRIMINAL JUSTICE

The Crime Control Model

As its name suggests, the **crime control model** (see Packer, 1968, pp. 158–163) views the suppression of criminal conduct—that is, controlling crime—as the most important function of the criminal justice system. The primary function of the system is to control crime by apprehending, convicting, and punishing those who violate the law. Failure to control crime, according to this perspective, leads to a breakdown in public order. If citizens believe that laws are not being enforced, they will have fewer incentives to obey the law, which will lead to an increase in crime and to a greater risk of victimization among law-abiding citizens. As Packer (1968) notes, failure to control crime eventually leads "to the disappearance of an important condition of human freedom" (p. 158).

According to the crime control model, *efficiency* is the key to the effective operation of the criminal process. A high proportion of offenders whose offenses become known must be apprehended, tried, convicted, and sentenced. Moreover, this must be accomplished in a system where the crime rate is high and resources for dealing with crime are limited. Thus, the model emphasizes *speed*, which depends on informality and uniformity, and *finality*, which means that there should be few opportunities for challenging outcomes. The requirement of informality means that cases should be screened by police and prosecutors to determine the facts and to separate the probably innocent from the probably guilty; judicial fact finding, which is more time consuming and thus less efficient, should be the exception rather than the norm. Uniformity means that officials should follow routine procedures in most cases. As Packer (1968) puts it, "The process must not be cluttered up with ceremonious rituals that do not advance the progress of the case" (p. 159).

The metaphor that Packer (1968) uses to describe the operation of the criminal process under the crime control model is that of an assembly line: "an assembly-line conveyor belt down which moves an endless stream of cases, never stopping, carrying the cases to workers . . . who perform on each case as it comes by the same small but essential operation that brings it one step closer to being a finished product . . . a closed file"

(p. 159). As this suggests, the goal is to move cases through the justice process as swiftly as possible. Suspects who are "probably innocent" are screened out early in the process by police and prosecutors; those who are "probably guilty" are moved quickly and perfunctorily through the remaining stages in the process and are convicted, usually by a plea of guilty, as expeditiously as possible. Thus, the system achieves the goal of controlling crime by separating the innocent from the guilty early in the process, by extracting early guilty pleas from those who are not screened out by police and prosecutors, and by avoiding trials.

A key to the operation of the crime control model is the **presumption of guilt**, which rests on a belief in the reliability of the screening process operated by police and prosecutors. That is, defendants who are not screened out early in the process by police and prosecutors are probably guilty and therefore can be passed quickly through the remaining stages in the process. It is important to point out that the presumption of guilt, which is descriptive and factual, is not the opposite of the presumption of innocence, which is normative and legal. The presumption of guilt is simply a prediction of outcome: Those not screened out early in the process are probably guilty and more than likely will plead guilty or be found guilty at trial. The **presumption of innocence**, on the other hand, means that until the defendant has been adjudicated guilty, that person is "to be treated, for reasons that have nothing whatever to do with the probable outcome of the case, as if his guilt is an open question" (Packer, 1968, p. 161).

In summary, the crime control model views the apprehension and conviction of criminals as the most important function of the criminal justice system. It characterizes the criminal process as an assembly line that moves cases forward in a uniform and predictable way. The model places great faith in the reliability of fact finding by police and prosecutors. It suggests that the process is operating with maximum efficiency if cases involving the probably innocent are screened out early by police and prosecutors and if the rest of the cases, which involve defendants who are presumed to be guilty, are disposed of as quickly as possible, preferably with guilty pleas.

The Due Process Model

Whereas the crime control model views the criminal process as an assembly line, the due process model sees the process as an obstacle course. Each stage in the process, according to Packer (1968, pp. 163–172), is designed not to move cases forward as expeditiously as possible but rather to throw up hurdles to carrying the case from one stage to the next. There are other differences as well. Whereas the crime control model stresses efficiency, the due process model stresses reliability and minimizing the potential for mistakes. And whereas the crime control model places great faith in the ability of police and prosecutors to separate the probably innocent from the probably guilty, the due process model contends that informal, non-adjudicatory fact finding carries with it a strong likelihood of error.

It is important to point out that the values underlying the due process model are not the opposite of those found in the crime control model. Like the crime control model, the due process model acknowledges the importance of controlling crime. However, the due process model rejects the premise that screening of cases by police and prosecutors is reliable. More to the point, the due process model stresses the likelihood of error in these informal screening processes. As Packer (1968) points out,

People are notoriously poor observers of disturbing events . . .; confessions and admissions by persons in police custody may be induced by physical or psychological coercion so that the police end up hearing what the suspect thinks they want to hear rather than the truth; witnesses may be animated by a bias or interest that no one would trouble to discover except one specially charged with protecting the interests of the accused (as the police are not). (p. 163)

Because of the strong possibility of mistakes in the early stages of the process, the due process model calls for fact-finding procedures that are formal, adjudicative, and adversarial. The case against the accused, in other words, should be "publicly heard by an impartial tribunal" and "evaluated only after the accused has had a full opportunity to discredit the case against him" (Packer, 1968, p. 164). The model also rejects the notion of finality; rather, there should be constant scrutiny of outcomes to ensure that mistakes have not been made.

There also are sharp differences between the two models in the degree to which mistakes can be tolerated. That is, there are differences in the weight given to reliability (a strong probability that factual guilt has been determined accurately) and efficiency (expeditious handling of the large number of cases that the system takes in). The crime control model is willing to sacrifice some reliability in pursuit of efficiency. It tolerates mistakes up to the level at which they interfere with the goal of preventing crime; if too many guilty people go free or if there is a general view that the system is not reliable, crime might increase rather than decrease. The due process model rejects this view, arguing that mistakes must be prevented and eliminated. To the extent that efficiency requires shortcuts that reduce the reliability of outcomes, efficiency must be sacrificed.

To ensure a high degree of reliability in the process, the due process model requires that both factual guilt and legal guilt be proved. Factual guilt simply means that the evidence shows that there is a high probability that the defendant committed the crime of which he or she is accused. Legal guilt, on the other hand, refers to the process by which determinations of guilt are made.

Defendants are not to be deemed guilty unless all the mandated procedures and rules designed to protect the rights of the accused have been followed. A defendant charged with an assault that was witnessed by a number of bystanders who are willing to testify against him may well be factually guilty of assault. His legal guilt at the time of charging, on the other hand, is an open question. If the determination of factual guilt is not made in a procedurally correct way, the defendant is not legally guilty and cannot be held accountable for the crime with which he is charged.

The due process model, then, resembles an obstacle course in which cases must navigate hurdles set up to ensure that determinations of guilt are reliable. The key to this is formal, adjudicative, and adversarial fact-finding procedures with constant scrutiny of outcomes to ensure that mistakes have not been made. Defendants are presumed to be innocent until proven guilty, legally as well as factually.

An Illustration of the Models in Action

A series of Supreme Court cases that illustrates the "tinkering" that goes on to modify the excesses that might arise with exclusive use of either model involves an escaped mental patient named Robert Williams who kidnapped, raped, and murdered a 10-year-old girl named Pamela Powers on Christmas Eve, 1968. Two days after the crime, Williams turned himself in to the police in Davenport, Iowa. Because the crime took place in Des Moines, a detective was dispatched to transport Williams from Davenport. Williams's lawyer secured the detective's agreement not to question Williams during the trip. However, the officer—concerned that if Pamela's body were not found before the snow fell, it would not be discovered until the following spring—engaged Williams in conversation, during which the officer made statements, but did not ask questions, about how important it was to the family to find Pamela's body so that they could give her a proper Christian burial. This "Christian burial speech" touched Williams, who then directed the detective to the girl's frozen body. On the basis of this evidence, Williams was convicted of murder in 1969.

The case reached the U. S. Supreme Court in 1977 (*Brewer v. Williams*, 1977). The Court overturned Williams's conviction by a vote of 5–4, stating that Williams had not waived his right to counsel during questioning and that the officer's "Christian burial speech" constituted custodial interrogation. It was reasoned that since Williams's confession was obtained in violation of his right to counsel, any evidence obtained on the basis of it (Pamela's body) was inadmissible under the exclusionary rule. The majority of the justices were focused on whether Williams had received a fair trial; concerns about crime control and efficiency were secondary.

Brewer v. Williams is an example of the potential excesses of the due process model. However, this case was one of a number of cases involving the boundaries of custodial interrogation from a time when the crime control model ran amok. The most famous of these cases was *Brown v. Mississippi* (1936), which involved the alleged murder of a White man by three Black men. All three men were sentenced to death on the basis of confessions obtained under torture (they were whipped and told that the whippings would not stop until they confessed). The injustice to the community inherent in the *Brewer* case can be viewed as one of a number of correctives to the injustices suffered by defendants and typified in the *Brown* case.

After Williams was retried, and again convicted, he appealed to the Supreme Court. This time, in *Nix v. Williams* (1984), which enunciated the inevitable discovery exception to the exclusionary rule, the Court upheld Williams's conviction, ruling that search parties looking for Pamela's body would have found it by lawful means eventually, and thus the fact that it was found sooner because of Williams's confession was irrelevant.

The Ongoing Battle

In an ideal world, judges and other criminal justice officials would balance due process and crime control ideals. They would strive for efficiency while insisting on reliability. In the real world, this is probably not possible; many decisions tip in one direction or another. High caseloads, limited resources, and concerns about protecting the community may lead to shortcuts that threaten reliability or to decisions that chip away at the procedural regulations that protect the rights of criminal defendants. Similarly, concerns about restraining the power of criminal justice officials may lead to decisions that make it more difficult for the criminal process to apprehend and convict those who commit crimes.

A good example of an issue where use of the crime control and due process models would lead to different conclusions is plea bargaining. According to the crime control model, the criminal process is operating most efficiently when defendants who are not screened out by police and prosecutors plead guilty at the earliest possible moment. The criminal process would break down if too many defendants insisted on taking their cases to trial. The crime control model thus sees nothing wrong with allowing prosecutors to reduce charges or drop counts in exchange for guilty pleas or permitting judges to make it clear to defendants that those who plead guilty will be treated more leniently than those who insist on a trial. Although plea bargaining may result in guilty pleas by those who are innocent, this type of mistake is likely to be rare, as those who have survived the screening process are in all probability guilty. Disposing of a large proportion of cases as quickly as possible via guilty pleas is, according to this model, the only feasible means of achieving the goal of crime control.

It is no surprise that use of the due process model leads to a different conclusion. According to this model, guilty pleas, which effectively preclude any oversight of the early, informal stages of the process, should be discouraged. The due process model values reliability and contends that mistakes are likely early in the process; because of this, guilty pleas that occur soon after the prosecutor makes a decision to charge have a high probability of producing unreliable factual determinations of guilt. In addition, the model does not allow prosecutors or judges to promise defendants leniency in return for a guilty plea. Defendants, no matter how overwhelming the evidence, have the right to have the charges against them tried using the procedures required by law; they should not be coerced to enter a guilty plea or punished for exercising their constitutionally protected rights. Moreover, before accepting a guilty plea, the judge adjudicating the case should be required to both establish the defendant's factual guilt and ensure that the process that brought the defendant into court has been free of mistakes. According to the due process model, it is only by following these rules that reliability of outcomes can be guaranteed and mistakes minimized.

JUDICIAL FUNCTIONS

Courts provide several functions. They provide a forum to settle disputes, either in civil court or criminal court. They make policy decisions that politicians may be unwilling to make for fear of not being reelected. They also serve to clarify the law through interpretation of statutes and the application of general principles to specific fact patterns. Courts are different from the other branches of government in many ways, but perhaps the most significant difference is that courts are reactive; that is, courts do not initiate cases but rather serve to settle controversies brought to them. In the process, courts are forced to choose one side over the other, or to interpret the law and apply it to a unique set of facts—this is sometimes referred to as "making law."

HOW JUDGES "MAKE LAW"

It is often said that our political system is a "government of laws, not men." This means that individuals in our system are governed by laws and not by the whims of those in power; it also means that the law applies to everyone—even to those in power—and that no one is above the law. Related to this is the notion that the law is "a set of

The Role of the Courts in America

Elizabeth Estess
Ada County Public Defender
Boise, Idaho

The role of the courts in America, as directed by its magistrates, judges, and Supreme Court justices, is to ensure fairness to individuals while attempting to ascertain the truth of the matter asserted. Achieving these two goals requires a balance of expertise, experience, and emphasis.

Expertise, in my opinion, largely consists of having the knowledge to hand down good oral or written opinions concerning the authenticity of the evidence and claims presented before the court. Experience means having a "seasoned," practical understanding that is based on personal observation from encountering and going *through* things in life as they occur over a long period of time. Emphasis requires that the court consider as important above all else the goal of ascertaining the truth, along with satisfying the defendant's constitutional right to a fair trial. If the court is properly emphasizing these goals, there should be a significant amount of stress between the adversaries as they attempt to present and defend their case.

rules transcending time, geography, and the circumstances surrounding specific cases" (Eisenstein, Flemming, & Nardulli, 1988, p. 5). According to this line of reasoning, judges simply apply the law in a rigid and mechanistic way to the specific cases that arise. Stated another way, judges "find" the applicable law and apply it to the case at hand.

The problem with this traditional view of law and the role of courts is that much of "the law" is broad and ambiguous. Thus, the judges who are charged with enforcing the law must first interpret it. They must decide what the law means and whether it is applicable in the given situation. Consider, for instance, a legislatively enacted statute that prohibits disturbing the peace, which is defined as "willfully disrupting the peace and security of the community." This statute, which does not define *willful* or offer examples of conduct that would "disrupt the peace and security," obviously leaves room for interpretation. Constitutional provisions, which are another source of law, have similar limitations. Take, for instance, the Fourth Amendment to the U.S. Constitution. It protects against unreasonable searches and seizures, but it does not define *unreasonable*. Because of these inherent ambiguities in criminal statutes, in state and federal constitutions, and in other sources of law, judges are called on to interpret the law. Judges' use of their position to interpret the law has a long history. It began during what is known as the common-law period in England. We discuss the development of the common law, as well as its associated principles, in the next section.

DEVELOPMENT OF THE COMMON-LAW SYSTEM

The Western legal tradition may be traced to the Code of Hammurabi. This is the first known written legal code, and it expressed a retributivist "eye for an eye" philosophy. The Roman Empire eventually adopted many of the principles of the Code of Hammurabi. The spread of the Roman Empire brought Roman law to Western Europe, but it had minimal impact on English common law. The Norman conquest of England in 1066, however, brought feudal law, which provided the basis for the common law, to England. During the following several hundred years, England slowly developed what came to be known as the common-law system. By the reign of Henry II (1154–1189), who is often referred to as the "father of the common law," a body of law had been developed and applied nationally. Decisions were written down, circulated, and summarized. The first systematic attempt to collect and explain these decisions was compiled under the supervision of Henry's chief justice, Ranulf de Glanvill, in a book titled *Treatise on the Laws and Customs of the Realm of England*, around 1188. This book details the transition from what was essentially the irrational decision making of pre-Norman England to adherence to formal legal rules. The result was a more unified body of law, which came to be known as the **common law** because it was in force throughout the country.

The next important document in the evolution of common law was the Magna Carta (or "Great Charter") of 1215. The Magna Carta was a document drawn up by English barons to limit the power of the sovereign (specifically, the notorious King John of Robin Hood fame) and to assert certain rights. Contained in the document are the first dim glimpses of many of the rights we take for granted today, such as the right to trial by jury, proportionality of punishment, and the privilege against self-incrimination. Although King John's acquiescence to the provisions of the charter was a victory for the barons, it meant little at the time for the common person.

Henry de Bracton's *On the Laws and Customs of England*, written between 1250 and 1260, furthered the development of the common law. Bracton was a judge in England who believed that the common law was based on case law, which was in turn decided based on ancient custom rather than on authoritative codes imposed on people from above. The common law is thus judge-made law. That is, it was law created by judges as they heard cases and settled disputes. Judges wrote down their decisions and, in doing so, attempted to justify their decisions by reference to custom, tradition, history, and prior judicial decisions. *On the Laws and Customs of England* was essentially a compilation of these judicial rulings made over the previous decades arranged to show how precedent may guide future rulings.

Originally, judges made decisions without referring to other cases or courts. They simply heard the case and decided the appropriate outcome, based on their understanding of the law as they had learned it through the reading of legal treatises. But as time went by, judges came to rely on prior decisions as a means of justifying their decision in a particular case. As judges began to rely on previous judgments, they developed the concepts of stare decisis and precedent.

Precedent

Under the common-law system, every final decision by a court creates a **precedent**. This precedent governs the court issuing the decision as well as any lower, or inferior, courts. The common-law system was brought to America by the early colonists. Many of the principles of the common law, including precedent and a belief in stare decisis, remain in force today in American courts. Thus, all courts in a state are bound to follow the

COMPARATIVE COURTS

The basic features of civil law are almost mirror opposites of the features of common law. France has a civil-law system. What follows is a list of some of the distinctive features of the French civil-law system:

1. *Civil law is written rather than unwritten.* As opposed to the common law's slow accumulation of case law derived from decisions based on local customs, the Napoleonic Code and its successors are all codes of conduct (statutes) written from above and imposed on citizens and subjects below.

2. *Precedent is not officially recognized.* The codes laid down in civil law are complete the day they are enacted and are not subject to judicial review. As such, there is no need to refer to past cases for guidance. In practice, however, no code is so complete as to provide unambiguous guidance in all matters coming before the courts, and civil-law judges often refer to case law and thus to precedent. The main difference between the common- and civil-law approaches is that in civil law, precedent is not binding.

3. *It is inquisitorial rather than adversarial.* This is the primary distinguishing feature of civil law vis-à-vis common law. The **inquisitorial system** is a system of extensive investigation and interrogations carried out to ensure that an innocent person is not subjected to trial. The term *inquisition* should be thought of as denoting "inquiry" as the term *adversarial* denotes "contest." The inquisitorial focus is on truth and not so much on procedure, so many of the procedural protections afforded suspects in common-law countries either do not exist or exist in modified form.

4. *It has traditionally made little use of juries.* There is some use of juries in civil-law countries in very serious criminal cases, but they don't have the same role that they have in common-law countries. In France, juries consist of 3 professional judges and 9 laypersons. In a jury trial, all jurors and judges are allowed to question witnesses and the accused. Jury deliberations are doubtless dominated by the professional judges on whom the laypersons must rely for explanations of law, but guilt or innocence is determined by a secret ballot in which all 12 votes are of equal importance. A verdict requires agreement of at least 8 of the 12 jurors rather than unanimity.

5. *Judicial review is used sparingly.* The French equivalent to the American Supreme Court in terms of dealing with constitutional issues is the Conseil Constitutionnel (the Constitutional Council). This entity is unique among national supreme courts in that it lies outside the judicial system (it is a council, not a court hearing cases forwarded to it from lower courts). The council's main function is to rule on the constitutionality of proposed legislation, not legislation already in effect, when requested to do so by leaders of the various political parties. Some civil-law countries tend to view the practice of judicial review of legislation as inherently antidemocratic and a violation of the separation of powers principle. The reason that the American model of judicial review is rejected in France is that the French believe that important decisions affecting large numbers of people should be made by legislators elected by and accountable to the voters, not by appointees with lifetime tenure.

While the French civil-law system has its benefits, it also has its limitations. The investigation of a crime often takes a long time, during which the accused is typically held in custody without bail. Bail is infrequently granted in France because it operates under a crime control model and because the accused is expected to be available to help with the inquiry. Also, by the time a case gets to trial, everyone involved basically knows what is going to happen because the trial is more a forum for a review of the known facts (of which all parties are aware) than a forum for fact finding. The system is one of professional bureaucracy that lacks the same measure of lay participation favored by common-law countries. The expectation of cooperation on the part of the defendant, as well as the negative conclusions that the judge and jurors can draw if he or she does not cooperate, is something that an American due process purist finds alarming.

Source: Reichel, P. (2005). *Comparative criminal justice systems: A topical approach* (4th ed.). Upper Saddle River, NJ: Prentice Hall.

decisions of the highest court in the state, usually known as the state supreme court. All courts in the federal court system are bound to follow the decisions of the U.S. Supreme Court. This is the notion of precedent.

Precedent is binding only on those courts within the jurisdiction of the court issuing the opinion. Thus, a decision of the Idaho Supreme Court is not binding on any court in Texas. Texas courts are not subject to the jurisdiction or control of Idaho courts and thus are free to interpret the law differently from Idaho courts, if they see fit to do so. Decisions from courts in other jurisdictions, although not binding, may be persuasive. This simply means that another court may give consideration and weight to the opinion of other courts. Thus, a Texas court may consider, if it chooses, the judgment of an Idaho court or any other state court. Courts may do this when faced with an issue that they have not dealt with before but that other courts have examined. Moreover, when judges look to the past or other jurisdictions and can find no guiding precedent, they must decide the case according to their interpretation of legal principles.

There also are situations where judges do not follow precedent, either because they believe that the facts in the case at hand distinguish it from cases decided previously or because they believe that the precedent, although once valid, should be overruled. In the first instance, the judge rules that facts in the case being decided are sufficiently different from those found in previous cases that the legal principles announced in these cases do not apply. In *Gideon v. Wainwright* (1963), for example, the U.S. Supreme Court ruled that Clarence Gideon, an indigent defendant who was charged with a felony in a Florida state court, should have been provided with an attorney to assist him with his defense. According to the Court, "In our adversary system of criminal justice, any person haled into court, who is too poor to hire a lawyer, cannot be assured a fair trial unless counsel is provided for him." Sixteen years later, however, the Court ruled in the case of *Scott v. Illinois* (1979) that an indigent defendant who was sentenced only to pay a fine was not entitled to an attorney. The Court's earlier ruling that the right to a fair trial required the appointment of counsel for "any person haled into court" notwithstanding, in this case, the Court stated that the Constitution required only "that no indigent defendant be sentenced to a term of imprisonment unless the state has afforded him the right to assistance of appointed counsel in his defense." What distinguished the two cases, in other words, was the fact that Gideon was sentenced to prison whereas Scott was not.

Occasionally, judges will decide that the precedent is no longer valid and should not be followed. They can handle this in two ways. They can simply ignore the earlier case and decide the case at hand as if there was no binding precedent, or they can overrule the earlier case. Often the process of overruling a precedent is gradual. The court finds more and more circumstances that distinguish new cases from the earlier case, until it becomes obvious that the precedent has outlived its usefulness. Former Supreme Court Justice William O. Douglas (1974) argued that this gradual erosion of precedent "breeds uncertainty" since "years of litigation may be needed to rid the law of mischievous decisions which should have fallen with the first of the series to be overruled."

According to Justice Douglas, then, it makes more sense for the court to overrule the outdated precedent as soon as it is clear that it has to go. The Supreme Court has done so on a number of occasions. In *Taylor v. Louisiana* (1975), for example, the Supreme Court considered a Louisiana law that gave women a blanket exemption from jury service; women who wanted to serve were required to ask that their names be placed on the lists from which jurors were chosen. The result was that few women volunteered, and most defendants, including Billy Taylor, were tried by all-male juries. In *Taylor*, which was decided in 1975, the Supreme Court struck down the Louisiana law and overruled a 1961 decision, *Hoyt v. Florida*, upholding a nearly identical Florida law.

In the *Hoyt* case, the Court ruled that women "are the center of home and family life" and therefore should be allowed to decide for themselves whether jury service was an unreasonable burden. According to the Court's decision in the *Hoyt* case, it is not "constitutionally impermissible for a State, acting in pursuit of the general welfare, to conclude that a woman should be relieved from the civic duty of jury service unless she herself determines that such service is consistent with her own special responsibilities." Fourteen years later, the Court changed its mind, ruling that "if it was ever the case that women were unqualified to sit on juries or were so situated that none of them should be required to perform jury service, that time has long since passed." Clearly, the Court's interpretation of the requirement that the jury pool must be drawn from a **random cross section of the community**, as well as its view of the role of women, had changed. (See Table 1.2 for examples of other instances in which the Supreme Court overruled its own decisions.)

The fact that statutes and constitutional provisions are ambiguous and that judges cannot always look to precedent for guidance in specific cases, then, means that judges are frequently called on to make law. Judges, in other words, do not simply "find the law." As the *Hoyt* and *Taylor* cases reveal, in interpreting the law, they often must choose between competing social, economic, and political values.

Stare Decisis

Stare decisis means "let the decision stand." Under the principle of stare decisis, if there is a prior decision on a legal issue that applies to a current case, the court will be guided by that prior decision and apply the same legal principles in the current case. In situations in which the law is ambiguous and the same issue has come up before, it makes sense to look to past decisions—that is, to precedent—to see how the matter was resolved previously.

TABLE 1.2 ■ Examples of Supreme Court Decisions Overruled by Subsequent Decisions	
Original Case	**Subsequent Decision**
Plessy v. Ferguson (1896) Upheld the constitutionality of racial segregation in public accommodations under the "separate but equal" doctrine.	*Brown v. Board of Education* (1954) Struck down a Kansas law that established racially segregated public schools and stated that the doctrine of "separate but equal" has no place in education: "Separate educational facilities are inherently unequal."
Bowers v. Hardwick (1986) Upheld the constitutionality of a Georgia sodomy law; held that the right to privacy found in the Fourteenth Amendment does not extend to this type of sexual conduct.	*Lawrence v. Texas* (2003) Struck down a Texas sodomy law; held that intimate consensual sexual conduct is protected by the Fourteenth Amendment.
Booth v. Maryland (1987) The Eighth Amendment bars the use of victim impact statements during the penalty phase of a capital case; information provided in them is not relevant to the blameworthiness of the defendant. *South Carolina v. Gathers* (1989) The Eighth Amendment precludes prosecutors from introducing evidence of the victim's character during the penalty phase of a capital case.	*Payne v. Tennessee* (1991) The Eighth Amendment does not bar the admission of victim impact evidence or prosecutorial argument regarding the victim's character during the penalty phase of a capital trial; "a state may legitimately conclude that evidence about the victim and about the impact of the murder on the victim's family is relevant to the jury's decision as to whether or not the death penalty should be imposed."
Arkansas v. Sanders (1979) A police search of personal luggage taken from a lawfully detained vehicle requires a warrant under the Fourth Amendment.	*California v. Acevedo* (1991) Police may search a container in a vehicle without a warrant if they have probable cause to believe that it holds contraband or evidence.

For instance, in deciding whether searches are "unreasonable" under the Fourth Amendment, it makes sense for judges to examine past decisions regarding the issue. Stare decisis is thus the judicial practice of looking to the past for pertinent decisions and deferring to them. As Benjamin Cardozo (1974), who was a Supreme Court justice from 1932 to 1939, put it, the first thing a judge does "is to compare the case before him with the precedents, whether stored in his mind or hidden in books . . . in a system so highly developed as our own, precedents have so covered the ground that they fix the point of departure from which the labor of the judge begins" (p. 26).

Stare decisis, then, is the principle behind establishing the value of prior decisions, or precedent. It is a principle that assures us that if an issue has been decided one way, it will continue to be decided that way in future cases. Through a reliance on precedent and the principle of stare decisis, common-law courts were able to provide litigants with some degree of predictability regarding the courts' decisions.

Precedent establishes a legal principle, but not every pronouncement that a court makes in a ruling establishes precedent. Pronouncements that do are known as **ratio decidendi** ("the reason for the decision"), which is the legal principle or rationale used by the courts to arrive at their decisions. Additional supporting statements are called **obiter dicta** ("things said by the way"), or simply dicta. These statements are other legal or nonlegal arguments used to support the ratio decidendi and do not constitute precedent.

Precedent is not necessarily unchangeable. Judge-made law may be set aside or overruled by an act of the legislature if the constitution permits the legislature to do so. In addition, the court that issued the precedent may overrule it, or a higher court may reverse the decision of a lower court. If an intermediate-level appeals court decides an issue one way and the losing party appeals to a higher appeals court (such as a state supreme court), that higher court may reverse the decision of the lower court. Higher level courts are not bound by the judgments of lower courts. They are bound only by the decisions of courts above them in the court structure.

Stare decisis, then, involves a respect for and belief in the validity of precedent. Precedent is simply the influence of prior cases on current cases. Understandably, courts are reluctant to reverse decisions they made previously because this is a tacit admission of error. Courts do so, however, when presented with a compelling justification. Thus, stare decisis is not an inflexible doctrine but merely the general rule. There are always exceptions, as with most areas of the law.

Alternatively, rather than expressly overrule a prior decision, a court may instead seek to *distinguish* the prior case from the present case on grounds that the facts are slightly different. By doing so, the court can avoid overruling a prior decision while coming to what it considers the proper result in the present case. Until a decision is expressly overruled, it stands as an accurate statement of legal principles, or "good law."

Judicial Review

What happens when two prior decisions are in conflict, and there is no clear precedent? Or when one law comes into conflict with another? In the United States, the answer to that question is the courts, through the power of judicial review. **Judicial review** simply means the court has the power to examine a law and determine whether it is constitutional. To make this determination, judges must examine the law and compare it with the Constitution. This requires them to interpret the language of both the statute and the Constitution. If the judge determines the law is constitutional, he or she upholds the law; if not, he or she declares it unconstitutional and therefore void.

For example, the Fourth Amendment prohibits "unreasonable" searches. Suppose a state legislature passes a law allowing police officers to search anyone they encounter on a public street. Is this law constitutional? Or does it violate the prohibition on unreasonable searches? To answer this question, judges must examine the history and meaning of "unreasonable" as contained in the Fourth Amendment. They do this by examining precedent.

Judicial review is not specifically provided for in the Constitution. Rather, judicial review is judge-made law. *Marbury v. Madison* (1803) established the authority of the

KEY CASES

MARBURY V. MADISON

Marbury v. Madison is perhaps the most important case ever decided by the Supreme Court because it established the authority of the high court. Article III of the Constitution created the Supreme Court, but it did not discuss whether the Supreme Court could review legislation or interpret the Constitution.

At the time of the adoption of the Constitution, there was heated debate concerning which branch of government had the authority to declare an act void. There were three suggestions on how to handle such a situation: (1) Each branch within its sphere of authorized power has the final say; (2) the Supreme Court has the final say, but only as to the parties in cases before the court; and (3) the Supreme Court has the final say. This controversy was finally resolved by the opinion in *Marbury*. An examination of the case provides insight into this controversy and how the Supreme Court handled the situation.

President Adams, a Federalist, appointed 42 of his fellow Federalists as justices of the peace for the District of Columbia just days before turning over the office to incoming President Thomas Jefferson, a Democrat. Adams's secretary of state, John Marshall, delivered most of the commissions to the newly appointed justices of the peace but failed to deliver Marbury's.

The newly elected president's secretary of state, James Madison, refused to deliver Marbury's commission, so Marbury applied directly to the Supreme Court for a **writ of mandamus** (a writ compelling public officials to perform their duty). The Supreme Court was granted original jurisdiction in such matters by the Judiciary Act of 1789. The Supreme Court agreed to hear the case but was unable to hear it for 14 months because Congress passed a law that stopped the Supreme Court from meeting.

In 1803, the Supreme Court reconvened, heard the case, and decided Marbury was entitled to his commission but that the Supreme Court could not issue a writ of mandamus. Chief Justice John Marshall (formerly Adams's secretary of state) wrote the opinion of the court. Marshall said:

1. Marbury was entitled to his commission because he had a legal right that was not extinguished by the change in office of president or the failure to deliver the already-signed commission.

2. A writ of mandamus was a proper legal remedy for enforcing Marbury's right.

3. However, the Supreme Court lacked the constitutional authority to issue such a writ. This was because the Judiciary Act of 1789 gave the Supreme Court original jurisdiction in such cases, but this grant of authority to the Supreme Court was unconstitutional because Article III of the Constitution defined Supreme Court jurisdiction.

The Judiciary Act of 1789 had the effect of changing (by enlarging) the jurisdiction of the Supreme Court, but Congress cannot pass a statute that changes the Constitution. The only way to change the Constitution is through a constitutional amendment. As stated by Chief Justice Marshall, "an act of the legislature, repugnant to the Constitution, is void." In other words, the Constitution is superior to congressional legislation.

Prior to the decision in *Marbury*, Democrats argued that the Supreme Court lacked the authority to declare acts of other branches of the federal government unconstitutional, while Federalists supported judicial review. If the Supreme Court had issued a writ of mandamus, it could not have forced Madison to honor it. The Supreme Court thus was faced with a serious challenge to its authority. Marshall's opinion saved the court's prestige while allowing the Democrats to claim a political victory

(Continued)

(Continued)

(not having to appoint any more Federalists as justices of the peace). What was more important in the long term, the decision established as law the idea that the Supreme Court has the authority to review the constitutionality of congressional activity (and presidential acts): This is judicial review.

This was obviously a major victory for the Supreme Court, and although opposed at the time, it was accepted at least in part because the result in the case was satisfactory to opponents of a strong Supreme Court. The Supreme Court did not use the power of judicial review to invalidate congressional legislation again until 1857.

U.S. Supreme Court to engage in judicial review of the acts of the other branches of government. The Supreme Court stated in *Marbury* that it was the duty of the judiciary (rather than the U.S. president or Congress) to interpret the Constitution and to apply it to particular fact situations. The Court also said that it was the job of the courts to decide when other laws (acts of Congress or state laws) were in violation of the Constitution and to declare these laws null and void if they were. This is the doctrine of judicial review.

THE ROLE OF COURTS IN THE CRIMINAL JUSTICE SYSTEM

It is misleading to view criminal courts as institutions isolated from the rest of the criminal justice system. Courts, which clearly are integral to the administration of justice, are but one part of the larger criminal justice system. However, the courts play two important and unique roles in the criminal justice system. The first and most common is **adjudication** of criminal offenses. The second is **oversight**.

Adjudication

The primary role played by the courts is to adjudicate criminal offenses—to process defendants who have been arrested by the police and formally charged with criminal offenses. Prosecutors decide who should be charged and then, provided a plea agreement does not circumvent trial, the defendant is brought to court. The state presents its case and so does the defense. The judge decides matters of law, and the judge or jury decides whether the defendant should be held accountable for the crime in question. If the defendant is convicted, the judge also imposes a sentence.

Both law enforcement and corrections officials play supporting roles in the adjudication of criminal offenses. The police determine who will be brought to court, and corrections officials make postsentencing decisions that affect offenders' punishment. However, "the official labeling of someone as a convicted criminal, and the determination of legitimate punishment can be done only by a court" (Eisenstein et al., 1988, p. 9). This adjudication function is most prevalent in limited and general jurisdiction courts at the state level and in U.S. district courts at the federal level. Moreover, adjudication is the most common court function. That is because there are many more trial courts than appellate courts and many more criminal defendants who must be processed than appeals that are filed.

Oversight

Courts, particularly the appellate courts, provide oversight, not just over the lower courts but over the criminal justice system in general. First, when cases are appealed to a higher level, the appellate court decides whether proper procedure was followed at the lower level. The appellate court may be asked to decide whether the procedures used to select the jury were appropriate, whether the defendant was denied effective assistance of counsel, or whether the trial court judge should have moved the case to another jurisdiction because of prejudicial pretrial publicity. The appellate decision may come months or even years after the trial that led to the appeal, but the very ability of the appellate court to influence what can happen or should have happened at the lower level is the essence of oversight.

Appellate courts also oversee the actions of other criminal justice officials. They decide whether the behavior of police, prosecutors, defense attorneys, and corrections officials comports with or violates laws and constitutional provisions. Consider, for instance, the Supreme Court's landmark 1985 decision in *Tennessee v. Garner*. The Court ruled that police officers cannot use deadly force to apprehend unarmed fleeing felons unless use of deadly force is necessary to prevent the suspect's escape *and* "the officer has probable cause to believe that the suspect poses a significant threat of death or serious physical injury to the officer or others." The Court held that the Tennessee statute that permitted officers to use "all the necessary means to effect the arrest" of a fleeing suspect was unconstitutional. Because of the Supreme Court's far-reaching jurisdiction, its decision had implications for police officers across the nation. The fact that the appellate courts—and particularly the Supreme Court—can tell criminal justice officials how to behave (so as to protect people's constitutional rights) is an important element of their oversight function.

MOVIES AND THE COURTS
A Man for All Seasons (1966)

The protections that fall under the heading "due process" are now taken for granted in the American court system. But these rights did not always exist, and the early courts were not infrequently used to advance political (and personal) agendas rather than to do justice. An infamous historical example is depicted in *A Man for All Seasons*. This movie tells the story of the conflict between King Henry VIII and Sir Thomas More, the English Lord Chancellor. Henry VIII, a Catholic, seeks a divorce from his first wife, Catherine of Aragon, so that he may marry Anne Boleyn, who, he hopes, will bear his child. Divorce is generally not permitted by the Catholic Church at this time (the 16th century). He seeks the support of Sir Thomas More. More is a devout Catholic and although More does not agree with the King's desire to divorce, he remains silent.

(Continued)

(Continued)

More's principles are further tested, however, when the king is named the head of the Church of England and subsequently when Parliament requires all to take an oath of allegiance to the Church of England or face a charge of treason. An expert in the law, More knows that if he does not state why he is opposed to taking the oath, he cannot be considered a traitor; More refuses to take the oath and is nonetheless arrested and imprisoned in the Tower of London. When More is finally brought to trial, he remains silent until after being convicted of treason on perjured testimony of Richard Rich. He is then informed that Rich has been promoted to attorney general as a reward for his testimony against More. More then abandons his silence and denounces the illegal nature of the king's actions, arguing the pope is the only true leader of the Catholic Church, not the king of England. He further declares that the immunity of the Church from State interference is guaranteed by the Magna Carta. More is condemned to death and eventually beheaded.

SUMMARY

In this chapter, we discussed the meaning of law, the purpose of law, and the judicial function. Law is a written body of rules of conduct applicable to all members of a defined community, society, or culture that emanate from a governing authority and are enforced by its agents by the imposition of penalties for their violation.

We have traced thinking across the centuries about various aspects of the law, from Hammurabi to the present day. The law was relatively well developed in Hammurabi's Code, replacing a system of personal vengeance with a system in which a neutral third party was charged with making decisions in both criminal matters and business transactions.

Most sociological students of the law conduct their analyses from one of the two general sociological models of society: the consensus model or the conflict model. The consensus model views society as an integrated network of institutions held together by a common set of values. The law is seen as a neutral protector of the continuity and stability of these institutions and values. This perspective also views society as basically good and just. The conflict model holds the opposite view: Conflict rather than consensus is the main characteristic of society, and the law serves the purposes of the ruling classes. This view is presented most forcefully in the works of Marx and Engels. We indicated that all societies are characterized by both conflict and consensus, with one process dominating at one time and the other at another time.

In discussing the relationship between law and justice, we noted that it is only through law that justice can be achieved. We began by discussing the role of equity in the evolution of the common law. Separate courts of equity evolved in England in the 13th century because the common law had become overly rigid and often at odds with justice. These courts of equity, or Courts of Chancery, were directed to be flexible and to decide cases based on standards of fairness rather than on rigid rules of law. It is important to note that equity supplemented rather than replaced common law and that both systems benefitted by the cross-pollination of ideas over the centuries.

The rule of law is the only way that we can reasonably ensure that we are integrating important aspects of justice into our legal systems. The rule of law contains three irreducible elements: (1) a nation must recognize the supremacy of certain fundamental values and principles, (2) these values must be committed to writing, and (3) a system of procedures holding the government to these principles and values must be in place. The first two principles are relatively unproblematic, but the third, requiring a nation to honor the first two in practice as well as in theory, is much more so. The third principle is best articulated by the concept of due process, which is procedural restitutive justice in practice.

Herbert Packer's (1968) two "ideal-type" models of criminal justice are the *crime control* and *due process* models. The former emphasizes the protection of the community from the criminal, and the latter emphasizes the protection of the accused from the state. No modern legal system completely conforms to either of these ideal types. Rather, each system lies on a continuum somewhere between the extremes. Both models can take their positions too far, requiring some legal adjustment.

Don't overlook the Student Study Site with its useful study aids, such as self-quizzes, eFlashcards, and other assists, to help you get more from the course and improve your grade.

DISCUSSION QUESTIONS

1. What do you think are the main differences between legal rules and other kinds of rules?

2. Give one or two examples of how changing values and/or technology have led to changes in the law.

3. Do you believe that the "ruling class" (decide for yourselves who these people may be) unfairly pass laws favorable to themselves and detrimental to the rest of us? If they do, what can we do about it?

4. In what ways can conflict be beneficial to a society? Can conflict actually support consensus?

5. Would you choose to live under a brutal dictator such as Hitler, Stalin, or Saddam Hussein or suffer the chaos of a society without any kind of law?

6. Why is law sometimes at odds with justice? Give an example.

7. Relate the rule of law to Packer's models of criminal justice.

8. Explain the concept of judicial review.

9. Why is *Marbury v. Madison* such an important decision?

10. What are some of the benefits of the common-law approach?

KEY TERMS

Adjudication 24
Code of Hammurabi 4
Common law 17
Conflict theorists 5
Consensus theorists 5
Crime control model 11
Due process 9
Due process model 10

Equity 7
False consciousness 7
Inquisitorial system 18
Judicial review 22
Law 4
Obiter dicta 22
Oversight 24
Precedent 17

Presumption of guilt 12
Presumption of innocence 12
Random cross section of the community 20
Ratio decidendi 22
Stare decisis 20
Writ of mandamus 23

INTERNET SITES

American Bar Association: www.americanbar.org/aba.html

The Common Law: www.lectlaw.com/def/c070.htm

Federal Judicial Center: www.fjc.gov

National Center for State Courts: www.ncsc.org

U.S. Department of Justice, Office of the Attorney General: www.usdoj.gov/ag

STUDENT STUDY SITE

Get the tools you need to sharpen your study skills. SAGE edge offers a robust online environment featuring an impressive array of free tools and resources.

Access practice quizzes, eFlashcards, video, and multimedia at **edge.sagepub.com/hemmens4e**

2

SOURCES OF LAW

SAGE edge™

Master the content at **edge.sagepub.com/hemmens4e**

INTRODUCTION

In this chapter, we discuss the sources of the law and the sources of individual rights. These foundational matters set the stage for our discussion of the criminal court system in following chapters. Courts serve, at the trial level in particular, as a forum for dispute resolution. But they also serve as interpreters of laws. Without courts to apply and interpret it, the law would be incomplete. The law is a social institution, and to study it is to gain valuable understanding of one's society, its heritage, its values, and its day-to-day functioning.

Law has always been considered of the utmost importance in American life. Law justly promulgated and justly applied is the bedrock of individual liberty and social progress. Law is a written body of rules of conduct applicable to all members of a defined community, society, or culture that emanate from a governing authority and are enforced by its agents by the imposition of penalties for their violation.

Law has several sources, including constitutions, statutes, and judicial opinions, or case law. Laws define the appropriate conduct for the members of a society and also provide protections for individuals from interference in their lives by other entities, including other people and the government. Even though legal scholars and philosophers debate endlessly the precise origin of various individual rights, it is clear that in America, a number of individual rights are either created by or enshrined in documents such as the federal and state constitutions and statutes. In this chapter we examine these documents and some of the most significant individual rights.

SOURCES OF LAW

Primary sources of law include judge-made law (also called common law) and statutory law (this includes the Constitution, statutes, ordinances, and administrative regulations). There are other sources for what constitutes appropriate conduct, such as religion and ethics; these are beyond the scope of this chapter.

Legislation is enacted by the legislature under the authority granted to it by the Constitution. A **constitution** creates a government; it literally *constitutes* the government. Legislatures are given authority to act in certain areas, and within these areas they may pass legislative enactments or bills, often referred to as statutes, which are collected into codes, such as the criminal code.

Legislators, sometimes referred to as lawmakers, quite literally make law. Acts of the legislature are not, however, lawful per se. In other words, just because a legislature passes a bill does not mean the bill is a lawful exercise of the legislature's authority. Acts of the legislature may not limit the constitution under which the legislation was created. For instance, the U.S. Congress may not lawfully pass legislation that abridges the Fourth Amendment.

Who decides when the legislature has acted beyond the scope of its authority? In the United States, the Supreme Court has the final say as to the constitutionality of statutes passed by either state or federal legislatures.

Administrative regulations are another form of legislation, which, under certain circumstances, may have the force of law. This means that they will be enforced by the courts just like a statute. Administrative regulations are issued either by agencies of the executive branch, which derive their authority from a delegation of power by the executive, or by independent agencies, created through a delegation of power from the legislature. Examples include regulations affecting food and drugs and occupational safety requirements. Both the federal government and state governments issue administrative regulations.

Statutes are frequently written in broad terms, leaving room for interpretation by those who must enforce them. This is also true of the U.S. Constitution. For example, the Eighth Amendment prohibits "cruel and unusual punishment." But what is cruel? What is unusual? There are no clear answers to these questions, and courts are forced to define the terms.

Why are statutes often vague? Why does the legislature not state precisely what it means? There are several reasons. First, it is difficult to clearly articulate in a statute precisely what conduct is or is not permitted, given the complexities of human behavior.

Second, drafting and enacting legislation requires legislators to work together to create a statute that can be supported by a majority. This often occurs when the statute deals with a controversial issue. The legislature may be forced to leave some things undefined, thereby forcing courts to interpret the terms of a statute.

SOURCES OF INDIVIDUAL RIGHTS

There are a number of sources of **individual rights** in the United States. These include the U.S. Constitution and state constitutions, case law, and federal and state statutes. Individual rights are defined as those that protect the individual citizen from other citizens as well as the federal or state government. Examples include the right to due process of law, the right to equal protections of the laws, and the right to be free from unreasonable searches and seizures. The Bill of Rights, which consists of the first ten amendments to the Constitution, provides a number of individual rights. States may provide additional rights in their constitutions, but they cannot restrict the rights provided in the U.S. Constitution.

The Constitution

In 1787, delegates from the 13 original states met in Philadelphia to write a new constitution to replace the Articles of Confederation. The Articles of Confederation, created in 1781, were widely regarded as a failure, as they left virtually all power in the hands of the individual states; as a result, it was difficult to establish a unified national government. The states were more akin to countries, acting in their own self-interest, than states that were part of a union.

The result of the convention was the development of the U.S. Constitution. The Constitution outlined the powers and limits of the federal government. Its focus was on how the new federal government would act, not on the relationship between the government and the individual citizen. There are only three individual rights mentioned in the Constitution: (1) the right to seek a **writ of habeas corpus** (a document challenging

COMPARATIVE COURTS

When the Union of Soviet Socialist Republics (USSR) collapsed and was split into separate countries, Russia had to develop a new constitution. This constitution was adopted in December 1993. It was the product of a contentious debate between the legislature (Duma) and then-president Boris Yeltsin. Following the adoption of the constitution, many observers predicted Russia would become a dictatorship, as the constitution gave much of the power to the president, at the expense of the legislative branch. As it turned out, however, President Yeltsin never used the power to dissolve the legislature granted to him in the constitution, and instead the branches of government (executive,

legislative, and courts) and government agencies have remained in place and intact. In fact, the Russian legislature on several occasions passed laws opposed by President Yeltsin and even voted "no confidence" in the executive branch.

The Russian constitution comprises nine sections; Section 7 contains the powers of the judiciary. The country has a civil law system. There is a Supreme Court, but it lacks the power to issue advisory opinions and can only issue opinions in cases that come before it, similar to the U.S. Supreme Court. Judicial opinions are written down and are generally available for examination, but it is unclear to what degree lower courts are expected to follow them.

the legality of a person's detention), (2) the prohibition of **bills of attainder** (legislation imposing punishment without a trial), and (3) the prohibition of **ex post facto laws** (legislation making prior conduct criminal).

When the proposed Constitution was submitted to the 13 states for ratification, a number of states were unwilling to ratify it without a clear detailing of the rights that individual citizens had against the federal government. Many people, remembering the excesses of the king under colonial rule, were afraid the federal government would be able to restrict individual rights such as the freedom of religion. In response to these concerns, 10 amendments, commonly referred to as the Bill of Rights, were added, and the Constitution was ratified in 1791.

The Bill of Rights

The **Bill of Rights** constitutes the first 10 amendments to the Constitution. There are 23 specific individual rights in the Bill of Rights. These rights originally applied only to the federal government, as it was not until the 20th century that the provisions of the Bill of Rights were applied to state governments via the Fourteenth Amendment (discussed later). This was done by the U.S. Supreme Court through a process referred to as incorporation, in a series of decisions stretching over a period of more than 50 years. To comprehend due process and individual rights in a criminal courts context, it is essential to examine the Bill of Rights further to delineate what rights defendants actually have throughout the adjudicative process. These rights, pursuant to some of the amendments within the Bill of Rights, are briefly discussed next.

First Amendment

The First Amendment includes a number of individual rights, among them the freedoms of religion, speech, press, and assembly. Each of these individual rights were very important to colonists, and it was their frequent abridgement by King George III of England that helped precipitate the American Revolution.

The First Amendment includes two clauses on religion. First, the government is forbidden from creating a state-supported religion. Second, the government is barred from interfering with individuals' religious practices. In essence, the federal government is not supposed to promote a particular religion or prevent the practice of religion.

The first clause is known as the Establishment Clause. This creates what the Supreme Court has referred to as a "wall of separation between church and state" (*Everson v. Board of Education,* 1947). According to the Supreme Court, any statute that affects religious practices is valid only if three conditions are met: (1) the statute has a secular (non-religious) purpose, (2) the primary purpose of the statute is neutral (meaning it neither promotes nor interferes with religious practice), and (3) the statute does not result in "excessive" government involvement with religion (*Lemon v. Kurtzman,* 1971).

> ### The First Amendment
>
> *Congress shall make no law respecting an establishment of religion, or prohibiting the free exercise thereof; or abridging the freedom of speech, or of the press; or the right of the people peaceably to assemble, and to petition the Government for a redress of grievances.*

This does not mean that there are no limitations whatsoever on the freedom of religion. The Supreme Court has held that a statute that incidentally restricts religious practices is constitutional. For example, a state may ban the use of mind-altering substances (including peyote) in prisons, despite the fact that doing so infringes on the legitimate religious practices of some Native American inmates.

Freedom of speech is one of the most valued individual rights. The right is not without limitations, however. At times in the past the Supreme Court has been willing to allow state limitations on a variety of forms of speech. The Supreme Court has held that the government can regulate obscene materials, including books and movies that

MOVIES AND THE COURTS
Inherit the Wind (1960)

The First Amendment protects the individual's right to exercise his or her religious beliefs and forbids the state from either interfering with religion or supporting a particular religion. The debate over the role of religion in American life has gone on since the first colonists arrived. One of the great battles, and one that is still going on in some states, is the role of religious beliefs in public education. If one's religious beliefs include the belief that evolution is not accurate, what is one to do? *Inherit the Wind* is a highly fictionalized account of the infamous Scopes Monkey Trial, as it was referred to, which dealt with the issue of whether a state could criminalize the teaching of evolution in high school. In the movie, set in the 1920s in Tennessee, schoolteacher Bertram Cates is put on trial for violating a state law that prohibits public school teachers from teaching evolution instead of creationism. At the trial, the attorneys for the state and for the defense spar over the meaning of the Bible. In real life, the two attorneys were Clarence Darrow (for the defense) and William Jennings Bryan (appearing on behalf of the state as an expert witness).

appeal to a "prurient" interest in sex (meaning an abnormal, as opposed to a "normal" interest in the activity) (*Miller v. California,* 1973). Commercial speech (such as advertising) may be regulated to a greater degree than so-called political speech (*Virginia State Board of Pharmacy v. Virginia Citizens Consumers Council, Inc.,* 1976).

In the latter part of the 20th century, however, the Court began to provide greater protection of freedom of speech. The Supreme Court has held that the freedom of speech includes the right to say things that may anger others. The Court also has held that the freedom of speech includes not just verbal statements (what we generally think of as "speech") but written statements (such as political protest signs) and some physical acts, such as burning the American flag to protest government intervention in South America (*Texas v. Johnson,* 1988). These acts are termed "symbolic speech" or "expressive conduct."

Second Amendment

The Second Amendment states that citizens have the right to "keep and bear arms" and that this right shall not be "infringed." Opponents of gun control legislation argue that this amendment prevents the state from enacting legislation that restricts in any manner the use and possession of firearms. Supporters of gun control legislation assert that the amendment was not intended to create an individual right to possess firearms, but instead to create a right for groups of citizens who wanted to form a militia to have firearms to protect themselves against oppression by the federal government. There was a great concern at the time of the passage of the Bill of Rights that the federal government might become oppressive (similar to the situation under the king of England), and allowing people to form militias would not be of much use if the federal government had outlawed weapons.

The Second Amendment

A well regulated Militia, being necessary to the security of a free State, the right of the people to keep and bear Arms, shall not be infringed.

In *District of Columbia v. Heller* (2008), the U.S. Supreme Court endorsed the view of opponents of gun control legislation, holding that the Second Amendment was intended to provide individual gun owners with a right to own firearms. The decision left some questions unanswered, however, as it appeared to allow for some degree of regulation but set no standard for evaluating that regulation. For example, Justice Scalia's opinion for the Court claimed that the decision was not meant to cast doubt on the constitutionality of "longstanding prohibitions" on gun ownership by felons. It remains to be seen precisely what limitations on firearm possession will withstand constitutional scrutiny.

The Third Amendment

No Soldier shall, in time of peace be quartered in any house, without the consent of the Owner, nor in time of war, but in a manner to be prescribed by law.

Third Amendment

The Third Amendment was a product of its times. During the American Revolution, English troops were frequently housed in the homes of citizens, against the wishes of the home's owner. The Third Amendment makes such a practice unconstitutional by expressly forbidding the "quartering," or housing, of soldiers in private homes without the permission of the homeowner.

Fourth Amendment

The Fourth Amendment forbids "unreasonable" searches and seizures by law enforcement officers and requires the existence of "probable cause" before arrest or search warrants may be issued. Warrants are required to describe the subject of their search with "particularity." The so-called particularity requirement was a response to the British practice in colonial times of issuing general warrants. General warrants allowed British customs inspectors to search without restriction on time or place for evidence of customs violations. Requiring warrant applications to describe precisely what was sought was an attempt to eliminate general warrants.

Similarly, requiring the police to have probable cause to believe there was something to seize or arrest was intended to limit the ability of the state to interfere at will in the lives of individual citizens without some justification. This amount of evidence of wrongdoing is **probable cause**. Probable cause is best defined as a fair probability that a crime has occurred. It is less than proof beyond a reasonable doubt but more than a mere guess.

The Supreme Court has determined that search and arrest warrants are not always required, however. The Reasonableness Clause allows the police to conduct a search or make an arrest so long as it is reasonable to do so. So what is reasonable and what is not? The Supreme Court has issued a number of decisions in an effort to define this phrase, but it remains less than crystal clear.

> **The Fourth Amendment**
>
> *The right of the people to be secure in their persons, houses, papers, and effects, against unreasonable searches and seizures, shall not be violated, and no Warrants shall issue, but upon probable cause, supported by Oath or affirmation, and particularly describing the place to be searched, and the persons or things to be seized.*

KEY CASES

MANUEL V. CITY OF JOLIET, ILLINOIS, ET AL. (2017)

In *Manuel v. City of Joliet, Illinois, et al.*, Manuel was found to be in possession of pills during a search incident to a traffic stop. The officers arrested him despite the field test showing that none of the pills tested positive for any illicit drug. The evidence technician at the station found the same results; however, in his report he claimed that one pill tested positive for ecstasy, which confirmed one of the officer's unfounded statements about the nature of the pills. Manuel was charged and detained prior to trial. Later, the Illinois police lab found that none of the pills tested positive. Nonetheless, Manuel remained in pretrial detention for 48 days! After his case was eventually dismissed, Manuel filed a lawsuit against the city and the officers, claiming that they violated his Fourth Amendment rights. The district court argued that the statute of limitation had run out in regard to his unlawful arrest claim and that precedent precluded any Fourth Amendment relief in cases where pretrial detention happened *after* the commencement of legal proceedings (i.e., the judge's determination that probable cause existed in order to detain him). The Seventh Circuit agreed with the lower court. The Supreme Court argued to the contrary, that the Fourth Amendment governs pretrial detention as well as arrests. Thus, Manuel could challenge his detention, as the Fourth Amendment covers his arrest *and* detainment. Also, the Court stated that unconstitutional pretrial detention can happen before and after the commencement of legal proceedings. Because probable cause is necessary to detain someone, when that probable cause is predicated on false statements, the individual's Fourth Amendment claims do not go away due to the commencement of the legal process.

The Fifth Amendment

No person shall be held to answer for a capital, or otherwise infamous crime, unless on presentment or indictment of a Grand Jury, except in cases arising in the land or naval forces, or in the Militia, when in actual service in time of War or public danger; nor shall any person be subject for the same offence to be twice put in jeopardy of life or limb; nor shall be compelled in any criminal case to be a witness against himself, nor be deprived of life, liberty, or property, without due process of law; nor shall private property be taken for public use, without just compensation.

Fifth Amendment

The Fifth Amendment includes a variety of individual rights, including the right to indictment by a grand jury, the prohibition of double jeopardy, the right to due process of law, and the privilege against self-incrimination. These rights are all related to criminal prosecutions. Many of the provisions of the Fifth Amendment were developed in reaction to brutal investigatory practices developed in Europe, such as torture and forced confessions.

The Fifth Amendment requires that a person be indicted by a grand jury before he or she may be put on trial. A **grand jury** comprises citizens who listen to the case presented by a prosecutor and decide whether there exists sufficient evidence to put the defendant on trial. The grand jury is intended to prevent the government from prosecuting people without some proof of guilt. Thus, the grand jury is meant to serve as a barrier between the citizen and an overzealous prosecutor.

An **indictment** is a legal document that charges a defendant with a crime. The requirement of an indictment before criminal prosecution is one of a handful of provisions of the Bill of Rights that has not been incorporated into the Fourteenth Amendment and applied to the states. In *Hurtado v. California* (1884), the Supreme Court held that the right does not apply to state criminal trials, and this decision never has been overruled. It is important to note that many states, per statute or state constitution, either require an indictment or give prosecutors the choice of seeking an indictment or proceeding through an information. An **information** is a substitute for an indictment, and it is a legal document filed directly with the court by the prosecutor.

The Fifth Amendment also prohibits putting a person in **double jeopardy**. This means a jurisdiction may not (a) prosecute someone again for the same crime after the person has been acquitted, (b) prosecute someone again for the same crime after the person has been convicted, or (c) punish someone twice for the same offense. This does not mean a state may not try someone again if the first trial results in a mistrial or a hung jury. A mistrial may be declared if a legal error occurs during a trial that unfairly prejudices the defendant and cannot be cured by the court. A **hung jury** occurs when the jury is unable to reach a unanimous verdict. A unanimous verdict is not a constitutional requirement (*Duncan v. Louisiana,* 1968), but most states still require it. In those states where a unanimous verdict is required, if the jury is deadlocked and the judge believes that further deliberations would not change the outcome, he or she may excuse the jury and order a new trial. When this happens, there has been neither an acquittal nor a conviction. An **acquittal** occurs when a jury votes unanimously that the defendant has not been proven guilty "beyond a reasonable doubt" by the prosecution. An acquittal does not necessarily mean that the jury believes the defendant is innocent of the crime charged; it simply means that the state was unable to meet the high burden of proof necessary for conviction. There is no such thing as a verdict of "innocent." Furthermore, if a conviction is overturned on appeal, the state may retry the person because a reversal on appeal is not an acquittal; it is merely a determination by the appellate court that the defendant did not receive a fair trial and that the trial must be redone.

While the Double Jeopardy Clause bars multiple punishments for the same offense, there are exceptions. Under the **dual-sovereignty doctrine**, a person may be prosecuted in both federal and state court for an act that is a crime under both state and federal law. For instance, if a person kills a postal worker in Idaho, he or she could be prosecuted in Idaho state court for murder or in federal court for the murder of a postal worker, which is a federal offense. Here, one act results in a crime in two different jurisdictions.

The Fifth Amendment also provides the privilege against self-incrimination. Although this is referred to as a *privilege* rather than a *right*, courts do not distinguish between the two terms. The privilege against self-incrimination allows a person to refuse to speak to police and to refuse to testify at trial. The individual cannot be compelled to speak if he or she does not wish to. The intent is to force the state to prove its case against a citizen without the cooperation of the citizen, unless the citizen chooses to cooperate. In addition, if a defendant chooses not to testify at trial, the prosecutor cannot comment on the defendant's silence, because doing so would limit the privilege against self-incrimination by suggesting that a defendant's assertion of a constitutional right was somehow evidence of something to hide (*Griffin v. California,* 1965).

The privilege against self-incrimination is not absolute, however. The Supreme Court has held that the privilege only applies to "testimonial communications," or spoken confessions (*Malloy v. Hogan,* 1964). The privilege does not apply to the obtaining of evidence from a suspect by other means, such as taking blood samples or fingerprints.

The Fifth Amendment also provides for due process of law. Exactly what constitutes due process of law is much debated. In general, due process refers to the procedures (such as an indictment or a fair trial) that the state must provide before it may deprive an individual of his or her life, liberty, or property. This applies not only to criminal trial but to situations where the state seeks to take private property for a public use through the process of condemnation.

Sixth Amendment

The Sixth Amendment contains a number of individual rights associated with the criminal trial. They include the right to a speedy trial, the right to a public trial, the right to a trial by an impartial jury, the right to notice of the charges against oneself, the right to representation by counsel, and the right to confront the witnesses against oneself.

The Sixth Amendment

In all criminal prosecutions, the accused shall enjoy the right to a speedy and public trial, by an impartial jury of the State and district wherein the crime shall have been committed, which district shall have been previously ascertained by law, and to be informed of the nature and cause of the accusation; to be confronted with the witnesses against him; to have compulsory process for obtaining witnesses in his favor, and to have the Assistance of Counsel for his defense.

The right to a speedy trial means that a defendant must be put on trial without "unnecessary delay" (*Barker v. Wingo,* 1972). In this case, the Supreme Court determined that there is no precise amount of time that constitutes "speedy" and that this must be determined on a case-by-case basis. In Barker's case, the Court held that a 5-year delay between arrest and trial was not an "unnecessary delay" because Barker had not objected to the delay during the 5 years prior to trial. The U.S. Congress responded to this decision by passing the Speedy Trial Act of 1974, which set a specific time limit of 100 days from arrest to trial. This act only applies to federal cases, but most states have enacted similar legislation.

The right to a public trial means defendants have a right to have the public attend the trial if they so desire. The right to notice of the charges against the defendant means the prosecution must inform the defendant prior to trial precisely what he or she is accused of so the defendant's attorneys can prepare a defense to the crime charged. This can occur through either an indictment by the grand jury or the filing of an information by the prosecutor. Both of these rights emanate from the traditional Anglo-Saxon distrust of secrecy in government as a menace to liberty.

The right to a trial by an impartial jury means the defendant has a right to a jury that is not predisposed to believe the defendant is guilty. The members of the jury are not expected to be unaware of the events that led to the trial, but they must be able to set aside what they have learned prior to trial and make a determination of the defendant's guilt or innocence based solely on the evidence presented at trial. Trial by jury is an ancient right mentioned in the Magna Carta (1215).

The Sixth Amendment also provides a defendant with the right to the assistance of counsel. The Supreme Court has interpreted this right to include representation not only during the trial but at any pretrial proceeding that is deemed to be a "critical stage" in the fact-finding process (*Kirby v. Illinois,* 1972). Precisely what constitutes a critical stage is subject to some dispute, but it includes the preliminary hearing, the arraignment, the trial itself, and the **right of appeal**.

The **right to counsel** includes the right of indigent persons who cannot afford to hire a lawyer to be provided with a lawyer at the state's expense (*Gideon v. Wainwright,* 1963). The Supreme Court has limited this to situations where the defendant faces the possibility of incarceration for 6 months or more, however (*Argersinger v. Hamlin,* 1972). In addition, the Supreme Court has held that the right to counsel includes the right to the *effective* assistance of counsel (*Strickland v. Washington,* 1984). This means an attorney must not be incompetent and must provide the defendant with an adequate defense. Although this sounds reasonable in theory, in practice the Supreme Court has been very reluctant to find that an attorney's conduct has been so bad as to be legally "ineffective."

The Seventh Amendment

In Suits at common law, where the value in controversy shall exceed twenty dollars, the right of trial by jury shall be preserved, and no fact tried by a jury, shall be otherwise reexamined in any Court of the United States, than according to the rules of the common law.

Seventh Amendment

The Seventh Amendment provides defendants in civil lawsuits filed in federal court with the right to a trial by jury. This amendment applies only to federal trials; it does not apply to civil lawsuits filed in state courts.

Eighth Amendment

The Eighth Amendment bars the state from several actions, including imposing excessive bail on a defendant prior to trial and engaging in cruel and unusual punishment. Both of these prohibitions are written vaguely, and the Supreme Court has at times struggled to interpret them in a consistent fashion.

> ### The Eighth Amendment
>
> *Excessive bail shall not be required, nor excessive fines imposed, nor cruel and unusual punishments inflicted.*

What constitutes excessive bail? The Supreme Court has determined that bail should be set at a figure no higher than necessary to ensure the presence of the defendant at trial (*Stack v. Boyle,* 1951). The amount of bail is not supposed to be based on the defendant's income level. The Eighth Amendment does not provide an absolute, unlimited right to bail, but every state provides for a right to bail in most cases. Bail does not have to be granted, and the Supreme Court has held that bail may be denied altogether if a person is found to be a threat to public safety (*United States v. Salerno,* 1987).

The prohibition on cruel and unusual punishment limits the type and method of punishment that may be imposed on a defendant by the state after conviction. It prohibits torture as well as punishment that is disproportionate to the offense (meaning the punishment should, in some sense, fit the crime and not be excessive). What constitutes inappropriate punishment has changed over time. For instance, at one time corporal punishment (such as whipping) was considered an acceptable form of punishment, but no state today allows the practice. The Cruel and Unusual Punishment Clause does not prohibit the death penalty because it is deemed to be in accord with contemporary standards of decency, and the death penalty existed at the time of the passage of the Eighth Amendment (*Gregg v. Georgia,* 1976).

Ninth Amendment

The Ninth Amendment simply states that the listing of some individual rights in the Constitution should not be construed as a listing of the only rights retained by citizens. In other words, the rights provided in the Bill of Rights should not be taken as the only rights that citizens have; they are merely some of the rights retained by the people. The obvious question is this: If the Bill of Rights is not all-inclusive, what exactly are the other rights retained by the people? The Supreme Court has struggled to provide a framework for delineating these rights, as the discussion on incorporation (later in this chapter) indicates.

> ### The Ninth Amendment
>
> *The enumeration in the Constitution, of certain rights, shall not be construed to deny or disparage others retained by the people.*

In at least one case, the Supreme Court expressly mentioned the Ninth Amendment as providing a basis for giving individual citizens other, unenumerated rights, such as a right to privacy (*Griswold v. Connecticut,* 1965). Griswold was the director of the Planned Parenthood League of Connecticut, and he and the league's medical director had been found guilty of dispensing birth control advice and devices (both then illegal in Connecticut) for which they were fined $100 each. In overturning their conviction, the Supreme Court affirmed that the right to privacy is a very important right while acknowledging that it is not specifically mentioned anywhere in the Constitution. Justice Douglas, who delivered the Court's majority opinion in *Griswold*, stated that the specific constitutional guarantees of the Bill of Rights "have **penumbras** [incompletely lighted areas] formed by emanations from these guarantees that help give them life and substance." In other words, although the right to privacy is not specifically mentioned in the Constitution, such a right can be logically deduced from the rights that are. *Griswold* was a very important step to *Roe v. Wade* (1973), which granted abortion rights to women under the principle of privacy, and to *Lawrence v. Texas* (2003), which outlawed sodomy statutes under the same principle.

The Tenth Amendment

The powers not delegated to the United States by the Constitution, nor prohibited by it to the States, are reserved to the States respectively, or to the people.

Tenth Amendment

The Tenth Amendment states that the rights not delegated to the federal government in the Constitution are reserved for the states or individual citizens. This is simply the principle of federalism; the federal government is a government of enumerated (or listed) powers. This means it has no authority to act unless so granted by the Constitution. And where the federal government has no authority, the states and individual citizens retain the authority.

The individual rights provided in the Bill of Rights are set forth in Table 2.1.

TABLE 2.1 ■ Individual Rights Contained in the Bill of Rights	
Amendment	**Rights**
First Amendment	Freedom of speech, press, and assembly, freedom of and from religion
Second Amendment	Right to bear arms
Third Amendment	Freedom from quartering soldiers
Fourth Amendment	Freedom from unreasonable searches and seizures; warrants must be based on probable cause and stated with specificity
Fifth Amendment	Grand jury indictment, freedom from double jeopardy and self-incrimination, rights to due process and to just compensation for takings
Sixth Amendment	Rights to speedy trial, to impartial jury, to be informed of charges, to obtain witnesses on one's behalf, to face accusers, and to an attorney
Eighth Amendment	Freedom from excessive bail or fines and from cruel and unusual punishment
Ninth Amendment	Listing of rights in the Bill of Rights does not imply the absence of other rights, such as the right to privacy

Due Process and the Fourteenth Amendment

In addition to the individual rights listed in the Bill of Rights, several other amendments include individual rights. These include the so-called Reconstruction Amendments (the Thirteenth, Fourteenth, and Fifteenth Amendments), which were passed shortly after the Civil War and intended to protect the recently freed slaves from abuse by the Southern states. While initially intended to prevent the Southern states from limiting the rights of the recently freed slaves, today these amendments, particularly the Fourteenth, are used to protect all citizens from state actions that impinge on constitutional rights.

Fourteenth Amendment

The Fourteenth Amendment is a very long amendment that has five sections. We include only the first section here, which has to do with individual rights. It is significant because it is the first amendment that applies to the states, as opposed to the federal government. Whereas the Bill of Rights was developed out of a fear of how the federal government might mistreat citizens, after the Civil War Congress recognized that individual states, particularly those in the South that had until recently allowed slavery, were just as capable of oppressing citizens as the federal government. Congress responded by enacting the Fourteenth Amendment, which forbids states from denying citizens due process of law or equal protection of the laws. These two clauses have dramatically altered the way that states may deal with citizens.

The Due Process Clause of the Fourteenth Amendment is identical to the Due Process Clause in the Fifth Amendment. It has been interpreted by the Supreme Court as incorporating (or applying) the various provisions of the Bill of Rights and making them applicable to the states. The Equal Protection Clause has been interpreted to prevent states from making unequal, arbitrary distinctions between people. It does not ban all discrimination by the state but requires that when the state treats people differently, it does so on the basis of reasonable classifications. It also bars discrimination on the basis of race, religion, or (in most instances) gender. These are referred to as **suspect classifications**. To put it another way, where the law limits the liberty of *all* persons, due process is involved; where the law treats *certain classes of people* differently, equal protection is involved.

Not all classifications by the state necessarily violate the Equal Protection Clause. States may treat people differently if they have a legitimate reason to do so. Thus, states may limit the practice of medicine to those who have a license or limit the age at which a person may lawfully consume alcoholic beverages. Classifications based on age are

> **The Fourteenth Amendment**
>
> *All persons born or naturalized in the United States, and subject to the jurisdiction thereof, are citizens of the United States and of the State wherein they reside. No State shall make or enforce any law which shall abridge the privileges or immunities of citizens of the United States; nor shall any State deprive any person of life, liberty, or property, without due process of law; nor deny to any person within its jurisdiction the equal protection of the laws.*

generally permitted based on the state's interest in the health and welfare of juveniles and because there exists no history of "invidious" discrimination against minors, as exists for minorities and women. Last, it is worth noting that the Equal Protection Clause does not prohibit discrimination of any kind, including discrimination based on race or gender, when the discrimination is practiced by private citizens. The Fourteenth Amendment applies only to state action, not to the actions of private citizens who are not affiliated in any way with the state.

STANDARD OF REVIEW

In constitutional law, the outcome of a case is often determined by the standard of review the court uses. Not all the individual protections set forth in the Bill of Rights are accorded the same level of protection by the courts. There exists a hierarchy of rights. Courts employ either strict scrutiny review or rational basis review, depending on whether a fundamental right is implicated or a suspect classification is affected. We discuss each of these terms here.

Fundamental rights are those individual rights the Supreme Court has determined are "essential to the concept of ordered liberty." By this the Court means these rights are the most important of all (*Palko v. Connecticut,* 1937). Examples include almost all the individual rights listed in the Bill of Rights, as well as the Fourteenth Amendment guarantees of due process and equal protection. A suspect classification is one that is presumed to be based on an unconstitutional basis. To date, the Supreme Court has held that only race and religion are suspect classifications in all circumstances.

CURRENT RESEARCH

It is one thing to have certain rights, such as the rights to remain silent and to have an attorney. It is another thing altogether to understand and be able to then assert these rights. The American Bar Association has called for **Miranda warnings** that can be understood by juveniles in police custody. In a study conducted by Rogers and colleagues (2012), the researchers sought to determine the degree to which juveniles understood their rights. In surveying prosecutors and public defenders, the researchers collected 293 juvenile Miranda warnings that were intended specifically for youthful offenders. Length and reading levels were analyzed and compared to an earlier survey. Nearly two thirds (64.9%) of these warnings were very long ($\rightarrow$175 words), which hinders Miranda comprehension. In addition, most juvenile warnings (91.6%) required reading comprehension higher than a 6th-grade level; 5.2% exceeded a 12th-grade reading level. More than half of juvenile Miranda warnings were found to be highly problematic because of excessive lengths or difficult reading comprehension. However, simple and easily read Miranda components were identified that could be used to improve juvenile advisements.

Source: "Juvenile Miranda Warnings: Perfunctory Rituals or Procedural Safeguards?" Richard Rogers, Hayley L. Blackwood, Chelsea E. Fiduccia, Jennifer A. Steadham, Eric Y. Drogin, and Jill E. Rogstad. *Criminal Justice and Behavior*, 39(3): 229–249, 2012.

Under **strict scrutiny** review, a statute that abridges a fundamental right or impacts a suspect classification will be determined to be unconstitutional unless (a) the state has a compelling interest, which justifies restricting a fundamental right, and (b) the legislation restricting that right is "narrowly tailored" so that the right is not limited any more than absolutely necessary to achieve the state's compelling interest. A criminal justice–related example of a compelling interest is the state's interest in the safe and secure operation of prisons.

This standard of review is referred to as strict scrutiny review because the court looks closely at the purpose and effect of the legislation rather than merely accepting the claims of the legislature that the statute is needed. The reason for employing a higher standard of review when a statute affects a fundamental right or suspect classification is that closer analysis is required when important individual rights are affected. The burden of proof is on the state to demonstrate the constitutionality of legislation under strict scrutiny review.

Laws involving quasi–suspect classifications (such as gender, legitimacy, and poverty) are reviewed under the **intermediate scrutiny** standard. A statute will be upheld if the Court finds that it is *substantially related* to an *important* government purpose. The burden of proof lies primarily with the state under this standard of review.

If neither a fundamental right nor a suspect classification is involved, a state may enact legislation abridging that right or affecting that class so long as there is a rational basis for the legislation. This standard of review is referred to as **rational basis** review since under it, the court will not strike down a statute that appears to have a rational basis. The court does not closely examine the effect of the legislation, unlike under strict scrutiny review. This standard of review is obviously a much easier one for the state to meet. The legislature need not choose the best possible means of achieving its goal; it must simply choose a means that is not entirely unrelated to the achievement of the legislative purpose.

INCORPORATION OF THE BILL OF RIGHTS INTO THE FOURTEENTH AMENDMENT

It was intended by the founding fathers that the Bill of Rights apply only to the federal government, because there was a fear of a strong centralized government when the Constitution was adopted. State governments were viewed with much less fear. In *Barron v. Baltimore* (1833), the Supreme Court expressly held that the Bill of Rights applied only to the federal government. The *Barron* case involved the Takings Clause of the Fifth Amendment that forbids governmental taking of private property without just compensation. Barron wanted this clause applied to the states because the city of Baltimore had essentially taken his property without providing him with compensation for it. The Supreme Court dismissed his claim, stating that the amendment did not apply to the states, and therefore the Court lacked jurisdiction in the matter. This case showed that without the application of the Bill of Rights to the states, individuals would have no recourse to higher authority if the states violated their rights.

After the Civil War and the failed attempt by the Southern states to secede from the Union, Congress passed the Fourteenth Amendment, in an effort to provide greater protections for individuals from the actions of state governments. There was in particular a fear that the Southern states would attempt to limit the ability of the recently freed slaves to become equal citizens. The Fourteenth Amendment contains three clauses: the Privileges and Immunities Clause, the Due Process Clause, and the Equal Protection Clause. The essence of each of these clauses is that they bar states, not the federal government, from infringing on individual rights. The amendment was expressly intended to control state action, but it was unclear exactly how far the amendment went. The original spur for it was a desire to protect the rights of the freed slaves, but the language of the amendment was broad and not specifically limited to state actions infringing on the rights of Blacks.

An early attempt to apply the language of the Privileges and Immunities Clause to persons other than the recently freed slaves failed in the *Slaughterhouse Cases* (1873). At issue was a Louisiana state statute passed by a highly corrupt state legislature granting one corporation a monopoly on slaughterhouse business. The petitioners (the person or persons bringing the suit) argued that the Privileges and Immunities Clause should be interpreted as prohibiting unreasonable restrictions on business because the restriction in question deprived them of their right to pursue their lawful trades. The Supreme Court sided with the monopoly, emphasizing that the Due Process Clause should not be a source enabling judges to nullify laws they considered unreasonable. (Despite the financial gain some legislators realized from the monopoly, there were genuine public health concerns involved.)

During the latter part of the 19th century, however, the Supreme Court began to use the Due Process Clause of the Fourteenth Amendment to strike down state action involving economic regulation. Due process rights are said to extend beyond procedural rights to encompass **substantive due process** as well. Under the principle of substantive due process, legislatures cannot pass laws that infringe on substantive rights such as free speech and privacy. (This is the legal theory under which the privacy rights applied in *Griswold v. Connecticut* and *Roe v. Wade* were based.) This sounds all very liberal

VIEW FROM THE FIELD

Erik Lehtinen
State Appellate Public Defender
Boise, Idaho

As a public defender with far too many clients and not nearly enough hours in the day, it's all too easy to give up on an argument when, after conducting your legal research, you discover that the U.S. Constitution has been interpreted in a way that is unfavorable to your client. But sometimes, when you just can't seem to get over how fundamentally unfair the existing law seems under the circumstances of your case, devoting some additional time to the issue may pay huge dividends for your client. In some of these cases, you may be able to argue that your state's constitution should be read to provide greater rights to your client than

does the U.S. Constitution (even if the two constitutions contain virtually identical language).

The difficulty with these arguments, of course, is that you have to use all your persuasive abilities to overcome the court's inclination to interpret the language of a given constitutional provision exactly as another court, perhaps even the U.S Supreme Court, has interpreted an identical provision, and you also have to use all your creativity to give the court a good reason (or, preferably, a host of good reasons) why, in this instance, the state constitution ought to be interpreted as providing greater protection than the U.S. Constitution. You're not going to win all the time, or hardly at all, but it's a tremendously gratifying experience when you do manage to prevail and improve the law—not just for your client but for everyone in your state.

until we realize that the Supreme Court used the principle to repeatedly hold that states could not impose regulations such as minimum wage laws and child labor laws on private businesses because doing so violated due process. The violation of due process consisted of the regulation or taking of a right such as the right to work or to enter into a contract (even if the "right" meant having to work long hours for low wages).

During the 1930s, the use of the Due Process Clause to protect economic interests fell into disfavor, in part because the Supreme Court used it to strike down much of President Roosevelt's New Deal legislation, which was intended to ease the Great Depression. At the same time, however, the Supreme Court began to use the Due Process Clause of the Fourteenth Amendment to protect individual rights from state action. Beginning in the late 1930s and continuing into the 1960s, the Supreme Court incorporated most of the various provisions of the Bill of Rights into the Fourteenth Amendment's Due Process Clause and applied them to the states.

By **incorporation**, we mean that the justices interpreted the Due Process Clause of the Fourteenth Amendment, which says no state shall deprive a person of life, liberty, or property without "due process of law," as prohibiting states from abridging certain individual rights. Many of these rights are included in the Bill of Rights, and hence these rights were included (or incorporated) in the definition of due process. Several approaches to incorporation are discussed next.

Total Incorporation

Under the **total incorporation** approach, the Due Process Clause of the Fourteenth Amendment made the entire Bill of Rights applicable to the states. In essence, the phrase "due process of law" was interpreted to mean "all of the provisions of the Bill of Rights." Justice Hugo Black advocated for this approach to incorporation, but he had few supporters on the Court.

Total Incorporation Plus

Under **total incorporation plus**, the Due Process Clause of the Fourteenth Amendment includes all the Bill of Rights as well as other, unspecified rights. One of the first advocates of this approach was Justice William Douglas, who claimed that the various provisions of the Bill of Rights limiting the ability of the government to intrude into a person's private life (such as the Fourth Amendment prohibition on unreasonable searches) created a general right to privacy, even though such a right is not expressly mentioned anywhere in the Constitution.

Fundamental Rights

Under the fundamental rights approach, there is no relationship between the Due Process Clause of the Fourteenth Amendment and the Bill of Rights. Rather, there are simply some rights that are essential to "due process" and that must therefore be protected. The Due Process Clause has an independent meaning that prohibits state action that violates rights that are deemed "fundamental" (*Palko v. Connecticut*, 1937). Exactly what constitutes a fundamental right is left to the Supreme Court to figure out. This approach provides justices with greater discretion, and they may interpret it either narrowly or broadly. The primary advocate of this approach was Justice Felix Frankfurter.

Selective Incorporation

The **selective incorporation** approach combines elements of the fundamental rights and total incorporation approaches in modified form. This approach favors a case-by-case approach. Selective incorporation rejects the notion that all the rights in the Bill of Rights are automatically incorporated in the Due Process Clause of the Fourteenth Amendment, but it looks to the Bill of Rights as a guide to determining the meaning of due process. The best-known advocate of selective incorporation was Justice William Brennan. Although selective incorporation accepted the idea that the Due Process Clause protects only "fundamental rights" and that not every right in the Bill of Rights is necessarily fundamental, over time it has led to the incorporation of virtually every individual right in the Bill of Rights.

It should be noted that because the Supreme Court has deemed incorporation necessary, it does not mean that most of these rights did not already exist in the states. Many states had rights in their state constitutions that were even more protective of individual rights than those in the Bill of Rights. For instance, a number of states had privacy rights in such matters as abortion and the bearing of arms long before the Court's "discovery" of "penumbras." Table 2.2 presents a summary of incorporation theories.

TABLE 2.2 ■ Summary of Incorporation Theories

Total Incorporation	Total Incorporation Plus	Selective Incorporation
Intent: To make all provisions of the Bill of Rights applicable to the states.	**Intent:** To protect rights enumerated in the Bill of Rights plus certain unenumerated rights.	**Intent:** To incorporate provisions of the Bill of Rights in a careful and discriminative way.
Justification: Due Process Clause of the Fourteenth Amendment.	**Justification:** The totality of the rights in the Bill of Rights created a penumbra over the law.	**Justification:** Only fundamental rights should be incorporated; nonfundamental rights should be left as state concerns.

SUMMARY

In this chapter, we discussed the sources of law. These include constitutions, statutes, administrative regulations, and case law. It is law that courts apply and, on occasion, interpret. Law serves as the reason for the existence of courts and as the body of rules and principles that courts apply to the infinite variety of human activity and interactions.

Individual rights come from many sources. Those rights most applicable to criminal courts are the rights found in the U.S. Constitution, particularly the rights enumerated in the Bill of Rights and applied to the states via the Due Process Clause of the Fourteenth Amendment. Crucial to our understanding of these individual rights is our understanding of how the U.S. Supreme Court applied these rights, originally intended to apply only to the federal government, to the state governments. This was a crucial step since so much of criminal justice and criminal law is handled at the state level.

Don't overlook the Student Study Site with its useful study aids, such as self-quizzes, eFlashcards, and other assists, to help you get more from the course and improve your grade.

DISCUSSION QUESTIONS

1. What are the primary sources of law?

2. How did the Bill of Rights come to be applied to the individual states?

3. Why was the Bill of Rights adopted, and what rights are contained in it?

4. What are the different standards of review in constitutional law, and when are they used?

5. Given the Supreme Court's "discovery" of penumbras in the Bill of Rights such as the right to privacy, should this right be extended to assisted suicide for terminally ill patients and/or access to marijuana for medical purposes? Why or why not?

6. How has the Equal Protection Clause of the Fourteenth Amendment been applied by the Supreme Court?

7. How has the Due Process Clause of the Fourteenth Amendment been applied by the Supreme Court?

8. Using strict scrutiny review, under what circumstances can a state abridge fundamental rights?

9. How has the Supreme Court interpreted the Second Amendment in recent years?

10. Why does the standard of review matter in constitutional law?

KEY TERMS

Acquittal 36
Administrative regulations 30
Bill of Rights 32
Bills of attainder 32
Constitution 30
Double jeopardy 36
Dual-sovereignty doctrine 37
Ex post facto laws 32
Fundamental rights 42
Grand jury 36

Hung jury 36
Incorporation 45
Indictment 36
Individual rights 31
Information 36
Intermediate scrutiny 43
Legislation 30
Miranda warnings 42
Penumbra 40
Probable cause 35

Rational basis 43
Right of appeal 38
Right to counsel 38
Selective incorporation 46
Strict scrutiny 43
Substantive due process 44
Suspect classification 41
Total incorporation 45
Total incorporation plus 45
Writ of habeas corpus 31

INTERNET SITES

The Bill of Rights: www.archives.gov/exhibits/charters/bill_of_rights.html

Federal Judicial Center: www.fjc.gov

Fourteenth Amendment: www.usconstitution.net/xconst_Am14.html

Incorporation Doctrine: www.law.cornell.edu/wex/incorporation_doctrine

STUDENT STUDY SITE

Get the tools you need to sharpen your study skills. SAGE edge offers a robust online environment featuring an impressive array of free tools and resources.

Access practice quizzes, eFlashcards, video, and multimedia at **edge.sagepub.com/hemmens4e**

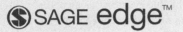

© Stockbyte/Thinkstock Images

3

TYPES OF LAW

Master the content at **edge.sagepub.com/hemmens4e**

INTRODUCTION

In this chapter, we discuss the elements of the criminal law, sometimes referred to as substantive law. Substantive law is the law of crimes, compared with procedural law, which is the rules the state must follow when investigating and prosecuting criminal activity. The criminal law is defined by statute, and it sets forth what is forbidden conduct and provides penalties for those who engage in such activity. It is the code of conduct that everyone in society is expected to follow. Criminal laws are enforced by the state, and violation of the criminal law is treated as an act against the state. The primary purpose of the criminal law is protecting the public from harm by either deterring or punishing unlawful acts.

So far, we have concentrated on law and justice as it pertains to criminal matters, but social order requires that the law also concern itself with other harmful acts that society has seen fit to regulate that are outside the purview of the criminal justice system. Civil law is private law in that it governs transactions between nongovernment entities such as corporations and private individuals. Public law involves the regulation of the various relationships between and among the government and private parties such as corporations and private individuals. Criminal law is part of public law, but we address only noncriminal administrative law in this chapter.

Many disagreements arise between and among citizens and institutions concerning matters such as property, contracts, and personal injuries. These disputes are resolved through the civil law, although certain harms may fall into both criminal and civil categories. Participants in the social contract must be willing to sacrifice some potential for personal gain to provide an environment conducive to the protection of important liberties for all. Civil law serves this important end, designed as it is to provide remedies for individuals harmed by others, manage social conflict, and restore social harmony. Reduced to its bare bones, civil law defines the rights and duties that all individuals owe to all other individuals.

Civil law is divided into five major categories: torts, property, contracts, family, and juvenile law. Although there is a great deal of overlap among these categories, each of the categories contains its own substantive law and procedures.

TYPES OF LAW: CRIMINAL AND CIVIL

There are two types of law: civil and criminal. Civil law is law designed to address private wrongs. A private citizen who believes that he or she has been injured in some way by another may sue that party for damages. Criminal law is designed to allow for the adjudication and punishment of those who violate society's rules, or criminal laws. The state is treated as the aggrieved party, and the alleged wrongdoer is the defendant.

Among the many differences between civil and criminal law, the most important is the criminal court requirement of "proof beyond a reasonable doubt" and the civil court "preponderance of the evidence" standard of proof. **Proof beyond a reasonable doubt** is the prosecution's burden of proof in a criminal trial. Each element of the offense charged must be proven "beyond a reasonable doubt" for the jury to return a guilty verdict. If the prosecution fails to establish this burden, then the jury must return a "not guilty" verdict. Determining whether the prosecution has failed to meet its burden of proof is different from determining whether the defendant is innocent. That is why the verdict delivered is "not guilty" rather than "innocent." Not guilty is a legal finding that the prosecution has failed to meet its burden of proof; it is not necessarily a factual description of reality. Proof beyond a reasonable doubt is a very high burden of proof, far higher than the **proof by a preponderance of the evidence** standard used in civil proceedings.

Criminal Law

The criminal law is sometimes referred to as substantive law. **Substantive law** is the law of crimes. It is defined by statute, and it prescribes (what we should do) and proscribes (what we should not do) various types of conduct. It is that code of conduct that all in a society are expected to follow, such as prohibitions on murder, assault, and robbery. Violation of the criminal law is treated as an act against the state as well as the individual victim. The primary purpose of the criminal law is thus to protect the public from harm by punishing harmful acts that have occurred and seeking to avoid harm by forbidding conduct that may lead to it.

What Is Crime?

Crime is (1) an *act* in violation of a (2) *criminal law* for which a (3) *punishment* is prescribed; the person committing it must have (4) *intended* to do so and to have done so without legally acceptable (5) *defense* or *justification*. Whereas not all actions classified as crimes are uniformly regarded as criminal (such as possession of marijuana or consumption of alcohol by persons between the ages of 18 and 21), there are some acts, such as murder and rape, that are universally condemned. These are referred to as **mala in se** crimes, or crimes that are inherently harmful. Less serious misdeeds, such as marijuana possession, for which there is no consensus they are harmful are referred to as **mala prohibita** crimes.

Whereas states may define crimes differently, there are a number of similarities, regardless of the jurisdiction. Common characteristics of the criminal law include a description of what conduct is forbidden, a list of the penalties for violations of the law, and the provision of defenses to criminal liability.

Sources of Criminal Law

The bulk of the criminal law is today located in state statutes, variously referred to as the penal code or criminal code. Many of the states' criminal codes are based on crimes created and defined by courts at common law. Criminal codes generally define the elements of a crime more precisely than was the case at common law. Courts in some states still recognize as crimes acts defined as crimes at common law even though these acts have not been written into the criminal code by the legislature. Another source of criminal law is federal statutes. Historically, there were relatively few federal crimes, because Congress left law enforcement to the states. But beginning in the early 20th century, Congress began to add a number of federal crimes, including kidnapping and drug possession and sale.

Limitations on the Criminal Law

There are a number of constitutionally derived limits on the criminal law. The Due Process Clause of the Fourteenth Amendment limits the state's ability to enact laws that infringe on constitutional rights, such as the freedom of assembly.

Other constitutional limitations on the criminal law include a prohibition on laws that are either overbroad or vague. A criminal law violates the **overbreadth doctrine** when

CURRENT CONTROVERSY
GETTING RID OF CRIME: THE ADULT USE OF MARIJUANA ACT (PROPOSITION 64)

In 2016 the state of California passed a voter initiative, Proposition 64, which legalizes the recreational use, possession, and cultivation, as well as the commercial sale, of recreational marijuana. The legal sale of recreational marijuana as well as licensure and regulation of marijuana businesses went into effect on January 1, 2018. Individuals who are over 21 years of age are allowed to possess one ounce (28.5 grams) of marijuana and cultivate up to six marijuana plants in their home or on their property. California is now the ninth province in the United States (eight states plus the District of Columbia) that has legalized recreational marijuana. The initiative also established taxes on the sale and cultivation of marijuana and renamed the Bureau of Medical Cannabis Regulation the Bureau of Marijuana Control, which is now responsible for overseeing and licensing businesses that sell, distribute, and produce marijuana. These changes to California law are substantial, in that California has the largest population of any U.S. state and, by extent, the largest potential market, thus potentially impacting the entire national marijuana market as well as legalization efforts. It took California almost two decades to legalize recreational marijuana after numerous failed efforts, despite legalizing medical marijuana in 1996. Consumers cannot use marijuana in public spaces or on school grounds, nor can they use it while driving or have an open container of it while in a motor vehicle. Individuals who are incarcerated for offenses that are now legalized or decriminalized under the proposition can petition the court for resentencing or dismissal of their sentence, as long as they do not pose a risk to society. Those who are in the same boat but have completed their sentences can petition the court for a dismissal and sealing of their conviction. These reflect changes in the criminal law and, as such, what constitutes a "crime."

Source: "Amendment to Statewide Initiative Measure," (2015); Ballotpedia (n.d.).

it fails to narrowly define the specific behavior to be restricted. For instance, banning the sale of obscene materials is permitted, but a statute banning the sale of all material that mentions or depicts sexual activity would be overbroad.

A statute is considered **void for vagueness** if it fails to clearly define the act prohibited and the appropriate punishment. A statute must give fair notice to citizens exactly what conduct is forbidden.

The Eighth Amendment bars "cruel and unusual punishment." This has been interpreted by the Supreme Court to prohibit punishments that are not proportionate to the crime committed. The concept of proportionality is not always entirely clear. For example, the Supreme Court has held that the death penalty is appropriate only in cases where a murder has been committed (*Gregg v. Georgia,* 1976), but the Court has upheld state statutes mandating a life sentence for repeat offenders, even when the felonies involved nothing more serious than obtaining a total of less than $230 through the fraudulent use of a credit card and writing bad checks in three separate incidents (*Rummel v. Estelle,* 1980). Whereas some have argued that a life sentence for a handful of minor thefts is disproportionate to the harm caused by these crimes, the Court has recognized the states' right to protect the public from habitual criminals.

Other constitutional limitations on the criminal law include a prohibition on ex post facto laws and bills of attainder. Ex post facto laws are laws that make an act that has already taken place a crime. For example, if a 22-year-old college student consumes alcohol in a state when the drinking age is 21 and the state subsequently passes a law raising the drinking age to 25 and making it a crime for anyone under the age of 25 to have consumed alcohol *before* the law was passed, such a law would be barred as ex post facto. Bills of attainder are laws that impose punishment for an act without requiring a conviction first. Bills of attainder existed at common law for crimes against the state such as treason and marked the accused as "attainted" (morally contaminated).

Elements of Criminal Liability

The commission of a harmful act does not automatically mean a crime has occurred. There are five elements of criminal liability, each of which must be established beyond a reasonable doubt, in order for criminal liability to exist. These five elements comprise the body of the crime, or **corpus delicti.**

The Five Elements of Criminal Offenses

Actus Reus (Criminal Act). There must be an act in order for there to be a crime. It is not a crime to merely have evil thoughts. There are three forms of the criminal act, or **actus reus,** meaning a guilty act: (1) voluntary bodily movements, (2) an omission when there is a legal duty to act, and (3) possession.

Voluntary movements are those that occur without coercion and with the actor's awareness of what he or she is doing. This excludes involuntary bodily movements such as reflexive actions or unconscious activity (such as sleepwalking). Words may constitute acts in some cases, such as solicitation to commit a crime or threatening someone with imminent harm. The state may not punish someone solely on the basis of his or her status, such as being an alcoholic (*Robinson v. California,* 1962), but it may criminalize conduct that is a consequence of that status, such as being drunk in public (*Powell v. Texas,* 1968).

An omission, or a failure to act, is generally not considered a crime, even if morally reprehensible, such as refusing to come to the aid of someone who is being assaulted. However, there are two narrow circumstances where failing to act may result in criminal liability. These include a failure to perform a legal duty (such as failing to pay income tax) and failure to intervene to prevent serious harm when there exists a special relationship between the parties that imposes a duty to act (as in the case of parents and children).

Possession of some items, such as cocaine, may constitute a crime if the person is aware that it is illegal to possess the item. Whereas possession is passive, the act of acquiring possession requires action on the part of the actor, and retaining possession when one is aware that it is unlawful to possess the item is similar to an omission.

Mens Rea (Criminal Intent). For criminal liability to exist, there must be a guilty mind, or **mens rea**. The rationale for this requirement is that society does not wish to punish people who did not intend to cause harm. Modern criminal law recognizes several levels of intent, with varying levels of punishment associated with each. Mens rea is determined by the circumstances surrounding the criminal act.

Criminal motive and criminal intent are different things. *Intent* refers to the defendant's mental state; **motive** is the reason why the act was committed. Some degree of intent is required for there to be criminal liability, but there is no requirement that the prosecution prove the defendant's motive, although it is commonly done in an effort to help the jury understand why the defendant did what he or she did.

There are four levels of intent in the **Model Penal Code**: purposeful, knowing, reckless, and negligent. A person who acts *purposefully* does so consciously, with the desire to commit a certain act. The person is virtually certain of the results of his or her conduct. A person acts *knowingly* when he or she is fairly certain of the result that will follow from this conduct but does not necessarily desire the result. A person acts *recklessly* when he or she acts with awareness of the risk involved but without the certainty of knowledge that harm will follow. A person acts *negligently* when he or she unconsciously creates a substantial risk of harm that a reasonable person would have been aware of.

Another form of intent is the doctrine of transferred intent. **Transferred intent** applies to situations where a person intended to harm *A* but in error harmed *B*. To prevent the defendant from escaping liability by claiming that he or she did not intend to hurt *B* and thus the element of intent is missing, courts developed the concept of transferred intent. This doctrine transfers the intent to harm *A* to *B*. Thus, if Craig shoots at David intending to kill him but misses and kills Bob instead, under the doctrine of transferred intent, Craig's intent to kill David is transferred to Bob, so Craig cannot claim he is not guilty of a crime because he did not intend to kill Bob.

Concurrence. **Concurrence** is the union of the criminal act and criminal intent. Both must exist. The criminal intent must set the criminal act in motion. Acts not generated by criminal intent do not constitute criminal conduct, and the intent to commit a crime, without action, does not constitute a crime.

Causation. There are two types of **causation**: factual and legal. Factual cause refers to the idea that "but for" the actor's conduct, the harm would not have occurred. It is an initial act that sets a series of other acts in motion that leads to some harm. Factual causation is a necessary but not sufficient element for the imposition of criminal liability. A legal cause also must exist.

Legal cause, also referred to as proximate cause, is a bit more complicated. In the vast majority of criminal cases, factual cause and legal cause are identical. The issue of legal cause becomes relevant only when some additional acts—not under the accused person's control or that he or she could not reasonably foresee—intervene between the factual cause and the harm ultimately caused. Consequences of an act that are not reasonably foreseeable to the actor are "intervening causes" and relieve the actor of some degree of criminal liability. An example might be if Bob got into his car and drove down the street, obeying all traffic laws and driving attentively. While he was driving down the street, a child ran out into the street from behind a parked car just as Bob was driving past the car. Bob could not stop his car in time and struck and injured the child. Bob was the factual cause of the child's injury; had he not been driving his car down the street that day, he would not have struck the child. But Bob's actions are not the legal cause of the child's injury, because there is an intervening cause—the action by the child of running into the street in such a manner that Bob could not avoid striking him. The child's action relieves Bob of criminal liability for his action.

Harm. **Harm** is simply the result of the act, the injury to another. The harm may be physical, as in an assault, or mental, as in frightening someone by threatening to strike him or her. Harm can also be economic (e.g., credit card fraud). There can be no liability without some form of harm. The state may criminalize acts that ostensibly harm only the actor, such as prostitution or drug abuse.

Liability Without Fault

There is one instance when criminal liability may exist without criminal intent. **Strict liability** imposes liability without criminal intent in situations where society deems it fair to do so. An example is selling alcohol to someone under the legal drinking age of 21. If a bartender sells alcohol to a person who is physically mature and appears to be older than 21, and who has false identification stating he or she is over 21, the bartender is nonetheless criminally liable. Society has determined that those who choose to sell alcohol must accept the responsibility for unintentionally selling it to a minor; imposing liability in these circumstances will, it is assumed, encourage alcohol sellers to be very careful. Such a scenario also exists for driving over the speed limit, as drivers are expected to adhere to existing traffic laws, regardless of intent.

Inchoate Crimes

An inchoate crime is one that is incomplete or that happens in preparation for another crime. Inchoate crimes are sometimes referred to as anticipatory or incomplete crimes, although the law treats them as completed crimes in which criminal liability exists even though the anticipated or planned crime never happens. There are three types of inchoate crimes: attempt, solicitation, and conspiracy.

Attempt. The doctrine of attempt was created in an effort to punish those who try but fail to commit a crime—why should someone escape criminal liability because they are an ineffective criminal? Merely thinking about committing a crime is not enough to constitute an attempt, however; there must be some evidence that the person has taken acts in pursuance of the intended crime. States vary in their definition of what constitutes an attempt. An example of an attempted crime is a man who plans to rob a bank, purchases a ski mask and shotgun and drives to the bank, puts on the ski mask in 100-degree weather, enters the bank with the shotgun, but then changes his mind and returns to his car. He has not committed bank robbery, but he has taken significant steps toward doing so.

Solicitation. **Solicitation** involves the intent to persuade another person to commit a crime. This is typically done by asking the person to commit a crime. Joking about committing a crime is not enough; there must be evidence that the person making the statement truly wants the other person to commit a crime. The solicited crime does not have to be committed for there to be solicitation. Thus, a crime has occurred as soon as Sue asks Joe to kill someone and gives him $10,000 to do it. Joe does not have to kill anyone or do anything for the solicitation to have taken place; the crime is in the asking.

Conspiracy. A **conspiracy** is an agreement between two or more people to commit a crime. If Frank and Joe make plans to rob a bank, they have conspired to commit bank robbery. A coconspirator may be held liable for the actions of others in the conspiracy, even if he or she is unaware of their offenses. Thus, criminals are advised to choose their partners carefully, as they are responsible for all acts in furtherance of the conspiracy.

Parties to Crime. Those who assist others in the commission of a crime may also be held liable, as an accomplice or party to crime. Parties to crime are often referred to as accessories to the crime; one can be an accessory before, during, or after the crime. An accessory before the crime is someone who helps prepare the crime, such as providing a weapon. An accessory during the crime is someone who helps commit the crime, such as driving a getaway vehicle after a bank robbery. An accessory after the crime is someone who helps after the crime has taken place, such as assisting someone in escaping from the police.

Defenses to Criminal Liability

It is possible that all the elements of criminal liability exist and still a person may be able to avoid punishment because he or she has a defense, or explanation, that precludes the imposition of criminal liability. Defenses to criminal liability include alibi, justification, and excuse. These are referred to as **affirmative defenses** because the defendant has the burden of production and the burden of persuasion. The **burden of production** refers to the duty to produce evidence. In a criminal case, the prosecution must introduce evidence showing the defendant committed the crime with which he or she has been charged. Failure to produce such evidence results in a dismissal of the case. The **burden of persuasion** refers to which side has to "prove" its case. In criminal cases, the prosecution has the burden of persuasion and must prove its case to the jury beyond a reasonable doubt. When the defense is asserting an affirmative defense, however, the defense bears the burden of producing evidence to support the defense and the burden of proof as well. The burden of proof for affirmative defenses is usually by a preponderance of the evidence, although in some states, a higher burden is imposed for certain defenses, such as the insanity defense (more on this later). Affirmative defenses may result in an acquittal or a reduction of the charge.

Alibi

An **alibi** defense is where a defendant asserts he or she is not the person who committed the act charged. An alibi is different from the other affirmative defenses because the defendant is claiming innocence, whereas the other defenses involve the defendant acknowledging committing the act for which he or she is being charged with a crime. There are two types: justification and excuse. These are discussed below.

Justification Defenses

A **justification defense** is one in which the defendant admits he or she has committed the act that occurred but claims that under the circumstances, the act was not criminal. Two examples of common justification defenses are self-defense and consent.

Self-Defense. **Self-defense** involves a claim by the defendant that he used force against another person only in response to an unprovoked attack and that the defendant reasonably believed he would be injured if he did not protect himself. There are a number of limitations and exceptions to the rules of self-defense. These include the **retreat doctrine**, which states that a person must retreat instead of using deadly force to repel an attack if it is safe to do so. The **castle doctrine**, on the other hand, states that when someone is attacked in her home (or castle) she may use deadly force even if she could have safely retreated—a person is not expected to flee her home. Self-defense also may apply to the defense of others and, in limited circumstances, to the defense of property.

Consent. **Consent** is a defense to a limited number of crimes. A majority of states allow a person charged with harming another to avoid criminal liability if the person charged can prove the person he harmed consented (i.e., agreed) to the conduct that led to the harm and that the victim's consent was voluntary, knowing, and intelligent. What harms a person can validly consent to suffer are quite limited, however. A person cannot consent to be killed or seriously injured. An example of voluntary, knowing, and intelligent consent is that of the professional athlete (such as a football player) who chooses to engage in a sport where injury similar to a physical assault is known to occur. This does not give license to harm, however; although a football player consents to being tackled and possibly injured, he does not consent to someone who acts well outside the established rules of conduct for the sport, such as a player running over to the opposing team before the game and punching a player in the face.

Excuse Defenses

An **excuse defense** is one in which defendants admit that what they did was wrong but argue that under the circumstances, they are not criminally liable for their conduct. Two examples are age and insanity.

Age. Historically, youth was treated as a defense to criminal liability on the grounds that children lack the mental capability to form mens rea or fully comprehend the consequences of their actions. Under the common law, there was a presumption that children under the age of 7 years were incompetent. Today, the age of adulthood, when full criminal liability attaches, is typically 18. Those under the age of 18 are dealt with in the juvenile justice system instead of the criminal justice system. The juvenile justice system was designed to focus more on rehabilitation of the offender (or delinquent, in juvenile justice parlance) than on retribution or deterrence. Today, most states have modified their juvenile justice code to allow for the transfer of juveniles who have committed more serious crimes or who are repeat offenders to the criminal court, on the assumption that the juvenile justice system is not effective for these individuals.

Insanity. **Insanity** is a legal term used to describe mental illness. Someone who is determined to be insane lacks the mens rea necessary to be criminally liable for his or her conduct. Mental illness and legal insanity are not the same. A person can be judged mentally ill by medical standards and sane by legal standards. The insanity defense is probably the most controversial of all defense strategies, although it is rarely used in practice. There are four different tests for insanity that have been developed over time.

- *M'Naghten rule:* Also known as the right–wrong test, the **M'Naghten rule** was created by an English court in *Rex v. M'Naghten* (1843). M'Naghten attempted to assassinate Robert Peel, the prime minister of England. M'Naghten missed Peel and hit Peel's secretary, who died. M'Naghten was found not guilty by reason of insanity after the court created a test for determining his sanity. Under this test, a defendant is insane and thus not criminally liable if he did not know what he was doing or that it was wrong to do it.

- *Irresistible impulse test:* The **irresistible impulse test** is defined as the inability to control one's conduct, even though one is aware that what one is doing is wrong. This test was developed in response to concerns that the right–wrong test did not account for the actions of those who acted under a compulsion, who could not stop themselves from doing something even though they knew it was a crime.

- *Durham rule:* This test is also known as the **product test**. The **Durham rule** is met when the act was the product of the defendant's mental illness. This test was developed by a court that felt the existing tests for insanity were too narrow; it has since been discarded by almost every state as too broad.

- *Substantial capacity test:* The **substantial capacity test** is when the defendant lacks substantial capacity to appreciate the wrongfulness of her conduct *or* the ability to control it. It is a combination and modification of the M'Naghten and irresistible impulse tests and is slightly easier for the defendant to establish, because she is not required to lack all capacity to understand or control her conduct, just substantial capacity.

After John Hinckley was found not guilty by reason of insanity for attempting to assassinate then-president Ronald Reagan, Congress and the states made a variety of changes to their insanity laws. A handful of states eliminated the defense entirely, and others adopted a "guilty but mentally ill" verdict. A number of states changed the burden of proof for the defense from a preponderance of the evidence to "clear and convincing evidence," a more difficult burden to meet.

VIEW FROM THE FIELD

Erik Lehtinen
State Appellate Public Defender
Boise, Idaho

Idaho is among those states that have eliminated the insanity defense. However, that is not to say that, in Idaho, the defendant's "insanity," or mental condition generally, can never be used to defend against a criminal charge. In those cases in which the state of Idaho is required to prove that the defendant acted with the specific intent to achieve a certain outcome, the defendant can still argue that his or her mental condition prevented him or her from forming the requisite level of intent.

Take, for example, the case of a paranoid schizophrenic who, after having been involuntarily committed to the state psychiatric hospital following a psychotic break, promptly escapes from the hospital, walks to a local convenience store, and asks the clerk for all the money in the register; if the clerk is frightened but refuses to hand over any money, and the man simply shrugs his shoulders and leaves, has the man committed an attempted robbery? In such a case, the jury would be allowed to consider all the evidence, including the man's mental illness, in determining whether the man acted with the specific intent to use force or fear to take the contents of the register from the clerk against his or her will, as would be required to support a conviction for attempted robbery under Idaho law (see generally, *State v. Beebe,* 2007).

Criminal Acts

Crimes are categorized based on the type of act. Under this approach, there are crimes against the person, crimes against property, and crimes against public order and morality. Each of these categories encompasses a wide range of conduct. Examples of each are provided here.

Crimes Against the Person. Crimes against the person include the most serious offenses. These include the following:

- *Murder.* Murder is a subcategory of **homicide**, a broad, all-inclusive term for any killing of another human being. Not all homicides are criminal—some are lawful, depending on the circumstances. Criminal homicides include murder and manslaughter. Under the common law, murder was defined as the killing of another person with malice aforethought. **Malice aforethought** means an intentional, premeditated (planned) killing. **Murder** is today defined by the Model Penal Code as a killing that occurs (1) purposefully, (2) knowingly, or (3) recklessly under circumstances exhibiting extreme indifference to human life. Because these comprise three distinct levels of intent, murder is graded into first degree and second degree. First-degree murder includes those killings that are deliberate and premeditated. Second-degree murder includes any killings that are intentional but not premeditated or planned.

- *Manslaughter.* **Manslaughter** is a second category of criminal homicide and includes both voluntary and involuntary manslaughter. Voluntary manslaughter is an intentional killing that occurs either (1) under a mistaken belief that self-defense permitted the use of deadly force or (2) in response to adequate provocation while in the sudden heat of passion. **Adequate provocation** is a concept that was developed at common law and applies to situations where a defendant uses deadly force without justification but under particularly stressful circumstances that could cause a reasonable person to react violently. Examples include catching a spouse in the act of committing adultery and being assaulted by someone who is not using deadly force. Words alone are not considered sufficient to create adequate provocation. The existence of adequate provocation does not eliminate criminal liability, but it does reduce the charge (and associated punishment) from first-degree murder to voluntary manslaughter. Involuntary manslaughter occurs when an unintentional killing results from a reckless act by the defendant.

Another type of murder is **felony murder**. Under the felony murder rule, an individual may be held liable for an unintended death that occurs during the commission of a dangerous felony, such as robbery, where the possibility of serious injury is reasonably foreseeable. An example is a bank robber who flees from the police in a vehicle, and during the high-speed chase, a police officer crashes and dies. The bank robber could be charged with felony murder for the death of the officer even though the bank robber did not do anything to directly cause the crash. The purpose of the felony murder rule is to hold people accountable for the consequences of their very dangerous acts. In most states, felony murder is treated as second-degree murder.

There are a number of offenses against the person aside from murder and manslaughter. These offenses, while less serious than killing, nonetheless are treated seriously in the criminal law because they involve harm of one form or another to a person. Among these are rape, assault, and robbery. These offenses, although different in form, all share the common denominator of direct harm to a person inflicted by the actor.

- *Rape.* Under the common law, **rape** was defined as carnal knowledge by a man of a woman who is not his wife, forcibly and without her consent. This definition created several gaps in the law: Only men were legally capable of rape, only women could be raped, men could not rape their wives, the only act that constituted rape was vaginal intercourse, and there must be evidence of both the use of force by the man and physical resistance by the woman.

The common-law gaps in the law of rape have been largely filled in. All 50 states have formally abolished the so-called *marital rape exception,* so men can be charged with rape if they engage in nonconsensual sex with their wife. Many states have rewritten their statutes using gender-neutral language so that the crime applies to acts committed by men and women, as well as acts committed against men and children. Perhaps most significantly, states have modified or completely eliminated the common-law requirement that a woman must physically resist her attacker on the grounds that requiring her to do so simply puts her at risk of additional harm. There also has been an attempt to limit the sort of evidence that can be introduced at trial. Rape shield statutes restrict the introduction into evidence of a victim's sexual history on the grounds that it is not relevant to whether consent was obtained in the present instance. Some states no longer use the term *rape* but instead use the phrase "sexual assault."

- *Assault.* Under the common law, there was a clear distinction between the offense of assault and the offense of battery. **Assault** was either (a) an attempt or (b) a threat to inflict immediate harm by a person who had the ability to carry out the threat. No physical contact was necessary for an assault to take place; it was enough if the victim reasonably feared for his safety. A completed assault, in which there was actual bodily contact, was considered a **battery**. A battery under the common law was defined as any intentional, unjustified, offensive physical contact, no matter how slight. It could be a blow from a fist, being spit on, or being shot. Today, many jurisdictions have merged the offenses of assault and battery, referring to both as assault.

- *Robbery.* Robbery is a form of larceny (theft) that involves the taking of property from another person, by force or threat of force. Robbery carries a more serious penalty than any other crimes except murder and rape because the act of taking property from someone who has it in her custody creates a strong risk of physical harm to the victim in addition to the loss of her property.

Crimes Against Property. Crimes against property include a variety of activities. The most common are burglary and theft. Whereas crimes against the person receive the bulk of media and public attention, the reality is that crimes against property occur far more often.

- *Burglary.* A person's home has always received special protection in the law; hence the common-law adage "A man's home is his castle." **Burglary** is a crime committed against the home. As such, the law surrounding it developed early in the common-law period, and its definition has changed substantially as society has changed. By the 17th century, burglary was defined as (1) the breaking and (2) entering of the (3) dwelling (4) of another (5) at night (6) with the intention of committing a felony inside the dwelling. Each of these six elements had its own unique meaning. Today, burglary is more broadly defined in most jurisdictions. It may occur at all hours of the day and is not limited to dwellings but also may occur in virtually any structure. It is important to note that burglary is not entry alone; there must be an *unlawful* entry accompanied by the present intent to commit another crime once inside. Thus, stealing a television from your neighbor's house is not necessarily burglary, unless you had the intent to remove the television *before* entering the house. Going into someone's house or simply onto their property unlawfully without the intention to commit any additional acts is the crime of trespass.

- *Larceny/Theft.* Under the common law, **larceny** was the unlawful taking and carrying away of another's personal property, with the intent to permanently deprive the rightful owner of its possession. This definition included takings that occurred by force (what we today call robbery) and takings that occurred without the knowledge or presence of the owner. It was not larceny if someone deprived some other person of property through fraud or deception. As society evolved and people began to rely on others to do business, personal property was placed in the custody of another for a limited purpose. Thus, Albert might give a clerk at the local drycleaners his laundry to be cleaned; if the clerk kept the clothes for himself and refused to return them to Albert there was no crime because Albert willingly handed over his clothing to the clerk. Courts responded by enlarging the definition of larceny. Larceny is defined broadly today and includes taking by stealth, by fraud, and by false pretenses. Under the common law, each of these was a separate offense, but today in many jurisdictions, they all are classified as larceny. Today, many states have done away with the variety of theft offenses and lump together all crimes involving the unlawful obtaining of property as larceny.

Most jurisdictions now grade larceny based on either the method of taking or the value of the property taken. According to the value of the item(s) stolen, larceny/theft is classified either as grand theft or petty theft, the former being a felony and the latter a misdemeanor. The distinction varies from state to state, but it is under $1,000 in every state.

Crimes Against Public Order and Morality. Crimes against persons and property have readily identifiable victims. There are other acts that are classified as crimes but for which the victim is less readily identifiable. These acts fall into one of two categories: crimes against public order and crimes against morality. Crimes against public order are those in which the injury is to the peace and order of society. These include disorderly conduct, unlawful assembly, and vagrancy. Crimes against morality are those in which the moral health of society is injured. These include consensual sexual acts such as adultery, prostitution, and obscenity.

Public order and morality offenses are frequently challenged as constitutionally invalid because they place limits on individual rights such as freedom of assembly and privacy. States must take care to carefully craft public order legislation so that it does not impermissibly limit constitutionally protected conduct. Statutes that do so often are struck down by courts on the grounds of vagueness or overbreadth.

According to early common-law decisions, it was a crime to disturb the public tranquility. This was referred to as breach of the peace. Today many states have codified it as **disorderly conduct**; this is a catch-all phrase and includes acts as diverse as public drunkenness, vagrancy, and fighting. Disorderly conduct in a group setting generally is referred to as **unlawful assembly**; this includes groups assembled in public without the necessary permits, as well as riots. Vagrancy was a crime developed in feudal England after the Black Death to control the peasants and tie them to their lords. Vagrancy laws made it a crime to move about the country without proof of employment. Today, courts often determine vagrancy statutes to be unconstitutionally overbroad (see *Papachristou v. City of Jacksonville,* 1972).

Public morals offenses involve acts committed by consenting adults but which society has chosen to prohibit as immoral even if freely engaged in. Examples include fornication, adultery, bigamy, and prostitution. Most morals offenses involve the regulation of sexual activity in some form. Although these acts all involve consenting adults, some argue that, in fact, consent is not freely given by some (as in the case of prostitution) or that such conduct diminishes the moral capacity of society and hence is deserving of criminalization as a means of eliminating or at least reducing such activity.

Civil Law

The criminal law is only one half of the court system. The other half involves civil law. Criminal law is designed to allow for the adjudication and punishment of those who violate society's rules, or criminal laws. The state is treated as the aggrieved party, and the alleged wrongdoer is the defendant.

Civil law is law designed to address private wrongs. A private citizen who believes that she has been injured in some way by another may sue that party for damages. The civil law primarily involves disputes between private parties, although the government can sometimes be involved. In civil cases, a person who has been injured by another may file a lawsuit. This person is referred to as the **plaintiff**; the person being sued is the defendant. There

COMPARATIVE COURTS

In September 1993, Michael Fay, an 18-year-old American living in Singapore, vandalized at least 18 cars. Fay pled guilty to two counts of vandalism and was sentenced to a fine, jail time, and six lashes of a rattan cane. Many Americans were appalled at what they considered the barbaric treatment of a juvenile because whipping is illegal in every state. Whatever people's opinions may have been on the matter, if they had one, they were engaging in thinking about comparative law.

Although whipping is a common penalty in Singapore, because an American was involved, it became a hot political issue in the United States in 1994. Twenty-four U.S. senators signed a letter condemning the sentence and appealing for **clemency.** Singaporeans resented such interference; many pointed out that Singapore was a safe and orderly society, whereas the United States had a much higher crime rate. Commentators in both the United States and Singapore pointed to differences in the legal penalties as causes for the differences in crime between the two countries. Although both countries are common-law countries, Singapore very much values the crime control model over the American due process model.

This is what comparative law is all about: How do two or more legal systems differ and how are they similar, and what are the consequences of those differences? Would the United States be a safer and more civic-minded country if it adopted a Singaporean attitude toward crime and punishment? Perhaps, but are we willing to go that far? If so, how about going further and cutting off the hands of thieves and executing adulterers as is done in some Islamic countries? These are some of the things to think about when we read about other systems and ask, "Why don't we do that?"

are no criminal penalties, such as incarceration, available; the primary remedy for harm in the civil law is money damages. The civil law is divided into four major categories: torts, property, contracts, and family law. Cases involving injury to person or property are called torts. Property law focuses on the ownership and acquisition of property. Contract law deals with the enforceability of private agreements between individuals and between organizations. Family law is the set of regulations involving marriage, child custody, and other issues arising in personal relationships, as well as laws regulating the behavior of minors.

Among the many differences between civil and criminal law, the most important is the criminal court requirement of "proof beyond a reasonable doubt" and the civil court "preponderance of the evidence" standard of proof. Proof beyond a reasonable doubt is the prosecution's burden of proof in a criminal trial. Under this standard, the prosecution is required to prove each element of the offense "beyond a reasonable doubt" for the jury to reach a guilty verdict. If the prosecution fails to establish this burden, then the jury must find the defendant "not guilty." Finding a defendant "not guilty" does not mean the defendant is "innocent." Not guilty is a legal finding that the prosecution has failed to meet its burden of proof; it is not necessarily a description of reality. Proof beyond a reasonable doubt is a very high burden of proof, far higher than the proof by a preponderance of the evidence standard used in civil proceedings, which roughly equates to a determination that the individual's actions *more likely than not* caused the harm suffered. It is essentially a weighing of the evidence to decide which direction the evidence tilts toward (i.e., liable or not liable).

Punitive damages are damages awarded in excess of compensatory damages and are intended to serve as a punishment and to discourage the conduct of the type the defendant displayed. **Involuntary commitment** is the use of legal means to commit someone to a mental institution against his will. Both punitive damages and involuntary commitment decisions against a civil defendant can be seen as quasi-criminal penalties in that persons are being deprived of liberty or property, and thus some states reason that a standard of proof closer to the criminal law standard is warranted.

The rights afforded criminal defendants under the Fourth, Fifth, and Sixth Amendments do not apply to civil defendants. Evidence that would be excluded in a criminal trial can often be introduced in civil cases. Defendants have no right to remain silent. There is no legal obligation for the state to provide an attorney for indigent defendants in civil cases because it is not the state that is bringing the case to court. A final important difference is that, whereas only the defendant can appeal an adverse decision in a criminal case, in civil law, either party can appeal given the presence of adequate legal grounds to do so. Table 3.1 summarizes the major distinctions between criminal and civil law.

Tort Law

Tort law is the body of law associated with harm caused to plaintiffs by the action or inaction of defendants other than breaches of contract, which are dealt with in contract law. A wide range of harms is covered under the tort rubric, such as invasion of privacy, personal injury, medical malpractice, product liability, and trespassing.

Tort law is similar to criminal law in that it deals with persons who have been harmed by other persons. Unlike the criminal law, however, tort law does not seek to punish the wrongdoer but to help the injured party become whole; this is usually accomplished by

TABLE 3.1 ■ Summary of Major Distinctions Between Criminal and Civil Law		
Distinction	**Criminal Law**	**Civil Law**
Who is the legal victim?	The state	The individual
Who initiates action?	State or federal prosecutor	Private party or parties, known as plaintiffs
Issue before the courts	Did the defendant violate a criminal code?	Did the defendant cause harm to the plaintiff(s)?
Standard of proof	Beyond a reasonable doubt	Generally, *preponderance of evidence*, sometimes extended to *clear and convincing evidence*
Who has the burden of proof?	The prosecution	Initially the plaintiff, but both parties must "prove" their cases
What is the remedy sought?	Punishment—probation, jail, prison, death	Money or other compensation, punitive damages, resolution of conflict
Rights of the defendant	All rights enumerated under the Fourth, Fifth, Sixth, Eighth, and Fourteenth Amendments	Amendments do not apply to private matters; they are rights owed only by the state to individuals
Who has the right to appeal an adverse decision?	The defendant	Both the plaintiff and the defendant

the awarding of money damages. Money damages are an imperfect remedy for many harms (e.g., how much money will compensate for a physical injury such as the loss of a limb?). In some instances, the remedy may be a court order to perform certain acts or to stop performing certain acts (an order to stop doing something is referred to as an injunction).

A person can be held liable, in both civil and criminal courts, for a harm done. This does not constitute double jeopardy because double jeopardy applies only to multiple criminal punishments; a civil suit and order to pay damages does not constitute "punishment." This does not mean that a plaintiff can again bring suit against the same person for the same tort in the event that she did not prevail in the case. The civil-law protection corresponding to the double jeopardy protection in criminal law is known as **res judicata** ("thing decided"). This principle means that once the case has been through all possible appeals, it is decided forever.

Tort Categories. There are three primary categories of torts: intentional acts, negligent acts, and acts for which strict liability exists. These categories are defined based on the intent of the defendant. Many of the defenses to criminal intent also serve as defenses to civil intent (such as self-defense).

Intentional torts include acts in which the defendant (referred to as the tortfeasor) deliberately causes harm to another person or a person's property. An example of intentional tort is a physical assault (again, a criminal matter that may also be pursued in civil court by victims seeking monetary compensation).

Negligence is conduct that falls below the standard established by law for the protection of others against unreasonable risks of harm. For negligence to exist, the plaintiff must prove that (a) the defendant had a duty to act in a certain way, (b) the defendant breached that duty, and (c) this breach of duty was the cause of the plaintiff's injury. The typical standard of care is referred to as **ordinary care**. This is the degree of care expected from the "reasonable person." Often, negligence cases hinge on the reasonable person standard. That is, did the defendant act the way a reasonable person should have acted to prevent the harm from occurring?

Another important element in tort cases is causation. In addition to the requirement that the tortfeasor owe a duty to the victim is the requirement that the victim be able to show that the tortfeasor's actions were the cause of the victim's injuries. As in criminal law, there are two types of causation—actual cause and proximate cause. **Actual cause** is also called "but for" cause. If the injury would not have occurred but for the defendant's action, then there exists actual cause. **Proximate cause** is also called legal cause. This is the requirement that the defendant's action be not only the actual cause but that society is willing to hold the defendant responsible. There can usually be no intervening causes; that is, the acts of a third person that come between the original negligent act and the harm do not excuse the original act.

Strict liability torts are those in which the plaintiff does not have to prove that the defendant acted intentionally or negligently. Liability is established if it can be shown that the plaintiff was injured and the defendant was the cause of the injury. Strict liability is typically applied to situations where a person chooses an activity that creates a risk of harm to others. An example of a strict liability tort involves harm done by a domestic animal, such as a pet dog. Generally, the owners of domestic animals are strictly liable for any injuries that their animals may cause even if they took all precautions against the animal getting loose.

Defenses to Liability. In addition to challenging issues such as causation and duty of care, tort defendants may raise other, affirmative defenses. These include contributory negligence, comparative negligence, and several other defenses. **Contributory negligence** is a doctrine that holds that if an injured party was even partially responsible for the injury he has suffered, he is barred from recovering damages from a tortfeasor. So, if two parties are both negligent, neither may sue the other. This doctrine has fallen out of favor as society has come to recognize that tortfeasors should not be completely excused from responsibility for the harm they have done to another simply because the person they injured was partially to blame.

Comparative negligence is a doctrine that attempts to apportion the responsibility among each party. For instance, if Jane is injured by Fred's negligent conduct, but the court determines Jane was also negligent (say 25% responsible), then she may only recover for the percentage of her injuries caused by Fred—in this case, 75%.

Defenses to torts include consent and immunity. A person may consent to being harmed by another person, although the law typically does not allow a person to give valid consent to serious harm. Some parties may be immune from suit. Historically, under the doctrine of **sovereign immunity**, governments could not be sued by their citizens. Most governments have relaxed this defense and now allow citizens to sue the government in many circumstances.

Property Law

Property law in the United States is largely a product of the English common law. Many of the legal doctrines used to decide property cases were first developed by the English courts in the 17th and 18th centuries, although many changes have since been made. Property law has been written and used primarily to protect the owners and possessors of property from harm to or the loss of their property by other persons or, in some instances, the government.

The legal term *property* varies somewhat from the common usage. In a legal sense, property means the right of possession or ownership. Property includes personal property, such as an automobile or a television, **real property**, defined as land or permanent attachments to land, and intellectual property, defined as unique ideas or concepts developed by an individual or group. In each case, legal property means the right of ownership or control over the item, land, or idea in question.

Interests in Real Property. At common law, a number of different types of interests (or rights) in real property were developed by the courts, largely in response to changes in how people used the land. Much of the law of property that developed at common law involved how land, and the buildings on it, could be transferred from one person to another, either during the owner's lifetime or upon his death. It is of course possible for more than one person to own an interest in real property, as when a husband and wife both own their home. When multiple parties each own an equal share of a piece of real property, they have a **tenancy in common**. If one of the parties dies, under the right of survivorship, that person's interest in the property may be transferred to the surviving party.

Other issues involving real property include air and subsurface rights. It is possible for a landowner to sell the rights to the air above her land or the right to use or extract materials from below the land (such as minerals or water). A landowner may also grant an easement to someone. An **easement** is a limited right to use the property of another for a particular purpose, without adversely affecting the ownership rights of the landowner. For example, if Fred owned some land that surrounded land owned by Alice, Alice could not legally cross Fred's land to get to her property. Fred could grant Alice an easement to cross his land, however. This easement could prescribe where Alice could cross Fred's land and for how long such a right would continue.

While real property is typically transferred either by gift or sale, it is possible for a person to acquire an interest in another's property simply by using it. Under the doctrine of **adverse possession**, if Smith openly and exclusively uses all or a portion of land owned by Jones for a specific period of time (traditionally for at least 7 years), then at the end of that time period, he may file suit to obtain the land. The purpose of adverse possession is to encourage people to use their property and to take steps to protect it from encroachment. Property owners are generally well protected by the law, however. Although the doctrine of adverse possession exists, it is very easy to prevent a claim of adverse possession.

At the same time that the rights of property owners are protected, the law does impose some duties on owners of real property. Under the **nuisance doctrine**, a property owner may not use her property in such a way that it has an unreasonable, adverse effect on other property owners. Thus, a homeowner may be prevented from operating a factory in a residential area, because such a use of the property does not comport with surrounding uses.

Property owners have a duty to keep their property in reasonably safe condition and to take reasonable steps to protect those who come onto the property, including trespassers, from harm. Until the 20th century, trespassers had no rights, and if they were injured while trespassing on another's property, they could not sue for damages. This is no longer the case, because courts have recognized that landowners have a duty to keep their property free of dangers that a trespasser could not be expected to discover.

Interests in Personal Property. Personal property includes any tangible item not connected to the land. This includes automobiles, books, televisions, money, and the like. These types of property are sometimes referred to as movables. It does not include land or items permanently attached to the land (such as trees or buildings) or intangible items, such as patents or copyrights. A person may own personal property and transfer that personal property permanently to another, either by sale or gift.

Personal property may also be the subject of a temporary transfer of possession. When a person transfers possession of an item to another for a particular purpose, with the understanding that the property will be returned at a later time, a **bailment** is created. A bailment involves the transfer of possession but not ownership. For example, when Craig takes his shirts to the cleaners, he gives the shirts to the clerk, who gives Craig a receipt. When Craig returns, he presents the receipt, pays the bill, and is given his shirts. Craig did not transfer ownership of his shirts to the cleaners, nor did he give the shirts to the cleaners to use as they see fit; he merely transferred possession to the cleaners for the limited purpose of having them cleaned.

Contract Law

Contract law is the law governing the conduct of business. Contracts are legally enforceable promises. They are formal agreements between two or more parties voluntarily undertaken that make certain promises in exchange for other specified promises. Thus, contract law is concerned with determining the legality of written and spoken agreements between citizens, groups, agencies, and corporations. Many thousands of contracts are arranged and agreed to in both public and private enterprises each day. Fundamental to the operation of any business is the ability to conduct business transactions. Imagine the chaos of a world in which there were no expectations about business agreements and what constitutes a legally binding contract. It would be very difficult to conduct any type of arranged deal without some common understanding of contracts. Contract law provides this common understanding. Much of the law concerning contracts is now guided by the **Uniform Commercial Code.** The Uniform Commercial Code is designed to standardize trade and contract practices among merchants and businesses. The Uniform Commercial Code codifies a variety of principles already established by common law.

Elements of a Valid Contract. Every contract has similar elements. These include at least two parties to the contract, both of whom are capable of signing a contract (meaning they have legal capacity). In addition, both parties must agree to the terms of the contract, and there must be a promise supported by consideration. Promises are the backbones of contracts and become legally binding when supported by legal considerations. Consideration is essentially the reliance by a party to the agreement. Put simply, a contract generally consists of two or more parties making promises to one another. It becomes legally binding when one or more of the parties relies on the promise of the other. Contracts can be either written or verbal.

Another concept crucial to the study of contract law is the notion of good faith. In most contract negotiations, there is an assumption that all the parties are making promises that they mean to keep and that these promises are made based on a common understanding of what will be required to meet the obligations incurred according to standards of fair dealing in trade. Finally, it is considered a breach of contract when the terms of a contract are not met.

Family Law

The family is the basic institution of any society. Because of this, we should expect all societies to have laws designed to protect the integrity of marriage. Family law is focused largely on the creation of and dissolution of marriages and other interpersonal relationships and the resultant changes in fiscal and personal responsibilities between the parties. Primary issues in family law are briefly addressed here.

Who May Marry Whom? Marriage is a legal contract that carries with it rights and responsibilities for both parties, and as a contract, it must meet certain requirements to be considered legally valid, just as any other contract. A person must be 18 years of age or older to get married without parental permission in almost all states. A person under legal age is considered incompetent to enter a marriage contract. Other incompetencies precluding the issuance of a marriage license include mental deficiencies such as insanity. Closely related persons such as brothers and sisters, parents and children, or cousins may not enter a marital contract. The final requirement is that neither party be currently married to someone else. If a person already married marries someone else, he or she is guilty of bigamy.

Common-Law Marriage. **Common-law marriage** may be established by couples cohabiting and acting in every way as though married (owning property in common, filing joint income taxes, etc.) even though they have not been through a formal wedding ceremony and have no license. Such marriages are recognized as valid if established in states allowing them. The vast majority of states allow common-law marriage.

Divorce and Annulment. Just as there are licensing requirements for marriage, the dissolution of the marital contract by divorce or annulment requires legal grounds. Grounds (legally acceptable reasons) for divorce are divided into no-fault (such as irreconcilable differences) and fault categories. All states now have **no-fault divorce**, meaning that there is no assumption of fault by either marriage partner for the marital breakup. Some states retain fault-based divorce in addition to their no-fault grounds. Fault grounds, which were traditionally such things as adultery, cruelty, desertion, insanity, and alcoholism, are used in states retaining fault for issues such as child custody and financial settlements, even if a no-fault divorce has already been granted.

Marriages may also be annulled. An **annulment** is a legal declaration that a marriage never existed because the legal requirements for a valid marriage were not met. An annulment can be obtained if someone lacked the legal ability to consent to marriage.

Dividing Property, Child Custody, and Spousal Support. Marriage is a partnership in the same sense that Smith and Jones's landscaping business is, and the dissolution of the partnership requires a determination of who gets what out of the partnership when it dissolves. Statutes governing property division vary by state, but they can generally be grouped into two types: dual-property and all-property models, with most following the dual-property model. In the dual-property model, the courts consider assets held jointly (acquired during the marriage) by the spouses and separate assets each brought with them to the marriage, inherited, or received as gifts during the marriage. If separate property is not commingled with joint assets, courts will typically recognize the separate ownership of the individual spouse, and it will not be divided along with joint marital assets. In all-property states, the courts typically divide all property owned by either spouse at the time of the divorce equally.

In marriages with children that end in divorce, the courts also have to decide the issue of child custody. In some cases, one spouse voluntarily gives up custody to the other spouse, but when a battle ensues, the courts are charged with making a decision that is in the best interests of the child. Child support is an area of family law that has grown in scope and consequence. Child support is based on the custodial status of the parents. That is, after the legal breakup of a family with children, the courts often are asked to require that the parent without primary physical custody assist with the financial burden placed on the parent with primary physical custody. Most often, the amount of support is based on a calculation of income and the costs associated with childrearing. Many states have complex formulas established to determine an equitable settlement that includes aggregate family income and time spent with each parent.

MOVIES AND THE COURTS
A CIVIL ACTION (1998)

One form of civil suit is a personal injury claim, or lawsuit involving a claim that the defendant's conduct caused harm to the plaintiff. This harm may be physical, emotional, or financial. *A Civil Action* tells the true story of a lawsuit brought by a group of residents of Woburn, Massachusetts, who alleged that several corporations dumped toxic waste into the city water supply, causing a number of children to get cancer. Jan Schlichtmann, a successful personal injury lawyer, and his small firm at first decline to take the case because it will

be costly to prove what caused the children to get cancer, but they change their minds when they realize there are two defendants (Beatrice Foods and Grace, two multinational corporations) with deep pockets.

A class action lawsuit is filed in federal court, with the families seeking a cleanup of the contaminated area and an apology. However, the attorneys for the parent corporations are not easy to intimidate, the judge makes a key ruling against the plaintiffs, and the cost of preparing the enormous amount of scientific evidence for trial ends up bankrupting the law firm, which covered all the costs in return for a percentage of the anticipated final settlement or judgment. After a lengthy trial, the case is dismissed against Beatrice, and the plaintiffs turned down a settlement offer of $20 million while the jury was deliberating. The plaintiffs are then forced to accept a settlement with Grace that barely covers the expense involved in trying the case. The families are very disappointed, because there will be no cleanup or public apology. A postscript to the story is that the Environmental Protection Agency later brought its own enforcement action against Beatrice and Grace, forcing them to pay millions to clean up the land.

SUMMARY

In this chapter, we discussed the basic elements of the criminal law as well as the purposes of the criminal law and sources and limitations on the criminal law. It is the criminal law that governs much of human activity today. According to social contract theory, when human beings abandoned their solitary existence for the benefits of living among others, they gave up some of their individual rights to the state in return for the benefits they gained from living in society. The criminal law is the formal means by which society attempts to control the conduct of individuals. Informal means of social control still exist and are often effective, but when informal means fail, the criminal law exists to deal with society's transgressors.

The criminal law has developed as society has developed. Definitions of crimes have changed, and new offenses have been created, in an attempt to maintain a rational set of rules by which society can function and individuals within society are protected from others. What is legal may vary across the years and by culture, but all societies with a written criminal law share many similarities.

The issues with which scholars, judges, and juries continue to struggle involve the limits of the criminal sanction. How much can society expect the criminal to accomplish? When is it fair and just to hold individuals accountable for their conduct and to subject them to criminal sanctions?

Determining when liability should attach and also the appropriate level of punishment are difficult choices involving policy considerations, legal doctrine, and morality.

In this chapter, we have attempted to explain what constitutes a particular crime such as murder or arson, why certain acts are crimes and others are not, and why we assess blame differently depending on the circumstances of each event and the mental state of the defendant. There are no easy answers in this area.

In this chapter, we also examined the primary areas of the civil law. Civil law is law designed to address private wrongs and is composed of tort, contract, property, and family categories. There are many differences between civil and criminal law, the most important being the lower "preponderance of evidence" standard of proof. Tort law is law regarding wrongs committed against private citizens, which may also be crimes that have already been prosecuted in criminal courts. A variety of tort categories mirror criminal categories (e.g., intentional vs. negligent wrongs) as well as a similar variety of defenses to liability.

Property law is law about the rights of ownership or possession of personal (movables, such as furniture and automobiles), real (buildings, houses), and intellectual (ideas, songs, abstract creations) property. It also has to do with the responsible use of property and how it can be used, disposed of, given away, or inherited.

Contract law is the law covering the conduct of business. A contract is a legally binding promise of one party to do or provide something to one party in exchange for a similar promise from the other party. A number of requirements must be met for a contract to be legal: two parties, capacity, assent, and legality. If the terms of a contract are not met, it is considered a breach of contract for which the injured party can seek legal redress.

Family law has to do with such issues as the legal requirements for a valid marriage, the duties and responsibilities of the parties in the marriage, the dissolution of the marriage, and issues of alimony and child support.

Don't overlook the Student Study Site with its useful study aids, such as self-quizzes, eFlashcards, and other assists, to help you get more from the course and improve your grade.

DISCUSSION QUESTIONS

1. What are some of the prominent limitations on the criminal law?

2. What are the five elements of the corpus delicti, and why must each be proven?

3. What is the difference between an excuse defense and a justification defense?

4. What are the major categories of crimes, and how are crimes classified?

5. How does the civil law differ procedurally from the criminal law?

6. Name and explain the different standards for the burden of proof.

7. What is a justification defense? Give three examples and explain them.

8. What is an excuse defense? Give five examples and explain.

9. Explain the M'Naghten rule.

10. Explain the differences between civil law and common law.

KEY TERMS

Actual cause 66
Actus reus 53
Adequate provocation 60
Adverse possession 67
Affirmative defenses 56
Alibi 56
Annulment 70
Assault 61

Bailment 68
Battery 61
Burden of persuasion 56
Burden of production 56
Burglary 61
Castle doctrine 57
Causation 54
Clemency 63

Common-law marriage 69
Comparative negligence 66
Concurrence 54
Consent 57
Conspiracy 56
Contributory negligence 66
Corpus delicti 53
Disorderly conduct 62

Durham rule 58
Easement 67
Excuse defense 57
Felony murder 60
Harm 55
Homicide 59
Insanity 58
Involuntary commitment 64
Irresistible impulse test 58
Justification defense 57
Larceny 62
Mala in se 51
Mala prohibita 51
Malice aforethought 59
Manslaughter 59
Mens rea 54
M'Naghten rule 58

Model Penal Code 54
Motive 54
Murder 59
Negligence 66
No-fault divorce 69
Nuisance doctrine 67
Ordinary care 66
Overbreadth doctrine 51
Plaintiff 63
Product test 58
Proof beyond a reasonable
     doubt 50
Proof by a preponderance of
     the evidence 51
Proximate cause 66
Punitive damages 64
Rape 60

Real property 67
Res judicata 65
Retreat doctrine 57
Self-defense 57
Solicitation 56
Sovereign immunity 67
Strict liability 55
Substantial capacity
     test 58
Substantive law 51
Tenancy in common 67
Tort law 64
Transferred intent 54
Uniform Commercial
     Code 68
Unlawful assembly 62
Void for vagueness 52

INTERNET SITES

American Bar Association: www.americanbar.org/aba.html

American Law Institute: www.ali.org

National Association of Criminal Defense Lawyers: www.nacdl.org

National District Attorneys Association: www.ndaa.org/

Sourcebook of Criminal Justice Statistics Online: www.albany.edu/sourcebook

STUDENT STUDY SITE

Get the tools you need to sharpen your study skills. SAGE edge offers a robust online environment featuring an impressive array of free tools and resources.

Access practice quizzes, eFlashcards, video, and multimedia at **edge.sagepub.com/hemmens4e**

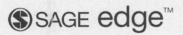

4

© Comstock/Stockbyte/Thinkstock Images

COURT ORGANIZATION AND STRUCTURE

Master the content at **edge.sagepub.com/hemmens4e**

INTRODUCTION

The United States has a dual court structure, with two distinct court systems: the federal court system and the 50 state courts (which also differ from each other in significant ways). In this chapter, we discuss the purpose and structure of both the federal courts and the state courts. The federal and state courts have a number of similarities and some important differences. Some examples of different court systems are provided to illustrate these similarities and differences. We include in the discussion trial and appeals courts as well as courts of limited jurisdiction. Frequently, issues arise concerning the interplay of federal courts and state courts.

After examining the various court structures, we briefly examine the court actors, focusing primarily on the judge, prosecutor and defense attorney, and the jury. It is these courtroom actors, or **courtroom workgroup**, who perform the tasks necessary for the court system to dispense justice. Each of these court actors will be discussed in greater depth in subsequent chapters.

Next, we provide a discussion of the pretrial process and the criminal trial. Although this process is covered in greater depth in later chapters, it is important that students have an understanding of the framework of the process before we begin to discuss in detail the various aspects of that process.

Before we examine the court personnel and structure, however, we need to discuss the jurisdiction of a court or court system. To appreciate how and why court systems are set up the way they are, one must understand the concept of jurisdiction.

JURISDICTION

Jurisdiction is a key component of any court system. The term **jurisdiction** comes from the Latin *juris* ("law") and *dicere* ("to speak") and denotes the legal authority or power of a court to hear a case. A court's jurisdiction is conferred by statute or constitution. There are four primary types of jurisdiction: personal, subject matter, geographic, and hierarchical.

Personal jurisdiction refers to the authority of a court over the person, or defendant. A court may have personal jurisdiction over a person if that person comes in contact with the court, either by being a citizen of the state or by committing an act within the state.

Subject matter jurisdiction refers to the authority of a court to hear a particular type of case. Some courts may hear only a specified type of case, such as a juvenile court or probate court. These courts are referred to as courts of **limited jurisdiction**. Other courts have broad subject matter jurisdiction and may hear both civil and criminal proceedings. These courts are referred to as courts of **general jurisdiction**. Different states allocate the subject matter jurisdiction of their courts differently, based on a variety of factors, including geography and population density.

Geographic jurisdiction refers to the authority of a court to hear cases that arise within specified geographical boundaries, such as a city, county, state, or country. This is also sometimes referred to as **venue**. For a court to have jurisdiction over an event, that event must have taken place within the geographic jurisdiction of the court. Thus, a person who assaults someone in Washington could not be prosecuted in Arizona for that assault. The proper forum is the state of Washington, and the appropriate court within Washington would be the court in the county in which the assault occurred.

Occasionally, a crime (or more accurately crimes) occurs in more than one jurisdiction. For instance, a person may be kidnapped in Iowa and taken to Florida. In this case, the kidnapping is what is known as a continuing offense; that is, a kidnapping occurs in each state into which the victim is taken. Furthermore, both Iowa and Florida may prosecute the kidnapper without violating the constitutional prohibition on double jeopardy, because each state is a separate sovereign government. This means each state derives its authority from a different source—its own state constitution. Most crimes, however, can only take place in one jurisdiction—where the crime occurred. An example is murder—a person can only be killed once, and it is the state in which the killing occurs that has the jurisdiction to prosecute the killer.

Hierarchical jurisdiction refers to the division of duties and roles among the various courts within a single jurisdiction. There is original jurisdiction and appellate jurisdiction, as well as limited and general jurisdiction. The trial court, where a case begins (or originates) and the trial is held, has **original jurisdiction**. After a verdict, the losing party in a civil case or the defendant in a criminal case (the prosecution is barred from appealing a trial court verdict) may seek review of the trial by another, higher court. Courts that are tasked with reviewing trial court verdicts have **appellate jurisdiction**. Appeals courts may affirm or reverse lower court judgments and either enter a new judgment or send the case back down to the lower court for reconsideration based on the appeals court's determination of error by the trial court. Appellate courts do not conduct a retrial; rather, they are generally limited to a review of the trial record to determine if there were any major legal errors. Rather than conducting a new trial, appeals courts read legal briefs and listen to oral arguments by the attorneys for each side and issue a decision, in a written document referred to as a judicial opinion, on these materials.

THE STRUCTURE AND JURISDICTION OF U.S. COURTS

It is somewhat misleading to talk about "the court system" in the United States. In reality, we have a dual court system that includes 50 separate state court systems, which differ from one another on a number of important dimensions, and the federal court system. Adding to the complexity is the fact that the jurisdiction of the federal and state courts may overlap, because what is a crime in a state may also be punishable under federal law in some circumstances. This makes our judicial system more complex than the systems found in other countries, most of which do not have complete sets of trial and appellate courts at both the state and federal levels. Rather, countries such as Germany and Austria have a single federal court.

In the sections that follow, we discuss the structure and jurisdiction of courts in the United States. We begin with the historical development of the federal court system, followed by a discussion of the federal courts and then the state courts.

A BRIEF HISTORICAL OVERVIEW

Article III of the U.S. Constitution provides that "the judicial power of the United States shall be vested in one supreme court, and in such inferior courts as the Congress may from time to time ordain and establish." The provision giving Congress the power to establish inferior courts represented a compromise between states' rights advocates (known as Anti-Federalists), who argued that state courts should hear all cases in the first instance and that the federal supreme court should only hear appeals from the state courts, and advocates for a strong national government (known as Federalists), who wanted a system of federal trial and appellate courts that would hear cases involving the national government or citizens from different states. By establishing only the Supreme Court but giving Congress the power to establish other "inferior" (meaning lower) federal courts, the framers of the Constitution, in essence, postponed debate on this contentious issue.

The debate was not postponed for long, however. When the first Congress convened in 1789, the first Senate bill introduced was the **Judiciary Act of 1789**, which created a federal judicial system composed of the Supreme Court (with six justices), three circuit courts, and 13 district (or trial) courts. Although the creation of a system of lower federal courts was a victory for the Federalists, passage of the act represented a compromise between the Federalists and the Anti-Federalists on a number of issues. For example, the act placed significant limitations on federal trial court jurisdiction, due to the Anti-Federalists' concerns about a too-powerful federal judiciary. Also, the act stipulated that the boundaries of the federal district and circuit courts were to be drawn along state lines. This structure was not achieved by accident; it reflected the Anti-Federalists' desire to see the federal courts connected in some sense to the political culture of each state. Finally, the act required that federal district judges be residents of the state in which the district court was located; this was intended to prevent out-of-state judges from serving, for fear they would not understand the local situation. Courts created under the authority of Article III of the Constitution are known as **Article III courts**.

The federal judicial system remained relatively unchanged until the late 1800s, when Congress responded to concerns that the growing country needed additional courts and judges to handle the increased number of both civil and criminal cases in federal courts. In 1891, Congress enacted the **Court of Appeals Act of 1891**, which created the circuit courts of appeal, a new layer of intermediate appellate courts that would hear appeals from the district courts, and gave the Supreme Court more discretion in deciding which cases to hear. The issue of discretionary appeal to the Supreme Court was also addressed in the Judges Bill, passed by Congress in 1925. This bill gave the district courts original jurisdiction to try cases involving federal statutes or the federal Constitution, with the right of appeal to the circuit courts. As a result of the passage of this bill, most cases can no longer be appealed as a matter of right to the Supreme Court.

Although Congress has continued to tinker with the structure and operation of the federal judiciary—creating, for example, U.S. magistrate judges in 1968 and charging the U.S. Sentencing Commission to develop sentencing guidelines in 1984—the basic structure and jurisdiction of the federal court system has not changed much since 1925.

The history of each state court system is beyond the scope of this book. However, it is important to note that state courts emerged more or less independently of the federal courts, even though the structure of the state courts looks quite similar to the federal court structure. State courts differ from the federal courts, however, in that they handle most criminal cases; that is, most criminal law enforcement and prosecution is handled by state and local agencies. Additionally, and perhaps most significantly, even before the writing of the Constitution in 1787, the colonies, as sovereign entities, already had their own constitutions—and their own court structures. This is the reason that state court structures do not necessarily mirror the federal court structure.

FEDERAL COURTS

The federal court system has three tiers: district courts, courts of appeal, and the Supreme Court. Each of these courts has different functions. The federal courts (see Figure 4.1, which illustrates the structure of the federal court system) have much more limited jurisdiction than do the state courts, especially with regard to criminal matters. Federal courts only hear cases in which the United States is a party, cases involving violations of the U.S. Constitution or a law passed by Congress, cases involving citizens of different states (referred to as diversity of citizenship), and some special types of cases such as bankruptcy cases and patent cases. In some cases, such as those involving citizens of different states, the federal courts have exclusive jurisdiction; these types of cases cannot be handled in a state court. In other cases—for example, criminal cases involving cross-border drug trafficking offenses—both the state and the federal courts have jurisdiction and the case can be tried in either type of court. Generally, however, if a criminal case involves a violation of a federal law, it will be tried in federal court. This means that when someone violates one or more provisions of the United States Code, that person will be prosecuted in federal court. For example, an individual who is arrested for failure to pay federal income taxes will be tried in federal court, as will an individual who is arrested for embezzling money from a national bank.

Until the latter part of the 20th century the federal court docket consisted primarily of civil cases, but this balance has shifted somewhat. Congress has dramatically increased the number of federal crimes. Consequently, whereas civil cases in federal district court still outnumber criminal cases, criminal cases take up a significant portion of the district court's time. In 2017 there were 367,937 cases filed with the federal district courts (Administrative Office of the U.S. Courts, 2017a). Crimes tried in federal courts include many types of white-collar crimes, kidnapping, bank robbery, mail fraud, and civil rights abuses. The "war on drugs" and the illegal immigration crisis have added greatly to the federal courts' burdens, together comprising about 60% of criminal cases heard by them. Because the Constitution requires a "speedy trial" in criminal cases, the prosecution of criminal cases takes precedence over the processing of civil cases when there is a conflict; as a result, civil cases may be delayed.

Federal judges are appointed for life: They hold office "during good behavior." Furthermore, their salary cannot be reduced during their term of office. This protects the independence of the federal judiciary and sets it apart from state court judges, most of whom are appointed or elected to a defined term of years.

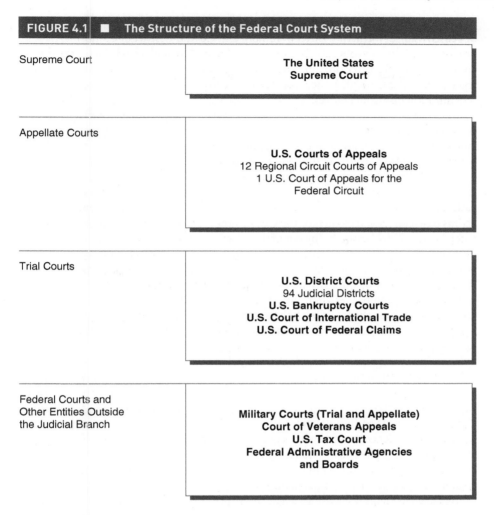

FIGURE 4.1 ■ **The Structure of the Federal Court System**

Supreme Court

> **The United States**
> **Supreme Court**

Appellate Courts

> **U.S. Courts of Appeals**
> 12 Regional Circuit Courts of Appeals
> 1 U.S. Court of Appeals for the
> Federal Circuit

Trial Courts

> **U.S. District Courts**
> 94 Judicial Districts
> **U.S. Bankruptcy Courts**
> **U.S. Court of International Trade**
> **U.S. Court of Federal Claims**

Federal Courts and
Other Entities Outside
the Judicial Branch

> **Military Courts (Trial and Appellate)**
> **Court of Veterans Appeals**
> **U.S. Tax Court**
> **Federal Administrative Agencies**
> **and Boards**

District Courts

The district court is the trial court, or court of original jurisdiction, for the federal court system. There are currently 94 U.S. district courts (including several in U.S. territories). Each state has at least one district court; some, such as California and Texas, have as many as four. With one exception (Wyoming, whose district court includes Yellowstone National Park, including the portion in Montana), no judicial district crosses state lines. Each district has more than one judge, but only one judge presides over a particular trial. There are approximately 677 federal district judges, all of whom are appointed for life. The number of judges in a district ranges from 2 to 29, depending on the population of the individual district. Several of the district courts (i.e., Vermont, Western District of Wisconsin, Northern District of Iowa, North Dakota, and Idaho) have only two authorized judgeships; other courts (i.e., Southern District of New York, Eastern District of Pennsylvania, Northern District of Illinois, and Central District of California) have 20 or more. Each district court also has a number of magistrate judges, who assist the district court judges in both civil and criminal cases. According to the Administrative Office of the U.S. Courts, as of 2014 (the most recent date for which data are available) there were 531 full-time magistrate judges.

Magistrate judges are subordinate judicial officers. These judicial officers conduct preliminary proceedings in cases before the district court and issue warrants. Judgments entered by magistrates are considered judgments of the district court. Federal magistrate courts are similar to courts of limited jurisdiction in state courts.

Federal district courts have jurisdiction to hear only those types of cases specified by acts of Congress, and Congress may authorize the district court to hear only those cases and controversies specified in Article III. Most cases in federal court deal with claims based on federal statutes or the Constitution. The other major category of cases in federal courts is civil cases arising out of the court's diversity jurisdiction. A federal court's diversity jurisdiction authorizes it to hear any civil matter, even if it involves only state law, if the amount in question exceeds $50,000 and the parties are diverse—meaning if they are citizens of different states. **Diversity of citizenship** refers to the situation where the opposing parties are from different states. Federal courts were given diversity jurisdiction because the founding fathers were concerned that state courts presented with a suit between a state resident and a nonresident would be biased in favor of their resident. Allowing the nonresident to shift the case to federal court on the basis of diversity of citizenship was seen as a means of ensuring a fair trial, because it was assumed federal courts would be neutral.

Most of the cases heard in federal courts are civil cases rather than criminal cases. In 2015, for example, 271,950 civil cases, but only 91,914 criminal cases, were filed in U.S. district courts (Administrative Office of the U.S. Courts, 2017a). Another criminal matter that district courts deal with is petitions for habeas corpus relief. Prisoners who are incarcerated enjoy the constitutional right to petition the federal courts (usually district courts) to review the constitutionality of their confinement. In 2006, the district courts responded to almost 55,000 such petitions.

As shown in Figure 4.1, there are a number of specialized trial courts in the federal system. They include the U.S. bankruptcy courts, the U.S. Court of International Trade, and the U.S. Court of Federal Claims. There also are courts that are outside the judicial branch of government: military courts, the Court of Veterans Appeals, and the U.S. Tax Court.

Courts of Appeals

The second tier in the federal system is the court of appeals. These courts are also referred to as circuit courts, because Supreme Court justices who were assigned to sit on them when the Supreme Court was not in session "rode circuit" as they traveled from court to court. Supreme Court justices are no longer required to sit on court of appeals panels, but the name remains in use. These courts handle appeals of decisions from the U.S. district courts in the circuit. Originally there were only three courts of appeals, but as the country grew, so too did the number of circuit courts. Today there are 13 courts of appeals: 11 for the 50 states, 1 for the District of Columbia, and 1 for the federal circuit.

The jurisdiction of the court of appeals for the federal circuit is limited to appeals from specified federal agencies and decisions of the U.S. Court of Federal Claims and the U.S. Court of International Trade, two specialized federal trial courts. The District of Columbia has its own appeals court in part because it is not a state and in part because of the large volume of cases filed in the District of Columbia (this is because so many federal agencies are located there and thus the court has geographic jurisdiction over suits involving these agencies). The 11 remaining courts of appeals are organized on a territorial basis, with each covering several states. For instance, the Third Circuit includes the states of Delaware, New Jersey, Pennsylvania, and the territory of the Virgin Islands, and the Seventh Circuit is composed of the states of Illinois, Indiana, and Wisconsin.

Both criminal and civil matters can be heard by the courts of appeals, and these appellate courts also hear a large number of habeas corpus petitions from inmates. In 2013, 57,777 appeals from U.S. district courts were filed in the courts of appeals; two thirds of these cases involved civil matters, and one third involved criminal matters.

There are 179 judges assigned to the circuit courts of appeals. The Ninth Circuit, which is the largest court of appeals and includes California, Arizona, Oregon, Washington, Nevada, Montana, Idaho, Alaska, and Hawaii, as well as Guam and the Northern Marianas Islands, is staffed by 29 judges. In contrast, the First Circuit, which is made up of Maine, Massachusetts, New Hampshire, and Puerto Rico, is staffed by only 6 judges.

Appeals are heard by three-judge panels, selected at random so that any of the judges on a particular court of appeal may sit with one judge on one case and a different judge on the next case. After reading written arguments and listening to oral arguments, the panel of judges discusses the case and votes whether to affirm or reverse the lower court ruling. In a criminal case in which an offender convicted in federal court is appealing his sentence for drug trafficking, for example, the judges would decide whether to uphold or strike down the sentence imposed by the district court judge. If two panels in the same circuit issue different opinions on a similar issue, the entire circuit may decide to sit **en banc** (meaning as a group) and rehear the cases and issue an opinion that is binding on the entire circuit. This can obviously be a bit unwieldy in those circuits that have a large number of judges; consequently, federal law permits courts of appeals with more than 15 judges to sit en banc with fewer than all its members. For example, the Ninth Circuit may hold en banc hearings with as few as 11 of its 29 judges.

The Supreme Court

The third tier in the federal court system is the Supreme Court. Because it is the final step in the federal court system and for any case involving the interpretation of a federal statute or the U.S. Constitution, it is sometimes referred to as the "court of last resort." The Supreme Court has original (meaning trial) jurisdiction over a very small number of situations, including suits between states, suits between the United States and a state, and suits between a state and a foreign citizen. These occur very rarely; when they do, the Court assigns the trial to a special master and then hears an appeal from the special master's decision. The bulk of the Court's docket consists almost entirely of cases taken on appeal from either the federal courts of appeals or state supreme courts.

The Court's appellate docket is almost entirely discretionary. The Court has the authority to choose which appeals it takes and which it refuses to hear. This is very different from trial courts and lower appeals courts, which must hear cases brought before them. The Supreme Court selects the cases it will hear from the many it is asked to review each year. In a typical year, the Court is asked to review approximately 9,000 cases but agrees to hear and decide fewer than 100. When someone asks the Court to hear an appeal, it submits a petition for a **writ of certiorari**. A writ of certiorari is an order issued by the Supreme Court to the lower court to send the record of the case up to the Supreme Court so that it may be reviewed.

When a litigant files a petition for a writ of certiorari, the justices review it and vote whether to grant it and hear the appeal. The Court comprises nine justices, but it takes only four votes for the appeal to be accepted for review by the Court. This is known as the **rule of four.** If four votes to accept are not obtained, the petition for a writ of

CURRENT CONTROVERSY

The addition of Neil Gorsuch to the U.S. Supreme Court was not without controversy. Gorsuch, a former federal judge for the Tenth Circuit Court of Appeals, was nominated and confirmed in early 2017 to replace recently deceased Antonin Scalia. Scalia, a staunch conservative member on the Court, passed away in early 2016. However, outgoing President Obama nominated chief judge of the D.C. Circuit Court of Appeals Merrick Garland. His nomination expired after 293 days following the conclusion of the 114th Congress, with no action being taken to confirm his nomination. Senate Republicans, which controlled the Senate during President Obama's tenure, declined to hold any hearings or votes on the subject of Garland's nomination, instead opting to wait for the nomination of the next president. This resulted in the longest pending nomination to the Supreme Court in history. Garland was considered to be a moderate (i.e., centrist) justice and was highly respected by both Republicans and Democrats. Nonetheless, following his presidential victory, Donald Trump nominated Gorsuch, as he shared many of the same interpretive ideologies as Justice Scalia. Despite the controversy surrounding the past year's events, the Senate voted 54–45 in favor of confirming Gorsuch. Justice Gorsuch officially assumed office on April 8, 2017, as the youngest appointee since Justice Clarence Thomas's appointment in 1991.

Franz Jantzen, Collection of the Supreme Court of the United States

The Justices of the United States Supreme Court, 2019. Front row, left to right: Associate Justice Stephen G. Breyer, Associate Justice Clarence Thomas, Chief Justice John G. Roberts, Jr., Associate Justice Ruth Bader Ginsburg, Associate Justice Samuel A. Alito. Back row: Associate Justice Neil M. Gorsuch, Associate Justice Sonia Sotomayor, Associate Justice Elena Kagan, Associate Justice Brett M. Kavanaugh.

certiorari is denied, and the decision of the lower court is left undisturbed. Refusal to accept a petition for a writ of certiorari is not considered a decision on the merits and has no binding precedential value. It does not mean the Court has found in favor of the winning side in the lower court; it simply means the Court, for an unknown reason, has decided not to hear the appeal. It may be the justices do not think the issue in the appeal is significant, or they may simply not want to address the issue, perhaps hoping they can avoid it and leave the solution to the lower courts or to the political process.

The Supreme Court has three main functions: (1) to resolve disputes between states, (2) to resolve conflicting opinions of lower federal and state courts, and (3) to resolve constitutional questions. The Court uses its discretionary docket to take only those cases that fit into one of these categories.

Whereas appeals to the federal courts of appeals come only from the U.S. district courts, the Supreme Court hears appeals from both courts of appeals and state supreme courts. The decisions of state supreme courts, however, will be reviewed by the Supreme Court only if they involve a "substantial federal question." An example of a criminal appeal from a state supreme court that the Court might agree to hear would be a case in which the defendant claimed that his constitutional rights were violated—for example, his jury was selected in a racially discriminatory manner (in violation of the Equal Protection Clause of the Fourteenth Amendment), or he did not receive effective assistance of counsel (in violation of the Sixth Amendment). Many of the landmark Supreme Court cases in the area of criminal procedure are cases that were appealed from state supreme courts.

It is important to emphasize that most disputed criminal and civil matters never come to the attention of the U.S. Supreme Court. As a result, there may be contradictory decisions from one state to the next, or from one federal circuit to the next. For example, the Court of Appeals for the Second Circuit may decide that a certain type of warrantless search is unconstitutional, but the Court of Appeals for the Sixth Circuit might decide otherwise. Only the Supreme Court can resolve the dispute, but again, only if it decides to hear a case involving this issue. That said, if there are conflicting decisions among the courts of appeals on an important legal question, the Supreme Court often agrees to hear a case and settle the conflict.

The Court is currently composed of nine justices, one of whom is designated the chief justice, and eight associate justices. John Roberts became Chief Justice in 2005 following the death of former Chief Justice William H. Rehnquist. Congress has the authority to either enlarge or reduce the number of justices on the Supreme Court (recall that Article III creates the Supreme Court but leaves the number justices on it to be determined by Congress, as was done with the Judiciary Act of 1791). During the 1800s Congress changed the number of justices from six to nine to ten and back to nine again, but Congress has not changed the number of justices in over 100 years, so it seems unlikely Congress would try to do so now, in the face of a longstanding tradition of having nine justices on the Court.

Created as the third branch of the federal government, the Supreme Court initially was largely overlooked and had little work to do. Because of the lack of work and the apparently low prestige, John Jay, the first chief justice, resigned to take a position as an ambassador. It was not until the term of John Marshall that the Supreme Court began to establish its role in the government, through the exercise of the power of judicial review.

The law is inherently conservative, and so are many of its servants. The conservatism of the law is plain in its emphasis on precedent and predictability (and hence the status quo). The conservatism of the Supreme Court is apparent in the composition of its members since the Court's beginning. As of 2018, there have been 113 justices, of whom 93 have been male, White, and Protestant. Forty-six years after its inception, the Court had its first Catholic, Roger Taney, appointed in 1835. Only eleven other Catholics have served on the Supreme Court, four of whom—John Roberts, Samuel Alito, Sonia Sotomayor, and Neil Gorsuch—are serving presently. It was not until 1916 that the first Jew, Louis Brandeis, was appointed. There have been five other Jewish justices, including two current members, Ruth Bader Ginsburg and Elena Kagan. It was not until 1965 that the first Black man, Thurgood Marshall, was appointed. On Marshall's retirement, the second Black justice, Clarence Thomas, was appointed. The first female, Sandra Day O'Connor, was appointed to the Court in 1981. Ruth Bader Ginsburg became the second female justice in 1993, and was joined in 2009 by Sonia Sotomayor, and in 2010 by Elena Kagan.

STATE COURTS

Although the federal courts, particularly the Supreme Court, receive much of the attention of legal scholars, politicians, and the public, the truth is the federal court system is a very small part of the U.S. court system. Each year, more than 100 million cases are processed in the state and federal courts; 98% of these cases are handled in the state courts. In 2004, the state court caseload included 54.7 million traffic cases, 20.7 million criminal cases, 16.9 million civil cases, 5.7 million domestic relations cases, and 2.1 million juvenile cases (National Center for State Courts, 2006, p. 15). These numbers increase every year.

The 50 states have created a variety of court structures. Some states, such as Illinois and Florida, have unified court systems, with a uniform three- or four-tier court structure for the entire state. Other states, such as New York and Texas, have more complicated systems with multiple layers of courts that often have overlapping jurisdiction. In the states without unified court systems, there may even be variations in court structure from one county to the next.

The most common state court systems have four tiers of courts. There are courts of limited jurisdiction, courts of general jurisdiction, intermediate appellate courts, and a final appellate court, or court of last resort. Each of these is discussed next. Because there is tremendous variation among the states, students should note that their state court structure may differ from our example.

Courts of Limited Jurisdiction

The first level of state courts includes courts of limited jurisdiction. Courts of limited jurisdiction are referred to by a variety of names, depending on the state, including justice of the peace court, magistrate's court, and municipal court. These lower courts handle a variety of matters, including minor criminal cases, traffic offenses, violations of municipal ordinances, juvenile delinquency hearings, and civil disputes under a certain dollar value. These courts may also be responsible for issuing search and arrest warrants and conducting the preliminary stages of felony cases, such as the arraignment and the preliminary hearing.

State courts of limited jurisdiction are quite common. There are some 13,500 such courts in the United States, and they are staffed by nearly 20,000 judicial officers. Six states (California, Illinois, Iowa, Minnesota, Missouri, and South Dakota) and the District of Columbia have no trial courts of limited jurisdiction; other states (e.g., Texas, New York) have more than 2,500 of these lower courts. A unique feature of limited jurisdiction courts is that they are often not part of the state court system. Most of them are controlled by the local governing authority—typically a county—that established them and funds them.

Proceedings in limited jurisdiction courts are often more informal in nature than they are in trial or appellate courts. There is usually no right to trial by jury provided in these courts; if a losing party wishes to appeal an adverse decision and have a jury trial, she must do so through a trial de novo in the trial court above the limited jurisdiction court. A **trial de novo** is not like a standard appeal, where the higher court concerns itself only with a review of any legal errors that may have occurred at trial. Instead, a trial de novo is an entirely new trial. Lower courts are not courts of record; that is, there is no constitutional requirement to provide an official, verbatim recording or transcript of the proceedings. The only official document is the judgment of the court.

Even though courts of limited jurisdiction receive little attention from scholars or the press, they are important for several reasons. First, for many citizens, they are the only experience that most people will ever have with the court system. Second, there are many of these courts, and they process a tremendous number of cases. Third, these courts are often involved in important parts of the pretrial process in criminal cases, such as the arraignment and preliminary hearing.

Courts of General Jurisdiction

The next level in a typical state court system is the courts of general jurisdiction. These are the trial courts for civil and criminal matters. They are typically authorized to hear any matters not exclusively designated for courts of limited jurisdiction; in some states, they may even have concurrent jurisdiction with lower courts on some matters, such as misdemeanors. The workload of these courts varies. In less populous areas, the trial court may hear a wide variety of cases, including civil and criminal. In more populated areas, there may be a greater specialization, with one court handling only felony trials and another handling only civil matters.

Depending on the state, general jurisdiction courts may be referred to as district courts, circuit courts, or superior courts. There are roughly 2,000 general jurisdiction courts throughout the 50 states, and they are staffed by more than 11,000 judges (Rottman, Flango, Cantrell, Hansen, & LaFountain, 2000). In 2004, the state courts of general jurisdiction and the unified courts (which handle both minor and major cases) processed 13.9 million traffic cases, 7.5 million civil cases, 6.5 million criminal cases, 4.1 million domestic relations cases, and 1.4 million juvenile cases (National Center for State Courts, 2006, p. 17).

Appellate Courts

At the next level of the state court system are the appellate courts. A century ago, the state court system included only a single appellate court—the state supreme court. As the number of cases appealed from the trial courts increased and threatened to overwhelm the state courts of last resort, states created intermediate appellate courts of appeals. Today, these courts—which may be referred to as appeals courts, appellate courts, appellate divisions, and courts of appeals—are found in 39 states. Larger states often have several such courts, and they may divide them into civil and criminal divisions.

The state appellate courts—like the federal circuit courts of appeals—hear civil and criminal appeals from the lower (trial) courts within their jurisdiction. Defendants who have been convicted and sentenced in a state trial court have the right to appeal to one higher court and to have the appeal heard by that court; this right of appeal is designed to ensure that the law was applied and interpreted correctly and that proper procedures were followed at every stage in the process. Interestingly, there is no right to appeal a guilty verdict provided in the U.S. Constitution, but all 50 states (and the federal government) provide for an appeal of right either by statute or state constitutional provision. Appellate courts do not decide matters of fact, such as whether a person convicted of a crime is in fact guilty. Appellate courts review the record from the trial court; they do not hear new testimony from the persons involved in the case, and they do not consider new evidence. Issues commonly raised on appeal include defects in the procedures used to select the jury, ineffective assistance of counsel, failure to exclude evidence that was obtained improperly, and coerced confessions or guilty pleas. The purpose of a state appellate court is to ensure a criminal defendant or a losing party in a civil case received a fair trial.

Appellate courts have both mandatory and discretionary jurisdiction. Mandatory jurisdiction means that the court must hear all properly filed appeals; discretionary jurisdiction means that the court can decide which cases it wants to hear. Intermediate appellate courts and supreme courts in states without an intermediate appellate court handle primarily mandatory appeals. State supreme courts in states with an intermediate appellate court, on the other hand, hear most cases under their discretionary jurisdiction. The National Center for State Courts compared the mandatory and discretionary caseloads of 22 states with both intermediate appellate courts and supreme courts. In 2004, 72% of the cases heard by the intermediate appellate courts in these states were mandatory appeals; in contrast, 86% of the cases heard by the supreme courts were discretionary appeals (National Center for State Courts, 2006, p. 75).

State Supreme Courts

The court of last resort in most states is referred to as the state supreme court. Forty-eight states have one court of last resort; two states (Oklahoma and Texas) have two: a court of last resort for civil cases and a court of last resort for criminal cases. The number of judges on the court of last resort varies by state from three to nine. As is the case with other courts in the state court system, the names of these courts vary from state to state: supreme court (43 states), court of appeals (2 states), supreme judicial court (2 states), court of criminal/civil appeals (2 states), and supreme court of appeals (1 state). We use the term *state supreme court* here.

State supreme courts usually hear the majority of appeals on a discretionary basis, similar to the U.S. Supreme Court. This allows them to focus on cases involving significant legal issues. The exceptions are those states that do not have an intermediate appellate court (usually the smaller, less populous states) and, in other states, death penalty cases. In states without an intermediate appellate court, the state supreme court is the only appellate court and thus is required to hear all appeals. Most states also require that their supreme court hear all appeals in cases involving the death penalty. This is provided as an extra safeguard in death penalty cases, because in these cases the punishment is the most severe possible and the states wish to be absolutely sure the defendant has received a fair trial.

For most cases, the state supreme court is as far as a case can go. The only option for a losing party in the state supreme court is to appeal directly to the U.S. Supreme Court, and to do so, the party must be able to identify a legal issue that involves the U.S. Constitution or a federal law. If there is no "federal question" involved, then the U.S. Supreme Court has no jurisdiction. Criminal defendants are often able to raise a claim based on a violation of one of the constitutional guarantees related to the investigation and prosecution of crime, however, so they may be able to file an appeal with the U.S. Supreme Court. Of course, recall that just because someone can file a petition for a writ of certiorari with the U.S. Supreme Court, there is no guarantee the Court will decide to accept the petition. Defendants who lose in state courts also have the option of filing a writ of habeas corpus in federal district court.

VIEW FROM THE FIELD

Molly J. Huskey
Idaho State Supreme Court Justice and former Idaho State Appellate Public Defender
Sara B. Thomas
Administrative Director of the Idaho Courts and former Chief, Appellate Unit, Office of the Idaho State Appellate Public Defender

The evidence is in, and the verdict has been rendered. Yet, not all convictions are just, and mistakes can be made during court proceedings. An appeal is often the defendant's only opportunity to present to the courts concerns with the process by which he or she was convicted. Removed from the immediacy of the trial, a transcript does not convey the emotions, inflections, or body language of the witnesses. The appellate attorney does not have all the facts or evidence, only that information placed in the record before the trial court. Neither can the appellate attorney add new evidence or do additional investigation in the case. Instead, the role of an appellate attorney is to review the already created record, identify any mistakes of law that were made, and ask the appellate court to remedy those errors.

Because the work of the appellate attorney is focused on ensuring that the law was followed, not arguing about the facts of the case, one can divorce oneself from the emotion and immediacy of a trial and address the broader impact of legal rulings. The appellate attorney compares and contrasts various possible rulings, researches prior cases with similar facts and the conclusions prior courts have reached, and presents argument on which of the various possible rules the appellate court should adopt as controlling in that state. Through this work, an appellate attorney has the ability to mold and shape the law, make innovative arguments, and advocate for individual clients. Although the focus is always on the individual client, the reality of practicing appellate law is knowing that your work and the court opinions that result can affect the entire legal system as they create precedent that will be followed in the cases to come.

COURT ACTORS

By court actors, we mean those who regularly appear in a trial or pretrial proceeding. Often referred to as "the courtroom workgroup" (Eisenstein & Jacob, 1977) or the courthouse "community" (Eisenstein et al., 1988), these are the individuals who work together day after day to process the civil and criminal cases that come before the court. The primary actors in a criminal case are, of course, the judge, the prosecutor, the defense attorney, and the jurors. The duties of each of the court actors are discussed briefly in this section of the chapter; in later chapters we examine more closely the role of the primary court actors, including the prosecutor, defense attorney, judge, criminal defendant, and victim.

Judge

The stereotypical view of the role played by a criminal court judge is that the judge presides over trials and imposes sentences. But judges make important decisions at all stages of the criminal process. They issue search warrants that allow police officers to search for contraband or evidence. After an arrest is made, **judges** decide whether bail is required and, if so, how much it should be, whether there is sufficient evidence to hold the defendant for trial, and whether pretrial motions filed by the prosecutor or the defense attorney should be granted. During the trial, judges play an important role in jury selection, in that they decide whether jurors can be excused for "cause" (i.e., because of bias or prejudice toward one side or the other or because a juror has already made up his mind about the defendant's guilt). Judges also are responsible for maintaining order in the courtroom and deciding whether to sustain or overrule objections to questions asked or evidence introduced. In **bench trials**—cases tried by the judge alone, without a jury—judges determine whether the prosecutor has proven the defendant's guilt beyond a reasonable doubt. If the defendant pleads guilty or is found guilty at trial, the judge determines what the sentence will be.

Judicial Selection Methods

Three common methods of selecting judges are appointment, election, and the merit system. Different states use different methods of selecting judges. Some states use more than one method, while others use only one method.

Appointment by the chief executive of the jurisdiction (the president of the United States or the governor of a state) is the oldest method of selecting judges. All 13 of the original colonies used it, and it is still used in the federal system and about 20 states.

Federal judges, including the justices of the Supreme Court, are appointed by the president, confirmed by the U.S. Senate, and serve life terms. (One exception is magistrate judges, who are appointed by the district court judges for terms of either 8 years [full-time judges] or 4 years [part-time judges].) Federal judges may be removed from the bench only if Congress determines, through a process known as **impeachment**, that they are guilty of "treason, bribery, or other high crimes and misdemeanors." Removal of federal judges, however, is rare; only 13 judges have been impeached (meaning that formal allegations were filed in the U.S. House of Representatives), and only 7 of the 13 were convicted by the Senate and removed from office. (Three other

KEY CASES

RIPPO V. BAKER (2017): THE IMPORTANCE OF JUDICIAL IMPARTIALITY

Michael Damon Rippo was convicted of murder in Nevada and was subsequently sentenced to death. Rippo found out during the trial that the judge was a target of a federal bribery investigation. Rippo sought to disqualify the judge, claiming that having a judge presiding over a case in which one of the parties—the county prosecutor's office—was investigating him biased his case and violated the Due Process Clause of the Fourteenth Amendment. The judge failed to recuse himself, and another judge, who stepped in following the prior judge's indictment, also refused to provide Rippo with a new trial. The Nevada State Supreme Court affirmed the lower court's decisions, stating that Rippo had not provided evidence that the state authorities were involved in the federal investigation. In seeking state postconviction relief, Rippo was able to demonstrate, via documents from the judge's trial, that the local prosecutor's office had participated in the federal investigation. Nonetheless, the court denied relief, and the Nevada Supreme Court affirmed in holding that the evidence did not demonstrate the judge was biased. The U.S. Supreme Court vacated the judgement of the Nevada Supreme Court, stating that "recusal is required when, objectively speaking, 'the probability of actual bias on the part of the judge or decisionmaker is too high to be constitutionally tolerable'" (citing *Withrow v. Larkin*, 421 U.S. 35, 47 [1975]) and that the Nevada Supreme Court had failed to properly follow precedent in answering this question. Whereas Rippo's guilt was never really up for debate, the impartiality of the judge presiding over his case was. This is a strong example of how important judicial impartiality is for the criminal process, even when guilt is obvious.

judges who were the subjects of investigations resigned before impeachment proceedings could begin.)

Election is the most commonly used form of judicial selection. The vast majority of state court judges are elected. Elections can be either partisan (the candidate's political party affiliation is listed on the ballot) or nonpartisan (no party affiliation is listed). In some states, judges first run in a partisan election and then stand for retention in subsequent elections; this means that the judge runs uncontested and the voters decide whether he or she should be retained in office.

Election of judges became popular during the 1830s, when Democrats, under the leadership of Andrew Jackson, gained control of Congress from the Federalists. Jackson and his supporters believed the Federalist system of appointing judges for life was both undemocratic and elitist. Georgia (1824) was the first state to implement judicial elections. Currently, 29 states use elections to select judges.

A third method of selecting judges is the **merit system**, also known as the **Missouri plan**, because it was first adopted by Missouri in 1940. The merit system gained in popularity slowly, but today 27 states use some form of it. The merit system consists of three stages. First, a nonpartisan nominating commission selects a list of potential candidates, based on the candidate's legal qualifications. Second, the governor makes a selection from this list, and this person becomes a judge. Finally, the person appointed by the governor stands for retention within a short time after they are selected, usually within one year. In a retention election the judge runs uncontested and the public simply votes whether the judge should continue to serve or not. If the vote is "no," then the judge is out of office and the process begins again.

Prosecutor

Prosecutors are found in both federal and state courts, and their primary responsibility is to bring criminal charges against individuals who are accused of crime and to represent the government's interest in court. Originally, there were no **prosecutors**. Instead, private citizens were responsible for litigating their criminal cases, similar to what a civil litigant does today. Private prosecution gave way to public prosecution as society came to view crime as an offense not just against the person but also against society. Today, private prosecution is no longer permitted. There are more than 25,000 prosecutors today, although about half of them are part-time (primarily in small jurisdictions).

In the federal court system, prosecution of criminal cases is the responsibility of the U.S. Department of Justice, which is headed by the U.S. Attorney General. The attorneys who prosecute cases in the federal courts are called U.S. attorneys. There are 93 U.S. attorneys—one for each of the district courts, with the exception of Guam and the Northern Mariana Islands, which share one attorney. These attorneys are appointed by the president and confirmed by the U.S. Senate. The 93 U.S. attorneys are assisted by more than 4,000 assistant U.S. attorneys.

Three types of prosecutors are found in state court systems. At the top of the hierarchy is the state **attorney general**, who is the state's chief legal officer. The attorney general represents the state in court when state laws and policies are challenged but plays a very limited role in criminal trials and does not supervise the activities of local prosecutors.

The attorneys who prosecute criminal cases are found at the local level. The chief prosecutor, who in all but five states is elected, and her deputies charge and prosecute those accused of crime at the local, typically the county, level. The lead attorney is frequently referred to as the district attorney (or DA). The district attorney is usually elected, with appointed assistants who do most of the trial work. The district attorney's duty is to prosecute cases on behalf of the citizens but also to do justice by pursuing only those who have in fact committed crimes.

Prosecutors in both state and federal courts enjoy a significant amount of unchecked discretionary power. The prosecutor decides who will be charged, what charge will be filed, who will be offered a plea bargain, and the type of bargain that will be offered. The prosecutor presents evidence designed to prove that the defendant is guilty beyond a reasonable doubt to the judge or jury and argues for the defendant's conviction.

The prosecutor also may make a recommendation to the judge regarding bail and often will recommend the sentence the offender should receive. If the defendant appeals his conviction, the prosecutor appears before the appellate court to argue that the conviction should not be overturned.

Defense Attorney

The Sixth Amendment to the U.S. Constitution states, "In all criminal prosecutions, the accused shall enjoy the right to have the assistance of counsel for his defense." Historically, this meant simply that a defendant who had the means to hire an attorney could bring the attorney along to defend her at trial. This was of little help to defendants who could not afford to hire their own attorneys. Recognizing this, the U.S. Supreme Court handed down a series of decisions requiring the appointment of counsel for indigent defendants.

Arguably, the most important of the Court's decisions regarding right to counsel was *Gideon v. Wainwright* (1963). Noting that "lawyers in criminal courts are necessities, not luxuries," the Court ruled that indigent criminal defendants charged with felonies are entitled to lawyers to assist them in their defense. In subsequent decisions, the Court expanded this right, holding that no person could be imprisoned longer than 6 months unless he was represented by counsel (*Argersinger v. Hamlin,* 1972) and that the right to counsel applies to all "critical stages" of the pretrial process.

The Court's decisions had a significant impact on state criminal justice systems, which had to devise ways of representing large numbers of poor defendants at trial and other critical stages in the criminal process. Today, states use one or more of the following systems: public defenders, assigned counsel, contract attorneys. **Public defenders**, like prosecuting attorneys, are salaried government employees; they are hired by the state (or by a county within a state) to represent indigent defendants. Public defender systems are most likely to be found in large urban jurisdictions with high caseloads. In jurisdictions that use an assigned counsel system, judges assign private defense attorneys to represent indigent defendants on a case-by-case basis. Under the contract model, jurisdictions enter into contracts with individual private attorneys or law firms; these attorneys agree to provide legal services to indigent defendants for a fixed sum.

All of the systems used to assign attorneys to indigent defendants have come under criticism. Much of the harshest criticism is directed at the public defender system. These attorneys tend to have large caseloads, and they are not always paid as well as either privately retained attorneys or prosecuting attorneys, so questions have arisen as to their ability to adequately defend their clients. Similar concerns have been voiced about the assigned counsel system. Critics charge that these systems, especially those that rely on lawyers who volunteer for indigent defense, do not necessarily result in the appointment of lawyers with the skills or the experience to defend those charged with crimes. The contract system has been criticized because of the concern that the contracts go to the lowest bidder and not necessarily to the most experienced attorneys.

Defense attorneys are expected to represent their client zealously, without regard for the client's guilt or innocence, while acting within the rules of court. It may be that the best a defense attorney can do for a client is have the charges reduced or the sentence shortened; if so, that is what they must try to do. Under the U.S. Constitution every defendant is entitled to the effective assistance of counsel, regardless of who the defendant is or what the defendant may have done.

Defense attorneys, whether hired by the defendant or appointed by the state, provide a number of services. They represent their clients at various (although not necessarily all) stages of the criminal process, sometimes even before criminal charges have been filed. They also participate in plea bargaining with prosecutors, defend the accused at trial, and otherwise act as their clients' advocates whenever the need arises. And just as prosecutors face certain constraints in their day-to-day activities, so do defense attorneys. The role of defense counsel is to (a) ensure the defendant's rights are not violated; (b) make sure the defendant has the information necessary to make an informed decision about a plea;

(c) investigate and prepare the defense; and, if necessary, (d) argue for the lowest possible sentence or the best possible plea bargain.

Although the Supreme Court has held that there is a right to counsel, the Court has not held that this means a right to the counsel of the defendant's choice in all cases. Defendants who can afford to hire a lawyer may do so and choose whomever they please; indigent defendants will be provided an attorney, but they have little or no say in who is selected to represent them. In addition, defendants may choose to represent themselves, if the court determines they are competent to do so. Representing one's self is referred to as proceeding **pro se**.

Jurors

Jurors clearly play an important role in the criminal process; they decide whether those charged with crimes are guilty and, in some jurisdictions, what the sentence should be if the defendant is convicted. Despite being a crucial component of the criminal justice system, juries are used relatively rarely, because most criminal cases result in a guilty plea rather than a jury trial.

The process of selecting a jury begins with the selection of the **jury pool** (sometimes referred to as the **venire**). The method of selecting names for the jury pool varies, but many states use voter registration lists, drivers' license lists, and other lists that are likely to include as many people as possible. Once the jury pool is created, people are selected from the list for jury service. Individuals selected from the jury pool for a particular case are usually called the **jury panel**. Members of the jury panel are called into court and, in a process known as **voir dire** (which is French for "to see to speak"), they are asked a series of questions by the judge, the lawyers, or both. These questions are, at least in theory, designed to determine whether the potential jurors are unbiased and can decide the case fairly and impartially. Potential jurors can be excused—or challenged—by either the prosecutor or the defense attorneys. Both sides have an unlimited number of **challenges for cause**; these challenges, which require the judge's approval, are used to excuse jurors who cannot be fair and impartial. In addition, each side has a limited number of **peremptory challenges**, which can be used to excuse potential jurors without giving any reason at all.

Other Actors

There are a number of other actors in the courts. These include the **bailiff**. This person is usually a law enforcement officer (often a sheriff's deputy) whose job is to maintain order in the courtroom and transport incarcerated defendants to and from court proceedings. At the federal level, bailiffs are U.S. marshals. Another court actor is the **court administrator**, who is responsible for facilitating the smooth flow of cases. The administrator maintains the court records, schedules hearings, and manages court personnel. The court administrator tends to work behind the scenes, but two court actors whose jobs are closely related to that of the court administrator are highly visible in court. One is the **court reporter**, whose job is to record all the court proceedings and to produce a transcript of the trial. The other is the **court clerk**, who maintains the records of all cases. The court clerk also prepares the jury pool, issues summonses for jury duty, and subpoenas witnesses who will testify at trial.

Another important actor is the expert witness. **Expert witnesses** are relied on to introduce scientific and other complicated forms of evidence, or to provide specialized knowledge to the jury that will assist the jury in reaching a verdict. The hope is that they can take a complicated matter, such as a DNA test, and explain it in simple terms for the jury. Unfortunately, though, expert witnesses hired by the prosecution and the defense often give conflicting testimony, which can deepen juror confusion.

Witnesses who are called to testify about what they know of the matter at hand, and who possess no specialized knowledge, are referred to as **lay witnesses**. What makes them different from expert witnesses is that they are not generally allowed to offer their opinion. Only expert witnesses can do this.

OVERVIEW OF THE CRIMINAL PROCESS

In this section, we provide an overview of the stages in a typical criminal prosecution. The process begins with the arrest of a suspect and ends with the verdict at trial or, potentially, an appeal.

Pretrial Proceedings

The criminal process begins with either the filing of a **complaint** or an **arrest**. A complaint is simply a legal document in which is made an accusation that a specific person committed a specified criminal act. If an arrest is made first, a complaint will be sworn out afterward, usually by the arresting officer. The complaint serves as the charging document for the preliminary hearing.

After a person is arrested, he or she is booked. **Booking** involves entering into the police blotter the suspect's name, arrest time, and offense charged, as well as the taking of fingerprints and a "mug shot."

The first appearance in court by the defendant is, not surprisingly, referred to as the **initial appearance**. The Supreme Court requires that the initial appearance take place soon after the arrest, or "without unnecessary delay." It is here that the suspect (now defendant) is informed of her constitutional rights as well as the nature of the charges against her, and a bail decision is made as to whether it will be granted and, if so, how much to set it at. There is no constitutional right to bail.

At the **arraignment**, the defendant enters a plea, which is the defendant's response to the charges. The arraignment and the preliminary hearing are in some states merged into one proceeding. Possible pleas include guilty, not guilty, no contest, and standing mute. **Standing mute** means refusing to enter any plea at all. When this happens, the judge enters a "not guilty" plea for the defendant. This is because, under the U.S. Constitution, there is a presumption of evidence and the state is required to overcome this presumption with proof of guilt beyond a reasonable doubt. Entering a "not guilty" plea thus preserves even the uncooperative defendant's right to trial. A **no contest** plea, also referred to as **nolo contendere**, means the defendant accepts whatever punishment the court would impose on a guilty defendant but refuses to admit criminal wrongdoing. This plea is frequently used by defendants who fear being exposed to civil liability for their criminal misdeeds—a guilty plea in a criminal court could be entered into evidence in a subsequent civil trial, where the burden of proof is lower.

A fourth possible plea, not accepted as a valid option in all states and rarely allowed in the federal system, is the **Alford plea**. An Alford plea (which comes from the case *North Carolina v. Alford,* 1970) is one in which the defendant enters a guilty plea but denies having committed the crime to which he is pleading. The reason that the Alford plea is not often accepted is that when a defendant enters a plea of guilty, she is expected to admit her guilt for the record. Judges do not take it lightly when defendants say they are guilty on one hand and then assert their innocence on the other. Nonetheless, it may be used in those rare instances when a defendant is willing to accept a plea bargain but not admit committing the crime, and the prosecutor is satisfied that a plea bargain is the best possible outcome.

The next stage in the proceedings is the **preliminary hearing**. At this hearing the prosecution presents evidence sufficient to convince the judge that there is probable cause to believe the defendant committed a crime. It is not a trial; it is a formal adversarial proceeding, and the defense attorney has the opportunity to question the witnesses (usually the arresting or investigating officer) and probe for weaknesses in the state's case.

If probable cause is established, the defendant is "bound over" for trial, which means that a trial date is set and the defendant is notified of the pending charges. There are two ways that charges may be filed against a defendant—either by an information filed by the prosecutor or by an indictment issued by a grand jury. The information is prepared and signed by the prosecutor. It is adequate if it informs the defendant of the facts and the elements of the offense charged. It is a substitute for a grand jury indictment and is a more efficient way to proceed, because it eliminates the need to organize a grand jury and present evidence.

The Fifth Amendment requires the federal government to proceed via an indictment, handed down by a grand jury. This clause of the Fifth Amendment is one of the few that has not been applied to the states, however, so states may use an information instead. A grand jury is by tradition composed of 23 people, and its proceedings are private. The only persons present aside from the members of the grand jury are the district attorney and any witnesses he calls. The rationale behind requiring indictment by a grand jury is that this body can act as a check on an overzealous prosecutor, preventing her from prosecuting cases for which there is not sufficient evidence. If the grand jury returns an indictment, it is referred to as a **true bill**. If the grand jury refuses to indict the defendant, it is referred to as a **no bill**.

Pretrial Motions

The period between arraignment and trial is referred to as the **discovery** period, because this is the time when both sides may seek to discover what evidence the other side has. This is typically done via a pretrial motion. These motions may cover a variety of issues. Common pretrial motions filed by the defense in criminal cases include a motion to compel discovery and a motion to suppress evidence. The judge will rule on these motions before the trial begins. The judge may hold a hearing during which the prosecution and defense can argue for why the motion should (or should not) be granted.

FIGURE 4.2 ■ What Is the Sequence of Events in the Criminal Justice System?

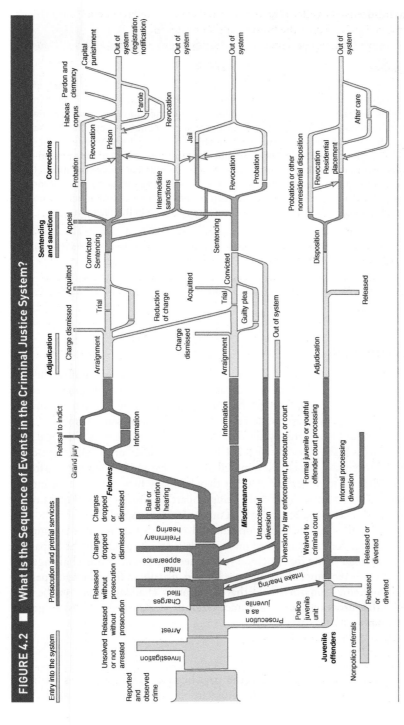

Source: Adapted from *The challenge of crime in a free society.* President's Commission on Law Enforcement and Administration of Justice, 1967. This revision, a result of the Symposium on the 30th Anniversary of the President's Commission, was prepared by the Bureau of Justice Statistics in 1997.

Note: This chart gives a simplified view of caseflow through the criminal justice system. Procedures vary among jurisdictions. The weights of the lines are not intended to show actual size of caseloads.

CURRENT RESEARCH

Just as there are different methods of selecting judges, there are different methods by which judges decide cases. There is a tremendous amount of research on judicial decision making. Recent studies have demonstrated that state supreme court judges' decision making is influenced by the type of selection mechanism that put them into office. In particular, judges are found to respond to the interests of those who have placed them on the bench. We extend this line of inquiry further by testing the effect of rules governing the retention of these judges in merit systems. Do these judges respond to the subtle differences in constituency that these rules establish? The researchers here find overwhelming evidence of the effects of these retention rules. In fact, we also conclude that judicial decisions are more influenced by the actor charged with retaining them than the actor who placed them on the bench in the first place.

Source: The Influence of Appointment and Retention Constituencies: Testing Strategies of Judicial Decisionmaking. Savchak, E. C., & Barghothi. A. J., State *Politics & Policy Quarterly* 7(4): 394–415, 2007.

Jury Selection

When defendants (suspects become defendants once indicted) plead not guilty, the next step in the process is the trial. Once a trial date is set, jury selection begins. The jury is selected from the eligible members of the community, who are selected at random, usually from voting records, automobile registration records, or some combination of records likely to include all or virtually all adults living in the jurisdiction. The legal term for summoning jurors is the *venire,* which is Latin for "to cause" or to "make come" (to the courthouse). Prospective jurors are examined by the judge and/or the attorneys for the prosecution and defense to determine whether they have any bias, prejudice, or interest that would prevent the potential juror from being impartial. This process of questioning the jurors is referred to as the *voir dire,* which means "to see to speak."

Jurors may be challenged for cause, or removed through the use of a peremptory challenge. A challenge for cause is based on evidence that a juror cannot be impartial. A peremptory challenge is one for which no reason need be given. While challenges for cause are unlimited, peremptory challenges are limited, usually to 6 (or, in death penalty cases, 12). The Supreme Court has held that peremptory challenges may not be used to exclude potential jurors on the basis of race (*Batson v. Kentucky,* 1986) or gender (*J. E. B. v. Alabama,* 1994).

The Trial

Once the jury is selected and sworn in, the trial begins. The first step is the making of **opening statements**—first by the prosecution and then by the defense. The prosecution goes first because it has the burden of proof. The defense may then speak, or choose to reserve its opening statement until after the prosecution has presented its evidence.

After opening statements, the prosecution presents the evidence supporting its claim that the defendant has committed a crime. This is referred to as the prosecution's case-in-chief. During this phase, the prosecution must establish each element of crime charged beyond a reasonable doubt.

Once the prosecution has presented its evidence and called its witnesses, the defense has an opportunity to present its case-in-chief. The defense is not required to put on any case, but if defense chooses to, it may raise several types of defenses. These include an alibi or an affirmative defense such as insanity or self-defense.

Witnesses may be called to testify by both the prosecution and the defense. The side that calls the witness to testify conducts what is called the **direct examination**. The other side conducts what is referred to as **cross-examination**.

After both the prosecution and defense have presented their evidence, the **closing arguments** take place. In closing arguments, each side has the opportunity to sum up its case. The prosecution goes last since it has the burden of proof. After closing arguments the judge will give the **jury instructions** on the applicable law. These include instructions on the elements of the crime charged, the presumption of innocence, and the burden of proof—which in criminal trials is "proof beyond a reasonable doubt."

Once the jury has received its instructions, it retires to the jury room to deliberate. It remains there until a verdict is reached. In most jurisdictions, criminal verdicts must be unanimous. Failure to achieve a unanimous jury (commonly referred to as a hung jury) means the case is declared a mistrial. If this occurs, the defendant may be retried, without violating the prohibition against double jeopardy.

Sentencing

If a jury returns a verdict of "not guilty," the defendant is set free. The constitutional prohibition on double jeopardy prevents the state from prosecuting the defendant again for the same act. If the verdict is "guilty," then a sentence of some sort will be imposed. In most instances, the judge imposes the sentence, the exception being death penalty cases, in which the jury must determine the sentence.

The sentence is usually not handed down immediately after the verdict. Instead, the judge orders a presentence investigation and sentencing recommendation, written by officers in a probation department. A number of different sentences are possible. These include probation, a suspended sentence, or a fine.

Appeals

Once a defendant has been convicted and sentenced, there are two ways to challenge the trial outcome. (Note the state can never challenge, or appeal, a not guilty verdict.) A defendant may file either a **direct appeal** or an indirect appeal, also known as a writ of habeas corpus. There is no federal constitutional right to an appeal, but every state allows a direct appeal, either by statute or state constitutional provision.

The writ of habeas corpus is considered an **indirect appeal** because it does not directly challenge the defendant's conviction but instead challenges the authority of the state to incarcerate the defendant. **Habeas corpus** translates as "you have the body," and the writ requires the person to whom it is directed to either release the person named in the writ or come to court to justify why the authority will not release the person from custody. Habeas corpus is one of the oldest legal remedies available to an incarcerated person, dating back to the Magna Carta in 1215.

SUMMARY

This chapter examined the structure of the federal and state courts. Both the federal and state court systems typically have three levels—the trial court, an intermediate appellate court, and a supreme court. The U.S. Supreme Court is the court of last resort, the final arbiter of legal disputes.

We also examined the court actors, focusing primarily on the judge, prosecutor and defense attorney, and the jury. It is these courtroom actors, or courtroom workgroup, who perform the tasks necessary for the court system to dispense justice.

Next, we provided a discussion of the trial process, focusing on the criminal trial. There are a number of steps in the trial process, which begins with an arrest or the filing of a complaint and the issuance of an arrest warrant. Each of these stages requires different actions by the courtroom actors.

Don't overlook the Student Study Site with its useful study aids, such as self-quizzes, e-Flashcards, and other assists, to help you get more from the course and improve your grade.

DISCUSSION QUESTIONS

1. Explain the concept of jurisdiction, and give four examples of the different types of jurisdiction.

2. How does a case get to the Supreme Court? What is the basis for acceptance of an appeal?

3. What is the Missouri plan, and how does it work?

4. When a trial begins, which side presents its case first, and why?

5. Briefly explain the different types of appeals.

6. What is voir dire?

7. What are the three different types of functions courts provide?

8. What is the Judiciary Act of 1789, and what did it do?

9. List the steps involved in pretrial proceedings in the order that they occur after arrest.

10. What is the purpose of a grand jury?

KEY TERMS

Alford plea 94
Appellate jurisdiction 76
Appointment 88
Arraignment 93
Arrest 93
Article III courts 77
Attorney general 90
Bailiff 92
Bench trials 88
Booking 93
Challenge for cause 92
Closing argument 97
Complaint 93
Court administrator 92
Court clerk 92
Court of Appeals Act of 1891 77
Court reporter 92
Courtroom workgroup 75
Cross-examination 97
Defense attorneys 91
Direct appeal 97

Direct examination 97
Discovery 94
Diversity of citizenship 80
Election 89
En banc 81
Expert witnesses 93
General jurisdiction 75
Geographic jurisdiction 75
Habeas corpus 98
Hierarchical jurisdiction 76
Impeachment 88
Indirect appeal 98
Initial appearance 93
Judges 88
Judiciary Act of 1789 77
Jurisdiction 75
Jury instructions 97
Jury panel 92
Jury pool 92
Lay witnesses 93
Limited jurisdiction 75
Magistrate judges 80

Merit system (Missouri plan) 89
No bill 94
No contest 93
Nolo contendere 93
Opening statement 96
Original jurisdiction 76
Peremptory challenge 92
Personal jurisdiction 75
Preliminary hearing 94
Pro se 92
Prosecutors 90
Public defenders 91
Rule of four 82
Standing mute 93
Subject matter jurisdiction 75
Trial de novo 85
True bill 94
Venire 92
Venue 75
Voir dire 92
Writ of certiorari 82

INTERNET SITES

Administrative Office of the U.S. Courts: www.uscourts.gov

American Bar Association: www.americanbar.org/aba.html

Federal Courts and What They Do: www.fjc.gov/content/federal-courts-and-what-they-do-2

Federal Judicial Center: www.fjc.gov

National Association of Criminal Defense Lawyers: www.nacdl.org

National Center for State Courts: www.ncsc.org

Sourcebook of Criminal Justice Statistics Online: www.albany.edu/sourcebook

STUDENT STUDY SITE

Get the tools you need to sharpen your study skills. SAGE edge offers a robust online environment featuring an impressive array of free tools and resources.

Access practice quizzes, eFlashcards, video, and multimedia at **edge.sagepub.com/hemmens4e**

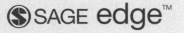

COURTROOM ACTORS AND THE COURTROOM WORKGROUP

CHAPTERS

© Comstock/Stockbyte/Thinkstock Images

5

PROSECUTORS

Master the content at **edge.sagepub.com/hemmens4e**

INTRODUCTION

The prosecutor is perhaps the most fascinating actor in the criminal justice system. The prosecutor is the government's representative in the criminal court process, yet this description does not begin to convey the complexity of the position and its level of importance in the functioning of the criminal courts and the criminal justice system as a whole.

This immense level of importance stems largely from the central position the prosecutor occupies in the criminal justice system. Law enforcement officers, judges, defense attorneys, and corrections officials are involved in limited, focused aspects of the criminal justice process. Each depends largely on the actions of others to begin or end their activity in a matter. The prosecutor, on the other hand, plays an active role in the investigation of crimes, the arrest of a suspect, the prosecution of the suspect, the sentence received following a conviction, and, in many jurisdictions, the termination of probation and parole.

Beyond the prosecutor's central position in the criminal justice system, it is the inherent contradictions involved in the job that make the position so fascinating. Consider the following contradictions:

- Prosecutors have nearly limitless discretion in the most critical matters they must consider, yet they are held to very high ethical standards.

- The prosecutor is a publicly elected official, yet most of the work performed by the office is done outside the public eye.

- Prosecutors have a duty to seek justice but operate in an adversarial rather than truth-seeking system.

This chapter examines how the prosecutor balances these contradictory demands. After examining the evolution of prosecution in the United States, we look at how prosecutors are selected and the way in which their offices are organized. We then examine the role prosecutors play in the system, the duties they perform on a daily basis, and their relationships with other members of the courtroom workgroup. In the last part of the chapter, we consider the ethical responsibilities placed on prosecutors and explore the evolving concept of community prosecution.

HISTORICAL EVOLUTION OF THE AMERICAN PROSECUTOR

The prosecutor's place in the U.S. criminal justice system is uniquely American. Like many aspects of American society, the prosecutor is a hybrid of British and European ancestry that evolved over time. To fully understand the role the prosecutor plays in the criminal justice system, one must briefly consider the historic origin and evolution of the position.

During the 17th century, the American colonies followed the English system of private prosecution of criminal cases. Each colony had an appointed attorney general, who served as counsel to the government and left the prosecution of crimes primarily to the victim. This system was ill suited for the vast colonies as victims had difficulty traveling to state capitals to pursue their claim. In addition, as sanctions imposed on conviction were severe, prosecutions were frequently initiated by individuals as a means of extorting financial compensation from an offender who would pay off the victim to avoid the punishment. To help alleviate these problems and as means to generate revenue, in the early 1700s, the colonies themselves began to routinely prosecute offenders.

As the population of the colonies grew, it became apparent that a centrally located public prosecutor was ill equipped to prosecute offenders across the colony. To ameliorate the workload, colonies appointed deputy attorneys general to handle prosecutions for a given county. This practice expanded throughout the 18th century. By the time of the American Revolution, each of the colonies conducted public prosecutions at the local level.

At the time the U.S. Constitution was ratified in 1789, the prosecutor was appointed by the government and straddled a line between the judicial and executive branches of government. In the federal government, the practice of executive appointment was put into law by the Judiciary Act of 1789. At the state and local levels, the appointment of prosecuting attorneys continued as a matter of local custom or pursuant to state constitutions.

In the 1820s, the populist movement (Jacksonian democracy) gained prominence. The rise of Jacksonian democracy brought with it an increase in the power of citizens to directly elect a number of government officials. As part of this wave, state after state amended their constitutions to provide for the election of local prosecutors. By the end of the 18th century, a majority of states had direct elections of prosecuting attorneys.

THE FEDERAL PROSECUTOR

As we have already seen, the United States has a dual system of criminal justice. Acts that violate federal statutes are prosecuted in the federal court system. Violations of state laws are prosecuted in the state where the act occurred. It should not be surprising, therefore, that prosecutors in the federal system and state-level prosecutors operate in different spheres.

In the federal court system, the government is represented by the **United States attorney**. The Judiciary Act of 1789 provided that within each judicial district, an attorney shall be appointed by the president as the United States attorney and represent the government in federal prosecutions. Today, there are 93 U.S. attorneys stationed throughout the United States, the U.S. Virgin Islands, Puerto Rico, Guam, and the Northern Mariana Islands. Each of the 93 federal judicial districts is assigned a U.S. attorney (except for Guam and the Northern Mariana Islands, which share a single U.S. attorney). U.S. attorneys are appointed by the president and are confirmed by the Senate. Generally, U.S. attorneys serve 4-year terms, but they may be removed from office at the will of the president. As the position is politically appointed, when a new president is elected into office, most if not all U.S. attorneys are replaced by appointees of the new president's choosing.

The day-to-day operations of each U.S. attorney's office are carried out by assistant U.S. attorneys. These are lawyers who often work as federal prosecutors for their entire career. Each U.S. attorney's office has anywhere from a dozen to several hundred assistants, who make charging decisions, conduct plea negotiations, appear in court, and perform tasks similar to those of local and state prosecutors. Assistant U.S. attorneys enjoy civil service protection and are expected to carry out their duties as prosecutors absent political considerations. Whereas U.S. attorneys are likely to be replaced when a new president takes office, assistant U.S. attorneys generally keep their positions and continue to represent the federal government in court.

STATE PROSECUTORS

Selection of the Local Prosecuting Attorney

State systems of prosecution are extremely decentralized. Normally, violations of state laws are prosecuted by a prosecutor's office located in the county or judicial district where the offense took place. The person in charge of the prosecutor's office is generally referred to as the district attorney, prosecuting attorney, state's attorney, commonwealth's attorney, or county attorney. In 45 of the 50 states, the chief local prosecuting attorney reaches office by way of popular election, generally for a 4-year term.

Not surprisingly, the specific tasks performed by the elected prosecuting attorney vary largely depend on the size of the jurisdiction. In 2001, there were 394 jurisdictions across the nation (average population 7,778), in which the elected prosecuting attorney was the only full-time attorney responsible for criminal prosecutions. Prosecutors in these counties regularly appear in court, represent the government at trial, and perform myriad other duties required of a prosecutor's office. Such an arrangement is only possible for areas with small populations and little criminal activity.

At the other extreme, large urban areas may have several hundred assistant prosecutors and budgets in the tens of millions of dollars. Facts about the 20 largest local prosecuting attorney offices in the nation are presented in Table 5.1.

The heads of these offices are more akin to a corporate CEO than a trial attorney. The typical prosecutor's office falls between these two extremes. The average office has a dozen assistant prosecutors and serves a jurisdiction of 100,000 people. In most offices, the elected prosecutor rarely works on specific cases or makes court appearances. Rather, his or her duty is to delegate day-to-day responsibility for the prosecution of cases to supervisors and assistant prosecuting attorneys, to manage the organization and long-term planning for the office, and to set overarching policies and priorities. As the chief prosecutor is an elected official in most locales, it should not be surprising that the policies and priorities instituted in the office are politically advantageous for the prosecutor and generally relate to crime control and fiscal efficiency.

These policies may involve having the office focus resources on particular types of crimes, implementing policies to increase efficiency, or promoting consistency in the treatment of defendants by restricting the discretion of assistant prosecutors to reduce charges or punishments as part of plea bargains (Green & Zacharias, 2004). Specific examples of policies set by some prosecutors' offices include mandatory prosecution of domestic violence arrests (Peterson & Dixon, 2005), a policy prohibiting assistant prosecutors from dropping sentence enhancements for crimes involving a firearm (Heumann & Loftin, 1979), bans on plea bargaining within 30 days of trial, and complete bans on plea bargaining in felony cases (Holmes, Daudistel, & Taggart, 1992). Specific policies in specific offices vary.

The chief prosecutor sets office policy, but the daily work of the office is usually handled by a number of assistant or deputy prosecuting attorneys. This work ranges from assisting law enforcement officers in their investigations to appearing on behalf of the government in court for hearings and trials.

Assistant prosecuting attorneys work in the trenches of the criminal court system. Whereas the chief prosecuting attorney and select supervisors set policy, it is the assistant prosecutors who appear in court, interview witnesses, oversee investigations, and negotiate with defense attorneys on a daily basis. Because of the hands-on nature of the job, many assistant

TABLE 5.1 ■ **Twenty Largest Prosecutor's Offices in the United States, 2005***

Location	Population Served	Full-Time Attorneys	Full-Time Staff	Annual Budget
Cook County, IL	5,327,777	897	1,893	$126,000,000
Los Angeles County, CA	9,937,739	887	1,959	$285,000,000
New York County, NY	1,562,723	442	1,139	$63,300,000
Kings County, NY	2,475,290	385	957	$63,000,000
Maricopa County, AZ	3,501,001	363	1,009	$72,220,855
Bronx County, NY	1,365,536	307	797	$42,106,635
Philadelphia County, PA	1,470,151	291	676	$48,113,158
Miami-Dade County, FL	2,363,600	289	1,154	$51,200,000
Queens County, NY	2,237,216	286	576	$39,200,000
King County, WA	1,777,143	246	485	$47,621,663
Harris County, TX	3,644,285	235	447	$44,063,572
Orange County, CA	2,987,591	228	694	$80,718,573
Riverside County, CA	1,871,950	225	633	$69,000,000
City of Baltimore, MD	636,251	215	400	$27,834,540
Broward County, FL	1,754,893	214	507	$33,231,705
San Bernardino County, CA	1,921,131	207	452	$47,827,736
Wayne County, MI	2,016,202	181	297	$33,884,100
Sacramento County, CA	1,352,445	175	447	$59,552,007
Dallas County, TX	2,294,706	170	376	$27,936,347
Suffolk County, NY	1,475,488	167	416	$30,059,066

Source: U.S. Department of Justice (2005).
*Most recent data available.

prosecutors are young attorneys from local law schools looking to gain extensive courtroom experience. Although prosecutors' offices do not pay salaries on par with most private law firms, they do provide an attorney with an opportunity to obtain a great deal of trial experience in a relatively short time. In addition, given the public nature of the job, many attorneys looking to enter state and local politics in the future start their careers as prosecutors. For these individuals, forgoing a higher salary in exchange for a government position that seeks to pursue justice and preserve the community is a tradeoff that is willingly made. The specific activities and duties of prosecutors are examined later in this chapter.

Organization and Operation of the Prosecutor's Office

Large prosecutors' offices maintain a bureaucratic organizational structure. Consider, for example, the organizational chart for the Philadelphia District Attorney's Office in Figure 5.1. The elected district attorney sits atop the organization, while everyday operations of the office are overseen by a first assistant and several deputies who oversee the five nonadministrative divisions maintained by the office. Each of these divisions represents a general area for which the office is responsible. Within each division are a number of units or teams that were established to help focus the regular operations of the office. Finally, within each unit, team, or task force, up to several dozen assistant district attorneys carry out specific duties for the office.

In many prosecutors' offices, units or teams are established to deal with the prosecution of specific classes of crimes. In Philadelphia, for example, the district attorney's office has units that deal only with prosecuting homicides, sexual assaults and acts of family violence, economic crimes, and repeat offenders. By having groups of prosecutors focus on specific types of crime, a district attorney's office builds up high levels of expertise in areas that are of significant seriousness and public importance.

Depending on how a particular office is organized, different methods of prosecuting cases can be implemented. Three general models are used by prosecutors' offices for prosecuting cases. Under a **horizontal model of prosecution**, assistant prosecutors are assigned to units that handle specific steps or functions in the judicial process that are routine in nature and involve limited discretion (see Figure 5.1). For example, regardless of the type of case (there are exceptions), one attorney or a group of attorneys may be responsible for all initial appearances, another for preliminary hearings, and others for arraignments, and so on. Horizontal prosecution is generally used in larger offices as it handles a large number of cases with great efficiency.

Under a **vertical model of prosecution**, a case is assigned to a single prosecutor who is responsible for the case at each step in the judicial process from initial appearance through a final disposition. This method is often used in smaller jurisdictions that lack the personnel to operate under a horizontal model. Although not as efficient as horizontal prosecution models, vertical prosecution has the advantage of allowing victims and witnesses to deal with only one attorney, adding to their level of comfort and trust in the prosecution as it goes forward.

In an effort to include the positive aspects of the two modes of prosecution, many jurisdictions have adopted a **mixed model of prosecution**. Under mixed models, most cases are handled in a horizontal manner. Specific crimes, however, such as homicide and sexual assaults, are handled at all steps along the process by a specialized unit. This approach meets the need of efficiency in handling "routine" crimes but permits the use of expertise and case ownership for more serious offenses.

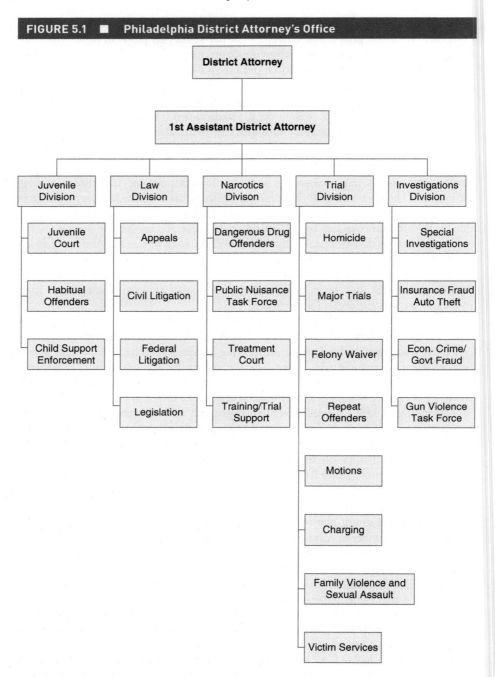

FIGURE 5.1 ■ Philadelphia District Attorney's Office

THE PROSECUTOR'S DUTIES

The overarching role of prosecutors in the criminal justice system is to represent the government in the prosecution of criminal offenses. That being said, prosecutors represent the government and governmental interests as well as specific needs of citizens beyond criminal prosecutions. Before examining the prosecutor's duties in the criminal justice system, we briefly describe the nonprosecutorial duties and responsibilities of local prosecutors.

Nonprosecutorial Duties

The locally elected prosecuting attorney is the government's attorney. This position requires the office to perform a number of duties on behalf of the local government, typically a county. The fundamental aspect of this duty is to provide legal assistance and advice to the various elected officials, boards, agencies, and employees of the county regarding official matters. This includes advising on personnel matters, annexations, commercial development and other land use issues, and procurement and other county contracts. In addition, the county attorney's office is also tasked with defending all lawsuits brought against the county and all city officers and employees named in lawsuits.

In addition to serving as the county's attorney in civil matters, most prosecutors' offices have a number of specific, nonprosecutorial duties for which they are responsible.

Juvenile and Dependency Matters

In addition to prosecuting delinquency matters involving juveniles accused of committing crimes, prosecuting attorneys' offices are also responsible for a number of duties relating to child welfare and dependency issues. These duties may include filing petitions to protect abused or neglected children, as well as vulnerable adults, including the elderly and developmentally disabled. In many states, local prosecutors are also frequently called on to file involuntary commitment actions to provide necessary treatment for individuals who are mentally ill, chemically dependent, or mentally handicapped.

Child Support Enforcement

Prosecutors' offices are normally responsible for enforcing child support orders. This involves taking legal steps to collect delinquent child support payments.

Victim Assistance

Most prosecutors' offices have programs or units to provide assistance to crime victims. The overarching mission of these services is to make the criminal justice system more responsive to the victims of crime. Services provided typically include victim notification of court proceedings, an orientation about the prosecutorial process, crisis intervention assistance, passing along information about counseling and advocacy resources, and assistance in obtaining restitution for financial losses and the return of seized property.

Civil Asset Forfeitures

State and federal laws provide for the seizure and civil forfeiture of items used to commit a crime or that represent the proceeds of a crime. Items that are routinely subject to civil forfeiture include guns, money, vehicles, and houses. As civil forfeiture proceedings are instituted separately from any criminal prosecution, they are usually conducted by the civil side of a prosecuting attorney's office.

Prosecutorial Duties

The primary role of the prosecutor's office is to oversee the adjudication of criminal matters. The duties associated with this role involve activities prior to the arrest of a suspect up through the time a convicted defendant is released from prison. The actual power the prosecutor has in fulfilling this role was eloquently articulated in 1940 by Supreme Court Justice Robert Jackson.

Prior to be being appointed to the U.S. Supreme Court in 1941, Robert Jackson served as U.S. Attorney General. In a speech given to the U.S. attorneys from across the nation, Justice Jackson laid out his perspective on the role and duties of the prosecutor in the American criminal justice system:

> It would probably be within the range of that exaggeration permitted in Washington to say that assembled in this room is one of the most powerful peacetime forces known to our country. The prosecutor has more control over life, liberty, and reputation than any other person in America. His discretion is tremendous. He can have citizens investigated and, if he is that kind of person, he can have this done to the tune of public statements and veiled or unveiled intimations. Or the prosecutor may choose a subtler course and simply have a citizen's friends interviewed. The prosecutor can order arrests, present cases to the grand jury in secret session, and on the basis of his one-sided presentation of the facts, can cause the citizen to be indicted and held for trial. He may dismiss the case before trial, in which case the defense never has a chance to be heard. Or he may go on with a public trial. If he obtains a conviction, the prosecutor can still make recommendations as to sentence, as to whether the prisoner should get probation or a suspended sentence, and after he is put away, as to whether he is a fit subject for parole. While the prosecutor at his best is one of the most beneficent forces in our society, when he acts from malice or other base motives, he is one of the worst. (Jackson, 1940, p. 3)

The following sections discuss in some detail the nature and importance of several of these functions and how they relate to the ideals expressed by Justice Jackson.

Assisting Law Enforcement Officers

Prosecutors frequently work closely with law enforcement officers during criminal investigations. As prosecutors are the government's attorneys, it is their responsibility to advise police on the legality of investigatory matters. This advice most often involves assessments regarding whether probable cause is present for an arrest or search warrant. Moreover, the prosecutor routinely prepares warrants and presents them to a judge for approval.

TABLE 5.2	■ Roles and Responsibilities of the Prosecutor in the Criminal Justice System
Before Arrest	Advise law enforcement during investigation.
	Help prepare arrest and search warrants.
	Work with law enforcement in developing cooperating witnesses.
After Arrest	Screen cases for prosecution.
	Make charging decision.
	Attend grand jury and preliminary hearing.
	Prepare charging documents.
	Evaluate strength of case and participate in plea negotiations.
	Assemble and evaluate potentially exculpatory evidence.
	Provide disclosure to defendant.
	Prepare and respond to pretrial motions.
	Oversee continued investigation.
	Interview witnesses.
	Represent the government at trial.
	Make sentencing recommendation.
	Present sentencing information, restitution amount, and victim impact statement to court during sentencing hearing.
	Represent government on appeals.
	Handle probation and parole revocation petitions and proceedings.

The prosecutor also plays an important role in deciding how investigations proceed. As the representative of the government in criminal matters, the prosecutor is in the best position to know what kind of evidence, as well as the amount of such evidence, is likely to be necessary to obtain a conviction. Accordingly, prosecutors routinely inform police investigators what is needed before prosecutors will go forward with filing charges. As prosecutors are the gatekeeper to the system and they alone have the ability to commence a prosecution, law enforcement officers generally take this information to heart and do what they can to obtain the evidence deemed necessary (Table 5.2).

Screening Cases and Making Charging Decisions

In the criminal justice system, it is the responsibility of the police to arrest individuals suspected of committing crimes. Whereas in a perfect world, only individuals worthy of prosecution would be arrested, and every arrest would lead to a prosecution, this is not the way in which the system operates. In fact, in the United States, between one third and one half of all arrests are not formally prosecuted.

There are several reasons for this. Prosecutors' offices do not have the capacity to prosecute every suspect arrested by police. Moreover, not every arrest is appropriate for prosecution. Following an arrest, the prosecutor has the duty of determining which of the arrestees should have formal charges brought against them and what those charges should be. This decision is made necessary because the prosecutor's office does not have the capacity to prosecute every individual arrested by police.

As prosecutors out of necessity must screen cases to determine which ones should be prosecuted, it is not surprising that how these decisions are made can be the source of controversy. What makes a **charging decision** more intriguing and controversial is the fact that in making this decision, the prosecutor has nearly limitless discretion. The Supreme Court has repeatedly held that courts should not review how and why charging decisions are made. So long as the decision is not based on the personal characteristics possessed by an individual (e.g., race, gender, religion) or for vindictive reasons (e.g., the exercising of a constitutional right or a prior acquittal), the prosecutor's charging decisions are beyond judicial review.

Whereas there are limited constitutional constraints on charging decisions, there are several ethical boundaries prosecutors are required to stay within. The appropriate limits of a prosecutor's discretion in making charging decisions are set out in Standard 3-3.9 of the American Bar Association Standards for Criminal Justice Prosecution Function (Exhibit 5.1). Under these standards, prosecutors may not file charges in cases where they do not have a belief that there is sufficient evidence to support a conviction. On the other hand, the standard explicitly states that prosecutors need not file charges if they determine it is not in the public interest to do so. As is evident from the numerous factors listed in the standard, the possibilities for this determination are virtually limitless.

How, then, does a prosecutor's office determine which cases to prosecute? Three key factors drive these decisions. The first is the seriousness and nature of the offense. Even though this would seem to be a straightforward consideration, it can be quite complex and controversial. Trying to measure the comparative seriousness of different crimes is not an easy task. Homicides are clearly at the top of the list, but how does one differentiate between armed robbery, residential burglary, attempted rape, child abuse, and the distribution of heroin? All are serious, yet people will differ in weighing their comparative seriousness. Though offenses that cause real harm to a person are often given priority, some nonviolent crimes, such as child pornography or large-scale narcotics distribution, may be considered to cause more harm to society than an isolated act of violence. In such cases, the nonviolent offenses may be prosecuted more readily than the crime of violence.

Relatedly, the nature of the offense given the specific community in which it occurs has an effect on whether it will be prosecuted. Recall that local prosecutors have autonomy on whether to file charges. Recall also that the prosecutor is an elected official, answerable to the voters in his or her community. These facts have a significant influence on what types of crimes, particularly minor offenses, are formally prosecuted. In a large city with the serious social and crime problems typically faced by cities, it is unlikely that charges will be filed against a college student drinking alcohol in public in violation of the law. However, in a small college town, where citizens want the police and prosecutor to assert control over local college students, a criminal prosecution of a minor in possession of alcohol is much more likely to occur. Such political realities inevitably enter into charging decisions.

A second factor that is considered in charging decisions is an offender's culpability. Crimes in which the offender acted intentionally or maliciously are more likely to be prosecuted than crimes resulting from a negligent or reckless act. This is because criminal prosecution is likely to have a greater impact on the future behavior of a person who intentionally broke the law as opposed to a person who simply made a mistake or error in judgment. In addition, a criminal who purposefully broke the law is more of a danger to society than a negligent offender. Prosecution of a deliberate offender, accordingly, serves to protect society.

Another aspect of culpability involves whether the offender has a prior criminal history. Repeat offenders are regarded as posing a greater danger to the community than a first-time offender. But that being said, should the prosecution of a habitual drug dealer take precedence over a first-time armed robbery suspect? It is largely the responsibility of the elected prosecuting attorney to set office policies in these determinations. Given the difficulty in making these distinctions and the potential for political repercussions, prosecutors' offices normally focus more on a third factor in deciding which cases to prosecute.

This third factor, the likelihood of being able to obtain a conviction at trial, has been repeatedly shown by research to be a critical factor in charging decisions (Albonetti, 1987; Frohmann, 1997). As discussed in the introduction to this section, members of the courtroom workgroup—the prosecutor, defense attorney, and judge—have the common goal of avoiding uncertainty. The most frequent and efficient way to decrease uncertainty from a prosecutor's perspective is to refrain from filing charges in cases where a conviction may be difficult to obtain. In making these assessments, prosecutors consider the amount and quality of evidence against the offender. Specific factors vary by type of crime, but key factors frequently include whether the offender confessed or made other incriminating statements, the believability of the victim, the presence of eyewitnesses, and the existence of physical evidence. In examining these items, prosecutors are less concerned about whether there is evidence to believe the offender probably committed the crime for which he or she was arrested than about whether the evidence is such that it is very likely to lead to a conviction.

Whereas this standard is logical from the prosecutor's perspective, it can be controversial in the eyes of outsiders. The cases in which the refusal to prosecute gives rise to the most controversy frequently involve sexual assault. The crime of sexual assault often occurs with no witnesses, little physical evidence showing compulsion, and conflicting accounts of what occurred between the victim and the accused. Absent evidence corroborating the victim's assertion, proving beyond a reasonable doubt that the offender committed the crime is unlikely. In such instances, prosecution is similarly doubtful. The decision to prosecute becomes even more controversial when one takes into account the perceived believability of the victim and offender. Remember, the prosecutor is deciding whether or not to file charges based largely on the level of certainty he or she has that a jury will find the defendant guilty at trial. If the victim is from a different racial, ethnic, or social background than most of the jurors are likely to be, whereas the offender is from a similar background as typical jurors, and if the prosecutor has had experience in such circumstances where the jury did not accept the victim's testimony as credible, prosecution is less likely than if the opposite background characteristics are present (Frohmann, 1997). While this may or may not be considered racism or classism, it is based on convictability, not prejudice. Nonetheless, it is a troubling component to charging decisions.

EXHIBIT 5.1 ■ Standard 3-3.9 Discretion in the Charging Decision

a. A prosecutor should not institute, or cause to be instituted, or permit the continued pendency of criminal charges when the prosecutor knows that the charges are not supported by probable cause. A prosecutor should not institute, cause to be instituted, or permit the continued pendency of criminal charges in the absence of sufficient admissible evidence to support a conviction.

b. The prosecutor is not obliged to present all charges which the evidence might support. The prosecutor may in some circumstances and for good cause consistent with the public interest decline to prosecute, notwithstanding that sufficient evidence may exist which would support a conviction. Illustrative of the factors which the prosecutor may properly consider in exercising his or her discretion are:

   i. the prosecutor's reasonable doubt that the accused is in fact guilty;
   ii. the extent of the harm caused by the offense;
   iii. the disproportion of the authorized punishment in relation to the particular offense or the offender;
   iv. possible improper motives of a complainant;
   v. reluctance of the victim to testify;
   vi. cooperation of the accused in the apprehension or conviction of others; and
   vii. availability and likelihood of prosecution by another jurisdiction.

c. A prosecutor should not be compelled by his or her supervisor to prosecute a case in which he or she has a reasonable doubt about the guilt of the accused.

d. In making the decision to prosecute, the prosecutor should give no weight to the personal or political advantages or disadvantages which might be involved or to a desire to enhance his or her record of convictions.

e. In cases which involve a serious threat to the community, the prosecutor should not be deterred from prosecution by the fact that in the jurisdiction juries have tended to acquit persons accused of the particular kind of criminal act in question.

f. The prosecutor should not bring or seek charges greater in number of degree than can reasonably be supported with evidence at trial or than are necessary to fairly reflect the gravity of the offense.

g. The prosecutor should not condition a dismissal of charges, nolle prosequi, or similar action on the accused's relinquishment of the right to seek civil redress unless the accused has agreed to the action knowingly and intelligently, freely and voluntarily, and where such waiver is approved by the court.

Source: American Bar Association (1993).

In addition to deciding which arrestees to have charges filed against, the prosecutor must also decide what specific charges will be filed. In most instances, a prosecutor will charge a defendant with the most serious level of crime for which there is probable cause to believe the defendant committed. There are several reasons behind this practice. First, a defendant cannot be convicted of a more serious offense than what he or she has been charged with. Whereas a matter that is overcharged can be corrected by the prosecutor or at trial to a lesser offense if need be, a crime that is undercharged cannot be ratcheted up later without significant effort, if at all. The second purpose behind charging the highest level offense is that it places the prosecutor in an advantageous position for the next critical decision point: plea bargaining.

CURRENT CONTROVERSY

As seen in this chapter, there are logical, resource-driven reasons behind decisions not to prosecute individual offenders despite strong evidence that a crime was committed. Case-by-case decision making of this sort is necessary for a prosecutor's office to function. A different question is raised when a prosecutor refuses to pursue charges against law violators because he or she strongly opposes the law in question. Over the past several years, a number of prosecutors have refused to prosecute individuals arrested for laws related to gun and weapon ownership and possession. In 2010, the District Attorney of Jackson County, Wisconsin, Gerald R. Fox, announced that he will no longer prosecute the state's laws prohibiting carrying concealed weapons, transporting uncased or loaded guns in vehicles, carrying guns in public buildings and taverns, and carrying switchblades and butterfly knives. In his statement, Mr. Fox wrote, "These so-called 'public safety' laws only put decent law-abiding citizens at a dangerous disadvantage when it comes to their personal safety, and I for one am glad that this decades-long era of defective thinking on gun issues is over" (Fox, 2010).

1. Should prosecutors be permitted to refuse to prosecute whole classes of crimes they disagree with?

2. What might be the impact of such a position?

3. Does the public have any recourse if a prosecutor takes such a position?

4. Is there any class of crime you would refuse to prosecute if you were an elected district attorney?

Plea Bargaining

In the United States, a vast majority of criminal prosecutions are settled through a plea bargain. The term *plea bargain* implies that the prosecution and the defense each give up something to reach a mutually acceptable disposition. Although this is generally true, it is the prosecutor that sets the ground rules for the bargain that is struck.

The prosecutor's control of the **plea bargaining** process is largely a result of the discretion possessed by the prosecutor in deciding what charges to file against a defendant. By charging a defendant with the highest level of crime possible, the prosecutor can agree to let the defendant plead guilty to a lesser offense. This usually results in a conviction and sentence at an acceptable level in the mind of the prosecutor, and charging defendants with the most serious offense possible places added pressure on defendants to avoid the sentence that would be imposed on conviction of the more serious crime.

The prosecutor has complete discretion in deciding whether to enter into a plea bargain. That being said, the prosecutor has strong internal incentives to avoid trials and the inherent uncertainty they present. Generally, the prosecutor and defense attorney will have a defendant enter into a plea agreement that sentences the defendant to the **going rate**—that is, the typical sentence for the crime charged. If the prosecution believes it has a case with weak evidence, it is likely to push for a plea agreement in which the defendant receives a better bargain than the going rate, yet the prosecution still obtains a conviction. On the other hand, if the prosecution has an airtight case, or a "slam dunk" against a defendant, it may be unwilling to offer any concessions in exchange for a guilty plea.

CURRENT RESEARCH

In 2014 Ronald Wright and Kay Levine published an article in the *Arizona Law Review* that examined how the attitudes and practices of prosecutors change as they gain experience. Wright and Levine conducted semistructured interviews of 217 prosecutors with varied levels of experience from eight distinct prosecuting attorney offices.

The article reports a number of very interesting differences between experienced and inexperienced attorneys. Based on their findings, the authors state that many inexperienced prosecutors suffer from "young prosecutors' syndrome." Young prosecutors were found to view themselves as "superheroes," eager to try any case fully at the drop of a hat with minimal interest in negotiating. Experienced prosecutors, on the other hand, viewed themselves as "arbiters, negotiators, 'BS meters', and advocates." The experience they obtained over years working with defense attorneys, judges, witnesses, and law enforcement gave them increased confidence to make more independent proportionate decisions depending on the circumstances of individual cases. While young prosecutors were eager to try and win cases, more seasoned prosecutors were more interested in fairness and efficiency.

The authors conclude that it is important to instill in young prosecutors the importance of negotiation, pragmatism, and the ability to evaluate cases realistically. Although most experienced prosecutors' attitudes varied significantly from those of neophyte colleagues, such evolution is not a given, and care must be taken to provide effective mentorship and guidance.

1. Should prosecutor offices screen applicants for "young prosecutor's syndrome" when they hire new attorneys? What characteristics or attributes might be warning signs exhibited by new attorney applicants that they might be prone to this syndrome?

2. What steps, policies, or actions do you think a prosecuting attorney's office could take to cure new attorneys of "young prosecutor's syndrome"?

Source: "The Cure for Young Prosecutors' Syndrome," Arizona Law Review, 56:1066-1028 (2014). Ronald Wright, Kay Levine.

Disclosure of Evidence

During a criminal investigation, law enforcement officers and investigators from the prosecutors' office obtain significant amounts of evidence concerning suspects and a criminal event. When formally charging a person, prosecutors have an ethical, statutory, and constitutional duty to disclose much of this evidence to the defendant. The prosecution, however, is not required to provide all of the evidence it possesses to the defendant.

Generally, there are three classes of evidence prosecutors are required to disclose to a defendant prior to trial. The first involves testimony and physical evidence the prosecutor intends to use at trial. This includes police reports, witness interviews, lab reports, and reports prepared by expert witnesses. The disclosure of these items is generally required by court rule, and failure to provide proper disclosure is likely to lead to their exclusion from use during a trial. The other two types of evidence that prosecutors are required to disclose to a defendant, exculpatory material evidence and impeachment evidence, are far less simple to identify.

Exculpatory evidence is evidence that is favorable to the defendant. Pursuant to the Supreme Court decision in *Brady v. Maryland* (1963), a prosecutor must disclose exculpatory evidence to the defendant if such evidence is considered to be material evidence. Two decades later, the Supreme Court stated that exculpatory evidence is material if there is a reasonable probability that the result of the proceeding would have been different had the evidence been disclosed. A reasonable probability of a different outcome is shown where suppression undermines confidence in the outcome (*United States v. Bagley,* 1985). The Supreme Court opinion in *Kyles v. Whitley* (1995) provides a vivid illustration of these standards.

In 1984, a woman was killed in a grocery store parking lot as she was putting her groceries in the trunk of her car. After the assailant shot the victim in the head, he took her keys and fled in her vehicle. Six eyewitnesses provided police investigators with statements, but these reports were inconsistent with one another with respect to the gunman's hair, height, and body type. Police also traced license plate numbers of the cars in the parking lot when the crime happened, but none of the plates were registered to the man later implicated, Curtis Kyles.

Police saw no real developments in the case until 2 days after the murder when they were contacted by a man known as "Beanie." Over the next few days, Beanie gave the police several statements suggesting the involvement of Curtis Kyles. While each statement implicated Kyles, each one also contradicted Beanie's other accounts on a number of factual details. Also questionable was that after Beanie's first statements to the police but before Kyles was arrested, Beanie visited Kyles's apartment several times. Two days following Beanie's first statement to investigators, Kyles was arrested in his apartment. While searching the apartment, police found the murder weapon and items taken from the victim. None of these materials bore Kyles's fingerprints. After Kyles's arrest, three of the eyewitnesses identified him as the assailant. Kyles was then indicted and tried for capital murder.

Before trial, Kyles's attorney filed a discovery motion requesting all exculpatory and impeachment evidence as required under *Brady*. The prosecution answered that there was no exculpatory evidence—despite the inconsistent reports of the eyewitnesses, the contradictory nature of Beanie's many written and recorded statements to the police, and evidence that Beanie was a suspect in other robberies.

Kyles argued at trial that he was framed by Beanie. The prosecution relied on the eyewitnesses and the evidence found in Kyles's apartment and chose not to call Beanie to testify. The trial resulted in a deadlocked jury. After the trial, Beanie met again with prosecutors and provided additional and contradictory statements against Kyles. Prosecutors used this new information at a second trial. As before, Kyles said that he was framed, and Beanie did not testify. This time Kyles was found guilty and sentenced to death.

Several years later, attorneys for Kyles found out about exculpatory evidence in the government's possession that had never been disclosed to the defense. This evidence included a computer printout of the license plate numbers of cars near the murder scene in which Kyles's car was not listed, the eyewitness accounts taken by police, and Beanie's recorded and written statements. Kyles argued that the prosecution's failure to disclose these items denied him due process. The district court and circuit court of appeals rejected Kyles's argument.

In a 5–4 decision, the Supreme Court reversed Kyles's conviction and ordered a new trial. The central issue was whether the undisclosed exculpatory evidence was material. Writing for the majority, Justice Souter held that the undisclosed evidence was material and that nondisclosure was unconstitutional. Kyles was arrested largely due to the statements made by Beanie. As Kyles's defense was based on his claim that Beanie framed him, evidence that supports that possibility, considered together with the discrepancies in the eyewitnesses' descriptions of the shooter, was found by the Court to be sufficient to create distrust in the verdict. Significantly, the Court also held that it is the prosecutor's duty to disclose material, exculpatory evidence that is in the hands of the police, even if the prosecutor does not know of its existence. The prosecutor is responsible for being aware of such evidence. Any other ruling would encourage police to obscure evidence from the prosecution and therefore a defendant.

Note that the identification of material evidence is left largely to the prosecutor. As prosecutors are the only ones who know what evidence is in their possession, it is their responsibility to determine what might be material and exculpatory. This is complicated by the facts that (a) this includes evidence in the possession of the police, (b) the prosecutor is presumed to know what is in the possession of the police, and (c) this decision must be made prior to trial.

It is important to remember that the same rules of disclosure for substantive evidence of criminal activity apply to **impeachment evidence**. Impeachment evidence is evidence that calls into question the credibility of a witness. For example, evidence that a witness who identified the defendant as the offender was previously sued in court by the offender and owed the offender a large civil judgment. This evidence of potential bias against the defendant would be usable to impeach the witness's testimony at trial. As such, if the prosecution had knowledge of the prior relationship between the witness and the defendant, it would be required to disclose it to the defendant's counsel.

The sanctions against a prosecutor for failing to disclose evidence to the defense can be severe. If a court finds that the failure to disclose was deliberate, it can dismiss the charges against a defendant. If it was an oversight or an error in judgment, the failure to disclose material evidence is likely to lead an appellate court to reverse a conviction and order a new trial. For these reasons, the need to disclose exculpatory evidence is taken very seriously by prosecutors. The Los Angeles County District Attorney's Office has gone so far as to establish a Brady Compliance Division to deal with exculpatory and impeachment evidence disclosure issues. In addition to providing counsel to local law enforcement and deputy prosecutors on specific cases, the Brady Compliance Division also maintains a database of prior acts by police officers that could be considered exculpatory evidence. In addition, a standardized form (see Exhibit 5.2), designed to identify potentially exculpatory evidence, has been put to use by the office in an effort to prevent nondisclosure issues from arising at trial.

CURRENT RESEARCH

The Los Angeles District Attorney's Office developed a specialized prosecution unit called Operation Hardcore to handle the prosecution of violent, gang-related offenses. Specialized units in prosecutor offices are developed in the hopes that the assigned prosecutors will gain specific knowledge and skills that will make them more effective in handling specific types of cases, the smaller caseloads will increase efficiency, and that the number of cases prosecuted and convictions secured will increase as a result. In 2011, a study was conducted that examined whether characteristics of the victim, suspect, and situational characteristics in the case influenced the charging decisions made by prosecutors in the specialized gang unit and whether the presence of the unit impacted the number of cases rejected.

The data used in the study was taken from the specialized prosecution unit in the Los Angeles District Attorney's Office over a 5-year period. The study examined prosecutor's charging decisions in 346 gang-related homicide cases. The victim and suspect characteristics (gender, race and ethnicity, gang affiliation, and number of victims and suspects) and situational characteristics (use of a firearm, whether the incident occurred after the unit was established and whether the unit prosecuted the case) were examined to determine their impact on whether the case was rejected or not.

The findings show that victim, suspect, and situational characteristics do impact the likelihood of case rejection. First, the results show that as the number of victims increased in the incident, the likelihood of the case being rejected significantly decreased. Second, the results show that cases involving female suspects and gang-affiliated suspects were more likely to be rejected by prosecutors. Last, the results show that gang-related homicides assigned to the specialized unit were more likely to be prosecuted compared to those gang-related homicides not assigned to the unit. Therefore, it appears that the existence of the specialized unit had one of the intended effects, in that it increased the likelihood that cases were fully prosecuted. Future research can build on the study by examining how decision making occurs in other specialized prosecution units for gang-related offenses and other types of crime. Furthermore, Los Angeles serves as an example to other cities considering implementing a specialized prosecution unit as a way to deal with their gang-related crime.

1. In your opinion, is it appropriate for the victim, suspect, and situational characteristics to have an impact on whether a case is prosecuted? How so?

2. Would you recommend that all cities establish a specialized gang-related prosecution unit?

Source: "Gang-related homicide charging decisions: The implementation of a specialized prosecution unit in Los Angeles," Criminal Justice Policy Review, 22(1), 3–26, (2011). David C. Pyrooz, Scott E. Wolfe, Cassia Spohn.

ASSISTANT PROSECUTORS AT WORK

Regardless of why young attorneys become assistant prosecutors, the transition from a law student, law clerk, or private attorney to being a prosecutor is frequently jarring. Prosecutors learn quickly that practicing law in the criminal justice system is much different than anything they learned in law school. Eloquent legal arguments are few and far between. What is observed is the rapid disposition of cases. Exactly how these decisions are made is not contained in a training manual but rather learned through informal courtroom observation and mentoring. The following section examines how assistant prosecutors do their jobs.

Working in the Courtroom Workgroup

One of the first things learned by a new prosecutor is that courts conduct business as a workgroup (Heumann, 1977). The court operates not unlike an assembly line, with each component anticipating what other components will do next. The new prosecutor learns that a member of the workgroup who disrupts the anticipated processes—that is, the efficient disposition of cases—is ripe for unofficial sanctioning by the judge.

Prosecutors have a great deal of control over a court's workload by their charging power and decisions regarding plea bargaining. The prosecutor's decisions regarding how cases are handled affect the workload placed on the members of the workgroup. Failure by a prosecutor to follow the informal workgroup guidelines makes every member suffer. In response to such actions, the judge is likely to take steps to teach the renegade prosecutor a lesson.

Consider the following example. Bob was arrested for driving while intoxicated. At the time of the arrest, his blood alcohol level was 0.24, three times the legal limit. To make matters worse, he had his 3-year-old twin sons in the car with him at the time. Peter Prosecutor has been on the job for 6 weeks. From observing and prosecuting 40 driving while intoxicated (also referred to as driving under the influence [DUI]) cases during this time period, he knows that first-time DUI offenders almost always receive no jail time in exchange for a guilty plea. The fact that Bob was so intoxicated and driving with his children disturbs Peter so much that he will only let Bob plead guilty if he receives a sentence of 10 days in jail. Bob's attorney explains that the going rate is no jail time and that even if he loses at trial, Bob will probably be sentenced to only 1 day in jail. Peter refuses to budge, and Bob rejects the plea offer.

Bob is later found guilty at trial and sentenced by Judge Julie to 1 day in jail. Afterward, Judge Julie asked the lawyers why they wasted her time by having a trial in a simple case. Bob's lawyer and Peter explain about the 10-day plea offer. The judge scolds Peter for wasting taxpayer money and says that he better learn not to do such a thing in the future. Although Peter understood the judge, his understanding grew even further over the next several months when every motion for a continuance (postponement) or time extension he requested, which previously had been granted as a matter of course, was

EXHIBIT 5.2 ■ **Los Angeles District Attorney**

Request Law Enforcement Conduct a Review of Its Files for Possible Brady Documents

The Office of the Los Angeles County District Attorney has determined that the following employees of your department may be material witnesses in:

People v._____   Case #_____

Therefore, it is requested that _____ review any files in your agency in order to locate any possible *Brady* documents for:

[Names of Employees]

Brady is information or evidence that (1) impeaches a prosecution witness, or (2) tends to exonerate a defendant. Evidence of conduct involving dishonesty or improper use of force or tending to show bias, which occurs in the course of exercising peace officer powers and while interacting with the public or when engaging in investigatory functions, may be deemed *Brady* documents.

If no *Brady* documents are found for the above-listed employees please indicate below and return form.

If *Brady* documents do exist for any of the above-listed employees, please identify the name, ID number and employment status of any such employee on this form and return it.

The obligation to provide *Brady* documents is ongoing. If your department receives any new *Brady* document regarding your above-listed employees, notify Deputy-in-Charge immediately.

_____ No document foreseen as being *Brady* documents exists for the above-named employees.

_____ Possible *Brady* documents exist for the following employees:

[Names of Employees]

Guidelines

Examples of possible impeachment evidence of a material witness include but are not limited to the following:

1. False reports by a prosecution witness.

2. Pending criminal charges against a prosecution witness. Parole or probation status of the witness.

3. Evidence contradicting a prosecution witness' statements or reports.

4. Evidence undermining a prosecution witness' expertise.

5. A finding of misconduct by a Board of Rights or Civil Service Commission that reflects on the witness' truthfulness, bias or moral turpitude.

6. Evidence that a witness has a reputation for untruthfulness.

7. Evidence that a witness has a racial, religious or personal bias against the defendant individually or as a member of a group.

8. Promises, offers or inducements to the witnesses, including a grant of immunity. An employee presently under suspension.

denied. With each denial, he was told that because he had so much time to try clear-cut DUIs, he shouldn't need any continuances. Peter has never bucked the workgroup's going rate in DUI plea offers again.

In his classic book *Plea Bargaining,* Milton Heumann (1977) explains that instances such as the one just described help lead all members of the workgroup to adapt to the workgroup's expectations. The other aspect that leads to prosecutors becoming melded with their workgroup is that it makes their lives easier. The workgroup operates to decrease uncertainty and increase efficiency. Given the large volume of cases handled by the criminal courts, without routine cooperation between prosecutors and defense attorneys, plea agreements would dissipate, and the number of trials, with their high levels of uncertainty and consumption of time, would increase. To avoid this unpleasantness, prosecutors generally play by the workgroup's informal rules.

THE EXPANSION OF THE PROSECUTOR'S DISCRETIONARY POWER

As you read throughout this chapter, discretion is an omnipresent force in the work of the prosecuting attorney. The vastness of the discretion possessed by prosecutors is based largely on the lack of effective checks on many of the decisions that are made by prosecutors, the fact that most of the decisions are made behind closed doors, and that the system relies on the prosecutor to exercise discretion to keep the system running. Over the past 25 years, every state and the federal government has adopted some form of sentencing guidelines or mandatory sentencing provision.

Mandatory sentencing laws, whether based on the type of crime, the number of prior convictions, or as part of a general determinate sentencing structure, have bolstered the discretionary power of prosecutors immensely. This increase in prosecutorial discretion comes at the expense of judicial discretion at sentencing (Woolridge & Griffin, 2005). By definition, mandatory sentencing laws require a judge to sentence an offender for a specified period of incarceration. Any prior sentencing discretion held by a judge is inapplicable in such cases. At the same time, the prosecutor maintains the discretion regarding what offenses with which to charge an offender. If a prosecutor thinks a mandatory life sentence is too extreme given the offender's conduct, he or she can choose not to allege prior convictions when charging the defendant and avert a mandatory sentence for repeat offenders. At the same time, the prosecutor can charge the defendant as a repeat offender with mandatory sentence on conviction and use the potential punishment as leverage during plea negotiations. Either approach is with the prosecutor's discretionary power.

PROSECUTORIAL ETHICS AND MISCONDUCT

As we have already seen, the prosecutor represents the government in criminal prosecutions. While the criminal court process operates under an **adversarial system**, with attorneys advocating for one side or the other, the roles of the prosecution and defense are

CURRENT CONTROVERSY

Prosecutors have a tremendous amount of discretion in deciding when to bring criminal charges against an individual and what those charges should be. This discretion is not without limitation. In the case of *Yates v. United States* (2015), the Supreme Court considered whether federal prosecutors overreached in prosecuting a commercial fisherman with violating a provision of financial crimes statute.

While conducting an offshore inspection of a commercial fishing vessel in the Gulf of Mexico, a federal agent found that the ships catch contained 72 undersized red grouper, in violation of federal conservation regulations. The officer instructed the ship's captain, John Yates, to keep the undersized fish segregated from the rest of the catch until the ship returned to port. After the officer left the ship, Yates had a crew member throw the undersized fish overboard. Yates was subsequently charged with violating 18 USC 1519, known as the Sarbanes–Oxley Act, which reads, "Whoever knowingly alters, destroys, mutilates, conceals, covers up, falsifies, or makes a false entry in any record, document, or tangible object with the intent to impede, obstruct, or influence the investigation or proper administration of any matter within the jurisdiction of any department or agency of the United States" is subject to imprisonment for up to 20 years. Yates argued to the trial court that 1519 was enacted to criminalize the destruction of incriminating documents and computer hard drives and not fish. The trial court rejected this argument and Yates was found guilty by a jury. The U.S. Court of Appeals for the Eleventh Circuit affirmed.

A divided Supreme Court (5–4) reversed the conviction, holding that prosecutors overreached in considering fish to be a tangible object under the Sarbanes–Oxley Act. Writing for a five-member majority, Justice Ginsburg found that the act had nothing to do with maritime regulations. It also noted that the caption of the relevant section is, "Destruction, alteration, or falsification of records in Federal investigations and bankruptcy." Additionally, the title of the section in which 1519 was originally placed, "Criminal penalties for altering documents," clearly indicated that Congress was referring only to financial records. Moreover, the text immediately surrounding "tangible object"—"falsifies or makes a false entry in any record [or] document"—indicates that Congress intended to restrict the term to documents and related items. The Court concluded that the prosecution overreached in charging a fisherman under this provision.

Justice Kagan wrote a dissenting opinion. She argued that the term "any tangible object" should be given its ordinary meaning and not arbitrarily limited by the Court. Given that the term means all items that possess a physical form, the dissent argued that fish should be covered under the statute.

1. Do you agree with the logic laid out by the majority or dissent? Why?

2. If a fish is a tangible object, and the statute prohibits destruction of "tangible objects," how can throwing the undersized fish off the boat not violate the statute?

The oral argument in *Yates v. United States* is available for you to listen to at https://www.oyez.org/cases/2014/13-7451.

quite different. Defense attorneys are duty-bound to do all they can do within the ethical rules to obtain a favorable outcome for their clients. This is the case even for clients they know are guilty.

The prosecutor, on the other hand, has a much different duty. The prosecutor represents the government and all of the citizens within the jurisdiction. Standard 3-1.2(c) of the American Bar Association's (1993) *Standards for Criminal Justice: Prosecution Function and Defense Function* simply states, "The duty of the prosecutor is to seek justice, not merely to convict." This plain statement provides a quick summary of the prosecutor's role in the criminal adjudication process. A more complete explanation of the extent of this duty was set forth by the Supreme Court in *Berger v. United States* (1935):

> The [prosecutor] is the representative not of an ordinary party to a controversy, but of a sovereignty whose obligation to govern impartially is as compelling as its obligation to govern at all; and whose interest, therefore, in a criminal prosecution is not that it shall win a case, but that justice shall be done. As such, he is in a peculiar and very definite sense the servant of the law, the twofold aim of which is that guilt shall not escape nor innocence suffer. He may prosecute with earnestness and vigor; indeed, he should do so. But, while he may strike hard blows, he is not at liberty to strike foul ones. It is as much his duty to refrain from improper methods calculated to produce a wrongful conviction as it is to use every legitimate means to bring about a just one. (p. 88)

The basis for this duty is twofold. First, as stated in *Berger*, it is simply wrong to convict an innocent person of a crime. Along with the presumption of innocence, which is the cornerstone of the American justice system, a prosecutor must operate with ethical safeguards to limit the chance of a wrongful conviction. The second basis revolves around the fact that the prosecutor represents the government rather than an individual. Private attorneys have an ethical duty to do all they can to achieve a favorable outcome for their clients. The prosecutor may have such a duty on behalf of the government, but that does not necessarily mean that prevailing in court is a favorable outcome. Society benefits from a fair outcome where justice is done. This includes having innocent defendants acquitted and rights of all parties—including the defendant—protected and upheld.

Relatedly, in representing the state, the prosecutor has a large effect on how citizens view their government. If prosecutors are perceived as operating outside the rule of law, respect for the government and court system's authority and legitimacy will be diminished.

> Recognizing a [prosecutor's] role as a shepherd of justice, we must not forget that the authority of the Government lawyer does not arise from any *right* of the Government, but from *power* entrusted to the Government. When a Government lawyer, with enormous resources at his or her disposal, abuses this power and ignores ethical standards, he or she not only undermines the public trust, but inflicts damage beyond calculation to our system of justice. (*In re Doe,* 1992, p. 480)

Ethical conduct, then, must be seen to be at the core of the prosecutor's role in the criminal justice system.

While no one disputes that prosecutors must seek to do justice, at times they lose sight of this duty. It is extremely rare for a prosecutor to deliberately try to have people convicted of a crime they did not commit. That being said, it is possible for a prosecutor, based on circumstantial evidence, to be convinced that a person is guilty of a crime when in fact the person did not commit the crime. It is such situations that give rise to breeches of a prosecutor's ethical duties and acts of **prosecutorial misconduct**.

Although it is atypical for prosecutors to deliberately act unethically, research has shown that such acts are committed from time to time across the country. The Center for Public Integrity is a nonprofit, nonpartisan organization that conducts research on public policy issues. In 2003, the center published the results from a multiyear study that examined appellate decisions in 11,452 cases in which prosecutorial misconduct was alleged. The study found that the appellate courts vacated the trial court outcome due to acts of prosecutorial misconduct in 2,012 cases (Weinberg, 2003). The center found that cases of misconduct occurred in a variety of areas, including the following:

- Courtroom misconduct (making inappropriate or inflammatory comments in the presence of the jury; introducing or attempting to introduce inadmissible, inappropriate, or inflammatory evidence; mischaracterizing the evidence or the facts of the case to the court or jury; committing violations pertaining to the selection of the jury; or making improper closing arguments)

- Mishandling of physical evidence (hiding, destroying, or tampering with evidence, case files, or court records)

- Failing to disclose exculpatory evidence

- Threatening, badgering, or tampering with witnesses

- Using false or misleading evidence

- Harassing, displaying bias toward, or having a vendetta against the defendant or defendant's counsel (including selective or vindictive prosecution, which includes instances of denial of a speedy trial)

- Improper behavior during grand jury proceedings

When misconduct is found to have occurred, a variety of sanctions can be ordered. If it is found that the misconduct was unintentional and did not affect the outcome of the case, there may be no sanction. On the other hand, if the act is intentional, it will likely lead to the reversal of a conviction, disciplinary action by a state bar association against the prosecutor, or both. For example, in the late 1990s, two first-degree murder convictions and death sentences were vacated by the Arizona Supreme Court when it was shown that during trial, the prosecutor intentionally presented false testimony, suborned perjury from a police detective, and argued facts to the jury that he knew were not true (*State v. McCrimmon*, 1996). The court ruled that due to egregious and intentional acts of misconduct by the prosecutor, retrial was barred by double jeopardy (*State v. Minnitt*, 2002). Finally, in 2004, the Court held that given the intentional and repeated nature of the misconduct, the serious harm (a death sentence) it gave rise to, and the fact that the prosecutor involved was very experienced, he should be disbarred and precluded from the practice of law (*In re Peasley*, 2004).

COMMUNITY PROSECUTION

Over the past two decades, the criminal justice system has seen consistent movement toward a community-based, proactive model of justice and crime control. Starting with community policing in the 1980s, various components of the criminal justice system shifted their focus away from arresting and prosecuting offenders and more toward dealing with underlying issues within the community in an effort to prevent crimes from occurring in the first place.

Since the 1990s, an increasing number of prosecutors' offices have engaged in what has been termed **community prosecution**. Community prosecution involves a partnership among the prosecutor's office, law enforcement, and the community, in which the authority and power possessed by the prosecutor's office are used to identify and solve problems, enhance public safety, and improve the quality of life in the community. Under a community prosecution model, the role of the prosecutor is redefined from a law enforcer in an adversary system to a member of a community partnership with the ability to facilitate **mediation**, galvanize community action, and impose civil sanctions and other nontraditional remedies in an effort to eradicate a problem faced by a community.

The American Prosecutors Research Institute (1995) identified five core elements to community prosecution:

- A proactive approach to crime

- A defined target area

- An emphasis on problem solving, public safety, and quality-of-life issues

- Partnerships between the prosecutor, the community, law enforcement, and others to address crime and disorder

- Use of varied enforcement methods

Community prosecution activities and programs are present in over half of the prosecutors' offices across the United States. These programs range from assigning prosecutors to geographic areas and having prosecutors responsible for attending community meetings to assigning prosecutors to work on specific community problems as identified by broad-based partnerships. What follows are two examples that show how community prosecution has been put into practice.

Albany, New York: Prisoner Reentry Program

Prisoners released from prison have a high recidivism rate. The faster former inmates take positive steps toward reintegrating into the community, the less likely they are to reoffend and be returned to prison. To foster this reintegration, the Community Prosecution Office of the Albany County District Attorney's Office established a prisoner reintegration program. Under the program, community prosecutors worked with nonprofit organizations to help 18- to 24-year-old former inmates living in high-crime neighborhoods obtain appropriate housing, employment, and health care. The partnership also helped former inmates obtain other necessities, such as driver's licenses, bank accounts, and clothing appropriate to wear on employment interviews. For several months following release, inmates met with a counselor to assess needs and obstacles.

In addition, the program established Reintegration Accountability Boards (RABs). RABs are panels of residents who meet with parolees and let them talk about past problems and future goals. The RAB also tells parolees what the community expectations are for their behavior and that the board is there to help with their reintegration. Parolees are given the chance to tell the board about community conditions that may have been a cause of prior criminal behavior and any current conditions that may lead to future problems. The RAB considers these items and takes steps to address them when possible.

Wayne County, Michigan: Drug Property Seizure and Abandoned Properties Program

The Wayne County, Michigan, Prosecutor's Office has an active community prosecution program. The office's focus has been to address quality-of-life issues in Detroit. In an effort to rid the community of drug dealers, community prosecutors, in partnership with community members, local police, and government agencies, initiated the Drug Property Seizure and Abandoned Properties Program to force slumlords to clean up or raze their buildings. The seizure policy forces landlords to fix up and police their properties. Failure to do so can lead to a court finding that the property is a danger or nuisance and ordering it razed and sold at auction. The program, which is used in a number of other cities, has been very successful in eliminating drug houses and reducing urban blight.

Programs such as these are being used by dozens of prosecutors' offices across the nation. It is fair to say that the use of community prosecution has increased to such a degree over the past decade that it is likely to be a permanent fixture in the criminal justice system.

SUMMARY

The prosecuting attorney is a critical cog in the criminal justice system. Decisions made by prosecutors at various stages of the criminal justice process have profound effects on the other actors in the system, individual members of society, and society as a whole. In the same speech quoted from previously in this chapter, Justice Robert Jackson (1940), in noting the power of the prosecutor in the American system of justice, concluded that it is individual prosecutors, as well as the way they view their position and make use of their authority, that determine how well the system will serve a community:

> The qualities of a good prosecutor are as elusive and as impossible to define as those which mark a gentleman. And those who need to be told would not understand it anyway. A sensitiveness to fair play and sportsmanship is perhaps the best protection against the abuse of power, and the citizen's safety lies in the prosecutor who tempers zeal with human kindness, who seeks truth and not victims, who serves the law and not factional purposes, and who approaches his task with humility.

The need for prosecutors with such qualities is compounded by the fact that prosecutors have almost limitless discretion in the decisions they make and the actions they take. That being said, they do not operate in a vacuum. Despite the power they wield, prosecutors do work in a system. As we will see in the coming chapters, for the court system to function effectively, prosecutors must work together with defense attorneys and judges to find a common ground and perform the joint duties called upon them by society. (p. 20)

Don't overlook the Student Study Site with its useful study aids, such as self-quizzes, eFlashcards, and other assists, to help you get more from the course and improve your grade.

DISCUSSION QUESTIONS

1. What role should politics play in the selection of U.S. attorneys?

2. Do you think local prosecuting attorneys should be elected or appointed? What are the pros and cons of each selection method?

3. What factors should voters consider in deciding if a prosecutor should be reelected?

4. In your opinion, should prosecutors' offices have to explain to the public why they declined to file charges in cases? What would be some ramifications of such a requirement?

5. Of the three models of prosecuting cases—horizontal model, vertical model, and mixed model—which do you think would be most appropriate for the prosecutor's office where you attend school?

6. What effect does being a member of the courtroom workgroup have on the way assistant prosecutors perform their jobs?

7. Is it fair to allow prosecutors to determine what evidence is exculpatory? What alternative methods (if any) would be better?

8. In *Griffin v. California* (1965), a case involving the rape and murder of a woman in a dark alley, the Supreme Court considered whether the following arguments by the prosecutor constituted prosecutorial misconduct and violated the defendant's rights:

> "The defendant certainly knows whether Essie Mae had this beat-up appearance at the time he left her apartment and went down the alley with her. . . ."

"He would know that. He would know how she got down the alley. He would know how the blood got on the bottom of the concrete steps. He would know how long he was with her in that box. He would know how her wig got off. He would know whether he beat her or mistreated her. He would know whether he walked away from that place cool as a cucumber when he saw Mr. Villasenor because he was conscious of his own guilt and wanted to get away from that damaged or injured woman."

"These things he has not seen fit to take the stand and deny or explain."

"And in the whole world, if anybody would know, this defendant would know."

"Essie Mae is dead, she can't tell you her side of the story. The defendant won't."

Do you think the prosecutor committed misconduct in making this argument?

9. Do you think community prosecution is an effective use of resources?

10. Think about the community where you live for a moment. Identify a quality-of-life problem in your community related to criminal behavior that may be a fitting target for a community prosecution effort. What is the problem? What might your community prosecution program include? What would be the desired outcome?

KEY TERMS

Adversarial system 122

Assistant prosecuting
    attorneys 106

Charging decision 112

Community prosecution 126

Going rate 115

Horizontal model of
    prosecution 107

Impeachment evidence 118

Mediation 126

Mixed model of
    prosecution 107

Plea bargaining 115

Prosecutorial misconduct 125

United States
    attorney 104

Vertical model of
    prosecution 107

INTERNET SITES

American Bar Association Prosecution Function Committee: www.abanet.org/dch/committee.cfm?com=CR204000

Association of Prosecuting Attorneys: www.apa-inc.org

National District Attorneys Association: www.ndaa.org

United States Department of Justice, Criminal Resource Manual: www.justice.gov/jm/criminal-resource-manual

Vera Institute of Justice: www.vera.org

STUDENT STUDY SITE

Get the tools you need to sharpen your study skills. SAGE edge offers a robust online environment featuring an impressive array of free tools and resources.

Access practice quizzes, eFlashcards, video, and multimedia at **edge.sagepub.com/hemmens4e**

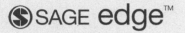

© Stockbyte/Thinkstock Images

6

DEFENSE ATTORNEYS

SAGE edge™

Master the content at **edge.sagepub.com/hemmens4e**

INTRODUCTION

The American court process is based on the adversarial system of justice. The cornerstone of an adversarial system is the presence of advocates representing opposing positions to the best of their ability. As we saw in the previous chapter, in the criminal court system, the government is represented by the prosecutor. On the flip side, as you know, a person accused of a crime is generally represented by a criminal defense attorney. The founding fathers recognized that for the adversarial system to function, persons accused of crimes needed to be represented by an advocate equally as skilled and educated as the opposing government prosecutor. To help ensure this balance, the Sixth Amendment to the Constitution provided that "in all criminal prosecutions the accused shall enjoy the right . . . to have the Assistance of Counsel for his defense."

In this chapter, we examine a number of aspects of this right. After we review the defense attorney's role in the criminal justice system and the historical underpinnings of the right to counsel, we consider the philosophical basis for the right to counsel as well as limitations placed on it by the Supreme Court. We then see what the right to counsel entails, the roles and duties of defense attorneys, and how states and local courts provide counsel for myriad defendants in criminal cases who cannot afford to pay an attorney. This chapter considers the level of effectiveness an attorney's performance must attain to provide constitutionally adequate assistance, the relationships between attorney and client, and whether a defendant unhappy with his or her attorney has the right to demand a new lawyer or even proceed without counsel. In considering these items, we repeatedly consider the manner in which defense attorneys fit into the operation of the criminal court system and processes.

DEFENSE ATTORNEY'S ROLE IN THE CRIMINAL JUSTICE SYSTEM

Criminal defense attorneys have a special role in the American justice system. As with all attorneys, they are officers of the court and must adhere to significant ethical standards. At the same time, however, defense attorneys must do all they can to promote the interests and protect the rights of their clients. This is far different from the roles and responsibilities faced by prosecutors.

As you may recall from the preceding chapter, whereas prosecutors, as representatives of the state, have an obligation to seek the truth and attain justice outcomes, criminal defense attorneys have no such obligation. Whereas a prosecutor may not seek to convict a person she believes to be innocent, a defense attorney has an ethical obligation to zealously defend a client he knows to be guilty. The reason for this duty is that for the American adversarial system of justice to work, it is necessary that actions and claims made by the government prosecutor be tested and challenged by a zealous advocate. If the prosecutor's case and evidence can withstand such scrutiny and be accepted beyond a reasonable doubt by a judge or jury, the likelihood of an innocent person being convicted of a crime she did not commit is considered remote.

To effectively put the prosecutor's case to the test, a defense attorney must be able to challenge the reliability of the evidence presented, cross-examine witnesses against the defendant, and raise matters involving violations of the defendant's rights regardless of whether the defendant is in fact guilty as charged. In describing the difference between a defense attorney's and a prosecutor's role in the system, Supreme Court Justice Byron White wrote,

> But defense counsel has no comparable obligation to ascertain or present the truth. Our system assigns him a different mission. He must be and is interested in preventing the conviction of the innocent, but, absent a voluntary plea of guilty, we also insist that he defend his client whether he is innocent or guilty. The State has the obligation to present the evidence. Defense counsel need present nothing, even if he knows what the truth is. He need not furnish any witnesses to the police, or reveal any confidences of his client, or furnish any other information to help the prosecution's case. If he can confuse a witness, even a truthful one, or make him appear at a disadvantage, unsure or indecisive, that will be his normal course. Our interest in not convicting the innocent permits counsel to put the State to its proof, to put the State's case in the worst possible light, regardless of what he thinks or knows to be the truth. Undoubtedly there are some limits which defense counsel must observe but more often than not, defense counsel will cross-examine a prosecution witness, and impeach him if he can, even if he thinks the witness is telling the truth, just as he will attempt to destroy a witness who he thinks is lying. In this respect, as part of our modified adversary system and as part of the duty imposed on the most honorable defense counsel, we countenance or require conduct which in many instances has little, if any, relation to the search for truth. (*United States v. Wade*, 1967, pp. 257–259)

Although not necessarily involving a search for the truth, defense attorneys play an important role in the search for justice. Beyond determining whether an individual committed a crime, the criminal court system operates to ensure that the government does not violate individual rights as guaranteed by the Constitution. The defense attorney's role in this process is to continuously challenge the government to ensure that all people's rights are honored; that suspects and defendants, regardless of who they may be, are treated equally under the law; and that a person is not convicted or punished until he pleads guilty before a judge or is proven to be guilty beyond a reasonable doubt before a jury.

HISTORICAL DEVELOPMENT OF THE RIGHT TO COUNSEL

As with many aspects of the American justice system, the role of counsel in criminal proceedings in 17th- and 18th-century England had a significant impact on the development of the right to counsel in the United States. Under English common law, a person charged with a crime was generally not allowed counsel in a prosecution for any felony or capital offense (Langbein, 1999; Tomkovicz, 2002). Not surprisingly, this practice was brought to the American colonies. During the colonial period, individuals were charged with crimes and tried before a court without the assistance of counsel. As discussed in the previous chapter, in the 1700s, the colonies moved increasingly toward the use of professional, state-funded prosecutors to prosecute criminal cases. Given the advantage a trained prosecutor had over a layperson defending himself, it became apparent that such a system was unfair to those charged with crimes. At the same time, more and more colonists were being prosecuted under British law without the rights and protections provided to English citizens. In light of these factors, individual colonies moved to provide defendants with the right to hire counsel to assist in their defense by law and, after the Declaration of Independence, by state constitution (Tomkovicz, 2002).

Shortly after the ratification of the U.S. Constitution, the right to counsel was included in the Bill of Rights presented to the First Congress. Specifically, the Sixth Amendment provided that "in all criminal prosecutions, the accused shall enjoy the right . . . to have the Assistance of Counsel for his defense." When the right to counsel was introduced and later adopted on the House and Senate floors during the First Congress, it was uncontroversial and adopted with little debate. In fact, the right to counsel generated minimal controversy until the 1930s.

The lack of controversy around the right to counsel was due to the limited scope of the right. Recall that in 18th-century England, defendants were not allowed to hire an attorney to represent them in most felony prosecutions. The Sixth Amendment's guarantee that individuals facing criminal prosecution had the right to hire an attorney to defend them was seen as an important constitutional right. Prior to 1933, the right to counsel was assumed to simply permit defendants to hire and to be represented by an attorney. In 1932, the Supreme Court addressed whether defendants who could not afford to pay for an attorney had the right to be represented by counsel at the government's expense.

In *Powell v. Alabama* (1932), the U.S. Supreme Court addressed for the first time whether indigent criminal defendants had a right to have an attorney provided to them at state expense. In *Powell,* nine African American youths, later known as the "Scottsboro boys," were charged with the rape of two White girls in rural Alabama. Under Alabama law, this crime was punishable by death. The trial court did not appoint counsel to the defendants until the morning of trial. Moreover, the defendants were not asked whether they were able to employ counsel or if they wished to have counsel appointed. After a one-day trial, eight of the defendants were convicted and sentenced to death.

In vacating the convictions rather than finding the defendants' right to counsel under the Sixth Amendment was violated, the Supreme Court ruled that the defendants were denied due process under the Fourteenth Amendment. In the majority opinion, Justice Sutherland wrote,

> The right to be heard would be, in many cases, of little avail if it did not comprehend the right to be heard by counsel. Even the intelligent and educated layman has small and sometimes no skill in the science of law. If charged with crime, he is incapable, generally, of determining for himself whether the indictment is good or bad. He is unfamiliar with the rules of evidence. Left without the aid of counsel, he may be put on trial without a proper charge and convicted upon incompetent evidence, or evidence irrelevant to the issue or otherwise inadmissible. He lacks both the skill and knowledge adequately to prepare his defense, even though he

may have a perfect one. He requires the guiding hand of counsel at every step in the proceedings against him. Without it, though he be not guilty, he faces the danger of conviction because he does not know how to establish his innocence. (pp. 68–69)

The Court concluded that given the seriousness of the charges and the special circumstances present, the lack of counsel denied the defendants due process under the law. Importantly, however, the Court emphasized a number of specific facts involved in the case, including that the case involved death sentences, as well as the age and "feeblemindedness" and ignorance of the defendants, in limiting the scope of its opinion. While Powell established a right to appointed counsel in capital cases, it did not require counsel be appointed in noncapital state prosecutions so long as the proceedings were not fundamentally unfair.

Six years later in *Johnson v. Zerbst* (1938), the Court expanded the reach of *Powell* in federal courts to include the right to counsel possessed by defendants who cannot afford to hire an attorney. The defendant in *Zerbst* was convicted without the assistance of counsel in federal court of "possessing and uttering" counterfeit money. The Court over-turned his conviction, basing its decision on the Sixth Amendment's guarantee of counsel "in all criminal prosecutions." Justice Hugo Black, writing for the majority, stated the Sixth Amendment "withholds from federal courts, in all criminal proceedings, the power and authority to deprive an accused of his life or liberty" unless he was represented by counsel at trial, or the right to counsel was waived by the defendant. The Court explicitly found that an indigent defendant appearing in court without an attorney suffers a marked disadvantage against the government. Moreover, the opinion stated that the right to counsel was "a constitutionally defined element of a criminal trial," and it was there-fore "the trial court's affirmative obligation to see that the accused was given this right."

Zerbst differed from *Powell* in several important aspects. Unlike *Powell*, *Zerbst* applied to all criminal defendants in federal court regardless of the particular circum-stances of individual cases. Furthermore, the rights announced in *Zerbst* were based on the Sixth Amendment right to counsel instead of the Due Process Clause. However, as *Zerbst* applied only to federal prosecutions, it did not alter *Powell*'s demands on the states. As such, states were still required to offer **court-appointed counsel** to indigent defendants only in capital cases or in particular situations that would offend all notions of due process.

In 1942, the Supreme Court considered whether the right to counsel as provided for in *Zerbst* should be applied to the state court prosecutions in *Betts v. Brady* (1942). *Betts* involved a robbery prosecution of a 43-year-old man of ordinary intelligence. Prior to trial, Betts requested counsel be appointed to aid in his defense. This request was denied, and he was subsequently found guilty by a jury and sentenced to prison.

In upholding the conviction, the Supreme Court held that the Fourteenth Amend-ment's Due Process Clause did not mandate counsel for an indigent defendant charged with a felony offense in state court. As it had done in *Powell,* the Court focused on the particular facts involved in the case: The defendant was an adult, he was familiar with the criminal process, and he was "of ordinary intelligence." On the basis of these facts, the Court found that Betts had the ability to adequately defend himself, and as such, the absence of counsel did not deprive him of a fair trial. In a broader sense, the holding in

Betts meant that states were not required to provide indigent defendants with an attorney absent special circumstances such as those present in *Powell.*

In a passionate dissent, Justice Black found the Court's ruling contrary to its prior holdings in *Powell* and *Zerbst.* He argued that depriving a defendant of counsel because of his indigent status is at odds with "common and fundamental ideas of fairness and right." Justice Black's dissenting opinion in *Betts* would lay the framework for the rejection of *Betts* two decades later.

On June 3, 1961, Clarence Gideon was arrested and charged with breaking and entering a poolroom with the intent to commit a misdemeanor, a felony under Florida law. Prior to his trial, Gideon, who was indigent, demanded that the state appoint him an attorney. The trial court judge refused, explaining that he "[could not] appoint Counsel to represent [Gideon] in this case. Under the laws of the State of Florida, the only time the Court can appoint Counsel to represent a Defendant is when that person is charged with a capital offense" (*Gideon v. Wainwright,* 1963). Gideon was convicted at trial and sentenced to 5 years in prison.

From his prison cell, Gideon, who had no formal education, sharpened his pencil and handwrote a petition for habeas corpus for submission to the Supreme Court. The Supreme Court receives thousands of pauper petitions annually, and it agrees to consider the merits of very few requests. Fortunately for Gideon, the Court agreed to hear his case and appointed attorney Abe Fortas, who would later be appointed to the Supreme Court, to represent him before the Court.

A unanimous Supreme Court explicitly overruled *Betts* and held that indigent defendants charged with a felony in state courts must have counsel provided to them at state expense. In the majority opinion, Justice Black, who had dissented in *Betts,* held that

> in our adversary system of criminal justice, any person hauled into court, who is too poor to hire a lawyer, cannot be assured a fair trial unless counsel is provided for him. This seems to us to be an obvious truth. Governments, both state and federal, quite properly spend vast sums of money to establish machinery to try defendants accused of crime. Lawyers to prosecute are everywhere deemed essential to protect the public's interest in an orderly society. Similarly, there are few defendants charged with crime, few indeed, who fail to hire the best lawyers they can to prepare and present their defenses. That government hires lawyers to prosecute and defendants who have the money hire lawyers to defend are the strongest indications of the widespread belief that lawyers in criminal cases are necessities, not luxuries. (p. 354)

The Court concluded that the right to counsel was essential to a fair trial and was therefore incorporated into the Fourteenth Amendment's Due Process Clause and was binding on the states. As groundbreaking as the *Gideon* decision was, it left several questions unanswered. Specifically, the Court did not address whether there is a right to counsel in all criminal prosecutions, including prosecutions of petty offenses and misdemeanors; at what point in the court process the right to counsel attaches; and whether the right to counsel applies to postconviction proceedings, such as appeals, habeas corpus filings, and probation and parole violation hearings. As discussed later, the Court addressed each of the matters over the next several decades.

Limits on the Right to Counsel

Read literally, this right would seem to apply equally to a person charged with murder and a person charged with littering. On the other hand, because *Gideon* involved a felony, it could be argued that the right to counsel applied only in cases involving felonies. Predictably, how individual states interpreted what constituted a criminal offense varied greatly. It wasn't until 1972, nine years after *Gideon* was decided, that the Supreme Court clarified under what circumstances indigent defendants charged with crimes that were not felonies were entitled to counsel at state expense.

Jon Argersinger, an indigent, was charged with carrying a concealed weapon, a misdemeanor punishable by imprisonment up to 6 months, a $1,000 fine, or both. Despite his request for an attorney, he was not provided with counsel. He was subsequently found guilty by a judge at a nonjury trial and sentenced to serve 90 days in jail. Argersinger brought a habeas corpus action in the Florida Supreme Court, alleging that his Fourteenth Amendment right to counsel as guaranteed in *Gideon* was violated. The Florida Supreme Court refused to provide relief, holding that a defendant has a right to counsel only if he is facing a potential period of incarceration longer than 6 months.

In an opinion written by Justice Douglas, the Supreme Court reversed (*Argersinger v. Hamlin,* 1972). The Court noted the vital role counsel plays in providing a defendant with a fair trial regardless of the seriousness of the charges being faced. Moreover, given the large number of misdemeanants prosecuted in local courts, the potential that indigent defendants in those courts face assembly-line justice is real. That being said, the Court acknowledged that this same large number of cases would make a requirement that all misdemeanants be provided with counsel largely unfeasible.

Facing these realities, the Court struck a balance, holding that absent a knowing and intelligent waiver, *no person may be imprisoned for any offense* unless the person is represented by counsel at a trial. Because Argersinger was convicted and sentenced to jail without being appointed counsel, his conviction and sentence were vacated.

The standard laid out in *Argersinger* was clarified 7 years later in *Scott v. Illinois* (1979). The Supreme Court in *Scott* explicitly recognized that a defendant may not be sentenced to jail or prison unless that person was represented by an attorney or voluntarily waived her right to counsel. If you think this standard would be awkward to implement, you would be correct. It essentially requires the trial judge and prosecutor to decide at an early stage of a prosecution whether they believe a defendant charged with a misdemeanor is deserving of a jail sentence if convicted. If a defendant is not provided an attorney, he may not be imprisoned if ultimately found guilty.

This places the prosecutor and judge in a situation where they must balance the ability to incarcerate a defendant on conviction against the cost of providing low-level offenders with counsel. Given the thousands of indigent defendants charged with misdemeanors each week across the country, if states and local governments were required to provide counsel in each case, the expense would be overwhelming.

Although the Supreme Court was unanimous in the finding that Argersinger's rights had been violated, several justices disagreed with the standard set forth in the majority opinion. The primary concern was that the criminal justice system would be overwhelmed with the new requirement for the appointment of counsel in thousands of new cases. These concerns have not come to fruition. As it tends to do, the criminal justice system adapted to this new requirement with minimal problems.

At What Point in a Proceeding Is There a Right to an Attorney?

Whereas *Argersinger* and *Gideon* laid out the types of cases in which a defendant has a right to counsel, they did not address the point in the prosecution process at which the right to an attorney attaches. The Supreme Court has held that the right to counsel for a defendant who would be entitled to an attorney under *Gideon* or *Argersinger* attaches at the initiation of formal adversarial proceedings. This occurs when a defendant is arrested and brought before a judge for an initial appearance or when the accused is indicted or formally charged with a crime by criminal complaint. Once the right to counsel has attached, a defendant has the right to an attorney at all *critical stages* in the court process. A critical stage is any stage of a criminal proceeding where substantial rights of a criminal accused may be affected. The basis for this definition centers on the fact that the core purpose behind the right to counsel was to provide assistance when the accused was confronted with both the intricacies of the law and the advocacy of the public prosecutor. For this reason, a defendant has a right to have a lawyer appear on her behalf at essentially all court proceedings following the commencement of a criminal prosecution. The Supreme Court has stated that a prosecution begins and the right to counsel attaches at a defendant's first appearance before a judicial officer, at which point the defendant is informed of the charges against him and has restrictions imposed on his liberty (*Rothgery v. Gillespie County,* 2008). In addition to having a right to counsel at court appearances, following the filing of formal charges, prosecutors, police, and investigators may not contact the defendant, let alone interrogate her, in the absence of counsel. Table 6.1 lists a number of stages of the criminal adjudication process and whether they require the presence of a defendant's lawyer.

TABLE 6.1 ■ Proceedings and the Right to Counsel	
Right to Counsel	**No Right to Counsel**
Custodial interrogation (Fifth Amendment per *Miranda v. Arizona*, 1966)	Noncustodial, preindictment interrogation
Preliminary hearing	Prearrest probable cause hearing
Lineup (postindictment)	Initial appearance
Postindictment court proceedings	Lineup (preindictment)
Plea bargaining negotiations	Grand jury
Trial	Probation and parole revocation if no incarceration
Sentencing	Discretionary appeals
Motion for new trial	Habeas corpus petitions (non–death penalty)
First appeal	
Probation or parole revocation if incarceration imposed	

The right to counsel does not end following the conviction and sentencing of a defendant. On the basis of the assumption that a defendant's right to appeal can be effective only if counsel is provided, the Supreme Court has held that indigent defendants have the right to the assistance of court-appointed counsel for their first appeal. This right does not extend to subsequent appeals, habeas corpus petitions, or other postconviction proceedings. Although there is no right to counsel under the U.S. Constitution for multiple appeals or petitions to the state and U.S. supreme courts, a number of states do provide for the assistance of counsel on request for other postconviction proceedings.

INDIGENT DEFENSE SYSTEMS

Recall that *Gideon* and *Argersinger* mandated that states provide counsel to indigent criminal defendants charged with felonies and misdemeanors in which a defendant may be sentenced to jail or prison if convicted. Given the fact that nearly 90% of criminal defendants are indigent, the magnitude of the responsibility placed on states to provide attorneys for indigent defendants cannot be overstated. Consider Table 6.2, which contains the expenditures associated with indigent defense services in the United States during 2012. In that one year alone, states spent between $108,000 and $214 million on indigent defense services.

Due in large part to these costs, state and local governments across the country work hard to provide counsel to indigent defendants as efficiently and inexpensively as possible. At the same time, however, it is morally and constitutionally required that a defendant be provided with competent representation. The best means of providing effective representation at a reasonable cost is widely debated. There are three primary indigent defense systems: assigned counsel programs, contract systems, and public defender offices.

Assigned Counsel Programs

Assigned counsel programs employ private attorneys to represent indigent defendants. Many attorneys, particularly those recently out of law school, welcome the opportunity to participate in an assigned counsel program because of the courtroom experience they can gain.

The most common type of assigned counsel system is the **ad hoc assigned counsel** program, under which the appointment of counsel is generally made by the court on an ad hoc basis; that is, lawyers are appointed to represent defendants on a case-by-case basis when necessary. Frequently, cases are assigned to whoever happens to be in the courtroom at a defendant's first appearance or arraignment. Under these systems, attorneys are usually paid on an hourly basis, for example, $40 an hour for work out of court and $50 an hour for work in court. In some states, attorneys are provided a flat fee per case. In most jurisdictions, private, court-appointed counsel must petition the court for funds for investigative services, expert witnesses, and other necessary costs of litigation. The ad hoc assigned counsel method is the predominant indigent defense system used in the country. It works particularly well in smaller, rural counties that have limited demand for indigent defense services. Drawbacks of ad hoc appointment systems are the lack of control over the experience level and qualifications of the appointed attorneys as well as the potential for judges funneling work to preferred lawyers.

The second type of assigned counsel program is referred to as the **coordinated assigned counsel** system. Under this system, attorneys apply to be included on a list of counsel to be appointed on an as-needed, rotational basis. As with the ad hoc appointment method, attorneys are paid on an hourly or per-case basis.

The coordinated assigned counsel system provides several benefits not available in the ad hoc model. A primary benefit is that it allows the court or a governing body to require attorneys to meet minimal qualification standards to be accepted into the program. By limiting appointments to attorneys who are prequalified to handle the case, both in terms of ability and desire to receive such appointment, problems associated with unqualified or unwilling attorneys being appointed cases are reduced if not eliminated. In addition, because the appointing authority knows the background and level of experience of each attorney eligible for appointment, experienced attorneys can be appointed to highly complex or serious cases, while less serious cases can be handled by less experienced lawyers. For these reasons, the coordinated assigned counsel model is generally recognized to be better than the ad hoc assigned counsel system.

Contract Attorney Programs

The second category of indigent defense systems is known as **contract attorney programs.** In contract programs, a state or county government (or judicial district administration) enters into a contract with one or more private attorneys, law firms, or nonprofit organizations to provide representation to indigent defendants. Such contracts are normally designated for a specific purpose within the court system, such as felonies, misdemeanors, or all cases where the public defender has a conflict of interest. Jurisdictions using contract systems to provide indigent defense services will periodically advertise requests for proposals under which attorneys, law firms, and nonprofit organizations can bid for the contract. Such bids generally state how much the attorney or firm will charge to handle the specified services.

Contract programs operate using either fixed-price contracts or fixed-fee-per-case contracts. Under a **fixed-price contract program**, a contracting lawyer or law firm agrees to accept an unknown number of cases within the contract period, normally one year, for a single flat fee. The contracting attorneys are usually responsible for the cost of overhead, support services, investigation, and expert witnesses. Even if the caseload in the jurisdiction is higher than was projected, the attorney is responsible for providing representation in each case for the original price.

Although the fixed-price contract program provides a level of certainty for a governmental agency trying to budget for indigent defense services, this approach comes with several negative components. The largest problems are (a) the inherent incentive for the attorney to spend as little time and expense on each case as possible and, relatedly, (b) the lack of oversight of the competence of the attorney handling each case for a law firm that has entered into the contract. Under such contracts, law firms have been known to have their least experienced attorneys handle a majority of cases involving indigent defendants, to refrain from employing investigators or expert witnesses, and to take all steps possible to dispose of cases prior to trial. In short, the quality of representation provided to indigent defendants suffers under fixed-price contract systems. It is for these reasons that the use of fixed-price contracts has been condemned by the American Bar Association.

TABLE 6.2 ■ State Indigent Defense Expenditures, 2012*			
State		**Total Expenditures**	
State	**Total Expenditures**	**State**	**Total Expenditures**
Alabama	$59,707,000	Montana	$23,335,000
Alaska	$24,916,000	Nebraska	$3,533,000
Arizona	$1,378,000	Nevada	$3,234,000
Arkansas	$37,600,000	New Hampshire	$18,038,000
California	$22,672,000	New Jersey	$117,628,000
Colorado	$100,714,000	New Mexico	$38,519,000
Connecticut	$64,002,000	New York	$62,700,000
Delaware	$18,792,000	North Carolina	$125,603,000
Florida	$214,526,000	North Dakota	$6,140,000
Georgia	$69,539,000	Ohio	$70,413,000
Hawaii	$9,275,000	Oklahoma	$16,581,000
Idaho	$1,990,000	Oregon	$112,269,000
Illinois	$20,266,000	Pennsylvania	$0
Indiana	$24,906,000	Rhode Island	$13,805,000
Iowa	$55,726,000	South Carolina	$21,938,000
Kansas	$22,714,000	South Dakota	$624,000
Kentucky	$43,586,000	Tennessee	$74,032,000
Louisiana	$67,964,000	Texas	$26,981,000
Maine	$14,448,000	Utah	$108,000
Maryland	$87,952,000	Vermont	$12,103,000
Massachusetts	$191,228,000	Virginia	$43,257,000
Michigan	$12,866,000	Washington	$25,564,000
Minnesota	$64,509,000	West Virginia	$42,681,000
Mississippi	$4,307,000	Wisconsin	$90,640,000
Missouri	$35,739,000	Wyoming	$10,258,000

Source: Bureau of Justice Statistics.
*Most recent data available.

Under **fixed-fee-per-case contract** systems, the contract entered into by the attorney or law firm and the local government entity agrees to a specific number of cases to be handled for a fixed fee per case. Typically, the contracting attorney or firm submits a monthly statement indicating the number of cases handled during the period. Once the predetermined number of cases has been reached, the option exists to renegotiate, extend, or terminate the contract.

The fixed-fee-per-case model is less common than the fixed-price model for jurisdictions that use a contract system for indigent defense. The main reason for this is that a number of jurisdictions have adopted the fixed-price contract model solely as a means to cut costs, often at the expense of the quality of the representation provided.

In recent years, the number of jurisdictions using contract programs has increased substantially. In most instances, contract programs have been introduced as an alternative to court-appointed attorneys handling conflict of interest cases in jurisdictions that have a public defender office. The primary appeal of contract systems to funding bodies is the ability to project costs for the upcoming year accurately by limiting the total amount of money that is contracted out. With an assigned counsel system, it is impossible to predict the total cost for the upcoming year. Variables affecting the cost of an assigned counsel system include the total number of cases assigned, whether any death penalty or complicated cases are filed, and whether there are drug sweeps resulting in multiple defendants for the same case. Counties and states using fixed-price contracts are not subject to these variables, so they can project with certainty what their indigent defense expenditures will be at the beginning of the year.

Public Defender Programs

A **public defender program** is a public or nonprofit institution designated to provide representation to indigent defendants in criminal cases. The defining characteristic of a public defender office is that it directly employs staff attorneys whose sole job is to provide representation to indigent defendants. The director of most public defender offices is normally appointed by a governing body (generally a county commission or a state's governor). Public defender offices employ full-time investigators and support staff and have budgets to hire expert witnesses as needed. Public defender offices are predominantly used in larger jurisdictions with a significant number of criminal prosecutions. Attorneys working in public defender offices range from those recently out of law school and admitted to the bar to veterans who have been public defenders for many years and even decades. Cases are usually assigned to individual public defenders based on the attorney's experience and the seriousness and complexity of the charges facing the defendant. In addition, public defenders normally handle all aspects of a case, from arraignment through sentencing.

Public defenders and their offices are routinely thought to provide less effective representation than attorneys in the private sector; however, this is not necessarily the case. Although notoriously overworked, public defenders and their offices have the capacity to handle large numbers of cases efficiently because of the fact that criminal defense in a single jurisdiction is the sole focus of their work. Familiarity with procedures increases efficiency and appearing before the same judges and with the same prosecutors on a daily basis also facilitates workgroup cohesion, which may lead to better outcomes for clients.

Another important benefit associated with being represented by a public defender is that public defender offices have investigators on staff and funds budgeted for expenses associated with expert witnesses. Generally, if a defendant being represented by a public defender needs investigatory work performed or would benefit from the testimony of an expert witness, these items will be accomplished as a matter of course. With assigned

CURRENT CONTROVERSY

Attorneys who work in an indigent defense system are notoriously overwhelmed by immense caseloads. Despite the fact that the American Bar Association and many states have explicit caseload limits of 150 felonies and 400 misdemeanors a year, these limits are routinely ignored, with attorneys' actual caseloads ballooning up to 200% more than what is authorized. Historically, this is because the caseload standards are advisory and contain no mechanism for enforcement.

In 2012, the Washington State Supreme Court took a giant step toward putting teeth into caseload limits by amending court rules on the appointment of attorneys to represent indigent defendants. In addition to reaffirming the caseload limits noted above, the court also enacted several important yet often ignored items associated with indigent defense. The court rules require attorneys possess specific levels of experience (years of practice and completed jury trials) before they can be assigned to specific classes of cases. Additionally, attorneys in private practice who also represent indigent defendants must adjust the number of cases they can be assigned to account for the percentage of time they spend representing private, fee paying clients. Moreover, the court also mandated that indigent defense attorneys and public defender offices have access to office space, support staff, and investigative resources, to effectively represent their clients.

While these items are important, the critical component of the standards involves how they are overseen and implemented. Rather than simply provide standards with no enforcement mechanism, the Washington Supreme Court requires attorneys to certify that they are in compliance with the standards four times a year (see Exhibit 6.1 for a sample certification form). These certifications must be filed with the courts in which they practice. What makes this system effective is its placing the burden of compliance on attorneys. Although the court has no rule making authority for cities and counties, it does have the authority to regulate attorneys who practice law in the state. As such, attorneys who certify their compliance with the guidelines when they are out of compliance may be subjected to discipline by the state bar and supreme court. Attorneys whose practice exceeds the number of assigned cases permitted run the risk of having their license to practice law in the state revoked.

The standards have been in effect for several years. Although it is too soon to tell what impact the new standards and procedures are having on the system, it appears cities, counties, and attorneys have effectively adapted to the new requirements imposed. For more information and updates visit the Washington State Office of Public Defense at http://www.opd.wa.gov.

1. Who should pay for the added expense of lowering public defender caseloads? Options include the state, the county, the public defense office, or the defendant.

2. Should the prosecuting attorney's office take any steps to help public defense offices reduce caseloads? How about local trial courts?

counsel or counsel appointed in a contract system, expenses for investigators and expert witnesses are either borne by the attorney as part of the contract or subject to court or administrative approval. Accordingly, an indigent defendant who is likely to need the testimony of an expert witness or further investigation beyond what is done by the police is probably better off being represented by a public defender than another type of appointed counsel.

EXHIBIT 6.1 ■ Certification of Appointed Counsel of Compliance With Standards

[ ] SUPERIOR COURT   [ ] JUVENILE DEPARTMENT

[ ] DISTRICT COURT   [ ] MUNICIPAL COURT

FOR

[ ] CITY OF [ ] COUNTY OF _____,

STATE OF WASHINGTON

[ ] No.: _____

[ ] Administrative Filing

CERTIFICATION BY:

[NAME], [WSBA#]

FOR THE:

[1ST, 2ND, 3RD, 4TH] CALENDAR QUARTER OF [YEAR]

CERTIFICATION OF APPOINTED COUNSEL OF COMPLIANCE WITH STANDARDS REQUIRED BY CRR 3.1 / CRRLJ 3.1 / JUCR 9.2

The undersigned attorney hereby certifies:

1. Approximately _____% of my total practice time is devoted to indigent defense cases.

2. I am familiar with the applicable Standards adopted by the Supreme Court for attorneys appointed to represent indigent persons and that:

   a. Basic Qualifications: I meet the minimum basic professional qualifications in Standard 14.1.

   b. Office: I have access to an office that accommodates confidential meetings with clients, and I have a postal address and adequate telephone services to ensure prompt response to client contact, in compliance with Standard 5.2.

   c. Investigators: I have investigators available to me and will use investigative services as appropriate, in compliance with Standard 6.1.

   d. Caseload: I will comply with Standard 3.2 during representation of the defendant in my cases. [Effective October 1, 2013 for felony and juvenile offender caseloads; effective January 1, 2015 for misdemeanor caseloads: I should not accept a greater number of cases (or a proportional mix of different case types) than specified in Standard 3.4, prorated if the amount of time spent for indigent defense is less than full time, and taking into account the case counting and weighting system applicable in my jurisdiction.]

   e. Case Specific Qualifications: I am familiar with the specific case qualifications in Standard 14.2, Sections B-K and will not accept appointment in a case as lead counsel unless I meet the qualifications for that case. [Effective October 1, 2013]

_____

Signature, WSBA#

_____

Date

PRIVATE VERSUS APPOINTED COUNSEL: WHICH IS BETTER?

While comparing the different forms of indigent defense systems is worthwhile, it is also important to consider whether defendants who are able to hire private attorneys at their own expense receive better representation than defendants with court-appointed counsel. The answer to this question depends largely on whom you ask and how you measure quality of representation.

From the perspective of the client, there is an overwhelming belief that defendants represented by private attorneys receive better assistance than that provided to defendants with appointed counsel (Casper, 1978; Feeney & Jackson, 1991; Wice, 2005). There are several reasons for this belief. First, public defenders and appointed attorneys are widely viewed as lawyers working for the government, just like the prosecutor. As such, many defendants view their appointed attorney as being in cahoots with the prosecutor and not having their best interests in mind. Relatedly, it is believed that people get what they pay for, and if they are getting an attorney for free, that attorney must not be very good; otherwise, that attorney would have a "real job" (Casper, 1978).

Although these perceptions are factually incorrect, research has shown that there are some differences in the way in which private and appointed attorneys do their jobs. One difference is the amount of time the different types of attorneys spend with their clients. Attorneys who are hired and paid by a defendant spend more time with their clients than attorneys who are appointed to represent defendants. This disparity is due to the large number of cases public defenders have and the number of clients they must see in a given day. Private attorneys, with smaller caseloads, are able to see their clients more frequently and respond to requests for meetings more expeditiously.

Research has also shown that private attorneys file more motions, attend more hearings, and meet with family members more often than do appointed counsel. Such actions demonstrate the level of effort these attorneys are putting into the cases and serve to justify the fee those attorneys are being paid. These efforts also make clients feel that someone is fighting for them and is doing everything possible to obtain a positive outcome. For these reasons, private attorneys, compared with court-appointed lawyers, consistently receive superior ratings on the quality of representation provided.

In terms of case outcomes, however, research has consistently indicated that there is little variation in case outcomes between privately **retained attorneys** and assigned counsel (Hanson, Hewitt, Ostrom, & Lomvardias, 1992; Wice, 2005). There is no significant difference in the rate of case dismissals, convictions, and sentences following conviction for defendants represented by appointed counsel and retained attorneys. Moreover, any differences found in case outcomes are due to items other than type of attorney, particularly the race, income, criminal history, and pretrial release status of the defendant. Although private attorneys generally file more motions and attend more hearings, these acts do not regularly generate better case outcomes. As discussed later in this chapter, while appointed attorneys fare just as well as retained counsel in the ultimate disposition of cases, achieving a positive result absent vivid displays of effort and adversariness is frequently unappreciated and dismissed.

CURRENT RESEARCH

As discussed in this chapter, research on the impact the type of attorney has on outcomes in criminal prosecutions are mixed. In "The Effect of Attorney Type on Bail Decisions," Marian Williams presents the results from a study that examined whether or not having a public defender or retained counsel representing a criminal defendant has an impact on bail and pretrial release decisions. Williams analyzed data involving over 4,000 cases from Florida's seven largest counties between 1990 and 2004 to address five research questions.

1. Is there is a relationship between type of counsel (retained or public defender) and whether or not defendants are denied bail?
2. Is there is a relationship between type of counsel and whether or not defendants are to be released prior to case outcome?
3. Is there is a relationship between type of counsel and the amount of bail set for defendants?
4. Is there is a relationship between type of counsel and the likelihood that a defendant is released on his or her own recognizance (ROR)?

5. Is there is a relationship between type of counsel and the likelihood that a defendant is given nonfinancial conditional release?

In the regression models she computed and analyzed, Williams included a number of relevant control variables related to the defendant and the offense. These include the number of charges, the most serious charge, and the defendant's age, race, prior failures to appear, prior convictions, prior arrests, and whether he or she was on active probation or parole.

The regression analyses produced mixed results. Defendants with public defenders had lower bail amounts set for them than those with retained counsel. Defendants with public defenders were also more likely to be given pretrial release with nonmonetary conditions (ROR or conditional release). On the other hand, defendants represented by retained counsel were more likely to be released prior to the case outcome and less likely to be detained through the entire case than were those represented by a public defender.

1. Do these results surprise you?
2. What factors do you think are behind these findings?

Source: "The Effect of Attorney Type on Bail Decisions." Marian R. Williams *Criminal Justice Policy Review*, 28(1): 3–17, 2017.

EFFECTIVE ASSISTANCE OF COUNSEL

By the 1970s, the Supreme Court clarified under what circumstances indigent defendants were entitled to the assistance of counsel at state expense. Less clear was the level of competence and ability required of attorneys appointed to represent indigent defendants. In 1970, the Supreme Court explicitly held that the right to counsel included the right to the effective assistance of counsel. As summarized by the Supreme Court in *McMann v. Richardson* (1970), "If the right to counsel guaranteed by the Constitution is to serve its purpose, defendants cannot be left to the mercies of incompetent counsel."

Although the Court clearly established that a defendant has a right to effective assistance, it did not define what level of performance is sufficiently effective. Up until the mid-1980s, a number of varying definitions and standards for what constituted effective assistance of counsel were used in federal and state courts. Criteria used by courts included whether the attorney's performance was "of such a kind as to shock the conscience of the court and make the proceedings a farce and mockery of justice," "reasonably competent," "[of] a minimum standard of professional representation," or "[characterized by] customary skills and diligence." As should be clear, these standards are so broad and ill defined as to be largely unusable.

In light of these varied measures, in the 1984 case of *Strickland v. Washington,* the Supreme Court set forth the standard to be used in evaluating ineffectiveness of counsel claims. Justice O'Connor, writing for a seven-member majority, noted that the standard for judging a claim of ineffectiveness is whether counsel's performance so undermined the proper functioning of the adversarial process that the trial cannot be relied on as having produced a just result. To determine whether this requirement was met, the Court established a two-pronged test.

1. Was the attorney's performance deficient?

2. If so, did the deficient performance injure (prejudice) the defendant?

In considering the first prong, the Court held that a court must evaluate whether, "in light of all the circumstances, the identified acts or omissions were outside the wide range of professionally competent assistance." The majority went on to hold that "counsel is strongly presumed to have rendered adequate assistance and made all significant decisions in the exercise of reasonable professional judgment." It is important to note that decisions made by the attorney about strategy will not be second-guessed in hindsight.

If counsel's performance is determined to have been below acceptable standards, a claim of ineffective assistance of counsel will not succeed unless it is also shown that counsel's ineffectiveness prejudiced the defendant. This prong requires proof that there is a reasonable probability that, except for counsel's unprofessional errors, the result of the proceeding would have been different. The Court went on to explain that a reasonable probability is "a probability sufficient to undermine confidence in the outcome."

The two-pronged standard established by the Court in *Strickland* has proven very difficult to meet. In particular, the prejudice prong of the test is difficult to pass. In most criminal trials, there is extensive evidence against the accused. In reviewing potential prejudice to a defendant caused by an attorney's ineffectiveness, a court will consider whether a competent attorney would have made a difference in the outcome. Specifically, a defendant must demonstrate that counsel's errors are so severe as to deny that defendant of a trial whose outcome is fair or reliable, not merely that the result would have been different. In the vast majority of cases in which ineffective assistance of counsel is raised, courts have found either that the performance of counsel was reasonable or that the outcome of the trial would have been the same regardless of the substandard performance and have denied relief.

There is a class of cases, however, for which prejudice need not be proven. These are cases involving claims of ineffective assistance of counsel in which a defendant was denied counsel during a critical stage of a prosecution or when the errors surrounding the representation "are so likely to prejudice the accused that the cost of litigating their effect in a particular case is unjustified" (*United States v. Cronic,* 1984). In *Cronic,* which was decided the same day as *Strickland,* the Supreme Court described such a circumstance: "If counsel entirely fails to subject the prosecution's case to meaningful adversarial testing, then there has been a denial of Sixth Amendment rights that makes the adversary process itself presumptively unreliable." For a presumption of prejudice to apply, it must be established that counsel failed to challenge any aspect of the prosecution's case, not simply some aspects. As such instances are extremely rare, it is almost always necessary that a defendant be able to establish prejudice to prevail on an ineffective assistance of counsel claim.

Right to Self-Representation

Gideon established that indigent defendants have the right to the assistance of counsel. It also gave rise to a new and related matter: Do criminal defendants have the right to represent themselves? The desire of a criminal defendant to proceed *pro se,* without counsel, raises several conflicting issues. As noted earlier in this chapter, the Supreme Court has found the assistance of an attorney to be critical to a person facing criminal prosecution, going so far as to hold that denying counsel to an indigent defendant makes the prosecution fundamentally unfair. As such, it would seem to be folly to permit a defendant to facilitate an unfair prosecution by demanding to represent himself. On the other hand, should the court force a criminal defendant to rely on an attorney when the defendant believes he can represent himself more effectively than appointed counsel?

CURRENT CONTROVERSY

Jae Lee moved to the United States from South Korea with his parents in 1982 when he was 13 years old. Lee never became a U.S. citizen but lived as a lawful permanent resident. In 2008, Lee was arrested and prosecuted for drug possession with the intent to distribute. Lee's counsel entered into plea discussions with the government. Lee repeatedly asked his attorney whether he would face deportation. Lee's attorney assured him that he would not be deported as a result of pleading guilty. Based on this assurance and given the strong case against him, including a confession, Lee accepted a plea bargain and was sentenced to a year and a day in prison.

Contrary to what his attorney told him, because his conviction qualified as "aggravated felony," Lee was subject to mandatory deportation under the Immigration and Nationality Act. When Lee learned this, he filed a motion to vacate his conviction and sentence, arguing that his attorney had provided constitutionally ineffective assistance. At an evidentiary hearing, Lee and his counsel testified that "deportation was the determinative issue" to Lee in deciding whether to accept a plea. Lee's counsel testified that if he had known Lee would be deported upon pleading guilty, he would have advised him to go to trial. The District Court denied this motion and Sixth Circuit Court of Appeals affirmed. The U.S. Supreme Court granted a writ of certiorari.

1. Was the performance of Lee's lawyer deficient?

2. Was Lee prejudiced?

3. Was Lee denied effective assistance of counsel?

4. Does the strength of the government's case impact whether or not he was prejudiced?

5. See how the Court decided *Lee v. United States*, 137 S.Ct. 1958 (2017).

CURRENT CONTROVERSY

In 2008, the Supreme Court considered whether a person who is mentally competent to stand trial (able to understand the proceedings and assist in his or her defense) may be prevented from criminal prosecution due to mental deficiencies (*Indiana v. Edwards*, 2008). Ahmad Edwards, diagnosed with schizophrenia, was charged with armed robbery and attempted murder. Prior to trial, he was found incompetent and ordered to be held in the state mental hospital for treatment to restore him to competency. After nearly a year, he was found competent to stand trial.

Prior to trial, he asked to fire his attorney and represent himself. The trial judge denied the request based on Edwards's mental illness. Edwards proceeded to trial with counsel and was convicted.

The Supreme Court took up Edwards's case to address the question of whether states may adopt a higher standard for measuring competency to represent oneself at trial than for measuring competency to stand trial.

Although the Court upheld the premise of *Faretta v. California* (1975) that there is a constitutional right to self-representation, the Court ruled against Edwards. The Court noted that one can be competent to stand trial but still lack the capacity to stand trial without the benefit of counsel. This is because mental illness is not a unitary concept but varies in degree and manifestations. As such, it would be inappropriate to mandate the use of a single competency standard. In addition, as the right to self-representation exists to affirm the dignity of a defendant who wants to proceed without counsel, a defendant suffering from mental illness may perform in such a manner that has the opposite effect and actually denies the defendant a fair trial. The Court did not spell out what standard should be used to determine if a person is competent to represent himself at trial. It simply ruled in this case, given Edwards's long history of mental illness, the trial court did not err in denying the request to proceed pro se.

1. Should the right to represent oneself in a criminal case be unlimited?

2. Should the right to represent oneself in a criminal case be limited to those individuals who can do so effectively?

In *Faretta v. California* (1975), the Supreme Court held that the Sixth Amendment may not be used to prevent a competent defendant from self-representation. While noting that a lawyer who represents himself or herself has a fool for a client, so long as a defendant knowingly, intelligently, and voluntarily waives his or her right to counsel, that person will be entitled to proceed pro se. That being said, courts are not powerless in dealing with pro se defendants. Typically, judges provide defendants who insist on proceeding pro se with "standby counsel." Standby counsel does not formally represent the defendant but acts as an adviser during the proceedings. This advice frequently involves procedural matters and issues involving rules of evidence that are unfamiliar to nonattorneys.

Right to an Attorney of One's Choosing

In the criminal justice system, the vast majority of defendants are indigent. Because they lack the means to hire an attorney, the government is required to provide one to indigent defendants. Not surprisingly, regardless of whether the defendant and the attorney like or trust each other, the experience level of the attorney, or the lawyer's reputation for effectiveness in prior cases, an indigent defendant has no right to choose whom she wants as counsel. The Constitution guarantees that an indigent defendant be given effective counsel, not the counsel of her choosing.

What happens if a defendant has the money to hire an attorney? Can the court place limits or restrictions on the attorney whom a defendant wants to hire with his own funds? If a nonindigent defendant is prevented from being represented by counsel of her choice and is forced to employ a different attorney, has the right to counsel been violated? Those questions were answered in *United States v. Gonzalez-Lopez* (2006).

Cuauhtemoc Gonzalez-Lopez was charged with conspiracy to distribute more than 100 kilograms of marijuana. His family hired attorney John Fahle to be his lawyer. Gonzalez-Lopez himself hired Joseph Low, a lawyer from California who had recently prevailed in a well-publicized drug sale case similar to the one facing Gonzalez-Lopez. At an evidentiary hearing shortly after arraignment, where Gonzalez-Lopez was represented by both attorneys, Low violated the court's orders by passing notes to Fahle. A short time later, Gonzalez-Lopez stated he wanted Low to be his only attorney. Because of the note-passing incident and alleged unethical conduct in unrelated cases, the judge denied Low's petition to represent Gonzalez-Lopez. The trial judge even refused Gonzalez-Lopez's new lawyer's request to let Low sit at counsel table during the trial; the judge made Low sit in the gallery and have no contact with Gonzalez-Lopez or his new attorney during the trial. The trial proceeded without Low's involvement, and Gonzalez-Lopez was convicted.

After several postconviction hearings and appeals, the case was heard by the Supreme Court regarding whether Gonzalez-Lopez's Sixth Amendment right to counsel was violated by the trial judge's refusal to allow him to hire an attorney of his own choosing. Two important points were stipulated by both sides by the time the appeal had reached the Supreme Court. First, it was agreed that the district court judge had committed error in denying Low's application to appear for the defendant. Second, it was agreed that Gonzalez-Lopez received a fair trial. Everyone agreed that the lawyer who represented Gonzalez-Lopez provided effective assistance of counsel.

With these stipulations in effect, the Supreme Court had to decide whether denying a defendant the counsel of his choice (this does not involve indigent defendants) is a reversible error absent a showing of ineffective representation or harm to the defendant. The Court held that denying a nonindigent defendant counsel of his choice violates the Sixth Amendment right to counsel, a fundamental right regardless of whether a fair trial took place. According to the Court, depriving a person of the attorney of his choice affects the entire context in which the trial is held, making it a structural error rather than simply a procedural error. Writing for the five-member majority, Justice Scalia stated that the Sixth Amendment right to counsel of choice requires "not that a trial be fair but that a particular guarantee of fairness be provided— to wit, that the accused be defended by the counsel he believes to be best." Moreover, the Court noted that the right at stake was the right to counsel of choice, not the right to a fair trial, and that right was violated because deprivation of counsel was erroneous. As such, no additional showing of prejudice was required to make the violation "complete." The four dissenting justices argued, on the other hand, that it made no sense to ignore the quality of the representation actually provided the defendant before deciding that his rights were violated.

It is important to note that no one argued that Gonzalez-Lopez was denied effective assistance of counsel or that he did not receive a fair trial. Rather, once Low was not permitted to represent Gonzalez-Lopez, the constitutional violation was complete, and reversal was mandated under the view of the majority. This would be the case even if the defendant were represented by the best attorney in the country but was denied the right to be represented by his cousin just out of law school. Justice Scalia would respond that there are intangible qualities possessed by individuals and that the attorney–client relationship can't and shouldn't be quantified.

ETHICS AND LAWYER–CLIENT RELATIONSHIPS

Often a criminal defense attorney is the only thing standing between a criminal defendant and a criminal conviction and lengthy prison sentence. In serving as a client's defender, a lawyer has a duty to provide diligent and competent representation for her client. This responsibility includes counseling the defendant, investigating items relevant to the case, pursuing a favorable disposition (plea bargain) prior to trial, zealously presenting the defendant's case in court, challenging the prosecution's evidence and cross-examining prosecution witnesses at trial, and, most of all, ensuring that the defendant's rights are honored and protected.

In more general terms, when representing a client, criminal defense attorneys are required to "serve as the accused's counselor and advocate with courage and devotion and to render effective, quality representation" (American Bar Association, 1993, Standard 4-1.2[b]). To facilitate the ability of an attorney to effectively represent a client, a number of ethical rules and standards regulate how a lawyer must relate to his clients. Beyond maintaining the integrity of the legal system, the overarching theme throughout these rules is the importance of fostering a defendant's trust in her attorney.

The most important component of building a client's trust in his attorney is the assurance that what is said between attorney and client will be kept confidential. Without the assurance of confidentiality, there is no reason to expect defendants to be candid with their lawyers about events surrounding the charges they face. Without such candor, the ability for a lawyer to effectively represent a client is greatly diminished.

Beyond assuring the client that all communications between them will be kept confidential, an attorney can do several other things to generally foster a good working relationship between client and lawyer:

- Meet with defendant as soon as practical following appointment or retention.

- Explain in detail the procedures that will take place as the case progresses.

- Promptly respond to the client's questions or requests for information.

- Keep the client informed of developments in the case on a regular basis.

Despite the importance of having defendants trust their attorneys and regardless of an attorney's efforts to build trust, research has shown that defendants are more often than not very distrustful of their lawyers. This distrust stems from (a) the environment and conditions under which a defendant is provided with an attorney, (b) the near autonomy with which the attorney makes strategic decisions on how to conduct the defendant's trial, and (c) the advice and counseling the lawyer provides that are less positive than the client envisioned and may include an attorney refusing to partake in unethical behavior on behalf of the client.

It is rare for criminal defense attorneys to meet with their clients under positive conditions. In the best of circumstances, the meeting occurs in a law office with the client seeking help and advice in dealing with potential or actual criminal prosecution. Alternatively, attorneys frequently meet their clients for the first time at the local jail where the client is being held following arrest. In either case, the client is likely to be scared of what may lie ahead, confused by the process, and leery of the attorney sitting across the table. To make matters worse, in a vast majority of cases, the attorney has been assigned by a court to represent the defendant. Keep in mind, in such cases, the client has no input into who will be appointed to be her lawyer, has no information about the lawyer's ability, and may well believe the court-appointed lawyer assigned to her is probably representing poor defendants because he is not capable enough to have a job as a "real" lawyer. To make matters worse, in the eyes of many indigent defendants, since the government is paying the salaries of both the prosecutor and the defense lawyer, the attorneys will be working together to get rid of the defendant's case as quickly as possible.

A second item that affects the amount of trust a client has in a lawyer involves the level of responsibility and autonomy given an attorney for strategic decisions made in defending a client. Once a criminal case reaches court, a defendant who is represented by an attorney has complete control over a limited number of basic, fundamental decisions about how his defense will proceed. Specifically, decisions that are reserved for the defendant to make include the following five items (see also Table 6.3):

- Whether to plead guilty

- Whether to accept a plea agreement

- Whether to waive a jury trial

- Whether to testify

- Whether to appeal

These items implicate specific constitutional protections, and thus a defendant has the right to make the relevant decisions. Decisions that must be made beyond these items are typically considered to be tactical or strategic in nature. These options commonly include the following:

- Whether to call specific witnesses to testify

- How to cross-examine prosecution witnesses

- Whether an affirmative defense, such as self-defense or insanity, should be raised

- Whether potential jurors should be challenged for cause or removed with a peremptory challenge (these matters are discussed at length in a future chapter)

- Whether to employ an expert witness

- Whether to give an opening statement or closing argument

Though an attorney should consult with a client before making tactical or strategic decisions, ultimately these decisions are left to the attorney to make. The logic behind this is that only a trained expert has the ability to comprehend the importance and implications of tactical decisions. Moreover, as many choices during a trial must be made rapidly, it is not practical to have a client weigh in on each question, objection, or strategic decision. As such, it is left to the attorney to do what she deems

KEY CASES

McCOY V. LOUISIANA

Was McCoy's right to effective assistance of counsel violated?

Robert McCoy was indicted on three counts of first-degree murder. Following arraignment, the State of Louisiana informed McCoy and the trial court that it would seek the death penalty. After initially being represented by the public defender's office, McCoy subsequently retained private counsel, Larry English.

Despite McCoy's insistence that he was innocent, English believed that the evidence against McCoy was "overwhelming" and encouraged him to plead guilty in exchange for a life sentence. McCoy rejected this suggestion, opting for a jury trial instead. As the trial approached, English told McCoy that he planned to tell the jury that McCoy had committed all three murders, in the hope that doing so would convince the jury to sentence McCoy to life in prison, instead of death. McCoy was dead set against this plan. Due to this disagreement, several days before the trial, McCoy asked permission to fire English and replace him with two new attorneys whom McCoy's parents had retained. The trial

court rejected the request as untimely. McCoy then tried to invoke his right to self-representation but was also denied by the court as being untimely. The trial took place as scheduled.

In his opening statement, English conceded his client's guilt and argued that McCoy had emotional issues that impaired his ability to function. During closing argument, English argued that McCoy was "crazy" and "lives in a fantasy world" and did not deserve a death sentence. The jury disagreed. McCoy was found guilty on all three counts of murder and sentenced to death. The Louisiana Supreme Court affirmed the convictions and sentence, and the U.S. Supreme Court granted certiorari to determine whether his trial lawyer's concession of guilt against his client's wishes violated the Sixth Amendment.

From the material covered in this chapter, do you think McCoy's right to effective assistance of counsel was violated by his attorney admitting his guilt to a jury in a strategic effort to avoid a sentence of death?

For the answer, see *McCoy v. Louisiana*, 584 U.S. ___ (2018).

TABLE 6.3 ■	Roles and Responsibilities of the Defense Attorney
Phase 1. **Arrest to** **Arraignment**	Obtain facts from client.
	Counsel client on procedures.
	Take steps to have in-custody client released from jail.
	Investigate the incident.
	Represent client at preliminary hearing and arraignment.
Phase 2. **Arraignment to** **Trial**	Interview witnesses, police officers, and alleged victims. Request discovery materials from prosecution. Provide discoverable materials and evidence to the prosecution. Advise client regarding case strategies and plea bargain options. Research, prepare, and argue pretrial motions. Conduct plea bargain negotiations. Make court appearances on behalf of client.
	Prepare for trial, including preparation of opening statement, closing argument, and development of direct and cross-examinations.
Phase 3. **Trial Through** **Sentencing**	Represent defendant at trial. Prepare presentence memorandum. Represent defendant at sentencing. File posttrial motions for new trial. File notice of appeal.
	Organize file and materials for appellate attorney.

best. As discussed earlier in this chapter, most decisions made by an attorney that hurt a defendant's case will not be a sufficient basis for reversal due to grounds of ineffective assistance of counsel. Only those decisions that are considered professionally unreasonable and are found to have prejudiced the defendant are grounds for reversal. Such legal parsing is of little consolation to a defendant who is convicted at trial.

The third area giving rise to defendants' distrust of their defense attorneys involves the counseling and advice conveyed from attorney to client. While a lawyer will counsel and advise clients on their best options, frequently an attorney must tell clients what they do not want to hear. This may include advising clients to enter into a plea bargain, telling them that their story of what occurred is unlikely to be believed by a judge or jury, and saying that, despite being willing to fight hard for the client's interests, there are limits to what an attorney is ethically permitted to do.

Often, the distrust felt by defendants is compounded by the fact that defense attorneys frequently have different opinions than their clients on how to proceed with a case. As discussed earlier, whereas the client has the right to make major, fundamental decisions regarding how to proceed with a case (plead guilty, testify), matters of strategy are left to the attorney. Moreover, an attorney has an overriding obligation to protect the integrity of the justice system. Although criminal defense lawyers must do all within their power to obtain favorable outcomes for their clients, lawyers must do so within the rules of the court and ethical standards laid out by state bar associations.

Above all else, while a defense attorney owes these (and other) duties to the client, a lawyer also has an obligation to be honest and candid with the court. An attorney cannot lie or misrepresent facts to the court or knowingly allow the admission of perjured testimony in a trial. These limitations apply even when the unethical or impermissible act is requested or demanded by a client.

In *Nix v. Whiteside* (1986), the U.S. Supreme Court considered how an attorney should handle a situation where he knows that a client intends to commit perjury while testifying in his own defense. In preparing for his trial on a murder charge, Emmanuel Whiteside consistently told his attorney, Gary Robinson, that he had not seen a gun in the victim's hand when he stabbed the victim. However, during preparation for his testimony the week before the trial was to begin, Whiteside, for the first time, told Robinson that he had seen "something metallic" in the victim's hand. When asked about this, Whiteside responded, "If I don't say I saw a gun, I'm dead." On Whiteside's insistence that he would testify that he saw "something metallic," Robinson told him that if Whiteside testified falsely, he would have to advise the court that he felt Whiteside was committing perjury. Whiteside ultimately testified truthfully, admitting on cross-examination that he had not actually seen a gun in the victim's hand. A jury convicted him of second-degree murder, and he was sentenced to 40 years in prison.

After his conviction was affirmed on appeal, Whiteside filed a writ of habeas corpus in the U.S. District Court for the Southern District of Iowa, alleging denial of effective assistance of counsel because Robinson's admonitions not to testify that he saw a gun or "something metallic" violated the *Strickland* standards. The district court ruled against Whiteside, but the Eighth Circuit Court of Appeals reversed. The eighth circuit found that while a criminal defendant's right to testify does not include a right to commit perjury, Robinson's warning that he would inform the court of the planned perjury constituted a threat to violate an attorney's duty to preserve confidentiality and therefore violated the standards of effective representation as stated in *Strickland v. Washington*.

The Supreme Court thought otherwise and reversed. The Court unanimously held that Robinson's actions fell "well within accepted standards of professional conduct ... under *Strickland*." The Court went on to state that whatever right a defendant has does not include the right to commit perjury. As such, his attorney acted appropriately given the situation.

Whereas all nine justices agreed that Whiteside's rights were not violated and also agreed that defense counsel should do all that he can to dissuade a client from committing perjury, only five justices joined in the majority's suggestions for dealing with potential client perjury. Chief Justice Burger wrote for the majority that an attorney faced with such a situation must reveal his client's conduct to the court and, if necessary, withdraw his representation. Under no circumstances should the lawyer permit or assist his client in giving false testimony.

REALITIES OF BEING A DEFENSE ATTORNEY

Recent graduates of law school become criminal defense attorneys for a variety of reasons, including the desire to help individuals in need, the determination to serve as a check on the government's power, or simply the desire to gain extensive trial and courtroom experience. Although being a public defender or attorney who represents indigent defendants provides the opportunity to accomplish each of these goals to a degree, new criminal defense attorneys learn in short order that the reality of their job is significantly different from what they envisioned.

The first aspect of the reality of criminal defense work is a lesson that newly minted criminal defense attorneys learn early on that, although they represent individual defendants, they operate within the confines of a courtroom workgroup. As such, rather than using their skills to defend people at trial, much of their time is spent meeting with clients, negotiating with prosecutors, and settling cases. Although criminal defense attorneys have the opportunity to conduct more trials than lawyers practicing civil law, the reality of the criminal court system is that 9 out of 10 cases are settled by a plea bargain. As such, within the confines of the workgroup—where the prosecution decides who to charge and what types of plea bargains to offer, and judges are interested in seeing just results achieved quickly—the defense attorney finds that a primary part of her job is to convince clients to accept plea offers made by the prosecution. Because the decision to plead guilty or go to trial belongs to the defendant, the defense attorney serves only as an adviser and negotiator. However, from experience with case outcomes and sentencing practices, the defense attorney is in a good position to determine if a case is winnable, the value provided in a plea bargain, and what action is in the client's best interest.

In fulfilling this role, the defense attorney is often viewed by his clients as a double agent who is lazy and does not want to do what is needed to have clients emerge from the system victorious. This perception is far from the truth. Because most criminal defendants are factually guilty of the offenses with which they are charged and will likely lose at trial and receive a sentence based on that crime, it is almost always in the client's best interest to accept a plea bargain to a reduced charge and less extreme sentence.

Despite being not very glamorous and seemingly antithetical, representing defendants at this stage in the process serves an important role in protecting their constitutional rights. By representing and advising criminal defendants before trial, the attorney makes sure that defendants' rights are being honored and that they understand the ramifications of pleading guilty or going to trial. In this manner, defense attorneys are an important component of the court system.

A second aspect of the reality of being a criminal defense attorney is that success is seldom clear and victories are infrequent. Because most criminal defendants are factually guilty and most trials result in convictions, success for criminal defense attorneys is relative. A successful outcome from their perspective is generally achieving as much of a reduction from the original charge and potential sentence as possible. Whether this involves a successful plea negotiation, the exclusion of some evidence, acquittals on the most serious charges a defendant faces, or a lower-than-expected sentence, determining whether an outcome is positive or negative is relative.

A third area where new criminal defense attorneys learn about the reality of their profession involves how people in the system and society as a whole view them. Although criminal defense attorneys play a critical role in the criminal justice system, they are vastly underappreciated. Their clients are likely to distrust them, to believe that they were sold out and coerced into entering into a disadvantageous plea bargain, or to believe that their attorneys were not sufficiently skilled or financed to present a winning defense. Prosecutors and police, while knowing the defense attorney has a job to do, resent being constantly and aggressively challenged and having their honesty questioned in the pursuit of a zealous defense. Judges may resent defense attorneys who file frequent legal motions, demand that time-consuming procedural rules be honored, and insist on lengthy and expensive jury trials for their clients. The general public views defense lawyers as obstacles to the truth who thrive on using their eloquence and flair to have factually guilty clients found not guilty and released back into society. Last, the vast majority of defense attorneys are paid significantly less than lawyers who practice in other areas, and public defenders are paid less than prosecutors with similar experience in the same jurisdiction.

Consider the following example posted on an online blog by a public defender under the heading "Why Public Defenders Have a Short Lifespan":

> I appeared with my client at a Jury Trial Management Hearing today. I told my client that the State agreed to dismiss the charges against him if he agreed to return ownership of a car to its original owner without contesting title (he was charged with buying a stolen car having reason to know it was stolen). My client asserted his innocence from the beginning, and I actually believe him, but the car would have gone back to the original owner anyway. If the case had gone to trial, he was facing 10-35 years.
>
> My client agreed to the dismissal and to relinquish any claim to valid title. Then he told me that he had no respect for me or confidence in me because he disagreed with the way we investigated the case on his behalf.
>
> I guess it wasn't enough that our investigation raised enough doubt *before* trial to eliminate his exposure to prison completely. A simple "thank you" would have sufficed; saying nothing would have sufficed, too. (Monday, November 17, 2008, AZ Public Defender at 5:17 PM, http://texansinaz.blogspot.com/2008/11/why-public-defenders-have-short.html)

Given this information about the realities of being a defense attorney, it is reasonable to ask why a lawyer would want to practice in the field of criminal defense. Despite and maybe in part because of the challenges, many defense attorneys enjoy their work. Compared to the work done by attorneys who never appear in court, criminal defense work is very exciting. It also provides attorneys with a chance to stand up for the little guy against the power of the state.

From a professional standpoint, criminal defense attorneys gain a large amount of courtroom and trial experience in a very short time. For young lawyers who want to be high-level litigators in the future, trying criminal cases is probably the best and most efficient manner in which to gain experience, skills, and a reputation as a skilled litigator. Also, beginning a legal career in an area that presents so many challenges and so little appreciation provides young attorneys with opportunities to prove their fortitude and abilities under pressure.

From a personal standpoint, it is out of a sense that someone has to do it. Someone must stand up for individuals who have no means to defend themselves. Someone must use their training to ensure that the government does not trample over a citizen's rights. Someone needs to ensure that innocent people have their day in court and guilty defendants are treated fairly under the law. For some criminal defense attorneys, knowing that they are doing this important work is its own reward. For others, the challenge of winning small victories in an uphill battle is invigorating. Still others view their job as a mission, with the objective of doing their little piece to improve society, promote equality, and serve as an obstacle to governmental oppression. Whatever their reason, defense lawyers are vital for the criminal justice system to work effectively.

SUMMARY

The Sixth Amendment provides that in all criminal prosecutions, the accused has the right to the assistance of counsel for his defense. Although this right is considered fundamental to the just operation of the criminal justice system, we have seen in this chapter that what is actually meant by the right to counsel is not as clear as one might think. In this chapter, we examined under what circumstances and at what point in a prosecution one is entitled to an attorney. We looked at whether a person has a right to represent herself and to employ an attorney of her own choosing as well as at what point is an attorney's performance so deficient as to violate the Sixth Amendment.

Beyond the right to counsel, the manner in which a lawyer is provided to an indigent defendant was also considered. We looked at the three primary systems of providing indigent defense services and discussed the relative benefits of each system as well as how having assigned counsel compares to employing a private attorney. We also looked at the ethical responsibilities faced by defense lawyers, how these affect the relationship between lawyer and client, and the difficult job faced by defense attorneys to balance the needs of their clients with the goals of the court system and the ethical rules they must abide by.

Don't overlook the Student Study Site with its useful study aids, such as self-quizzes, eFlashcards, and other assists, to help you get more from the course and improve your grade.

DISCUSSION QUESTIONS

1. Do you think the rule announced in *Scott v. Illinois* (1979), that a defendant may not be sentenced to jail or prison unless he was represented by an attorney or voluntarily waived his right to counsel, is good for the judicial system, or is it too difficult to implement?

2. Given that 90% of criminal defendants are indigent, do you think more of an effort should be made to increase the money that is paid to counsel appointed to represent these people to ensure that they receive competent representation?

3. What do you think of the ability of judges to choose the attorney who will represent an indigent defendant in the ad hoc assigned counsel system? Should there be some other method to ensure that judges don't funnel work to preferred lawyers?

4. Which assigned counsel method do you find to be the better method for appointing lawyers?

5. Which contract attorney program, either fixed price or fixed fee, do you think is better? Can you think of any other way that a contract program could operate?

6. Which system do you think ensures that the best possible representation is provided to indigent defendants—assigned counsel, contract, or public defender?

7. Do you think more of an effort should be made to increase public perception of public defenders given the amount of criticism they receive?

8. Given that research shows that there is little difference in the outcome achieved when a client is represented by a private attorney as opposed to an appointed one, why would someone prefer to hire counsel? What advantages do you see between the two?

9. If you were a defense attorney and thought that your client was guilty, how would you weigh this against your duty to ethically represent your client and safeguard this person's rights?

10. Do you think the two-pronged test announced in *Strickland v. Washington* (1984) creates too high of a standard by which to judge the effectiveness of assistance of counsel?

11. Given that indigent defendants have no right to choose the counsel that is appointed to them, what do you think should be the solution if they do not like the attorney appointed them or cannot work with them? Should new counsel be provided?

12. Should the court be allowed to refuse to allow an attorney to represent someone?

13. Should clients be allowed to play more of a role in strategizing their case? What if you were an attorney and you knew that it would be better for your client to plea out, but your client insisted on bringing the case to trial—how would you balance your personal belief with your ethical obligation?

14. Do you think some form of counsel should be provided for every offense? For example, should it be required that an attorney be available for advice on how to proceed with a traffic infraction?

15. Do you think that if a client can afford representation, that client should be forced to hire private counsel to reduce the workload that public defenders face?

KEY TERMS

Ad hoc assigned counsel 139

Assigned counsel programs 139

Contract attorney programs 140

Coordinated assigned counsel 140

Court-appointed counsel 135

Fixed-fee-per-case contract 141

Fixed-price contract program 140

Public defender program 142

Retained attorneys 145

INTERNET SITES

American Bar Association Criminal Justice Section: www.abanet.org/crimjust/home.html

American Bar Association Standing Committee on Legal Aid and Indigent Defendants: www.americanbar .org/groups/legal_aid_indigent_defendants.html

American Civil Liberties Union Indigent Defense: www.aclu.org/issues/criminal-law-reform/effective -counsel/indigent-defense

Criminal Defense BlogSpot: http://criminaldefenseblog.blogspot.com

National Association of Criminal Defense Lawyers (NACDL): www.nacdl.org

National Center for State Courts Indigent Defense Resource Guide: www.ncsc.org/Topics/Access-and -Fairness/Indigent-Defense/Resource-Guide.aspx

National Legal Aid & Defender Association: www.nlada.org

Washington State Office of Public Defense: www.opd.wa.gov

STUDENT STUDY SITE

Get the tools you need to sharpen your study skills. SAGE edge offers a robust online environment featuring an impressive array of free tools and resources.

Access practice quizzes, eFlashcards, video, and multimedia at **edge.sagepub.com/hemmens4e**

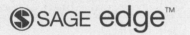

7

© Jupiterimages/Creatas/Thinkstock Images

JUDGES

INTRODUCTION

Judges are public officers authorized by law to hear legal disputes, administer the law, and preside over courts of justice. This technical definition, although accurate, does not begin to convey the importance of the position or the varied roles and duties placed on members of the judiciary. In the eyes of many people, judges are expected to personify justice. Judges are the human face the public associates with the American court system. They are portrayed by the media and seen by the public as the wise people in black robes sitting above everybody else in the courtroom. The decisions judges make and the manner in which they are made affect individual lives and also how the justice system is perceived throughout a community and across the nation, if not the world. In reality, judges are mere human beings doing the best they can to facilitate the administration of justice in the American court system.

In this chapter, we look at the role judges play in the functioning of the criminal courts. Before examining the duties performed by judges, we consider the different types of judges across the various levels of the courts. We see who judges are, where they come from, and how they become judges. After discussing these items, we examine the specific duties carried out by judges throughout the criminal justice process. From issuing a warrant for a search to sentencing a convicted murderer to death to restoring a person's rights following completion of a prison sentence, we examine the roles and duties performed by judges throughout the prosecution and adjudication system.

ROLES AND DUTIES OF JUDGES

Most people view the judge as the most powerful and important actor in the criminal court system. After all, people neither rise to their feet out of respect when a prosecutor enters a courtroom nor address defense attorneys as "your honor." These symbols of respect are bestowed only on judges.

Beyond these symbols of deference, however, the power and actions of trial court judges are greatly limited by the criminal court system's structure, procedures, and other actors. Specifically, prosecutors have virtually limitless authority in deciding what alleged crimes will be formally prosecuted. Moreover, the prosecutor determines what the specific charges will be and whether a plea bargain will be offered to a defendant. The defendant and defense counsel have control over whether a plea agreement will be entered into, whether a jury trial will be demanded, and whether one or more motions to dismiss a prosecution or exclude evidence from trial will be filed and heard.

Whereas the scene of judges presiding over a trial in a grand courtroom is the vision of the judiciary portrayed on television and in the movies, most of their time is spent performing other duties. As illustrated in Figure 7.1, trial court judges are active participants at multiple stages of the criminal justice system's processes, from before a suspect is arrested until after a convicted defendant has completed serving a prison sentence.

Prearrest Judicial Roles

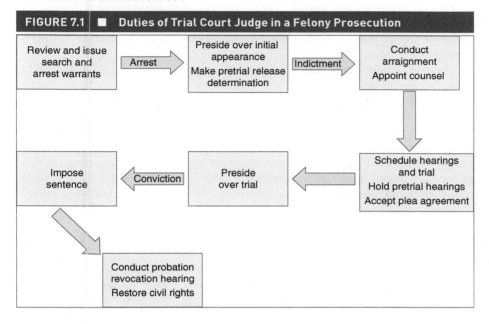

FIGURE 7.1 ■ Duties of Trial Court Judge in a Felony Prosecution

The Fourth Amendment of the U.S. Constitution states,

The right of the people to be secure in their persons, houses, papers, and effects, against unreasonable searches and seizures, shall not be violated, and no Warrants shall issue, but upon probable cause, supported by Oath or affirmation, and particularly describing the place to be searched, and the persons or things to be seized.

Search and arrest warrants must be signed by a judicial officer. Rather than simply rubber-stamping warrant applications submitted by police or prosecutors, judges have an obligation to review each application to determine if it provides probable cause to justify the requested search or arrest. Moreover, in considering search warrant applications, a judge must ensure that the place to be searched is clearly articulated and that the items or class of items sought are stated and described with "sufficient specificity." In addition, a judge may be asked to allow the police to conduct the search at nighttime or to enter the place to be searched without knocking on the door, requesting entry, or announcing their presence.

Postarrest/Pretrial Roles

Following the arrest of a suspect, the focus of the criminal justice system moves from the law enforcement arena to the court system. A person placed under arrest and held in custody must be brought before a judge for an initial appearance within a reasonable time period. Generally, this will take place within one to two days of arrest. At the initial appearance, the judge informs the defendant of the nature of the charges associated with the arrest. (Recall that a defendant is not formally charged until he or she is indicted by a grand jury or bound over for prosecution at a preliminary hearing.)

The most important decision a judge has to make at an initial appearance is what conditions should be imposed for an arrestee to be released from custody. In making this decision, a judge must consider what conditions are necessary to reasonably ensure the defendant's reappearance at further court proceedings as well as what conditions may be necessary to protect the safety of individuals or the community at large. Conditions of release may include the posting of a bond as bail, as well as behavioral requirements such as not consuming alcohol, not contacting the alleged victim, not leaving the state, or regularly reporting to a pretrial services officer. Judges must balance the need for public safety and the administration of justice against the rights of a defendant—who is presumed innocent but also has yet to be formally charged with committing a crime— not to be incarcerated or have his freedom unnecessarily restricted.

Once a defendant is formally charged with an offense and arraigned, whether by indictment or information, the case is assigned to a judge. The judge who is assigned the case schedules deadlines for motions to suppress evidence or dismiss some or all the charges. Frequently, motions to suppress or dismiss require the testimony of police officers or other witnesses germane to the specific issues under consideration. The judge presides over the hearings, referred to as evidentiary hearings, and makes rulings on the motions based on the evidence and legal arguments presented in court and on written materials prepared by the prosecution and defense, filed in the form of legal memoranda in support of or opposition to a motion.

Prior to a trial, judges also frequently do what they can to encourage a plea agreement be reached between the parties. While judges rarely become directly involved in plea negotiations, they often encourage the prosecutor and defense attorney to consider the standard "going rates" for the charges involved as established by the courtroom workgroup over time (Eisenstein & Jacob, 1977). The judge may also imply that a prosecutor who fails to offer a reasonable plea bargain or a defendant/defense attorney who refuses to accept such an offer may be informally sanctioned by the judge (Heumann, 1977). Such sanctioning may include adverse rulings on procedural motions, such as for continuances or scheduling matters, or an increased sentence for a defendant convicted after demanding a trial.

Judicial Roles at Trial

The most visible role played by trial court judges is presiding over jury trials. In this role, judges make numerous rulings on admissibility of evidence and objections made during the presentation of testimony and arguments of the attorneys. In addition, judges instruct the jurors on the law they are to apply in reaching a verdict.

Following the presentation of the prosecution and defense cases, the judge has the duty to consider whether there has been sufficient evidence presented for a jury to find that the defendant is guilty of each charge beyond a reasonable doubt. If the evidence has not reached this standard, the judge should direct a verdict of acquittal for the defendant before deliberations begin. Should the jury convict the defendant, the judge retains the ability to enter a directed verdict of not guilty if she believes there was insufficient evidence to support a conviction.

Beyond these specific legal duties, judges presiding over jury trials have a more overarching duty. As stated in Standard 6-1.1 of the American Bar Association's (2000) *Standards for Criminal Justice,*

> The trial judge has the responsibility for safeguarding both the rights of the accused and the interests of the public in the administration of criminal justice. The adversary nature of the proceedings does not relieve the trial judge of the obligation of raising on his or her initiative, at all appropriate times and in an appropriate manner, matters which may significantly promote a just determination of the trial.

While it is critical that judges protect the interests of the prosecution and defense, they are responsible for seeing that the proceedings are conducted in a way that upholds the dignity of the proceedings and the appearance of fairness in the eyes of the public. Promoting such an environment is essential to convey the trustworthiness and legitimacy of the court to the general public. If a judge fails to maintain control of the proceedings and to take all necessary steps to ensure a fair trial, the court may be ridiculed, the proceedings may fall into disrepute, and the potential for an unjust verdict increases considerably. This is exactly what happened in the notorious prosecution of Sam Sheppard for the murder of his wife.

On July 4, 1954, Dr. Sam Sheppard, a well-known member of Cleveland society, called the police to report that his pregnant wife had been beaten to death in their upscale home. Sheppard told police that he fought off and chased the assailant as best he could but was knocked unconscious and could not identify the attacker. From the outset, the police and media suspected Sheppard of killing his wife. In the days following the murder, newspapers editorialized about Sheppard's guilt, reported that he was not cooperating with the police investigation and that he refused to take a lie detector test, and published information about evidence publicized by the police that was never used at trial. The coroner's inquest into the cause of death lasted 3 days, was held in a gymnasium, was conducted in front of hundreds of spectators, and was broadcast live on television and radio. After repeated calls for his arrest, Sheppard was taken into custody by local police on July 30 and charged with the murder of his wife.

The trial itself was a media circus. Prior to the trial, the media published the names and addresses of all the prospective jurors. During the trial, the media overran the courtroom. In addition to assigning nearly all the available seats in the courtroom to the media, the trial judge had an extra table placed behind the defendant for an additional 20 members of the media to sit. Photographers were permitted to take pictures of jurors during the trial; the jury even posed for newspaper photographers while on a lunch break during deliberations. Special telephone and telegraph equipment was installed and made available to the media throughout the floor of the courthouse where the trial was held. The judge even permitted a radio station to broadcast live from a room next to the jury room while the jury took recesses and deliberated. Despite the potential problems with disruption to the courtroom, the repeated inflammatory headlines and articles in the media regarding Sheppard's guilt, and the effect the atmosphere and media coverage were having on the jury, the trial judge took no steps to limit press access to the trial and jurors' access to media reports on the trial. After several months of testimony, Sheppard was found guilty of murder and sentenced to life in prison.

Several years after Sheppard's conviction, the Supreme Court, acting on habeas corpus review, vacated the conviction on the grounds that the massive pretrial publicity and carnival atmosphere denied him his right to a fair trial (*Sheppard v. Maxwell,* 1966). The Court repeatedly chided the trial court judge for losing control of his courtroom. The Court stated that the trial judge should have taken whatever steps were necessary to isolate the jury from prejudicial material and outside influences and prevent the court from taking on a "carnival atmosphere." The Court further criticized the trial judge for failing to "control the release of leads, information and gossip to the press by police officers, witnesses, and the counsel for both sides."

The Court noted that the judge could have taken a number of remedial actions to prevent the situation from getting out of control. These measures included placing gag orders on the trial participants, limiting media access to the courtroom to normal spectator confines, prohibiting media broadcasts from within the courthouse, protecting the privacy and identity of jurors, investigating whether jurors were exposed to and influenced by the media coverage, moving the trial to another county, sequestering the jury, and continuing the trial until the furor died down. As the trial court took none of these steps, and the defendant was prejudiced as a result, the Court ruled it had no choice but to vacate the conviction.

In November 1966, Sam Sheppard was retried for the murder of his wife. Following 16 days of testimony, a jury found him not guilty. The case against Sam Sheppard has grown in notoriety since the 1954 trial. The saga of Sam Sheppard inspired the television show and movie *The Fugitive,* which involved a respected doctor, his murdered wife, and an alleged intruder in their suburban home. For an excellent depiction of the Sheppard case, see the book *Mockery of Justice: The True Story of the Sheppard Murder Case* (Cooper & Sheppard, 1995), which was coauthored by Sam Sheppard's son.

Judicial Roles Posttrial

Following a conviction, whether by plea bargain or trial, it is the judge's duty to impose a sentence. The sentence a judge imposes is limited to what is permissible under the statute on which the conviction is based. The flexibility afforded judges in determining an appropriate sentence in a specific case varies depending on the sentencing schemes employed by individual states. In states that have a determinate sentencing system with explicit sentencing guidelines, the discretion possessed by a judge regarding the length of time a defendant may be sentenced to prison is restricted to a range of time. In states that do not have sentencing guidelines but use an indeterminate sentencing system, a judge is likely to have wide discretion in deciding how long a prison sentence is appropriate in a given case.

Regardless of the type of sentencing system present, when judges sentence defendants to probation, judges have a great deal of discretion in deciding what conditions of probation a defendant must abide by to avoid incarceration. Judges may make the following items conditions of probation: regular drug or alcohol testing, substance abuse treatment, counseling, education, employment, payment of fines and restitution, and limitations on places a defendant may go or people a defendant may associate with.

The involvement of a trial court judge in a case is not necessarily over once a sentence has been imposed. If a convicted defendant sentenced to probation violates one or more conditions of probation, a probation officer may file a motion with the judge who sentenced the defendant to have his probation revoked or modified. If such a request is made, the judge must consider (a) whether the conditions of probation were in fact violated and (b) if so, what would be an appropriate sanction to impose on the probationer. This often involves a probation revocation hearing at which the judge hears testimony from the probation officer, other witnesses, and the probationer. From the evidence submitted, the judge must make a factual and legal determination as to whether the conditions of probation were violated.

If the judge determines that a probation violation occurred, she may revoke the granting of probation and impose a prison sentence within the range permitted for

CURRENT RESEARCH

In 2010, Lydia Tiede, Robert Carp, and Kenneth Manning published the results of a study that examined whether personal characteristics and backgrounds of federal judges had an impact on their sentencing decisions. The Sentencing Reform Act of 1984 tasked the U.S. Sentencing Commission with developing federal sentencing guidelines with the intention of reducing sentencing disparity. Under the original federal sentencing guidelines, the guidelines were to be mandatory for judges, with departures allowed only under very strict circumstances. In *United States v. Booker* (2005), the U.S. Supreme Court ruled that the guidelines could not be mandatory and judges were allowed to depart from the guidelines when they deemed it "reasonable" to do so.

To explore what impact personal characteristics of judges had on the use of sentencing departures (either for or against a defendant), the study examined data from criminal sentencing decisions made by U.S. district court judges from 1997 to 2008.

The findings show that some judicial attributes significantly impact judges' departures from the guidelines. Judges who were appointed by a Democrat president were significantly more likely to issue departures that favored the defendant. Additionally, female judges were significantly more likely to decide against defendants, which is contrary to the belief that female judges are more lenient in their sentences. Interestingly, a judge's race and the number of years he or she had served on the bench did not significantly impact sentencing decisions.

1. Do the results from this study affect your feelings about the need for a diverse judiciary?

2. Should judges be made aware of findings akin to those from this study? Should it be part of their training to enhance their ability to render justice?

Source: "Judicial Attributes and Sentencing-Deviation Cases: Do Sex, Race, and Politics Matter?" The Justice System Journal, 31(3), 125–148 (2010). Lydia Tiede, Robert Carp, Kenneth Manning.

the crime on which the original conviction was based. The judge may also modify the conditions of probation by imposing more stringent supervision, sentencing the probationer to a short period of incarceration in the local jail, or extending the duration of the probationary period.

Administrative Duties

Apart from the role judges play and the duties they perform in the prosecution and adjudication process, judges serve an important administrative purpose in the functioning of the court system. Most courts have a presiding judge, a court administrator, and a court clerk; however, the individuals who occupy these positions have limited control over how each judge operates and manages his own courtroom. In most jurisdictions, individual judges manage their own courtroom and support staff. This management may involve allocation of duties, job performance evaluations, and personality conflicts.

In addition to managing their staff, judges have the freedom and responsibility to set their court schedules. This involves establishing routine starting and ending times as well as setting hearing and trial dates. The more predictable a judge's scheduling is, the smoother the judge's courtroom, as well as the entire court, is likely to function. The ability of judges to maintain consistent and predictable schedules is complicated by the fact the attorneys who appear before them have their own scheduling needs and obstacles. Furthermore, it is not always easy to predict how long hearings or other matters will take to complete. For every hearing that runs past its allotted time, any number of matters waiting to be heard by the judge will be delayed and perhaps rescheduled.

VIEW FROM THE FIELD

Hon. Cheryl Cesario
Former Associate Judge,
Circuit Court of Cook County,
Illinois

As a judge assigned to a dedicated domestic violence court call, the most difficult aspect of my job was balancing the concern for the victim with the need to protect the constitutional rights of the accused. On the one hand, it is impossible not to feel sympathy for the victim of a crime, particularly when the victim has been physically injured and you see the person in a compromised position (i.e., still bloody, black and blue, swollen, scarred, or with fresh stitches). That being said, it is vital that I keep in mind that the person charged with the crime, the defendant, is presumed to be innocent and begin each bond hearing, motion, or trial with an open mind. Our Constitution requires the state to prove guilt beyond a reasonable doubt. As such, even if I might suspect that a defendant is guilty, I must hold the state to the requisite standard of proof. While a not guilty finding may be hard to explain to the victim, above all else my job is to uphold the law faithfully and even-handedly.

JUDICIAL SELECTION

The method used to select judges has been hotly debated in the United States for well over 200 years. At the heart of the different judicial selection methods are the concepts of judicial independence and judicial accountability. An independent judiciary is one that is free to make decisions without interference from the other branches of government or concern for the popularity or the political consequences. Judicial accountability, on the other hand, involves the ability of society or the government to observe the performance of judges and remove from office those who are performing below acceptable standards.

Proponents of a strongly independent judiciary argue that the role of judges is to faithfully interpret laws and the Constitution without considering outside factors such as politics or popular sentiment. Advocates of increased judicial accountability maintain that since judges make policy on behalf of the government, they should be directly accountable to somebody, preferably the electorate.

In reality, it is necessary that judges be both independent and accountable. Judges must be free to interpret and apply the law fairly. On the other hand, there must be an effective method of accountability of a judge who abdicates her role as a detached, neutral jurist or makes decisions based on individual beliefs or opinions rather than the law and the Constitution. The debate centers on what point of the independence–accountability continuum is appropriate. This decision is at the crux of how federal and state court judges are selected across the nation.

As you consider the methods used for selecting judges, first federal judges and later state judges, keep the debate between judicial independence and accountability in mind.

Federal Judicial Selection

To understand how judges are selected in the United States, it is helpful to look at how judges were selected in colonial America. During the colonial era, judges in the American colonies were appointed by the king of England and served at his will. The control the king had over the judiciary and the direct control he had over the decisions handed down by colonial judges were sources of great concern and frustration for the colonists. The injustices brought about by this system angered the colonists to the extent that the lack of judicial independence of colonial judges was one of the enumerated grievances raised in the Declaration of Independence.

Given the colonial experience, it should not be surprising that the system of government established by the Constitution, which was premised on separation of powers and checks and balances, would provide for a judiciary that was on equal footing with and independent of the legislative and executive branches. In an effort to meet these objectives, the U.S. Constitution provides that judges are to be appointed for life by the president and must be confirmed by a majority vote in the Senate. This method of selecting judges was designed to give both the president and the Senate a voice in who would serve on the bench. Furthermore, by providing for lifetime appointments, the Constitution ensures that judges and the judiciary will be independent of the other branches and not beholden to them to maintain their judgeships.

Although the plain text of the Constitution seems to clearly state how judges are to be chosen, in practice, their selection, particularly that of district court judges, is a bit more involved. When a federal court vacancy arises, the president's staff and officials at the justice department search for potential candidates from the state or circuit where the vacancy is located. During this search, input is obtained from party leaders, prominent attorneys and judges, and campaign supporters. In addition, in the case of a vacancy on the district court, the unofficial practice of senatorial courtesy will take place. **Senatorial courtesy** is a process whereby the president defers to the wishes of a senator from the state where a vacancy is located in nominating a person for a district court judgeship.

Once the president has settled on a candidate, the person's name is put in nomination and forwarded to the Senate for consideration and, it is hoped, confirmation. Typically, the nomination is referred to the Senate Judiciary Committee. The committee sends the nominee questionnaires about his background and writings, which are scrutinized by the committee. In addition, since the 1950s, the American Bar Association (ABA) has rated nominees for federal judgeships. Whether a judicial nominee has been rated "well qualified," "qualified," or "not qualified" is considered by the Judiciary Committee. (ABA ratings and related materials can be viewed on the Internet at https://www.americanbar .org/groups/committees/federal_judiciary/ratings.html.)

In addition to these written materials, often the nominee may be asked to appear at hearings where she is questioned by members of the committee. Following this testimony and considering other information collected on the nominee, the committee makes a recommendation to the full Senate, which votes on whether to confirm or reject the appointment.

The judicial confirmation process is taken seriously by all involved. This is because, unlike elected offices, federal judgeships involve lifetime appointment. There is only one way under the Constitution that federal judges can be removed: The House of Representatives can vote to impeach a federal judge for "treason, bribery or other high crimes or misdemeanors." If impeached, the judge is tried by the Senate. To remove the judge, two thirds of the Senate must vote to convict. In the nation's history, only 13 federal judges have been impeached by the House, and only 7 have been convicted by the Senate. In each case, the judge was convicted for committing illegal acts, not for making unpopular decisions or for holding a particular judicial philosophy.

Proponents of appointing judges argue that it protects judicial independence by insulating judges from the pressure of public opinion and the need to be reelected, factors that may have an effect on the decisions judges make on the bench. Also, proponents argue that appointing judges results in the selection of "better" judges. This argument is based on the proposition that voters lack the necessary background to comprehend what qualities make a "good" judge and are unqualified to intelligently select their judges.

The appointive method of selecting judges has largely succeeded in meeting the aim of providing an independent judiciary. As we will see, the level of independence provided judges under the federal selection system has not always been seen as a good thing by the 50 states in the development of their own judiciaries.

State Judicial Selection

In contrast to the relatively straightforward system for selecting federal court judges, the methods used to select state court judges are quite diverse. The four general methods of selecting judges are appointment, **partisan elections, nonpartisan elections,** and **merit selection plans.** The general systems used by states to select appellate court judges and judges sitting in trial courts of general jurisdiction, typically superior or county courts, are presented in Table 7.1. While four general methods are used to select judges, each of the 50 states employs systems that have slight nuances that differentiate one from the others. These state-specific systems exist because of a combination of state history, the political environment, and state constitutional impediments to reforming how judges are selected. In the following sections, we examine these items and various methods used to select state judges.

Appointment

At the founding of the nation, judges in each of the 13 original states were appointed to the bench. Like their federal counterparts, drafters of state constitutions were highly distrustful of a powerful executive, be it a king, president, or governor. Unlike the drafters of the federal constitution, a majority of the states' founders were unwilling to give appointing authority to the executive—in the case of states, the governor. Rather, eight states placed the power of judicial appointments in the hands of the legislature. The other five states provided for gubernatorial appointment subject to approval of the legislature or a council.

Over time, the willingness to permit elected officials to appoint judges eroded. People came to believe appointed judges were not sufficiently accountable to the people and were beholden to the politicians who appointed them to the bench.

Currently, fewer than 10 states still select their judges by appointment. Of those states, most employ appointment by the governor with confirmation by the legislature. Two states, however, give the legislature the power to appoint a segment of their judiciary. As can be seen in Table 7.1, all the states that use executive or legislative appointments are on the East Coast and were among the original 13 states.

TABLE 7.1 ■ Initial Selection of State Trial Court Judges				
Nonpartisan Election	**Partisan Election**	**Merit Selection**	**Appointment**	**Combined**
Arkansas	Alabama	Alaska	Maine	Arizona
California	Illinois	Colorado	New Jersey	Kansas
Florida	Indiana	Connecticut	South Carolina	Missouri
Georgia	Louisiana	Delaware	Virginia	
Idaho	New York	Hawaii	Rhode Island	
Kentucky	Ohio	Iowa		
Michigan	Pennsylvania	Maryland		
Minnesota	Tennessee	Massachusetts		

(Continued)

TABLE 7.1 ■ (Continued)

Nonpartisan Election	Partisan Election	Merit Selection	Appointment	Combined
Mississippi	Texas	Nebraska		
Montana	West Virginia	Nevada		
North Carolina		New Hampshire		
North Dakota		New Mexico		
Oklahoma		Rhode Island		
Oregon		Utah		
South Dakota		Vermont		
Washington		Wyoming		
Wisconsin				

Source: American Judicature Society. Available online at http://www.ajs.org/selection/docs/Judicial%20Selection%20Charts.pdf.

Popular Elections

During the nation's first several decades, no state selected judges through elections. In the 1820s, however, the United States entered a historical period known as the Jacksonian era. During this period, government at all levels was greatly influenced by reformers seeking to open up government to greater popular control. It was as part of this movement that the election of judges took root. The theory behind electing judges is that because judges make policy, they should be accountable to the people. Furthermore, it is contended that an appointed judiciary consists of political elites with political connections. When elections are used to select judges, anyone who meets the statutory requirements to be a judge has an opportunity to do so. As such, beyond being able to hold judges accountable, election systems open up opportunities for the average citizen or attorney.

In 1830, Mississippi became the first state to use judicial elections to choose its judges. As of 2008, more than half of the states use popular elections to select at least a portion of their judiciaries. Judicial elections are either partisan or nonpartisan. Partisan judicial elections are similar to other elections in that candidates are selected by and affiliated with political parties. Nonpartisan judicial elections, in contrast, require candidates to campaign unaffiliated with any political party, and they appear on the ballot without a party designation. Whereas similar in that they place the choice of judges in the hands of voters, there are some important differences between the two modes of elections.

At one time, a majority of states used partisan elections to select judges. During and immediately after the Jacksonian era, popular control over all aspects of the government was a dominant political philosophy in the United States. As elections traditionally involved political parties, it seemed logical that judicial elections should be partisan in nature as well.

Such a system would allow the parties to select candidates and run campaigns, thereby giving voters clear choices among opposing candidates from competing parties.

During the early part of the 20th century, the use of partisan elections came under a great deal of criticism. Political parties were implicated in corruption scandals, and big city political machines were viewed as having too much control over the selection of judges. Rather than making judges independent from politicians, partisan judicial elections had caused judges to become responsive to the same forces as those exerted on other elected officials. By the beginning of the 20th century, these concerns led to a shift away from partisan election of judges.

This shift away from partisan judicial elections was generally in the direction of a nonpartisan election process wherein judges would be selected according to their own attributes rather than on the basis of their political connections. Currently, more than a dozen states use nonpartisan elections as a means of judicial selection.

In addition to greatly reducing the influence party politics have on judicial elections, nonpartisan elections remove party identification as a basis for voters to cast their ballots. Without information related to party identification and with little other information about a judicial candidate, voters have been found to base their votes on such items as gender, ethnicity, ballot position, or name recognition. Furthermore, voter participation tends to be lower in nonpartisan elections than in partisan contests.

Whether or not judges should be elected is a hotly debated topic on philosophical as well as practical grounds. The American legal system gives judges the responsibility of dispensing justice equally and dispassionately, regardless of their personal beliefs or what a majority of voters believe would be in their best interests. Moreover, the judiciary was set up to protect individuals from unjust oppression by the government or the attitudes of the majority. Having to campaign for office and answer to the public for correct legal rulings that may not be popular forces judges to face a conflict between upholding the law and doing what is politically beneficial.

Although having judges be accountable to the people they represent is desirable, there are doubts as to whether popular elections provide this accountability. Most adults have very little knowledge about the performance of either sitting judges or judicial candidates in their community. Because of this lack of knowledge, only a relatively small percentage of voters who cast votes in a presidential election will even vote in judicial elections that are on the same ballot. Research has also shown that the people who do vote in judicial elections often do not possess any information about the candidates' qualifications (Sheldon & Lovrich, 1999). As noted earlier, citizens often cast votes based on such considerations as name recognition, ethnicity, gender, or location on the ballot.

Judicial selection systems that make use of popular elections provide little accountability in large part because of the manner in which they operate and are administered. The most important of these administrative components is the way in which midterm vacancies are addressed. If a judge retires, dies, or decides to resign before the end of his term, the judgeship needs to be filled. In states that select judges by elections, an interim judge is appointed either by the governor or through a merit selection process. The newly appointed judge is then given the opportunity to run for reelection as part of the normal election process but with the advantage of running as a sitting judge.

Although this process is seemingly appropriate and may well be necessary, it is widely used to transform the elective system into an appointment system. In 2008 in the state of

Washington, which uses nonpartisan elections to select its judges, 60% of sitting judges originally gained their position not by winning a nonpartisan election but by being appointed by the governor.

What makes this situation especially troubling is the fact that very few sitting judges are challenged in contested elections. In such instances, the unchallenged judge is automatically certified to remain on the bench for another full term. Once again, using Washington State as an example, in 2008, 84% of judges were unopposed and therefore automatically maintained their position. It is safe to say that a system that automatically retains 84% of its judges does not effectively promote accountability.

KEY CASES

CAPERTON V. A. T. MASSEY COAL CO.

In 2002, a West Virginia jury returned a verdict of $50 million against A. T. Massey Coal Company for fraudulent misrepresentation, concealment, and interference with contractual relations against Hugh Caperton and Harmon Mining Company. While the appeal was still pending, Massey's CEO, Don Blankenship, spent $3 million to have Brent Benjamin elected to the West Virginia Supreme Court. (This figure was three times more than was provided by all other Benjamin supporters.) In November 2004, Benjamin was elected to the court.

By the fall of 2005, the appeal of the case reached the West Virginia Supreme Court. Because of the level of campaign support Justice Benjamin received from Blankenship, Caperton asked Justice Benjamin to disqualify himself from the case. Justice Benjamin refused, and in a 3–2 opinion, with Justice Benjamin voting with the majority, the West Virginia Supreme Court vacated the verdict against Massey Coal. Caperton appealed this decision to the U.S. Supreme Court, arguing that it was a violation of the Due Process Clause for Justice Benjamin to have heard the case.

On June 8, 2009, the U.S. Supreme Court, in a 5–4 decision, ruled in favor of Caperton and reversed the West Virginia Supreme Court's decision (*Caperton v. A. T. Massey Coal Co., Inc.*, 2009). Writing the majority opinion, Justice Anthony Kennedy wrote that a judge must be disqualified from hearing a case when a campaign contribution to elect a judge creates "a serious risk of actual bias based on objective and reasonable perceptions" (p. 2263). Justice Kennedy went on to state that such a risk is present "when a person with a personal stake in a particular case had a significant and disproportionate influence in placing the judge on the case by raising funds or directing the judge's election campaign when the case was pending or imminent" (pp. 2263–2264).

In finding that Justice Benjamin should have refrained from hearing the case, the Court emphasized that "not every campaign contribution by a litigant or attorney creates a probability of bias, but this is an exceptional case" (p. 2263). Moreover, the Court emphasized that its opinion was limited to the extraordinary facts presented in the case, noting that "application of the constitutional standard implicated in this case will thus be confined to rare instances" (p. 2267).

Although the decision in *Caperton* is limited to the specific facts presented, its import cannot be overstated. If the Supreme Court had ruled otherwise, it would be difficult to imagine a situation when a judge would be required to disqualify herself from a case involving campaign donors or supports.

In another case involving judicial elections, the U.S. Supreme Court recently considered whether judicial candidates have a right to personally solicit funds in support of an election campaign.

Most states that elect some or all its judiciary have rules of judicial conduct that prohibit judicial candidates from personally soliciting campaign contributions. States that prohibit judicial candidates from directly soliciting campaign contributions require the candidate establish a campaign committee that deals with fundraising matters. Lower federal and state courts have issued conflicting opinions about whether these restrictions violate the First Amendment right of freedom of speech of judicial candidates. In 2015, the U.S. Supreme Court considered the constitutionality of these rules in the case of *Williams-Yulee v. The Florida Bar* (2015).

Lanell Williams-Yulee ran as a candidate in the election for Hillsborough County judge in 2009. As part of her campaign, Williams-Yulee signed a letter soliciting campaign contributions in support of her candidacy. The Florida Bar filed a complaint against Williams-Yulee alleging that this personal campaign solicitation violated Canon 7C(1) of the Florida Code of Judicial Conduct. This canon provides that a candidate "for a judicial office that is filled by public election between competing candidates shall not personally solicit campaign funds." Williams-Yulee was found to have violated the canon and was issued a public reprimand. Williams-Yulee appealed the reprimand, arguing that the prohibition against personal solicitation of campaign funds by judicial candidates was an impermissible infringement of freedom of speech. The Florida Supreme Court upheld the sanction, and Williams-Yulee petitioned the U.S. Supreme Court to consider the matter.

In a 5–4 opinion written by Chief Justice John Roberts, the Court upheld the sanction and the limitation of judicial campaigning. So long as the restriction on free speech is closely tailored to foster a compelling state interest, such restrictions are constitutional. The Court held that the Florida restriction serves the compelling state interest of preserving public confidence in the integrity of the judiciary and is sufficiently narrowly tailored to that interest. The Court found the restriction provides an appropriate balance between the need of candidates to get their message out to voters and raise campaign funds to do so and the state's interest in promoting the integrity of the court system.

The oral argument for *Caperton* can be found at https://www.oyez.org/cases/2008/08-22 and *Yulee* at https://www.oyez.org/cases/2014/13-1499.

1. Should judges be given an unlimited right of free speech as part of an election campaign?
2. What specific limits do you think should be placed on a judicial candidate's speech?
3. Should there be limits on the amount of money a person can donate to a judicial campaign? How would you set that limit?

Merit Selection Plans

By the early part of the 20th century, concern about electing judges was growing in legal circles. In 1906, Roscoe Pound, a leading legal scholar, addressed the American Bar Association on "The Causes of Popular Dissatisfaction With the Administration of Justice." In the address, he stated, "Putting courts into politics, and compelling judges to become politicians, in many jurisdictions has almost destroyed the traditional respect for the Bench" (p. 415). Other leading scholars, attorneys, and judges condemned the need for judges to conduct political campaigns to reach or stay on the bench. Out of these concerns, "merit plans" for selecting judges were designed and debated.

Under merit selection plans, when a judicial vacancy arises, a bipartisan, broad-based commission (made up of lawyers and nonlawyers) interviews and evaluates candidates for judicial positions and recommends three candidates to the governor.

The governor is then required to appoint one of the people recommended by the commission. During the next general election following the appointment, the new judge must stand for a retention election at which voters are asked, "Should Judge _____ be retained in office?" A majority of voters must vote that the judge be retained for the judge to stay on the bench. Under the merit system, judges continue to face periodic retention elections in which voters decide whether each judge should remain in office.

The merit system was first used by Missouri in 1940. Today, most states use a merit selection system to select at least some of their judges. Its proponents maintain that it increases the likelihood that high-quality, nonpolitical people will be chosen to serve as judges. Such individuals will be identified and screened by a nonpartisan commission and nominated based on their legal abilities rather than their political connections or ability and willingness to jump into an election campaign. At the same time, it is argued that the system provides the public with the ability to hold poorly performing judges accountable through **retention elections.**

Although the merit selection plan seems to reach a reasonable middle ground between pure appointment and contested election systems, in practice, some of the same problems with the other methods emerge. Critics of the merit system argue that politics enter into the makeup of the nominating commissions. While commission members are selected by a variety of individuals within a state, it is possible that commission members are selected for their political ideologies or leanings. Based on these and other items, different commission members may have different views on how to judge a candidate's "merit." Because different states have different methods of selecting who serves on a nominating commission, it is difficult to generalize about the actual impact politics has on the process.

Another concern raised by critics of the merit system is the level of accountability achieved through retention elections. In theory, retention elections provide voters with the opportunity to hold poorly performing judges accountable. Although this may be true, since 1980, less than 1% of judges standing for retention election were voted out of office. Relatedly, contested judicial elections have low levels of participation, and this problem is exacerbated in retention elections.

Diversity on the Bench: The Effect of the Selection System on Who Becomes a Judge

Despite the claims regarding judicial independence and accountability, diversity on the bench, and judicial excellence made by proponents of the different systems for selecting judges, research on the effect judicial selection methods have on the makeup of a state's judiciary has been inconclusive. No system has been found to produce a greater proportion of minority or female judges. Moreover, there is no indication that the selection system employed by a state has an effect on incidents of judicial error or misconduct.

That being said, how judges are selected affects whether an individual will become a judge. Some appointed judges would not have had the political connections or desire to run in a contested election. Other judges, who connect with people and enjoy election campaigns and were elected to the bench, would not have been able to secure an appointment from the governor. Beyond the individual case, however, judicial selection methods do not have a significant impact on the makeup of the judiciary.

Regardless of how states select their judges, the vast majority of judges in the United States are White men. That being said, the number of women and minority judges is increasing across the nation. As can be seen in Table 7.2, three out of four state court judges sitting in appellate courts or trial courts of general jurisdiction are men. Moreover, roughly 90% of state court judges are White.

Although these numbers are heavily skewed toward White men, the American judiciary is currently more diverse than ever. Between 1985 and 2005, the number of non-White male judges and the number of female state appellate court judges increased by approximately 20%. In addition, similar increases were found in the number of federal courts of appeals judges (Hurwitz & Lanier, 2008). In a detailed analysis of these changes, Mark Hurwitz and Drew Lanier (2008) found that these changes are not associated with the system used to select judges. Rather, the increases are due to a combination of an increased pool of female and minority attorneys to serve on the bench, an increase in the public's acceptance of non-White men in positions of authority, and any number of immeasurable reasons.

TABLE 7.2 ■ Diversity in the State Courts			
	Appellate Court Judges	**Trial Court Judges**	**All Judges**
Male[a]	877 (66.9%)	11,582 (72.2%)	12,459 (71.8%)
Female[a]	435 (33.1%)	4,473 (27.8%)	4,908 (28.2%)
State court judges' race/ethnicity[b]			
African American	75 (8%)	662 (7%)	769
Asian/Pacific Islander	13 (1%)	140 (2%)	157
Latina/o	34 (4%)	364 (4%)	408
Native American	1 (<1%)	12 (<1%)	13
Other	8 (1%)	80 (1%)	89
Total minority judges	131	1,258	1,436

[a] Irvine (2008).
[b] American Bar Association (2009).
Note: Most recent data available.

CURRENT RESEARCH

In an effort to learn more about why some attorneys become judges, several years ago, Margaret Williams surveyed several hundred practicing attorneys and sitting judges in the state of Texas, which uses partisan elections to select judges. As part of the survey, judges and lawyers were asked a number of questions about their backgrounds to see if there were systematic differences between the two groups.

The items that differentiate the backgrounds of sitting judges from practicing attorneys in Texas revolve around the political activity of judges prior to their ascension to the bench. Williams reports that when compared to practicing attorneys, judges were significantly more likely to have had previous experience running for elected office, held a political office, and been active in state and local party politics. Beyond their political activity, the surveys showed that judges were more moderate in their ideological positions than were attorneys, therefore giving them broader appeal across the electorate.

It is important to note that this study was conducted in one state that has partisan judicial elections. Future research needs to be conducted to determine if similar items are present in other states and whether the manner in which judges are selected in individual states is related to the prejudicial backgrounds of the judiciary.

1. In your opinion, what is the best way to select judges? Does it matter what your priorities are?

2. Do you think the results for replications of this study will vary state by state? What factors do you think might lead to different results?

Source: "In a Different Path: The Process of Becoming a Judge for Women and Men," Judicature, 90, 104–113 (2006). Margaret S. Williams.

JUDICIAL SOCIALIZATION AND DEVELOPMENT

Once a person becomes a judge, he is faced with the task of performing a job for which he has little specific training. After all, there are no classes in law school on how to be a judge. New judges were most likely successful attorneys who possess sharp legal minds. Excellent legal ability is just one of the qualities we expect of our judges. Some of the qualities are innate, whereas others have to be learned through experience.

The newly selected judge faces a period of rapid adjustment that is frequently a rude awakening—that being a judge might not be exactly what was expected. The judge learns on the job to perform the fundamentals of judging, such as how to maintain order in hearings and trials, administer a docket and calendar, be decisive in her actions, and present a commanding presence on the bench while still treating others with respect. This process involves seeing herself as a judge without becoming afflicted with "black robe disease," an overwhelming sense of grandeur, wisdom, and power.

Training and orientation can be either formal or informal. Most states have judicial education programs designed to help new judges adapt to the bench. These programs focus on procedural issues and matters of professionalism rather than items of substantive law. Figure 7.2 is a description of the New Judge Orientation curriculum provided to new judges in Ohio.

In addition to state programs, the National Judicial College (NJC), located in Reno, Nevada, provides training in many areas for judges at all levels of experience. In an effort to make this training available to judges from across the country and in jurisdictions with limited financial resources, the NJC offers training seminars and programs on site in Reno as well as over the Internet and through other media.

As with many other jobs, the vocation of judging is often not exactly as described in course materials. Although areas involving judicial demeanor, court management, and communication skills may be similar in any court, every court and jurisdiction has its own nuances that new judges must adapt to or attempt to change. In his classic book *Plea Bargaining,* Milton Heumann (1977) describes in detail how judges adapt to plea bargaining in the Connecticut trial courts. Heumann describes the process as "drifting along," where "judges adapt to the court on a case-by-case basis. As a problem crops up, they seek guidance and information" (p. 134). New judges are repeatedly "grasping for information from prosecutors and veteran judges" (p. 134). In seeking such guidance, the new judge implicitly learns to operate under the accepted procedures and routines of the local court.

FIGURE 7.2 ■ **Ohio Judicial College New Judge Orientation Program**

Ohio Judicial College

New Judge Orientation

The transition to the bench for a new judge is a challenging experience. To equip new judges to meet these challenges, the Supreme Court of Ohio Judicial College offers a new Judge Orientation Program. The program is provided in two parts entitled New Judge Orientation, Parts I and II. All new judges (appointed or elected) are required to participate in New Judge Orientation. . . .

Part I is offered annually following the November general election but before the commencement of the terms of newly elected judges. Part I is a week-long course that all newly elected judges are required to attend prior to taking the bench. This beginning course is followed within six months by Part II which is another week-long course.

Course Content

Part I of the program is intended to prepare the new judge for the first weeks on the bench. The course includes instruction in two primary areas:

(1) how to get started, which will address establishing your reputation, staff relations, local judicial culture, whom to turn to for what you need to know, and critical scripts, checklists, and forms; and (2) essential judicial skills and knowledge, which concerns ethics and professionalism, decision-making, trial skills, sentencing, and other issues including jurisdictional specific information.

Part II addresses issues that arise after most judges have been on the bench for a few months. Consequently, the focus is on more substantive law that the new judge is expected to know and apply to the judge's cases.

In addition, experienced judges will share the tricks of the trade that are learned from their years on the bench and, again, new judges learn more information specific to their jurisdiction(s).

Source: Originally authored by Teresa Liston, retired judge, Franklin Co. Municipal Court, and John Meeks, former director, Ohio Judicial College. Updated by Milt Nuzum, director, and Christy Tull, manager, of Curriculum Development, Ohio Judicial College, November 2008.

Aside from the procedural and administrative aspects of being a judge, what makes the adjustment to becoming a new judge even more difficult is the varying areas of the law judges are required to master. Attorneys generally specialize in one or two areas of law: criminal, personal injury, corporate, family, and so on. Courts and judges hear cases in each of these and dozens of other areas of law. When judges deal with cases in areas of law that are new to them, it is up to the judge to put in the extra work to get up to speed in the specific areas so as to provide just and informed decisions that are fair to the parties involved. This challenge is compounded when judges are assigned to court departments that hear specific types of cases, such as family law or juvenile, in which they have no experience. While judges learn the substantive law over time, it can be a harrowing experience as this knowledge is gained. Like successful college students who had to adapt and endure growing pains during their first year in college, almost all judges survive this growth process and develop into excellent jurists.

JUDICIAL ACCOUNTABILITY AND JUDICIAL INDEPENDENCE

Judicial accountability involves the ability of an entity to remove or discipline judges who do not perform their jobs in an acceptable manner. While in our system of government, a level of judicial accountability is expected, it is important that it not interfere with judicial independence. **Judicial independence** entails ensuring that judges are free to decide cases fairly and impartially based on the facts and the law without consideration of public, political, financial, or other outside pressure.

How is it possible to protect judicial independence while maintaining the ability to hold judges accountable? To foster both items appropriately, two distinct forms of judicial accountability—decisional and behavioral—must be considered. **Decisional accountability** involves holding judges answerable for judicial rulings. Were a judge to deliberately ignore the stated law and binding precedent, the judge should be held accountable. However, if a decision was within the bounds of the law and based on precedent, the desire to hold a judge answerable for an unpopular ruling is fraught with peril. Because most rulings fall into the second category, decisional accountability is generally inappropriate.

Behavioral accountability, on the other hand, involves holding individual judges answerable for their conduct on the bench. Because judges are the human element of the justice system, conduct that reflects badly on the integrity and impartiality of the justice system is likely to decrease public trust in the judiciary and should be deterred. Explicit statements, acts of bias and partiality, rudeness, and a lack of respect for parties or counsel are examples of actions for which a judge may be held accountable. Acts related to behavioral accountability, which may involve acts of judicial misconduct, are universally accepted as being appropriate components of judicial accountability and do not restrict appropriate aspects of judicial independence. The following sections discuss two means of increasing behavioral accountability without infringing on judicial independence.

COMPARATIVE COURTS

Judges in Japan

Judges in Japan are held in high esteem and treated with great respect. Under the Constitution of Japan, judges are guaranteed independence "in the exercise of their conscience" and to be "bound only by this Constitution and the laws." Judges cannot be disciplined by any executive office, nor can they be removed unless judicially declared incompetent. This independence is fostered by the fact that the Japanese judiciary is set up as an autonomous national organization. The judges themselves administer the nationwide system of courts. Judicial appointments and advancement are decided by a central office managed by peers, a practice that is customary in many other large Japanese institutions.

Judges are selected based largely on their merit. A person interested in being a judge must perform well on a highly competitive national judicial examination. The top scorers on this exam are admitted to the court-run Legal Training and Research Institute. While there, they are assigned to a district court prosecutor's office, to both criminal and civil sections of a district court, and to a law firm. They also attend two extended periods of classroom lectures and training. After 2 years' study, new graduates can apply to the Supreme Court for placement as assistant judges.

New assistant judges serve for a 10-year term, at the end of which they are qualified to be appointed as full judges. Terms for full judges are also 10 years, and reappointment is the norm. Judges' careers often span 30 to 40 years, with the majority working until retirement at age 65.

JUDICIAL PERFORMANCE EVALUATIONS

As discussed earlier, a key factor in how states have chosen to select their judges involves the notion of judicial accountability. Both popular elections and merit selection systems with retention elections are theoretically based on the premise that citizens can hold poorly performing judges accountable via the ballot box. The ability for voters to do this, however, requires a means for them to be informed about which judges are not performing at an acceptable level.

In general, voters have very little information about judicial candidates. This leads to high levels of voter *falloff,* people who vote for president, governor, or other major office who do not vote in judicial elections. Furthermore, as previously noted, people who do vote in judicial elections often base their votes on such items as gender, ethnicity, ballot position, or name recognition because of a lack of information on the judge's performance on the bench.

To address this lack of information, a number of states operate **judicial performance evaluation** (JPE) programs. Typically, JPE programs are based on evaluations of how well a judge demonstrates a number of qualities expected of an excellent jurist submitted by individuals who have experience appearing before the judge. Importantly, they focus exclusively on items related to the judge's behavior and not to case outcomes. These items generally fall into the categories of legal ability, integrity, communication, judicial temperament, and administrative ability. The keys to JPE systems are that they

(a) involve information only from individuals who have firsthand knowledge, through observation, of a judge's performance; and (b) expand the sources of information beyond attorneys to include laypersons, jurors, witnesses, and court staff who have had the ability to personally observe the judge's performance. This information is then provided to the public in a condensed form for use in considering how to vote in judicial elections.

Research has found that the existence of JPE programs is related to increased voter participation and judicial accountability, with judges receiving poor evaluations either being removed from office by the voters or at least receiving lower vote levels than judges receiving favorable evaluations (Brody, 2008). Judicial performance evaluation programs are currently used to provide voters with information about judges in eight states that use the merit system with retention elections. Moreover, several states and large counties that use nonpartisan elections are developing plans to implement such programs in the near future.

ACCOUNTABILITY FOR JUDICIAL MISCONDUCT

Given their position in the justice system, it should not come as a surprise that judges are held to a high ethical standard. After all, how could the public be expected to trust and rely on a system in which the judges who are the system's decision makers are unethical? The federal and state governments use a number of methods to foster high ethical standards among their judges, as well as to hold judges who act improperly accountable.

Whereas the Constitution provides that federal judges are appointed for life, it also allows for their removal for "treason, bribery, or other high crimes and misdemeanors." Complaints of misconduct rarely involve such allegations and are handled internally by the court system. In the federal system, most allegations of judicial misconduct are dealt with by judicial councils that were established by the Judicial Councils Reform and Judicial Conduct and Disabilities Act of 1980. Under the act, procedures are laid out for filing a complaint against a judge, and means are provided for disciplining a judge if the council deems it necessary. The council may also refer the matter to the House of Representatives with a recommendation that impeachment proceedings be commenced. Such an outcome is rare. In the history of the nation, only 13 federal judges have faced impeachment trials, and only 7 were convicted and removed from office.

In addition to the federal system, each of the 50 states has organizations established to investigate allegations of misconduct by state court judges. The organizations, referred to as judicial conduct commissions, **judicial disciplinary commissions** and disability commissions, or judicial qualifications commissions, are created by the state supreme court and are generally made up of a combination of judges, attorneys, and nonattorney citizens. (A list of the organizations from each state established to investigate allegations of misconduct by state court judges is maintained by the American Judicature Society and can be found at http://americanjudicaturesociety.org/category/key-issues/judicial-ethics/.) These commissions investigate complaints against state judges to determine if they have merit. If the commission finds a complaint to be meritorious, it may recommend the imposition of discipline against the judge. Sanctions may include a private or public censure, suspension, or removal from the bench. Ultimately, it is up to the state supreme court to make a final determination on an appropriate sanction and to impose punishment.

SUMMARY

"The quality of our justice in America patently hinges, in large measure, on the quality of our judges" (Special Commission on Evaluation of Judicial Performance, 1985). There is little doubt that this statement is as true today as when it was initially written. That being said, given the broad range of expectations placed on the nation's judiciary, exactly what qualities, backgrounds, practices, and strengths lead to high-quality judges are not easy to define.

Being an excellent judge requires more than being highly intelligent, extremely understanding, or unquestionably fair. More than 2,000 years ago, Socrates described the traits required for a person to be an outstanding judge: "Four things belong to a judge: to hear courteously, to answer wisely, to consider soberly, and to decide impartially." Despite the complex substantive nature of the tasks judges are asked to perform, to maintain the public trust, judges must exhibit these qualities in dealing with each case and individual appearing before the bench. For, as the English Lord Chief Justice Hewart wrote, "Justice should not only be done but should manifestly and undoubtedly be seen to be done" (*Rex v. Sussex Justices*, 1924, p. 259).

Don't overlook the Student Study Site with its useful study aids, such as self-quizzes, eFlash-cards, and other assists, to help you get more from the course and improve your grade.

DISCUSSION QUESTIONS

1. The notorious trial of Sam Sheppard is discussed in the chapter as an example of the failure of a trial judge to adequately perform his duties. What kind of impact do you think a case such as this has on the public's perception of the judiciary?

2. What do you think should be done to make trial judges more accountable when they fail to adequately ensure that the rights of the accused are safeguarded? Should the public have a say in the sanctioning of judges?

3. Do you think that there should be more cooperation or sharing of administrative responsibilities either among the court staff or among judges to improve the scheduling and timing problems?

4. Which system of electing judges, partisan or nonpartisan, do you think is better for preserving the goals of the judicial system?

5. Do you think judges should be elected at all considering that most of the public is not educated in the ways of the legal system?

6. If all judges were appointed, how would the public be able to hold them accountable for the rulings they make?

7. Which interest do you think is more important when determining how to select judges: judicial accountability or judicial independence?

8. Which system for selecting judges do you find achieves the best balance of accountability and judicial independence:

pure appointment, election, or merit selection? Why?

9. The chapter speaks of state programs and the National Judicial College, which provides training to judges to help them be more effective on the bench. Should participation in these programs be mandatory for all first-time judges?

10. Given that most judges were attorneys who specialized in only one or two areas of law, should they be required to learn (take classes on) other areas of law?

KEY TERMS

Behavioral accountability 180

Decisional accountability 180

Judicial accountability 180

Judicial disciplinary commission 182

Judicial independence 180

Judicial performance evaluation 181

Merit selection plans 171

Nonpartisan elections 171

Partisan elections 171

Retention elections 176

Senatorial courtesy 170

INTERNET SITES

American Bar Association Judicial Division: www.americanbar.org/groups/judicial.html

American Bar Association Standing Committee on Federal Judiciary: www.americanbar.org/groups/committees/federal_judiciary.html

American Judges Association: www.aja.ncsc.dni.us

American Judicature Society: www.ajs.org

National Association of State Judicial Educators: www.nasje.org

National Association of Women Judges: www.nawj.org

National Center for State Courts: www.ncsc.org

National Judicial College: www.judges.org

STUDENT STUDY SITE

Get the tools you need to sharpen your study skills. SAGE edge offers a robust online environment featuring an impressive array of free tools and resources.

Access practice quizzes, eFlashcards, video, and multimedia at **edge.sagepub.com/hemmens4e**

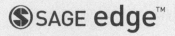

8

© iStock.com/RichLegg

CRIMINAL DEFENDANTS AND CRIME VICTIMS

Master the content at **edge.sagepub.com/hemmens4e**

INTRODUCTION

In the previous three chapters we examined the key actors in the criminal court system. The members of the courtroom workgroup—the prosecutor, defense attorney, and judge—are central to the workings of the criminal court system. Yet, they are not the only people who play a direct role in criminal prosecutions. Criminal defendants, crime victims, and witnesses have prominent roles to play in a majority of prosecutions. Additionally, despite having disparate interests in the proceedings, they share several common attributes. Neither defendants nor victims work within the criminal court system. Despite being central to the consideration of a particular case, they are kept at the periphery of procedural and administrative aspects of proceedings. In fact, although they could be considered the court's "clients" or "customers," they are frequently treated as an afterthought, if not a nuisance, by members of the courtroom workgroup.

In this chapter we explain the role each plays in the adjudication process. As you consider the rights provided to them and their role in the system, bear in mind that both crime victims and criminal defendants are people caught up in a confusing, complicated system, which they know little about. With this in mind, consider how well the system balances the duty it owes to the individual defendants and victims against the need to have the court process operate in a fair and efficient manner.

CRIMINAL DEFENDANTS

Once a person suspected of committing a crime is arrested, he transforms from being a suspect to being a criminal defendant. Criminal defendants are the hub around which the criminal court system rotates. The determination of a defendant's guilt and the pronouncement of his punishment are the foundational roles of the criminal courts. The protection of each defendant's constitutional rights is required of the system. Even the names of cases are based on the individual defendant.

In this section we examine, in general terms, who are criminal defendants, what constitutional rights they possess, and what role they play in the operation of the criminal courts.

Defendants in Court

The defendant plays both minor and major roles in the criminal court process. As discussed in Chapter 6, the defendant has the ability and right to make major decisions regarding her defense, particularly whether to enter into a plea bargain and whether to testify. Beyond these items, a defendant's attorney is charged with making strategic and tactical decisions. Although attorneys must consult with their clients on important strategic matters and are frequently given unsolicited input from their clients, attorneys tend to trust their own ability to make tactical decisions.

The primary role of a defendant is to focus on his demeanor and appearance before the judge and jury. Attorneys instruct their clients to be well groomed and wear neat clothes during a jury trial. Attorneys frequently have their office staff assist defendants who are in custody obtain clothes prior to trial.

Beyond looking good, it is important that defendants display an appropriate demeanor while in court. This includes looking interested in what is happening, not scowling, and having a concerned yet pleasant expression when possible. Defendants should not acknowledge or talk to witnesses or victims as they appear in court. It is also important that defendants not react emotionally to what they hear from the witness stand or the prosecution. Even if testimony is untrue and inflammatory, it is critical that defendants refrain from showing any reaction to what they hear. This includes resisting the urge to repeatedly whisper in their attorney's ears. Most attorneys will have their clients write down items that they would want to bring to the lawyer's attention and wait to discuss it until requested. This allows the attorney to concentrate on the proceedings and not appear like she is ignoring the defendant.

Defendant Characteristics

Criminal defendants come from all backgrounds and possess a full range of demographic characteristics. That being said, individuals from several segments of society and backgrounds sit as criminal defendants at levels greater than in the general population. As shown in Table 8.1, gender, race/ethnicity, and level of education represent three areas where individuals from specific backgrounds appear in court as defendants at disproportionately high levels.

Data collected by the Bureau of Justice Statistics (BJS) indicated 83% of defendants prosecuted for felonies in the 75 largest counties in the United States in 2006 were male. BJS also reported that a majority of defendants were non-White. More specifically, 24% of the defendants were Hispanic, and 45% were Black/African American. The age of defendants was fairly evenly distributed across age groups. The numbers of defendants were evenly split between those younger and older than age 30, with the median age being 32 years old.

A majority of the defendants tend not to be well educated. As shown in Table 8.1, nearly half of defendants prosecuted in federal courts did not graduate from high school. Moreover, 20% attended college, with only 5.4% earning a college degree. Not surprisingly, as discussed in Chapter 6, the overwhelming majority of defendants are indigent and are represented by publicly financed attorneys (DeFrances & Litras, 2000; Wolf-Harlow, 2000).

TABLE 8.1 ■ Felony Defendants in Large Urban Counties, 2009*	
Gender	
Male	83%
Female	17%
Race	
White, Non-Hispanic	30%
Black, Non-Hispanic	45%

(Continued)

TABLE 8.1 ■ (Continued)	
Other, Non-Hispanic	2%
Hispanic, Any Race	24%
Age	
Under 21 Years	18%
21–29	34%
30–39	23%
40 Years or Older	26%
Prior Convictions	
No Prior Convictions	40%
1 Prior Conviction	11%
2–4 Prior Convictions	20%
5–9 Prior Convictions	15%
10 or More Prior Convictions	14%
Educational Level	
Less Than High School Graduate	51.1%
High School Graduate	28.9%
Some College	14.4%
College Graduate	5.6%

Source: U.S. Department of Justice, Bureau of Justice Statistics. (2013, December); U.S. Department of Justice, Bureau of Justice Statistics. (2015). Table 4.4.

*Most recent data available.

Perhaps the most troubling item reported in Table 8.1 is that for a significant majority of criminal defendants in the counties studied, the 2009 prosecution they faced was not the first time they sat as a defendant in a criminal court. This fact speaks volumes about the apparent revolving door system of justice that exists across the nation. The reason for this and how to address it are well beyond the scope of this book. It is important to note, however, that the huge caseloads in many of the nation's courts—as well as the limited amount of attention given to individual cases, defendants, and victims—are due in large part to this problem.

Defendant Rights Prior to Prosecution: The Exclusionary Rule

Beyond rights enjoyed by defendants during court proceedings, the courts have the authority to sanction the government for acts that violate individual rights and have led to the discovery of evidence to be used in a criminal prosecution. The exclusionary rule is a judicially created remedy for violations of the Fourth Amendment. It provides that any evidence obtained by law enforcement officers in violation of the Fourth Amendment guarantee against unreasonable searches and seizures is not admissible in a criminal trial to prove guilt. The rule was applied to the states by the U.S. Supreme Court in *Mapp v. Ohio* (1961).

The primary purpose of the exclusionary rule is to deter police misconduct. Whereas some proponents argue that the rule emanates from the Constitution, the Supreme Court has indicated it is merely a judicially created remedy for violations of the Fourth Amendment. Without a means of enforcing the prohibition on unreasonable searches and seizures through deterrence of police misconduct, the Fourth Amendment is reduced to a "form of words," because police have no incentive to act lawfully.

The exclusionary rule is perhaps the most controversial legal issue in criminal justice. Application of the rule may lead to the exclusion of important evidence and the acquittal of persons who are factually, if not legally, guilty. Consequently, the exclusionary rule has been the subject of intense debate. Proponents argue it is the only effective means of protecting individual rights from police misconduct, while critics decry the exclusion from trial of relevant evidence. Despite calls for its abolition and shifts in the composition of the Supreme Court, the exclusionary rule remains entrenched in American jurisprudence. But although the rule has survived, it has not gone unscathed. Supreme Court decisions over the years have limited the scope of the rule and created several exceptions.

The History of the Exclusionary Rule

In 1914, the Supreme Court held that evidence illegally obtained by federal law enforcement officers was not admissible in federal criminal prosecutions (*Weeks v. United States*, 1914). Because the *Weeks* decision applied only against the federal government (the Fourth Amendment had not yet been incorporated), state law enforcement officers were still free to seize evidence illegally without fear of its exclusion in state criminal proceedings.

In addition, evidence seized illegally by state police could be turned over to federal law enforcement officers for use in federal prosecutions because federal law enforcement officers were not directly involved in the illegal seizure. This was known as the silver platter doctrine because illegally seized evidence could be turned over to federal law enforcement officers "as if on a silver platter." In *Elkins v. United States* (1960), the Court put an end to this practice, prohibiting the introduction of illegally seized evidence in federal prosecutions regardless of whether the illegality was committed by state or federal agents.

In 1949, the Supreme Court applied the Fourth Amendment against the states, incorporating it into the Due Process Clause of the Fourteenth Amendment. However, the Court refused to apply the remedy of the exclusionary rule to the states (*Wolf v. Colorado*, 1949). Just 3 years later, the Court modified its position somewhat, holding in *Rochin v. California* (1952) that evidence seized in a manner that "shocked the conscience" must be excluded as violative of due process. Exactly what type of conduct shocked the conscience was left to be determined on a case-by-case basis. The exclusionary rule thus became applicable to state criminal proceedings, but its application was uneven.

Finally, in 1961, in *Mapp v. Ohio*, the Court took the step it failed to take in *Wolf* and explicitly applied the remedy of the exclusionary rule to the states. The Court did so because it acknowledged the states had failed to provide an adequate alternative remedy for violations of the Fourth Amendment. Although there was language in *Mapp* that suggested the exclusionary rule originated from the Constitution and was not merely a judicially created remedy, subsequent decisions indicate the Court views the rule not as part of the Constitution but rather a means of enforcing the Fourth Amendment prohibition against unreasonable searches and seizures.

Exceptions to the Exclusionary Rule

The Supreme Court in *Mapp* stated that the exclusionary rule serves at least two purposes: the deterrence of police misconduct and the protection of judicial integrity. In recent years, however, the Court has emphasized almost exclusively the deterrence of police misconduct, leading to the creation of several exceptions to the rule. In addition, the Court has held that the exclusionary rule does not apply to a variety of proceedings other than the criminal trial.

In 1984, the Court held, in *Massachusetts v. Sheppard* and *United States v. Leon*, that evidence obtained by the police acting in good faith on a search warrant issued by a neutral and detached magistrate, which is ultimately found to be invalid, may nonetheless be admitted at trial. The Court stressed that the primary rationale for the exclusionary rule—deterrence of police misconduct—did not warrant exclusion of evidence obtained by police who act reasonably and in good faith reliance on the actions of a judge. By "good faith," the Court meant the police are unaware that the warrant is invalid.

The Court emphasized that the good faith exception did not apply to errors made by the police, even if the errors were entirely inadvertent. The exception applies only to situations where the police relied on others who, it later turns out, made a mistake. Subsequent cases reiterated this point. In 1987, in *Illinois v. Krull,* the Court extended the good faith exception to the exclusionary rule to instances where the police act in reliance on a statute that is later declared unconstitutional. In 1995, in *Arizona v. Evans,* the Court refused to apply the exclusionary rule to evidence seized by a police officer who acted in reliance on a computer entry, made by a court clerk, which was later found to be in error.

The rationale for the good faith exception is that excluding evidence obtained by police who have not knowingly violated the Fourth Amendment and who relied in good faith on other actors in the criminal justice system does not serve the purpose of deterring police misconduct, the primary goal of the exclusionary rule.

The Court has also established the inevitable discovery exception to the exclusionary rule. This exception, developed in *Nix v. Williams* (1984), permits the use at trial of evidence illegally obtained by the police if they can demonstrate that they would have discovered the evidence anyway by legal means. The burden is on the police to prove they would in fact have discovered the evidence lawfully even if they had not acted illegally. Police have only infrequently been able to successfully establish this exception, however.

Both the *Weeks* and *Mapp* decisions involved criminal trials. The Supreme Court has been reluctant to extend the exclusionary rule to other proceedings even if there is a potential for loss of liberty. The Court has held that illegally seized evidence may be admitted in a criminal trial if the purpose for admitting the evidence is not to prove guilt. Thus, illegally obtained evidence may be used to impeach a defendant's testimony or to determine the appropriate sentence. The Court has consistently refused to apply the exclusionary rule to evidence seized by private parties, if they are not acting in concert with, or at the behest of, the police. The rule does not apply to evidence presented to the grand jury. An unlawful search does not bar prosecution of the arrestee, because the exclusionary rule is an evidentiary rule rather than a rule of jurisdictional limitation.

Defendant Rights in the Court Process

The Bill of Rights was adopted in an effort to protect individual freedoms and liberties from an overzealous government. Beyond protecting rights that directly impact all citizens, such as freedom of speech and freedom of religion, a significant number of the amendments contained in the Bill of Rights include the rights afforded individuals charged by the state with violating criminal statutes. Table 8.2 lists a number of rights provided to criminal defendants once they enter the court system. In the following section we discuss several of these rights in more detail.

TABLE 8.2 ■ Important Defendant Rights Before and During Trial	
Pretrial Rights	
Reasonable Bail	Eighth Amendment
	Stack v. Boyle (1951)
Notice of Charges	Sixth Amendment
	In re Oliver (1948)
Right to Counsel	Sixth Amendment
	Gideon v. Wainwright (1963)
Rights at Trial	
Speedy Trial	Sixth Amendment
	Barker v. Wingo (1972)
Public Trial	Sixth Amendment
	Waller v. Georgia (1984)
Trial by Jury	Sixth Amendment
	Duncan v. Louisiana (1968)
Remain Silent	Fifth Amendment
	Griffin v. California (1965)
Testify	Sixth Amendment
	Rock v. Arkansas (1987)
Compulsory Process	Sixth Amendment
	Washington v. Texas (1967)
Present at Trial	Sixth Amendment
	Illinois v. Allen (1970)
Confrontation	Sixth Amendment
	Pointer v. Texas (1965)
	Davis v. Alaska (1974)

Right to a Speedy Trial

One basic principle of the American criminal justice system is that a person must be considered innocent until proven guilty. It is therefore logical, if not essential, that a person accused of a crime should have the opportunity to have the cloud of accusation removed as quickly as possible. This is particularly true if the person is being held in custody until disposition of the charges. Based largely on this premise, the Sixth Amendment explicitly guarantees the right to a speedy trial in all criminal prosecutions. Although this general maxim is not controversial, it has been difficult, if not impossible, to quantify what constitutes a denial of a defendant's speedy-trial rights.

Congress and state legislatures have established specific, formal time limits within which a defendant has a right to be tried. Typical time periods, which begin to run at the time of arrest to arraignment, are 60 to 90 days for defendants held in custody, 90 to 120 for those who are not. Standard 12-1.1 of the American Bar Association's (2006) *Standards for Criminal Justice: Speedy Trial and Timely Resolution of Criminal Cases* provides for 90 days if in custody and 180 days when on pretrial release.

In reality, these time limits are rarely met. Consider the information presented in Table 8.3. The median time from arrest to sentencing for defendants convicted of felonies in 2006 was 265 days. Moreover, one out of three cases takes longer than a year to complete. As a result, the enforcement of these time limits rarely takes place. Not only are the time limits not met, they are surpassed exponentially.

The reason for this is that defendants are generally free to waive their right to a speedy trial and, as indicated in Table 8.3, frequently do. They do this largely for strategic reasons. Defendants, especially those on pretrial release, normally prefer increased delay before standing trial. Not only does the passage of time allow for increased time to prepare a defense, more importantly it increases the chance the prosecution will lose a witness or have some other unforeseen event take place that can damage its case.

There are times, however, when a defendant's demand for a speedy trial is not acted on. For a constitutional violation to be found, it is necessary that a defendant affirmatively and clearly request a speedy trial and not waive his right to one. If such a demand is made, and the authorized time limit has passed, courts will consider a possible constitutional violation on a case-by-case basis. The Supreme Court has held that no specific length of time automatically triggers a violation; instead, it has adopted a balancing test that takes into account the specific circumstances present, as articulated in *Barker v. Wingo* (1972). The factors a court will consider are the length of delay, the reason for delay, the defendant's assertion of his right, and any prejudice to the defendant caused by the delay (p. 530). Not surprisingly, delays that harm the defendant and are deliberate on the part of the prosecution have constitutional implications. That being said, the Court has held that the factors do not have to be given equal weight. For example, in *Barker*, the Court found that a 5-year delay, even if attributable to the prosecution, did not violate Barker's rights because he did not make a demand for a speedy trial and he did not suffer any prejudice as a result of the delay.

Right to Be Present at Trial

The Supreme Court has held that a criminal defendant has a right to be present at her trial. This right is based on two constitutional rights: the Confrontation Clause

TABLE 8.3 ■ Time Between Arrest and Sentencing for Felons Convicted in State Courts, 2006*				
	Median Time (in Days)	**Sentenced Within 3 Months**	**Sentenced Within 6 Months**	**Sentenced Within 1 Year**
All Offenses	265	14%	33%	67%
Violent Offenses	295	9%	26%	62%
Property Offenses	237	15%	38%	70%
Drug Offenses	271	15%	32%	66%

Source: U.S. Department of Justice, Bureau of Justice Statistics, Felony Sentences in State Courts, 2006—Statistical.
*Most recent data available.

of the Sixth Amendment and the Due Process Clause of the Fourteenth Amendment. The Confrontation Clause (discussed in more detail later) provides defendants with the right to confront, generally face-to-face, witnesses who provide testimony for the prosecution at trial. To do this, logic dictates that the defendant be present at the trial.

Beyond the right to confront witnesses, the Supreme Court has found that a defendant's right to be present at trial and other significant court proceedings is also guaranteed by the Due Process Clause of the Fourteenth Amendment (*Illinois v. Allen,* 1970). The rationale for this is that it would be unfair and against the spirit of an open criminal court system, where defendants are presumed innocent, to conduct any significant part of a trial without the defendant being present. In addition to raising questions in the eyes of the jury, the absence of a defendant from trial would take away his ability to communicate with and provide input to his attorney.

The right to be present in court extends to hearings "whenever his presence has a relation, reasonably substantial, to the fullness of his opportunity to defend against the charge" (*Snyder v. Massachusetts,* 1934, p. 106). Note that the Court did not say a defendant has an absolute right to be present at all times during the trial. Rather, the Court said the defendant has a right to be present when being present has a "reasonably substantial" relationship to her ability to effectively defend the charges. Thus, the general right to be present at trial does not necessarily extend to pretrial hearing on procedural matters, meetings between the judge and attorneys regarding evidentiary items, or those rare instances when the court takes the jury outside the courtroom to view a relevant scene or locale.

Courts have also found that the right to be present at trial may be forfeited or waived by the defendant. There are two primary ways that this takes place. First, if a defendant absconds either before or during his trial, he may be tried *in absentia* (*Taylor v. United States,*1973). Before a court conducts a **trial in absentia**, the court must determine that the absence is voluntary and deliberate. So long as the defendant had notice of the time the proceedings were to begin, intentional absence is presumed, and the trial will likely proceed without the defendant being present.

The second circumstance where defendants forfeit their right to be present at trial is when they repeatedly disrupt the proceedings by their unruly, loud, and disruptive conduct. *Illinois v. Allen* (1970) dealt explicitly with whether a defendant can lose his or her right to be present at trial because of such behavior. At his trial for robbery, Allen chose to represent himself. Throughout the early part of the trial, Allen was highly disruptive, used vile language, threatened the judge, and ripped up a court file. The judge warned him several times that if he did not behave, he would be removed from the courtroom and the trial would continue without him. After one such warning, Allen responded by yelling at the judge, "There's not going to be no trial, either. I'm going to sit here and you're going to talk and you can bring your shackles out and straight jacket and put them on me and tape my mouth, but it will do no good because there's not going to be no trial" (p. 341). Allen was subsequently removed from the courtroom and the trial proceeded without him. Following his conviction, Allen appealed, arguing his right to be present at trial was violated.

The Supreme Court held that by behaving as he did, Allen forfeited his right to be present at his trial. In considering the balance between a defendant's right to be present at trial and the need for the court system to operate efficiently with some decorum, Justice Black wrote,

> It is not pleasant to hold that the respondent Allen was properly banished from the court for a part of his own trial. But our courts, palladiums of liberty as they are, cannot be treated disrespectfully with impunity. Nor can the accused be permitted by his disruptive conduct indefinitely to avoid being tried on the charges brought against him. It would degrade our country and our judicial system to permit our courts to be bullied, insulted, and humiliated and their orderly progress thwarted and obstructed by defendants brought before them charged with crimes. As guardians of the public welfare, our state and federal judicial systems strive to administer equal justice to the rich and the poor, the good and the bad, the native and foreign born of every race, nationality, and religion. . . . [I]f our courts are to remain what the Founders intended, the citadels of justice, their proceedings cannot and must not be infected with the sort of scurrilous, abusive language and conduct paraded before the Illinois trial judge in this case. (pp. 346–347)

When a defendant such as Mr. Allen must be removed from the courtroom, courts are typically equipped so the defendant can watch the trial and communicate with counsel via electronic means. Once the defendant agrees to behave properly, he must be given an opportunity to return to the trial.

In addition to having the right to be present at trial, defendants have the right to appear at their trial in civilian clothes and without visible restraints. In *Estelle v. Williams* (1976), Chief Justice Burger held that having a defendant appear at trial in jail or prison clothes is likely to dilute the presumption of innocence in the eyes of the jury. That being said, courts will not force defendants to wear civilian clothes to court. For a constitutional violation to be found, the defendant must prove that she was compelled to appear before the jury in identifiable prison clothing and that she notified the judge of the problem. Without meeting these two conditions, a later appeal based on appearing before the jury in prison clothes or restraints will be unsuccessful.

KEY CASES
AKE V. OKLAHOMA (1985) AND *McWILLIAMS V. DUNN* (2016)

In *Ake v. Oklahoma* (1985), the Supreme Court considered whether a criminal defendant had a right to the assistance of an expert witness in preparing his defense. The Court held that "when a defendant demonstrates to the trial judge that his sanity at the time of the offense is to be a significant factor at trial, the State must, at a minimum, assure the defendant access to a competent psychiatrist who will conduct an appropriate examination and assist in evaluation, preparation, and presentation of the defense" (p. 83).

Later that year James McWilliams was charged with committing rape and murder. McWilliams's appointed attorney requested a psychiatric evaluation of McWilliams. The trial court granted this request and ordered the Alabama Department of Corrections conduct an evaluation. McWilliams was found to be competent to stand trial and had not been suffering from mental illness at the time of the alleged offense. He was convicted of capital murder and the jury recommended a death sentence. Prior to sentencing, McWilliams's counsel asked that the client be given neurological and neuropsychological testing. The court granted the request and McWilliams was examined by Dr. John Goff, a neuropsychologist employed by the State's Department of Mental Health. Two days before the sentencing hearing, Dr. Goff filed a report with the court, concluding that McWilliams was probably exaggerating his symptoms but did suffer from genuine neuropsychological problems. Just before the hearing, counsel also received updated and previous requested mental health records. Defense counsel requested the hearing be continued to allow him to review the new material; counsel also asked for the assistance of someone with expertise in psychological matters to review the findings. The trial court denied both requests, and McWilliams was sentenced to death.

McWilliams appealed, arguing that the trial court denied him the right to meaningful expert assistance guaranteed by *Ake*. The Alabama Court

of Criminal Appeals affirmed the conviction and sentence, holding that Dr. Goff's examination satisfied *Ake*'s requirements. This was affirmed by the Alabama State Supreme Court. On federal habeas review, the District Court also found that the Goff examination satisfied *Ake* and denied relief. The Eleventh Circuit Court of Appeals affirmed.

The U.S. Supreme Court granted certiorari, and in a 5–4 decision written by Justice Stephen Breyer, reversed *McWilliams v. Dunn* (2017). The majority held that once it is established that a defendant is indigent and that his mental condition is relevant and in question, *Ake* requires the state to provide a defendant with access to a mental health expert who is sufficiently available to the defense and independent from the prosecution to effectively "conduct an appropriate examination and assist in evaluation, preparation, and presentation of the defense." The Court went on to state that the limited exam and assistance given to McWilliams by a doctor employed by the state were insufficient to satisfy the requirements mandated by *Ake*.

Ake requires more than just an examination. It requires that the state provide the defense with "access to a competent psychiatrist who will conduct an appropriate (1) examination and assist in (2) evaluation, (3) preparation, and (4) presentation of the defense" (p. 83).

Even assuming that Alabama met the examination requirement, it did not meet any of the other three requirements. No expert helped the defense evaluate the Goff report or McWilliams's extensive medical records and translate these data into a legal strategy. No expert helped the defense prepare and present arguments that might, for example, have explained that McWilliams's purported malingering was not necessarily inconsistent with mental illness. No expert helped the defense prepare direct or cross-examination of any witnesses or testified

(Continued)

(Continued)

at the judicial sentencing hearing. Because Alabama's provision of mental health assistance fell so short of *Ake*'s requirements that an independent expert be provided to the defendant if needed, the Alabama courts' decision affirming McWilliams's sentence was erroneous.

1. What are your thoughts on the Court's opinion?

2. Should an expert appointed by the court to assist the defense work solely for the defense? Can such an expert be neutral and work for both parties?

3. Who should pay for an appointed expert? Should the expense enter a court's consideration of whether to appoint an expert to assist the defense?

Oral arguments in *McWilliams v. Dunn* can be found at https://www.oyez.org/cases/2016/16-5294.

Right to Compulsory Process and to Present a Defense

The **Compulsory Process Clause** of the Sixth Amendment to the U.S. Constitution provides, "In all criminal prosecutions, the accused shall enjoy the right … to have compulsory process for obtaining witnesses in his favor." While this seems quite straightforward and limited in scope, the Supreme Court has interpreted it to provide defendants with a variety of rights.

This explicit right provided to defendants by the Compulsory Process Clause is the right to compel individuals to appear in court and testify as witnesses for the defense. To do this, the defense obtains a subpoena from the court. A **subpoena** is simply a court order that requires an individual to appear at a specific time and place to testify as a witness. A subpoena is issued by the court and must be personally served (delivered) to the person whose appearance is sought. After being served with a subpoena, an individual who fails to appear in court as ordered is likely to be held in contempt of court. An important component of this right is to have individuals in prison or jail brought to court by law enforcement officials to testify.

Beyond facilitating the defendant's ability to secure witnesses for trial (or pretrial proceedings), the Supreme Court has found that the Compulsory Process Clause provides defendants with a number of less obvious rights. One of the most important of these is the right to put on a defense at his or her trial.

It may seem obvious that a defendant has a right to present evidence and a defense at his or her trial, but states often have rules of evidence and statutes that can preclude evidence the defendant seeks to present to the jury. For example, in *Washington v. Texas* (1967), the Court considered a Texas law that prohibited individuals charged or convicted as coparticipants in a common crime from testifying on behalf of one another. As such, at his trial for murder, Washington was precluded from having his codefendant testify that it was he, and not Washington, who fired the gun that killed the victim.

The Supreme Court held that regardless of the basis for the Texas law, when it precludes a person from presenting a defense, it violates the Sixth and Fourteenth Amendments. The Court explained the underlying basis for this right in the following manner:

The right to offer the testimony of witnesses, and to compel their attendance, if necessary, is in plain terms the right to present a defense, the right to present the defendant's version of the facts as well as the prosecution's version to the jury, so it may decide where the truth lies. Just as an accused has the right to confront the prosecution's witnesses for the purpose of challenging their testimony, he has the right to present his own witnesses to establish a defense. This right is a fundamental element of due process of law. (p. 19)

It is important to bear in mind that a defendant does not have an absolute right to present any and all evidence or testimony she desires. For evidence and testimony to be admissible, it must at a minimum be relevant and trustworthy in the eyes of the judge. Evidence is considered relevant if (a) it has any tendency to make a fact more or less probable than it would be without the evidence, and (b) the fact is of consequence in determining the action (Federal Rule of Evidence 401). The case of *Crane v. Kentucky* (1986) provides an interesting example of the balance between letting a defendant present a complete defense and requiring such evidence to be relevant to the issues in question.

Crane was on trial for a murder he committed when he was 16 years old. Prior to his trial, Crane moved to suppress a confession he had given the police. The trial court found that the confession was voluntary and allowed it to be presented to the jury. Hoping to discredit the confession, Crane then sought to introduce testimony regarding the length of the interrogation and how it was conducted. The trial court found that the testimony pertained only to the issue of voluntariness, which had previously been decided, and therefore ruled it to be irrelevant for the determination of guilt. Crane was subsequently found guilty.

The U.S. Supreme Court vacated the conviction, holding that the trial court prevented Crane from having a fair opportunity to present a defense. The Court found that evidence about the way a confession is obtained, in addition to bearing on its voluntariness, often bears on its credibility, a matter that is exclusively for the jury to assess. According to the Court, the physical and psychological environment associated with a confession can also be of substantial relevance to the ultimate factual issue of a defendant's guilt or innocence, especially in a case where there apparently was no physical evidence to link the defendant to the crime.

The fact that evidence a defendant wishes to present at trial may be **relevant** is not enough to ensure its admissibility. The rules of evidence (federal and state) give the trial court judge discretion to preclude the admission evidence that may fall within the definition of relevance. For example, Rule 403 of the Federal Rules of Evidence provides,

> The court may exclude relevant evidence if its probative value is substantially outweighed by a danger of one or more of the following: unfair prejudice, confusing the issues, misleading the jury, undue delay, wasting time, or needlessly presenting cumulative evidence.

It is interesting to note that it is not a violation of the Sixth Amendment for a judge to preclude testimony offered by the defense that fits into one of the previously mentioned categories (*Montana v. Egelhoff,* 1996).

Right to Testify

A criminal defendant has the right to testify on her own behalf. Despite this fact, it is interesting to note that this right is actually not stated in the Constitution or Bill of Rights. In fact, although it was never really questioned, it wasn't until 1987 and the case of *Rock v. Arkansas* that the U.S. Supreme Court specifically held that such a right exists.

Vikki Rock was charged with killing her husband. Prior to her manslaughter trial, Rock participated in two hypnosis sessions. Following hypnosis, she remembered that her husband was killed as a result of an accidental shooting. At her trial, when she attempted to testify about the hypnotically refreshed memories, the prosecution objected on the grounds that such testimony was prohibited by an Arkansas law that precluded hypnotically refreshed testimony from being presented at trial. The trial court agreed, ruling "testimony of matters recalled by Defendant due to hypnosis [will] be excluded because of inherent unreliability and the effect of hypnosis in eliminating any meaningful cross-examination on those matters." Rock was subsequently found guilty of manslaughter.

The U.S. Supreme Court reversed the conviction, holding that the trial court's actions violated Rock's right to testify on her own behalf. The Court stated that a criminal defendant's right to testify is found within the Due Process Clause of the Fourteenth Amendment (fundamentally unfair to prevent a defendant from testifying), the Compulsory Process Clause of the Sixth Amendment (right to call witnesses and present evidence must include having defendant testify), and the Fifth Amendment's privilege against self-incrimination (right not to testify implies and requires a right to testify).

While supporting the right to testify, the Court noted that it was not without limits, stating "the right 'may, in appropriate cases, bow to accommodate other legitimate interests in the criminal trial process'" (*Rock* at 55–56). These include procedural and evidentiary rules designed to ensure fairness and reliability. These rules, however, must not be arbitrary or disproportionate. As Arkansas's rule prohibited all posthypnotic testimony without consideration of the specific facts in a given case, the Court found using it to limit Rock's testimony was an arbitrary restriction on her right to testify.

It is important to remember that a defendant's right to testify may be restricted so long as the restrictions are not arbitrary or disproportionate. Defendants may only testify about otherwise admissible evidence. Just as with other witnesses, testimony that is not relevant to the trial or viewed as unreliable may be precluded by the judge.

Whether or not a defendant testifies on his own behalf is the most critical decision for the defense to make at trial. As discussed in Chapter 6, whereas the defendant has the final word as to whether he testifies, the Supreme Court has held that the right to testify does not include the right to commit perjury (*Nix v. Whiteside,* 1986). Accordingly, the right to testify is not violated if a defendant's attorney or the trial judge refuses to allow the offering of false testimony.

Right to Confront and Cross-Examine Witnesses

The **Confrontation Clause** of the Sixth Amendment provides, "In all criminal prosecutions, the accused shall enjoy the right . . . to be confronted with the witnesses against him." Simply put, the Confrontation Clause guarantees the defendant's right to face and confront any witness or evidence offered by the prosecution in a criminal trial or other proceedings substantially related to her ability to defend against the charges faced. The clause involves two distinct concepts: (a) the right to confront one's accusers face-to-face and (b) the right to cross-examine witnesses called by the prosecution.

The purposes behind the Confrontation Clause were summed up by Supreme Court Justice Byron White in 1970.

> In addition to requiring witness's physical presence before criminal defendant, the Confrontation Clause also (1) insures that witness will give his statements under oath, thus impressing him with seriousness of matter and guarding against lie by possibility of penalty for perjury, (2) forces witness to submit to cross-examination, the greatest legal engine ever invented for discovery of truth, and (3) permits jury that is to decide defendant's fate to observe demeanor of witness in making his statement, thus aiding jury in assessing his credibility. (*California v. Green,* 1970, p. 158)

The opportunity to cross-examine prosecution witnesses is the crux of the Confrontation Clause. Aside from the right to counsel, it is perhaps the most important right possessed by defendants standing trial. Cross-examination gives defendants the ability to challenge the evidence against them. By asking witnesses questions that probe their accuracy, veracity, biases, and consistency, defendants (through counsel) can challenge the prosecution's case by discrediting the testimony of witnesses and associated evidence.

This can be done by attacking two critical components of a witness's testimony. The first involves the capacity of a witness to observe what she is testifying about. In challenging a witness's capacity, the defense is not saying that the witness is lying, just that she is mistaken. This frequently occurs in cases involving eyewitness identifications of direct observations of specific acts. In such cases, witnesses generally testify (and genuinely believe) that they are "positive" about what they observed (Loftus, 1979). In fact, they are very often mistaken. Through cross-examination, the defense can inform the jury about items that may decrease the capacity for observation and memory and therefore lower the weight given to the testimony. Questions about the physical items that might impact the witness's cognitive abilities, such as the use of drugs, medications, or alcohol; fatigue; quality of vision; and use of prescribed glasses during the incident are typical areas addressed. Other areas frequently addressed include the length of time for observation, the witness's emotional state (e.g., fear), distractions, and focus of attention. Additionally, witnesses are questioned about prior statements or descriptions they may have given officials that are different from their court testimony.

The second component of cross-examination is impeachment. Impeachment is the process of challenging the truthfulness and credibility of a witness. Under the rules of evidence, a number of specific items can be used for impeachment. These include prior inconsistent statements, items showing bias or a motive for testifying against the defense, prior felony convictions, and questions about the witness's character that would make the jury question his testimony.

The ability to cross-examine prosecution witnesses also provides the defense with the opportunity to focus jurors' attention on its theory of the case and the facts it wants the jury to think about. As discussed in the next section, the ability to do this and protect the right to confront witnesses requires in-court testimony that can be challenged.

Hearsay and the Right of Confrontation

Over the past decade, the Supreme Court has had a dramatic shift in the enforcement of the Confrontation Clause as it pertains to hearsay, out-of-court statements made by witnesses who are not available to testify at the defendant's trial. After all, if the ability to cross-examine one's accusers is critical to arriving at the truth and the key to the right of confrontation, should statements made by people who will not testify at trial, and therefore not be cross-examined, be admitted into evidence? Historically, under the rules of evidence (not the Sixth Amendment), such statements were generally inadmissible at trial unless they fell under one of the 23 exceptions to the hearsay rule.

Prior to 2004, the Supreme Court took a very flexible approach in considering this relationship between the Sixth Amendment and the rules of evidence. The Court took the view that the Confrontation Clause was not an end itself but simply a method of promoting fairness to the defendant and the establishment of the truth. As such, if the out-of-court statements were of a trustworthy nature and deemed reliable by the judge, they could be admitted without having the speaker testify and be cross-examined. Over time it became the Court's practice to assume that a hearsay statement made by a person unavailable at trial would be admissible if it fit within one of the 23 exceptions to the hearsay rule (*Ohio v. Roberts,* 1980). A statement fitting into such an exception bore sufficient "indicia of reliability" to warrant its admission into evidence. Under this standard, victim statements, forensic reports, and many other types of hearsay statements were ruled to be admissible at trial because they were found by the trial judge to fall within a hearsay exception and to be reliable. In other words, the right to confront the speaker could be ignored if the statement were admissible under the rules of evidence. This flexible, permissive approach to the use of hearsay statements in criminal trials was applied up to 2004.

The basis of how issues related to hearsay and the Confrontation Clause was reevaluated by the Supreme Court in the case of *Crawford v. Washington* (2004). In 1999, Michael Crawford stabbed a man who allegedly tried to rape his wife. When questioned by police, his wife Sylvia said that the victim was unarmed when Michael stabbed him. This statement, which was recorded, was contrary to Michael's claim of self-defense and was very damaging to him at trial. At Michael's trial, Sylvia refused to testify, citing Washington's marital privilege rule. Over objection, the trial judge admitted the tape of her statement into evidence pursuant to a valid hearsay exception. Michael was convicted of assault and attempted murder. The U.S. Supreme Court agreed to hear the matter to consider whether the use of the hearsay statement violated the Confrontation Clause.

In a unanimous decision the Supreme Court explicitly overruled *Ohio v. Roberts* (1980) and in the process turned the manner in which questions about the right of confrontation were examined for over a century on its head (*Crawford v. Washington,* 2004). Writing for the Court, Justice Scalia stated that the rules of evidence and reliability of a statement have no relation to a defendant's right to confront witnesses against the defendant. He disparagingly wrote, "Dispensing with confrontation because testimony is obviously reliable is akin to dispensing with jury trial because a defendant is obviously guilty" (p. 62). He went on to state, "Where testimonial statements are at issue, the only indicium of reliability sufficient to satisfy constitutional demands is the one the Constitution actually prescribes: confrontation" (pp. 68–69).

The Court held that the key question to be considered is whether an out-of-court statement was given for testimonial purposes. If so, it is inadmissible unless the defendant had an opportunity to cross-examine the declarant. The *Crawford* Court did not specifically define what makes statements testimonial beyond saying that formal statements made for the purpose of proving a fact and which are likely to be used by the prosecution at trial are testimonial. Justice Scalia went on to say, "We leave for another day any effort to spell out a comprehensive definition of 'testimonial.' Whatever else the term covers, it applies at a minimum to prior testimony at a preliminary hearing, before a grand jury, or at a former trial and to police interrogations" (p. 68).

In 2006, the Court clarified what differentiates testimonial and nontestimonial statements.

> Statements are nontestimonial when made in the course of police interrogation under circumstances objectively indicating that the primary purpose of the interrogation is to enable police assistance to meet an ongoing emergency. They are testimonial when the circumstances objectively indicate that there is no such ongoing emergency, and that the primary purpose of the interrogation is to establish or prove past events potentially relevant to later criminal prosecution. (*Davis v. Washington*, 2006, p. 822)

Under this definition, a 911 call made during the commission of a crime, an ongoing emergency, is not testimonial. On the other hand, responses to questions posed by the police of other government officials after the emergency has subsided are testimonial and subject to the *Crawford* restrictions. The analysis set forth in *Davis* was later reaffirmed by the Court in *Michigan v. Bryant* (2011).

In 2009, the Supreme Court continued to strengthen criminal defendants' confrontation rights in a manner that has the potential to be disruptive to the entire criminal justice system. While *Crawford* and *Davis* involved verbal statements made by a witness in response to questioning, testimonial evidence may also consist of written reports prepared by forensic scientists as part of a criminal investigation that will be presented as evidence at trial. In *Melendez-Diaz v. Massachusetts* (2009), the Supreme Court held that forensic science reports, such as those prepared as part of the testing of substances, particularly narcotics, are part of the "core class of testimonial statements." Accordingly, for such reports to be admissible at trial, the person who conducts the forensic tests and prepares the report must appear in court and be subjected to cross-examination by the defense. Prior to *Crawford*, such reports were routinely admitted into evidence without the testimony of the forensic analyst because they fit under a recognized hearsay exception and were deemed reliable as required by *Ohio v. Roberts*. It was widely feared that requiring the individual analyst who conducted the tests to appear at trial and be available to be cross-examined for dozens of trials a year would have serious impacts on the criminal court system (Hines, 2010).

In 2011, the Court expounded on the requirements announced in *Melendez-Diaz v. Massachusetts*. *Bullcoming v. New Mexico* (2011) involved a prosecution for aggravated driving while intoxicated. At trial, the prosecution submitted into evidence the certified blood-analysis report that indicated the defendant was intoxicated. Rather than have the crime analyst who conducted the blood-alcohol analysis and prepared the report testify, the prosecution had the analyst's supervisor authenticate the report. The evidence was admitted and Bullcoming was convicted.

The Supreme Court reversed the conviction. The Court held that Bullcoming's confrontation right had been violated because prosecutors were allowed to offer a crime lab report analyzing Bullcoming's blood sample without having the lab analyst who did the tests and prepared the report testify. The Court held that producing such a substitute, or "surrogate," witness is insufficient to satisfy the Sixth Amendment confrontation right.

VICTIMS AND THE CRIMINAL COURTS

Crime victims are an important yet frequently overlooked aspect of the criminal court system. Beyond the need for victim cooperation to successfully prosecute many crimes, the courts and the people that work in them have a moral obligation to treat victims with respect and dignity. Unfortunately, far too often, victims have been ignored and viewed as a nuisance to the people who work in the system on a daily basis.

This has not always been the case. The role played by the victim in the U.S. criminal justice system has changed drastically over time. Prior to the American Revolution, the legal system in the American colonies was based primarily on the English common law. Under this system, which viewed crime as a private harm, victims were required to investigate and prosecute matters themselves under civil law.

Following the establishment of the United States as a nation, state and federal governments moved away from private prosecution and adopted a system of public prosecution of crimes. With this shift, the preferences of victims became increasingly less important in how criminal laws were enforced and crimes prosecuted.

Throughout most of the 19th and 20th centuries, crime victims were treated as an afterthought, and frequently a nuisance, by the court system. Although specific issues faced by victims vary greatly based on the offense involved, victims face several challenges, frustrations, and impediments as they seek justice.

Challenges Faced by Crime Victims

Victims of crime face a number of challenges and obstacles in working with the criminal courts. The basis for these challenges is the lack of sensitivity to the plight of crime victims among actors in the court system. This led to victims frequently being double or triple victimized as their case travailed the court process. In this section we discuss a number of challenges faced by the court system that gave rise to the victims' rights movement.

Lack of Input Into Decisions

Historically, victims have had minimal if any input into how a criminal prosecution is adjudicated. Input from victims was seen as an unnecessary complication that can inhibit the efficient functioning of a prosecutor's office and courtroom workgroup. Victims are interested in justice related to the offender who victimized them. Courtroom actors, on the other hand, have to consider going rates for dozens if not hundreds of cases. Considering, let alone following, the desires of a victim would increase uncertainty among the actors as to how an individual case should be and will be resolved. As such, historically, input from victims on how cases should be adjudicated, what a fair plea agreement would look like, and what would be an appropriate punishment for the offender was not sought or desired.

Lack of Information About Case

Prior to the codification of victims' rights, crime victims had difficulty tracking the progress of their case. With no formal mechanism in place, the only news victims would hear about their case was when the police or prosecution needed something from them or when they received a subpoena to testify in court. Moreover, given the frequency in which hearings and trials are continued and rescheduled, keeping current on pending matters is extremely difficult for anyone not working in the system.

Pretrial Revictimization and Invasion of Privacy

Prior to victims' rights, in the run-up to trial, a victim is likely to be questioned extensively by the police, prosecutor, and defense attorney. From the police and prosecution perspective, it is important that they are confident in the victim's veracity and ability to withstand cross-examination. To achieve this, prosecutors pose difficult questions to the victim and look to find any damaging information from the victim's past that could be used by the defense to attack her credibility. Although necessary, this forces the victim to relive the offense.

More troubling is the way some defense attorneys would treat the victim. Defense attorneys would use interviewing the victim about the crime for purposes beyond gathering information. One goal would be to badger and confuse the victim to the point where he gives conflicting answers to questions. This information is then used during cross-examination to give the impression that the victim is changing stories, being deceitful, and should not be believed.

It is also likely that a defense attorney will attempt to dig into the victim's past for helpful information. This may include criminal histories, psychiatric records, and medical records. It also may involve friends, family members, coworkers, and acquaintances of the victim being interviewed in attempts to uncover damaging information that can be used at trial.

These acts serve to advance several nefarious objectives pursued by defense attorneys. Ultimately, some defense attorneys will do what they can to intimidate the victim to the point where she decides it not worth it to pursue the case. This could be done through yelling and berating the victim during the interview; intimating that past acts, misdeeds, or other facts will be used in court to disparage and humiliate; and generally put the victim on trial rather than the defendant.

Logistical and Financial Obstacles Faced by Victims

Victims who participate in the court process often face logistical barriers that make participation very difficult. These barriers can include repeated rescheduling of necessary court appearances, being forced to wait for hours on end at the courthouse waiting to testify, having to pay for and arrange transportation and parking at the courthouse, and work missed and wages lost because of being at court. The expenses associated with these obstacles can mount and lead a victim to conclude that pursuing a case is not worth the time and aggravation.

The Rise of the Victims' Rights Movement

The challenges faced by crime victims came to prominence toward the end of the 20th century. Like many aspects of American society, in the 1970s, grassroots activities began to impact the way crime victims were treated by the criminal justice system. During the 1970s, crime victims, victims' families, and average citizens began to organize locally and establish victim advocacy organizations. In the early part of the decade, organizations such as Aid for Victims of Crime in St. Louis, Missouri, the Bay Area Women Against Rape in San Francisco, California, and the Rape Crisis Center in Washington,

CURRENT CONTROVERSY
VICTIMS' RIGHTS VERSUS DEFENDANTS' RIGHTS

In 1980 Wisconsin enacted the first crime victims' bill of rights in the nation. Since that time, all 50 states and the federal government have passed statutes or amended their constitutions to protect the rights of crime victims. These rights, many of which are discussed in this chapter, provide critical protections for crime victims and have become an important part of the criminal justice system.

If a conflict exists between the rights guaranteed a criminal defendant and the rights provided to victims, whose rights should take precedence? The Arizona Court of Appeals considered this question in the case of *State ex rel. Romley v. Superior Court* ("Roper") (1992).

Ann Roper was charged with aggravated assault for stabbing her husband with a knife. Roper argued that she acted in self-defense. She claimed that "she ha[d] been the victim of horrendous emotional and physical abuse by her husband during their marriage; that the victim is a mental patient with a multiple personality disorder who, on the date of the alleged aggravated assault, was manifesting one of his violent personalities, a personality who was resisting 'integration' during treatment by his psychiatrist and by a Christian pastor" (p. 450). She further claimed that "the victim is a violent and psychotic individual who has been treated for multiple personality disorder for at least 12 years in most local hospitals and by a number of local psychiatrists and psychologists" (p. 450).

Roper filed a motion asking the trial court to compel the victim to make available all past and present medical records based on the premise that the records would contain exculpatory evidence related to the victim's psychiatric disorders relevant to her claim of self-defense. The trial court granted the defense motion and ordered the records be provided to the court for *in camera* review. The state appealed on the grounds that the Arizona Victim's Bill of Rights, which states in part that a victim of crime has a right "to refuse an interview, deposition, or other discovery request by the defendant" precludes the trial court from compelling disclosure of a victim's medical records.

The case required the court to resolve a conflict between a victim's right to privacy and a defendant's right to due process and fundamental fairness.

The Court of Appeals held that

> if the trial court determines that *Brady* and due process guarantees require disclosure of exculpatory evidence and, further, if the court determines that the medical records *are* exculpatory and are essential to presentation of the defendant's theory of the case, or necessary for impeachment of the victim relevant to the defense theory, then the defendant's due process right to a fundamentally fair trial and to present the defense of self-defense overcomes the statutory physician–patient privilege on the facts as presented here, just as the due process right overcomes the Victim's Bill of Rights on these facts. (p. 452)

The court ordered the trial court to conduct an in-camera review of the medical records and determine which, if any, are exculpatory and essential to Roper's ability to present a defense. The court concluded,

> The Victim's Bill of Rights was appropriately amended to the Arizona Constitution as a shield for victims of crimes. However, the amendment should not be a sword in the hands of victims to thwart a defendant's ability to effectively present a legitimate defense. Nor should the amendment be a fortress behind which prosecutors may isolate themselves from their constitutional duty to afford a criminal defendant a fair trial. (p. 454)

1. On what basis could Roper argue that her husband's medical records are exculpatory?

2. What is an in-camera review? Why would it be used in this case?

3. Do you agree with the court's conclusion?

D.C., were established. Several years later, national organizations, including the National Organization for Victim Assistance (NOVA) and Mothers Against Drunk Drivers (MADD), were established and rapidly became powerful political voices.

In response to the expanding victims' rights movement, local, state, and federal policy makers became interested in the issue. In 1982, the federal government established a Task Force on Victims of Crime. The task force held public hearings in six cities across the nation and sharpened the national focus on the needs of crime victims. The task force's final report became the basis for many policies and standards that currently exist and helped lead to the creation of the Office for Victims of Crime in 1984.

With the growing attention and acceptance that something needed to be done to protect and serve crime victims, since the mid-1980s federal and state governments have enacted laws and amended their constitutions in the name of victims' rights. These efforts include the establishment of victim assistance programs, emotional support networks, and victim advocacy offices. The rest of this section focuses on the establishment of victims' rights and their presence and impact on the criminal court system.

Since the 1980s, the rights and protections provided to crime victims have grown exponentially. Today, every state as well as the federal government have enacted laws designed to protect and provide assistance to victims of crime. Moreover, a number of states have amended their constitutions to include victims' rights provisions. In 1982,

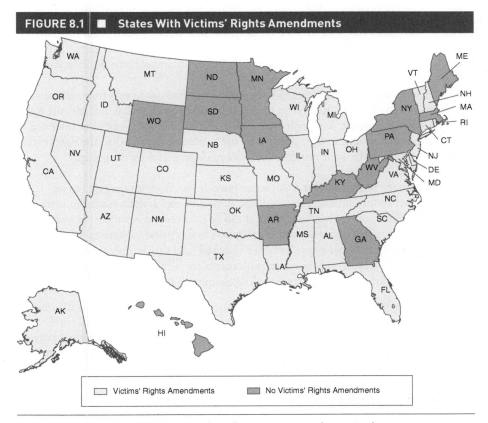

FIGURE 8.1 ■ States With Victims' Rights Amendments

Victims' Rights Amendments   No Victims' Rights Amendments

Source: Adapted from Klaas Kids Foundation (http://www.klaaskids.org/vrights.htm).

TABLE 8.4 ■ Crime Victims' Rights Act of 2004, 18 U.S.C.A. § 3771
(a) Rights of crime victims—A crime victim has the following rights:
1. The right to be reasonably protected from the accused.
2. The right to reasonable, accurate, and timely notice of any public court proceeding, or any parole proceeding, involving the crime or of any release or escape of the accused.
3. The right not to be excluded from any such public court proceeding, unless the court, after receiving clear and convincing evidence, determines that testimony by the victim would be materially altered if the victim heard other testimony at that proceeding.
4. The right to be reasonably heard at any public proceeding in the district court involving release, plea, sentencing, or any parole proceeding.
5. The reasonable right to confer with the attorney for the Government in the case.
6. The right to full and timely restitution as provided in law.
7. The right to proceedings free from unreasonable delay.
8. The right to be treated with fairness and with respect for the victim's dignity and privacy.

California became the first state to adopt a victims' bill of rights. Since then, more than 30 other states have followed suit (Figure 8.1). Because a state's constitution and associated amendments carry greater weight than statutory protections and rights, they carry with them a sense of permanence and provide symbolic importance by indicating the essential rights valued by a state's citizenry.

The rights provided in these statutes and constitutional provisions vary from state to state. The federal Crime Victims' Rights Act of 2004, presented in Table 8.4, includes the rights common across the nation. As a preliminary matter, victims have the right to be informed of the rights they possess and services available for use as needed. Beyond that, the rights specifically associated with the court system can be broken down into three categories.

1. *The Right to Be Informed.* All states provide victims with the right to be notified about important proceedings, decisions, and actions related to their case. These generally include the right to be informed about the time and place of court proceedings, release of a defendant from custody, dismissal of charges, negotiated plea agreements, sentence imposed, and the defendant's final release from confinement. Additionally, prosecutors are required to make reasonable efforts to inform victims of scheduling changes in a timely manner.

2. *The Right to Attend.* All jurisdictions provide victims with the right to attend court proceedings. These generally include pretrial hearings, the trial itself, sentencing, and parole hearings. An area of controversy involves whether victims should have the right to be present in court throughout a trial at which they will be testifying as a witness. In criminal trials, witnesses are generally prohibited from being in the courtroom until they have completed their testimony. This is designed to prevent them from having their testimony influenced by the testimony of other witnesses. Whereas some states provide that the victim's right

to be present at trial supersedes this practice and allow for the victim to attend the entire trial, most states do not provide for such an exception.

3. *The Right to Be Heard.* Victims' rights provisions across the states provide opportunities for victims to be heard at a variety of stages and settings in the court process. States frequently require prosecutors inform victims and consider their opinions prior to entering into a plea agreement or dismissing the charges. Although the prosecutor is not required to do what the victim wants, strenuous objections from a victim about how the government wishes to dispose of a case may cause the prosecutor to think twice about how he will proceed.

Prior to sentencing, victims are given the opportunity to address the judge, either verbally or in writing, through what is called a **victim impact statement.** All 50 states permit victim impact statements, but states vary as to whether they are done verbally and in person at the sentencing hearing, submitted in writing, or presented via a video recording. The victim impact statement permits victims to explain the pain, trauma, financial hardships, or other effect the crime has had on their life. Victims are permitted to provide input on the sentence they believe would be appropriate as well as provide information about any restitution or financial compensation they deem appropriate.

The following is a victim impact statement submitted to court in the prosecution of Robert Owens on behalf of the murder victim, J. T. Codd. As you read it, consider what impact it might have on the trial court judge deciding how to sentence Mr. Codd's killer.

Your Honor, I am writing to share with you some of my thoughts and feelings about JT Codd, a great man who was admired by many and loved by all. A man whose life was brutally taken by a loathsome and perverse individual. My hope is that you will take my words into consideration as this case moves forward.

To say that JT was a special human being would be an understatement of epic proportions. He meant so much to so many, did so much for anyone and everyone, and left an enormous impact on countless lives. He was a huge part of my own life for close to 30 years—yet it wasn't nearly long enough.

JT was much more than just a friend. He was the most honest, caring and generous person I have ever known. He was my business partner, the best man at my wedding and in every possible way, my big brother. There wasn't anything I couldn't talk with him about. No problem he couldn't solve. No obstacle too big for him to conquer. And it was the same for so many others. From his closest friends to total strangers, JT was JT, as genuine as a man could be. The stories about JT, his exploits, his perspective, his generosity, make him sound like a mythological creature, a legend—larger-than-life. But the truth is that he was larger-than-life.

He really did these things and thought that way and gave that much. I was there. I saw it with my own eyes. There was no one stronger. Whether it was spiritual strength—like the time he chose to live homeless for a year as an example of his unrelenting empathy for those less fortunate, or physical strength—like the time he caught a shark with his bare hands while kayaking, and shared shark-steaks with the rest of us. There was no one kinder.

JT's heart was a bottomless well, filling bucket after bucket for those around him. His door was always open to anyone in need of a shower, a decent meal or just a place to keep warm in the winter or cool in the summer. His phone was always on and I never once saw him glance at an incoming call and send it to voicemail. He ALWAYS picked up. Nobody gave more or expected less.

The sacrifices JT was willing to make for the people around him knew no bounds. Money, time, muscle or effort—if you needed it, it was yours with no questions asked and no strings attached. There was no one wiser. JT had an incredibly focused and honest way of viewing the world and the people in it. He was constantly asking the deeper questions—What is our purpose? Why do people treat each other so poorly? How can we leave this world a better place than we came into it? But he didn't just talk about inequities and injustice, he fought them wherever and whenever he could. And most of the time, he won.

Robert Jason Owens is a murderer. He took the lives of my brother, JT Codd, his wife, Cristie Schoen and their unborn baby daughter, Skylar. And while there could never be any true justice for his cowardly and evil acts, it is my opinion that anything less than life in a maximum-security prison without the opportunity for parole would be an absolute injustice.

This was not an accident. This was not his first time. The Sheriff knows it. The DA knows it and Robert Jason Owens knows it. Owens is a career criminal, a damaged and deranged killer who must be held accountable for his actions and, more importantly, must be kept from tearing apart any more families with his heinous atrocities. Forever.

No parent should ever have to hear about the gruesome murders of their children and grandchildren, or grizzly details of how their bodies were dismembered and disposed of by a deranged maniac. So, I understand why the families would accept a plea deal. But I implore Your Honor to please remember, the families and friends of Owens' victims are victims as well. And while my deepest and most sincere hope is that the outcome of this case will bring Faith, Joe and the rest of the Codd family the possibility of some kind of peace, I also ask that you consider the hideous and inhumane nature of Owens' crimes and subsequent attempted cover-up of his crimes when rendering your final decision.

Thank you for your time and consideration in this matter.

Sincerely,

Perry Sachs

As noted earlier, all 50 states provide rights to victims in one form or another. In an effort to allow people to become aware of the specific rights and services available to crime victims, the Office for Victims of Crime maintains several websites with extensive, practical information. These sites (see specific Internet addresses listed at the end of this chapter) include Victim Law (database with search engine for specific state and topics), the Directory of Crime Victim Services, and U.S. Resource Map of Crime Victim Services and Information, an extensive library and multimedia resource center. We encourage you to explore what your state's victims' rights laws are and what resources are available in your community.

Federal Victims' Rights

Since the 1980s the U.S. government has been very supportive of the crime victims' rights movement. Overseeing much of the government's efforts is the Office for Victims of

Crime (OVC). The OVC was established as part of the 1984 Victims of Crime Act. The OVC administers and distributes funds to local and state agencies that deal directly with victim services. Since the OVC's inception, the federal government, through the OVC, has distributed billions of dollars to support crime victims.

Over the past 30 years, Congress has enacted and amended hundreds of statutory provisions aimed at supporting and protecting crime victims. These laws range from the Crime Victims' Rights Act of 2004, which mandates that federal crime victims be provided with specific rights, to 8 U.S.C. § 1154, which authorizes and regulates the granting of favorable immigration status for international victims of human trafficking.

Given the clear support of protecting the interests of crime victims by policy makers, and the large number of states that have amended their constitutions to guarantee victims' rights, it is not surprising that there have been attempts to similarly amend the U.S. Constitution. Despite this support, efforts over the past couple of decades to adopt such an amendment have largely stalled. In 2012, Congress entered into the early stages of considering the adoption of such an amendment.

Victims' Advocates Offices

Local prosecutors have been given primary responsibility for the implementation of a significant number of the provisions contained in victims' rights measures. As a result, nearly all prosecuting attorney offices in the United States maintain some type of victim services or advocacy program. These programs employ trained victim advocates to work with victims and their families throughout the criminal justice process. Their primary mission is to ensure

CURRENT RESEARCH

The courtroom workgroup functions in a closed environment in an effort to maintain control of the workflow and operation of the court. In a 2011 article, Englebrecht explored how members of the workgroup viewed the participation of crime victims in the court process. To do this she interviewed 44 individuals who were either part of the workgroup or worked closely with victims.

The researcher found that although prosecutors viewed themselves as representatives of the victim, they chose to selectively make use of victim input. Prosecutors were protective of maintaining the discretion they possess and were leery of victims and their advocates pushing for a contrary case resolution.

They acknowledged that victims come away dissatisfied when their input is not acted on by the prosecutor. As long as the elected prosecuting attorney and the law permit courtroom prosecutors to exercise their discretion with limited regard for the opinion of the victim, prosecutors will continue to do so.

1. What are the downsides of giving victims more control over case-related decisions?

2. Do you think allowing victims increased decision-making power regarding their case would have any impact of the overall functioning of the court?

Source: "The Struggle for 'Ownership of Conflict': An Exploration of Victim Participation and Voice in the Criminal Justice System." *Criminal Justice Review*, 36: 129–151 (2011). Christine Englebrecht.

that victims are made aware of their rights and are treated fairly and with respect. Although specific services performed by advocates vary by jurisdiction, there are some common services:

- Keeping victims informed about their case status and progress

- Accompanying a victim to court proceedings and investigative interviews

- Speaking on the victim's behalf in court and with other officials

- Preparing victims for pending court hearings by informing them of procedures

- Providing contact information for local resources and counseling referrals

- Assisting victims in recovering stolen property and in obtaining restitution or compensation for expenses incurred as a result of the criminal act

Victim advocates have proven to be a tremendous resource to the court system and of great service to crime victims across the country. Without organized, professional victim support program staff, whose job is to look out for the victim and have limited concern for the rest of the court system, the implementation of victims' rights would not be feasible.

SUMMARY

Despite entering the criminal court process from opposite perspectives, crime victims and criminal defendants share the experience of being outsiders in a confusing, fast-paced system. Both have rights that need to be protected and interests that need to be considered by members of the courtroom workgroup. In this chapter, we touched on some of these rights and means used for their protection. As we move on to the next several chapters, we explore how these items fit into specific processes and stages in a criminal prosecution.

Don't overlook the Student Study Site with its useful study aids, such as self-quizzes, eFlashcards, and other assists, to help you get more from the course and improve your grade.

DISCUSSION QUESTIONS

1. Is it fair to try a defendant in absentia? What are some possible alternatives?

2. What might explain the long period of time it takes to complete criminal prosecutions?

3. Why is cross-examination of prosecution witnesses such an important right?

4. Can you think of a circumstance when a defendant's rights and the rights of a victim may come into conflict? What should a court do in such a situation?

5. Should the Supreme Court consider the practical implications of its Confrontation Clause decisions?

6. Why might people be opposed to a Victims' Rights Amendment to the U.S. Constitution?

KEY TERMS

Compulsory Process
  Clause 196
Confrontation Clause 198

Hearsay 199
Relevant 197
Subpoena 196

Trial in absentia 193
Victim impact
  statement 207

INTERNET SITES

The Confrontation Blog: www.confrontationright.blogspot.com/

Office for Victims of Crime: www.ovc.gov/

Office for Victims of Crime, Directory of Crime Victim Services: http://ovc.ncjrs.gov/findvictimservices/

Office for Victims of Crime, Library & Multimedia: www.ovc.gov/library/index.html

Office for Victims of Crime, U.S. Resource Map of Crime Victim Services & Information: www.ovc.gov/map.html

Victim Law Info: www.victimlaw.org/victimlaw/start.do

STUDENT STUDY SITE

Get the tools you need to sharpen your study skills. SAGE edge offers a robust online environment featuring an impressive array of free tools and resources.

Access practice quizzes, eFlashcards, video, and multimedia at **edge.sagepub.com/hemmens4e**

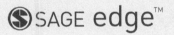

© Comstock/Stockbyte/Thinkstock Images

9

THE JURY

Master the content at **edge.sagepub.com/hemmens4e**

INTRODUCTION

Trial by jury has been an integral part of the American criminal justice system for well over 200 years. In serving to temper the power of the government to judge individuals to be in violation of the rules of society, the jury lets members of society itself determine if a person is worthy of condemnation. As explained by Supreme Court Justice Byron White in *Duncan v. Louisiana* (1968),

> A right to jury trial is granted to criminal defendants in order to prevent oppression by the Government. Those who wrote our constitutions knew from history and experience that it was necessary to protect against unfounded criminal charges brought to eliminate enemies and against judges too responsive to the voice of higher authority. The framers of the constitutions strove to create an independent judiciary but insisted upon further protection against arbitrary action. Providing an accused with the right to be tried by a jury of his peers gave him an inestimable safeguard against the corrupt or overzealous prosecutor and against the compliant, biased, or eccentric judge. If the defendant preferred the common-sense judgment of a jury to the more tutored but perhaps less sympathetic reaction of the single judge, he was to have it. Beyond this, the jury trial provisions in the Federal and State Constitutions reflect a fundamental decision about the exercise of official power—a reluctance to entrust plenary powers over the life and liberty of the citizen to one judge or to a group of judges. Fear of unchecked power, so typical of our State and Federal Governments in other respects, found expression in the criminal law in this insistence upon community participation in the determination of guilt or innocence. (p. 156)

Although it is generally agreed that juries serve an important function in the criminal justice system, over the past several decades, they have come into some disrepute. Verdicts of not guilty in the high-profile trials of O. J. Simpson, Lorena Bobbitt, Marion Barry, Robert Blake, and the Los Angeles police officers who were videotaped beating Rodney King have raised outrage among members of the public and media. Critics complain that the system allows wealthy individuals with unlimited funds to hire top criminal defense attorneys to trick and manipulate the unfortunate 12 who weren't able to get out of jury duty into gaining acquittals. At the same time, it is argued that many criminal defendants, who are poorly educated, non-White individuals living at or below the poverty line and being represented by an overworked public defender, have little hope of gaining an acquittal from a jury made up of people from the "other side of the tracks."

In this chapter, we consider various aspects and some of the complexity surrounding the criminal trial jury. After exploring the historical roots of trial by jury and the role it played in the founding of the United States, we examine some of the nuts and bolts of serving on a jury. This includes the manner in which average citizens become jurors, the responsibilities and duties faced by jurors in criminal trials, and modern reforms to the jury system designed to make jurors more effective. In addition, we consider the role the jury plays in the criminal justice system and where the act of jury nullification fits in fulfilling this function.

HISTORY OF JURY TRIALS

Employing juries to decide the guilt or innocence of their fellow citizens is not an American invention. In fact, juries were used hundreds of years before America was even discovered. Whereas the use of average citizens to decide the fate of individuals charged with criminal offenses goes back more than 2,000 years to ancient Athens and Rome, the foundation of the modern jury has its origin in England. During the Middle Ages, the guilt or innocence of a person charged with a crime was determined through **trial by ordeal** (Bartlett, 1986). Under this process, the defendant would be required to perform a perilous task, such as walking across burning coals or removing a rock from boiling water. If the defendant performed these tasks and emerged without being harmed, he was judged innocent, for surely God had intervened and provided protection. If the defendant were injured during the trial, he was adjudged guilty.

Over time, the trial by ordeal gave way to trial by a jury of citizens. In 1215, under pressure from a group of noblemen, King John signed the Magna Carta, which provided that "no freeman shall be taken, or imprisoned, or disseized, or outlawed, or exiled, or in any way harmed—nor will we go upon or send upon him—save by the lawful judgment of his peers or by the law of the land." Initially, this right applied only to nobility, but over time, it was construed to apply to all men equally.

The role of the jury as an independent decider of guilt was cemented in 1670. At this time, two young Quaker activists, William Penn and William Mead, were accused of unlawful assembly for preaching Quaker beliefs that were contrary to the views espoused by the Church of England. At their trial—which was highly publicized and closely watched by the public, the government, and the monarchy—despite urging from the judge, the jury returned verdicts of not guilty. At that time, jurors could be and routinely were fined and imprisoned if it was determined that they returned an "erroneous" verdict. Believing the jurors were wrong in refusing to convict Penn and Mead, the trial judge ordered the jurors fined and imprisoned until they paid off their fines.

Although the jurors were eventually released, one juror, Edward Bushell, filed a lawsuit over his being imprisoned. The Court of Common Pleas ruled that jurors cannot be punished for their decisions. The court's ruling stated that jurors must be free from coercion to decide a case independent from any intimidation or pressure from the government or the court. The jury was thusly guaranteed the power and freedom to acquit individuals wrongly prosecuted by the government.

The English jury system was established in colonial America long before the signing of the U.S. Constitution. The basic structure of the colonial jury system was similar to the English system, but as time passed by and colonists viewed themselves increasingly as Americans rather than Englishmen, the American jury became more American. By the 18th century, the right to trial by jury and the protection it provided from the strong arm of the government became a factor in the colonists' declaring independence from England.

The divergence between the two jury systems began to take root in 1735 with the trial of John Peter Zenger. Zenger was the publisher of a small newspaper in New York that was critical of the king's appointed governor. After repeated warnings, Zenger was arrested and charged with the crime of seditious libel. Under English law, the prosecution needed only to present evidence establishing the fact that Zenger published the newspaper that contained criticisms, a fact that was not in dispute. At trial, Zenger's attorney argued to the jury that Zenger was no different from each of them and, like all citizens, should have the right to criticize the government without fear of punishment. As such, he argued, regardless of English law, the jury should find Zenger not guilty. The jury, despite being instructed by the judge that the only issue for them to decide was whether or not Zenger published the newspaper, returned a not guilty verdict in only 5 minutes.

Following the trial of John Peter Zenger, juries in the colonies increasingly refused to convict individuals charged with political crimes. In response, the English Parliament took steps to assert control of the court and jury system, ultimately implementing a law that required jurors be selected from names provided by the English government. This assault of the colonists' perception of justice and wresting away control of the jury system was a significant factor in the move toward independence.

By the time America gained its independence from England, the founding fathers had general distrust regarding a government's power over individuals. In their eyes, the jury was an essential safeguard against the power of the state. This attitude was illustrated by Thomas Jefferson (1789), who went so far as to write, "I consider trial by jury as the only anchor yet imagined by man, by which a government can be held to the principles of its constitution" (p. 269). Considering this was a common belief at the time the United States was founded, it is not surprising that the Constitution and the Bill of Rights made explicit mention and protection of the right to a trial by jury.

Specifically, Article III, Section 2 of the Constitution states that "the Trials of all crimes, except in cases of Impeachment, shall be by Jury; and such Trial shall be held in the State where the said Crimes shall have been committed." The particular requirements attendant to trial by jury in criminal matters were expounded on in the Sixth Amendment to the Constitution.

The Sixth Amendment guarantees that a person accused of a crime shall have the right to a trial "by an impartial jury of the State and district wherein the crime shall have been committed." Several items with the text of the amendment are interesting to note. First, recall that a concern raised by the founding fathers' experiences with the jury system under English rule was the use of individuals handpicked by the English Crown to make up jury pools in the colonies. In response to this, the Sixth Amendment required that a jury be impartial and not stacked by the government. Second, because of general distrust of central government, individuals were guaranteed the right to be tried in the state where the crime occurred. This assurance was seen as an important protection against the government uprooting an individual charged with a crime and having him tried in a distant part of the country by jurors from different backgrounds.

Even though the Constitution and Sixth Amendment clearly guarantee the right to trial by jury in all prosecutions, a number of matters associated with juries were not spelled out at the founding of the nation. Items such as exactly what crimes involve the right to a jury trial, the jury's permissible and required roles and actions during a criminal trial, and the composition of the jury, both in terms of size and the demographic background of jurors, were left to courts and legislatures to consider.

THE ROLE OF THE JURY

The jury's role in a criminal trial is both simple and complex, logical and illogical. Under the law, the jury's role in the process is that of fact finder. Individual jurors are to consider the evidence and testimony presented to them, much of which will be conflicting, and determine what the true facts are. This involves deciding which witnesses to believe and what evidence to trust as being reliable. While the individual jurors come to personal conclusions, it is during the give-and-take of deliberations that the jury reaches the ultimate determination of what really happened in the incidents giving rise to the criminal prosecution.

The jury has virtually unlimited discretion in how it interprets the evidence and establishes the facts of a case. If members of the jury believe a witness is lying, they can discount or reject all her testimony. If they don't accept the reliability of a scientific test, they can reject its results.

There are, however, some restrictions on what a jury can do in its role as fact finder. The jury is permitted to consider only facts presented in court as evidence. Jurors are not permitted to conduct their own investigations, look up information about the case in newspapers, or read scientific journals or other scholarly materials to weigh the validity of forensic evidence. In addition, jurors are to consider only evidence properly admitted in the case. If items were raised at trial but excluded by the judge, jurors are instructed to "disregard" that evidence. In reality, it is difficult for jurors to disregard what they actually hear in court. Such a process is commonly referred to as trying to unring a bell. That said, such items are not to be considered by a jury in its deliberations, and it is expected that the group dynamic of the deliberation process will keep individuals from considering items that are deemed inappropriate.

The most important restriction on what the jury can consider in establishing the facts of a case is prohibition of their considering a defendant's failure to testify at trial. Because the Fifth Amendment gives a defendant the right to refrain from testifying, it would be wrong for a jury to infer anything from the exercise of this right. Judges normally (although not always) instruct juries not to consider the defendant's refusal to testify, and defense attorneys will emphasize this restriction and possible reasons for their client's silence in their closing arguments.

Finally, the jury is not permitted to consider possible punishments. Because the jury is to determine the facts of the case based solely on the evidence presented, and the consequences of their verdict are clearly outside this factual determination, juries are expressly instructed not to consider what will happen to the defendant should they vote to convict. Such considerations have no impact on what happened in the past and are therefore irrelevant to a dispassionate evaluation of the evidence.

Once a jury has established the facts of a case, the jury's job is to apply the facts to law. The law is provided to the jury in the form of jury instructions. Jury instructions are read to the jury by the judge at the close of the trial. There are two central components of jury instructions. One section of these instructions is general in nature and applies to most criminal trials. These instructions may include items related to the burden of proof, the need for guilt to be proven beyond a reasonable doubt, the presumption of innocence, and the defendant's right not to testify along with the jury's obligation not to consider this fact. The second component of the jury instructions involves the specific elements of the crimes and affirmative defenses that are at issue in the trial.

Jury instructions can be dozens of pages in length and very complex. Over the past 20 years, extensive efforts have been made to require that jury instructions be written in "plain English," language easily understood by nonattorneys (American Bar Association, 2005). Research has shown that the movement toward using jury instructions with less legalese has a significant impact on the ability of the jury to fulfill its role in the system (Lieberman & Sales, 1997; Steele & Thornburg, 1988–1989).

LIMITS ON THE RIGHT TO TRIAL BY JURY

As has been discussed several times in this book, the rights guaranteed in the Bill of Rights are not directly applicable to states but only to the federal government. Unless the Supreme Court determines that a right is a fundamental right and applicable to the states via the Fourteenth Amendment, the specific liberty interest involved is not germane to state prosecutions. Unless the Supreme Court considered a right to be implicit in the concept of ordered liberty and basic to our system of jurisprudence, states would not be required to respect it.

For nearly 200 years, the Supreme Court did not consider whether the Sixth Amendment right to trial by jury in criminal matters was a fundamental right and therefore applicable to state prosecutions. That being said, throughout the nation's history, every state provided defendants charged with certain kinds of offenses with the right to a jury trial through their state constitutions. Specifically, the types of cases, however, varied from state to state. It was not until the late 1960s, at the height of the Warren Court's expansion of defendants' rights under the U.S. Constitution, that the Sixth Amendment right to trial by jury was made applicable to the states.

The case of *Duncan v. Louisiana* (1968) involved a prosecution for simple battery, a misdemeanor punishable by up to 2 years in prison. Under Louisiana law, only defendants charged with crimes with a potential punishment of death or imprisonment at hard labor were entitled to a jury trial. Duncan was convicted at a bench trial and sentenced to 60 days in jail. After losing his appeal to the Louisiana Supreme Court, he sought review at the U.S. Supreme Court on the grounds that his right to a trial by jury for a crime punishable by 2 years in prison was violated.

The Supreme Court agreed to hear the case and held that the right to trial by jury for serious offenses was a fundamental right and applicable to the states. For prosecutions involving petty crimes, however, the Court ruled that there was no right to a jury trial. The Court refused to define what a serious or petty offense is, holding only that the case before it, where the defendant faced up to 2 years in prison, involved a serious offense.

Two years later, the Court clarified when an offense is to be considered petty or serious. In *Baldwin v. New York* (1970), the Court ruled that "no offense can be considered petty for purposes of the right to trial by jury where incarceration for over six months is authorized."

The Supreme Court has held firmly to this standard in considering when a person has a right to a jury trial. For example, in 1996, the Court held that a person charged with several minor, **petty offenses** whose cumulative period of incarceration on conviction could be longer than 6 months is not entitled to a jury trial (*Lewis v. United States,*

1998). Similarly, the Court held in *Muniz v. Hoffman* (1975) that regardless of how large a monetary fine may be, if an offense involves a potential period of imprisonment of 6 months or less, it is considered petty.

JURY SIZE AND UNANIMITY REQUIREMENTS

Two aspects of the use of juries in criminal trials not addressed in the Constitution are how many jurors are needed to conduct a fair trial and whether all the jurors must agree on a verdict before a person can be convicted or acquitted. Before we examine the constitutional requirements regarding these items, it is important to understand why they are important.

The importance of size and unanimity requirements hinges on the role of the jury in the criminal justice system. Because the jury serves as the conscience of the community and speaks for society in considering a defendant's fate, it is important that efforts be made to ensure that the jury represents the community for which it is speaking. The arguments in favor of requiring unanimous verdicts focus on these questions: If all members of the jury who represent various aspects of the community are not persuaded by the facts presented at trial to reach a certain verdict, is it appropriate to ignore the minority opinion and allow a nonunanimous verdict? Would accepting nonunanimous verdicts encourage the majority of jurors to ignore or discount the input of the minority? Is there a minimum number of jurors needed to foster meaningful group deliberations? Would such a system truly have the jury represent the community as a whole? On the other hand, jury trials are expensive. Requiring unanimity as opposed to a substantial majority verdict (10–2) does not necessarily improve the accuracy of jury verdicts and costs the taxpayers significant expense in necessary retrials.

Relatedly, the number of jurors needed for jury trial also involves a balance of expense versus fulfilling the ideal of trial by jury. Because juries deliberate as a group, a process that involves significant give-and-take, it is argued that juries with more members will have more constructive deliberations. In addition, larger juries are likely to have broader demographic representation and therefore be more representative of the community they represent. On the other hand, unnecessarily large juries are an added expense to an already burdened system. Requiring larger juries also entails an increased number of citizens to be called in for jury duty and increased costs in assembling and administering juries.

These factors have been key considerations in the size and unanimity requirements established by the U.S. Supreme Court, state supreme courts, and state legislatures.

Jury Size

Since the 14th century, juries in England have been made up of 12 jurors. The use of 12 jurors in the American colonies was generally accepted as the correct size to fairly sit in judgment at a criminal trial and was the accepted standard at the time the nation was founded. More than 200 years later, juries made up of 12 people are still the norm.

Although Rule 23(b) of the Federal Rules of Criminal Procedure, which states that juries must consist of 12 persons, governs federal prosecutions, the use of 12 jurors is not constitutionally mandated. In *Williams v. Florida* (1970), the Supreme Court ruled that juries do not have to be made up of 12 people to be constitutional. In considering the matter, the Court found that the tradition of juries having 12 members was a "historical accident, wholly without significance except to mystics." Rather, the minimum number of jurors required under the Constitution should be determined by examining the function of the jury in the American system of justice, to ensure that the judgment of the community stands between the state and the defendant. This requires that the number of jurors be "large enough to promote group deliberation, free from outside attempts at intimidation, and to provide a fair possibility of obtaining a representative cross section of the community." The Court concluded that six-person juries did not prevent the fulfillment of this function and were therefore constitutional.

As you might have guessed, once the Court ruled that six-person juries were allowed, the Court would be asked to consider whether even smaller juries were constitutional. In *Ballew v. Georgia* (1978), the Court unanimously held that six was the fewest number of jurors permissible. The Court based this holding on research that smaller juries have less collective recall of trial testimony, are less likely to "foster effective group deliberation," and are less likely to be representative of the community or include racial or ethnic minorities. While acknowledging that there is no clear distinction between five- and six-person juries, the Court held that juries with fewer than six members were unconstitutional.

Despite the Court ruling that juries of fewer than 12 people are constitutional, not all states have opted to use smaller juries. Only six states use juries with fewer than 12 members for trials involving a felony, while 35 states use 6- or 8-person juries to hear misdemeanors.

Unanimous Verdicts

As with the use of 12-person juries, the requirement that a jury reach a unanimous verdict was also firmly established in England and the United States. Having all jurors agree on a verdict serves to legitimize the decision, thereby providing society a sense that the verdict must be correct. Despite the general sense that unanimous verdicts are a necessary component of the jury system, by the 20th century, several states permitted the use of nonunanimous verdicts in criminal prosecutions.

In 1972, the Supreme Court decided two cases that held that there was no constitutional requirement that jury verdicts in criminal trials be unanimous. In *Apodaca v. Oregon* (1972), the Court held that Oregon's law permitting 10–2 verdicts in noncapital cases did not diminish the function of the jury as it articulated in *Williams* 2 years before. Similarly, in *Johnson v. Louisiana* (1972), the Court held that Louisiana's statute permitting 9–3 verdicts in noncapital cases did not diminish the validity or reliability of the decision. Interestingly, since *Johnson* and *Apodaca* were decided, no other states have abandoned the requirement for unanimity. Moreover, the Court has not been asked to consider the constitutionality of verdicts with less than a 75% majority, but in 1979, the Supreme Court held that when a six-person jury is used, the verdict must be unanimous (*Burch v. Louisiana,* 1979).

THE SELECTION OF JURORS

A critical component of any court system that uses juries to determine guilt is how individuals are selected to be jurors. The makeup of a jury has the potential to affect the outcome of an individual trial, and the representativeness of the people asked to participate in the jury system as jurors also has an impact on the perceived fairness and legitimacy of

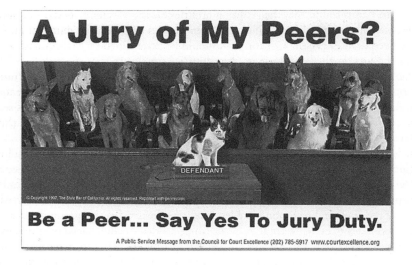

the process. In addition, as is discussed next, to satisfy the Sixth Amendment, courts and states must take steps to ensure that their jury selection system provides the defendant with a trial before an impartial jury.

Consider the unfortunate defendant depicted in the photo above. Undoubtedly, a cat would not feel comfortable being judged by a jury of 12 dogs. Although the trial of a cat is clearly fictional, it illustrates important concerns with who sits on juries, how they are selected, and what impact the makeup of juries has on the criminal justice system.

As you reflect on the cat's predicament, ask yourself, "Would a man being judged by a jury of 12 women feel as uneasy as our cat defendant? How about a member of a minority group being judged by an all-White jury? Going beyond how individual defendants feel about their jury, are such juries constitutional?" These questions are paramount in considering how jurors are selected.

The jury selection process is designed to achieve two goals. First, it must ensure that a fair cross section of the community is included as potential jurors. Second, it must permit the seating of individual jurors who are unbiased with regard to the case on which they serve. To achieve these goals, the jury selection process is performed in three stages.

Stage 1: Developing a Master Jury List

The first step in the jury selection process involves a jurisdiction establishing a **master list**, or "**jury wheel**," of all potential jurors within its jurisdictional boundaries who can be chosen at random to report for jury duty as needed. The master lists developed in the 21st century are very broad and inclusive in their scope, but this was not always the case.

Up until the 1960s, most courts used a "**key-man**" **system** to choose their jurors. Under this system, court clerks and jury commissioners would consult with civic and political leaders (the "key men") for input on who should be placed on the master list of potential jurors. Predictably, these "blue-ribbon" juries were not representative of the community and included a disproportionately high number of middle- and upper-class middle-aged White men. As Blacks began gaining civil rights, the makeup of juries in cases involving Black defendants came under increased scrutiny to determine whether defendants were being denied their Sixth Amendment right to an "impartial jury" and their Fourteenth Amendment right to "equal protection of the laws." As this scrutiny increased, the use of the key-man system began to wane.

A major step toward making jury lists more representative was taken with the enactment of the **Jury Selection and Service Act**. Under this legislation, all litigants in the federal courts entitled to trial by jury have the right to juries "selected at random from a fair cross section of the community in the district or division wherein the court convenes." Importantly, the act further provided that all citizens must have the opportunity to serve on juries. To achieve these goals, the law required that a master jury list be drawn in each jurisdiction from the list of registered or actual voters as well as from other representative sources.

Several years later, in *Taylor v. Louisiana* (1975), the Supreme Court declared that the Sixth Amendment required that juries be selected from an impartially drawn jury panel representing a cross section of the community. This mandate does not require that each jury actually be representative of the community. Rather, it requires that there be no government actions or practices that serve to systematically exclude a segment of the community. In *Taylor,* for example, the law in Louisiana provided that a woman could not be selected for jury service unless she submitted to the state a written declaration stating her desire to serve on a jury. The Supreme Court held that this process systematically excluded women, an obviously major segment of the community, from the jury pool and consequently violated the fair cross section of the community requirement.

Following the passage of the Jury Selection and Service Act and the decision in *Taylor,* most states abandoned use of the key-man system. While the Supreme Court has ruled that a key-man system may be constitutional if done in a fair manner, the use of master wheels developed pursuant to state requirements was seen as significantly fairer and is now nearly universal.

When initially established, jury wheels were developed primarily from voter registration lists. The lists were chosen largely because they are administratively convenient to determine the location of where citizens reside, thereby making organization and selection at the county or jurisdictional level easier. It was soon recognized, however, that voter registration lists tend to be unrepresentative of the community at large. Because individuals who are non-White, young, poor, and less educated tend to register to vote at much lower rates than the population as a whole, members of these groups would be left off the jury wheel at a disproportionate level. In an effort to make the jury wheel more representative, most states now use a combination of source lists, including driver's licenses, utility and telephone directories, and fishing and hunting licenses, to compile a master list.

Once the components of the various source lists are merged and placed into the jury wheel, when the clerk of court or jury commissioner determines the number of jurors that will be needed for a time period, names from the wheel are selected at random and sent a summons to report for jury duty at a specific time and place in the courthouse. Not all individuals who are selected off the jury wheel and sent a summons report to jury duty. In fact, in many places, a majority of those summoned do not report. Juror yields (i.e., the percentage of jurors summoned who report for jury duty) have been as low as 5% in Los Angeles; 20% in Washington, D.C.; 22% in Maricopa County, Arizona; and 26% in Baltimore, Maryland.

These shockingly low yield rates are due to several factors. The primary reason for the low yield rates involves the staleness of the master jury lists. The names and addresses of potential jurors are obtained from lists updated on a periodic basis. Depending on the source and how often the list is updated, a significant portion of individuals will no longer reside at the address indicated on the master list. Because jury summonses are generally not forwarded to a different address, these summonses get returned as undeliverable. In many places, one out of every four jury summonses sent out are returned to the court as undeliverable.

A second cause for low juror yields is the presence of statutory exemptions. Half of American states have laws stating that members of certain professions are exempt from serving as jurors. These professions generally involve public safety responsibilities or direct work with the criminal justice system. As can be seen in Table 9.1, others involve less obvious professions or even classes of personal responsibilities. Regardless of the merits of specific exemptions, the names of exempt persons are still kept on the jury wheel, and they are still likely to receive a jury summons. Although they are able to notify the court of their exempt status without having to physically report to jury duty, the fact that summons are still sent to them adds to the costs of the jury system and low juror yields.

CURRENT CONTROVERSY

As discussed in this chapter, a significant percentage of individuals summoned to report for jury duty fail to report as directed. The lack of jurors has caused the rescheduling of trials, increasing the costs of administering the jury system in courts across the nation. In an effort to decrease the number of no-shows, more and more judges are taking the drastic step of holding people who do not report for jury duty in contempt of court. Along with contempt citations, judges have issued arrest warrants, and, in rare instances, individuals who ignored repeated summonses and entreaties have been sentenced to jail.

These actions by courts have received mixed reviews. On one hand, crackdowns on those not reporting for jury duty have been associated with increased participation rates in the weeks and months following the actions. On the other hand, individuals, some of whom were exempt from jury duty or who did not receive a jury summons, have been shocked to be served with arrest warrants and fined up to $100 per day. An additional concern is the effect of having individuals who are "coerced" into appearing for jury duty actually sit on a jury. It is possible that these individuals will be bitter and unhappy about being on a jury and will take their anger out on one of the parties.

1. What steps do you think courts should take to improve response rates for jury summonses?

2. What are possible downsides to your suggestions?

3. Should people be able to pay money to the court to be excused from jury duty?

TABLE 9.1 ■ State Exemptions From Jury Service	
Exemption	Number of States With Exemption
Political officeholders	16
Law enforcement	12
Judicial officers	9
Health care professionals (including dentists and veterinarians)	7
Sole caregivers (child care, elder care, and special needs persons)	7
Attorneys	6
Active military	5
Other exemptions, including clergy, teachers, journalists, mariners, accountants, and individuals with specific religious designations	12

Beyond these two factors, low juror yields are related to the inconvenience of jury service. Whether it be the inability to miss work or school to attend, the unavailability of transportation or parking, the low amount of compensation paid, or anticipated unpleasantness, perceived hardships lower juror yields. Over the past several decades, states have taken steps to address these items. In a number of states, jury fees have been increased to $50 a day, with additional payment (up to $300 per day) for trials that last longer than 1 week. Jurors are now typically provided reimbursement for transportation costs associated with jury duty and are provided with free parking. Many courts have implemented on-site child care programs or provide vouchers to help pay for child care if needed.

Last, a number of courts have implemented systems in which jury service lasts only one day or one trial, eliminating lengthy terms of jury service that have caused problems in the past. These measures have a positive effect on juror yields and have been part of an overall movement to reform the jury system, which is discussed later in this chapter.

Stage 2: From Venire to Jury Panel

The group of individuals who report for jury duty at a given time is known as the venire, or jury pool. In midsize and large jurisdictions, it is typical for more than one jury trial to be scheduled to begin on the same day or in the same week. To fill this need, dozens and even hundreds of summoned jurors may be asked to report to the courthouse at the same time. On reporting, members of the venire are likely to be asked to fill out a questionnaire and administrative paperwork and to receive information about matters such as parking, scheduling, and the payment of fees for jury service. In addition, they are given an orientation about the jury system, their role as jurors, and what they should expect.

Following these preliminary matters, members of the venire wait in the jury assembly room until the jury commissioner's staff is given notice that a court is ready to select a jury. At this point, a set number of members of the venire are selected at random to report to the given courtroom. This group of individuals is referred to as the jury panel. The size of a jury panel will vary depending on the number of jurors needed and the nature of the

CURRENT CONTROVERSY
THE USE OF ANONYMOUS JURIES

The Sixth Amendment provides, "In all criminal prosecutions, the accused shall enjoy the right to a speedy and public trial, by an impartial jury of the State and district wherein the crime shall have been committed." A key component of this process is jury selection and the use of voir dire. In selecting a jury, attorneys are allowed to consider information provided by potential jurors in making challenges for cause based on bias, and peremptory challenges based largely on gut feelings. Information used in jury selection is generally obtained from questionnaires that have jurors provide their name and other biographical information, and answers provided by jurors to questions posed during voir dire. Charged with overseeing this process, trial court judges are granted extensive discretion in deciding what information will be asked for, collected, and released to the attorneys and public. In exercising this discretion, judges can limit the information jurors must provide, and, on rare occasions, keep all biographical information confidential. By doing this, judges create what is referred to as an "anonymous jury."

The first use of an anonymous jury was in the 1977 prosecution of Leroy Barnes and his associates. Barnes was the boss of the largest heroin distribution network in New York. In 1977 he was tried with 14 codefendants on myriad charges, including narcotics distribution, conspiracy, engaging in a criminal enterprise, and firearms violations. Prior to trial one witness was murdered and another was threatened. Fearful that the jurors might be threatened, the trial court judge ordered the names, addresses, and ethnicity be withheld from public disclosure. Barnes and 10 codefendants were convicted. On appeal, the Second Circuit affirmed the convictions, holding that limits on biographical information about jurors is not prohibited by the Constitution of federal law. The court discussed the potential dangers involved in organized crime investigations, possibility of jury tampering, media harassment of jurors, and the discretion a trial judge possesses in conducting a trial. It concluded that juror anonymity "comported with [the Court's] obligation to protect the jury, to assure its privacy, and to avoid all possible mental blocks against impartiality."

Since 1979 the use of anonymous juries has expanded and is now used in all federal circuits and approximately half of the states. Although infrequent, the use of anonymous juries based on concerns for juror safety, juror privacy and freedom from harassment by the media, and protection from potential juror tampering has been approved by state and federal courts. When they are used, it must be for a specific reason.

Although specific standards vary by jurisdiction, courts have generally held that an anonymous jury may be used if two conditions are met. First, the court must find that there is a need to protect the jury from threats, harassment, or actual danger. If this is found, the court must take reasonable precautions to ensure that the defendant's rights are protected.

At first, the use of anonymous juries was limited to organized crime prosecutions. In recent years it has been expanded to cases involving high-profile defendants (O. J. Simpson, Bill Cosby, and Illinois Governor Rob Blagojevich), as well as notorious, widely publicized crimes (Casey Anthony, the Los Angeles police officers charged with beating Rodney King, the World Trade Center bombers, and George Zimmerman). Note that the reason for use of anonymous juries has expanded well beyond juror safety and now focuses largely on protecting jurors from media harassment.

The use of anonymous juries has been controversial. Opponents of their use argue that anonymous juries eliminate juror and jury accountability to the community, impose a prejudicial effect on the defendant, create an assumption that the defendant is a danger to the community, and limit public access to the trial. It is also argued that anonymous juries restrict the ability to conduct meaningful voir dire that limits a defendant's ability to select an impartial jury. Even though these arguments have been successful in a limited number of cases, generally when the use of an anonymous jury is requested, it occurs.

1. What do you think about the use of anonymous juries?

2. Do they infringe on a defendant's rights to a fair trial? In what way? Should their use be encouraged or discouraged? When is it appropriate?

3. Can you think of any upcoming trials where the use of an anonymous jury should be considered?

case. Generally it ranges from 20 people for cases using 6-person juries to 40 people when a 12-person jury is to be selected.

Stage 3: Voir Dire

Once prospective jurors report to a courtroom, they participate in what is known as voir dire ("to see to speak"). The voir dire involves prospective jurors being questioned under oath by the attorneys and the judge to help determine their appropriateness to sit as a juror for a specific trial. The "official goal" is to select jurors who can consider the case in a fair, impartial, and unbiased manner. Although this is true to a degree, in reality attorneys want jurors who are predisposed to rule in their favor.

At the beginning of voir dire, the judge is likely to introduce the jury to the attorneys and the defendant. The judge will also read the names of people who are expected to testify at the trial. Jurors who know any of these individuals are asked to make this fact known and are typically removed from the jury panel. Next, the judge will explain the nature of the offense and acts involved in the case as well as ask if there is anything about these items that might make it difficult to consider the evidence and render a verdict fairly and impartially. For example, a person who is a member of Mothers Against Drunk Driving may find it difficult to be impartial in a prosecution for driving while intoxicated. Jurors who acknowledge being unable to consider the evidence and law presented to them impartially are likely to be removed from the jury panel, in what is known as a challenge for cause, which we discuss later.

Following these preliminary items, jurors are asked to provide more personal information, such as their occupation, marital status, the part of a town or city in which they reside, and any experiences they may have had with the criminal justice system. They will be asked a wide range of questions designed to identify predispositions, ideological leanings, or hidden perspectives of the case or criminal justice system. Potential jurors are frequently asked for their opinion on such items as a defendant being presumed innocent, the state's burden to prove guilt beyond a reasonable doubt, whether they would trust the testimony of a police officer more than other witnesses, and whether they would hold against a defendant if he did not testify. These types of questions are asked not only to ensure that a juror is willing to follow the law but also to provide the attorneys and judge to observe the jurors' demeanor, body language, and other items that may indicate attitudes and predispositions. Depending on what answers are given, follow-up questions may be asked to obtain more detailed information.

The questioning during voir dire can be conducted by the attorneys, the judge, or both. Voir dire conducted by attorneys is generally considered more effective and productive that when the questioning is done solely by the judge. That being said, allowing attorneys to question the jury panel can be very time-consuming and routinely leads to both sides doing what they can to influence potential jurors. As a result, judges frequently conduct voir dire by themselves. As an alternative to having attorneys do the questioning, judges permit the attorneys to submit questions they would like the judge to ask. Judges have a great a deal of discretion in how voir dire is conducted and are generally free to ask all or none of the requested questions.

Challenges for Cause and Peremptory Challenges

As noted earlier, attorneys use voir dire to identify jurors who have a bias that prevents them from being fair and impartial, as well as to identify people who are believed to be predisposed to their client's position in a case. Based on the information obtained during the voir dire, there are two means by which potential jurors can be removed from the jury panel. If an attorney believes a potential juror is biased and cannot be fair and impartial, the attorney may make a challenge for cause. In making such a challenge, the attorney needs to provide the judge with a legal reason as to why the potential juror is unfit to serve on the jury. A judge will uphold a challenge for cause if she is convinced that the juror is biased and will not be fair or impartial. This may involve items such as being a victim, having a family member who was the victim of the type of crime involved in the trial, being strongly opposed to the law that is the basis for the criminal charge, having a close family member in law enforcement, being a member of an organization whose purpose involves advocating for issues related to the crimes under consideration (e.g., Mothers Against Drunk Drivers or the National Organization for the Reform of Marijuana Laws), or an explicitly stated racial, gender, or other form of bias.

The prosecution and defense are not limited in the number of challenges for cause they are allowed to make. Because voir dire is used to identify jurors who cannot be fair and impartial, it is only logical that there should be no limit on the number of potential jurors who may be removed for cause. That being said, challenges for cause are routinely denied by the trial judge. Because potential jurors will rarely make an explicit statement about being biased, if the judge does not think there is sufficient evidence of bias present, the challenge will be denied. That does not necessarily mean the person will be seated on the jury.

After challenges for cause have been resolved and voir dire has been completed, the attorneys are given the opportunity to have a certain number of potential jurors removed from the panel without having to state a reason. This act is known as a peremptory challenge. Peremptory challenges give each side the opportunity to remove a limited number of potential jurors whom the attorney believes will have a negative view toward his client or positive predisposition toward the other party. They are often used to remove a

KEY CASES

IMPEACHING A JURY'S VERDICT

Miguel Peña-Rodriguez was charged with and convicted of harassment and unlawful sexual contact with two teenage girls. Following the trial two jurors told Peña-Rodriguez's lawyers that during deliberations a third juror had made racially biased remarks about Peña-Rodriguez and his main witness, both of whom are Latino. Based on this information, Peña-Rodriguez moved for a new trial. The trial court denied the motion on the ground that Rule 606(b) of the Colorado Rules of Evidence ("No Impeachment Rule"), which is used by the federal courts and a majority of state courts, generally prohibits a juror from testifying as to statements made during deliberations in a proceeding inquiring into the validity of the verdict. The Colorado Court of Appeals and Colorado Supreme Court affirmed based on the premise that racially biased remarks made during deliberations fell within the No Impeachment Rule.

The U.S. Supreme Court granted certiorari and reversed *Peña-Rodriguez v. Colorado* (2017). Justice Kennedy wrote the majority opinion (5–3). He noted that the No Impeachment Rule promoted candor in jury deliberations by generally prohibiting evidence of the content of deliberations from court proceedings. That being said,

the Court provided that the rule is not absolute and may be subject to carefully delineated exceptions. The Court held that one such exception is when a juror's verdict is based on racial bias. The Court explained that for the No Impeachment Rule to be circumvented a defendant must show "that one or more jurors made statements exhibiting overt racial bias that cast serious doubt on the fairness and impartiality of the jury's deliberations and resulting verdict. To qualify, the statement must tend to show that racial animus was a significant motivating factor in the juror's vote to convict."

The Court remanded the matter to the trial court for consideration of whether this threshold had been met, and if so, to apply the standard laid out by the Court.

1. How could one show that "racial animus was a significant motivating factor in the juror's vote to convict"?

2. The Court held that evidence of racial bias may overcome the No Impeachment Rule. Why? Can you think of other areas of bias where it would be appropriate to circumvent the No Impeachment Rule?

potential juror who has a perceived bias but whose predisposition cannot be shown with sufficient certainty to warrant a challenge for cause. By allowing each side to remove a set number of jurors, peremptory challenges allow for a fairer, more balanced jury.

Peremptory challenges are frequently based on an attorney's hunches, experience, and intuition based on information learned during the voir dire. This may be based on pure intuition or on the juror's background, education level, or life experiences made known during voir dire. For example, a defendant may not want a person whose father was a police officer to serve on the jury out of fear that the juror will be predisposed to believe the testimony of law enforcement officers. Conversely, the prosecution may not want a person who works as a social worker who assists individuals and families on a daily basis for fear that sympathy for people such as the defendant will have an impact on that potential juror's decision making.

The number of peremptory challenges allowed is generally regulated by state statute. Typically, the prosecution and defense in noncapital cases are provided with four to six challenges. Frequently, however, this number is altered through an agreement between the parties and the judge. Additionally, in trials with multiple defendants, each of whom receives a set number of peremptory challenges (which, in the aggregate, is at least double the number given the prosecution), the prosecutor is given additional challenges to make up for this discrepancy.

Attorneys are given wide discretion in deciding how to use the peremptory challenges, but this discretion is not limitless. In 1986, the Supreme Court, in the case of *Batson v. Kentucky,* held that a prosecutor's use of peremptory challenges based on race violated the Equal Protection Clause of the Fourteenth Amendment. In *Batson,* the prosecution used its peremptory challenges to remove all four Black members of the jury panel. Batson's attorney objected, arguing that the deliberate removal of all members of the defendant's race violated his rights to a jury selected from a fair cross section of the community as well as equal protection under the law. The judge denied the motion, stating that the parties were entitled to use their peremptory challenges as they saw fit. Batson was subsequently convicted by an all-White jury.

The Supreme Court held that although a defendant does not have a right to a jury composed of any particular racial makeup, the Fourteenth Amendment does prohibit the prosecution from excluding potential jurors solely on the basis of their race. If it is alleged that the prosecution systematically used peremptory challenges to remove potential members of the jury based on their race, the prosecution must be able to present a race-neutral basis for the challenge. If the judge is satisfied that the challenge was made for a reason not related to the juror's race, the challenge will be permitted. If the reason is not accepted, the removed juror will be placed back on the jury. In practice, objections based on *Batson* are rarely sustained. Regardless of appearances, race is rarely the sole basis to want a person off of a jury, and as long as a race-neutral reason is articulated, the *Batson* objection will be denied.

Since 1986, the *Batson* rule has been expanded significantly. In 1992, the Supreme Court held that the rule applies to the prosecution as well as the defense (*Georgia v. McCollum,* 1992). The Court has also found that in addition to race, the use of peremptory challenges to remove potential jurors based on the gender of a juror is also unconstitutional (*J. E. B. v. Alabama,* 1994).

REFORMS TO THE JURY SYSTEM

Over the past quarter century, several aspects of the jury system have been of concern to various groups of citizens, policy makers, and scholars. Seemingly irrational verdicts in high-profile trials have given rise to concern over the competence of jurors. Shockingly low juror yield and participation rates in many cities have raised concerns about the continued viability of the jury system.

Since the early 1990s, efforts have been under way in a number of states to reform a number of aspects of the jury system. In this period, 38 states have created statewide commissions to consider ways of improving the jury system. These commissions have made various recommendations to state policy makers, resulting in myriad reforms. The reforms can be placed into two general categories: jury management and trial practices. Several of the jury management reforms have been discussed previously in this chapter.

A central theme among the trial practices reforms has been to make changes that enhance the ability of jurors to accurately consider the evidence presented to them and apply it to the law. The following are reforms being used by a number of courts around the nation in criminal trials.

Allowing Jurors to Take Notes

A major jury reform over the past 20 years has been permitting jurors to take notes during trial. It may seem logical to you that jurors should be permitted to take notes during a trial for use during later deliberations, but historically, under the common law, jurors were prohibited from taking notes during trial. The reason for this was twofold. First, as a practical matter, before the 20th century, most jurors were illiterate and therefore unable to take notes. This led to a legitimate concern that those jurors who could and did take notes would dominate the jury's deliberations.

Although concerns still exist that jurors who have detailed notes from the trial will dominate deliberations, with near universal literacy, today it is assumed that all jurors have the ability to take notes. Not surprisingly, most courts allow jurors to take notes during criminal trials.

The drive toward this reform is based on research that has shown that there are a number of benefits to allowing jurors to take notes (Horowitz & Forster Lee, 2003; Rosenhan, Eisner, & Robinson, 1994). These benefits include increased active participation of jurors during testimony and deliberations, increased levels of alertness and focus during the trial, and increased confidence in the factual accuracy of the jury's verdict.

Allowing Jurors to Question Witnesses

One of the most controversial jury reforms involves allowing jurors to submit questions to be asked to witnesses. The basis for allowing jurors to question witnesses is the fact that as the ultimate fact finders, it would seem logical that they should be allowed to ask witnesses what they consider to be important. Moreover, it encourages active listening and engagement.

Allowing jurors to question witnesses is not without potential problems and must be facilitated carefully. Just as with traditional testimony, questions posed by jurors should only be asked if they are relevant and likely to elicit admissible testimony. Frequently, questions jurors seek to ask are deliberately omitted from an attorney's questioning because they are likely to lead to answers that will not be admissible into evidence.

Because of this problem, it is important that juror questions be submitted to the judge in writing rather than simply posed by a juror directly to a witness. The judge can then consult with the attorneys and decide if the question should be posed to the witness. If it is appropriate, the judge should ask the question. If not, the judge should explain to the jury why the court decided not to ask the question. This process can be time-consuming and has the potential to bog down a trial. This fact must be weighed against the potential benefits of permitting jurors to ask questions of witnesses.

Providing Written Copies of Instructions for Each Juror

Since the 1990s, a number of courts have begun providing each juror with an individual copy of the jury instructions to read along when the court presents them orally and to use during deliberations. Because most people comprehend oral instructions better when they are able to read along, providing each juror with written instructions is likely to improve the quality of deliberations. Furthermore, letting each juror have a copy of the jury instructions during deliberations allows each juror equal access to them, thereby improving the deliberative process.

Providing Jurors With a Trial Notebook

In recent years, courts have begun providing jurors with individual trial notebooks. Trial notebooks contain items such as jury instructions, a list of witnesses with photographs, and copies of key documents and exhibits that have been admitted into evidence. Having these items in one place makes it easier for each juror to follow the trial, recall specific testimony, and conduct deliberations more effectively and efficiently.

The Use of Jury Reforms

In an effort to develop a picture of the status of jury reforms across the country, the National Center for State Courts, Center for Jury Studies conducted the *State-of-the-States Survey of Jury Improvement Effort* (National Center for State Courts, 2007). A central component of this research involved surveying nearly 12,000 judges and attorneys from across the country regarding practices related to jury reform efforts. Table 9.2 presents the outcome of this survey.

As is evident from the results, there are mixed levels of use of jury reforms. Two items stand out from these findings. First is the fact that 31.8% of respondents reported that jurors were not permitted to take notes during the trial. Second, in 31.6% of the cases, the jury was not given written copies of the jury instructions to use during its deliberations. Given the seeming unobtrusiveness of providing these conveniences to jurors, these findings are somewhat startling.

The implementation of jury reforms varies greatly across the country. Whereas some states, such as Arizona, Colorado, and Indiana, have been aggressive in implementing reforms, only a few jury reforms have been adopted by every state. The practices of permitting jurors to take notes, allowing jurors to ask questions, and providing each juror with written jury instructions are used to varying degrees in each state. Importantly, the results of the survey indicate that individual judges in each state may permit one item to be used during a trial but not others. Moreover, it is important to bear in mind that regardless of changes in state law, individual judges in local courts from across the nation have implemented a number of jury reforms.

TABLE 9.2 ■ Judges and Attorneys Reporting Jury Reform Practice Permitted During Trial	
Trial Practice	**Percentage**
Jurors allowed to take notes	69.2
Jurors given notebook	6.2
Jurors allowed to ask questions in criminal trial	13.8
Jury provided with at least one copy of jury instructions	69.4
All jurors given copy of written instructions	33.6

CURRENT RESEARCH

The "*CSI* effect" hypothesizes that jurors who watch television shows such as *CSI* will expect strong forensic evidence to be presented during the trial. If the forensic evidence is not present or is seen as weak, then jurors will not be convinced that the defendant committed the crime. To test if a *CSI* effect exists, Rebecca Hayes-Smith and Lora Levett conducted a study that examined the impact of watching crime-related television shows, such as *CSI*, on jurors' considerations of evidence and their verdicts.

The study used actual jurors who reported to a courthouse in a southern city for jury duty but were dismissed from jury selection. To measure their television watching behavior, the jurors were asked to report how many hours, in general, they watch television per day and per week and how many hours of crime-related television shows they watch per day and per week. The jurors were then presented with a trial vignette based on an actual case, which provided detailed information about the case. In order to determine how different levels of forensic evidence may shape the juror's opinions, the amount of forensic evidence described in the vignette was varied across three different levels: no forensic evidence, low forensic evidence, and high forensic evidence. However, the other details of the case remained constant throughout each vignette. After reading the trial vignette, the jurors were asked to give a verdict of guilty or not guilty, how confident they were with their verdict, and how confident they were that the defendant had committed the crime. The jurors were also asked to rate the strength of the evidence that was described in their vignette.

The authors found that the jurors' television watching behavior had a strong impact on their decisions concerning considerations of evidence and their verdicts. Jurors who reported watching crime dramas perceived the evidence in the cases differently from those jurors who did not watch crime dramas. Jurors who reported watching more hours of crime dramas rated themselves as less confident in their verdict when there was no forensic evidence compared to jurors who watched fewer hours of crime dramas, thus supporting the idea of the *CSI* effect. However, there was also some support for the theory that just watching more television in general is responsible for differences in jurors' perceptions of the evidence. For example, jurors who watched more hours of television in general were less likely to give a guilty verdict when there was little forensic evidence compared to those jurors who watched less television. It is possible that being exposed to more hours of television in general, not just crime dramas, results in the skewing of a person's overall perception of reality.

1. Can anything be done to limit the impact of the *CSI* effect?

2. How might the potential for the presence of the *CSI* effect be dealt with during jury selection?

Source: "Jury's Still Out: How Television and Crime Show Viewing Influences Jurors' Evaluations of Evidence." *Applied Psychology in Criminal Justice,* 7(1), 29–46 (2011). Rebecca M. Hayes-Smith, Lora M. Levett.

JURY NULLIFICATION

At the beginning of this chapter, we noted that the jury's role in the trial process is to apply the facts presented during the trial to the law as given by the judge. Although jurors are instructed to follow the law as given to them by the judge, at times jurors are faced with situations involving a particular case in which they believe strictly applying the law would bring about an injustice. In such circumstances, what can and should jurors do?

The answer to this question is not simple and involves an issue that dates back to the trial of John Peter Zenger. Recall the jury in Zenger's trial for seditious libel refused to return a guilty verdict despite indisputable evidence that Zenger violated the law as it was written. The jury did this because it felt Zenger had a right to publish a newspaper, and, as a jury, it would not hold him criminally responsible for doing so.

As Justice White wrote in *Duncan v. Louisiana,* the jury in a criminal trial serves as the conscience of the community. Rather than the government having the final say regarding whether a person has violated a criminal law, it is the jury, made up of typical citizens, that has the job of finding a defendant guilty of a criminal act. "If the defendant preferred the common-sense judgment of a jury to the more tutored but perhaps less sympathetic reaction of the single judge, he was to have it" (*Duncan v. Louisiana,* 1968). The use of ordinary people, who rather than strictly applying the law as provided may allow sympathy and common sense to enter into their deliberations and verdict, is a foundation of the jury system. It has also caused problems for the courts in the form of **jury nullification**.

Jury nullification occurs when a jury, based on its sense of justice and fairness, refuses to abide by the law and convict in a particular case even though the defendant is unquestionably guilty under the law. It occurs when a jury refuses "to apply a law in situations where strict application of the law would lead to an unjust or inequitable result" (Scheflin & Van Dyke, 1980, p. 54). What makes jury nullification so troubling for courts is the fact that the exercise of this authority is unreviewable due to the constitutional prohibition against "double jeopardy"—the retrying of an acquitted defendant for the same offense. It is important to note that jury nullification cannot be used to convict a person despite a lack of evidence. If there is insufficient evidence to sustain a conviction beyond a reasonable doubt and a jury returns a guilty verdict, the judge has a duty to override the verdict and enter a judgment of acquittal.

Although jury nullification is often viewed negatively, there are times when a jury's exercise of its nullification power is desirable. Examples include juries refusing to convict in cases involving Northerners violating fugitive slave laws by harboring runaway slaves in the 1800s, Vietnam War protesters who refused to register for the draft, and battered women who kill their batterer in a situation not falling under the doctrine of self-defense. The use of nullification by a jury is rare, but it does occur. The types of cases giving rise to jury nullification today are likely to involve the medical use of marijuana, mercy killings or euthanasia, and instances when the jury knows or senses that a defendant will face an unfairly long prison sentence if convicted because of "three strikes and you're out" laws and other offenses involving mandatory sentences.

Despite its occasional benevolent and appropriate use, jury nullification is viewed harshly by American courts. Jurors are told they must apply the law as contained in the jury instructions. In fact, if a juror or jury asks the judge about jury nullification and their right to go beyond the letter of the law in reaching a verdict, judges tell the jury that jury nullification is not allowed and that they must follow the law. Moreover, jurors who refuse to apply the law may be removed from the jury if this fact is uncovered prior to a verdict being reached (*United States v. Thomas,* 1997).

Although a legal argument can be made as to why jurors should be instructed about their right and power to partake in jury nullification, nearly all federal and state courts that have considered the issue have held that such an instruction is not required by the Constitution (Brody, 1995; Conrad, 1998). Whereas it is acknowledged that jury nullification is appropriate in rare instances, courts are loath to encourage it and are willing to accept its occurrence when juries come to such a result on their own. For an excellent depiction of jury nullification in action, the 1986 episode of the PBS series *Frontline* titled "Inside the Jury Room" is highly recommended. The report presents the deliberations of an actual jury in which jury nullification becomes a central issue.

SUMMARY

Since colonial times, the jury has played an important role in shaping how the American court system is viewed by society. The use of a jury, made up of average citizens, to determine the guilt of a person charged with committing a crime helps infuse the conscience and values of the community into how the criminal law is to be enforced. Regardless of the aims and actions of the government, if a body of average citizens refuses to find a defendant guilty, the government is powerless to impose a conviction and punishment.

The philosophical underpinning of the right to trial by jury has stayed the same for more than 200 years, but significant reform to the jury system has taken place, particularly over the past several decades. By implementing reforms designed to improve the ability of jurors to digest and consider testimony, physical evidence, and the law, states are striving to make serving on a jury less frustrating and more rewarding. Because jury trials are an essential part of the criminal justice system, the implementation of reforms to improve their functionality, effectiveness, and efficiency is critical and necessary.

Don't overlook the Student Study Site with its useful study aids, such as self-quizzes, eFlashcards, and other assists, to help you get more from the course and improve your grade.

DISCUSSION QUESTIONS

1. Should juries be given less discretion to interpret evidence and establish the facts of the case? How do you ensure that a juror doesn't get influenced by the media?

2. Should the right to a trial by jury be limited to only *serious offenses,* or should it be guaranteed regardless of the level of offense?

3. What are your thoughts on the way the Supreme Court has attempted to define what constitutes a *serious offense* versus a *petty crime*? Should there be a more concrete definition?

4. Should all verdicts be required to be unanimous or only a substantial majority? What are the advantages and disadvantages to both?

5. What are your thoughts on the "key-man" system for selecting juries versus current methods?

6. Should statutory exemptions for serving on a jury be declared illegal on a nationwide basis rather than letting each state choose whether to have this type of law?

7. Should jurors be allowed to take notes, or can this distract them from what's going on in the trial?

8. Should there be greater attention paid to the racial and gender makeup of a jury to ensure that it reflects every viewpoint of the community?

9. Should jurors be provided a copy of the jury instructions? What do you see as the advantages of giving these to them? Disadvantages?

10. Given the low level of juror yield rates, what else do you think should be done to improve the level of citizen participation?

11. If a jury serves as the conscience of the community, what can jurors do if they feel that applying the law would bring about injustice? Should they simply disregard the law and vote based on their own belief?

12. Is jury nullification always a bad thing? When might it be a correct outcome?

KEY TERMS

Jury nullification 232

Jury Selection and Service
   Act 221

"Key-man" system 220

Master list ("jury wheel")
   220

Petty offenses 217

Trial by ordeal 214

INTERNET SITES

Commission on the American Jury Project: www.americanbar.org/groups/judicial/american_jury.html

Fully Informed Jury Association: https://fija.org

Jury Blog: http://juryblog.blogspot.com

National Center for State Courts, Center for Jury Studies: www.ncsc-jurystudies.org

STUDENT STUDY SITE

Get the tools you need to sharpen your study skills. SAGE edge offers a robust online environment featuring an impressive array of free tools and resources.

Access practice quizzes, eFlashcards, video, and multimedia at **edge.sagepub.com/hemmens4e**

COURT PROCESSES

SECTION III

© Comstock/Stockbyte/Thinkstock Images

10

PRETRIAL PROCEDURES

INTRODUCTION

In this chapter, we provide an overview of the steps in the pretrial process. The process begins with the arrest of a suspect and ends with the criminal trial. There are a number of steps in this process, and each serves a different purpose. At many of these points in the process, the defendant has the opportunity to challenge the sufficiency of the evidence against him, but the prosecution is not required to demonstrate proof of the defendant's guilt beyond a reasonable doubt; that standard applies only at the trial. Typically, it is sufficient if the prosecution can provide evidence adequate to create "probable cause" that the defendant committed the crime for the court to continue the proceedings.

Although the prosecution's burden is not as heavy during the pretrial process as it is during trial, the defendant nonetheless has the opportunity to examine the case against him through a variety of procedures, generally known as discovery. During the pretrial period, the defendant may also seek to have evidence the prosecution wishes to use against him suppressed, or excluded from evidence, via the exclusionary rule.

Once the pretrial maneuvering is complete, the last task before the trial starts is the selection of the jury. This process varies from jurisdiction to jurisdiction, but in general, both the prosecutor and defense attorney participate in selecting which individuals will (and will not) be selected to serve on the jury.

ARREST

The criminal process begins either with the filing of a complaint or an arrest. A complaint may be filled out by a police officer, a prosecutor, or a private citizen. If an arrest is made first, a complaint will be sworn out afterward, usually by the arresting officer. The complaint serves as the charging document for the preliminary hearing.

The criminal process usually begins with an arrest. Virtually all arrests are made by a police officer, although a private citizen can, in limited circumstances, make a "citizen's arrest." For an arrest to be made, a police officer must have probable cause to believe a crime has been committed and that the person being arrested committed the crime or was in some way involved in the criminal activity. An arrest may be made by an officer either with or without an arrest warrant.

Search and arrest warrants are obtained by police officers, who first must fill out an **affidavit** stating the facts relied on to create what is called probable cause. There must be probable cause to arrest or search. Probable cause is a legal concept referring to the amount of proof a police officer must have to search or arrest someone.

BOOKING

Suspects who are arrested will be booked at the arresting officer's station. Booking consists of filling out paperwork that records who is arrested, the time of the alleged offense, the facts involved, and so on. Fingerprints will be taken, and so will photographs. Then the suspect may be placed in a holding cell and allowed to contact family and/or an attorney. Many suspects are promptly released, especially if the offense in question is minor and there is no concern that the suspect won't show up for court proceedings.

THE CHARGING DECISION

None of the discretionary decisions made by the prosecutor are more critical than the initial decision to prosecute or not, which has been characterized as "the gateway to justice" (Kerstetter, 1990). Prosecutors have wide discretion at this largely invisible stage in the process; there are no legislative or judicial guidelines on charging in most jurisdictions, and a decision not to file charges ordinarily is immune from review. As the Supreme Court noted in *Bordenkircher v. Hayes* (1978), "So long as the prosecutor has probable cause to believe that the accused committed an offense defined by statute, the decision whether or not to prosecute, and what charge to file or bring before a grand jury generally rests entirely in his discretion."

In most prosecutors' offices, there are no explicit criteria or concrete guidelines for prosecutors to use in deciding whether to charge or what charges to file. Although the American Bar Association (ABA) has promulgated "Standards on Charging" (American Bar Association, 1993), the standards are relatively broad. For example, the ABA's standards state that

> a prosecutor should not institute, or cause to be instituted . . . criminal charges when the prosecutor knows that the charges are not supported by probable cause [and that] the prosecutor should not bring or seek charges greater in number or degree than can reasonably be supported with evidence at trial or than are necessary to fairly reflect the gravity of the offense. (p. 23)

These provisions require prosecutors to dismiss the case if the evidence is not sufficient to support the charges and prohibit overcharging, but they provide little guidance regarding how the determination of probable cause or the decision regarding the number and type of charges is to be made.

There are a number of reasons why prosecutors might decide not to file charges against a suspect who has been arrested by the police. One reason might be that the prosecutor believes that the suspect is not guilty of the crime with which she is charged. The prosecutor is a representative of the government who is supposed to ensure that justice is done. If the evidence does not support the charges, the case against the suspect should not be pursued.

Another reason—in fact, a more likely reason—for charge dismissal is that the prosecutor believes that the suspect is guilty but doesn't believe that he can get a conviction in the case. Even though the prosecutor is supposed to see that justice is done, he is nonetheless concerned about the possibility of conviction. Because prosecutors are evaluated—by other members of the courtroom workgroup and by the public—on their record of securing convictions, they are sensitive to losing. Therefore, prosecutors evaluate the evidence and attempt to predict how the case will be viewed by the judge or jurors who will be asked to assess the suspect's guilt. If the prosecutor believes that the police investigation has not produced sufficient evidence to prove the case beyond a reasonable doubt or that the victim or other essential witnesses either will refuse to cooperate as the case moves forward or will not be viewed as credible by the judge or jury, the prosecutor may decide to dismiss the case rather than risk losing at trial.

Some researchers assert that prosecutorial charging decisions are not simply a product of individuals exercising discretion but rather reflect departmental policies that dictate—or at least influence—how cases will be evaluated. Joan Jacoby (1980), for example, argues that prosecutors' offices operate within one of four distinct types of prosecutorial policies: legal sufficiency, trial sufficiency, system efficiency, and defendant rehabilitation. Prosecutors operating under the **legal sufficiency policy** accept all cases in which the legal elements of the crime are present. Because prosecutors operating under this policy do not necessarily "screen out" cases where the evidence is weak, there is both a high proportion of cases that are accepted for prosecution and a large percentage of cases that are dismissed at preliminary hearings and trials.

Prosecutors operating under a **trial sufficiency policy**, on the other hand, evaluate cases in terms of their likelihood of conviction at trial; they file charges only if the odds of conviction at trial are good (see "Charging Policies and Practices in Sexual Assault Cases: A Focus on Los Angeles" for an example of this type of policy). Thus, this policy produces both a high rate of rejection at initial screening and a high prosecution rate for the cases that are not screened out.

The remaining two policies are less concerned with either legal sufficiency or convictability. The **system efficiency policy**, which emphasizes case screening as a way of decreasing office workload, is characterized by high levels of referrals to diversionary programs and by overcharging (for the purpose of enhancing the prosecutor's power in plea negotiations). By contrast, the **defendant rehabilitation policy** is based on the notion that most defendants—particularly first-time offenders accused of nonviolent crimes—should not be processed through the criminal justice system; the focus of this policy is on early diversion of defendants and the use of noncriminal justice alternatives. According to Jacoby (1980), then, the factors that motivate prosecutors to file or reject charges depend to some extent on formal and informal departmental policies.

Charging Policies and Practices in Sexual Assault Cases: A Focus on Los Angeles

A study of sexual assault case processing in Los Angeles (Spohn & Tellis, 2014) focused on police and prosecutorial decision making in these types of cases. Since 2001, the Los Angeles County District Attorney's Office has had a specialized sex crimes unit, the Victim Impact Program (VIP), which vertically prosecutes sexual assault. The standard used by the Los Angeles County District Attorney's Office in screening cases is a trial sufficiency standard (Jacoby, 1980). That is, the assistant district attorney will file charges only if there is sufficient evidence to prove the case beyond a reasonable doubt at a jury trial. Moreover, the policy in sexual assault cases is that charges will not be filed without some type of corroboration of the victim's testimony—DNA evidence that establishes the identity of the perpetrator, injuries to the victim, witnesses who can corroborate the victim's testimony, or physical or medical evidence that is consistent with the victim's account of the incident.

Although there are some exceptions, a prefiling interview designed to assess the victim's credibility and willingness to cooperate in the prosecution of the case also is required. According to Cassia Spohn and Katharine Tellis (2014), many of the respondents that they interviewed for this project emphasized that rejection is likely if the incident is a "she said/he said" situation, in which the victim is claiming that she was forced to engage in sexual relations but the suspect contends that the sexual acts were consensual and there is no corroboration of the victim's allegations. In fact, when asked whether there are any types of "she said/he said" cases that would be filed without corroboration of the victim's allegations, most admitted that there were not. As one assistant district attorney replied, "No. That would be a violation of office policy. There are cases where I would like to, but no."

The policies and practices in sexual assault cases prosecuted in Los Angeles conform to Jacoby's trial sufficiency standard.

Factors Affecting Prosecutors' Charging Decisions

Studies of the charging process demonstrate that prosecutors exercise their discretion and reject a significant percentage of cases at screening (Frazier & Haney, 1996; Spears & Spohn, 1997; Spohn, Beichner, & Davis-Frenzel, 2001; Spohn, Gruhl, & Welch, 1987; Spohn & Holleran, 2001). A classic study of the deterioration of felony arrests in New York City, for example, found that 43% of the cases were dismissed by the prosecutor (Vera Institute of Justice, 1977). A more recent study of charging decisions in sexual assault cases in three large urban jurisdictions found that the rejection rate was 50.6% in Philadelphia, 42.5% in Kansas City, and 41.4% in Miami (Spohn & Holleran, 2001). Most studies of the charging process also conclude that prosecutors attempt to "avoid uncertainty" (Albonetti, 1986, 1987) by filing charges in cases where the odds of conviction are good and by rejecting charges in cases where conviction is unlikely. The results of these studies reveal that prosecutors' assessments of convictability are based primarily, but not exclusively, on legally relevant factors such as the seriousness of the offense, the strength of evidence in the case, and the culpability of the defendant.

A second fairly consistent finding is that prosecutors' assessments of convictability, and thus their charging decisions, also reflect the influence of legally irrelevant characteristics of the suspect and victim. Some researchers suggest that prosecutors attempt to predict how the background, behavior, and motivation of the suspect and victim will be interpreted by other decision makers, especially jurors. Lisa Frohmann (1997), for example, contends that prosecutors' concerns about convictability create "a 'downstream orientation' in prosecutorial decision making—that is, an anticipation and consideration of how others (i.e., jury and defense) will interpret and respond to a case" (p. 544). Other studies conclude that the race of the suspect (Spohn et al., 1987; for a review, see Kutateladze, Lynn, & Liang, 2012) or the racial composition of the suspect/victim pair (Keil & Vito, 1989; LaFree, 1989; Paternoster, 1984; Radelet & Pierce, 1985; Sorensen & Wallace, 1996) affects the prosecutor's decision to charge, especially in sexual assault and homicide cases; charging is more likely if the defendant is non-White, and, especially, if the defendant is Black and the victim is White. Other research indicates that prosecutors are more likely to file charges against men (Spohn et al., 1987) and those who are unemployed (Schmidt & Steury, 1989).

Victim characteristics also play a role in the charging process. Elizabeth Stanko (1988), in fact, concludes that "the character and credibility of the victim is a key factor in determining prosecutorial strategies, one at least as important as 'objective' evidence about the crime or characteristics of the defendant" (p. 170). In assessing victim credibility, prosecutors rely on stereotypes about appropriate behavior (Frohmann, 1991); they attribute credibility to victims "who fit society's stereotypes of who is credible: older, White, male, employed victims" (Stanko, 1988, p. 172). The relationship between the victim and the suspect also affects case processing; several studies conclude that prosecutors are less likely to file charges if the victim knew the offender (Albonetti, 1987; Hepperle, 1985). These studies suggest that a prior relationship with the offender may cause the prosecutor to question the truthfulness of the victim's story and may lead the victim to refuse to cooperate as the case moves forward (Vera Institute of Justice, 1977).

A number of other extralegal factors besides suspect and victim characteristics could also help explain prosecutors' charging decisions. Such factors may include limited resources, a lack of motivation on the part of the prosecutors' office, and, with respect to domestic violence, "the questionable wisdom of state intervention in family affairs" (Schmidt & Steury, 1989, p. 488). In fact, some researchers have found that prosecutors will pursue some types of charges more aggressively when the case is brought to them by the police rather than by a crime victim or other concerned citizen (Ford & Burke, 1987). As one team of researchers put it, "Citizen-invoked complaints of domestic violence stand a slim chance of producing criminal charges because of their lower legal visibility and because, as critics claim, prosecutors view such cases as more appropriate for social service agencies" (Schmidt & Steury, 1989, p. 489).

The theoretical perspectives guiding research on prosecutorial decision making are not as well developed as those that guide research on judicial decision making. Researchers generally agree that prosecutors' charging decisions reflect, first and foremost, their assessments of the likelihood of conviction. Spohn et al. (2001) elaborate on this, arguing that prosecutors' charging decisions, like judges' sentencing decisions, are guided by a set of "focal concerns" (Steffensmeier, Ulmer, & Kramer, 1998). According to the focal concerns perspective, judges' sentencing decisions reflect their assessment of the blame-worthiness or culpability of the offender, their desire to protect the community by incapacitating dangerous offenders or deterring potential offenders, and their concerns about the practical consequences or social costs of sentencing decisions.

Spohn and her colleagues (2001) maintain that the focal concerns that guide prosecutors' charging decisions are similar but not identical to those that guide judges' sentencing decisions. Prosecutors, like judges, are motivated by the practical constraints on and consequences of decisions. They are more likely to file charges when the crime is serious, when it is clear that the victim has suffered real harm, and when the evidence against the suspect is strong. Prosecutors' concerns, however, are somewhat different from those of judges. Although both sets of officials are concerned about maintaining relationships with other members of the courtroom workgroup, prosecutors' concerns about the practical consequences of charging decisions focus on the likelihood of conviction rather than the social costs of punishment. In other words, prosecutors' **downstream orientation** (Frohmann, 1997) forces them to predict how the victim, the suspect, and the incident will be interpreted and evaluated by the judge and jurors. Other scholars contend that because prosecutors' predictions are inherently uncertain, they develop a "perceptual shorthand" (Hawkins, 1981; Steffensmeier et al., 1998, p. 767) that incorporates stereotypes of real crimes and genuine victims. As a result, prosecutors consider the legally relevant indicators of case seriousness and offender culpability as well as the background, character, and behavior of the victim; the relationship between the suspect and the victim; and the willingness of the victim to cooperate as the case moves forward.

In summary, the strength of evidence against the defendant plays a key role in prosecutors' charging decisions, but other legal and extralegal factors also influence the decision to file charges or not. Prosecutors, particularly those operating under a trial sufficiency screening policy, are concerned about the likelihood of conviction. As a result, characteristics of the suspect and the victim inevitably come into play.

Constraints on Prosecutorial Discretion

As emphasized previously, prosecutors exercise very broad discretion in deciding whether to file formal charges against those who have been accused of crimes, and their decisions to charge (or not to charge) are rarely challenged. Those who object to the prosecutor's refusal to file charges can raise the issue with the prosecutor's supervisor or before a judge at a court hearing (see, e.g., *NAACP v. Levi,* 1976), but it is unlikely that the decision would be overturned. The Supreme Court, in fact, has argued that judges should not be allowed to overrule a prosecutor's failure to press charges. According to the Court, judicial oversight of charging decisions should be avoided because "such factors as the strength of the case, the prosecution's general deterrence value, the Government's enforcement priorities, and the case's relationship to the Government's overall enforcement plan are not readily susceptible to the kind of analysis the courts are competent to make" (*Wayte v. United States,* 1985, p. 606). This suggests that judges and other criminal justice officials should defer to the prosecutor's judgment that charges should not be filed.

At the same time, the Supreme Court has stated that the discretion of prosecutors, while broad, "is not unfettered" (*United States v. Batchelder,* 1979). The Court has ruled that the decision to prosecute may not be "deliberately based upon an unjustifiable standard such as race, religion, or other arbitrary classification" (*Bordenkircher v. Hayes,* 1978, p. 364). Thus, prosecutors cannot single out racial minorities or men for prosecution or selectively prosecute only persons from certain religious groups. Similarly, a prosecutor cannot file charges vindictively or with revenge as a motive. Doing so violates the Due Process Clause of the Fourteenth Amendment, which states that "no state shall deprive any person of life, liberty, or property, without due process of law."

This was the decision reached in *Blackledge v. Perry* (1974), a case in which the defendant was convicted in a lower court for misdemeanor assault with a deadly weapon. After the defendant filed an appeal with the county superior court, the prosecutor obtained an indictment charging the offender with *felony* assault for the same conduct. The defendant pled guilty to this offense and was sentenced to 5 to 7 years. The Supreme Court, stating that "a person convicted of an offense is entitled to pursue his statutory right to [appeal his conviction] without apprehension that the State will retaliate by substituting a more serious charge for the original one" (p. 32), overturned his conviction on the felony offense. The Court also stated that "vindictiveness against a defendant for having successfully attacked his first conviction must play no part in the sentence he receives after a new trial" (p. 33).

It needs to be emphasized that the Supreme Court's *Blackledge* decision is limited; it applies only after the charged individual exercises his or her legal right to appeal and the prosecutor "ups the ante" in response. If the prosecutor threatens the defendant with more serious charges during the *pretrial* phase—for example, if the prosecutor threatens more serious charges if the defendant refuses to plead guilty—the Fourteenth Amendment will not be violated (*Bordenkircher v. Hayes,* 1978). There is nothing inherently wrong with such a practice because it is possible, for instance, that additional evidence could become available prior to trial, thus justifying a more serious charge. However, if the more serious charge is purely motivated by revenge, it will not be allowed (*United States v. Goodwin,* 1982).

Prosecutors also are expected to follow professional standards of conduct. The standards regarding charging are spelled out in the American Bar Association's (1993) *Standards for Criminal Justice: Prosecution Function and Defense Function.* Standard 3-3.9(b), for example, states that "the prosecutor is not obliged to present all charges which the evidence might support" and delineates the factors that the prosecutor "may properly consider in exercising his or her discretion." Included are such things as reasonable doubt that the accused is guilty, the harm caused by the offense, improper motives of a complainant or reluctance of the complainant to testify, and the cooperation of the accused in the apprehension or conviction of other offenders. Such standards help prosecutors decide which cases are worthy of prosecution, and they also help prosecutors decide which charges to pursue.

A highly publicized example of a situation in which the prosecutor's decision to file charges was called into question is the 2006 case involving three members of the Duke University lacrosse team. In April 2006, Durham County (North Carolina) District Attorney Mike Nifong filed first-degree forcible rape, first-degree sexual offense, and kidnapping charges against the players after a woman who had been hired as a stripper for a team party claimed that she had been repeatedly raped. The charges were filed despite the fact that the complainant's story changed several times and that DNA tests failed to connect any of the accused to the alleged sexual assault. In the weeks and months following the filing of charges, District Attorney Nifong gave dozens of interviews to local and national media. He stated repeatedly that he was "confident that a rape occurred" ("Duke Suspends," 2006), and he called the players "a bunch of hooligans" whose "daddies could buy them expensive lawyers" (Schorn, 2006).

The case against the three Duke University students began to unravel during the summer and fall of 2006. In mid-December, it was revealed that Nifong had withheld exculpatory DNA evidence (i.e., evidence that proved none of the three men accused of the assaults was involved) from defense lawyers, and on December 22, Nifong dropped the rape charges but not the sexual offense and kidnapping charges. Six days later, the North Carolina Bar Association filed ethics charges against Nifong, alleging that he had engaged in "conduct that involves dishonesty, fraud, deceit or misrepresentation, as well as conduct that is prejudicial to the administration of justice" ("Duke DA," 2007). In January 2007, Nifong asked to be taken off the case, which was then turned over to North Carolina Attorney General Roy Cooper. After conducting his own investigation,

Cooper dropped all the remaining charges on April 11. Cooper stated that his office "believed these three individuals are innocent of these charges." He also alleged that the charges resulted from a "tragic rush to accuse and a failure to verify serious allegations" and showed "the enormous consequences of overreaching by a prosecutor" (Beard, 2007).

Nifong resigned from his position as Durham County district attorney on June 18, 2007. Two days earlier, he had been disbarred after a disciplinary hearing committee of the North Carolina Bar ruled that he had committed numerous violations of the state's rules of professional conduct. In August, Nifong was held in criminal contempt of court and sentenced to one day in jail for his actions in the case.

As this case illustrates, prosecutors have an ethical obligation to "do justice." Their charging decisions cannot be motivated by "personal or political advantages or disadvantages which might be involved" or by "a desire to enhance [their conviction records]" (American Bar Association, 1993).

INFORMATION

The charges filed against the defendant are delineated in an information or an indictment. In states that do not use a grand jury, the prosecutor files an information, which is a written statement of the charges the defendant will face. The information must inform the defendant of the facts in the case and of the elements of the offense charged. It is a substitute for a grand jury indictment and is a more efficient way to proceed because it eliminates the need to organize a grand jury and present evidence.

INDICTMENT

The Fifth Amendment to the U.S. Constitution requires the federal government to proceed via an indictment, handed down by a grand jury. This clause of the Fifth Amendment is one of the few in the Bill of Rights that has not been applied to the states, however, so states may use an information instead. Fewer than half of the states require an indictment, and only four of these states require indictment by a grand jury for all felonies and misdemeanors. Twelve states require indictment by a grand jury only for felonies, and three states require indictment by a grand jury only for capital offenses.

At the federal level, the grand jury is composed of 23 people, and proceedings are not open to the public. Some states follow the federal model and seat grand juries of 23 members; other states seat anywhere from 6 to 23 members. The only persons present aside from the members of the grand jury are the prosecutor and any witnesses the prosecutor calls.

The rationale behind requiring indictment by a grand jury is that this body can act as a check on an overzealous prosecutor, preventing her from prosecuting cases for which there is not sufficient evidence. In reality, the grand jury today is unlikely to refuse to indict anyone (but see "Current Controversy" box, "Grand Jury Refuses to Indict Police Officer Who Shot Michael Brown"). This does not necessarily mean it is not achieving its purpose of preventing improper prosecutions, however, because its very existence may prevent prosecutors from taking shaky cases to the grand jury. In this way, the grand jury

CURRENT CONTROVERSY
GRAND JURY REFUSES TO INDICT POLICE OFFICER WHO SHOT MICHAEL BROWN

In August 2014, Michael Brown, an unarmed Black teenager, was shot and killed by Darren Wilson, a White police officer in Ferguson, Missouri. The shooting led to widespread protests and prompted St. Louis County Attorney Robert P. McCulloch to take the case to a grand jury tasked with determining whether there was sufficient evidence to charge the officer with a crime. In November 2014, the grand jurors, who heard over 60 witnesses—including Officer Wilson, who claimed that he shot Michael Brown in self-defense—over a 3-month period, determined that there was not probable cause to indict the officer. After concerns were raised about the fairness of the grand jury proceedings, the NAACP's Legal Defense and Educational Fund in January 2015 asked a Missouri judge to convene a new grand jury to consider charges against the Ferguson police officer who fatally shot the teenager. The judge refused to do so. In March 2015, the U.S. Department of Justice reported the results of its own investigation, which cleared Officer Wilson of violating Michael Brown's civil rights in the shooting. The Department of Justice concluded that Wilson shot Brown in self-defense.

checks the prosecutor's power. If the grand jury returns an indictment, it is referred to as a true bill. If the grand jury refuses to indict the defendant, it is referred to as a no bill.

INITIAL APPEARANCE

If a suspect is arrested, booked, and charged, she will then be brought before a lower court judge for what is known as an initial appearance. Once a person is arrested, she must be brought before a magistrate "without unnecessary delay." The initial appearance, which is usually held within a few hours or, at most, a few days of arrest, serves to advise the suspect why she is being detained and to explain what the suspect's rights are. The judge will read the charges filed against the accused and will explain the penalties for each charge. The judge also will inform the suspect of the right to a trial by jury and the right to counsel, including the right to have an attorney appointed if the suspect is indigent.

Suspects charged with misdemeanors typically enter a plea at this stage in the process. If the accused pleads guilty, the judge either imposes a sentence immediately (typically, a fine, probation, or a jail term) or sets a date for sentencing; if the accused enters a not guilty plea, the judge sets a date for trial. Felony suspects, on the other hand, do not enter a plea at the initial appearance; judges in courts of limited jurisdiction generally are not authorized to accept pleas in felony cases. Instead, the judge informs the suspect of the right to a preliminary hearing, explains the purpose of the preliminary hearing, and sets a date for the hearing.

Bail

Decisions regarding bail may be made at the initial appearance or at a bail hearing that will be scheduled soon after the initial appearance. The judge must decide whether to release the suspect on bail and, if so, the type and amount of bail to impose. When a judge concludes that a suspect poses a significant risk of flight or of harm to others, bail will not be granted. But if the suspect's appearance at trial is not a concern and he is not seen as dangerous, the suspect may either be released on his own recognizance (i.e., without paying bail) or required to pay monetary bail. Interestingly, there is no constitutional right to bail. The Eighth Amendment only provides that "excessive bail shall not be required." This means that bail should be an amount that is not unreasonable but that will guarantee the defendant's appearance at trial. In many jurisdictions, judges follow bail schedules, except in cases of serious or unusual offenses.

When a defendant does not have the money to post bail, she may pay a bail bondsman a fee (usually 10% of the bond), who posts the bond for the defendant. In an attempt to reduce the number of defendants detained in jail prior to trial, many jurisdictions have implemented a system of court-administered bail. In these jurisdictions, the defendant pays 10% of the bond set to the court; if she shows up for all court appearances, most (typically, 90%) of the fee is returned to the defendant. If a defendant cannot raise the money to post bail or to hire a bondsman, then she will remain in jail until trial. This is a common fate for many indigent criminal defendants.

ARRAIGNMENT

After the grand jury or the judge at the initial appearance has decided that there is sufficient evidence to proceed with the case, the defendant will be arraigned. The purpose of arraignment is to formally notify the defendant of the charge(s) and to ask the defendant to enter a plea. At the arraignment, the defendant enters a plea. Possible pleas include guilty, not guilty, no contest, and *standing mute*. Standing mute means refusing to plead; in these instances, the court enters a "not guilty" plea for the defendant, thus preserving the defendant's constitutional right to trial. A no contest plea, also referred to as *nolo contendere*, means "I do not desire to contest the action." This plea resembles a guilty plea but is different in one important respect: It cannot be used against the defendant in any later civil litigation arising from the acts that gave rise to the initial criminal charge. Also, a plea of nolo contendere means that the defendant does not admit to the crime. A guilty plea, by contrast, requires that the defendant admit and *explain* (known as allocution) what happened.

A fourth possible plea, not accepted as a valid option in all states and only conservatively allowed in the federal system, is the Alford plea. An Alford plea is one in which the defendant enters a guilty plea but denies having committed the crime to which he is pleading. The reason that the Alford plea is not recognized in some states and only reluctantly accepted in special circumstances in others is that when a defendant enters a plea of guilty, he is expected to state so on the record. Judges do not take it lightly when defendants say they are guilty on one hand and then assert their innocence on the other.

DISCOVERY

Discovery is the process by which both parties to the case learn of the evidence the opposing side will use. Rule 16 of the Federal Rules of Evidence provides, for example, that the defendant may, on request, discover from the prosecution "any written statements or transcriptions of oral statements made by the defendant that are in the prosecution's possession; (2) the defendant's prior criminal record; and (3) documents, photographs, tangible items, results from physical and mental evaluations, as well as other forms of real evidence considered material to the prosecution's case."

There is considerable variation among the states in the types of information that are discoverable by the defense and the prosecution. In some states, only the defendant's statements and physical evidence need be disclosed to the defense; in other states, there is a presumption that the prosecutor, with only narrow exceptions, will disclose most of the evidence against the defendant. The defendant has a constitutional right to any exculpatory evidence. According to the Supreme Court's decision in *Brady v. Maryland* (1970), prosecutors are not allowed to conceal exculpatory evidence, which is evidence tending to show that the defendant is innocent.

Some states also require reciprocal discovery; that is, the defense is required to turn over certain types of evidence to the prosecutor. Generally, the defense is required to notify the prosecutor if the defendant is going to enter an insanity plea or use an alibi defense; in the latter situation, the defense may have to provide a list of witnesses who will support the alibi defense so that the state can be prepared to cross-examine them.

PRETRIAL MOTIONS

Before the trial commences, each side may file one or more pretrial motions, which are then ruled on by the judge hearing the case. The party filing the motion must state in writing the grounds on which the motion is based and the type of relief requested. For example, the prosecuting attorney might file a motion asking the judge to rule that one of the key witnesses for the defense—a homeless woman who has a history of mental illness—is not competent to testify and therefore should be excluded as a witness at trial. If there has been substantial pretrial publicity about the case, the defense attorney might file a motion for a **change of venue**; in the motion, the defense would argue that it will be difficult to obtain an impartial jury and that therefore the trial should be moved to a jurisdiction where there has been less publicity. If the defense attorney believes that the police did not have probable cause to arrest the defendant or that there is insufficient evidence to justify the charges filed by the state, the attorney can move for a dismissal of the charges.

Pretrial motions—or, more accurately, the judge's rulings on pretrial motions—set the boundaries of the case and may play an important role in determining whether the case goes to trial at all and, if so, what the outcome will be. If the defense attorney's case rests entirely on the testimony of a witness who will provide an alibi for the defendant and the prosecutor's motion to exclude that witness is successful, the defense attorney may have little recourse but to try to convince the defendant to plead guilty. Similarly, if the state's case against a drug dealer hinges on the introduction of drugs and drug paraphernalia seized from the defendant at the time of her arrest and the judge grants the defense attorney's motion to exclude that evidence on the grounds that it was illegally obtained, the prosecutor may not want to take the case to trial and may instead offer the defendant a plea bargain. If the defendant in the first case insists on going to trial, the judge's ruling that the alibi witness cannot testify will make it difficult for him to win the case. And if the defendant in the second case refuses the plea bargain, the prosecutor may decide to dismiss the charges rather than risk losing at trial.

A variety of pretrial motions can be filed in a criminal case. Some of the more common motions are the following:

Motion for Dismissal of Charges. Motion to dismiss the charges against the defendant on the grounds that there was not probable cause for the police to make an arrest or there is insufficient evidence to support the charges filed by the state.

In February 2008, lawyers for O. J. Simpson, who was charged with 12 crimes after he and five other men took items at gunpoint from two men who were selling Simpson memorabilia, filed a motion to dismiss 6 of the 12 charges. Simpson's lawyers contended that the prosecution did not have sufficient evidence to charge him with kidnapping, robbery, and conspiracy. The judge denied the motion, and in October 2008, Simpson was convicted of all 12 charges.

Motion for a Change of Venue. Motion to move the case to another jurisdiction because of prejudicial pretrial publicity about the case. Only the defendant, and not the prosecution, may file a motion for a change of venue. This is because the Sixth Amendment provides that the accused in a criminal trial has the right to be tried "by an impartial jury of the State and district wherein the crime shall have been committed." By filing a motion for a change of venue, the defendant waives this right.

In 2014, the judge assigned to hear the case of Dzhokhar Tsarnaev, who was charged in the 2013 bombing of the Boston Marathon, denied Tsarnaev's attorneys' motion for a change of venue. The defense team asked that the trial be moved from Boston because of extensive and prejudicial pretrial publicity in the case. In their motion for a change of venue, the defense attorneys handling the case argued that it would be difficult, if not impossible, to select jurors who were impartial and who had not made up their minds about their client's guilt or innocence. In denying the motion, the judge hearing the case stated, "The court has confidence that a sufficient number of qualified, impartial jurors will be identified and ultimately sworn as jurors," He added that if that were not the case, the question of transferring the trial could be revisited.

Motion for Discovery. Motion filed by the defense attorney requesting that the prosecution provide documents and evidence that will be used against the defendant at trial as well as a list of witnesses who will be called to testify. In many states, there is reciprocal discovery, which means that the prosecution can request certain types of evidence from the defense. Although the evidence that must be disclosed by the defense varies from state to state, most states require the defense to notify the prosecution if the defendant plans to plead not guilty by reason of insanity or to enter an alibi defense. Other types of evidence that fall under the reciprocal discovery rule include results of physical and mental examinations of the defendant, the names and addresses of witnesses the defense intends to call, and any witness statements.

In March 2015, the Court of Appeals for the Ninth Circuit overturned the conviction of Debra Milke, who spent 22 years on death row after being convicted in Arizona of murder, conspiracy to commit murder, child abuse, and kidnapping of her 4-year-old son. The jury convicted Milke based largely on the testimony of the detective who allegedly took her confession. The detective had a well-documented history of misconduct and resulting disciplinary action. Milke appealed her conviction, arguing that the failure of the prosecution to turn over evidence of the officer's misconduct violated the prosecution's obligation to turn over exculpatory evidence. The Ninth Circuit agreed and held that the state had acted contrary to established precedent when it failed to disclose information regarding the history of misconduct of one of the state's key witnesses.

Motion to Suppress Evidence. Motion to exclude evidence obtained illegally—that is, evidence obtained as a result of an illegal search or interrogation. The so-called exclusionary rule prohibits the introduction at trial of evidence obtained illegally; such evidence, which is referred to as the "fruit of the poisonous tree," is inadmissible because it is tainted and therefore is not credible or trustworthy.

The prosecuting attorney dismissed the charges in a drug case after a judge in Bradenton, Florida, granted a defense attorney's motion to suppress evidence that was seized during a warrantless search. Police officers responding to a report of a home invasion discovered illegal drugs in the home when they searched the home to make sure that the suspects were no longer there. They did not have a warrant authorizing the search, and the suspect did not consent to the search (Alund, 2009).

Motion for Severance of Defendants. Typically, codefendants in a case are tried together. This saves the court time and money and avoids a situation in which witnesses have to testify about the same matter multiple times. However, there may be situations when it is not in a defendant's best interest to be tried with her codefendants. For example, there may be evidence against one defendant that is not applicable to the other defendants in the case, or the testimony of one defendant may incriminate the others. In this case, the defense attorney may file a motion for separate trials of codefendants in the case.

In 1997, a defendant charged with armed robbery in Clayton County, Georgia, filed a motion to sever his case from that of his codefendants. He argued that because his codefendants were apprehended at or near the scene of the crime and he was not, the evidence against them was more substantial than was the evidence against him. He further asserted that trying them together would mean that the evidence against his codefendants would have an improper "spillover effect" on the case against him. The judge hearing the case denied the motion (*Maloy v. The State,* 1999).

Motion for a Determination of Competency. Motion to determine if the defendant is competent to stand trial. According to the U.S. Code, the motion is to be granted "if there is reasonable cause to believe that the defendant may presently be suffering from a mental disease or defect rendering him mentally incompetent to the extent that he is unable to understand the nature and consequences of the proceedings against him or to assist properly in his defense" (U.S. Code, Title 18 §4241). If the motion is granted, the defendant's competency is evaluated by a psychiatrist or a clinical psychologist.

In 2009, a Pennsylvania superior court judge ruled that Wiley M. Smith was not competent to stand trial. Smith was charged with murder after he allegedly smothered

The Pretrial Process

Elizabeth Estess
Ada County Public Defender
Boise, Idaho

If left on their own, it is the "norm" for indigent clients to meet us for the first time on the date and time set for pretrial conference. Therefore, the biggest challenge in the pretrial process is "discovering" our client.

First, is he incarcerated? Where is he incarcerated? Should he be incarcerated? If not, how can we get him out of jail earlier than the dates set by the court? What is his version of the facts? Does he agree with the statements made in the police report? Why or why not? Is there an audio available of his statements made to law enforcement officers? Why was he apprehended in the first place? How was he treated by law enforcement? How should I "read between the lines" of the report to discover any suppressible evidence?

Second, what state of mind is the client in? Is he competent to proceed? Does he understand the proceedings? Can he communicate with me adequately for purposes of representing him in court? Is he struggling with substance abuse or mental illness? Has he ever been treated before? Where? How long ago and for how long? Who is his primary doctor? What is his criminal history?

Yes, the pretrial process for me consists of attempting to answer many questions. No one is looking out for these folks. They are poor and are considered the "dregs of society." Yet, we *must* ensure that justice applies to all. All persons are entitled to a fair trial and fair representation notwithstanding bad first impressions made up of fairly reasonable concerns and stereotypes. In criminal law, each case is a unique and creative person that "We, the People" cannot simply throw away. We must respectfully address the concerns we are confronted with by individuals within our society. To respect the law, the individual must first be respected.

his mother with a pillow. The ruling came after years of competency hearings in which doctors reported that Smith suffered from severe paranoid schizophrenia. The judge ordered Smith civilly committed to a state psychiatric hospital for continued treatment of his mental illness, noting that he cannot "rationally assist in his own defense and lacks the judgment and insight into what's happening as a result of his mental illness." "There is no likelihood that he will regain competency in the reasonably foreseeable future," the judge added. "He continues to be mentally ill. If he is not hospitalized, he remains a danger to himself and others. He needs hospitalization and care" (Camilli, 2009).

PLEA BARGAINING

The predominance of jury trials in television dramas such as *Law and Order* and *Suits* notwithstanding, most criminal convictions result from guilty pleas, not trials. In fact, about 94% of state-level felony convictions and 97% of convictions in federal courts result from guilty pleas. Although the actual number of guilty pleas that result from plea bargains is unknown, most experts would argue that some type of negotiation between the prosecutor and the defendant (or her attorney) occurs prior to the entry of the guilty plea.

Article II, Section 2 of the U.S. Constitution provides that "the trial of all Crimes, except in Cases of Impeachment, shall be by Jury." The Sixth Amendment also declares that "in all criminal prosecutions, the accused shall enjoy the right to a speedy and public trial, by an impartial jury." Although the founding fathers may have expected that "all crimes" would be tried by juries, in the United States today, very few criminal cases are settled by jury trials. As one commentator has noted, "Our system of criminal dispute resolution differs enormously from the one that the Sixth Amendment was designed to preserve" (Alschuler & Deiss, 1994).

Historically, jury trials were the norm, not the exception, in the United States. In fact, courts initially were reluctant to accept guilty pleas from persons charged with serious crimes. An example is the 1804 case of *Commonwealth v. Battis* (1804), which involved a 20-year-old Black man who was accused of raping and murdering a 13-year-old White girl. When the defendant notified a Massachusetts court that he wanted to plead guilty as charged, the court "informed him of the consequence of his plea" and explained that "he was under no legal or moral obligation to plead guilty" (*Commonwealth v. Battis,* 1804, p. 95). When the defendant refused to withdraw his plea, the court sent the defendant back to jail to think about the effects of pleading guilty. When the defendant returned to court, he again pled guilty, which prompted the court to examine "under oath, the sheriff, the jailer, and the justice [who had conducted the preliminary examination of the defendant] as to the sanity of the prisoner; and whether there had been tampering with him, either by promises, persuasions, or hopes of pardon if he would plead guilty" (*Commonwealth v. Battis,* 1804, p. 96). In this case, then, the Massachusetts court made an oblique reference to the practice of plea bargaining; the court wanted to be assured that the defendant had not been promised anything in exchange for his guilty plea.

Following the Civil War, plea bargaining became increasingly common. By the beginning of the 20th century, it was the dominant method of resolving criminal cases, especially in large urban jurisdictions. As can be seen in the language of an 1878 Michigan court decision, most of the early commentary on the practice of plea bargaining was negative. In *Edwards v. People* (1878), the court discussed a Michigan statute that set forth various plea bargaining requirements. The court observed that Michigan passed the statute "for the protection of prisoners and of the public" in response "to serious abuses caused by [prosecutors] procuring prisoners to plead guilty when a fair trial might show they were not guilty, or might show other facts important to be known" (*Edwards v. People,* 1878, p. 761). The court also pointed out that it was "easy to see that the Legislature thought there was danger that prosecuting attorneys would procure prisoners to plead guilty by assurances they have no power to make, of influence in lowering the sentence, or by bringing some other unjust influence to bear on them" (*Edwards v. People,* 1878, p. 762).

As plea bargaining proliferated and concerns about its fairness increased, many states impaneled crime commissions to study the operation of the criminal justice system. Nearly every report published by these commissions reported an increase in the practice of plea bargaining. For example, the Georgia Department of Public Welfare (1924) reported that guilty plea rates increased 70% from 1916 to 1921. A report from New York revealed that between 1839 and 1920, the guilty plea rate rose to 90% of all cases (Moley, 1929). These commissions also stated that plea bargains were too common and recommended that more cases should go to trial. One early critic of the practice called plea bargaining an "incompetent, inefficient, and lazy method of administering justice" (Alschuler, 1979, p. 211).

Why did plea bargaining increase so dramatically during the 1800s and early 1900s? One school of thought is that plea bargaining emerged during the mid-19th century as a result of the increasing professionalism of the criminal court system (Langbein, 1979).

That is, trials became more complex and adversarial, and defendants were more likely to have competent attorneys to represent them; as a result, prosecutors turned to plea bargaining as a way of reducing the uncertainty of case outcomes. According to this view, "plea bargaining should be viewed as a natural outgrowth of a progressively adversarial criminal justice system" (Guidorizzi, 1998). Another explanation holds that the growth of plea bargaining as a means of resolving criminal cases can be attributed to case pressure. This explanation suggests that plea bargaining was a natural response to increasing caseloads and limited resources to deal with them (Fisher, 2003).

In a book on the origins of plea bargaining, Michael McConville and Chester Mirsky (2005) refute both of these arguments. They argue that the political context in which criminal courts were operating, rather than professionalism or case pressure, explains the increase in plea bargaining that began in 1850. According to these authors, the advent of the elected district attorney, coupled with the influx of large numbers of immigrants, led district attorneys to search for effective and politically palatable ways of controlling the immigrant population. As they note, district attorneys allowed defendants to plead guilty to less serious charges "to avoid the discontent that harsh terms of punishment would engender among the immigrant underclass, who, under the movement for universal suffrage, had become part of the newly formed electorate" (McConville & Mirsky, 2005, p. 197).

Regardless of whether the growth of plea bargaining is explained as a result of an increasingly professional criminal court system, caseload pressure, or the political context in which elected district attorneys were operating, it is clear that it has become a key feature of the American criminal justice system. In the words of the U.S. Supreme Court, plea bargaining is "an essential component of the administration of justice" (*Santobello v. New York,* 1971).

Defining Plea Bargaining

It is important to understand that although all plea bargains involve guilty pleas, not all guilty pleas result from plea bargains. A guilty plea occurs when a defendant admits committing a crime. When a guilty plea is entered, the defendant usually will be required to explain what happened to the judge. This process is known as allocution. A guilty plea can be entered without any type of plea bargaining; that is, the defendant can plead guilty to the original charge without any concessions or promises from the prosecutor. A defendant who believes that the state's evidence is overwhelming or who is plagued by guilt might simply decide to admit involvement in the crime. These types of guilty pleas are the exception, however. Most guilty pleas are preceded by plea bargaining.

> What exactly is plea bargaining? *Black's Law Dictionary* (1990) defines it as the process whereby the accused and the prosecutor in a criminal case work out a mutually satisfactory disposition of the case subject to court approval. It usually involves the defendant pleading guilty to a lesser offense or to only some of the counts of a multicount indictment in return for a lighter sentence than the sentence possible for the graver charge. (p. 1152)

The problem with this definition is that it fails to capture the range of concessions prosecutors may offer. They can offer more than just reductions in charges and counts or favorable sentencing recommendations. We consider some of these in the "ad hoc" plea bargaining section. A better, more all-encompassing definition of plea bargaining is this: "the defendant's agreement to plead guilty to a criminal charge with the reasonable expectation of receiving some consideration from the state" (Miller, McDonald, & Cramer, 1978, pp. 1–2).

There are several different forms of plea bargaining, and they can be used alone or in combination with one another. Consider the following scenario: A 19-year-old man holds a gun to the head of a convenience store clerk, demands money, and escapes on foot with a bag containing over $1,000. Thirty minutes later, he is spotted and arrested by the police. The prosecutor reviewing the case charges the defendant with one count of aggravated robbery, which is punishable by 3 to 10 years in prison, and one count of use of a weapon during the commission of a felony, which adds an additional 2 years to the sentence. The plea negotiations in this case might center on the charges that have been filed. If the defendant agrees to plead guilty, the prosecutor might reduce the aggravated robbery charge to a less serious charge of robbery or might dismiss the weapons charge. Both types of **charge reductions** would reduce the potential sentence that the defendant is facing.

The plea negotiations also might revolve around the sentence. In exchange for a guilty plea, the prosecutor might agree to recommend a sentence of 3 years on the aggravated robbery and 2 years on the weapons charge, with the sentences to be served concurrently rather than consecutively. Alternatively, the prosecutor might agree "to stand mute at sentencing" or might agree to a "sentence lid." In the first instance, the prosecutor would not recommend any particular sentence or challenge the defense attorney's presentation of mitigating evidence and recommendation for leniency; he would, in other words, say nothing about the sentence the defendant should receive. In the second instance, the prosecutor would recommend that the judge impose a sentence that does not exceed the sentence lid; in this case, for example, he might state that the sentence should be no greater than 3 years in prison.

Both charge reductions and sentence agreements limit the judge's options at sentencing. Judges have little if any recourse if the prosecutor decides to reduce the number or the severity of the charges in exchange for a guilty plea. Because the charging decision "generally rests entirely in his [the prosecutor's] discretion" (*Bordenkircher v. Hayes,* 1978), the judge ordinarily cannot refuse to accept the plea to a reduced charge and force the defendant to go to trial. In *United States v. Ammidown* (1973), for example, the U.S. court of appeals ruled that a judge who rejected a plea agreement because he believed that the "public interest" required that the defendant be tried on a more serious charge "had exceeded his discretion." Although the justices stated that the trial court should not "serve merely as a rubber stamp for the prosecutor's decision," they ruled that the judge cannot reject the agreement reached between the prosecution and defense unless he determines that the prosecutor abused her discretion. Moreover, the Court said that "the question is not what the judge would do if he were the prosecuting attorney, but whether he can say that the action of the prosecuting attorney is such a departure from sound prosecutorial principle as to mark it an abuse of prosecutorial discretion" (*United States v. Ammidown,* 1973).[1]

Sentence agreements also reduce the judge's discretion, even though the prosecutor does not have any official authority to impose a sentence. If, for example, the prosecution and the defense negotiate an agreement whereby the defendant agrees to plead guilty and the state agrees that a probation sentence is the appropriate disposition, the judge must either accept the plea agreement and place the defendant on probation or reject the agreement and allow the defendant to withdraw his guilty plea.[2] As the Supreme Court stated in the case of *Santobello v. New York* (1971), "When a plea rests in any significant degree on a promise or agreement of the prosecutor so that it can be said to be part of the inducement or consideration, such promise must be fulfilled." Moreover, judges face organizational pressure to approve plea agreements. Like other members of the courtroom workgroup, they view guilty pleas as an efficient and effective method of case disposition. As a result, they are unlikely to reject the sentence agreements that make a high rate of guilty pleas possible.

Ad Hoc Plea Bargaining

Although plea negotiations usually produce charge and/or sentence reductions, other practices fall within the definition of plea bargaining. Joe Colquitt (2001) used the term **ad hoc plea bargaining** to refer to the unusual concessions defendants agree to make during the plea negotiation process. He states,

> Ad hoc bargains exist in at least five forms: (1) the court may impose an extraordinary condition of probation following a guilty plea, (2) the defendant may offer or be required to perform some act as a quid pro quo for a dismissal or more lenient sentence, (3) the court may impose an unauthorized form of punishment as a substitute for a statutorily established method of punishment, (4) the State may offer some unauthorized benefit in return for a plea of guilty, or (5) the defendant may be permitted to plead guilty to an unauthorized offense, such as a "hypothetical" or nonexistent charge, a nonapplicable lesser-included offense, or a nonrelated charge. (p. 712)

There are numerous examples of these five forms of ad hoc plea bargaining. Defendants have been given the option of providing charitable contributions in lieu of fines or jail terms (see, e.g., *Ratliff v. State,* 1992, p. 243; *State v. Stellato,* 1987, p. 1349) and have agreed to relinquish property ownership in exchange for leniency (see, e.g., *United States v. Thao Dinh Lee,* 1999, p. 1278). Other defendants have agreed to not work in particular professions or to surrender professional licenses (see, e.g., *United States v. Hoffer,* 1997, p. 1199). One defendant consented to undergo voluntary sterilization (*State v. Pasicznyk,* 1997), and another agreed to enlist in the army (see *State v. Hamrick,* 1999, p. 494). Defendants have also opted to perform shaming punishments, such as affixing a bumper sticker labeling the driver of a car as a convicted DUI offender (see, e.g., *Ballenger v. State,* 1993). Defendants have even agreed to surrender profits, such as from books written about their crimes (*Rolling v. State ex rel. Butterworth,* 1999), or to be banished to another location (see, e.g., *Phillips v. State,* 1999; *State v. Culp,* 1976).

Arguments for and Against Plea Bargaining

Arguments in favor of plea bargaining are really arguments about the *benefits* of plea bargaining. Most people would agree that the primary benefit of plea bargaining is that it enables courts to dispose of large numbers of criminal cases quickly. As we have already seen, the crime control model contends that a high rate of guilty pleas—which implies a high rate of plea bargaining—is necessary if the system is to operate with maximal efficiency. The Supreme Court, which recognized the legitimacy of plea bargaining more than 40 years ago, has also emphasized the economic benefits of plea bargaining. The Court noted that "if every criminal charge were subject to a full scale trial, the states and the Federal Government would need to multiply by many times the number of judges and court facilities" (*Santobello v. New York,* (1971), pp. 260–261).

Plea bargaining clearly benefits prosecutors, who are concerned about securing convictions and avoiding acquittals at trial. Like other public officials, prosecutors are faced with limited resources. They cannot prosecute every criminal case, and they certainly cannot take all the cases they prosecute to trial before juries. The cases that go to trial are likely to be high-profile cases or those in which defendants are facing harsh potential sentences. Less serious cases, or cases with evidentiary or witness problems, are prime candidates for plea bargains. Giving the defendant in a less serious or weaker case some type of concession in exchange for a guilty plea allows the prosecutor to secure a conviction and sentence without risking an acquittal at trial. Plea bargaining, in other words, may be favored by the prosecution because it allows the courtroom workgroup to further its "mutual interest in avoiding conflict, reducing uncertainty, and maintaining group cohesion" (Weninger, 1987, p. 265).

Other actors in the criminal court system also benefit from plea bargaining. Defense attorneys, including public defenders, have high caseloads and limited resources and, like prosecutors, are concerned about disposing of cases quickly and efficiently. In addition, plea bargaining allows defense attorneys to mitigate the harshness of the sentence their clients would face following conviction at trial. In this sense, plea bargaining also benefits defendants, who receive more lenient sentences by pleading guilty to less serious charges or to fewer counts. As the Supreme Court itself has noted, plea bargaining affords the defendant the opportunity of "avoiding the anxieties and uncertainties of trial" (*Blackledge v. Allison,* 1977, p. 71). Finally, victims may benefit from plea bargaining; if the defendant pleads guilty, the victim will not have to testify at the trial or face the possibility that the prosecution will not succeed in obtaining a conviction (Demarest, 1994).

There are many arguments against plea bargaining. One is that plea bargaining allows prosecutors and defense attorneys to effectively decide matters of guilt; no judge and no jury are involved. Another criticism is that in an effort to secure a guilty plea, the prosecutor may start with the most serious charge and work down from there; the prosecutor may "overcharge" as a first step in the bargaining process. If, for example, the prosecutor believes that the appropriate charge in a case is simple assault, he may initially file a charge of aggravated assault and then offer to reduce the charge to simple assault if the defendant agrees to plead guilty. In this situation, the effect of the charge reduction is symbolic rather than substantive.

Critics also charge that plea bargaining is inefficient. This criticism rests on two assumptions. The first is that defense attorneys attempt to draw out the negotiations in an attempt to get prosecutors to offer better deals. As one researcher observed, "Defense attorneys commonly devise strategies whose only utility lies in the threat they pose to the court's and prosecutor's time" (Alschuler, 1968, p. 50). The second assumption is that plea bargaining is unnecessary to induce guilty pleas. That is, critics of plea bargaining contend that most defendants would plead guilty without any concessions or promises of leniency if they think it is likely that they would be found guilty at trial (Arenella, 1983).

One of the most pervasive criticisms of plea bargaining is that it undermines the integrity of the criminal justice system. Plea bargaining, which amounts to deciding guilt without trial, circumvents the "rigorous standards of due process and proof imposed during trials" (Worden, 1990, p. 336). The prosecutor is not required to prove the defendant's guilt beyond a reasonable doubt, and the defendant does not have an opportunity to cross-examine the witnesses against her or otherwise test the prosecutor's case. Plea bargaining also may result in convictions and sentences that do not accurately reflect the seriousness of the crime committed by the defendant. A defendant who commits a robbery with a gun, but whose charge is reduced from armed robbery to robbery during plea negotiations, may receive a more lenient sentence than he deserves. Finally, critics of plea bargaining claim that innocent individuals may be coerced to plead guilty. As one of the staunchest critics of plea bargaining has stated, plea bargaining "darkens the prospect of going to trial as it brightens the prospect of pleading guilty" (Kipnis, 1976, p. 94).

An example of the type of pressure to plead guilty that defendants face can be found in the case of *North Carolina v. Alford* (1970). In its opinion in this case, the Supreme Court reprinted a statement made by the defendant, who pled guilty to second-degree murder to avoid the death penalty:

> I pleaded guilty on second degree murder because they said there is too much evidence, but I ain't shot no man. . . . We never had an argument in our life and I just pleaded guilty because they said if I didn't they would gas me for it, and that is all. (p. 28)

In this case, the Court ruled that it was not a violation of due process to accept the plea despite Alford's insistence that he was innocent because there was a strong factual basis for his guilt. The Constitution, according to the Court, does not preclude "imposition of a prison sentence upon an accused who is unwilling expressly to admit his guilt but who, faced with grim alternatives, is willing to waive his trial and accept the sentence" (*North Carolina v. Alford,* 1970, p. 28). Justice Brennan, one of the dissenting justices in the case, disagreed with the Court's assessment regarding the voluntariness of the plea. He wrote that the facts in the case demonstrated that "Alford was 'so gripped by fear of the death penalty' that his decision to plead guilty was not voluntary but was the product of duress."

In summary, plea bargaining is an issue that continues to evoke controversy and spark debate. Advocates, many of whom see plea bargaining as a "necessary evil," argue that it is an essential element of an overburdened court system and that it benefits most, if not all, of the participants in the court process. Opponents counter that it perverts justice, undercuts the protections afforded to criminal defendants, and coerces innocent defendants to plead guilty and should therefore be restricted or eliminated.

Attempts to Restrict or Ban Plea Bargaining

Given the controversy surrounding plea bargaining, it is not surprising that a number of jurisdictions have attempted to restrict or even eliminate it. In 1975, for example, the

Alaska attorney general issued an order that banned all forms of plea bargaining. Under this policy, prosecutors could not reduce charges or dismiss counts in exchange for guilty pleas; they also were not supposed to ask the court to impose a particular sentence if the defendant agreed to plead guilty. The attorney general imposed the ban on plea bargaining in an effort to increase convictions and restore public confidence in the justice system (Carns & Kruse, 1992). An evaluation of the impact of the ban found that explicit sentence bargaining disappeared and that charge bargaining continued for a few months and then "dried up" (Rubinstein & White, 1979). The evaluation also revealed that, contrary to predictions that defendants would refuse to plead guilty and that the Alaska criminal justice system would therefore grind to a halt, guilty pleas did not decrease and trials did not increase dramatically. Although the authors of the study concluded that the Alaska experience showed that "the incidence of plea bargaining *can* be substantially reduced without wrecking a criminal justice system," they also cautioned that the results of the Alaska reform could not necessarily be generalized to other, larger jurisdictions (Rubinstein & White, 1979, p. 382).

A number of other jurisdictions have taken a more modest approach with respect to limiting the practice of plea bargaining. One such method is to impose cutoff dates that prohibit plea bargaining after a case has been under way for a certain amount of time. As an example of this, the Brooklyn district attorney has adopted a cutoff date of 74 days after indictment (Mirsky, 1994). Prior to the deadline, plea bargaining is acceptable, but after the deadline, plea negotiation is prohibited. If the case goes to trial before the cutoff period passes, plea bargaining could even take place during trial or during jury deliberations. Some jurisdictions have also experimented with banning plea bargaining for certain offenses. For example, the Bronx County district attorney enacted a ban on plea bargaining whenever a grand jury returned a felony indictment. This was a controversial move on the district attorney's part, but he justified it by stating that plea bargaining "means that society has ceded control to those it has accused of violating its laws; and it means that our system is running us, instead of the other way around" (R. T. Johnson, 1992).

Another approach to restricting plea bargaining is the Philadelphia jury waiver. The jury waiver gives defendants the opportunity to engage in plea negotiations in exchange for giving up their right to a jury trial. This is something of a hybrid approach, with elements of plea bargaining and trial. Defendants get their day in court, but to receive concessions from the prosecutor, they cannot demand a jury trial. This practice is known as the **slow plea of guilty**, which reflects the fact that it does not result in the disposition of a case prior to trial. According to Martin Levin (1977),

> Slow pleas are informal and abbreviated, and consist largely of the defense's presentation of statements concerning the defendant's allegedly favorable personal characteristics. . . . The defense presentation is not concerned with guilt or innocence since it usually is implicitly assumed by all parties involved in the process that the defendant is guilty of at least some wrongdoing. (p. 143)

Other states have used the initiative process to restrict plea bargaining. In 1982, for example, California voters passed a referendum (now codified as Cal. Penal Code 1192.7) that imposed the following restrictions: no plea bargaining in any case involving

(1) a serious felony, (2) a felony where a firearm was used, or (3) the offense of driving under the influence. Plea bargaining is permissible, however, if the prosecution's evidence is weak, witnesses are unavailable, or a plea agreement does not result in a significantly reduced sentence (*People v. Brown,* 1986).

El Paso, Texas, also experimented with plea bargaining restrictions. There, two state district judges adopted a policy of prohibiting all plea negotiations in their courts as a method of ensuring equal treatment for similarly situated defendants (Weninger, 1987). Maricopa County (Phoenix, Arizona) superior court judges adopted a policy that prohibited plea agreements based on "stipulated" (i.e., agreed-on) sentences. In other words, the judges refused to accept plea agreements that included a negotiated sentence. They felt that sentencing should be a decision left to the trial courts. These and other efforts to restrict plea bargaining have become fairly common, but it is difficult to argue that they are much more than symbolic gestures.

The Predictors of Plea Bargaining: Does Race Matter?

There is relatively little research on the factors that affect prosecutors' plea bargaining decisions. In part, this reflects the fact that plea negotiations typically take place "behind closed doors." Generally, there are no written records that document the concessions that were offered or the promises made. Although it may be possible to measure count or charge reductions, sentence agreements and the types of ad hoc plea agreements mentioned earlier are difficult, if not impossible, to document.

The research that does exist reveals that prosecutors' plea bargaining decisions are determined by the strength of evidence against the defendant, the defendant's prior criminal record, and the seriousness of the offense (Mather, 1979). Prosecutors are more willing to offer concessions to defendants who commit less serious crimes and have less serious prior records. They also are more willing to alter charges when the evidence against the defendant is weak or inconsistent. These findings are not surprising, given the prosecutor's desire to avoid uncertainty and secure convictions.

There also is some evidence that examines the impact of the defendant's race/ethnicity on plea bargaining outcomes. A number of studies conclude that White defendants are offered plea bargains more frequently and get better deals than racial minorities. A study of the charging process in New York, for example, found that race did not affect charge reductions if the case was disposed of at the first presentation. Among defendants who did not plead guilty at the first opportunity, on the other hand, African Americans received less substantial sentence reductions than Whites (Bernstein, Kick, Leung, & Schultz, 1977). An analysis of 683,513 criminal cases in California concluded that "Whites were more successful in getting charges reduced or dropped, in avoiding 'enhancements' or extra charges, and in getting diversion, probation, or fines instead of incarceration" (Weitzer, 1966, p. 313). A more recent study of plea bargains in misdemeanor marijuana cases adjudicated in New York City examined whether offenders received plea offers for lesser charges or sentence offers for noncustodial punishment (Kutateladze, Andiloro, & Johnson, 2014). Initial analyses revealed that Blacks were less likely than Whites to receive plea offers for lesser charges and that both Blacks and Hispanics were more likely than Whites to receive sentence offers for custodial sentences. Although controlling for legally relevant indicators of crime seriousness, the defendant's prior record, and the strength of evidence in the case eliminated most of these differences, Blacks still were more likely than Whites to receive sentence offers that included some time in jail or prison.

An analysis of plea bargaining under the federal sentencing guidelines also concluded that Whites receive better deals than racial minorities (Maxfield & Kramer, 1998). This study, which was conducted by the U.S. Sentencing Commission, examined sentence reductions for offenders who provided "substantial assistance" to the government. According to §5K1.1 of the *Guidelines Manual,* if an offender assists in the investigation and prosecution of another person who has committed a crime, the prosecutor can ask the court to reduce the offender's sentence. Since the guidelines do not specify either the types of cooperation that "count" as substantial assistance or the magnitude of the sentence reduction that is to be given, this is a highly discretionary decision.

The Sentencing Commission estimated the effect of race/ethnicity on both the probability of receiving a **substantial assistance departure** and the magnitude of the sentence reduction. They controlled for other variables such as the seriousness of the offense, use of a weapon, the offender's prior criminal record, and other factors deemed relevant under the sentencing guidelines. They found that Blacks and Hispanics were less likely than Whites to receive a substantial assistance departure; among offenders who did receive a departure, Whites received a larger sentence reduction than either Blacks or Hispanics (Maxfield & Kramer, 1998). According to the commission's report, "The evidence consistently indicated that factors that were associated with either the making of a §5K1.1 motion and/or the magnitude of the departure were not consistent with principles of equity" (Maxfield & Kramer, 1998, p. 21).

Two studies found that race did not affect plea bargaining decisions in the predicted way. An examination of the guilty plea process in nine counties in Illinois, Michigan, and Pennsylvania revealed that defendant race had no effect on four measures of charge reduction (Nardulli, Eisenstein, & Flemming, 1988). The authors of this study concluded that "the allocation of charge concessions did not seem to be dictated by blatantly discriminatory criteria or punitive motives" (Nardulli et al., 1988, p. 238). A study of charge reductions in two jurisdictions found that racial minorities received more *favorable* treatment than Whites. In one county, Blacks received more favorable charge reductions than Whites; in the other county, Hispanics were treated more favorably than Whites (Holmes, Daudistel, & Farrell, 1987). The authors of this study speculated that these results might reflect devaluation of minority victims. As they noted, "If minority victims are devalued because of racist beliefs, such sentiments could, paradoxically, produce more favorable legal outcomes for minority defendants." The authors also suggested that the results might reflect overcharging of minority defendants by the police; prosecutors may have been forced "to accept pleas to lesser charges from Black defendants because of the initial overcharging" (pp. 248–249).

In sum, the evidence concerning the factors that affect prosecutors' plea bargaining decisions is both scanty and inconsistent, especially regarding the effects of the defendant's race/ethnicity. Given the importance of these decisions, these contradictory findings "call for the kind of scrutiny in the pretrial stages that has been so rightly given to the convicting and sentencing stages" (Spohn et al., 1987, p. 189).

COMPARATIVE COURTS

Contrast the adversarial system with the inquisitorial system found in most countries on the European continent. Inquisitorial systems are the opposite of adversarial systems in many respects. For one thing, the parties to the case provide all the relevant evidence to the court, and the judge, not the attorneys for the state or the defense, calls and examines witnesses. As Nancy Goldberg and Marshall Hartman (1983) have noted, "The European trial is considered more like an investigation than competition between two opposing sides. Underlying the theory of this system is faith in the fairness and good will of the judges" (p. 69). An example of an inquisitorial system is France. There, a *juge d'instruction* (i.e., an investigating magistrate) engages in fact finding and investigation in cases of serious and complex crimes. The goal of the judge is to determine the truth—what actually happened—and therefore he or she looks for both exculpatory and incriminating evidence. If the judge determines that there is sufficient evidence against the defendant, the case is referred to court for trial.

The court to which the case is referred may be the *cour d'assises*, which relies on jurors but not in the same way American criminal courts do. Instead, nine lay jurors sit with three professional judges, deliberate with them, and vote with them. Each vote carries equal weight, and a majority of eight is necessary to convict. This approach is limited to serious offenses, however, such as murder, rape, and armed robbery. Juries are thus the exception. But it is also possible for an adversarial system to avoid juries. The key to distinguishing between adversarial and inquisitorial systems, though, does not require a focus on juries. Simply put, adversarial systems pit the prosecution and defense against each other in the pursuit of truth. The attorneys in inquisitorial systems are much more passive, and judges take on a more prominent role in the pursuit of truth.

JURY SELECTION

When defendants (suspects become defendants once officially indicted) plead not guilty, the next step in the process is the trial itself. Once a trial date is set, jury selection begins (see Chapter 9 for a more detailed discussion of the jury selection process). The jury is selected from the eligible members of the community, who are selected at random, usually from voting records or automobile registration records. These records are used to obtain as complete a list as possible of all the residents of a community.

The legal term for summoning jurors is the *venire*, which is Latin for "to cause" or to "make come" (to the courthouse). Prospective jurors are examined by the judge and/or the attorneys for the prosecution and defense to determine whether they have any bias, prejudice, or interest that would prevent them from being impartial. This process of questioning the jurors is referred to as the *voir dire*, which literally means "to see to speak."

It should be noted that while the purpose of the voir dire is to obtain an unbiased jury, in reality each side seeks to excuse potential jurors who are biased against their side as well as keep on the jury those individuals who are biased toward their side. Attorneys sometimes employ the services of professional **jury consultants** to help them determine what type of person is more likely to favor the prosecution or defense.

Challenges to the Jury

Jurors may be challenged for cause or removed through the use of a peremptory challenge. A peremptory challenge is one for which no reason need be given. Whereas challenges for cause are unlimited, peremptory challenges are usually limited to a certain number. The Supreme Court has held that peremptory challenges may not be used to exclude potential jurors on the basis of race (*Batson v. Kentucky,* 1986) or gender (*J. E. B. v. Alabama,* 1994).

The Supreme Court has also held that the jury need not be composed of the traditional 12 members. Juries as small as six have been approved for both civil and criminal trials (*Williams v. Florida,* 1970). Furthermore, there is no constitutional requirement that the jury verdict be unanimous, even in criminal cases. The Supreme Court has approved both 9 to 3 and 10 to 2 verdicts (*Apodaca v. Oregon,* 1972; *Johnson v. Louisiana,* 1972). However, a 6-person jury must be unanimous.

Finally, the requirement of a "jury of one's peers" has been interpreted simply to require the jury be randomly selected from the community where the crime takes place. It does not mean the members of the jury must share any characteristics (including race and ethnicity) or traits with the defendant.

KEY CASES

During the jury selection process, or voir dire, jurors may be challenged for cause or removed through the use of a peremptory challenge. A peremptory challenge is one for which no reason need be given by the attorney who is using it. Whereas challenges for cause are unlimited, peremptory challenges are usually limited to a certain number; in many jurisdictions, each side has 6 peremptory challenges in most criminal cases and 12 in capital murder cases. Although historically, there was no opportunity for an attorney to object to the use of a peremptory challenge by her opponent, this has changed recently. The Supreme Court held, in *Batson v. Kentucky* (1986), that a peremptory challenge may not be used to exclude a potential juror on the basis of race. In *J. E. B. v. Alabama* (1994), the Court held that peremptory challenges could not be used to exclude a potential juror on the basis of gender.

As a result of the Court's decisions in *Batson* and *J. E. B.,* courts have been forced to deal with objections to the use of peremptory challenges. There have been a number of appeals where one side claimed the other was misusing a peremptory challenge. When this objection is raised, the trial court must determine if the peremptory challenge is being used for an improper reason. This is done by requiring the attorney seeking to use the peremptory challenge to provide some race- or gender-neutral explanation for the challenge. This may be difficult for an attorney to articulate because the idea behind peremptory challenges is that an attorney uses them to excuse jurors who have not displayed a clear reason for being excused but whom the attorney has a "bad feeling" about. The key is the attorney has to show that his "bad feeling" is not based on race or gender. The Supreme Court dealt with this issue in *Snyder v. Louisiana* (2008). Snyder was sentenced to death by an all-White jury. He argued on appeal that the prosecutor had improperly used his challenges to remove all Blacks from the jury. When the defense objected, the prosecutor was required, per *Batson,* to provide a race-neutral explanation for his peremptory challenges. He said he struck the jurors because they seemed nervous

(Continued)

(Continued)

and expressed concern that the trial would take a long time and interfere with their studies or job. The trial judge accepted the explanation even though several White jurors had expressed similar concerns and the prosecutor had not challenged them. The Supreme Court overturned the conviction, noting that the prosecutor's explanations for removing Black jurors were unfounded and that White jurors with similar issues were not excused from the jury, suggesting race was indeed the motivation for excusing the Black jurors. When *Batson* was decided, it was criticized for not establishing a standard to evaluate the race neutrality of peremptory challenges, and lower courts have struggled with this issue. Here, the Court provided some guidance and made it clear that total deference to the determinations of the trial court judge is not appropriate.

SUMMARY

The idealized adversarial model of the criminal courts suggests that prosecutors and defense attorneys are in constant battle with one another. In reality, criminal case processing is characterized more by cooperation and consensus than by conflict. This reflects in large part the fact that trials are rare, and thus the opportunities for conflict are limited. It also can be attributed to the fact that both prosecutors and defense attorneys are part of a courtroom workgroup with common goals (i.e., efficient and expeditious case processing) and agreed-on procedures for attaining those goals.

Researchers interested in the roles played by prosecutors have focused on identifying the factors that influence charging and plea bargaining decisions by prosecutors. These studies reveal that these highly discretionary and largely invisible decisions reflect a mix of (a) legally relevant measures of case seriousness and evidence strength and (b) legally irrelevant characteristics of the victim and suspect.

The American criminal justice system is dominated by guilty pleas, not trials. The members of the courtroom workgroup develop case processing routines designed to ensure that cases are handled as efficiently and expeditiously as possible. Plea negotiations—which may involve a reduction in the severity of the charge, a reduction in the number of counts, a sentence agreement, or some other type of concession—produce high rates of guilty pleas and limit the number of cases that go to trial. Supporters of plea bargaining argue that the system benefits both defendants and members of the courtroom workgroup; critics counter that plea bargains pervert justice, undercut the protections afforded to defendants, and coerce innocent defendants to plead guilty. Although a number of jurisdictions have attempted to eliminate or restrict plea bargaining, the effects of these reforms are symbolic rather than instrumental. It thus seems likely that for the foreseeable future, courts in the United States will continue to process most criminal cases using negotiated guilty pleas.

Don't overlook the Student Study Site with its useful study aids, such as self-quizzes, eFlashcards, and other assists, to help you get more from the course and improve your grade.

DISCUSSION QUESTIONS

1. What is the meaning of probable cause?

2. What is the difference between an information and an indictment?

3. What are the "focal concerns" that guide prosecutors' charging decisions?

4. What factors influence prosecutors' charging decisions?

5. Explain how the legal sufficiency charging policy and the trial sufficiency charging policy would produce different outcomes in criminal cases.

6. What are the types of pleas, and how do they differ?

7. Do you think plea bargaining should be eliminated? Why or why not?

8. What is the purpose of bail?

9. What is the purpose of discovery?

10. Why are there so few trials and so many plea bargains?

11. What is the difference between a challenge for cause and a peremptory challenge? Why is the use of the peremptory challenge controversial?

KEY TERMS

Ad hoc plea bargaining 254
Affidavit 237
Change of venue 247
Charge reduction 253
Defendant rehabilitation policy 239

Downstream orientation 241
Jury consultant 260
Legal sufficiency policy 239
Sentence agreement 253
Slow plea of guilty 257

Substantial assistance departure 259
System efficiency policy 239
Trial sufficiency policy 239

INTERNET SITES

Federal Grand Jury: https://corporate.findlaw.com/litigation-disputes/federal-grand-jury-crash-course.html

National Center for State Courts: www.ncsc.org

U.S. Courts: www.uscourts.gov

Voir Dire: Creating the Jury: www.crfc.org/resource-center/voir-dire-creating-jury

STUDENT STUDY SITE

Get the tools you need to sharpen your study skills. SAGE edge offers a robust online environment featuring an impressive array of free tools and resources.

Access practice quizzes, eFlashcards, video, and multimedia at **edge.sagepub.com/hemmens4e**

ENDNOTES

1. However, it should be noted that other appellate courts have adopted a less restrictive standard. In *United States v. Bean* (1977), the Court of Appeals for the Fifth Circuit ruled that "a decision that a plea bargain will result in the defendant's receiving too light a sentence under the circumstances of the case is a sound reason for the judge's refusing to accept the agreement."

2. Rule 11 of the Federal Rules of Criminal Procedure, which applies to cases adjudicated in federal court, states that "if the court accepts the plea agreement, the court shall inform the defendant that it will embody in the judgment and sentence the disposition provided for in the plea agreement . . . If the court rejects the plea agreement, the court shall, on the record, inform the parties of this fact, advise the defendant personally in open court . . . that the court is not bound by the plea agreement, afford the defendant the opportunity to then withdraw his plea, and advise the defendant that if he persists in this guilty plea . . . the disposition of the case may be less favorable to the defendant than that contemplated by the plea agreement."

11

© Comstock/Stockbyte/Thinkstock Images

THE CRIMINAL TRIAL

SAGE edge™

Master the content at **edge.sagepub.com/hemmens4e**

INTRODUCTION

In August 2006, Samuel Dieteman and Dale Hausner were charged with a series of random shootings in the Phoenix metropolitan area. Authorities alleged that the two roommates killed 8 people, wounded 17 more, and killed several animals in a 16-month crime spree that terrorized Phoenix and surrounding communities. In April 2008, Dieteman pled guilty to two of the murders and agreed to testify against Hausner at his trial. Hausner, who was facing eight counts of first-degree murder as well as dozens of other charges, pled not guilty and went on trial in September 2008. Hausner's jury trial, which lasted nearly 6 months, featured testimony by dozens of victims who survived the shootings, stabbings, and arsons that Hausner was charged with committing. It also featured the testimony of a jailhouse informant who claimed that Hausner had confessed to one of the shootings while they were in jail together and evidence of Hausner's involvement in the crimes that was provided by Samuel Dieteman. Dale Hausner spent several days on the stand; he denied that he had any role in the attacks and claimed that he had alibis for some of the dates when the crimes occurred.

The case went to the jury in late February 2009. After deliberating for more than 2 weeks, the jury found Hausner guilty of 80 crimes, including six counts of first-degree murder. During the penalty phase of the trial, the jury found 22 aggravating circumstances that justified sentencing Hausner to death. Hausner then waived his right to present mitigating evidence in support of a sentence of life in prison and indicated to the judge that he did not intend to fight for a life sentence. On March 28, 2009, Dale Hausner was sentenced to death.

The trial of Dale Hausner, which attracted the attention of the national media, was in many ways not your typical criminal trial. For example:

- Hausner was arrested in August 2006, but his trial did not conclude until March 2009, almost 3 years later. By contrast, the typical felony case is disposed of within 85 days. Even for violent crimes, the average time from arrest to adjudication is only 130 days (Bureau of Justice Statistics, 2010).

- Hausner pled not guilty, and his case was tried by a jury. But more than 90% of all convictions of felony defendants in large urban counties are the result of guilty pleas. Jury trials are the exception, not the rule.

- Hausner testified in his own defense, despite the fact that the Fifth Amendment to the U.S. Constitution provides that a defendant cannot "be compelled in any criminal case to be a witness against himself." Many defendants exercise their right to remain silent at trial.

- The jury deliberated for more than 2 weeks before finding Hausner guilty. This no doubt reflects the complexity of the charges the jurors had to consider; they had to decide whether Hausner was guilty of 87 crimes, and they had to vote on each charge separately. Although there are no national data on the length of time that juries deliberate, one study of criminal trials in Oregon found that no jury deliberated for more than 8 hours and 20 minutes (Brunell, Chetan, & Morgan, 2007). The jury that found Dzhokhar Tsarnaev, the so-called Boston Marathon Bomber, guilty of all 30 counts against him deliberated for less than 12 hours.

● Hausner was sentenced to death, which is a punishment that is rarely applied. In 2013, more than 10,000 persons were arrested for murder and nonnegligent manslaughter (Federal Bureau of Investigation, 2014), but only 83 persons were sentenced to death (Death Penalty Information Center, 2014).

Although the highly publicized trials of defendants such as Dale Hausner are not typical, they nonetheless are the trials that capture the public's attention and, in many ways, define what people believe about the process of trial and adjudication in the United States. They also are the trials that are most likely to involve clashes between the prosecution and the defense over the selection of the jury, the admissibility of evidence, and the testimony and examination of witnesses. In short, they are the trials that best symbolize the adversarial nature of the criminal court system.

The purpose of this chapter is to describe the criminal trial, from the opening statements by the prosecutor and the defense attorney to the verdict by the judge or jury.

OPENING STATEMENTS

After the judge has ruled on pretrial motions and the jury has been selected and sworn in, the trial begins with opening statements by the prosecutor and the defense attorney. Although neither side is required to make an opening statement and the statements themselves are not considered evidence, the prosecutor will almost always make at least a brief statement that explains the charges that have been filed and the evidence that is likely to be produced as the trial progresses. In his statement, the prosecutor might describe the crime, the defendant's motivation for committing the crime, and the impact that the crime has had on the victim or the victim's family. The prosecutor also might walk the jury through the evidence, explaining the relevance of the evidence and demonstrating how the evidence will prove the defendant's guilt. For example, Joseph Hartzler was the attorney who prosecuted Timothy McVeigh for the bombing of the Murrah Federal Building in Oklahoma City that left 168 people dead, including 19 children from a day care center in the building. He concluded his opening statement by promising to meet the burden of proving Timothy McVeigh guilty beyond a reasonable doubt:

> It's our burden to prove each of the elements for each of the counts. We will meet that burden. We will make your job easy. We will present ample evidence to convince you beyond any reasonable doubt that Timothy McVeigh is responsible for this terrible crime. You will hear evidence in this case that McVeigh liked to consider himself a patriot, someone who could start the second American Revolution. The literature that was in his car when he was arrested included some that quoted statements from the founding fathers and other people who played a part in the

American Revolution, people like Patrick Henry and Samuel Adams. McVeigh isolated and took these statements out of context, and he did that to justify his anti-government violence. Well, ladies and gentlemen, the statements of our forefathers can never be televised to justify warfare against innocent children. Our forefathers didn't fight British women and children. They fought other soldiers. They fought them face to face, hand to hand. They didn't plant bombs and run away wearing earplugs. (Entire opening statement available online at www.famous-trials.com/oklacity/727-hartzleropening)

The defense attorney also has the opportunity to make an opening statement at the beginning of the trial. Often, the defense will remind the jurors that the defendant is presumed innocent until proven guilty and that the prosecution bears the burden of proving the defendant's guilt beyond a reasonable doubt. The defense may also remind the jurors that their duty is to ensure that justice is done and ask them to keep an open mind until they have heard all the evidence in the case. In the Timothy McVeigh case, defense attorney Steven Jones began his opening statement by stating that the evidence would prove not McVeigh's guilt but his innocence:

I have waited two years for this moment to outline the evidence to you that the Government will produce, that I will produce, both by direct and cross-examination, by exhibits, photographs, transcripts of telephone conversations, transcripts of conversations inside houses, videotapes, that will establish not a reasonable doubt but that my client is innocent of the crime that Mr. Hartzler has outlined to you. (Entire opening statement available online at www.famous-trials.com/oklacity/722-defenseopen)

In many jurisdictions, the defense attorney has the option of reserving the opening statement until the state has concluded its case and the defense case is about to begin. The advantage of this is that it allows the defense to size up the state's case, point out evidence that the state promised in its opening statement but failed to deliver, and generally respond more effectively to the evidence (or lack thereof) presented by the prosecution. On the other hand, deferring the opening statement means that the defense attorney does not get the opportunity early on in the trial to present his or her version of the case or to persuade the jury to keep an open mind or to view the evidence from the defense perspective.

THE PRESENTATION OF EVIDENCE

The introduction of evidence in the case begins with the prosecutor presenting the case for the state. This is because the prosecutor has the burden of proving the defendant's guilt beyond a reasonable doubt; the defendant is presumed to be innocent and therefore is not required to prove her innocence. It is important to point out that the presumption of innocence is not a prediction of the outcome of the case: Presuming the defendant's innocence does not equate to an expectation that the defendant will be found not guilty. Rather, as Herbert Packer (1968) pointed out, the presumption of innocence means that until there has been an adjudication of guilt by someone with the authority to make such a determination (i.e., the judge or jury), the suspect is to be treated as if his guilt is an open question.

In making a case against the defendant, the prosecutor must prove the defendant's guilt "beyond a reasonable doubt." Although the U.S. Constitution does not explicitly address this issue, the Due Process Clause has been interpreted to mean that every element of the offense in a criminal prosecution must be proved beyond a reasonable doubt. But what does this—beyond a reasonable doubt—mean? Jurors are typically informed that "reasonable doubt is a doubt based on reason, a doubt for which you can give a reason. It is not a fanciful doubt, or a whimsical doubt, nor a doubt based on conjecture" (Tanford, 1990, p. 78). In other words, the state is not required to prove its case with absolute certainty by eliminating all doubt—no matter how unreasonable—regarding the defendant's guilt from the jurors' minds. The U.S. Supreme Court, in the case of *In re Winship* (397 U.S. 358, 1970), emphasized the importance of the proof beyond a reasonable doubt standard, noting that

> a society that values the good name and freedom of every individual should not condemn a man for commission of a crime when there is reasonable doubt about his guilt. Moreover, use of the reasonable-doubt standard is indispensable to command the respect and confidence of the criminal law. It is critical that the moral force of the criminal law not be diluted by a standard of proof that leaves people in doubt whether innocent men are being condemned. It is also important in our free society that every individual going about his ordinary affairs have confidence that his government cannot adjudge him guilty of a criminal offense without convincing a proper fact finder of his guilt with utmost certainty.

To prove its case, the prosecution calls witnesses and introduces various types of evidence (see later in this chapter for a discussion of the types of evidence and the rules for presenting evidence). After the prosecution has presented its direct case against the defendant—that is, the evidence designed to prove beyond a reasonable doubt that the defendant committed the crime—the defense presents its case. Often, the defense attorney will first move for a directed verdict of not guilty, which in some states is referred to as a judgment of acquittal. Essentially the defense attorney is asking the judge to rule that the prosecution has not proven the defendant's guilt beyond a reasonable doubt. If the judge grants the motion, the defendant is discharged and the case is over. If, as is more likely, the judge rejects the motion, the case continues with the presentation of evidence, if any, by the defense.

Like the state, the defense may call witnesses and introduce evidence. However, the defense is not required to do so; as noted earlier, the defense attorney does not have to prove the defendant's innocence. If the defendant does not have a valid defense and is not going to testify in his own defense, the defense attorney's strategy will be to create doubt in the minds of the jurors through cross-examination of the witnesses called by the prosecution.

Each witness who is called to testify in the case is questioned first by the side that called the witness. This is referred to as the direct examination of the witness.

KEY CASES
SOUTH CAROLINA V. ARNOLD, OPINION NO. 25892 (2004)

A Directed Verdict in a Murder Case

In 2004, the South Carolina Supreme Court upheld a lower court decision overturning the conviction of Eddie Lee Arnold for the murder of a Savannah child psychologist. The lower appellate court ruled that the judge should have granted the defense attorney's motion for a directed verdict of acquittal at the conclusion of the state's case. The South Carolina Supreme Court agreed, noting that the circumstantial evidence against Arnold was not sufficient to prove his guilt. The court was particularly critical of the fact that there was no evidence at all that put the defendant at the scene of the crime.

The lawyer for the opposing side then has an opportunity to cross-examine the witness. The attorney doing the cross-examination may try to discredit the testimony of the witness by getting the witness to contradict what she said on direct examination, by pointing out inconsistencies with statements made by other witnesses, by raising questions about the witness's motivation in testifying, or by getting the witness to admit to a criminal record or other facts that raise questions about the witness's credibility. Alternatively, the attorney simply may attempt to get the witness to say things that are consistent with the attorney's version of the facts. The cross-examination of the witness may be followed by a redirect examination, in which the side that originally called the witness is allowed to question the witness again so as to clarify or explain issues that were raised during the cross-examination. If an issue not raised before comes out during the redirect examination, the judge may allow a re-cross-examination.

To illustrate how this might work, assume that the prosecutor has called a witness in a criminal case involving the sexual assault of a woman by a man she met at a local bar. The witness is the victim, who testifies on direct examination that she met the suspect at the bar and, after a couple of drinks, agreed to accompany him to his apartment, where he sexually assaulted her. She describes the sexual assault and testifies that she asked the suspect to stop. She also testifies that the suspect drove her home after the attack. On cross-examination, the defense attorney asks her how much she had to drink at the bar and whether she was impaired when she arrived at the suspect's apartment; he also asks her a series of questions designed to elicit what she did to rebuff the defendant's advances and to establish doubt in the jurors' minds that the sexual contact was nonconsensual. He focuses on the fact that the victim willingly went to the suspect's apartment and allowed the suspect to drive her home after allegedly being sexually assaulted. During the redirect examination, the prosecutor asks the victim questions designed to establish that she was not impaired by alcohol or drugs at the time and asks her to clarify why she went to the suspect's apartment and allowed the defendant to drive her home.

It is important to point out that the defendant in a criminal case has a *right* to cross-examine witnesses against him or her. This right is found in the Sixth Amendment to the Constitution, which states that a defendant has the right "to be confronted with the witnesses against him." This has been interpreted to mean, among other

THE LAWYER WHO ASKED ONE QUESTION TOO MANY

Inexperienced lawyers often commit the common error of cross-examining every witness, even interrogating witnesses whose direct testimony has done no damage to their case. Eventually most lawyers learn to leave witnesses alone if there is nothing to be gained from them. Knowing when to stop asking questions is sometimes learned from painful lessons of having gone on too long. [President Abraham] Lincoln was fond of telling the story of the young lawyer who asked one question too many: "If you now admit not having seen the defendant bite the young man's ear, how can you tell this jury that he really did bite that ear off?" "Because," the witness answered, "I saw him spit it out."

Source: Wishman (1986, pp. 179–180).

things, that the defendant must have an opportunity to question all witnesses called by the prosecution so as to test the accuracy and credibility of the witness's testimony. As the U.S. Supreme Court stated in *California v. Green* (1970), the purpose of the Confrontation Clause is to ensure that "the trier of fact [has] a satisfactory basis for evaluating the truth of the prior statement."

Generally, the right to confront witnesses has been interpreted to mean that the witnesses who testify against the defendant must appear at trial and confront the defendant face-to-face. In fact, in 1988, the U.S. Supreme Court ruled that an Iowa statute that allowed children who were victims of child abuse to testify from behind a screen violated the defendant's constitutional right to a face-to-face confrontation with accusing witnesses (*Coy v. Iowa*, 1988). The Court returned to this issue 2 years later (*Maryland v. Craig*, 1990). In this case, the issue was whether a child victim of sexual assault could testify by closed-circuit television. The justices, who noted that the Confrontation Clause does not guarantee criminal defendants an absolute right to a face-to-face confrontation with witnesses against them at trial, also stated that face-to-face confrontation can be dispensed with "only where denial of such confrontation is necessary to further an important public policy and only where the reliability of the testimony is otherwise assured." The Court found that the Maryland procedure, unlike the one struck down in Iowa, did ensure the reliability of the testimony; the defendant was able to cross-examine the witness, and the judge and jurors were able to observe the demeanor and body language of the witness as he or she testified. The Court concluded that "a State's interest in the physical and psychological well-being of child abuse victims may be sufficiently important to outweigh, at least in some cases, a defendant's right to face his or her accusers in court." Although a number of state courts have held that these types of procedures violate their state constitutions, they are not necessarily *precluded* by the Sixth Amendment of the U.S. Constitution.

CALLING WITNESSES

The Sixth Amendment gives the defendant in a criminal case the right to cross-examine witnesses against him or her and also "to have compulsory process for obtaining witnesses in his favor." This means that the defendant can compel witnesses to come to court and testify in the case. This is done by subpoena, which is a court order requiring the individual to come to court and testify as a witness. The subpoena form used by the U.S. District Court for the Northern District of California, for example, states,

> YOU ARE COMMANDED to appear in the United States District Court at the place, date, and time specified below, or any subsequent date and time set by the court, to testify in the above referenced case. This subpoena shall remain in effect until you are granted leave to depart by the court or by an officer acting on behalf of the court.

The subpoena can be used to compel witnesses to give pretrial depositions to explain what they know about the crime and the defendant's role in the crime, to testify at the trial itself, and/or to bring specified evidence or documents to court. If the individual subpoenaed does not appear on the date specified, the judge has the power to find the person in contempt of court, which may result in a jail sentence or fine.

Privileged Communications

Certain categories of individuals generally cannot be compelled to testify in criminal cases. For instance, husbands and wives cannot be forced to testify against each other, priests cannot be compelled to testify about things told to them in confidence by parishioners, doctors cannot be forced to testify about their patients, and lawyers cannot be forced to reveal information provided by their clients. Each of these types of communication—referred to as **privileged communication**—is an exception to the general rule that all relevant evidence is admissible at trial. The rationale behind these privileges, none of which is absolute, is that each of these relationships involves an expectation of privacy and confidentiality. Husbands and wives assume that things told to one another in confidence will not be revealed. Similarly, those who confess to a priest or confide in a doctor or lawyer have an expectation of confidentiality.

Regarding the spousal or marital privilege, the Supreme Court in 1934 held that "the basis of the immunity given to communications between husband and wife is the protection of marital confidences, regarded as so essential to the preservation of the marriage relationship as to outweigh the disadvantages to the administration of justice which the privilege entails" (*Wolfe v. United States,* 1934). However, the marital privilege does not apply if the victim of the crime was the spouse or a child of the defendant or if the statements were made in the presence of a third party. The privilege can be waived if the spouse is willing to testify in the case. If the spouse claims the privilege and refuses to testify against his or her partner, the prosecution cannot comment on the spouse's failure to testify.

A highly publicized case involving the spousal privilege was the trial of Michael Derderian, who, along with his brother, was charged with involuntary manslaughter after 100 people died in a 2003 fire at a Rhode Island nightclub, which the brothers owned. Kristina Link, who was the office manager for the nightclub at the time of the fire, initially testified before the grand jury that indicted the brothers. She later married Michael Derderian and, when subpoenaed to testify at his trial, indicated that she would invoke the marital privilege and would refuse to testify. Both of the brothers eventually pleaded no contest to involuntary manslaughter.

Privilege Against Self-Incrimination

The other person who cannot be called to the stand to testify in a criminal case is the defendant. The Fifth Amendment states that "no person . . . shall be compelled in any criminal case to be a witness against himself." This **privilege against self-incrimination** means that the prosecutor cannot call the defendant as a witness and question this person about her involvement in the crime with which she is charged. Although critics charge that the privilege helps guilty people avoid conviction for their crimes, Supreme Court Justice Arthur Goldberg saw it as a protection of individual rights. In *Murphy v. Waterfront Commission of New York* (1964), Goldberg wrote, "The privilege [of avoiding self-incrimination] while sometimes a shelter to the guilty, is often a protection to the innocent."

The defendant's failure to take the stand and tell his side of the story obviously will raise questions in the minds of the judge and, especially, the jurors. The jurors will wonder why, if the defendant is innocent, he is unwilling to testify under oath that he played no role in the crime with which he is charged. However, the defendant does not have to explain the decision to remain silent, and the prosecutor cannot comment on the defendant's refusal to testify. The prosecutor cannot say, in her closing argument, for example, "If the defendant is innocent, as he claims, why doesn't he take the stand and tell us what he knows? What is he hiding?" In fact, the defendant can request that the judge instruct the jurors not to infer anything from the defendant's failure to testify. As the Supreme Court stated in the case of *Carter v. Kentucky* (1981),

> A trial judge has a powerful tool at his disposal to protect the constitutional privilege—the jury instruction—and he has an affirmative constitutional obligation to use that tool when a defendant seeks its employment. No judge can prevent jurors from speculating about why a defendant stands mute in the face of a criminal accusation, but a judge can, and must, if requested to do so, use the unique power of the jury instruction to reduce that speculation to a minimum.

If the defendant waives the privilege against self-incrimination and takes the stand in her own defense, the defendant, like all other witnesses, is subject to cross-examination by the prosecutor. This means that the prosecutor can attempt to impeach the defendant's credibility by asking, for example, if the defendant has ever been convicted of a crime. Moreover, the defendant cannot pick and choose the questions to answer and must testify truthfully or face the prospect of prosecution for perjury.

A related issue is whether defendants have a right to testify in their own defense and whether the scope of their testimony can be limited. The Supreme Court has ruled that the Fourteenth Amendment's guarantee that no one should be "deprived of life, liberty, or property without due process of law" includes defendants' right to offer testimony in their own defense (*Faretta v. California,* 1975). This right is also found in the Sixth Amendment provision giving defendants the right to call witnesses and in the defendant's right to serve as his own lawyer. As the Court stated in a 1987 case, "A defendant's opportunity to conduct his own defense by calling witnesses is incomplete if he may not present himself as a witness" (*Rock v. Arkansas,* 1987). However, the introduction of the defendant's testimony is governed by the same rules of evidence that apply to the testimony of other witnesses.

EVIDENCE AND RULES OF EVIDENCE

During the trial of Dale Hausner, the Phoenix serial shooter convicted and sentenced to death in 2009 for six murders and more than 70 other crimes, prosecutors trying the case introduced the testimony of dozens of victims who allegedly were targeted by Hausner as well as the testimony of the police and paramedics who responded to the crimes. They used this testimony to lay out the facts of every shooting, stabbing, and arson that Hausner was accused of committing. They also introduced transcripts of secret wiretap conversations between Hausner and Samuel Dieteman (who was charged along with Hausner and who testified against him) and several hours of the videotaped interrogation of Hausner by Phoenix police detectives. A police fingerprint analyst testified that Hausner's fingerprints were not found on either of the shotguns seized from Hausner's property the night of his arrest, but a police DNA analyst testified that his DNA was found on a pair of latex gloves that also had gunshot residue on them. Hausner's ex-wife also testified for the prosecution; she claimed that Hausner had violent tendencies and that he attacked her on two occasions. Hausner testified in his own defense, arguing that he had alibis for many of the times when the crimes occurred.

As this case illustrates, a criminal trial may involve the introduction of various types of evidence. To prove the defendant's guilt, the prosecution introduces evidence designed to prove the elements of the crime and to convince the judge or jury that the defendant is the person who committed the crime. Likewise, the defendant may introduce evidence that challenges the prosecution's version of the crime and raises questions about the evidence presented by the prosecution.

Types of Evidence

The evidence introduced at trial may be either real evidence or testimonial evidence (Scheb & Scheb, 1999). **Real evidence** consists of fingerprints or DNA linking the suspect to the crime, stolen property, clothing worn by the victim, documents, photographs of the victim or the crime scene, guns or knives used in the crime, and other tangible items. **Testimonial evidence** is the sworn statements of witnesses, including the victim, eyewitnesses to the crime, and the police officers who investigated the crime. It also includes the testimony of experts who are called to testify about things such as the defendant's sanity; the scientific tests that were conducted on fingerprints, DNA, or a recovered weapon; or the cause of the victim's death. Although there are some exceptions, lay witnesses generally are not allowed to express their opinions or draw conclusions. They are required to state what they saw, heard, felt, tasted, or smelled. By contrast, expert witnesses may express their opinions about things that are within the area of their expertise: A psychiatrist might testify that, in his opinion, the defendant suffers from paranoid schizophrenia; a handwriting expert might testify that the defendant forged the victim's signature on a check; and a forensic scientist might testify about the "match" between the defendant's DNA and the DNA found in a semen sample taken from the victim of a sexual assault. To testify as an expert, the witness must be accepted by the trial court as an expert on the topic about which the witness is to testify. In 2018, for example, a forensic psychiatrist named Barbara Ziv testified as an expert witness in the retrial of comedian Bill Cosby, whose first trial on sexual assault charges ended in a hung jury. Ziv was called to testify about the prevalence of rape myths—pervasive misconceptions about the behavior and comportment of "genuine" victims of sexual assault—to counteract defense allegations that the victim in the crime was lying because she failed to make a prompt report and that she maintained contact with Cosby following the attack. In April 2018 Cosby was convicted of three counts of sexual assault.

Evidence can be either direct or indirect. **Direct evidence** includes eyewitness testimony, the confession of the defendant, or testimony by the victim of the crime; it is evidence that, by itself, proves (or disproves) a fact that is at issue in the case. **Indirect evidence**, or circumstantial evidence, is evidence that requires the judge or jury to make inferences about what happened at the scene of the crime or judgments about the defendant's role in the crime. An eyewitness who testifies that she saw the defendant force the victim out of a car at gunpoint is giving direct evidence. By contrast, evidence that the defendant's fingerprints were found on the steering wheel of the car is circumstantial evidence; the existence of the fingerprints establishes that the defendant was in the car but does not establish that the defendant is the person who committed the crime. Evidence can be both direct and circumstantial. For example, a credit card receipt for the purchase of the gun that was used in the crime is direct evidence that the defendant owned the gun but only circumstantial evidence that the defendant is the person who used the gun during the commission of the crime.

Rules of Evidence

The introduction of witness testimony and other types of evidence is governed by the rules of evidence. The two most important of these rules concern the relevance and the competence of the evidence. According to Rule 401 of the Federal Rules of Evidence, "'Relevant evidence' means evidence having any tendency to make the existence of any fact that is of consequence to the determination of the action more probable or less probable than it would be without the evidence." Evidence that does not meet this standard is irrelevant and is therefore inadmissible. For example, assume that a defendant is charged with burglary of a residence. It would be relevant to show that the defendant's fingerprints were found in the house, that a laptop computer and jewelry stolen during the burglary were sold to a pawnshop, and that the owner of the pawnshop paid the defendant, whom he can identify, for the items. Evidence that the defendant had once been arrested for driving while intoxicated or that the defendant had a child out of wedlock would be irrelevant; this evidence would not help the judge or jury decide whether the defendant is the person who burglarized the home.

Evidence must also be competent. The competence of real evidence is established by showing that the evidence really is what it is purported to be; that is, that the gun is, in fact, the gun that was found at the scene of the crime, that the bullets are the actual bullets that were recovered from the body of the victim, and the letter from the defendant to the victim is the original letter and not a photocopy. The police officer who found the gun would testify that the gun was found in a particular place and would explain what he did with the gun after finding it and where it has been since it was recovered. The medical examiner who removed the bullets from the victim's body similarly would present testimony designed to establish that the bullets being entered as evidence in the case are the actual bullets recovered during the postmortem examination of the victim.

CURRENT CONTROVERSY
NATIONAL ACADEMY OF SCIENCES REPORT ON FORENSIC EVIDENCE

In 2009, the National Academy of Sciences issued a highly critical report on the forensic evidence that police and prosecutors often rely on in criminal trials, including fingerprints, firearms identification, and analysis of bite marks, blood spatter, hair, and handwriting (National Research Council, 2009). The report noted that, with the possible exception of DNA evidence, there was little scientific basis for the claims made about the reliability or infallibility of forensic evidence. For example, the report stated that claims that fingerprint analyses have a zero error rate are "not scientifically plausible" and that the scientific basis for bite mark evidence is "insufficient to conclude that bite mark comparisons can result in a conclusive match." The authors of the report also charged that many of the nation's crime labs, which they characterized as "a system in disarray," were underfunded, beholden to law enforcement agencies, and lacked oversight and consistent standards. The report called for a number of reforms, including the creation of a new federal agency, the National Institute for Forensic Science, which would fund scientific research, disseminate standards for use and interpretation of forensic evidence, and certify expert witnesses and forensic analysts. U.S. Court of Appeals Judge Harry Edwards, who cochaired the panel, said, "There are a lot of people who are concerned, and they should be concerned. Forensic science is the handmaiden of the legal system. . . . If you claim to be science, you ought to put yourself to the test."

Testimonial evidence also must be competent. The witness who is testifying must be competent to testify. This standard requires that the witness testify under oath and swear (or affirm) that the testimony the witness is about to give is "the truth, the whole truth, and nothing but the truth." This, in turn, requires that the witness understand what it means to tell the truth. The witness also must have personal knowledge about the subject of his testimony (i.e., he saw, heard, felt, tasted, or smelled something relevant to the case) and must be able to recollect and describe what happened. Under this standard, a very young child might not be competent to testify; a child of age 3 or 4 might not understand the meaning of telling the truth and might not have the language skills to be able to accurately describe what she saw or heard. Similarly, a person with a mental illness or an eyewitness to a crime who was under the influence of alcohol or drugs at the time of the crime might be ruled incompetent to testify. If there are questions about the competence of a potential witness, the judge hearing the case must determine whether the witness is competent.

Objecting to Introduction of Evidence or Questions Asked

The admissibility of evidence can be established either before trial—through the judge's rulings on motions to suppress evidence—or during the trial—through the judge's ruling on objections to evidence raised by either the prosecutor or the defense. The attorney making the objection will say, "Your honor, I object," and will then state the reason for the objection. Either side can object to the introduction of evidence on the grounds that the evidence is not relevant, that the witness is not competent to testify or is being asked to give an opinion that the witness is not qualified to give, or on some other grounds. The judge either will rule immediately on the objection—either sustaining it or overruling it—or will ask the opposing attorney to respond to the objection. The judge also may send the jury out of the courtroom before hearing arguments from the two sides.

A common reason for objecting to the admission of evidence is that the evidence is hearsay. **Hearsay evidence** is evidence given by a witness that is based on information provided to the witness by someone else. This type of evidence generally is not admissible. For example, a witness who states in court, "I know that the defendant owned a gun like that because my brother told me that he saw the gun in the defendant's car," would be giving hearsay testimony. The witness has no direct knowledge that the defendant owned a gun. If the prosecutor wants to prove that the defendant owned such a gun, the prosecutor must call the witness's brother to the stand to testify.

There are a number of important exceptions to the hearsay rule. In fact, the Federal Rules of Evidence list more than 20 situations in which hearsay evidence can be admitted. This includes the so-called dying declaration exception, which allows, for example, a third party to testify about statements made by a homicide victim as the victim was dying. If the victim identified or described the perpetrator of the crime before dying and if a nurse attending the victim heard what the victim said, the nurse would be allowed to testify about what he heard. Related to this is the excited utterance exception, which allows third parties to testify about emergency 911 telephone calls or about statements made to a police officer arriving at the scene of the crime. The assumption is that statements made by a person who has just been the victim of a crime or who has just witnessed a crime will be spontaneous and trustworthy. As one court put it, "The test is whether the utterance was made before there has been time to contrive and misrepresent—that is, while the nervous excitement may be supposed still to dominate and the reflective powers to be yet in abeyance" (*People v. Brown,* 1987).

Restricting the Introduction of Evidence: Rape Shield Laws

Significant changes in rape laws have occurred in the past several decades (Spohn & Horney, 1992). These changes came after feminists, social scientists, and legal scholars charged that the laws and the rules of evidence unique to rape encouraged criminal justice officials and jurors to base their decisions on legally irrelevant evaluations of the victim's character, reputation, and relationship with the accused.

Reformers were particularly critical of evidentiary rules that allowed the defense attorney to introduce evidence of the victim's past sexual conduct or reputation for promiscuity. Under common law, evidence of the victim's sexual history was admissible to prove that she had consented to intercourse and to impeach her credibility as a witness. The notion that the victim's prior sexual conduct was pertinent to whether she consented was based on the assumption that chastity was a character trait and that, therefore, an unchaste woman would be more likely to agree to intercourse than a woman without premarital or extramarital experiences. Some courts also admitted evidence of the victim's lack of chastity on the issue of credibility, which they justified on the grounds that unchaste women are apt to lie (see, generally, Estrich, 1987; Spohn & Horney, 1992).

Those who championed rape law reform insisted that this two-pronged evidentiary rule be eliminated or modified. Some pointed to the law's inherent double standard; nonmarital sexual activity could not be used to impeach the defendant's credibility if he took the stand but could be used to call the victim's truthfulness into question. Many critics argued that the rule was archaic in light of changes in attitudes toward sexual relationships and toward the role of women in society. This type of evidence, according to critics of the evidentiary rule, was simply irrelevant to either the issue of nonconsent or the credibility of the victim as a witness.

Confronted with arguments such as these, state legislatures enacted rape shield statutes designed to limit the admissibility of evidence of the victim's past sexual conduct. The laws range from the less restrictive, which permit evidence of sexual conduct to be admitted if it is shown to be relevant, to the most restrictive, which prohibit such evidence unless it involves a prior sexual relationship between the victim and the defendant. Between these two extremes are statutes that attempt to balance the interests of the victim against the rights of the defendant by delineating a number of exceptions to the general presumption against admission of evidence of sexual conduct. Among the more common exceptions are (a) evidence of the complainant's prior sexual activity with third persons to show that a third person was the source of semen, pregnancy, or disease and (b) evidence to rebut sexual conduct evidence introduced by the prosecutor.

Rape shield laws are controversial. The main point of contention between advocates and opponents of the laws is whether evidence of the victim's past sexual behavior is, in fact, relevant evidence. Reformers argue that what a woman has done in the past with other people or in other situations is not relevant to her behavior with the defendant in the situation being contested. Some civil libertarians and legal scholars, on the other hand, argue that the evidence is relevant if it reveals a pattern of behavior or a propensity to engage willingly in a particular type of behavior. If this is the case, according to critics of the laws, the evidence is relevant to whether the victim consented to the behavior in question and should be admitted.

Consider a case in which the victim has accused the defendant of sexual assault. She testifies that she met the defendant at a singles' bar, danced and drank with him, and accepted his offer to drive her home. She also testifies that he walked her to the front door of her apartment and, when she opened the door, forced his way in and raped her. The defendant admits that he and the victim had sexual relations but claims that it was consensual. He wants to introduce evidence that the victim previously had consented to intercourse with casual acquaintances that she met at singles' bars.

What do you think? Is the evidence of the victim's prior sexual conduct relevant? Can the defendant get a fair trial if the evidence is excluded?

CLOSING ARGUMENTS

After all the evidence in the case has been presented, each side is allowed to make a closing argument. As is the case with the opening statements, what the attorneys say during closing arguments is not considered evidence. The prosecutor usually goes first, followed by the defense attorney, with the prosecutor having an opportunity to make a concluding argument. The purpose of the closing argument is to summarize the case for the jury and to persuade the jury to either convict or acquit

SOWING SEEDS OF REASONABLE DOUBT IN THE MINDS OF THE JURORS

During a closing argument, a defense attorney is said to have told the jury, "In the next few seconds, you will see the alleged murder victim walking into the courtroom." After every juror had turned to look in the direction of the door, the lawyer continued, "Although the victim has not appeared, I have proved that you must have a reasonable doubt in your minds that the victim is even dead, much less murdered. Otherwise you would not all have looked at the door of the courtroom."

Source: Wishman (1986, pp. 223–224).

CURRENT CONTROVERSY

PLAYING THE "RACE CARD" IN A CRIMINAL TRIAL

In 1994, O. J. Simpson, a Black actor and former All-American football star, was accused of murdering his ex-wife, Nicole Brown Simpson, and Ronald Goldman, a friend of hers. On October 4, 1995, a jury composed of seven Black women, two White women, one Hispanic man, and one Black man acquitted Simpson of all charges. Many commentators attributed Simpson's acquittal at least in part to the fact that his attorney, Johnnie L. Cochran Jr., had "played the race card" during the trial. In fact, another of Simpson's attorneys, Robert Shapiro, charged that Cochran not only played the race card but "dealt it from the bottom of the deck" (Kennedy, 1997, p. 287).

Cochran was criticized for attempting to show that Mark Fuhrman, a Los Angeles police officer who found the bloody glove that linked Simpson to the crime, was a racist who planted the evidence in an attempt to frame Simpson. He also was harshly criticized for suggesting during his closing argument that the jurors would be justified in nullifying the law by acquitting Simpson. Cochran encouraged the jurors to take Fuhrman's racist beliefs into account during their deliberations. He urged them to

"send a message" to society that "we are not going to take that anymore" (Kennedy, 1997, pp. 286–290).

Although appeals to racial sentiment—that is, "playing the race card"—are not unusual in U.S. courts, they are rarely used by defense attorneys representing Blacks accused of victimizing Whites. Much more typical are *prosecutorial* appeals to bias. Consider the following historical examples:

- An Alabama prosecutor who declared, "Unless you hang this Negro, our White people living out in the country won't be safe" (*Moulton v. State*, 1917)
- A prosecutor in North Carolina who dismissed as implausible the claim of three Black men that the White woman they were accused of raping had consented to sex with them. The prosecutor stated that "the average white woman abhors anything of this type in nature that had to do with a black man" (*Miller v. North Carolina*, 1978)
- A prosecutor in a rape case involving a Black man and a White woman who asked the jurors, "Gentlemen, do you believe that she

(Continued)

(Continued)

would have had intercourse with this black brute?" (*State v. Washington*, 1915)

- A prosecutor in a case involving the alleged kidnapping of a White man by two Black men who said in his closing argument that "not one *white* witness has been produced" to rebut the victim's testimony (*Withers v. United States*, 1976, emphasis added)

- A prosecutor who stated, during the penalty phase of a capital case involving Walter J. Blair, a Black man charged with murdering a White woman, "Can you imagine [the victim's] state of mind when she woke up at 6 o'clock that morning, staring into the muzzle of a gun held by this black man?" (*Blair v. Armontrout*, 1990)

All of these appeals to racial sentiment, with the exception of the last, resulted in reversal of the defendants' convictions. A federal court of appeals, for example, ruled in 1978 that the North Carolina prosecutor's contention that a White woman would never consent to sex with a Black man was a "blatant appeal to racial prejudice." The court added that when such an appeal involves an issue as "sensitive as consent to sexual intercourse in a prosecution for rape . . . the prejudice engendered is so great

that automatic reversal is required" (*Miller v. North Carolina*, 1978, p. 708).

A federal court of appeals, on the other hand, refused to reverse Walter Blair's conviction and death sentence. Its refusal was based on the fact that Blair's attorney failed to object at trial to the prosecutor's statement. The sole dissenter in the case suggested that the court should have considered whether the defense attorney's failure to object meant that Blair had been denied effective assistance of counsel. He also vehemently condemned the prosecutor's statement, which he asserted "played upon white fear of crime and the tendency of white people to associate crime with blacks" (*Blair v. Armontrout*, 1990, p. 1351).

According to Harvard law professor Randall Kennedy, playing the race card in a criminal trial is "virtually always morally and legally wrong." He asserted that doing so encourages juries to base their verdicts on irrelevant considerations and loosens the requirement that the state prove the case beyond a reasonable doubt. As he noted, "Racial appeals are not only a distraction but a menace that can distort interpretations of evidence or even seduce jurors into believing that they should vote in a certain way irrespective of the evidence" (*Kennedy*, 1997, pp. 256–257).

the defendant. The attorneys can only discuss issues that were raised during the trial and cannot comment on evidence that was not presented. The prosecutor cannot comment on the fact that the defendant failed to testify in his or her own defense or make inflammatory remarks to the jury. Although defense attorneys may be given wider latitude in making closing arguments to the jury, they too are prohibited from crossing the line by, for example, challenging the integrity of the prosecutor or referring to the state's witnesses in derogatory terms.

Both the prosecutor and the defense attorney generally will begin the closing argument by thanking the members of the jury for their attention and their patience. Each side then will recollect and evaluate the evidence that was presented and attempt to connect the evidence to the theory of the case that was developed during the trial. The prosecutor will discuss the elements of the crime and will argue that the evidence proves the defendant's guilt beyond a reasonable doubt; the defense will argue just the opposite. Although each side may urge the jury to "do its duty" by either convicting or acquitting the defendant, it is inappropriate for either side to express a personal belief in the defendant's guilt or innocence.

INSTRUCTING THE JURY

Before the jurors begin their deliberations, the judge instructs them about the law and how they are to apply the law. This is because the jurors determine the facts in the case, but the judge determines the law that is to be applied. As the Supreme Court stated in 1895, "It is the duty of juries . . . to take the law from the court and apply that law to the facts as they find them to be from the evidence" (*Sparf v. United States,* 1895).

In the instructions to the jury, the judge reminds the jurors that the defendant is presumed innocent and that the prosecutor bears the burden of proving the defendant's guilt beyond a reasonable doubt. The judge defines each of the elements of the crime(s) with which the defendant is charged and, if the defendant has raised a defense such as insanity or self-defense, explains the meaning of the defense based on the law in that jurisdiction. The judge may also instruct the jurors regarding the procedures they are to follow as they deliberate. The judge might say, for example,

> Each juror should listen, with a disposition to be convinced, to the opinions and arguments of the other jurors. It is not intended under the law that a juror should go into the jury room with a fixed determination that the verdict shall represent his opinion of the case at that particular moment. Nor is it intended that he should close his ears to the discussions and arguments of his fellow jurors who are assumed to be equally honest and intelligent. (Wishman, 1986, p. 222)

If a unanimous verdict is required, the judge will explain what this means and will instruct the jury on the procedures to be followed if they cannot reach unanimity.

One of the criticisms of jury instructions is that, because they are crafted by lawyers, they are full of legal jargon and therefore are difficult for laypeople to understand. As Jerome Frank, who served as a U.S. court of appeals judge from 1941 to 1957, wrote in 1930,

> Time and money and lives are consumed in debating the precise words which the judge may address to the jury, although everyone who stops to see and think knows that those words might as well be spoken in a foreign language. (p. 181)

A lawyer who served on a jury was similarly critical of the instructions he and his fellow jurors received, noting that "those instructions did not, in the ordinary or familiar use of that plain English word, instruct us in any way to do anything that could have been digestible to an adult without a legal training" (Kraft, 1982, p. 593).

This issue—the degree to which jurors are able to comprehend the instructions on the law given by the judge—has been the subject of a considerable amount of research. Most of this research concluded that jurors do not understand the judge's instructions (Steele & Thornburg, 1988–1989). For example, one early study of persons summoned for jury service in Florida found that only half of the jurors understood

EXHIBIT 11.1   ■   Examples of Standard Jury Instructions: State of Florida

Plea of Not Guilty: Reasonable Doubt and Presumption of Innocence

The defendant has entered a plea of not guilty. This means you must presume or believe the defendant is innocent. The presumption stays with the defendant as to each material allegation in the [information] [indictment] through each stage of the trial unless it has been overcome by the evidence to the exclusion of and beyond a reasonable doubt.

To overcome the defendant's presumption of innocence, the State has the burden of proving the crime with which the defendant is charged was committed and the defendant is the person who committed the crime.

The defendant is not required to present evidence or prove anything.

Whenever the words "reasonable doubt" are used you must consider the following:

A reasonable doubt is not a mere possible doubt, a speculative, imaginary or forced doubt. Such a doubt must not influence you to return a verdict of not guilty if you have an abiding conviction of guilt. On the other hand, if, after carefully considering, comparing and weighing all the evidence, there is not an abiding conviction of guilt, or, if, having a conviction, it is one which is not stable but one which wavers and vacillates, then the charge is not proved beyond every reasonable doubt and you must find the defendant not guilty because the doubt is reasonable.

It is to the evidence introduced in this trial, and to it alone, that you are to look for that proof.

A reasonable doubt as to the guilt of the defendant may arise from the evidence, conflict in the evidence, or the lack of evidence.

If you have a reasonable doubt, you should find the defendant not guilty. If you have no reasonable doubt, you should find the defendant guilty.

Lesser Included Crimes

In considering the evidence, you should consider the possibility that although the evidence may not convince you that the defendant committed the main crime[s] of which [he] [she] is accused, there may be evidence that [he] [she] committed other acts that would constitute a lesser included crime [or crimes]. Therefore, if you decide that the main accusation has not been proved beyond a reasonable doubt, you will next need to decide if the defendant is guilty of any lesser included crime.

Source: Florida Supreme Court, Standard Jury Instructions.

that the judge's instruction on presumption of innocence meant that the defendant did not have to present any evidence of his or her innocence (Strawn & Buchanan, 1976). There also has been research designed to determine if juror comprehension is affected by the language used in the jury instruction. One **mock jury study** found higher comprehension rates for instructions that were written in clear, nontechnical language (Elwork, Alfini, & Sales, 1987).

The results of this research prompted many jurisdictions to adopt patterned jury instructions—that is, standard instructions that apply in most criminal cases (see "Examples of Standard Jury Instructions: State of Florida" for examples of Florida's standard jury instructions). Typically, the judge consults the prosecutor and the defense attorney about the instructions that will be given and allows each side to suggest supplemental instructions. This is usually done during a charging conference. If the judge rejects one of the defense attorney's proffered instructions, the attorney will object to the judge's decision, which preserves the issue for appeal.

JURY DELIBERATIONS AND VERDICT

What goes on in the privacy of the jury room? Stated another way, what makes juries tick? This is a topic that has long fascinated legal scholars, social scientists, and others interested in criminal trials. The mystery surrounding the jury deliberation process stems from the fact that jurors deliberate in secret and are neither required nor allowed to explain why they arrived at the verdict they did. It also stems from the fact that jurors are more or less on their own in terms of the procedures they will follow in arriving at a verdict: Do they take an initial vote prior to deliberating? Should the votes be by secret ballot or by a show of hands? Should the judge's instructions be read and discussed before deliberations begin? Should they review the evidence and, if so, who should lead the discussion? All these issues are left to the jurors' discretion.

After receiving the judge's instructions, the jurors retire to the jury room. In many states, they are allowed to take a copy of the instructions with them and usually are provided with written forms for all possible verdicts in the case. Typically, the first step is to select one of the jurors as the foreperson or presiding juror, whose job it is to preside over the deliberations and votes and deliver the jury's verdict to the judge. If the jurors have questions about the evidence or need clarification of legal issues, they can send a note to the judge. Although the judge can refuse to answer the question, it is more likely that the judge will either respond immediately or call the jury (and the defendant and the lawyers for both sides) back into the courtroom for additional instructions or to read back the part of the transcript about which the jurors have questions.

The Verdict: Guilty or Not Guilty?

An important assumption underlying the jury trial is that the jurors will be able to accurately determine the facts in the case; that is, that the jurors, both individually and collectively, will arrive at a just decision (but see "Wrongful Conviction and Exoneration of the Innocent" for a discussion of wrongful convictions, many of which resulted from jury verdicts). This assumption, in turn, rests on the jurors' ability to assess the credibility of witnesses, to disregard testimony or evidence that the judge ruled inadmissible, to ignore their sympathies and/or biases toward the defendant or other witnesses, and to interpret and apply the law to the facts in the case.

As numerous commentators have pointed out (Levine, 1992), the adversarial process—which in theory should illuminate the truth—is more likely to produce juror uncertainty than certainty about the facts in the case. This is because jurors usually hear two versions of the facts, one told by the prosecutor and the other told by the defense attorney. The same set of facts, in other words, may be given two completely different interpretations by the adversaries in the case. For example, the fact that the defendant ran when confronted by the police, which the prosecutor might interpret as evidence of guilt, might be explained away by the defense attorney as evidence of fear of the police in poor neighborhoods. This is compounded by the fact that the law itself is ambiguous and vague. For instance, a key element of the crime of sexual assault is nonconsent by the victim. But what does this mean? The judge's instruction that "consent means a freely given agreement to the act of sexual penetration" notwithstanding, how will the jurors know whether the victim did or did not consent?

Because jury deliberations are conducted behind closed doors, researchers are unable to observe the actual deliberation process. Instead, they use mock juries or mock trials that involve hypothetical scenarios. These may be actual mock trials, such as in a university classroom, or simple written scenarios wherein people (often college students) are asked to decide a hypothetical defendant's fate. Then the researchers compare people's demographic characteristics to the decisions they hand down. One problem with this approach is that the hypothetical situations presented are not real, and therefore no one's liberty is at stake. In addition, the vignettes are typically short and provide very limited information about the crime, the defendant, and the victim. The decisions that "jurors" make in these situations may or may not be the same as decisions they would make in actual trials.

Research on jury decision making generally has focused on the effects of procedural characteristics, juror characteristics, case characteristics, and deliberation characteristics (Devine, Clayton, Dunford, Seying, & Pryce, 2001). Procedural characteristics refer to such factors as jury size, juror involvement during the trial, and jury instructions. Juror characteristics refer to demographic factors, such as age, race, gender, employment status, and other individual variables. Case characteristics refer to variables associated with specific trials, such as the charges involved or the strength of the evidence. Finally, deliberation characteristics refer to such factors as polling procedures or participation in deliberation.

In an extensive review of the literature, Dennis Devine and his colleagues (2001, pp. 700–701) drew several conclusions regarding juror decision making. Not surprisingly, the studies revealed that juror decisions are affected by the quality and the quantity of the evidence; jurors are more likely to convict when the evidence is strong and conclusive. The personal characteristics of the participants (i.e., the mock juror, the victim, the defendant), on the other hand, do not reliably predict juror verdicts. These factors come into play primarily in cases where the evidence is ambiguous and the outcome is therefore less predictable. This has been explained using the **liberation hypothesis** (Kalven & Zeisel, 1966), which suggests that when the evidence is uncertain, jurors are "liberated" from the constraints imposed by the law and therefore feel free to take legally irrelevant factors into consideration. Research also reveals that the deliberation process produces a reversal of the verdict preference initially favored by the majority in 1 of every 10 trials. Finally, the studies conducted to date indicate that jurors' decisions reflect their past experiences, their stereotypes about crime and criminals, and their beliefs about what is right, wrong, and fair.

Two studies of jury verdicts in actual cases addressed the issue of the factors that influence verdicts, reaching somewhat contradictory conclusions (see also the "Current Research" box, later in this chapter, which summarizes the results of a study of jury decision making in federal death penalty cases). Martha Myers (1979) analyzed jury verdicts in 201 felony trials in Marion County, Indiana. Her objective was to determine the extent to which the jury's verdict was affected by various types of evidence, indicators of witness credibility, and legally irrelevant characteristics of the victim and defendant. She found that juries were more likely to convict if a weapon was recovered, if there were several witnesses, if the defendant had a lengthy prior record or was unemployed, if the defendant or an accomplice testified, and if the victim was young. The likelihood of conviction, on the other hand, was not affected by eyewitness identification of the defendant, expert testimony, the relationship between the victim and the defendant, or the race of either the victim or the defendant. In these cases, then, the jury's decision to convict or acquit the defendant was predicted primarily by legally relevant indicators of the strength of evidence in the case, the victim's vulnerability, and the defendant's credibility.

A study of jury verdicts in 38 sexual assault trials in Indianapolis similarly found that the likelihood of a guilty verdict was affected by the strength of evidence in the case: whether a weapon was recovered, whether there was evidence that the victim suffered collateral injuries, other physical evidence, and eyewitness testimony (Reskin & Visher, 1986). However, the jurors' perceptions of the victim also played a role. Jurors were less likely to convict the defendant if they believed that the victim had not exercised sufficient caution at the time of the alleged assault or if they had questions about the victim's moral character. Consistent with Harry Kalven and Hans Zeisel's (1966) liberation hypothesis, the study also revealed that these legally irrelevant victim characteristics came into play only in weak cases—that is, in cases with no more than one of the four types of hard evidence. This led the authors to conclude that "the influence of extralegal factors [was] largely confined to weak cases in which the defendant's guilt was ambiguous because the prosecution did not present enough hard evidence" (p. 436).

WRONGFUL CONVICTION AND EXONERATION OF THE INNOCENT

In 1997, Orange County (California) Superior Court Judge Everett Dickey reversed Geronimo Pratt's 1972 conviction for first-degree murder, assault with intent to commit murder, and robbery (Olsen, 2000). Pratt, a decorated Vietnam War veteran and a leader in the Black Panther Party, was accused of killing Caroline Olsen and shooting her ex-husband Kenneth Olsen on the Lincoln Park tennis court in Santa Monica. Pratt, who claimed he had been in Oakland on Panther business at the time of the crime, was convicted based in large part on the testimony of another member of the Black Panther Party, Julius Butler. It was later revealed that Butler had been a paid police informant and that police and prosecutors in Los Angeles conspired to keep this information from the jury hearing Pratt's case.

Over the next 25 years, Pratt's lawyers filed a series of appeals, arguing that Pratt's conviction "was based on false testimony knowingly presented by the prosecution" (Olsen, 2000, p. 367). Their requests for a rehearing were repeatedly denied by California courts, and the Los Angeles District Attorney's Office refused to reopen the case. Then, in May 1997, Judge Dickey granted Pratt's petition for a writ of habeas corpus and reversed his conviction. Citing errors by the district attorney who tried the case, Judge Dickey stated, "The evidence which was withheld about Julius Butler and his activities could have put the whole case in a different light, and failure to timely disclose it undermines confidence in the verdict" (Olsen, 2000, p. 465). Geronimo Pratt, who spent 25 years in prison—including 8 years in solitary confinement—was released on June 10, 1997. In April 2000, Pratt's lawsuit for false imprisonment and violation of his civil rights was settled out of court: The city of Los Angeles agreed to pay Pratt $2.75 million, and the federal government agreed to pay him $1.75 million. Pratt's attorney, Johnnie Cochran Jr., described the settlement as "unprecedented" and praised Pratt for "the relentless pursuit of justice." Cochran also stated that the settlement puts "to rest a matter that has dragged on for more than three decades."

During the past two decades, the issue of wrongful convictions has appeared on the national political and public agendas. Highly publicized exonerations of individuals—such as Geronimo Pratt—convicted of murder, sexual assault, and other serious crimes have led to questions about the accuracy and fairness of the procedures used to investigate and adjudicate criminal cases. These concerns are based in part on the fact that a large number of the exonerees, many of whom were facing sentences of death or life in prison, were freed as a result of DNA tests that either were unavailable or were deemed unnecessary when their cases were being investigated and tried; this, in turn, has led some critics to suggest that the documented cases of wrongful conviction (according to the National Registry of Exonerations, there were 1,535 exonerations from 1989 through 2014) are only "the tip of the iceberg" (Gross, Jacoby, Matheson, Montgomery, & Patil, 2005, p. 531). Concerns about false convictions also are based on research showing that a disproportionate number of those exonerated have been racial minorities and that the disparity is particularly stark in cases of interracial sexual assault (Gross et al., 2005). Together, these concerns have raised questions about the legitimacy and integrity of the criminal justice process.

There is compelling evidence that conviction of the factually innocent occurs in court systems throughout the United States (Garrett, 2008), but the rate of wrongful convictions is difficult to estimate. Although some scholars have placed the number at around 7,500 annually (Huff, 2004), practitioners generally provide lower estimates. Two separate studies found that practitioners assume about a 0.5% to 1% rate of wrongful conviction in their own jurisdictions versus a more liberal estimate of 1% to 3% nationwide (Ramsey & Frank, 2007; Zalman, Smith, & Kiger, 2008). Even a conservative estimate of 0.5% nationally extrapolates to approximately 5,000 wrongful convictions and 2,000 innocent persons incarcerated annually (Zalman et al., 2008). When only considering capital murder–rape cases during the 1980s (a crime for which DNA evidence can be expected), D. Michael Risinger (2007) estimated, based on cases of factual innocence established through DNA evidence, a minimum base rate of erroneous convictions of 3.3%.

Several studies have attempted to investigate the reasons for erroneous convictions. C. Ronald Huff (2004) cites the following as leading predictors of wrongful conviction: false or mistaken eyewitness identification; unethical or overzealous practices among criminal justice actors, including prosecutors and the police; illegally obtained and/or false confessions; use of unreliable informants, especially "jailhouse snitches"; inadequate assistance of counsel; forensic errors and/or malfeasance (see National Research Council, 2009); and an uber-focus on legal versus factual guilt. James S. Liebman (2002) suggests that the high rate of invoking capital punishment throughout the United States (relative to other industrialized countries) raises the probability of executing factually innocent persons. Furthermore, he argues that political exigencies for elected judges maintain a high rate of death sentences (see also Bright & Keenan, 1995), which in turn enhances the probability of executing the innocent.

Rape, Race, and Misidentification

An analysis of 340 exonerations in the United States from 1989 to 1990 revealed that DNA exonerations were especially prevalent in rape cases (Gross et al., 2005). These cases also were characterized by eyewitness misidentification. In fact, in 107 of the 121 exonerations for rape, the defendant was the victim of eyewitness misidentification, and in 105 of these cases, the defendant was eventually cleared by DNA evidence. About half (102 of 205) of the exonerations in murder cases also involved eyewitness misidentification, but only 39 of the 205 defendants were cleared as a result of DNA evidence.

Although the percentages of Blacks, Hispanics, and Whites who were exonerated for all crimes were similar to the percentages of each group incarcerated in state prisons, this was not the case for rape. In 2002, 58% of all persons incarcerated for rape were White, 29% were Black, and 13% were Hispanic. Among defendants who were convicted of rape but later exonerated, the percentages were reversed: 64% were Black, 28% were White, and 7% were Hispanic. Blacks, in other words, comprised only 29% of all persons incarcerated for rape but 64% of all defendants exonerated for rape (Gross et al., 2005, p. 547).

The authors of this study suggested that the key to the explanation for the over-representation of Blacks among defendants falsely convicted for rape "is probably the race of the victim" (Gross et al., p. 547). As they pointed out, the race of the victim was known in 52 of the 69 exonerations of Blacks for rape. In 78% of these cases, the victim was White. As they noted, "Interracial rape is uncommon, and rapes of white women by black men in particular account for well under 10% of all rapes. But among rape exonerations for which we know the race of both parties, almost exactly half (39 of 80) involve a black man who was falsely convicted of raping a white woman" (p. 548).

The authors, who admitted that there were many possible explanations for this finding, stated that the "most obvious explanation for this racial disparity is probably also the most powerful: the perils of cross-racial identification" (Gross et al., p. 548). Almost all the exonerations in the interracial rape cases included in their study were based at least in part on eyewitness misidentification.

There is substantial evidence that cross-racial eyewitness identifications, particularly eyewitness identifications of Blacks by Whites, are unreliable (Meissner & Brigham, 2001; Rutledge, 2001). What seems to happen, then, is that a White victim of a rape case mistakenly identifies a Black man as the perpetrator of the crime, the defendant is found guilty at trial based at least in part on the eyewitness identification, and the defendant is exonerated when DNA evidence reveals that he was not the man who committed the crime. This line of research (see also S. Walker, Spohn, & DeLone, 2018) suggests that racial disparity in the criminal justice system remains an unresolved issue.

Requirement of Unanimity

In most jurisdictions, the jury verdict must be unanimous. This reflects the fact that the jury's role is to determine the truth, and there can be but one "true" version of the facts. It also reflects an assumption that a verdict rendered by a jury that speaks with a single voice will be more likely to be accepted as authoritative and final (Jonakait, 2006). These arguments notwithstanding, in 1972, the U.S. Supreme Court ruled that the Sixth Amendment to the Constitution did not require unanimous verdicts in criminal cases. In doing so, the court upheld an Oregon law that permitted criminal defendants to be convicted

CURRENT RESEARCH

In 1976, the U.S. Supreme Court upheld the new death penalty statute enacted in Texas following the Court's ruling in *Furman v. Georgia* that the death penalty as it was then being administered violated the constitutional prohibition against cruel and unusual punishment. The new statute required jurors to determine "Whether there is a probability the defendant would commit criminal acts of violence that would constitute a continuing threat to society." In *Jurek v. Texas*, the Court expressed confidence in the ability of jurors to make such judgments, noting, "It is, of course, not easy to predict future behavior. The fact that such a determination is difficult, however, does not mean that it cannot be made . . . . The task that a Texas jury must perform in answering the statutory question in issue is basically no different from the task performed countless times each day throughout the American system of criminal justice."

Mark D. Cunningham, Jon R. Sorensen, and Thomas J. Reidy (2009) argue that confidence in jurors' ability to predict future dangerousness "may not be well placed" (p. 226). Noting that rates of prison violence are low, the authors point out that "it is much more difficult to predict which offender will exhibit a low base rate behavior" (p. 227). That is, it is unlikely that jurors in capital cases will be able to identify, with any degree of accuracy, the relatively rare offender who will engage in serious violence while incarcerated.

To test this, the authors use data on 72 male federal capital defendants for whom juries made a determination of the defendants' likelihood of committing future acts of violence; 37 of the defendants were sentenced to life in prison with no possibility of parole (LWOP) and 35 received a sentence of death. They used data from the Federal Bureau of Prisons to determine whether each offender had committed any serious violent disciplinary violations, including homicide, attempted homicide, serious assault (which was defined as assault with the potential to result in

serious injury), attempted serious assault, participating in a riot, or taking a hostage.

When they examined the characteristics of offenders in the two groups—that is, the offenders for whom the jury found that future violence was likely and the offenders for whom the jury found that future violence was not likely—the authors found that offenders did not differ by race/ethnicity, mean age at conviction, or the elements involved in the capital offense. In fact, the only statistically significant difference was the sentence that was imposed; not surprisingly, cases in which the jury determined that the offender did have a probability of future violence were substantially more likely to result in a death sentence.

When they examined the in-prison behavior of the offenders in their study, the authors found that the frequency and prevalence rates of serious violence were low and that "even among infractions defined as serious assaults . . . the actual level of harm resulted in only minor injuries in each case" (p. 238). More importantly, they also found that there was little correspondence between jury predictions of future violence and actual violence. As they noted, "for both the LWOP-sentenced group and the death-sentenced group, predictions of future violence were wrong far more often than right" (p. 239). In fact, jury predictions of future dangerousness were incorrect 9 out of 10 times and "their performance was no better than random guesses" (p. 240).

These findings led the authors of this study to conclude that the jurors in these cases were engaging in arbitrary decision making and that the outcomes of the decision-making process are not reliable. According to their analysis, "Whatever its salience to capital jurors and intuitive attractiveness to legislatures, there is a chasm between the predictions of capital jurors that serious violence is likely in the future and the science demonstrating that capital jurors cannot reliably make this prediction" (pp. 231–232).

Source: "Capital Jury Decision Making: The Limitations of Predictions of Future Violence," Psychology, Public Policy and Law, 14, 223–256 (2009). Mark D. Cunningham, Jon R. Sorensen, Thomas J. Reidy.

by a 10–2 vote (*Apodaca v. Oregon,* 1972) and a Louisiana law that allows conviction by a 9–3 vote (*Johnson v. Louisiana,* 1972). The Court stated that unanimity was not required for the jury to exercise its "commonsense judgment."

Seven years later, the Court returned to this issue, ruling in *Burch v. Louisiana* (1979) that a Louisiana law permitting conviction by a vote of 5–1 in felony cases tried with 6-person juries did violate the Sixth Amendment. In his opinion for the Court, Justice Rehnquist stated that "lines must be drawn somewhere if the substance of the jury trial right is to be preserved," adding that "conviction for a nonpetty offense by only five members of a 6-person jury presents a threat to preservation of the substance of the jury trial guarantee and justifies requiring verdicts rendered by such juries to be unanimous."

The Court's decisions allowing nonunanimous verdicts notwithstanding, today only two states—Oregon and Louisiana—allow a defendant to be convicted of a felony by a nonunanimous verdict. Unanimity also is required in all federal criminal cases. In 2014, defense attorneys for Ortiz V. Jackson, who was found guilty of second-degree murder by a 10–2 vote of a Louisiana jury, asked the U.S. Supreme Court to review his case and overrule their decision allowing nonunanimous verdicts. The Supreme Court refused to hear the appeal.

Jury Nullification

Most jury trials result in convictions. A jury's decision to acquit the defendant usually means that the state has failed to prove its case beyond a reasonable doubt. Sometimes, however, the jury votes to acquit despite overwhelming evidence that the defendant is guilty. In this case, the jury ignores, or nullifies, the law.

Jury nullification, which has its roots in English common law, occurs when a juror believes that the evidence presented at trial establishes the defendant's guilt, but nonetheless the juror votes to acquit. The juror's decision may be motivated either by a belief that the law under which the defendant is being prosecuted is unfair or by an objection to the application of the law in a particular case. In the first instance, a juror might refuse to convict a defendant charged in a U.S. district court with possession of more than 5 grams of crack cocaine, based on a belief that the long prison sentence mandated by the law is unfair. In the second instance, a juror might vote to acquit a defendant charged with petty theft but also charged as a habitual criminal and facing a mandatory life sentence, not because the juror believes the law is unfair but because the juror believes that this particular defendant does not deserve life in prison (Dodge & Harris, 2000).

Although nullification allows the jury to be merciful when it believes that either the punishment or a criminal conviction is undeserved, it also allows the jury to make arbitrary or discriminatory decisions. For example, there is evidence that southern juries have—and some would say, still do—refused to convict White defendants charged with offenses against Black victims, even in the face of convincing evidence of their guilt (Hodes, 1996). Nullification can also be used to make a political statement, such as to express dissatisfaction with a policy. Some have alleged that O. J. Simpson's acquittal reflected in part the jurors' beliefs that the Los Angeles Police Department was racist (Rosen, 1996). An even darker form of jury nullification has been called jury vilification (Horowitz, Kerr, & Niedermeier, 2001). According to Irwin Horowitz and colleagues (2001, p. 1210), "Juries may return verdicts that reflect prejudiced or bigoted community standards and convict when the evidence does not warrant a conviction."

Jurors clearly have the power to nullify the law and vote their conscience (for a discussion of this, see "Current Controversy: Race-Conscious Jury Nullification"). If the jury votes to acquit, the Double Jeopardy Clause of the Fifth Amendment prohibits reversal of the jury's decision. The jury's decision to acquit, even in the face of overwhelming evidence of guilt, is final and cannot be reversed by the trial judge or an appellate court. In most jurisdictions, however, jurors do not have to be told that they have the right to nullify the law (see, e.g., *United States v. Dougherty,* 1972).

There is no way to know with any certainty how often jury nullification occurs. However, researchers have sought to identify the circumstances under which jurors will disregard the law. Some experimental evidence shows that as penalties become more severe, jurors are less likely to convict and in fact apply higher standards of proof (Kerr, 1978). Keith Niedermeier, Irwin Horowitz, and Norbert Kerr (1999), for example, reported on an experiment they conducted wherein a physician was accused of knowingly transfusing a patient with blood he knew hadn't been screened for HIV. Holding everything else constant (e.g., the evidence), the authors found that mock jurors were less likely to declare the physician guilty when the penalty was severe (25 years in prison relative to a $100 fine). The findings from these studies show that jurors are influenced by something other than the facts of the case as laid out by the prosecution and defense.

Hung Juries

If the jury cannot reach a unanimous verdict (or a 9–3 verdict in Louisiana or a 10–2 verdict in Oregon), the jury is said to be deadlocked, or hung. This ends the trial, and the prosecutor has to decide whether to dismiss the charges, offer the defendant a plea bargain, or try the defendant again before a new jury.

There are limited data on the frequency of hung juries. One study of jury trials in the 10 largest counties in California in the early 1970s found that 12.2% of the trials resulted in hung juries (Planning and Management Consulting Corporation, 1975). This study also found that 26% of the cases involving deadlocked juries were dismissed, 41% were resolved with a plea agreement, and 33% resulted in a new trial. A more recent study by the National Center for State Courts (2002) found that many states did not compile data on interim dispositions such as hung juries. The rate in the 30 jurisdictions that did compile such data was 6.2%. Like the earlier research in California, this study also found that only a third of the cases that resulted in a deadlocked jury were retried to a new jury.

According to the research conducted by the National Center for State Courts (2002), three factors were significant predictors of the likelihood of a hung jury: (1) the complexity of the case and the ambiguity of the evidence; (2) the group dynamics of the jury deliberation process, including the level of conflict among the jurors, the extent to which the deliberations were dominated by one or two individuals, whether the jury took an early vote, and whether the members of the jury had previously served on a jury (jurors with previous experience were more likely to deadlock); and (3) juror concerns about the fairness of the process that brought

CURRENT CONTROVERSY
RACE-CONSCIOUS JURY NULLIFICATION

In a provocative essay published in the *Yale Law Journal* (Butler, 1995) shortly after O. J. Simpson's acquittal, Paul Butler, a Black professor of law at George Washington University Law School, argued for "racially based jury nullification." That is, he urged Black jurors to refuse to convict Black defendants accused of nonviolent crimes, regardless of the strength of the evidence mounted against them. According to Butler, "it is the moral responsibility of black jurors to emancipate some guilty black outlaws" (p. 679).

Butler's position on jury nullification is that the "black community is better off when some nonviolent lawbreakers remain in the community rather than go to prison" (p. 679). Arguing that there are far too many Black men in prison, Butler suggested that there should be "a presumption in favor of nullification" (p. 715) in cases involving Black defendants charged with nonviolent, victimless crimes such as possession of drugs. Butler claimed that enforcement of these laws has a disparate effect on the Black community and does not "advance the interest of black people" (p. 714). He also suggested that White racism, which "creates and sustains the criminal breeding ground which produces the black criminal" (p. 694), is the underlying cause of much of the crime committed by Black Americans. He thus urged Black jurors to "nullify without hesitation in these cases" (p. 719).

Butler did not argue for nullification in all types of cases. In fact, he asserted that defendants charged with violent crimes such as murder, rape, and armed robbery should be convicted if there is proof beyond a reasonable doubt of guilt. He contended that nullification is not morally justifiable in these types of cases because "people who are violent should be separated from the community for the sake of the nonviolent" (p. 716). Violent Black offenders, in

other words, should be convicted and incarcerated to protect potential innocent victims. Butler was willing to "write off" these offenders based on his belief that the "black community cannot afford the risks of leaving this person in its midst" (p. 719).

The more difficult cases, according to Butler, involve defendants charged with nonviolent property offenses or with more serious drug-trafficking offenses. He discussed two hypothetical cases, one involving a ghetto drug dealer and the other involving a thief who burglarizes the home of a rich family. His answer to the question "Is nullification morally justifiable here?" is "It depends" (p. 719). Although he admitted that "encouraging people to engage in self-destructive behavior is evil" and that therefore most drug dealers should be convicted, he argued that a juror's decision in this type of case might rest on the particular facts in the case. Similarly, although he is troubled by the case of the burglar who steals from a rich family because the behavior is "so clearly wrong," he argued that the facts in the case—for example, a person who steals to support a drug habit—might justify a vote to acquit. Nullification, in other words, may be a morally justifiable option in both types of cases.

Randall Kennedy's Critique

Randall Kennedy (1997) raised a number of objections to Butler's proposal, which he characterized as "profoundly misleading as a guide to action" (p. 299). Although he acknowledged that Butler's assertion that there is racial injustice in the administration of the criminal law is correct, Kennedy nonetheless objected to Butler's portrayal of the criminal justice system as a "one-dimensional system that is totally at odds with what black Americans need and want,

(Continued)

(Continued)

a system that unequivocally represents and unrelentingly imposes 'the white man's law'" (p. 299). Kennedy faulted Butler for his failure to acknowledge either the legal reforms implemented as a result of struggles against racism or the significant presence of Black officials in policy-making positions and the criminal justice system. The problems inherent in the criminal justice system, according to Kennedy, "require judicious attention, not a campaign of defiant sabotage" (p. 301).

Kennedy objected to the fact that Butler expressed more sympathy for nonviolent Black offenders than for "the law-abiding people compelled by circumstances to live in close proximity to the criminals for whom he is willing to urge subversion of the legal system" (p. 305). He asserted that law-abiding Black Americans "desire more rather than less prosecution and punishment for all types of criminals" (pp. 305–306), and suggested that, in any case, jury nullification "is an exceedingly poor means for advancing the goal of a racially fair administration of criminal law" (p. 301). He claimed that a highly publicized campaign of jury nullification carried on by Black Americans will not produce the social reforms that Butler

demands. Moreover, such a campaign might backfire. Kennedy suggested that it might lead to increased support for proposals to eliminate the requirement that the jury be unanimous in order to convict, restrictions on the right of Black Americans to serve on juries, or widespread use of jury nullification by White jurors in cases involving White-on-Black crime.

According to Kennedy, the most compelling reason to oppose Butler's call for racially based jury nullification is that it is based on "an ultimately destructive sentiment of racial kinship that prompts individuals of a given race to care more about 'their own' than people of another race" (p. 310). He objected to the implication that it is proper for Black jurors to be more concerned about the fate of Black defendants than White defendants, more disturbed about the plight of Black communities than White communities, and more interested in protecting the lives and property of Black than White citizens. "Along that road," according to Kennedy, "lies moral and political disaster." Implementation of Butler's proposal, Kennedy insisted, would not only increase but legitimize "the tendency of people to privilege in racial terms 'their own'" (p. 310).

the defendant to court to face criminal charges. By contrast, the study found no relationship between the likelihood of a deadlock and the racial, ethnic, gender, or socioeconomic composition of the jury. Although the authors of this report stated that eliminating the unanimity requirement would reduce the number of hung juries, doing so

> would address the symptoms of disagreement among jurors without necessarily addressing the actual causes—namely, weak evidence, poor interpersonal dynamics during deliberations, and jurors' concerns about the appropriateness of legal enforcement in particular cases. (p. 86)

Announcing the Verdict

After the jury has reached a verdict, the jurors return to the courtroom to deliver their verdict. All the other key players—the judge, the prosecutor, the defense attorney, and

COMPARATIVE COURTS

Prior to 1984, there were no female judges on the Magistrates' Courts in Victoria, Australia. A series of controversial decisions in rape cases, however, led to public protests and calls for the appointment of women to the bench. From 1984 to 1992, 30% of the new appointees were women. By the mid-1990s, women comprised 15% of all judges on the Victoria Magistrates' Court. The chief magistrate was also a woman.

Kathy Laster and Roger Douglas (1995) examined the impact of this "sudden and dramatic" change (p. 181) in the gender composition of the Victoria Magistrates' Court, which handles about 90% of all criminal cases. The researchers interviewed 6 female judges and 24 male judges regarding their perceptions of the changes that had taken place on the court.

Laster and Douglas (1995) state that the "most striking" finding of their study "is the ready acceptance of women as appropriate appointees to the bench" (p. 184). A number of the male judges reported that "there had been some initial shock when the first women were appointed to the bench" (p. 185). Generally, however, the men believed that the women had made positive contributions to the work environment and had proven themselves to be competent, professional, and hardworking. The male judges, for example, reported that the female judges were "good fun," that they had "livened things up," and that female judges were a "boon" to the working environment (p. 186). Some of them indicated that the women were more sensitive, more understanding, and more empathic in their decision making. The male judges also believed that their female colleagues had been accepted and integrated into the organizational culture. According to Laster and Douglas, "Within a relatively short period, the female members of the bench had managed to impress their male colleagues. They seem to have proved to them that if there is any 'difference' between male and female magistrates, the qualities that women bring to the job make them eminently suitable for the career" (p. 190).

The women magistrates maintained that "gender in the courtroom was irrelevant" (p. 194). Although some noted that witnesses seemed uncomfortable when they had to repeat indecent language and that their gender might be commented on by those who were unhappy with the outcome, most of the women magistrates believed that "no one seems to be conscious that you're a man or a woman" (p. 194). Moreover, the attitudes of the men and women toward standards of proof, sentencing standards, and other aspects of the magistrate's job "were marked more by congruence than by divergence" (p. 200). The women magistrates also stated that the overall style of the court reflected feminine values and that both the men and the women on the bench "have female ways of doing things" (p. 201).

Laster and Douglas (1995) conclude that the "feminization of the bench" was part of a more general change in perceptions about the administration of justice. "Women did not change practice; rather, politicians allowed women into the all-male preserve because the political imagination suddenly could conceive of them as exercising power under a new ideological regime" (p. 201).

the defendant—also reassemble in the courtroom. The judge will ask the foreperson of the jury if they have reached a verdict; the foreperson will reply that they have and will hand the verdict to the bailiff, who will hand it to the judge. The defendant will be asked to stand and face the jury, and the judge (or, sometimes, the foreperson of the jury) will read the verdict.

A defendant who is found not guilty is released. The judge cannot overrule the jury's decision, and the state cannot appeal it. The jury's decision is final. If the jury finds the defendant guilty, the defendant has the right to appeal the decision. In addition, the defense attorney may ask the judge for a directed verdict of acquittal;

in essence, the defense attorney is asking the judge to set aside the jury's guilty verdict. If the judge decides to do so, the prosecutor can appeal the judge's decision. If the guilty verdict stands, the judge either will sentence the defendant immediately or, more likely, will schedule a date for a sentencing hearing.

SUMMARY

The criminal trials that capture the attention of the national media clearly influence public perceptions of what goes on in criminal court. However, these highly publicized trials are distortions of reality. Most of them involve defendants charged with very serious crimes—often multiple murders or sexual assaults—and teams of lawyers for the prosecution and the defense. Jury selection takes days, if not weeks; the presentation of each side's case is a long, drawn-out process in which the attorneys constantly raise objections to the admission of testimony or evidence; and the jury deliberates for days, not hours. The *typical* criminal trial bears little resemblance to this "idealized" view. The charges that the defendant is facing are less serious, the proceedings are much shorter, the defense may or may not present a case, and the jury is unlikely to spend days deliberating on a verdict.

The purpose of this chapter is to describe the typical criminal trial, from the opening statement by the prosecutor to the announcement of the verdict by the jury. The process begins when the prosecution gives an opening statement, which generally outlines the facts in the case and the evidence that will be presented to prove beyond a reasonable doubt the state's case against the defendant. After the prosecutor delivers the opening statement, the defense attorney is allowed but not required to present his or her side of the case from the perspective of the defendant.

Following opening statements, evidence is presented by the prosecutor in the form of witness testimony and real evidence. Once the prosecutor has finished presenting the state's case, the defense has an opportunity to present evidence designed to raise doubts in the minds of the jurors. It is possible that the defense attorney will not present any evidence; this might be the strategy if the defense attorney believes that the prosecutor has failed to establish guilt beyond a reasonable doubt or if the defendant has no alibi or other defense to the charges. Typically, however, the defense calls its own witnesses to the stand and admits its own evidence in hopes of establishing reasonable doubt in the minds of the judge or jury.

Closing statements come at the end of the trial, and they provide both the prosecutor and the defense attorney an opportunity to summarize their arguments to the judge and jury a final time. Next, the judge provides the jury with instructions on how to interpret and apply the relevant law of the case, and the jury is dismissed to deliberate. On completion of deliberations, the jury reports its verdict to the judge. If the defendant is found not guilty, she or he is free to leave. If the verdict is guilty, the judge then sentences the defendant or schedules a sentencing hearing for a later date.

While rare, criminal trials in the United States symbolize the rule of law for the American form of criminal justice. On completion of the trial, the case may not end because there are opportunities to appeal, which is the topic of a subsequent chapter.

Don't overlook the Student Study Site with its useful study aids, such as self-quizzes, eFlashcards, and other assists, to help you get more from the course and improve your grade.

DISCUSSION QUESTIONS

1. Do you believe that individuals such as the defendant's spouse, priest, doctor, or lawyer should or should not be compelled to testify against the defendant? What are the arguments in favor of designating these "privileged communications"? What are the arguments in favor of forcing these individuals to testify?

2. Take into consideration the cases cited in the discussion of "playing the race card" and pay close attention to the years in which the cases occurred. Are you surprised that such discrimination emerges in contemporary courtrooms? How do you feel about attorneys "playing the race card" during trial? What could judges do to prevent it?

3. What are the consequences of jury instructions being given in technical legal terms to jurors? What are the pros and cons to making the jury instruction process more comprehensible to laypeople?

4. Should jurors be allowed to base a decision to sentence an offender to death rather than to life in prison on predictions of future dangerousness? Why or why not?

5. What problems could arise from requiring all juries to return a unanimous verdict in order to convict an individual of a crime? Allowing nonunanimous verdicts?

6. Should juries be notified by the judge that they are allowed to nullify the law? Are there situations when jury nullification can be justified? Where it produces injustice rather than justice?

7. Do you agree or disagree with Paul Butler's call for "race-conscious jury nullification"? What are the dangers inherent in allowing jurors to nullify the law based on the race of the defendant?

8. Why do you believe criminal trials in the United States follow such an orderly sequence of events such as that described in this chapter?

KEY TERMS

Direct evidence 275

Hearsay evidence 277

Indirect evidence 275

Liberation hypothesis 284

Mock jury study 282

Privilege against self-incrimination 273

Privileged communication 272

Real evidence 274

Testimonial evidence 274

INTERNET SITES

Bureau of Justice Statistics: www.bjs.gov

Fully Informed Jury Association (American Jury Institute): www.fija.org

National Academy of Sciences Committee on Law and Justice: http://sites.nationalacademies.org/dbasse/claj/index.htm

National Center for State Courts: www.ncsc.org

University of Missouri–Kansas City School of Law: https://law.umkc.edu

STUDENT STUDY SITE

Get the tools you need to sharpen your study skills. SAGE edge offers a robust online environment featuring an impressive array of free tools and resources.

Access practice quizzes, eFlashcards, video, and multimedia at **edge.sagepub.com/hemmens4e**

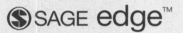

© Brand X Pictures/Stockbyte/Thinkstock Images

12

SENTENCING

Master the content at **edge.sagepub.com/hemmens4e**

INTRODUCTION

Seated on a raised bench, clothed in black robes, and wielding a gavel that he uses to maintain order in the courtroom, the judge pronounces sentence on the offender, who has been found guilty of armed robbery. "After considering all the facts and circumstances in the case," he states, "I have decided to impose the maximum sentence—15 years in prison. I believe that this is the appropriate sentence, given the heinousness of the crime and the fact that you have a prior conviction for aggravated assault."

Scenes such as this are played out every day in courtrooms throughout the United States. Judges must decide what the appropriate punishment is for offenders convicted of crimes, some of which are serious and merit imprisonment and others of which are minor and deserve fines or other alternatives to incarceration. In determining what the sentence should be, judges attempt to tailor sentences to fit both crimes and the offenders convicted of them. They also attempt to fashion sentences that are designed to meet one or more of the goals of punishment. In doing so, they consider the seriousness of the crime and the offender's criminal history as well as other offender and case characteristics that they believe are relevant. Although these decisions generally result in similar sentences for similarly situated offenders, the discretion inherent in the process sometimes produces sentences that are disparate or discriminatory.

In this chapter, we focus on judges' sentencing decisions. We begin by discussing the philosophical justifications for punishment. We then discuss the judges' options at sentencing. This is followed by a discussion of the factors that affect judges' sentencing decisions. We conclude the chapter with an overview of sentencing as an "inexact science."

THE GOALS OF SENTENCING

Consider the following hypothetical situation. A federal district court judge sentences William Kelly, a repeat offender who has been convicted of selling 100 grams of powder cocaine to an undercover narcotics officer, to 10 years in prison. When asked why she imposed the sentence she did, the judge replies, "Ten years is the mandatory sentence under the federal **sentencing guidelines**—it is the sentence prescribed by the law." Is this a sufficient justification for the punishment imposed? It is certainly true that the judge has the legal authority to impose the prescribed penalty. This does not explain, however, why this punishment—indeed any punishment at all—is justified in this case. The judge's response tells us nothing about the purpose(s) for which the punishment is imposed.

Why Punish?

What should be done with an individual who has been found guilty of a crime? Should the offender be punished? If so, what is the purpose of the punishment? If punishment is justified, what should the punishment be? Should the offender be required to pay a fine or provide restitution to the victim? How much should the payment be? Should the offender be placed on probation? If so, for how long and under what conditions? Should the offender be incarcerated in jail or prison? How long should the sentence be? Or should the offender receive the "ultimate punishment" and be sentenced to death?

Questions such as these have been pondered and debated by philosophers and legal scholars since the beginning of time. Although answers to the question, "Why do we punish those who violate the law?" vary widely, they can be classified into two distinct categories: retributive (desert-based) justifications and utilitarian (result-based) justifications. According to retributive theory, an offender is punished because he has done something wrong—something blameworthy—and therefore deserves to be punished (Hospers, 1977; H. Moore, 1968; von Hirsch, 1976). **Retributive justifications for punishment,** in other words, "rest on the idea that it is right for the wicked to be punished; because man is responsible for his actions, he ought to receive his just deserts" (Packer, 1968, p. 37). By contrast, **utilitarian justifications for punishment** emphasize the prevention of crimes in the future (Bentham, 1970). Punishment is seen as a means of deterring the offender from reoffending or discouraging others from following his example (deterrence), preventing the offender from committing additional crimes by locking him up (incapacitation), or by reforming the offender (rehabilitation). Whereas retributive theorists equate punishment with desert, then, utilitarian theorists justify punishment by the results it is designed to achieve. We discuss these justifications for punishment in more detail next.

Retribution: The "Just Deserts" Theory of Punishment

The retributivist's answer to the question, "Why punish?" is straightforward. We punish those who violate the law because they have done something wrong; justice demands that they be punished. Stated another way, "We are justified in punishing because and only because offenders deserve it" (M. S. Moore, 1992, p. 188). The basis for this principle—that is, the answer to the question, "Why do the guilty deserve to be punished?"—is more complex. One school of thought holds simply that there is "intrinsic good in the guilty suffering" (Braithwaite & Pettit, 1990, p. 157). Just as those who believe in an afterlife think that it is morally justified that those who lead good lives will be rewarded whereas those who lead wicked lives will suffer, advocates of this position believe that punishment of those who violate the law is inherently right (Kant, 1887). Man, in other words, "is a responsible moral agent to whom rewards are due when he makes right moral choices and to whom punishment is due when he makes wrong ones" (Packer, 1968, p. 9).

Another school of thought holds that all members of a civilized society agree—either explicitly or implicitly—to follow the rules that govern the society (Finnis, 1980; H. Moore, 1968; J. G. Murphy, 1979; Sadurski, 1985). They agree that they will not attack or kill one another, steal one another's property, or behave in other ways that cause harm. This agreement benefits all members of the society. Therefore, someone who violates the rules—by killing or stealing, for example—gains an unfair advantage over law-abiding members of society. Punishment, by penalizing the offender, rectifies this unfair advantage; it restores the equilibrium. As Nigel Walker (1991) noted, "Penalties put matters right, either by removing what the offender has gained or by imposing a disadvantage" (p. 25).

In summary, the retributive justification for punishment focuses on what the offender "deserves" as a result of her criminal behavior. It is a backward-looking approach that focuses exclusively on the offender's wrongdoing as the reason for punishment.

Utilitarian Justifications for Punishment

In contrast to desert theory, which is a backward-looking approach, the utilitarian justifications for punishment—deterrence, incapacitation, rehabilitation, and restoration—are forward looking. Rather than looking back to the crime that has been committed, these justifications focus on the future criminal behavior of both the person being punished and other members of society. Punishment thus does not occur simply because a crime has been committed and the offender deserves to be punished for it; rather, "the punishment is in order to promote good (and/or prevent evil) in the future" (Hospers, 1977, p. 25). According to the utilitarian theorist, if punishment cannot achieve this, "it is immoral; merely the adding of one evil (punishing) to another (the crime)" (Hospers, 1977, p. 25). Strictly speaking, then, if no "good consequences" would result from punishing an individual, no punishment would be justified.

One of the utilitarian justifications for punishment is **deterrence**. As developed by 18th-century utilitarian philosophers such as Jeremy Bentham and Cesare Beccaria, deterrence theory suggests that crime results from a rational calculation of the costs and benefits of criminal activity. Individuals commit crimes, in other words, when the benefits outweigh the costs. Since an important "cost" of crime is apprehension and punishment, deterrence theorists suggest that potential offenders will refrain from committing a crime if they believe that the odds of getting caught and being severely punished are high and are not outweighed by any anticipated gain from the crime. Deterrence can be either specific or general. **Specific deterrence** occurs when someone who has been legally punished ceases offending because of a fear of future punishment. **General deterrence** occurs when potential offenders "learn of the consequences of criminal involvement [for actual offenders] and decide not to risk subjecting themselves to such punishment" (Durham, 1994, p. 134). If, for example, a young woman is sentenced to 30 days in jail for drunk driving and, as a result of being punished, never again gets behind the wheel of a car after she has been drinking, we would say that specific deterrence has occurred. If those who learn of her sentence similarly resolve to refrain from drinking and driving, we would conclude that general deterrence has occurred.

A second forward-looking utilitarian justification of punishment is **incapacitation**, which is sometimes referred to as isolation, neutralization, or predictive restraint. Incapacitation involves locking up—or otherwise physically disabling—dangerous or high-risk offenders to prevent them from committing crimes in the future. This justification for punishment can rest on two related but conceptually distinct views of incapacitation. The first is **collective incapacitation**, which refers to the incapacitation of all offenders found guilty of a particular type of crime, without regard to their prior record or other personal characteristics. Offenders convicted of certain types of crimes—armed robberies, aggravated rapes, or drug sales involving large amounts of crack cocaine, for example—are deemed dangerous and are locked up to protect society from them.

Selective incapacitation focuses on the offender as well as the crime. Whereas collective incapacitation means incarcerating those whose crimes are deemed dangerous, selective incapacitation involves incarcerating primarily "those who, when free, commit the most crimes" (J. Q. Wilson, 1992, p. 152). It involves predicting that an individual offender, or offenders with certain characteristics, will commit additional crimes if not locked up.

Rehabilitation is the third utilitarian justification for punishment. Sometimes referred to simply as treatment, rehabilitation refers to "any measure taken to change an offender's character, habits, or behavior patterns so as to diminish his criminal propensities" (von Hirsch, 1976, p. 11). Like deterrence and incapacitation, the goal of rehabilitation is crime prevention. Rehabilitation achieves this goal not by making offenders fearful of additional punishment (deterrence) or by isolating them so that their opportunities for crime are limited (incapacitation) but by reforming them. The techniques used to reform or rehabilitate offenders include such things as individual or group counseling, education, job training, substance abuse treatment, and behavior modification programs. The advocate of rehabilitation, then, justifies punishment on the grounds that it will "'cure' an offender of his or her criminal tendencies" (von Hirsch & Ashworth, 1992, p. 1).

The final utilitarian justification for punishment is restoration or restorative justice. Unlike the other three utilitarian perspectives, all of which emphasize punishment for crime prevention and focus almost exclusively on the offender, restorative justice views punishment as a means to repair the harm and injury caused by the crime and focuses on the victim and the community as well as the offender (Bazemore, 1998; Braithwaite, 1998; Kurki, 1999). The goal of restorative justice "is to restore the victim and the community and to rebuild ruptured relationships in a process that allows all three parties to participate" (Kurki, 1999, p. 236). Restorative justice achieves its goals through a variety of practices. These practices include victim–offender mediation, family group conferencing, sentencing circles, and citizen supervision of probation. What typically occurs is a face-to-face meeting involving the victim, the offender, the victim's and offender's families, and other members of the community. Participants in the process discuss the effects of the crime on the victim, the offender, and the community and attempt to reach a collective agreement regarding the most appropriate sanction.

In summary, punishment, which involves the intentional infliction of harm or suffering, must be morally justified. It does not suffice to say that punishment is justified because it is prescribed by law. This is a *legal* justification for punishment, not a *moral* justification. A moral justification for punishment rests on ethical principles, not legal rules. Punishment is justified either because of the offender's guilt and blameworthiness (retribution) or in order to achieve good results (utilitarianism). The retributivist looks backward to the crime and the criminal and argues that punishment is justified because it is deserved. Punishment is deserved either because it is inherently right that the guilty suffer for their wrongdoing or because those who violate the rules gain an unfair advantage over those who abide by the rules. The utilitarian, on the other hand, looks forward to future consequences or results and argues that punishment is justified because it leads to good results: It prevents future crime, reforms the offender, or helps the victim and the community heal. The harm done to the offender in the name of punishment, in other words, is outweighed by the good consequences that result from punishment.

How Much to Punish?

Having defined punishment and discussed the various justifications for punishment, we now turn to a related question: How much punishment is justified? Each of the theoretical perspectives would answer this question differently. In fact, if we asked a panel of judges, each of whom represented a different philosophy of punishment, to determine the appropriate punishment for a particular offense, the resulting sentences probably would vary widely. As Andrew von Hirsch (1976) stated, "Deciding how much to punish is an agonizing process in which conflicting aspirations compete" (p. 59).

In the sections that follow, we explain how each theoretical perspective would determine the amount of punishment. The principles that guide each theory's approach to this issue are summarized in Exhibit 12.1.

How Much to Punish: The Retributive Approach

The retributivist, who justifies punishment on the grounds of desert, uses the *principle of proportionality* to determine the amount of punishment (von Hirsch, 1976; von Hirsch & Ashworth, 1992). Simply stated, this principle holds that the amount of punishment imposed on the offender should be equal to the amount of harm done by the offender. If the harm is great, the punishment should be severe; if the harm is minor, the punishment should be lenient. Disproportionate penalties—a death sentence for a minor crime such as drug possession or probation for a serious crime such as armed robbery—are undeserved; as such, they are unjustified.

Another way of expressing the retributive principle is "the punishment should fit the crime" (Hospers, 1977, p. 23). This does not mean, however, that the punishment must "resemble" the crime or that the punisher should inflict on the offender what he has inflicted on his victim. Although this "mirror image" theory often is used to justify capital punishment—that is, if someone takes another's life, then his life should be taken—it is not necessarily consistent with desert theory (Walker, 1991). Even if the punishment resembles the crime, in other words, it is not necessarily what the offender deserves.

EXHIBIT 12.1 ■ How Much Should We Punish Those Who Violate the Law?

Retribution

The amount of punishment imposed on the offender should equal the amount of harm done by the offender. The punishment should be proportionate to the seriousness of the crime and the culpability of the offender.

Deterrence

The punishment should be sufficient to outweigh the benefits of the crime. The amount of punishment should be enough (and no more) to dissuade the offender from reoffending and to discourage potential criminals.

Incapacitation

The amount of punishment should be proportionate to the risk posed by the offender. Dangerous, high-risk offenders should be punished more severely than nonviolent, low-risk offenders.

Rehabilitation

The nature and duration of the punishment should be based on the offender's need for treatment and potential for reform. The punishment should continue until the offender has been rehabilitated.

Consider the case of a woman who runs a red light and crashes into a car, breaking both of the driver's legs. Although the retributivist would agree that she deserves to be punished for her negligent behavior, he would not agree that she deserves to have her legs broken in a similar fashion. That punishment, according to the retributivist, would be disproportionately severe.

To say, as retributive theory does, that the amount of punishment should be proportionate to the harm done implies a rank ordering of crimes and punishments. It implies that the most serious offense should be matched to the most severe punishment and that the least serious offense should be matched to the most lenient punishment. But how are we to determine which offense is most (least) serious and which punishment is most (least) severe? With respect to the determination of crime seriousness, retributive theory suggests that crimes should be rank-ordered based on the harm done or risked by the offense and the culpability of the offender. Although this seems fairly straightforward, measuring harm and determining culpability are complicated. For example, most people would agree that armed robbery is a more serious crime than burglary; both involve theft of property, but armed robbery poses a much greater risk of serious injury than burglary. But how would we rank-order the theft of a car from a shopping center parking lot and a nighttime burglary in which only an inexpensive stereo system is taken? The thief who steals a car has taken a more valuable piece of property, but the nighttime burglar has violated the occupants' privacy and threatened their sense of security. How about the offender who plants a bomb in a crowded subway station, but the bomb is defused before it causes any damage? Is this crime—which risks a great deal of harm—more or less serious than an assault that seriously injures one person but poses no risk to anyone else?

There are similar problems in determining an offender's culpability, which is defined as the degree to which the offender may be blamed or held responsible for the consequences (or risked consequences) of the act. Most people would agree that someone who commits an intentional act is more blameworthy than someone who is reckless or negligent. The woman who commits a cold-blooded, premeditated murder is more culpable—and therefore her crime is more serious—than the woman who impulsively grabs a kitchen knife and stabs her husband during a domestic disturbance. Other issues, however, are more contentious. For example, should intoxication or mental capacity be taken into consideration in determining culpability? Should the offender's motivation for the crime or the degree to which the victim precipitated the crime matter? Should the offender's blameworthiness depend on whether she was a key player or an accomplice? Clearly, determining culpability, like measuring crime seriousness, is complicated.

Even if retributivists could agree on the relative seriousness of offenses, which is by no means assured, they still might not agree on what the specific punishment for each offense should be. Premeditated murder is, arguably, the most serious offense. As such, the retributive theorist would insist that it be punished with the most severe penalty. But what should that penalty be? Death? Life in prison with no possibility of parole? A prison sentence of a fixed number of years? If the most serious offense is punished by a sentence of death, what is the appropriate sentence for a crime in the middle of the seriousness scale? How about the least serious crime? To say, as the retributivist does, that the punishment should be neither disproportionately severe nor disproportionately lenient does not tell us how we should answer these questions.

To the retributive theorist, then, a just punishment is a deserved punishment, which is a punishment proportionate to the harm caused by the offense. Although disagreements regarding the measurement of crime seriousness, the relationship between crimes and penalties, and the role played by prior criminal record complicate the process, they do not alter this basic principle.

How Much to Punish: The Utilitarian Approach

The utilitarian, who justifies punishment on the basis of the positive results it produces, would give a variety of answers to the question, "How much should we punish?" Utilitarians generally would agree that the amount of punishment should be the amount that would be needed to prevent the offender and other potential criminals from committing crimes in the future. However, each of the three traditional utilitarian approaches—deterrence, incapacitation, and rehabilitation—would use somewhat different criteria to determine how much punishment would be needed to prevent future crime.

If deterrence is viewed as the justification for punishment, then the amount of punishment should be sufficiently "costly" to outweigh the potential benefits of the crime. Deterrence theorists contend that the costs of punishment reflect its certainty, severity, and celerity; potential offenders "will refrain from committing crimes if they perceive that they are certain to be punished, with a severe penalty, and soon after the offense has been committed" (Paternoster, 1991, p. 219). This suggests that the punishment should be harsh enough to dissuade the offender from reoffending and to discourage would-be criminals from following the offender's example. But how much is that? Would a lot or a little punishment be required to prevent the rapist from repeating his crime and to deter potential rapists? How about the petty thief? What if it could be shown that a relatively lenient punishment is all that is needed to deter the rapist but a fairly severe punishment is needed to prevent petty theft? Would a penalty structure based on deterrence, which might not be calibrated to the seriousness of the offense, be "just"?

The advocate of incapacitation would use a somewhat different calculus in determining the appropriate punishment. Because the goal of incapacitation is to prevent future crime by isolating dangerous or high-risk offenders, the amount of punishment would be proportionate to the risk posed by the offender. An offender whose predicted risk of reoffending is high would be punished more severely than one whose predicted risk is low. Again, this would not necessarily result in a punishment scheme that reflects the seriousness of the offense. Murderers, for example, seldom repeat their crimes, whereas those who use drugs have high recidivism rates. Does this mean that the murderer should receive a mild punishment and the drug offender a severe one? Related to this, if incapacitation requires that we lock up offenders until the end of their "crime-prone" years, how do we predict when that will be? If their crimes stem from an addiction or compulsion that they cannot control, will they need to be locked up forever (Packer, 1968)? Even if we assume that predictions about future criminality are reasonably accurate (a highly questionable assumption), is it justified to punish someone more severely for what that person is predicted to do in the future?

If rehabilitation is regarded as the justification for punishment, the nature and duration of the punishment will depend on what is needed to reform the offender. Offenders' punishments, in other words, will be individualized treatment programs designed to alter the forces that caused their criminality; they will be punished (treated) until they are "cured." Because we can't accurately predict how long it will take to reform an offender, the duration of the punishment is not known in advance. Thus, like punishment for deterrence and selective incapacitation, there is not necessarily a correlation between the seriousness of the crime and the amount of punishment. Consider, for example, the case of an offender who commits a serious crime but who does not need any type of rehabilitation at all. Since this person doesn't need to be reformed, should she simply be released? What about the minor offender who has serious psychological problems or is a long-time heroin addict? Should this person be held indefinitely because he can't be reformed? Would either of these outcomes be fair?

In summary, the three traditional utilitarian perspectives have similar but not identical views regarding the amount of punishment that is appropriate, and judges using these perspectives would not necessarily arrive at the same sentence (see "Key Cases: Justifying the Punishment"). The utilitarian regards the purpose of punishment as crime prevention; therefore, the amount of punishment needed is the amount necessary to prevent crime by the offender and by other members of society. This implies that the punishment should be individualized. It should be tailored not just to the seriousness of the offense but to each offender's likelihood of recidivism, dangerousness, or need for treatment. This implies, in turn, that similarly culpable offenders who commit the same crime may receive different sentences, depending on the amount of punishment that is needed to deter, incapacitate, or rehabilitate.

KEY CASES

JUSTIFYING THE PUNISHMENT

In January 2009, Lillo Brancato Jr., a first-time felony offender and acknowledged drug addict who had appeared on *The Sopranos*, stood before Judge Martin Marcus of the State Supreme Court of the Bronx (New York) for sentencing. He had been convicted of attempted burglary for his role in a crime that led to the death of an off-duty police officer. The officer was killed when he went outside to investigate a possible break-in at a neighbor's house. During the ensuing confrontation, Brancato's accomplice, Steve Armento, shot and fatally wounded the officer. Armento was convicted of murder and sentenced to life in prison without parole.

Prosecutors originally charged Brancato with felony murder, arguing that although he was unarmed and did not fire the shots that killed the officer, he knew that Armento had a gun and therefore was culpable. A jury acquitted Brancato of felony murder, finding instead that he was guilty of only attempted burglary. Brancato was facing a sentence of from 3.5 to 15 years.

If you were Judge Marcus and believed that the purpose of punishment was retribution, what sentence would you impose? What sentence would you impose if you believed that the purpose of punishment was deterrence or incapacitation or rehabilitation?

On January 9, 2009, Judge Marcus sentenced Lillo Brancato, who had been locked up for 3 years, to 10 years in prison. He was released in December, 2013.

Source: Eligon (2009).

THE JUDGE'S OPTIONS AT SENTENCING

An individual who has been convicted of a crime faces a number of different sentence alternatives, depending on the seriousness of the crime, the offender's prior criminal record, and the willingness of the judge to experiment with alternative sentences. The judge has more discretion and thus more opportunities to tailor the sentence to fit the individual offender, if the crime is a misdemeanor or a less serious felony and the offender has not been convicted previously of a crime. In this situation, the judge might impose a fine, order the offender to perform community service, place the offender on probation, or impose some other alternative to incarceration. The judge's options are more limited if the crime is serious or if the offender has a lengthy prior criminal record. In these circumstances, a jail or prison sentence is likely; the only question is how long the offender will serve.

In this section, we discuss the options available to the judge at sentencing. We begin with the death penalty, which is the ultimate sanction that society can impose on the guilty. We then discuss incarceration and the various alternatives to incarceration.

The Death Penalty

In the United States, 30 states and the federal government have statutes that authorize the death penalty. States without the death penalty are Alaska, Connecticut, Delaware, Hawaii, Illinois, Iowa, Maine, Maryland, Massachusetts, Michigan, Minnesota, Nebraska, New Jersey, New York, North Dakota, Rhode Island, Vermont, Washington, West Virginia, and Wisconsin; the death penalty is also outlawed in the District of Columbia. Once imposed for a variety of offenses, including armed robbery and rape, the death penalty today is imposed almost exclusively for first-degree murder. It is, however, a penalty that is rarely applied. In 2016, more than 11,700 persons were arrested for murder and nonnegligent manslaughter (Federal Bureau of Investigation, 2018), but only 31 persons were sentenced to death (Death Penalty Information Center, 2018).

A sentence of death does not necessarily mean that the offender will be executed. The offender's conviction or sentence might be overturned by a higher court, the sentence might be commuted to life in prison by the governor, or the offender might die in prison. Of the 8,124 prisoners under sentence of death between 1977 and 2013, 17% were executed, 6% died by causes other than execution, and 40% received some other type of disposition; the remaining inmates were still incarcerated. The average amount of time the 39 inmates executed in 2013 had been on death row was 15.5 years (Bureau of Justice Statistics, 2014).

Current death penalty statutes have a number of common features. Most are what is referred to as **guided discretion statutes**, which allow the death penalty to be imposed only if at least one statutorily defined aggravating circumstance is present. Although the aggravating circumstances vary among jurisdictions, the list typically includes such things as murder for hire, murder of more than one person, murder of a police officer, murder that involves torture, or murder during the commission of another crime such as armed robbery or sexual assault. Most jurisdictions also require a bifurcated trial in capital cases. The first stage involves the determination of the defendant's guilt or innocence. If the defendant is convicted of a capital crime—that is, a crime for which the death penalty is an option—a separate sentencing proceeding is held. At this stage, evidence regarding the aggravating and mitigating circumstances of the case is presented. The jury and/or the judge weigh the evidence and decide whether the defendant should be sentenced to death or should receive a lesser sentence of life without parole, life, or a specified term of years. Finally, most death penalty statutes also provide for automatic review of the conviction and death sentence by the state's highest court. If either the conviction or the sentence is overturned, the case can be sent back to the trial court for retrial or resentencing.

Constitutional Issues

Although the Supreme Court has never ruled that the death penalty per se is cruel and unusual punishment in violation of the Eighth Amendment to the Constitution, in 1972, the Court ruled in *Furman v. Georgia* (1972) that the death penalty, as it was being administered under then-existing statutes, was unconstitutional. The majority opinions in the 5–4 decision focused on the procedures by which convicted defendants were selected for the death penalty. The justices ruled that because the statutes being challenged offered no guidance to juries charged with deciding whether to sentence convicted murderers or rapists to death, there was a substantial risk that the death penalty would be imposed in an arbitrary and discriminatory manner.

The impact of the *Furman* decision was dramatic. The Court's ruling "emptied death rows across the country" and "brought the process that fed them to a stop" (Gross & Mauro, 1989, p. 215). Many commentators argued that *Furman* reflected the Supreme Court's deep-seated concerns about the fairness of the death penalty process; they predicted that the Court's next step would be the abolition of capital punishment. The Court defied these predictions, deciding to regulate capital punishment rather than abolish it.

Also as a result of the *Furman* decision, the death penalty statutes in 39 states were invalidated. Most of these states responded to *Furman* by adopting new statutes designed to narrow discretion and thus to avoid the problems of arbitrariness and discrimination identified by the justices in the majority. These statutes were of two types. Some required the judge or jury to impose the death penalty if a defendant was convicted of first-degree murder. Others permitted the judge or jury to impose the death penalty on defendants convicted of certain crimes, depending on the presence or absence of aggravating and mitigating circumstances.

The Supreme Court ruled on the constitutionality of the new death penalty statutes in 1976. The Court held that the mandatory death penalty statutes enacted by Louisiana and North Carolina were unconstitutional (*Roberts v. Louisiana,* 1976; *Woodson v. North Carolina,* 1976), both because they provided no opportunity for consideration of mitigating circumstances and because the jury's power to determine the degree of the crime (conviction for first-degree murder or for a lesser included offense) opened the door to the type of "arbitrary and wanton jury discretion" condemned in *Furman*. The justices stated that the central problem of the mandatory statutes was their treatment of all defendants "as members of a faceless, undifferentiated mass to be subjected to the blind infliction of the penalty of death" (*Woodson v. North Carolina,* 1976, p. 305).

By contrast, the Supreme Court ruled that the guided discretion death penalty statutes adopted by Georgia, Florida, and Texas did not violate the Eighth Amendment's prohibition of cruel and unusual punishment. In *Gregg v. Georgia* (1976), the Court held that Georgia's statute—which required the jury to consider and weigh 10 specified aggravating circumstances, allowed the jury to consider mitigating circumstances, and provided for automatic **appellate review**—channeled the jury's discretion and thereby reduced the likelihood that the jury would impose arbitrary or discriminatory sentences. According to the Court,

> No longer can a jury wantonly and freakishly impose the death sentence; it is always circumscribed by the legislative guidelines. In addition, the review function of the Supreme Court of Georgia affords additional assurance that the concerns that prompted our decision in *Furman* are not present to any significant degree in the Georgia procedure applied here. (*Gregg v. Georgia*, 1976, pp. 206–207)

Since 1976, the Supreme Court has handed down additional decisions on the constitutionality of the death penalty. The Court has ruled that the death penalty cannot be imposed on a defendant convicted of raping an adult woman (*Coker v. Georgia*, 1977) or a child (*Kennedy v. Louisiana*, 2008) and that the death penalty can be imposed on an offender convicted of felony murder if the offender played a major role in the crime and displayed "reckless indifference to the value of human life" (*Tison v. Arizona*, 1987). In 2002, the Court ruled that the execution of the mentally retarded is cruel and unusual punishment in violation of the Eighth Amendment (*Atkins v. Virginia*, 2002), and in 2005, the Court ruled 5–4 that the Eighth and Fourteenth Amendments forbid the imposition of the death penalty on offenders who were under the age of 18 when their crimes were committed (*Roper v. Simmons*, 2005). In 2008, the Court ruled that the lethal injection procedures used by Kentucky (which are similar to those used in many other states) did not violate the Eighth Amendment's prohibition on cruel and unusual punishment (*Baze v. Rees*, 2008). In 2015, the Supreme Court heard oral arguments in a case challenging the use of the drug midazolam as part of the lethal injection procedure (*Glossip v. Gross*, 2015). Opponents argued that the drug did not provide proper sedation of those to whom it was administered and that therefore executions using this drug violated the Eighth Amendment's prohibition against cruel and unusual punishment. In June 2015, the Supreme Court ruled 5–4 that the use of the drug did not constitute cruel and unusual punishment. Justice Breyer, joined by Justice Ginsburg, filed a separate dissenting opinion, in which he stated that he believed that it was "highly likely that the death penalty violates the Eighth Amendment."

A recent case that explicitly challenged the constitutionality of the death penalty is *Hidalgo v. Arizona* (Docket No. 17-251, 2018). Arizona is a state with a guided discretion statute. The statute identifies 14 aggravating circumstances that make a defendant charged with first-degree murder eligible for the death penalty, including whether the defendant was convicted for a serious offense committed on the same occasion of the homicide; whether the defendant created a risk of death to another person or persons; whether the offense was committed as a consideration for the receipt of anything of pecuniary value; whether the defendant committed the offense in an especially heinous, cruel, or depraved manner; and whether the defendant committed the offense while on probation for a felony offense. Abel Daniel Hidalgo was sentenced to death based on three aggravating factors: that he agreed to kill the victim for a $1,000 payment from a gang member, that he also killed a bystander, and that he committed another serious crime.

In 2014, Hidalgo's lawyers in Maricopa County (Phoenix) filed a motion arguing that the Arizona death penalty statute was unconstitutional, in that it failed to sufficiently narrow the cases eligible for the death penalty and therefore resulted in unconstitutionally arbitrary and capricious decisions to seek and impose the death penalty. In support of their motion, they introduced evidence from a study conducted by researchers at Arizona State University. The researchers examined 866 first-degree murder cases from 2002 to 2012, finding that 856 (98.8%) of these cases had at least one aggravating circumstance. The Arizona death penalty statute, in other words, did not narrow the cases eligible for the death penalty and, therefore, the prosecuting attorney had almost unfettered discretion in making the decision whether to seek the death penalty or not.

In March 2018 the U.S. Supreme Court turned down Hidalgo's request for a hearing on the case. In doing so, however, the Court wrote that Arizona's capital sentencing system may well be unconstitutional and invited the state to mount a further challenge with additional evidence. According to Justice Breyer (who was joined in his statement by three other justices), the evidence presented by Hidalgo's lawyers, which was unrebutted by the state, "points to a possible constitutional problem . . . Evidence of this kind warrants careful attention and evaluation."

Incarceration

Unlike the death penalty, which can be imposed only for first-degree murder and a handful of other offenses, a jail or prison sentence is an option in most criminal cases. This includes misdemeanors as well as felonies. The Texas penal code, for example, categorizes misdemeanors as Class A, Class B, or Class C; Class A misdemeanors are the most serious, Class C the least serious. Although offenders convicted of Class C misdemeanors cannot be sentenced to jail, those convicted of Class B offenses can be confined in jail for up to 180 days, and those found guilty of Class A offenses can be sentenced to jail for as long as 1 year. In most jurisdictions, sentences of less than 1 year are served in a local jail, but those of a year or more are served in a state prison. All offenders who are tried in U.S. district courts and who receive a prison sentence are incarcerated in a federal prison; there are no federal jails.

For some offenses, a prison sentence is not simply an option; it is required. All jurisdictions in the United States now have laws that prescribe mandatory minimum terms of incarceration for selected crimes. Almost all states have mandatory sentences for repeat or habitual offenders and for crimes involving possession or use of a deadly weapon. Most states also require minimum prison sentences for certain types of drug offenses: trafficking, selling drugs to minors, or selling drugs within 1,000 feet of a school. At the federal level, more than 100 crimes are subject to laws requiring from 2- to 20-year minimum sentences. Although mandatory minimum provisions can be circumvented by prosecutors who refuse to charge an offense that triggers a minimum sentence or by judges who either refuse to convict or ignore the statute and impose something less than the **mandatory minimum sentence**, these "tough-on-crime" laws limit the options available to the judge at sentencing. They generally require the judge to sentence the offender to prison for a specified period of time.

Judges' options also are limited by the type of sentencing system used in the jurisdiction (see Exhibit 12.2, "Sentencing Systems in State and Federal Jurisdictions"). Some state laws require judges to impose **indeterminate sentences**. In these states, the legislature specifies a minimum and a maximum sentence for a particular offense or category of offenses. In sentencing an offender, the judge either imposes a minimum and maximum sentence from within this range or, alternatively, determines only the maximum sentence that the offender can serve. Assume, for example, that the sentence range for armed robbery is 5 to 20 years. In the first scenario, the judge would determine both the minimum and the maximum sentence; he might sentence the offender to 5 to 10 years, 10 to 15 years, 5 to 20 years, or any other range of years within the statutory minimums and maximums. In the second scenario, the judge would determine only the maximum penalty; the minimum penalty would be applied automatically. Regardless of whether the maximum penalty was 10 years, 15 years, or 20 years, in other words, the minimum would always be 5 years. In either case, the actual amount of time the offender will serve is determined by the parole board, based on its judgment of whether the offender has been rehabilitated or has simply served enough time. An armed robber sentenced to an indeterminate sentence of 5 to 10 years, then, will serve at least 5 years but no more than 10 years, depending on the parole board's assessment of her case.

In other states, judges impose **determinate sentences**, which are fixed-term sentences that may be reduced if the offender behaves himself while incarcerated (i.e., through so-called good time credits). The offender's date of release is based on the sentence imposed minus any good time credits. Parole officers may supervise offenders who have been released from prison, but the parole board does not determine when offenders will be released. In states that have adopted this type of system, the legislature provides a presumptive range of confinement for various categories of offenses. Although some offenses are nonprobationable, for most crimes, the judge has discretion to determine whether the offender will be incarcerated and, if so, for how long. If, for example, the

---

EXHIBIT 12.2 ■ Sentencing Systems in State and Federal Jurisdictions

Indeterminate Sentence: The legislature specifies a minimum and maximum sentence for each offense or class of offenses. The judge imposes either a minimum and a maximum term of years or the maximum term only. The parole board decides when the offender will be released from prison.

Determinate Sentence: The legislature provides a presumptive range of confinement for each offense or class of offenses. The judge imposes a fixed term of years within this range. The offender serves this sentence, minus time off for good behavior.

Mandatory Sentence: The legislature requires a mandatory minimum prison sentence for habitual offenders and/or for offenders convicted of certain crimes. Examples include use of a weapon during the commission of a crime, drug trafficking, and selling drugs to minors.

Sentencing Guidelines: A legislatively authorized sentencing commission establishes voluntary or presumptive sentencing guidelines. The guidelines typically are based on the seriousness of the offense and the offender's prior record. Judges in states with presumptive guidelines are required to follow the guidelines or explain in writing why they did not.

FIGURE 12.1 ■ The Minnesota Sentencing Guidelines Grid

Presumptive sentence lengths are in months. Italicized numbers within the grid denote the discretionary range within which a court may sentence without the sentence being deemed a departure. Offenders with stayed felony sentences may be subject to local confinement.

SEVERITY LEVEL OF CONVICTION OFFENSE (Example offenses listed in italics)		CRIMINAL HISTORY SCORE						
		0	1	2	3	4	5	6 or more
Murder, 2nd Degree (intentional murder; drive-by shootings)	11	306 *261–367*	326 *278–391*	346 *295–415*	366 *312–439*	386 *329–463*	406 *346–480[2]*	426 *363–480[2]*
Murder, 3rd Degree Murder, 2nd Degree (unintentional murder)	10	150 *128–180*	165 *141–198*	180 *153–216*	195 *166–234*	210 *179–252*	225 *192–270*	240 *204–288*
Assault, 1st Degree Controlled Substance Crime, 1st Degree	9	86 *74–103*	98 *84–117*	110 *94–132*	122 *104–146*	134 *114–160*	146 *125–175*	158 *135–189*
Aggravated Robbery, 1st Degree Controlled Substance Crime, 2nd Degree	8	48 *41–57*	58 *50–69*	68 *58–81*	78 *67–93*	88 *75–105*	98 *84–117*	108 *92–129*
Felony DWI	7	36	42	48	54 *46–64*	60 *51–72*	66 *57–79*	72 *62–84[2]*
Controlled Substance Crime, 3rd Degree	6	21	27	33	39 *34–46*	45 *39–54*	51 *44–61*	57 *49–68*
Residential Burglary Simple Robbery	5	18	23	28	33 *29–39*	38 *33–45*	43 *37–51*	48 *41–57*
Nonresidential Burglary	4	12[1]	15	18	21	24 *21–28*	27 *23–32*	30 *26–36*
Theft Crimes (over $5,000)	3	12[1]	13	15	17	9 *17–22*	21 *18–25*	23 *20–27*
Theft Crimes ($5,000 or less) Check Forgery ($251–$2,500)	2	12[1]	12[1]	13	15	17	19	21 *18–25*
Sale of Simulated Controlled Substance	1	12[1]	12[1]	12[1]	13	15	17	19 *17–22*

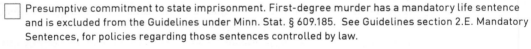

Presumptive commitment to state imprisonment. First-degree murder has a mandatory life sentence and is excluded from the Guidelines under Minn. Stat. § 609.185. See Guidelines section 2.E. Mandatory Sentences, for policies regarding those sentences controlled by law.

Presumptive stayed sentence; at the discretion of the court, up to one year of confinement and other non-jail sanctions can be imposed as conditions of probation. However, certain offenses in the shaded area of the Grid always carry a presumptive commitment to state prison. Guidelines sections 2.C. Presumptive Sentence and 2.E. Mandatory Sentences.

[1] 12[1]=One year and one day

[2] Minn. Stat. § 244.09 requires that the Guidelines provide a range for sentences that are presumptive commitment to state imprisonment of 15% lower and 20% higher than the fixed duration displayed, provided that the minimum sentence is not less than one year and one day and the maximum sentence is not more than the statutory maximum. Guidelines section 2.C.1-2. Presumptive Sentence.

Source: Minnesota Sentencing Guidelines Commission.

presumptive range of confinement for robbery is 4 to 15 years and the statute does not specify that offenders convicted of robbery must be sentenced to prison, the judge could impose either a probation sentence or a prison sentence of anywhere from 4 to 15 years. If the sentence was 10 years in prison, the offender would serve that time, minus credit for good behavior.

In still other states and at the federal level, judges' incarceration options are limited by voluntary or presumptive sentencing guidelines. In jurisdictions that use this model, a sentencing commission develops guidelines based on the seriousness of the offense and the offender's prior criminal record. The offender's crime receives a crime seriousness score, and the offender receives a criminal history score; the intersection of these two scores on the sentencing guidelines grid determines the sentence range. Although judges in states with voluntary or advisory guidelines are not required to follow the guidelines, judges in states with presumptive or mandatory guidelines are required to impose a sentence within the guideline range or explain in writing why they did not. For example, under the 2012 Minnesota sentencing guidelines (see Figure 12.1), an offender convicted of aggravated robbery would receive an offense seriousness score of 8 (on a scale that ranges from 1 to 11, with 11 being most serious). If this offender had a criminal history score of 3 (the scores range from 0 to 6, with 6 being the most serious), the presumptive sentence would be 78 months in prison, but the judge would be able to impose a prison sentence of 67 to 93 months.

Although most jurisdictions allow judges to depart from the guidelines and impose a more or less severe sentence than the guidelines require, the circumstances under which departures are justified are narrowly defined, and judges must provide a written justification for the departure. In most jurisdictions, judges are allowed to depart if there are specified aggravating or mitigating circumstances. Some states also list factors that should not be used to increase or decrease the presumptive sentence. For example, the Minnesota guidelines state that the offender's race, gender, and employment status are not legitimate grounds for departure. In North Carolina, on the other hand, judges are allowed to consider the fact that the offender "has a positive employment history or is gainfully employed" (Bureau of Justice Assistance, 1996, pp. 79–80). The judge's decision to depart either upward or downward can be appealed, generally to a state or federal appellate court. (See the "Current Controversy" box, which appears later in this chapter, for a discussion of a current controversy concerning the roles played by the judge and the jury in jurisdictions that use determinate sentencing or sentencing guidelines.)

As shown in Table 12.1, most offenders convicted of felonies are incarcerated; fewer than one third receive "straight probation" (i.e., probation only, not jail or prison followed by probation). In 2006 (this is the latest date for which data on sentences imposed in state courts are available), 35% of all offenders convicted of felonies in state courts located in large urban counties were sentenced to prison, 36% were sentenced to jail, and 25% were placed on probation. The mean sentence imposed on those who were incarcerated was 49 months. Not surprisingly, the proportion of offenders sentenced to prison was higher for violent offenses (55%) than for drug offenses (36%) or property offenses (38%); violent offenders also were sentenced to longer terms of incarceration (an average of 94 months) than were drug offenders (34 months) or property offenders (38 months).

The proportion of federal offenders sentenced to prison was even higher. In 2017, 88% of all federal offenders convicted of felonies and 93% of those convicted of drug trafficking were sentenced to prison. The average prison sentence was 45 months for all offenders and 70 months for offenders convicted of drug trafficking. Incarceration, then, is a widely prescribed and frequently imposed sentencing option. In the United States, in fact, it is now the "option of choice" for offenders convicted of felonies in both state and federal courts. (See "Comparative Courts: Sentences in the United States, England, and Wales" for a comparison of sentences imposed in the United States, England, and Wales.)

Limiting Incarceration: Public Safety Realignment in California

Skyrocketing prison populations and ballooning correctional budgets prompted many states to consider ways to reduce the number of offenders incarcerated in their correctional institutions. In 2011 the California Legislature passed the Public Safety Realignment Act (AB 109/117), which transferred responsibility for supervising low-level inmates and parolees from the California Department of Corrections and Rehabilitation (CDCR) to counties. The legislation, which took effect in October of 2011, (a) provides that offenders sentenced after October 1, 2011, on nonserious, nonviolent, and non-sex offenses are, with certain limited exceptions, no longer eligible for state prison sentences; (b) shifts the responsibility for postrelease community supervision of prison inmates serving sentences for nonserious, nonviolent, and non-sex offenses from the state to the county; and (c) as of July 1, 2013, transfers responsibility for revocation hearings from the State Board of Parole Hearings to the county court system.

TABLE 12.1 ■ Sentences Imposed on State (2006)* and Federal (2017) Felony Offenders

	Type of Sentence			
	Prison (%)	Jail (%)	Probation (%)	Mean Prison Sentence
Offenders convicted in state courts				
All offenses	35	36	25	49
Violent offenses	55	26	18	94
Drug offenses	36	32	31	34
Property offenses	38	37	23	38
Offenders convicted in federal courts				
All offenses	88	—	7	45
Drug trafficking	93		3	70

Source: Bureau of Justice Statistics (2009); United States Sentencing Commission (2018).
*The Bureau of Justice Statistics discontinued the *Felony Sentences in State Courts* series after publishing the 2006 data; most recent data available.

The law was designed to reduce the state prison population in California by diverting low-level offenders from prison to jail. As the California Department of Corrections and Rehabilitation (CDCR) noted in a report issued in December 2013, "The intent of Realignment is to encourage counties to develop and implement evidence-based practices and alternatives to incarceration to limit future crimes and reduce victimization. In addition, the Realignment Act is based on the premise that the provision of community-based support services will increase offenders' potential to successfully reintegrate into their communities" (CDCR, 2013, p. 1).

Early research on realignment revealed that the legislation was being implemented inconsistently across counties in California. The research also found, however, that the prison population in California declined, the number of inmates housed in local jails increased, and the arrest and conviction rates of offenders released from prison before and after realignment were very similar (CDCR, 2013).

Probation

The primary alternative to incarceration is **probation**. A straight probation sentence does not entail confinement in jail or prison. Rather, the judge releases the offender into the community and imposes a set of conditions that the offender agrees to abide by. The conditions of probation typically include regular meetings with a probation officer and a requirement that the offender obey all laws; other conditions might include drug testing, substance abuse treatment, and enrollment in educational programs. The court retains control over the offender while the offender is on probation; if the offender violates the conditions of probation, the judge can modify the conditions or revoke the offender's probation and sentence that person to jail or prison. Revocation of probation is more likely if the offender is arrested for a new offense, particularly a felony offense, than if the offender is cited for violating the conditions of probation.

COMPARATIVE COURTS

Sentences in the United States, England, and Wales

There are both similarities and differences in sentencing policies and procedures and in judges' sentencing decisions in the United States and in England (including Wales) (Bureau of Justice Statistics, 1998). Unlike the United States, England does not have the death penalty or life sentences without the possibility of parole, and until 1992, all sentences under 10.5 months were indeterminate. Since 1992, England has used a determinate sentencing system; the only sentences that are indeterminate are those that are 4 years or more.

As noted earlier, sentencing procedures vary widely among the states in the United States; judges in some states impose indeterminate sentences, whereas judges in other states and the federal system operate under either determinate sentencing systems or presumptive sentencing guidelines.

With the exception of offenders convicted of murder or rape, courts in the United States are more likely than those in England to sentence offenders to prison. In the mid-1990s, for example (Bureau of Justice Statistics, 1998, p. 23):

- 79% of U.S. robbers and 67% of English robbers were incarcerated;

- 62% of U.S. offenders convicted of assault were incarcerated, compared with only 27% of English offenders convicted of assault;

- 60% of U.S. burglars and 38% of English burglars were incarcerated; and

- 55% of U.S. offenders convicted of motor vehicle theft, but only 30% of English offenders convicted of motor vehicle theft, were incarcerated.

For the less serious crimes of assault, burglary, and motor vehicle theft, then, the likelihood of incarceration in the United States was 1.5 to 2 times greater than it was in England.

Prison sentences in the United States also are longer than those in England. Compared with sentences imposed in England, sentences imposed in the United States average about 4 years longer for rape (123 months vs. 77 months) and robbery (89 months vs. 40 months), 3 years longer for murder (266 months vs. 230 months) and assault (48 months vs. 14 months), 2 years longer for burglary (43 months vs. 15 months), and 1 year longer for motor vehicle theft (24 months vs. 9 months). Stated another way, sentences in the United States are about 3 times longer than those in England for assault and burglary, are more than twice as long for robbery and motor vehicle theft, and are 1.5 times as long for rape (Bureau of Justice Statistics, 1998, p. 31).

1. As these figures clearly demonstrate, offenders convicted of felonies in the United States—especially those convicted of crimes other than murder—are punished more harshly than are offenders convicted of these crimes in England. What might explain these differences?

Although the proliferation of statutes requiring mandatory minimum prison sentences has reduced the number of offenses for which probation is an option, judges retain wide discretion in deciding between prison and probation for offenses that are not subject to mandatory minimums. Most state statutes allow the judge to impose probation *unless* she believes that (a) the offender is likely to commit additional crimes if released, (b) the offender is in need of treatment that can be provided more effectively in jail or prison, or (c) probation would be inappropriate given the seriousness of the offender's crime. Probation was developed primarily as a means of diverting juvenile offenders and adults convicted of misdemeanors and nonviolent felonies from jail or prison, but it is not reserved for these minor crimes. As shown in Table 12.1, 18% of all offenders convicted of violent offenses in state courts in 2006 were sentenced to probation.

Intermediate Sanctions

Although incarceration—in jail or in prison—and probation are the principal sentences imposed on criminal offenders in the United States, they are not the only sentencing options. Indeed, a variety of **intermediate sanctions** are available: boot camps, house arrest and electronic monitoring, day reporting centers, community service, restitution, and fines. These alternative punishments are intended to fill the void between routine probation and protracted imprisonment. A detailed discussion of each of these alternatives is beyond the scope of this chapter. Instead, we provide a brief introduction to four intermediate sanctions: boot camps, house arrest and electronic monitoring, community service, and monetary penalties.

Correctional **boot camp**, or shock incarceration, programs target young, nonviolent felony offenders who do not have extensive prior criminal records (for a detailed description, see MacKenzie & Herbert, 1996). Modeled on the military boot camp, the correctional boot camp emphasizes strict discipline, military drill and ceremony, and hard labor and physical training. Most also provide substance abuse counseling and educational and vocational training. Offenders selected for these programs, which typically last from 3 to 6 months, are separated from the general prison population. They live in barracks-style housing, address the guards by military titles, and are required to stand at attention and obey all orders. Although the structure and focus of the programs vary widely, their primary goal is to divert young offenders from "a life outside the law using the same tactics successfully employed by the military to turn civilians into soldiers" (MacKenzie & Herbert, 1996, p. vii).

Prison boot camps began in Georgia and Oklahoma in 1983. Today, these programs are found in more than half of the states. Most serve young adult males, but programs that target women and juvenile offenders are becoming increasingly popular (Bureau of Justice Statistics, 2000, Table 47). Most programs limit eligibility to offenders who are under age 30, but some have a higher upper age limit. Georgia, which has one of the largest programs, admits offenders ages 17 to 35, and Massachusetts takes offenders as old as 40. About a third of the programs restrict eligibility to first offenders; the others admit first-time felony offenders or those without a prior prison sentence.

House arrest, with or without **electronic monitoring**, is an alternative sanction used primarily for nonviolent offenders. Offenders placed on house arrest, which is also referred to as home confinement, are ordered to remain at home for a designated period of time. They are allowed to leave only at specified times and for specific purposes—to obtain food or medical services, to meet with a probation officer, and, sometimes, to go to school or work. Both back-end and front-end programs exist. In some jurisdictions, such as Oklahoma, house arrest is a back-end program; offenders are released early from jail or prison sentences if they agree to participate in a home confinement program. In other jurisdictions, such as Florida, house arrest is a front-end program in which offenders who otherwise would be sentenced to jail or prison are confined to their homes instead. Both types of programs "aim simultaneously to offer a community sentence that is seen as burdensome and intrusive … and to reduce pressure on overcrowded prisons and jails" (Morris & Tonry, 1990, p. 213).

Offenders who are placed on house arrest often are also subject to electronic monitoring, which is a means of ensuring that offenders are at home when they are supposed to be. The most popular system today is one in which the offender is fitted with a wrist or ankle bracelet that she wears 24 hours a day. The bracelet serves as a transmitter; it emits a constant radio signal to a home monitoring unit, which is attached to the offender's home phone. The monitoring unit informs the monitoring center when the offender enters and leaves her home; it also sends a message if she tampers with or attempts to remove the bracelet. The monitoring officer is informed if the offender deviates from the preapproved schedule—if, for example, the offender returns from school at 9 p.m. when she is expected at 4 p.m. Ideally, the officer will respond immediately to a violation notice. The offender can be terminated from the program for tampering with the device, for repeated unauthorized absences from home, and for a variety of other violations.

An underused but potentially important intermediate sanction is the **community service** order. Rather than being sentenced to jail or placed on routine probation, offenders are ordered to perform a certain number of hours of unpaid work at schools, hospitals, parks, and other public and private nonprofit agencies. Thus, an accountant convicted of fraud might be sentenced to provide advice to poor taxpayers, a baseball player convicted of a drug offense might be required to lecture to junior high school students on the dangers of using drugs, and traffic offenders might be required to pick up trash along highways or in public parks.

Community service is not widely used as an alternative punishment in the United States, especially for adult offenders. The primary use of community service is as a condition of probation or as a punishment for minor traffic offenses or for juvenile offenders. The reluctance of judges to use this alternative as a stand-alone sanction for misdemeanors and less serious felonies may reflect a belief that requiring an offender to perform community service is not adequate punishment for most crimes. Judges may believe, in other words, that removing graffiti or cleaning up parks for 200 hours is not as onerous as even a short stint in jail. Those who advocate wider use of intermediate sanctions disagree. They contend that community service should not be regarded as merely a "slap on the wrist." Rather, it is a constructive and burdensome penalty "that is inexpensive to administer, that produces public value, and that can to a degree be scaled to the seriousness of crimes" (Tonry, 1996, p. 121).

Monetary penalties—fines, fees, and restitution to the victim—are frequently imposed on offenders convicted of misdemeanors and felonies in American courts. Every year, millions of offenders convicted of traffic offenses and less serious misdemeanors are ordered to pay fines that are, to some degree, calibrated to the seriousness of the crime. Offenders placed on probation are required to pay fees for probation supervision, for substance abuse treatment, for urinalysis, and for use of electronic monitoring equipment. And offenders who steal or damage someone else's property or cause physical or emotional injuries are ordered to pay restitution to the victim, often as a condition of probation.

Although these types of monetary penalties are common, their use as a stand-alone sentence is not. Fines, for example, are seldom used as an alternative to incarceration for offenders convicted of less serious felonies and are often used only in conjunction with probation for more serious misdemeanors. Although the fine is "unambiguously punitive" (D. C. McDonald, Greene, & Worzella, 1992, p. 1), studies reveal that judges do not regard it as "a meaningful alternative to incarceration or probation" (Cole et al., as cited in Morris & Tonry, 1990, p. 127). Use of fines also poses dilemmas for the courts. If the amount of the fine is commensurate with the seriousness of the offense, with no consideration given to the ability of the offender to pay the fine, then fines will be relatively more burdensome to the poor than to the rich. To avoid this potential problem, a number of jurisdictions use what is referred to as a **day fine**. Originating in Europe and Latin America, the day fine is calibrated both to the seriousness of the offense and to the offender's ability to pay. Rather than requiring all offenders convicted of shoplifting to pay $1,000, for example, judges determine how many "punishment units" each offender deserves. Typically, each punishment unit is equal to one day's pay, or some fraction of one day's pay. Two offenders convicted of shoplifting might each be ordered to pay 5 punishment units, equal to 5 days' pay. If one offender made $50 per day while the other earned $500 per day, the fines paid by the two offenders would differ; the first would pay $250, the second $2,500.

The day fine has obvious advantages over the traditional fine. Because it can be tailored more precisely to an offender's ability to pay, the day fine is more equitable. It also is more likely to be paid in full, which means that offenders are less likely to be called back to court or sentenced to jail for nonpayment. But there are disadvantages as well. Courts that use the day fine must define a unit of punishment other than time in jail or dollars to be paid, establish the range of units to be imposed on offenders convicted of various offenses, and devise a means of translating these units into dollars. Implementing a system of day fines, in other words, involves "changing—or, at least accommodating—existing habits, customs, and laws" (D. C. McDonald et al., 1992, p. 5).

The Future of Intermediate Sanctions

As we approach the third decade of the 21st century, prison, jail, and probation sentences remain the dominant forms of punishment imposed on criminal offenders—especially those convicted of felonies. In fact, state and federal prison statistics suggest that the trend over time has been one of increasing reliance on imprisonment. In the United States, the rate of incarceration was relatively stable from 1925 through 1975, but it skyrocketed from 1980 to 2000. Despite stable or falling crime rates, the number of offenders incarcerated in state and federal prisons ballooned from 329,821 in 1980 to 1,381,892 in 2000—an increase of more than 300%! At the end of 2016, the number of prisoners in the United States was 1,572,600, an increase of almost 13% from 2000 (Bureau of Justice Statistics, 2018). In 2016, more than 6.5 million people, or 2.6% of the U.S. adult population, were on probation, in jail or prison, or on parole in the United States (Bureau of Justice Statistics, 2018). Rather than replacing incarceration and probation with "a portfolio of intermediate punishments," the United States "has been engaged in an unprecedented imprisonment binge" (Austin & Irwin, 2001, p. 1) in the past two decades.

The question, of course, is why this is so. Some scholars suggest that it can be attributed in large part to the public's fear of drugs and crime, which led to a movement for more punitive sentences for felony offenders in general and for drug offenders in particular (Austin & Irwin, 2001, pp. 4–7). Michael Tonry (1996) argues that it also reflects a view on the part of judges and policy makers that "only imprisonment counts" as punishment. He suggests that this emphasis on absolute severity "frustrates efforts to devise intermediate sanctions for the psychological (not to mention political) reason that few other sanctions seem commensurable with a multiyear prison sentence" (p. 128). If, in other words, the philosophy of just deserts demands that felony offenders be punished harshly, and only incarceration is regarded as harsh punishment, then nonincarceration sentences will be viewed as inappropriately lenient. Unless these attitudes change, it seems unlikely that intermediate sanctions will play anything more than a supporting role in sentencing policies and practices in the United States.

The conclusion that incarceration will remain the punishment of choice for felony offenders—especially drug offenders—is called into question by recent legislation that either decriminalizes or legalizes adults' recreational use of marijuana, reduces drug possession offenses from felonies to misdemeanors, and modifies or eliminates mandatory minimum sentences for certain types of offenses.

CURRENT CONTROVERSY
THE U.S. SUPREME COURT AND SENTENCING

Since 2000, a series of important decisions by the U.S. Supreme Court have reshaped the sentencing process, particularly in jurisdictions with determinate sentencing or sentencing guidelines. More to the point, these decisions, which rest on the Sixth Amendment right to trial by jury and the Due Process Clause of the Fifth and Fourteenth Amendments, have constrained the role of the judge and enhanced the role played by the jury.

The first ruling handed down by the Supreme Court was *Apprendi v. New Jersey* (2000). This case involved an offender, Charles Apprendi Jr., who fired several shots into the home of a Black family. At the time of his arrest, Apprendi made a number of statements, which he later retracted, suggesting that he had fired into the home because he did not want the family living in his neighborhood. Apprendi pled guilty to possession of a weapon for an unlawful purpose, which carried a term of imprisonment of 5 to 10 years. The prosecutor then filed a motion for an enhanced sentence under the New Jersey hate crime statute. The judge in the case found by a preponderance of the evidence that the shooting was racially motivated and sentenced Apprendi to 12 years in prison. Apprendi appealed, claiming that the Due Process Clause of the Constitution required the state to prove the allegation of bias to the jury beyond a reasonable doubt. The Supreme Court ruled in Apprendi's favor, stating that any fact that increases the penalty for a crime beyond the prescribed statutory maximum, other than the fact of a prior conviction, must be submitted to a jury and proved beyond a reasonable doubt. In 2002, the justices similarly ruled that a jury—not a judge—must find the aggravating circumstances necessary for imposition of the death penalty (*Ring v. Arizona*, 2002).

The Court reiterated this position in subsequent decisions involving defendants who were challenging sentences imposed under state and federal sentencing guidelines. In 2004, for example, the court ruled in *Blakely v. Washington* (2004) that the judge's decision to impose a sentence more severe than the statutory maximum allowed under the Washington sentencing guidelines violated the defendant's Sixth Amendment right to trial by jury.

The Court revisited this issue 6 months later. This time, the issue was the power of federal judges to impose sentences more severe than called for under the U.S. sentencing guidelines. In *United States v. Booker* (2005), the Court ruled, consistent with its decisions in *Apprendi* and *Blakely,* that the jury must determine beyond a reasonable doubt any fact that increases the defendant's sentence beyond the maximum sentence allowed under the sentencing guidelines. The facts in this case were similar to those in *Blakely.* Booker was found guilty of a drug offense that, under the guidelines, carried a sentence of 210 to 262 months. At the sentencing hearing, however, the judge found additional facts that justified a harsher sentence; he sentenced Booker to 360 months in prison. The court held that the 30-year sentence imposed by the judge violated the Sixth Amendment right to a jury trial and ordered the district court either to sentence Booker within the sentencing range supported by the jury's findings or to hold a separate sentencing hearing before a jury. The Court also ruled that the federal sentencing guidelines were advisory, not mandatory.

The next decision handed down by the Supreme Court was *Cunningham v. California* (2007), which addressed sentences imposed under California's determinate sentencing law. The California law at issue allowed judges to choose one of three specified sentences for people convicted of particular offenses. The judge was supposed to choose the middle term unless there were aggravating or mitigating

(Continued)

(Continued)

circumstances that justified imposing the higher or lower terms. In this case, the judge sentenced John Cunningham to the higher term, based on six aggravating circumstances that the judge found by a preponderance of the evidence during a posttrial sentencing hearing. In striking down Cunningham's sentence, the Court stated that it had "repeatedly held that, under the Sixth Amendment, any fact that exposes a defendant to a greater potential sentence must be found by a jury, not a judge, and established beyond a reasonable doubt, not merely by a preponderance of the evidence."

In the *Cunningham* case, the Supreme Court also explained how states with structured sentencing procedures could comply with the Court's rulings. One way is to require the prosecutor to include facts that increase the defendant's sentence exposure in the charging document and then to require the jury—either at trial or in a postconviction sentencing hearing—to find these facts beyond a reasonable doubt. This is the approach taken by most jurisdictions with legally binding guidelines (Frase, 2007, p. 426). Another remedy is to permit judges to exercise broad discretion within a statutory sentencing range; in this situation, the judge does not need to show that there are aggravating factors that justify a sentence at the top of the range. This is the approach taken by California; under SB 40, which Governor Arnold Schwarzenegger signed into law in April 2007, the judge in each case can choose between the lower, middle, or upper term provided by the law for the particular crime.

The Supreme Court's decisions in these sentencing cases enhance the role played by the jury in both capital and noncapital cases. The decisions emphasize that the jury, not the judge, is to determine the facts in the case; that juries must determine the existence of aggravating factors that justify the imposition of the death penalty; and that sentences cannot exceed the maximum sentence based on the facts that were admitted in a guilty plea or found by the jury.

Another issue addressed by the Supreme Court was the constitutionality of life in prison with no possibility of parole (otherwise known as LWOP) for juvenile offenders. In *Miller v. Alabama* (132 S. Ct. 2455, 2012), the Court ruled 5–4 that the Eighth Amendment precludes a sentencing scheme that requires LWOP for juvenile homicide offenders. At issue in this case were the sentences imposed on two offenders who were 14 years old when they were convicted of murder and sentenced to a mandatory term of life imprisonment without the possibility of parole. The justices in the majority reasoned that "the Eighth Amendment's prohibition of cruel and unusual punishment 'guarantees individuals the right not to be subjected to excessive sanctions.' That right 'flows from the basic precept of justice that punishment for crime should be graduated and proportioned' to both the offender and the offense." They also noted that "children are constitutionally different from adults for sentencing purposes," citing their lack of maturity, underdeveloped sense of responsibility, and vulnerability to outside influences and peer pressure. The Court's decision in this case invalidated LWOP terms for certain juvenile homicide offenders in 29 jurisdictions.

HOW DO JUDGES DECIDE? MODELING THE SENTENCING PROCESS

William Spence pled guilty to two felonies in the circuit court of Jackson County, Missouri: assault in the first degree and armed criminal action. Spence, who had heard from a friend that Bill Smith had been harassing his girlfriend at the restaurant where she worked, shot Smith five times in the leg with a .38-caliber revolver. Smith was seriously injured. According to Missouri law, assault in the first degree is a Class A felony; the range of punishment is 10 to 30 years or life in prison. Armed criminal action is also a Class A felony; it is punishable by a mandatory prison term of 3 years to life.

William Spence was 18 years old and lived with his grandmother. His parents were divorced. He was not married, had no children, and had completed only 2 years of high school. He had been employed off and on at the fast-food restaurant where his girlfriend worked. In his early teens, he was hospitalized in a psychiatric unit for about a month because of behavior problems at school. He had been arrested at age 17 for petty larceny but had no previous felony convictions.

Judge Ann Harding presided at the guilty plea proceeding. Judge Harding questioned Spence to ensure that he understood the nature of the charges against him and the range of penalties for each charge. She also asked him a series of questions designed to ensure that (a) he was pleading guilty voluntarily and (b) he understood that, in doing so, he was giving up his right to a trial by jury. After stating that the court was accepting the defendant's guilty plea, Judge Harding sentenced William Spence to 10 years in prison for assault in the first degree and to 3 years in prison for armed criminal action. The sentences were to be served concurrently.

How did Judge Harding arrive at this decision; that is, how did she determine that this was the appropriate punishment for this offender convicted of these crimes? What factors do judges generally consider as they attempt to decide whether an offender should be sentenced to prison and, if so, the length of time that he or she should be incarcerated? Do sentences depend on the nature of the crime or the characteristics of the offender and victim? If so, which are most important? In this section, we address these questions. Our goal is to explain how judges decide—that is, to explain how judges arrive at the appropriate sentence for a particular offender (see "View From the Field" for one judge's account of the sentencing process).

VIEW FROM THE FIELD

Sentencing by a U.S. District Court Judge

In 2001, Judge Gerard E. Lynch, a U.S. district judge for the Southern District of New York, published an article titled "Sentencing Eddie" in the *Journal of Criminal Law and Criminology* (Lynch, 2001). Judge Lynch used the case of "Eddie," the first person he sentenced after taking office as a federal district judge, to illustrate the injustices produced by sentencing statutes that required lengthy minimum sentences for offenders convicted of drug offenses.

Judge Lynch described Eddie as a "somewhat marginal member" of a drug distribution network.

He was identified during the course of a major investigation of his supplier; law enforcement officials heard him negotiating with the supplier, whose phone was tapped. Unlike his codefendants, Eddie refused to plead guilty; he was convicted at trial of conspiring to sell 500 grams or more of cocaine. Eddie spent a year in prison in his youth for armed robbery and, after age 40, was convicted of a number of minor drug offenses, followed by a conviction, at age 49, for a more serious drug offense (conspiracy to purchase cocaine), for which he was sentenced to probation. Eddie was 53 years old; he was married, was supporting three teenagers, and had been steadily employed since being honorably discharged from the military.

(Continued)

(Continued)

According to Judge Lynch, the favorable aspects of Eddie's life history did not outweigh his involvement in a serious crime. As he noted, "I assume most judges, and most citizens would regard Eddie as a candidate for a reasonably severe sentence.... He has broken a law that our legislators and citizens want treated with particular seriousness.... Among the ranks even of drug violators, his prior record must rank him among the less sympathetic offenders: not only was he a recidivist but he was one who had benefited from leniency on his most recent arrest, and returned immediately to dealing" (Lynch, 2001, pp. 554–555).

These statements notwithstanding, Judge Lynch was not convinced that the appropriate sentence was the one required—a mandatory minimum sentence of 10 years in prison. As he noted,

> But if we agree that Eddie does not deserve leniency, we still are left to ask, what should his sentence actually *be*? . . . I can pick a number as well as anyone else, and before 1987 that's more or less what judges were asked to do—pick the number that they thought, taking all of the above facts and more into account, was the fairest sentence. But I don't have a lot of confidence, and I doubt that any of your more intelligent and thoughtful friends will have much either, that the number that any of us picks represents some objectively correct just desert. (p. 555)

Although Judge Lynch stated that he could not say with any degree of certainty that Eddie's sentence, while certainly very harsh, was too severe, he did point out that his sentence would only have been 6.5 years in prison if it had been calculated using the federal sentencing guidelines. The fact that Eddie was convicted of a crime that required a minimum sentence, in other words, meant that his sentence was 3.5 years longer than it would have been absent the mandatory minimum sentencing statute.

Judge Lynch, who acknowledged that Eddie was not "the poster child of the movement to repeal mandatory minimum sentences" and who reiterated that he did not believe that Eddie should be treated lightly (p. 564), nonetheless stated that he believed that there had been some "injustice" in Eddie's case. He urged his readers to consider exactly how the federal mandatory minimum sentences for drug crimes operate as well as what the sentences imposed under that regime actually mean in particular cases, and then to consider whether—at least in the federal system, which already has a comprehensive guidelines regime— the statutory minimum provisions are just or unjust, desirable or not, worth the price we pay for them, or unnecessarily costly.

Judge Lynch concluded that although he did not expect to feel good about sentencing people to prison, he was "sorry and surprised to find that the very first sentence I imposed felt like an injustice" (p. 566).

Modeling the Sentencing Process

Researchers have conducted dozens of studies designed to enhance our understanding of judges' sentencing decisions and to identify the factors that predict sentence outcomes. These studies generally use data on actual cases decided by judges in a particular jurisdiction (examples include Albonetti, 1997; B. D. Johnson, 2003; Spohn, Gruhl, & Welch, 1981–1982; Steffensmeier, Ulmer, & Kramer, 1995, 1998; Ulmer, 1997). Researchers collect information about the crime, the offender, and the case from court files or electronic databases. They analyze the data using statistical techniques that allow them to isolate the effect of one factor—the offender's prior criminal record, for example—while controlling for other factors that influence sentence severity—crime seriousness, the offender's background characteristics, whether the offender pled guilty or went to trial, whether the offender was free on bond or detained in jail prior to trial, whether the offender had a private attorney or a public defender, and so on.

Researchers typically analyze the decision to incarcerate or not and the length of sentence imposed on those who are incarcerated separately. They assert that sentencing is in fact a two-stage process: Judges first decide whether the offender should be incarcerated and then decide how long the sentence should be. They also argue that different case attributes may affect each decision. In the following sections, we discuss the results of empirical research on judges' sentencing decisions. We focus on the role played by characteristics of the offense, the offender, the victim, and the case.

Offense Seriousness and Prior Record

Studies of judges' sentencing decisions reveal that these decisions are based, first and foremost, on the seriousness of the offense and the offender's prior criminal record. Offenders who commit more serious crimes are sentenced more harshly than those who commit less serious crimes. Offenders with more extensive criminal histories receive more severe sentences than those with shorter criminal histories. As the National Academy of Sciences Panel on Sentencing Research concluded in 1983, offense seriousness and prior criminal record are the "key determinants of sentences" (Blumstein, Cohen, Martin, & Tonry, 1983, p. 83).

This is not surprising. Legislators devise penal codes or sentencing guidelines based explicitly on these two factors. Offenders who commit more serious crimes or who repeat their crimes are legally eligible for more punishment than first-time offenders or those who commit less serious crimes. Moreover, judges who see retribution as the primary purpose of punishment believe that sentences should be proportionate to the seriousness of the crime and the culpability of the offender. Even utilitarian judges would not contend that these two factors are irrelevant to the sentence that should be imposed. Judges, in other words, are legally and morally justified in taking crime seriousness and prior record into account in making sentencing decisions.

There are a number of ways to measure crime seriousness and criminal history. Crime seriousness, for example, might be defined by the type of crime (e.g., armed robbery or drug trafficking), the statutory classification of the crime (e.g., first-degree felony, second-degree misdemeanor), whether the offender used a gun, the degree of injury to the victim, the amount of property stolen, whether the offender victimized a stranger or a nonstranger, and so on. Similarly, there are a number of indicators of the offender's past criminal history that judges might take into consideration: whether the offender was previously incarcerated, whether the offender was previously convicted of a misdemeanor or felony, whether the offender was ever convicted of a violent crime, whether the offender was on probation or parole at the time of arrest for the current crime, or whether the offender's crimes were increasing in frequency or seriousness. Researchers often include multiple indicators of these legally relevant variables in their models of the sentencing process.

Regardless of the way in which they are measured, there is compelling evidence that crime seriousness and prior criminal record are important determinants of sentence severity. Research consistently reveals that judges impose harsher sentences on offenders who commit more serious crimes and who have more serious prior criminal records.

Offender Characteristics

Prior criminal record is not the only offender characteristic that affects judges' sentencing decisions. Studies have shown that the sentences offenders receive may depend on their demographic characteristics (gender, age, and race/ethnicity), their socioeconomic status (education and income), and their social stability (employment history, marital status, responsibility for dependent children, history of drug or alcohol abuse). For example, there is evidence that men are sentenced more harshly than women (for reviews of this research, see Daly & Bordt, 1995; Daly & Tonry, 1997; Steffensmeier, Kramer, & Streifel, 1993), that young adults are sentenced more harshly than either teenagers or older adults (Spohn & Holleran, 2000; Steffensmeier et al., 1995, 1998), and that Blacks and Hispanics are sentenced more harshly than Whites (for reviews of this research, see Mitchell, 2005; Spohn, 2000). In fact, some studies concluded that the harshest sentences are imposed on young Black and Hispanic males (Spohn & Holleran, 2000; Steffensmeier et al., 1998). (See "Current Research" for the results of a study examining the sentences imposed on Black, White, and Hispanic drug offenders in U.S. district courts.) There also is evidence that the offender's education (Albonetti, 1997), income (Smith, 1991), and employment status (Nobiling, Spohn, & DeLone, 1998) affect sentence severity: Harsher sentences are imposed on the less educated, the poor, and the unemployed.

CURRENT RESEARCH

The results of the state and federal sentencing studies conducted to date highlight the importance of attempting to identify the contexts in which legally irrelevant factors affect sentence outcomes and suggest that stereotypes of dangerousness and threat are linked in complicated ways to race/ethnicity, gender, and other offender characteristics. Evidence of this comes from a study of sentences imposed on drug offenders in Washington State (Steen, Engen, & Gainey, 2005) that examined the relationships among images of threat, the race of offenders, and criminal sentences. Drawing on both the racial stereotypes approach and the case processing approach, Sara Steen and colleagues (2005) predicted that judges' attributions of dangerousness, culpability, and threat would vary depending on the offender's sex, criminal history, and offense type; they expected these variables "to interact and their effects on sentencing decisions to be contextualized by race" (p. 444).

Central to the work of Steen and her colleagues are the concepts of stereotypical offenders and "normal" crimes. In previous research, these researchers suggested that criminal justice decision makers develop stereotypes of dangerous drug offenders based on three factors: the offender's sex, the offender's prior record, and the type of drug offense for which the offender was convicted. Images of threat were most closely associated with males, lengthy criminal histories, and convictions for drug delivery. To the degree that drug offenders conform to this stereotype of a "dangerous" offender, then, they will receive harsher sentences than females, offenders with no priors, and offenders convicted of drug possession. Steen and her colleagues asserted, however, that judges' decisions regarding the appropriate sentence also would be affected by stereotypes about normal crimes. Cases that comported with officials' notions of normal crimes would be dealt with expeditiously using routine procedures and patterned responses; cases that were at odds with these notions, on the other hand, would require different, and more complex, decision rules.

Using this integrated perspective, the researchers hypothesized that cases that fully matched the stereotype of the dangerous drug offender—that is, male drug dealers with prior convictions—would be treated more harshly than cases that did not. However, they also hypothesized that the effect would be larger for White offenders than for Black offenders. They reasoned that White drug dealers with priors would be seen as "atypical" offenders by decision makers and that "in these atypical cases, the presumed social advantage of white offenders will increase judges' estimates of their culpability and therefore will increase their sentence severity relative to other whites" (Steen et al., 2005, p. 446). In contrast, Black drug dealers with prior convictions would be seen as "typical" drug offenders; their cases, therefore, would not merit extensive judicial scrutiny and their crimes would not be deemed worthy of harsher punishment. The results of their analyses confirmed these hypotheses. Matching the stereotype of the dangerous drug offender increased the odds of incarceration 23 times for White offenders but only 3 times for Black offenders; matching the stereotype had no effect on sentence length for Black offenders but increased sentence length by 13% for White offenders.

Cassia Spohn and Lisa Sample (2008/2013) built on these results using data on drug offenders convicted in three U.S. district courts. They extended the study conducted by Steen and her colleagues by (a) using data on federal, rather than state, drug offenders; (b) including Hispanics as well as Blacks in the analyses; (c) using a definition of the dangerous drug offender that reflects the nature of the drug caseload in the federal court system; and (d) examining whether the effects of stereotypes of dangerousness varied by type of drug.

Because there were only 23 drug offenders in their data file who were convicted of an offense other than drug trafficking, Spohn and Sample could not differentiate between offenders convicted of drug delivery and those convicted of simple possession. Instead, they defined the dangerous drug offender in federal court as a male offender with a prior conviction for drug trafficking who used a weapon during the current crime. They hypothesized that offenders who perfectly matched the stereotype—that is, males with prior trafficking convictions who used a weapon—would receive longer sentences than all other offenders. They also predicted that the effect of matching the stereotype of a dangerous drug offender would not vary by race/ethnicity and that the effect of being a dangerous drug offender would vary by the type of drug involved in the case and by the race/ethnicity of the offender. They hypothesized that the effect of being a dangerous drug offender would be confined to crack cocaine cases for Black offenders and to methamphetamine cases for White and Hispanic offenders.

Spohn and Sample (2008/2013) found that Black offenders were more likely than either White offenders or Hispanic offenders to have the characteristics of a dangerous drug offender; they also found that White offenders were more likely than Hispanic offenders to match the characteristics of a dangerous drug offender (see also Spohn, 2006). Consistent with these findings, Blacks were overrepresented in the most serious category of the offender groups. Fourteen percent of the Black offenders, but only 5% of the White offenders and 2% of the Hispanic offenders, were male offenders with prior drug trafficking convictions who used weapons in the current offense.

Although Spohn and Sample found partial support for their hypothesis that offenders who perfectly matched the stereotype of a dangerous drug offender would be sentenced most harshly, their results were inconsistent with their hypothesis that the effect of matching this stereotype would not vary by race/ethnicity. They found that there were no significant differences in the sentences imposed on the

(*Continued*)

(Continued)

most dangerous offenders and the five categories of less dangerous offenders for Whites or Hispanics. There were, on the other hand, significant differences in the prison sentences imposed on the most dangerous Black offenders and offenders in all five categories of less dangerous Black offenders. Partitioning the data by type of drug further clarified these relationships. Matching the stereotype of the dangerous drug offender had no effect on sentence severity for White or Hispanic offenders in either methamphetamine cases or cases involving other types of drugs or for Black offenders in cases involving drugs other than crack cocaine. In contrast, fitting the dangerousness stereotype significantly affected the length of the prison sentence for Black offenders convicted of offenses involving crack cocaine but had no effect on sentence length for Black offenders convicted of offenses involving other types of drugs. At least in these three U.S. district courts, images of dangerousness and threat affected the length of the prison sentence only for Black offenders who were convicted of trafficking in crack cocaine.

Spohn and Sample noted that although the results of their study conflicted with the substantive findings from Washington State, they were nonetheless consistent with Steen and her colleagues' conclusion that "the meaning of race ... will vary depending on other offender and offense characteristics, and that differences in treatment within race may therefore be as large as differences between races."

Source: "The Dangerous Drug Offender in Federal Court: Stereotyping Blacks and Crack Cocaine," Crime & Delinquency, published online in 2008. Cassia Spohn, Lisa Sample

Relatively few studies test for the effects of offender characteristics such as marital status, responsibility for dependent children, or a history of drug or alcohol abuse. Kathleen Daly's (1987, 1989) research on gender bias in sentencing suggests that judges do take offenders' family circumstances into consideration in making pretrial release and sentencing decisions. She found that defendants who were living with a spouse, living with parents or other relatives, or caring for young children were treated more leniently than "nonfamilied" defendants. According to Daly, this more lenient treatment of familied defendants reflects judges' beliefs that these offenders have more informal social controls in their lives as well as judges' concerns about maintaining families and protecting innocent children, which she labels the "social costs of punishment" (Daly, 1989, p. 138). One study of the effect of the offender's substance abuse history and use of drugs at the time of the crime found that although the offender's history of drug use did not affect sentence length, offenders who were using drugs at the time of the crime received longer sentences both as a direct consequence of their drug use and because drug use at the time of the crime increased the odds of pretrial detention and decreased the likelihood of receiving a substantial assistance departure (Spohn, Kim, Belenko, & Brennan, 2014). Spohn and her colleagues also found that the effects of drug use varied depending on whether the offender was using crack cocaine or some other drug.

In summary, judges do appear to take offenders' background characteristics into consideration when determining the appropriate sentence. Race/ethnicity, gender, and social class clearly are illegitimate considerations; judges are legally precluded from using these "suspect classifications" in sentencing. Indicators of the offender's "social stability" or measures of the degree to which the offender has "informal social control" in his life, on the other hand, may be legally and/or practically relevant. Judges who believe that punishment serves purposes other than retribution and who therefore attempt to individualize sentences may believe that the offender's social and economic circumstances are not irrelevant. Michael Tonry (1995, p. 154) contends that judges ought to consider offenders' social and economic disadvantages at sentencing. He argues that allowing judges to use "social adversity" as a mitigating consideration is not incompatible with a "just sentencing system." In fact, he has called for the repeal of all sentencing policies "that forbid mitigation of sentences on grounds of the offenders' personal characteristics or special circumstances." He argues that these policies "damage disadvantaged and minority offenders, especially those who have to some degree overcome dismal life chances" (Tonry, 1995, p. 195).

Characteristics of the Victim

In attempting to determine the appropriate sentence, do judges consider the characteristics of the victim or the behavior of the victim at the time of the crime? Are offenders who victimize Whites, especially White females, treated differently from those who victimize Blacks? Are offenders who victimize strangers sentenced differently than those who victimize relatives, friends, or intimate partners? Do judges mitigate the sentence if the victim "provoked" or "precipitated" the crime?

Evidence regarding the effect of victim characteristics on sentence severity comes primarily from research regarding the imposition of the death penalty and from research examining sexual assault case outcomes. There is a substantial body of research demonstrating that Blacks who murder Whites are much more likely to be sentenced to death than Blacks who murder Blacks or than Whites who murder Blacks or Whites (see Baldus, Woodworth, & Pulaski, 1990; Gross & Mauro, 1989; Paternoster, 1991). The most widely cited of these studies found that defendants convicted of killing Whites in Georgia were more than 4 times as likely to receive a death sentence as defendants convicted of killing Blacks (Baldus et al., 1990). David C. Baldus and his colleagues (1990) also found that Blacks who killed Whites had the greatest likelihood of receiving the death penalty. There also are a number of studies that find that Black men convicted of sexually assaulting White women are sentenced more harshly than other race-of-offender/race-of-victim pairs (LaFree, 1989; Spohn, 1994; Walsh, 1987). Some death penalty research finds that those who murder White females have substantially higher odds of being sentenced to death than those who murder Black males, Black females, or White males (Williams, Demuth, & Holcomb, 2007).

Other evidence of the role played by victim characteristics is found in research examining the legal processing of sexual assault cases. This research provides evidence that supports the claims of feminist theorists, who assert that outcomes of rape cases reflect decision makers' beliefs about acceptable and unacceptable behavior by women or their stereotypes of sexual assault (Estrich, 1987; LaFree, 1989). Although sentences in sexual assault cases, like those in other types of cases, are strongly influenced by legally relevant factors, such as the seriousness of the crime and the offender's prior criminal record, victim characteristics also come into play. A number of studies, for example, reveal that sexual assault case processing decisions—including decisions regarding sentence severity—are affected by the victim's age, occupation, and education (Kingsnorth, MacIntosh, & Wentworth, 1999; McCahill, Meyer, & Fischman, 1979); by "risk-taking" behavior such as hitchhiking, drinking, or using drugs (Kingsnorth et al., 1999; Spohn & Spears, 1996); and by the reputation of the victim (McCahill et al., 1979). Sexual assault case outcomes also are affected by the relationship between the victim and the offender; men convicted of sexually assaulting women who are strangers to them are sentenced more harshly than men convicted of sexually assaulting women who are relatives or friends (Kingsnorth et al., 1999; Spohn & Spears, 1996).

In summary, victim characteristics do affect the sentences that judges impose. Offenders who murder or sexually assault Whites—and particularly Blacks who murder or sexually assault Whites—are sentenced more harshly than offenders who murder or sexually assault Blacks. The sentences imposed on offenders convicted of sexual assault are less severe if the victim's character, reputation, or behavior suggests that she is not a "genuine victim."

Case Processing Factors

Three case processing attributes have been linked to sentence severity: the type of disposition (plea vs. trial), the defendant's pretrial status (released or in custody prior to trial), and the type of attorney representing the defendant (private attorney vs. public defender). Critics of the sentencing process charge that defendants who plead guilty are treated more leniently than those who are tried by a judge or jury, that defendants who are released pending trial are sentenced more leniently than those who are detained in jail prior to trial, and that defendants represented by a private attorney receive more lenient sentences than those represented by a public defender. Some critics (Holmes, Hosch, Daudistel, Perez, & Graves, 1996) suggest that these findings reflect discrimination against the poor. That is, indigent defendants who are unable to make bail or hire an attorney to defend them are sentenced more harshly than nonindigent defendants.

Although there is little evidence that defendants represented by public defenders receive harsher sentences than those represented by private attorneys, studies of sentencing outcomes reveal that both the type of disposition in the case and the defendant's pretrial status affect sentence severity. Evidence of a **trial penalty/jury tax** comes from studies conducted in both federal and state courts. Two studies of sentences imposed on drug offenders in U.S. district courts, for example, found that pleading guilty reduced both the likelihood of a prison sentence and the length of sentence imposed on offenders who were incarcerated (Albonetti, 1997; Kautt & Spohn, 2002). Research in Pennsylvania also uncovered a substantial trial penalty (B. D. Johnson, 2003; Steffensmeier & Hebert, 1999). For example, one study found that defendants tried by a jury were 25% more likely than those who pled guilty to be sentenced to prison; they also received prison sentences that averaged 19 months longer than those imposed on defendants who pled guilty (Steffensmeier & Hebert, 1999).

A number of studies also demonstrate that offenders held in jail prior to trial get harsher sentences than those who are released pending trial. A study of sentencing decisions in two Florida counties, for example, found that defendants who were held in jail prior to trial were significantly more likely to be incarcerated following conviction, even after controlling for other predictors of sentence severity (Chiricos & Bales, 1991). Moreover, pretrial detention increased the odds of incarceration for offenders convicted of drug offenses, property crimes, and violent crimes. A study of sentencing decisions in Chicago, Miami, and Kansas City reached a similar conclusion (Spohn & DeLone, 2000). In each city, offenders who were released prior to trial faced substantially lower odds of imprisonment than those who were detained. In Chicago, the probability of incarceration for offenders who were released was 41.7% less than the probability for offenders who were in custody. The difference in the probability of imprisonment was 32.0% in Kansas City and 10.2% in Miami. The harsher sentences imposed on offenders detained prior to trial may reflect the fact that defendants held in jail in the months prior to trial are less able to assist in their own defense and/or the fact that judges and jurors assume that defendants locked up prior to trial are more dangerous and pose greater risks than those who are free.

MOVIES AND THE COURTS
DEAD MAN WALKING (1995)

Every crime has a defendant and a victim. Many crimes have more than one victim, and many argue that some criminal defendants are themselves victims of an unjust criminal justice system that favors the rich and well educated over the poor and less educated. The death penalty is a controversial subject, with strong advocates for and against it. In the film *Dead Man Walking*, the impact of murder on the victims and victims' families, as well on the murderer, are depicted. The movie is a fictionalized, composite story based on a book by Sister Helen Prejean, who has spent years counseling murder victims' families and death row inmates.

In the movie, Matthew Poncelet has been on Louisiana's death row for 6 years, awaiting execution for his role in the murder of a young couple. Poncelet committed the crimes with another man, who received life imprisonment. He writes to Sister Prejean for help with his appeal, and they meet and talk about the murder and Poncelet's life. At first he claims to be innocent. Over time, they establish a special relationship. At the same time, Sister Prejean gets to know Poncelet's mother and the victims' families. The families do not understand Sister Helen's efforts to help Poncelet. Poncelet's appeal and request for a pardon are denied, and Poncelet asks her to be his spiritual advisor. Sister Helen tells Poncelet that his redemption is possible only if he takes responsibility for what he did. Just before he is taken from his cell, Poncelet admits to Sister Prejean that he killed the couple. During his execution, he appeals to the boy's parents for forgiveness. At his burial, the murdered boy's father attends the ceremony and begins to pray with Sister Helen.

SUMMARY

The sentencing decision results from a process of gathering and interpreting information about the offense and the offender. Judges use this information to evaluate the harm done by the crime and to paint a portrait of the offender. As John Hogarth (1971) wrote more than 30 years ago, sentencing "is a cognitive process in which information concerning the offender, the offense, and the surrounding circumstances is read, organized in relation to other information and integrated into an overall assessment of the case" (p. 279).

As they attempt to fashion sentences that fit individual offenders and struggle to impose just punishments, judges consider the harm done by the crime, the blameworthiness and culpability of the offender, and the offender's potential for reform and rehabilitation. Their assessment of harm rests squarely on the nature and seriousness of the crime. It rests on both the statutory seriousness of the offense and the gravity and consequences of the crime. Thus, armed robbers will be sentenced more harshly than those who steal cars or write bad checks, and offenders who use deadly weapons or inflict serious injuries on their victims will receive more severe punishment than those who do not. Similarly, offenders who play a primary role in the crime will be punished more harshly than accomplices or those who play secondary roles. The punishment imposed by the judge, in other words, will be proportionate to the harm done by the crime; the punishment will "fit the crime."

Judges also attempt to fashion sentences that "fit the offender." Their evaluation of the offender rests primarily but not exclusively on the offender's prior criminal record. In attempting to understand the offender, assess her blameworthiness, and predict her future dangerousness, the judge examines the offender's past criminal behavior as well as her life history and current circumstances. The judge considers the offender's educational history, family and work situation, community ties, and conduct since she was arrested. The judge also attempts to determine the offender's motivation for the crime, the extent to which the offender feels remorse for her behavior, and the degree to which the offender cooperated in the prosecution of her (or another's) case. Assessing the offender in this way "allows judges to make substantial and refined distinctions between offenders who might appear quite similar if one looked only at the legal wrong committed and the harm it caused" (S. Wheeler, Mann, & Sarat, 1988, p. 120).

To tailor sentences to the facts and circumstances of each case, the judge needs detailed information about the crime and the offender. Although cases tried before a jury may provide the judge with the information he needs, most convictions result from guilty pleas, not trials. Thus, the judge may know little more about the case than the facts necessary to support a guilty plea. A presentence investigation might fill in some of the details about the crime and offender, but the offender might waive the investigation or the probation department might conduct a cursory review. And if the prosecutor and the defense attorney have negotiated a deal that affects the sentence, the judge may believe that gathering additional information about the case would be a waste of the court's resources. Consequently, the judge may have incomplete information about the crime and the offender.

The fact that the information judges have is typically incomplete and the predictions they are required to make are uncertain helps explain why offender characteristics—including the legally irrelevant characteristics of race, gender, and social class—influence sentencing decisions. Because they don't have all the information they need to fashion sentences to fit crimes *and* offenders, judges may resort to stereotypes of dangerousness and threat that are linked to offender characteristics (Hawkins, 1981). Thus, men may be perceived as more dangerous than women, younger offenders may be regarded as more crime prone than older offenders, gang members may be viewed as more threatening than nongang members, the unemployed may be seen as more likely to recidivate than the employed, and those who abuse drugs or alcohol may be viewed as less amenable to rehabilitation than those who abstain from using drugs or alcohol. Similarly, racial minorities—particularly those who are also male, young, members of gangs, and unemployed—may be seen as more dangerous and threatening than Whites. Judges use these perceptions to simplify and routinize the decision-making process and to reduce the uncertainty inherent in sentencing. As a result, men may be sentenced more harshly than women, Blacks and Hispanics may be sentenced more harshly than Whites, the unemployed may be sentenced more harshly than the employed, and so on.

The sentences judges impose also may reflect the fact that they are part of a courtroom work-group (Eisenstein & Jacob, 1977) or courthouse community (Eisenstein et al., 1988) with common goals and shared expectations about how cases should be handled and the types of sentences that should be imposed. The members of the courtroom workgroup, for example, may believe that efficiency demands a high rate of guilty pleas; consequently, plea bargaining will be encouraged, and defendants who cooperate by pleading guilty will be rewarded. The members of the courthouse community also may believe that there are "normal penalties" (Sudnow, 1965) or "going rates" (Eisenstein et al., 1988, pp. 30–31) for particular types of crimes or particular types of offenders. They may agree on the appropriate penalty for the run-of-the-mill burglary or for the offender who repeatedly appears in court on drug charges. Because judges are concerned about maintaining relationships with other members of the courtroom workgroup and ensuring the smooth flow of cases through the criminal justice system, these expectations will constrain their discretion and affect the sentences they impose.

The ambiguity and uncertainty inherent in the sentencing process, coupled with the fact that judges exercise considerable discretion in deciding what the sentence will be, means that we cannot conclusively determine how a judge arrived at a particular sentence in a particular case. We know that judges' sentencing decisions rest, to a considerable degree, on their assessments of harm and blameworthiness and their predictions of dangerousness, but we don't know with certainty how these assessments and predictions are made. Sentencing, in other words, is an inexact science.

Don't overlook the Student Study Site with its useful study aids, such as self-quizzes, eFlash-cards, and other assists, to help you get more from the course and improve your grade.

DISCUSSION QUESTIONS

1. How would a judge using a retributive justification for punishment answer the question, "Why do we punish those who violate the law?" How would a judge using a utilitarian justification answer the question?

2. According to retributive theory, why do those who violate the law deserve to be punished?

3. What problems do each of the philosophical perspectives on sentencing—retribution, deterrence, incapacitation, rehabilitation— encounter in attempting to determine how much to punish?

4. Why did Judge Lynch conclude that the sentence he was required to impose on

"Eddie" was "unjust"? Do you agree or disagree with his conclusion?

5. What are the most common types of sentences imposed by judges in state and federal courts in the United States? Why are intermediate sanctions used so infrequently?

6. How do researchers model the sentencing process?

7. What are the key determinants of judges' sentencing decisions? Why are these two factors so important?

8. What explains the fact that offenders convicted of crimes in the United States

are sentenced more harshly than those convicted of crimes in England and Wales?

9. Should judges take the characteristics of the victim or the relationship between the victim and the offender into consideration when determining the appropriate punishment? Why or why not? According to research on the death penalty and on sentencing decisions in sexual assault cases, do judges take these factors into account?

10. Is it legitimate for judges to impose a trial penalty or jury tax on defendants who refuse to plead guilty? What are the arguments in favor of the trial penalty? Against the trial penalty?

11. Why is sentencing referred to as an "inexact science"? Could it be made more "exact"? Should it be?

KEY TERMS

Appellate review 308

Boot camp 315

Collective incapacitation 300

Community service 316

Day fine 317

Determinate sentence 310

Deterrence 300

Electronic monitoring 316

General deterrence 300

Guided discretion statutes 306

House arrest 316

Incapacitation 300

Indeterminate sentence 310

Intermediate sanction 315

Mandatory minimum sentence 309

Probation 314

Rehabilitation 301

Retributive justifications for punishment 299

Selective incapacitation 300

Sentencing guidelines 298

Specific deterrence 300

Trial penalty/jury tax 328

Utilitarian justifications for punishment 299

INTERNET SITES

Mackenzie, D. L. (2001, July). *Sentencing and corrections in the 21st century.* www.ncjrs.gov/pdffiles1/nij/grants/189089.pdf

National Criminal Justice Reference Service, Publications and Reports: www.ncjrs.gov/App/Publications/alphaList.aspx?alpha=S

United States Sentencing Commission: www.ussc.gov

STUDENT STUDY SITE

Get the tools you need to sharpen your study skills. SAGE edge offers a robust online environment featuring an impressive array of free tools and resources.

Access practice quizzes, eFlashcards, video, and multimedia at **edge.sagepub.com/hemmens4e**

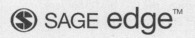

13

Florida Supreme Court

THE APPELLATE PROCESS

Master the content at **edge.sagepub.com/hemmens4e**

INTRODUCTION

In February 1985, two Florida residents were convicted of disorderly conduct and fined $500 each for sunbathing nude on a beach in Daytona Beach, Florida. Following their conviction, their attorney stated in court that he intended to appeal, noting that he would pursue the case "all the way to the Supreme Court in Washington if necessary" ("Attorney Says He'll Appeal," 1985, p. 4B).

Although statements such as these—"We will appeal this case all the way to the U.S. Supreme Court"—are common in criminal cases, they represent little more than grandstanding on the part of losing attorneys. There is no right to appeal to the U.S. Supreme Court, and very few cases make it to the Court's docket. In fact, most criminal cases are not appealed, and those that are typically are appealed to only one higher court.

In this chapter, we examine the appellate process and procedures. We discuss the appellate courts to which criminal offenders direct their appeals. We also discuss the "right" to appeal to one higher court and the reasoning behind the right, and we explore the procedures that appellate courts use in deciding cases.

APPEALING TO A HIGHER COURT

When a person convicted of a crime appeals a conviction, she asks a higher court to examine the trial court's decisions to determine whether the proper procedures were followed. In other words, the offender argues that the trial court made a legal error (or several legal errors) that prevented the offender from receiving a fair trial. The offender asks the appellate court to correct those errors by overturning the decision of the trial court. For example, the offender might argue that the trial was not fair because of prejudicial pretrial publicity that prevented the selection of an impartial jury or because the judge allowed the prosecutor to use the peremptory challenge to remove all the Blacks and Hispanics in the jury pool. Or the offender might assert that the judge's rulings during the trial were incorrect—the judge refused to suppress evidence that the offender contends was obtained illegally or the offender believes that the judge inappropriately allowed a witness to give hearsay testimony. What the offender cannot do, however, is argue that the judge or jury made incorrect findings of fact and that she therefore should not have been convicted. This is because the scope of appellate review is confined to questions of law, not findings of fact.

Most offenders who challenge their convictions were convicted at either a bench or a jury trial; in fact, in many jurisdictions, defendants who plead guilty explicitly waive the right to appeal the conviction. However, there are some grounds on which offenders who plead guilty can appeal. An offender might ask the appellate court to set aside his guilty plea, arguing that the plea was not voluntary or was the result of ineffective assistance of counsel. The Supreme Court has repeatedly ruled that defendants who enter guilty pleas must do so knowingly, intelligently, and voluntarily (see, e.g., *Boykin v. Alabama,* 1969). Moreover, the Court has reiterated that defendants who plead guilty voluntarily and unconditionally cannot later appeal a ruling made by the trial court judge or a decision made by the prosecutor prior to entry of the guilty plea. According to the Court's decision in *Tollett v. Henderson* (1973), "When a criminal defendant has solemnly admitted in open court that he is in fact guilty of the offense with which he is charged, he may not thereafter raise independent claims relating to the deprivation of constitutional rights that occurred prior to the entry of the guilty plea. He may only attack the voluntary and intelligent character of the guilty plea."

Pre- and Postadjudication Appeals

A criminal defendant can appeal at one of two stages during the adjudication process: prior to the reading of the verdict or following adjudication. The prosecutor can also appeal some decisions made by the judge during the pretrial process or the trial. Appeals filed prior to announcement of the final judgment in the case are known as **interlocutory appeals.**

Although the general rule (i.e., the **final judgment** rule) is that the parties to the case must wait until the case has been decided before appealing decisions made by the judge during pretrial proceedings or during the trial, there are some situations in which interlocutory appeals can be filed in criminal cases. Examples of these situations would be those in which the decision being contested (a) involves substantial rights, (b) may materially affect the final decision in the case, or (c) involves a situation in which a determination of the correctness of the order will better serve the administration and interests of justice. Thus, the prosecutor might be allowed to appeal a judge's ruling that the defendant's confession or a critical piece of incriminating physical evidence is inadmissible. This would be allowed if the prosecutor could show that the judge's ruling was wrong and that without the evidence, the state is unable to proceed with the case against the defendant. This reflects the fact that if the evidence is improperly excluded and the defendant is acquitted, the prosecution would not be able to retry the defendant because of the Double Jeopardy Clause. Because the prosecutor cannot appeal a not guilty verdict, in other words, a judge's decision that effectively prevents conviction of the defendant may be appealable.

The defendant also has the right to file an interlocutory appeal, but again, the reasons for allowing this type of appeal are very limited. In *Cohen v. Beneficial Industrial Loan Corp* (1949), the Supreme Court held that only a few interlocutory appeals are likely to succeed—namely, those that involve "a small class [of preadjudication decisions] which finally determine claims of right separable from, and collateral to, rights asserted in the action, too important to be denied review and too independent of the cause itself to require that appellate consideration be deferred until the whole case is adjudicated" (p. 546). Two cases illustrate this ruling. In *Stack v. Boyle* (1951), the Court held that the defendant could appeal a judge's decision rejecting his argument that bail was excessive, in apparent violation of the Eighth Amendment. In another case (*Abney v. United States,* 1977), the Court held that a defendant's appeal of a preadjudication order denying dismissal of his indictment on double jeopardy grounds was permissible. Both of these preadjudication appeals dealt with important constitutional questions, which is why they were allowed.

Appeals filed *after* adjudication, by contrast, are subject to few restrictions. As already discussed, appeals focus on matters of law, not the facts in the case. Postadjudication appeals can raise any number of issues, perhaps challenging such actions as the following:

- An involuntary guilty plea
- The use of a coerced confession

- The use of evidence obtained as a result of an unconstitutional search or seizure

- The use of evidence obtained as a result of an unlawful arrest

- A violation of the privilege against self-incrimination

- The failure of the prosecution to disclose to the defendant evidence favorable to him or her

- A violation of the Fifth Amendment's Double Jeopardy Clause

- A conviction based on a jury that was unconstitutionally selected and impaneled

- Denial of effective assistance of counsel

- Denial of rights to speedy trial and appeal

All these issues focus on the procedures that were used to adjudicate the case and whether these procedures were fair. That is, they address the question of whether the offender received a fair trial. They do not question the defendant's guilt or innocence.

The Appellate Court's Options

When an appeal is heard, the appellate court will either affirm or reverse the lower court's decision to convict the defendant. An appellate court decision to overturn the defendant's conviction means not that the defendant is acquitted and, if confined, set free but that the defendant is entitled to a new trial. The appellate court sends the case back to the trial court (i.e., "remands" the case) for further proceedings consistent with its opinion. Essentially, the appellate court orders the lower court to "do it again the right way." The lower court then has the option of retrying the defendant or dismissing the charges.

Consider a situation in which an offender convicted of drug trafficking appeals his conviction to the state's intermediate appellate court, arguing that evidence used to convict him was obtained illegally and that the judge therefore should have excluded it. The appellate court could rule that the trial judge erred when he refused to suppress the evidence and that the offender's conviction should therefore be overturned. The case will then be sent back to the trial court. If the prosecutor wants to retry the case, she must do so without the evidence that the appellate court has ruled inadmissible. If the case cannot be tried without the evidence that was illegally seized by the police, the prosecutor may have little choice but to dismiss the charges. The appellate court also could rule that the evidence was properly admitted and that the offender's conviction should not be over-turned. In either scenario, the losing party may decide to appeal the court's decision to the state court of last resort; however, this court is not required to hear the appeal.

The Harmless Error Rule

An appellate court that agrees with the defendant's contention that procedural errors were made during the pretrial process or at trial may nonetheless decide not to reverse the defendant's conviction. The court may decide that the errors were "harmless" errors that did not affect the outcome of the case. The so-called **harmless error rule** is designed to prevent an unnecessary new trial in a situation where correcting the error would not result in a different outcome. According to the U.S. Supreme Court, harmless error rules "serve a very useful purpose insofar as they block setting aside convictions for small errors or defects that have little, if any, likelihood of having changed the result of the trial" (*Chapman v. California,* 1967).

For example, in *Chapman v. California* (1967), the Supreme Court considered whether a trial court made a harmless error by permitting the prosecutor, during closing arguments, to repeatedly refer to the defendant's refusal to take the stand and testify. (Although this was allowed under California law that existed at the time, the law was struck down by the Supreme Court in *Griffin v. California,* 1965.) The Court stated that for an error to be ruled harmless, the court must be convinced beyond a reasonable doubt that the error did not contribute to the defendant's conviction. In this case, the Court ruled that the error was not harmless. The Court reversed the defendant's conviction, claiming that "though the case in which this occurred presented a reasonably strong 'circumstantial web of evidence' against petitioners, it was also a case in which, absent the constitutionally forbidden comments, honest fair-minded jurors might very well have brought in not guilty verdicts" (pp. 25–26). In this case, then, the fact that the state's case against Chapman was weak, coupled with the violation of the defendant's privilege against self-incrimination, led the Court to conclude that the error may have affected the outcome of the case and that Chapman therefore was entitled to a new trial.

In the *Chapman* case, the Supreme Court also stated that some rights, including the right to counsel and the prohibition against coerced confessions, were so important to ensuring a fair trial that violations of them would never be treated as harmless error. In a later case, however, the Court retreated from this position, ruling 5–4 that a coerced confession could be admitted as evidence under some circumstances (*Arizona v. Fulminate,* 1991). Writing for the Court, Chief Justice Rehnquist noted that "the admission of an involuntary confession . . . is similar in both degree and kind to the erroneous admission of other types of evidence." According to the Court, if evidence other than the confession was strong enough to convict the defendant, the verdict should stand. For Rehnquist, only "structural defects," such as a biased judge or failure to provide a defendant with assistance of counsel, were absolutely excluded from the harmless error analysis. The dissenting judges took a different view, noting that "the majority today abandons what until now the Court has regarded as the axiomatic [proposition] that a defendant in a criminal case is deprived of due process of law if his conviction is founded, in whole or in part, on an involuntary confession, without regard for the truth or falsity of the confession."

Based on this decision, there are only two constitutional violations—denial of the right to counsel and trial before a biased judge—that are never harmless errors and that, if proven, result in an automatic reversal of the defendant's conviction. All other violations may or may not be harmless, depending on the court's assessment of whether the error had an effect on the verdict and whether the evidence against the defendant is overwhelming and untainted.

Appealing the Sentence

All of the issues previously listed concern decisions made during the pretrial process or during the trial itself. The ability of appellate courts to alter sentences imposed by trial court judges is more limited. The U.S. Supreme Court has ruled that "review by an appellate court of the final judgment in a criminal case . . . is not a necessary element of due process of law, and that the right of appeal may be accorded by the state to the accused on such conditions as the state deems proper" (*Murphy v. Com. of Massachusetts,* 1900). According to the Court, then, due process of law does not require that offenders be allowed to appeal their sentences.

Although all states with death penalty statutes provide for automatic appellate review of death sentences, only half of the states permit appellate review of noncapital sentences that fall within statutory limits (Bureau of Justice Statistics, 2006). The standards for review vary. In some states, appellate courts are authorized to modify sentences deemed "excessive," but in other states, only sentences determined to be "manifestly excessive," "clearly erroneous," or "an abuse of discretion" can be altered (Miller, Dawson, Dix, & Parnas, 1986, p. 1106). A defendant sentenced under the federal sentencing guidelines can appeal a sentence that is more severe than the guidelines permit. Federal law also allows the government to appeal a sentence that is more lenient than provided for in the guidelines.

If an offender appeals her sentence and the appeal is sustained, the sentence must be corrected. An appellate court decision to vacate the sentence does not mean, however, that the offender will escape punishment. As the Supreme Court stated in 1974, "The Constitution does not require that sentencing should be a game in which a wrong move by the judge means immunity for the prisoner" (*Bozza v. United States,* 1947). Thus, the case will be sent back to the trial court for resentencing.

CURRENT CONTROVERSY
WRONGFUL CONVICTION AND THE INNOCENCE PROTECTION ACT OF 2004

In 1993, Kirk Noble Bloodsworth became the first death row inmate in the United States to be exonerated by DNA tests. Bloodsworth was convicted of the rape and murder of a 9-year-old girl and was sentenced to death in Baltimore County, Maryland, in 1985. The Maryland Court of Appeals overturned Bloodsworth's conviction in 1986, ruling that the prosecutor had withheld important evidence from the defense. He was retried, again convicted, and sentenced to two terms of life in prison. This conviction and sentence was upheld by the Maryland courts in 1988.

Four years later, Bloodsworth obtained court approval for DNA tests on biological material from the crime that had been collected and preserved. The results of these tests established conclusively that Bloodsworth was innocent of the crime for which he had been twice convicted. In 1994, he was granted a full pardon by the governor of Maryland.

Bloodsworth's story is not unique. In fact, the past several decades have witnessed the exoneration of more than 350 prisoners, many facing long terms of incarceration or death sentences, as a result of DNA tests (Innocence Project, n.d.). As the number of exonerations has increased and as the accuracy and availability of DNA testing have improved (Houck & Budowle, 2002), states have had to grapple with the problem of creating statutory guidelines for DNA testing and for exoneration procedures (Steinbeck, 2007; Swedlow, 2002). However, some states have not implemented clear guidelines (Steinbeck, 2007), and those that have guidelines often restrict the use of postconviction DNA testing to defendants who pleaded not guilty and to individuals convicted for a major felony such as murder or sexual assault (Borteck, 2004; Swedlow, 2002).

In an attempt to remedy some of these problems, in 2004 Congress passed the Innocence Protection Act, a comprehensive package of criminal justice measures designed to reduce the risk that innocent persons may be executed. Part of the larger Justice for All Act that was signed into law by President George W. Bush, the Innocence Protection Act aims to ensure that defendants in death penalty cases have access to counsel and, where appropriate, access to postconviction DNA testing necessary to prove their innocence. The act created the Kirk Bloodsworth Post-Conviction DNA Testing Program and authorized funding to help states pay the costs of postconviction DNA testing. One of the primary sponsors of the reauthorization of the Justice for All Act, Senator Patrick Leahy of Vermont, had this to say about the effect of the act:

> The Innocence Protection Act and the funding it provides for post-conviction DNA testing has played a critical role in helping the innocent clear their names and receive the exonerations they deserve. These cases happen more often than people might think. In the first six months of 2016, at least four people have been exonerated by DNA testing after spending a combined 100 years in prison for crimes they had not committed. (Leahy, 2016)

Documented cases of wrongful conviction, which many legal scholars believe significantly underrepresent the true population of false convictions, raise questions about the legitimacy and integrity of the American criminal justice system. The sheer number of cases also calls into question assertions that wrongful convictions are rare and that "the ghost of the innocent man convicted" is an "unreal dream" (*United States v. Garsson,* 1923). In March 2009, the U.S. Supreme Court heard oral arguments in an Alaska case centering on whether an inmate's right to postconviction DNA testing is constitutional in origin. Alaska was one of four states that did not have a law providing offenders access to DNA testing. In June 2009, the Court ruled that there was not a constitutional right to DNA testing. Today, all 50 states have postconviction DNA access statutes, but the statutes vary in terms of scope and restrictiveness.

THE APPELLATE COURTS

An offender convicted of a crime in a state or federal court files an appeal with an appellate court in the system (state or federal) where the case was tried. An offender convicted in a state court must first appeal to the next highest court in the state court system; in fact, the offender must exhaust all appeals in the state court system before appealing to the U.S. Supreme Court. As explained in more detail in this section, the grounds on which an offender can appeal from a state court of last resort to the U.S. Supreme Court are limited to cases that fall under the jurisdiction of the federal courts. Offenders convicted of crimes in a U.S. district court appeal to the court of appeals for the circuit in which the district court is located.

State Appellate Courts

A century ago, the state court system included only a single appellate court—the state court of last resort. Because of the right to appeal to at least one higher court, this meant that the state supreme court was required to hear and consider all appeals from state trial courts. As the number of cases appealed from the trial courts increased and threatened to overwhelm the state courts of last resort, states created intermediate courts of appeals (Marvell, 1989). Today, these courts—which go by such names as appeals courts,

FIGURE 13.1 ■ The Structure and Jurisdiction of Arizona State Courts

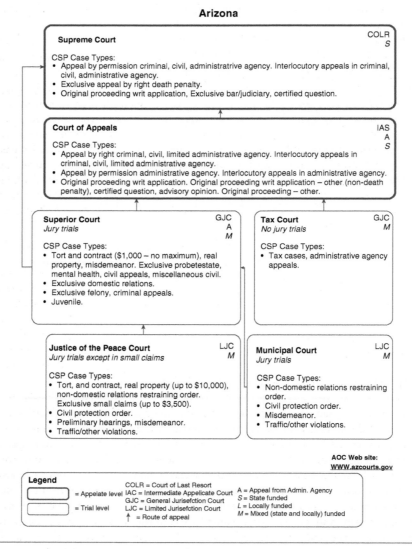

Arizona

Supreme Court   COLR
                                                                            S
CSP Case Types:
• Appeal by permission criminal, civil, administratrive agency. Interlocutory appeals in criminal, civil, administrative agency.
• Exclusive appeal by right death penalty.
• Original proceeding writ application, Exclusive bar/judiciary, certified question.

Court of Appeals   IAS
                                                                            A
                                                                            S
CSP Case Types:
• Appeal by right criminal, civil, limited administrative agency. Interlocutory appeals in criminal, civil, limited administrative agency.
• Appeal by permission administrative agency. Interlocutory appeals in administrative agency.
• Original proceeding writ application. Original proceeding writ application – other (non-death penalty), certified question, advisory opinion. Original proceeding – other.

Superior Court   GJC   **Tax Court**   GJC
Jury trials   A   *No jury trials*   M
                                      M
CSP Case Types: CSP Case Types:
• Tort and contract ($1,000 – no maximum), real   • Tax cases, administrative agency
  property, misdemeanor. Exclusive probetestate,   appeals.
  mental health, civil appeals, miscellaneous civil.
• Exclusive domestic relations.
• Exclusive felony, criminal appeals.
• Juvenile.

Justice of the Peace Court   LJC   **Municipal Court**   LJC
Jury trials except in small claims M   *Jury trials*   M

CSP Case Types: CSP Case Types:
• Tort, and contract, real property (up to $10,000), • Non-domestic relations restraining
  non-domestic relations restraining order.   order.
  Exclusive small claims (up to $3,500).   • Civil protection order.
• Civil protection order.   • Misdemeanor.
• Preliminary hearings, misdemeanor.   • Traffic/other violations.
• Traffic/other violations.

AOC Web site:
WWW.azcourts.gov

Legend
☐ = Appelate level   COLR = Court of Last Resort   A = Appeal from Admin. Agency
                       IAC = Intermediate Appelicate Court   *S* = State funded
☐ = Trial level   GJC = General Jurisefction Court   *L* = Locally funded
                       LJC = Limited Jurisefction Court   *M* = Mixed (state and locally) funded
                       ↑ = Route of appeal

Source: National Center for State Courts. Available online at courtstatistics.org.

appellate courts, appellate divisions, and courts of appeals—are found in 40 states. Some states have two **intermediate appellate courts,** one for civil appeals and the other for criminal appeals (Bureau of Justice Statistics, 2006). These courts are required to hear and rule on appeals properly brought by criminal offenders.

State supreme courts are the highest courts—or the courts of last resort—in each state. As is the case with other courts in the state court system, the names of these courts vary from state to state: supreme court (43 states), court of appeals (2 states and the District of Columbia), supreme judicial court (2 states), court of criminal/civil appeals (2 states), and supreme court of appeals (1 state). Texas and Oklahoma have two courts of last resort, one for criminal appeals and one for civil appeals (Bureau of Justice Statistics, 2006). The number of judges also varies, from a low of five to a high of nine (National Center for State Courts, 2006). (See Figure 13.1, which shows the structure of the Arizona court system and the routes of appeal from one court to another.)

The role of the state court of last resort in the appellate process differs, depending on whether or not the state has an intermediate appellate court. In states with these intermediate courts, the supreme court generally has discretionary jurisdiction in criminal cases. That is, the court has discretion to accept or not accept cases appealed from the intermediate appellate court(s). The one exception to this is cases in which the offender has been sentenced to death, which are automatically appealed to the state supreme court and which that court must hear. In the 10 states without intermediate appellate courts, the state supreme court is required to hear properly filed appeals in criminal cases. The National Center for State Courts compared the mandatory and discretionary caseloads of 22 states with both intermediate appellate courts and supreme courts, finding that 72% of the cases heard by the intermediate appellate courts in these states were mandatory appeals; by contrast, 86% of the cases heard by the supreme courts were discretionary appeals (National Center for State Courts, 2006, p. 75).

Federal Appellate Courts

Offenders who are convicted of crimes in the federal courts appeal their convictions to the federal appellate courts. As is the situation in most states, there are two layers of federal appellate courts. The first layer includes the U.S. courts of appeals, which, as their name implies, handle appeals of decisions handed down by the U.S. district courts in the circuit. There are 13 courts of appeals (see Figure 13.2), including one for the federal circuit and one for the District of Columbia. These courts, which originally were called *circuit courts of appeals,* were renamed, and now each individual court is called the United States Court of Appeals for the _____ Circuit.

Both criminal and civil matters can be heard by the courts of appeals. In 2017, 50,506 appeals from U.S. district courts and other federal courts and administrative agencies were filed in the courts of appeals; of these cases only 20% involved criminal matters (Administrative Office of the U.S. Courts, 2017b). There are 179 authorized judges on the courts of appeals. The Ninth Circuit, which includes California, Arizona, and five other western states, is staffed by 29 judges. By contrast, the First Circuit, which is made up of Maine, Massachusetts, New Hampshire, and Puerto Rico, is staffed by only 6 judges.

Not all matters are resolved at the level of the circuit courts of appeals. Sometimes decisions of those courts (and of other courts) are appealed to the U.S. Supreme Court, the highest court in the land (and often called simply "the Court"). However, there is, with only very few exceptions, no right to appeal to the U.S. Supreme Court. The Supreme Court has discretion to select the few cases it will hear from the many it is asked to review each year. In fiscal year 2012, 5,362 petitions for appellate review (including 1,122 that involved criminal cases) were filed with the Supreme Court; of these, only 117 (37 of the criminal appeals) were granted and only 79 were argued before the court during the 2013 court term.

Cases reach the Supreme Court through the writ of certiorari, which is an order to the lower court to send the records in the case forward for review. In deciding whether to issue the writ, the justices follow the "rule of four"; the case will be heard and the writ issued if four of the nine justices agree to hear the appeal (Murphy, Pritchett, Epstein, & Knight, 2006, p. 626). It is important to point out that the Supreme Court's refusal to hear a case does not mean that the Court agrees with the lower court's decision. As Justice Felix Frankfurter said in *State v. Baltimore Radio Show* (1950), it means only that four of the nine justices did not, for whatever reason, believe that the case was important enough or timely enough to justify a hearing before the Court. Nonetheless, refusing to grant certiorari "does lend some credence to the lower court's ruling" (Murphy et al., 2006, p. 627).

Whereas appeals to the federal courts of appeals come only from the U.S. district courts, the Supreme Court hears appeals from both U.S. courts of appeals and state supreme courts. However, the decisions of state supreme courts are reviewed by the Supreme Court only if they involve a "substantial federal question." An example of a criminal appeal from

FIGURE 13.2 ■ Map of the U.S. Courts of Appeals

Note: Numbers and shading represent regional circuits.

a state supreme court that the Court might agree to hear would be a case in which the defendant claimed that his constitutional rights were violated; that is, he was denied a fair trial or a speedy trial, his jury was selected in a racially discriminatory manner, or he did not receive adequate representation by his defense attorney. In fact, many of the landmark Supreme Court cases in the area of criminal procedure are cases that were appealed from state supreme courts (see "Clarence Earl Gideon's *in forma pauperis* Appeal to the United States Supreme Court," which describes the appeal of Clarence Earl Gideon to the U.S. Supreme Court and the landmark case, *Gideon v. Wainwright,* 1963).

It is important to emphasize that most disputed criminal and civil matters never come to the attention of the U.S. Supreme Court. As a result, there may be contradictory decisions from one state to the next, from one federal district to the next, or from one federal circuit to the next. For example, the Court of Appeals for the Ninth Circuit may decide that a certain type of search is unconstitutional, but the Court of Appeals for the Fifth Circuit might decide otherwise. Only the Supreme Court can resolve the dispute, but again, only if it decides to hear a case involving this issue. That said, if there are conflicting decisions among the courts of appeals on an important legal question—such as the meaning of the Fourth Amendment's prohibition against unreasonable searches and seizures—the Supreme Court often agrees to hear a case and settle the conflict. This is what happened in 2014, when the Supreme Court agree to hear oral arguments in a series of cases regarding the constitutionality of same-sex marriage. The Court's decision was prompted by the fact that several of the U.S. Courts of Appeals had ruled in favor of same-sex marriage, but the Court of Appeals for the Sixth Circuit ruled that state-level bans of same-sex marriage were constitutional. The Court heard oral arguments in April 2015 and in June 2015 held that same-sex marriage was constitutional, resolving the circuit split (*Obergefell v. Hodges*).

KEY CASES

CLARENCE EARL GIDEON'S *IN FORMA PAUPERIS* APPEAL TO THE UNITED STATES SUPREME COURT

In August 1961, Clarence Earl Gideon appeared in a Florida state court facing a felony charge of breaking and entering into a poolroom with the intent to commit a misdemeanor. Because he was indigent, he asked the court to appoint an attorney to represent him. The judge hearing the case, Judge Robert L. McCrary Jr., denied his request. The following is the exchange that took place between Judge McCrary and Mr. Gideon:

> *The Court* (Judge Robert L. McCrary Jr.):
> The next case on the docket is the case of the State of Florida, Plaintiff, versus Clarence Earl Gideon, Defendant.

What says the State, are you ready to go to trial in this case?

Mr. Harris (William E. Harris, Assistant State Attorney): The state is ready, your Honor.

The Court: What says the Defendant? Are you ready to go to trial?

The Defendant: I am not ready, your Honor.

The Court: Did you plead not guilty to this charge by reason of insanity?

The Defendant: No Sir.

The Court: Why aren't you ready?

(*Continued*)

(Continued)

The Defendant: I have no counsel.

The Court: Why do you not have counsel? Did you not know that your case was set for trial today?

The Defendant: Yes sir, I knew that it was set for trial today.

The Court: Why, then, did you not secure counsel and be prepared to go to trial?

The Defendant: Your Honor, I said: I request this Court to appoint counsel to represent me in this trial.

The Court: Mr. Gideon, I am sorry, but I cannot appoint counsel to represent you in this case. Under the laws of the State of Florida, the only time the court can appoint counsel to represent a defendant is when that person is charged with a capital offense. I am sorry, but I will have to deny your request to appoint counsel to defend you in this case.

The Defendant: The United States Supreme Court says I am entitled to be represented by counsel.

The Court: Let the record show that the defendant has asked the court to appoint counsel to represent him in this trial and the court denied the request and informed the defendant that the only time the court could appoint counsel to represent a defendant was in cases where the defendant was charged with a capital offense. The defendant stated to the court that the United States Supreme Court said he was entitled to it.

Because the laws of Florida said that he was not entitled to an attorney, Gideon defended himself. As

the Supreme Court explained in the decision handed down in his case (*Gideon v. Wainwright,* 1963):

"Gideon conducted his defense about as well as could be expected from a layman. He made an opening statement to the jury, cross-examined the State's witnesses, presented witnesses in his own defense, declined to testify himself, and made a short argument emphasizing his innocence to the charge contained in the Information filed in this case."

Predictably, the six-man jury hearing Gideon's case handed down a guilty verdict. He was sentenced to 5 years in prison.

From his prison cell, Gideon, who steadfastly maintained his innocence, applied to the Florida Supreme Court for a writ of habeas corpus. In his petition, he challenged his conviction and sentence on the ground that the trial court's refusal to appoint an attorney to defend him violated his constitutional rights. The Florida Supreme Court denied his petition without issuing an opinion. Gideon then filed a five-page, handwritten petition for a writ of certiorari with the U.S. Supreme Court. He filed *in forma pauperis,* meaning that because he was poor, he was not required to pay the normal court costs or fees for filing an appeal. The Supreme Court agreed to hear Gideon's case and appointed Abe Fortas, a partner at a prestigious Washington, D.C., law firm, to argue Gideon's case.

In a landmark—and unanimous—decision, the U.S. Supreme Court reversed Gideon's conviction and ruled that the court's refusal to appoint an attorney to represent him violated the Sixth Amendment right to counsel. As Justice Black put it, "Reason and reflection require us to recognize that in our adversary system of criminal justice, any person haled into court, who is too poor to hire a lawyer, cannot be assured a fair trial unless counsel is provided for him. This seems to us to be an obvious truth" (p. 344).

Clarence Earl Gideon was retried by a Florida court on August 5, 1963. This time, he had a lawyer to assist him in his defense. After one hour of deliberation, the jury acquitted Gideon of all charges.

Source: A detailed account of this case can be found in *Gideon's Trumpet* by Anthony Lewis (1964). To listen to the oral arguments in the Supreme Court case, go to http://www.oyez.org/cases/1960-1969/1962/1962_155/.

COMPARATIVE COURTS

In Italy, issues of constitutional law are decided by the Constitutional Court, which was established with the enactment of the Italian Constitution in 1948. The Constitutional Court is also called *La Consulta*—a name that reflects the Court's official residence at the Palazzo della Consulta in Rome.

According to Article 34 of the Italian Constitution, the Constitutional Court is charged with (1) judging the constitutionality of laws enacted by national and regional governments, (2) resolving conflicts of jurisdiction between the national government and regional governments, (3) settling disputes between regional governments, and (4) serving as the court of impeachment when charges are brought against the president, the prime minister, or a cabinet minister.

Unlike the U.S. Supreme Court, which is composed of 9 judges, including the chief judge, who are appointed for life by the president with the advice and consent of the Senate, the Italian Constitutional Court is made up of 15 judges who serve 9-year terms and whose terms cannot be renewed or extended. Five of the judges are appointed by the president, 5 are elected by Parliament, and 5 are selected by a committee made up of judges selected from the highest courts in Italy. The President of the Court is elected by the judges and serves a 3-year renewable term of office.

The first decision handed down by the Court involved the constitutionality of a 1931 law that required permission from the police to distribute leaflets or to put up posters, which, those who challenged the law argued, violated the right to freedom of expression guaranteed by the 1948 Constitution. At issue in this case was whether the Court had jurisdiction to review the constitutionality of laws passed prior to the enactment of the Constitution. The Court ruled that all laws, including those enacted before 1948, could be reviewed. More recently, the Constitutional Court agreed to rule on the contentious issue of gay marriage. The case arose when the mayor of Venice refused to proceed with the publication of the notice of marriage, which in Italy is the first step to entering into a civil marriage, filed by a same-sex couple.

Note: Information on the Constitutional Court can be found at http://www.lexadin.nl/wlg/courts/nofr/eur/lxctita.htm. Detailed information can be found in the senior thesis written by Samuel Alito (now a justice of the U.S. Supreme Court) as an undergraduate student at Princeton University, which is also available online at http://www.princeton.edu/~mudd/news/Alito_thesis.pdf.

THE "RIGHT" TO APPEAL

The U.S. Constitution requires that a criminal defendant receive *due process of law.* This term is obviously vague, but it has consistently been interpreted by courts and legislatures to mean that a criminal defendant must have a fair trial. The appeals process helps ensure this right; it helps ensure that the law is applied correctly and that the procedures used to secure the conviction were fair. However, the U.S. Supreme Court has never held that appeals are constitutionally required. In fact, the Court stated more than 140 years ago that "a review by an appellate court of the final judgment in a criminal case, however grave the offense of which the accused is convicted, was not at common law, and is not now, a necessary element of due process of law" (*McKane v. Durston,* 1864). Despite this ruling, state governments and the federal government have rules providing that a defendant in a criminal case whose guilt or innocence was determined at trial has a right to at least one appeal. (As noted earlier, in most jurisdictions, defendants who plead guilty waive their right to appeal on issues other than those that relate to the guilty plea process.)

The prosecutor, on the other hand, does not have the right to appeal a not guilty verdict. The Fifth Amendment to the Constitution states that no person shall "be subject for the same offense to be twice put in jeopardy of life or limb." The **Double Jeopardy Clause** prevents the state or federal government from prosecuting an individual for the same crime more than once. As the Supreme Court stated in *Ashe v. Swenson* (1970), "When an issue of ultimate fact has once been determined by a valid and final judgment, that issue cannot again be litigated between the same parties in any future lawsuit." In this case, the Court ruled that the state could not charge the defendant, who had been acquitted of robbing one of six poker players, with robbing a second victim of the same crime. According to the Court, "Since, on the record in this case, the jury in the first trial

KEY CASES
WARREN MCCLESKEY'S ODYSSEY THROUGH THE APPELLATE COURTS

Warren McCleskey, a Black man, was convicted and sentenced to death in Georgia for killing a White police officer during the course of an armed robbery. McCleskey claimed, among other things, that the Georgia capital sentencing process was administered in a racially discriminatory manner. In support of his claim, he offered the results of a study conducted by David Baldus and his colleagues (Baldus, Woodworth, & Pulaski, 1985). This study found that Blacks convicted of murdering Whites had the greatest likelihood of receiving the death penalty.

Here is a summary of the appeals and the appellate court decisions in McCleskey's case.

1978: McCleskey was convicted of two counts of armed robbery and one count of murder in the Superior Court of Fulton County. He was sentenced to death on the murder charge and received two consecutive life sentences on the armed robbery charges.

1980: The Georgia Supreme Court affirmed McCleskey's convictions and sentences.

1980: The U.S. Supreme Court denied McCleskey's petition for a writ of certiorari.

1980: The Superior Court of Fulton County denied McCleskey's motion for a new trial.

1981: The Superior Court of Butts County denied McCleskey's petition for a writ of habeas corpus.

1981: The Georgia Supreme Court denied McCleskey's application to appeal the superior court's denial of his petition for a writ of habeas corpus.

1981: The U.S. Supreme Court again denied McCleskey's petition for a writ of certiorari.

1984: McCleskey filed a petition for a writ of habeas corpus with the U.S. District Court for the Northern District of Georgia. In his petition, he claimed, among other things, that the Georgia capital sentencing process was administered in a racially discriminatory manner in violation of the U.S. Constitution. The district court denied his petition.

1985: The Court of Appeals for the Eleventh Circuit, sitting en banc, affirmed the denial by the district court of McCleskey's petition for a writ of habeas corpus.

1986: The U.S. Supreme Court granted McCleskey's petition for a writ of certiorari. In *McCleskey v. Kemp* (1987), the Court affirmed the ruling of the court of appeals.

1987: McCleskey filed a second petition for a writ of habeas corpus with the U.S. District Court for the Northern District of Georgia. This time, he claimed that the trial court erred when it allowed the testimony of a jailhouse informant, who stated that McCleskey admitted that he shot the police officer during the robbery. The district court ruled in McCleskey's favor, and the state appealed the ruling.

1989: The Court of Appeals for the Eleventh Circuit reversed the ruling of the district court.

1991: The U.S. Supreme Court granted McCleskey's petition for a writ of certiorari. In *McCleskey v. Zant* (1991), the court affirmed the ruling of the court of appeals.

1991: Warren McCleskey was executed on September 25, 1991.

had determined by its verdict that petitioner was not one of the robbers, the State . . . was constitutionally foreclosed from relitigating that issue in another trial."

The defendant's right to appeal is not unlimited. Most jurisdictions require that appeals be filed within a certain period of time following the final judgment in the case. For example, Arizona requires that a written appeal be filed with the trial court within 20 days, and California requires that the appeal be filed within 60 days (Flango & Rottman, 1998, Table 2.1). In addition, the defendant can only appeal on issues that were properly raised by the defense attorney during the trial. This is referred to as *preserving the issue for appeal*. Thus, if the defense attorney believes that evidence in his client's favor has been erroneously excluded, the attorney must object to its exclusion on the record and state why the evidence should have been admitted. Failure to do so would prevent the attorney from raising the issue on appeal since there would be nothing in the record to indicate why the attorney believed that the evidence was relevant. Finally, a defendant must file a single appeal in which all appealable issues are raised. The defendant is not allowed to file an appeal on one issue and then, after the courts rule against her, file another appeal on a different issue (see "Key Cases: Warren McCleskey's Odyssey Through the Appellate Courts").

Protections Afforded to Appellants

The appellate process has evolved to the point that the U.S. Supreme Court has granted a number of protections to appellants. These protections are intended to ensure access to trial transcripts, the right to counsel, and the right to be free from government retaliation for successful appeals. For example, in *Griffin v. Illinois* (1956), the Supreme Court decided that indigent defendants must be given access to trial transcripts. It held that the government cannot act "in a way that discriminates against some convicted defendants on account of their poverty" (p. 18). Why is access to the transcripts important? It is because they form the basis for an appeal. When a court reporter documents the trial, a record of the trial is produced. If, say, the defense attorney objects to the introduction of some testimony or a piece of physical evidence, that objection will be noted in the record. Such objections often provide the basis for an appeal.

The Supreme Court has also required that counsel be provided to indigent defendants on appeal, as a matter of either equal protection or due process. This decision was reached in the case of *Douglas v. California* (1963), where the Court concluded that the government must provide indigent defendants with counsel to assist in their appeals of right. According to the Court, "Where the merits of the *one and only* appeal an indigent has as of right are decided without benefit of counsel . . . an unconstitutional line has been drawn between rich and poor" (p. 357). The Court has also held that more than just counsel is necessary; the counsel needs to be effective (*Evitts v. Lucey,* 1985).

It is also important that the government not retaliate following successful appeals. This was the decision reached in *North Carolina v. Pierce* (1969), a case where a defendant was reconvicted after a successful appeal but punished more harshly the second time around. The Court concluded that due process required that the "defendant be freed of apprehension of such a retaliatory motivation on the part of the sentencing judge" (p. 725). A similar decision was reached in *Blackledge v. Perry* (1974), where the Supreme Court held that a prosecutor's decision to increase the charge against a defendant who was convicted but appealed was unconstitutional.

THE WRIT OF HABEAS CORPUS

The appeals discussed thus far are direct appeals; that is, they are appeals that directly challenge the defendant's conviction (or sentence) on procedural grounds. An offender who is incarcerated can also file an indirect appeal by filing a petition for a writ of habeas corpus with an appellate court. *Habeas corpus,* which is Latin for "you have the body," requires the person to whom the writ is directed to either produce the person challenging his confinement or release that person from custody. The writ of habeas corpus is considered an indirect appeal because it does not directly challenge the defendant's conviction but instead challenges the authority of the state to incarcerate the defendant. Unlike a direct appeal, the right to petition an appellate court for a writ of habeas corpus is a constitutional right, which is spelled out in Article I of the U.S. Constitution.

The Origins of Habeas Corpus

Habeas corpus is an ancient legal remedy, dating back at least to the Magna Carta (Federman, 2004; Pursley, 1995). Also referred to as the Great Writ, it was initially intended to prevent the king of England from locking people up without ever filing charges. As early as the 13th century, courts were given the power to summon individuals imprisoned by the executive authority to determine whether they were being held unlawfully. Later, the authority of the courts to summon those imprisoned was expanded to include individuals who had been convicted by trial courts. According to Cary Federman (2004), "In part because of the writ's historic association with the Magna Carta, many jurists and legal scholars consider habeas corpus as a tool of liberty in the fight against governmental oppression" (p. 317).

The importance of the writ of habeas corpus is revealed in the fact that the founding fathers included it in the Constitution itself. Article, I, Section 9 states that "the Privilege of the Writ of Habeas Corpus shall not be suspended unless when in Cases of Rebellion or Invasion the public safety can require it." Reflecting its origins in English common law, the writ initially was viewed solely as a means of protecting citizens from unlawful detention by the state. This changed after the Civil War. As Pursley (1995) explained, Congress was concerned that the Southern states would retaliate against the Northern states by locking up the reconstructionists who were attempting to restore order in the South. These concerns prompted the passage of an 1867 law that authorized federal courts to issue writs of habeas corpus on behalf of any person being held in custody in violation of the constitution. With this law, "the machinery was set in place for the writ to evolve into what it has primarily become today: a postconviction remedy to challenge trial judgment" (Pursely, 1995, p. 117).

Postconviction Review Through Habeas Corpus

How does habeas corpus work? Whereas anyone convicted of a crime has the right to file a direct appeal, only offenders who are incarcerated can seek a writ of habeas corpus, which is a type of postconviction review. If the prisoner chooses to do so, she petitions a state or federal court, most often a federal district court, and asks it to issue a writ of habeas corpus. If the court decides to issue the writ, the prisoner (called the petitioner) is brought before the court so that the constitutionality of her confinement can be reviewed. Importantly, the Constitution provides only the right to petition for habeas review, not the right to a hearing. The court has discretion to decide if it wants to grant a hearing.

There are other differences between the appellate process and the habeas corpus process. First, because habeas corpus petitions are collateral rather than direct attacks on trial court judgments, offenders must exhaust all direct appeals before challenging the judgment of the trial court via habeas corpus. Second, habeas corpus petitions filed in federal courts must raise constitutional questions, such as ineffective assistance of counsel (a common ground for filing habeas corpus petitions), racial discrimination in the selection of the jury, or suppression of exculpatory evidence by the prosecutor. A third difference is that, unlike direct appeals, petitions for writs of habeas corpus can raise issues that were not brought up and objected to during the trial; they can be used to challenge the fact, length, or conditions of confinement. Finally, because habeas corpus petitions are discretionary appeals, the Supreme Court has ruled that indigent offenders filing petitions do not have to be provided with attorneys to assist them (*Ross v. Moffitt,* 1974). The Court also ruled, however, that states cannot prohibit prisoners from helping each other prepare and submit habeas corpus petitions (*Johnson v. Avery,* 1969).

Expanding and Restricting Habeas Corpus

Decisions handed down by the U.S. Supreme Court have altered the availability of habeas corpus remedies to state prison and jail inmates. Under the leadership of Chief Justice Earl Warren, who served as chief justice from 1953 to 1969, the Court expanded habeas corpus and made it easier for state inmates to challenge their convictions in the federal courts. These rulings were subsequently modified by cases decided by the more conservative Burger (1969–1986) and Rehnquist (1986–2005) Courts and by the Antiterrorism and Effective Death Penalty Act of 1996.

Three 1963 decisions greatly expanded the right of imprisoned offenders to use the habeas corpus process to obtain review of their convictions and confinement (*Fay v. Noia,* 1963; *Sanders v. United States,* 1963; *Townsend v. Sain,* 1963). In the first case, Noia and two codefendants were convicted of felony murder and sentenced to life imprisonment; the only evidence against the three men was their confessions. Noia did not appeal, but his codefendants did, and an appellate court ruled that their confessions were coerced and ordered their release. Because Noia had missed the deadline for filing an appeal, the U.S. District Court for the Southern District of New York denied his petition for a writ of habeas corpus; the district court ruled that Noia had failed to exhaust all available state remedies before filing his petition.

The Court of Appeals for the Second Circuit reversed the ruling of the district court and ordered that Noia's conviction be overturned and that he either be discharged from custody or given a new trial. The U.S. Supreme Court affirmed the decision of the court of appeals, ruling that it was "intolerable" to imprison someone based on a conviction that resulted from a coerced confession and that habeas corpus was the appropriate remedy. According to the Court, "The basic principle of the Great Writ of habeas corpus is that, in a civilized society, government must always be accountable to the judiciary for a man's imprisonment; if the imprisonment cannot be shown to conform with the fundamental requirements of law, the individual is entitled to his immediate release" (*Fay v. Noia,* 1963, p. 399).

As a result of this decision and the other two decisions handed down in 1963, both of which also expanded the right of prisoners to use the habeas corpus process to bring challenges in federal court, the number of petitions for writs of habeas corpus filed by state prison inmates skyrocketed from about 1,000 in 1961 to 12,000 in 1992 (Pursley, 1995). As Pursley noted, "Although a significant portion of this increase can be accounted for by the simple fact that state inmate populations have increased so drastically, even factoring in the increase in the number of state prison inmates over this period cannot alone account for such a proportional increase" (p. 118).

More recent Supreme Court decisions have gone in the opposite direction. These decisions have restricted the ability of state prisoners to use habeas corpus to secure federal court review of their convictions and sentences. In a series of decisions that commenced in 1976, the Supreme Court

- Ruled that "where the State has provided an opportunity for full and fair litigation of a Fourth Amendment claim," a federal court should not issue a writ of habeas corpus to a petitioner who alleges that the evidence used against him or her was obtained as a result of an unconstitutional search and seizure violation (*Stone v. Powell*, 1976). This decision meant that an offender who claimed that illegally seized evidence was admitted at trial and whose appeals on this issue were heard and decided by state courts could no longer use the habeas corpus process to challenge his or her conviction.

- Held that an offender cannot use the writ of habeas corpus to obtain review in federal court based on rules of criminal procedure (i.e., the rule regulating the use of peremptory challenges to remove racial minorities from juries that was announced in *Batson v. Kentucky*, 1986) that did not exist at the time that the offender's case was decided on direct appeal (*Teague v. Lane*, 1989).

- Ruled that a prisoner who files a habeas corpus petition that involves new claims (i.e., claims not raised in the first petition) must be able to provide a legitimate reason to explain the failure to raise the claim in the earlier petition and must demonstrate that the errors cited had a prejudicial effect on the outcome of the case. Thus, the Court ruled that Warren McCleskey (see "Key Cases: Warren McCleskey's Odyssey Through the Appellate Courts") could not challenge the state's use of a jailhouse informant in a second habeas action (*McCleskey v. Zant*, 1991).

- Held that a death row inmate was barred from filing a habeas appeal in federal court because his lawyers had filed notice that they would appeal a state habeas decision 3 days after the deadline (*Coleman v. Thompson*, 1991). According to Justice O'Connor, Coleman had his "'one and only appeal' as to the claims in question, since the County Circuit Court fully addressed and denied those claims."

- Ruled that a death row inmate's claim of "actual innocence" did not entitle him to federal habeas relief unless there was an accompanying federal constitutional violation. As the majority opinion noted, "Federal habeas courts do not sit to correct errors of fact but to ensure that individuals are not imprisoned in violation of the Constitution. Thus, claims of actual innocence based on newly discovered evidence have never been held to state a ground for federal habeas relief absent an independent constitutional violation occurring in the course of the underlying state criminal proceedings" (*Herrera v. Collins*, 1993).

In these more recent decisions, the Supreme Court has argued in favor of the finality of state court decisions and against allowing the federal courts to overturn those decisions if there are not compelling reasons to do so. Consider, for example, Justice O'Connor's opening statement in the *Coleman v. Thompson* (1991) case mentioned in the preceding list: "This is a case about federalism. It concerns the respect that federal courts owe the States and the

CURRENT CONTROVERSY
THE FEDERAL COURTS AND "FRIVOLOUS" APPEALS

Prior to the Supreme Court's 1991 decision limiting the ability of offenders to file repeated habeas corpus petitions, some prison inmates filed appeal after appeal in an attempt to get their convictions overturned.

One such offender was Billy Roy Tyler, an inmate of the Nebraska State Penitentiary who filed 149 lawsuits in federal court during 1986 and 1987. This included 17 petitions for writs of habeas corpus challenging his conviction on virtually the same grounds. Because Tyler had no money, all his appeals were filed *in forma pauperis*.

In 1987, the U.S. District Court for the District of Nebraska, which noted that many of his appeals

"used foul and disgusting language" and called judges and other court officials "racially derogatory names," issued a ruling that limited the number of appeals that Billy Roy Tyler could file *in forma pauperis* with the district court to one per month. The court also prohibited Tyler from drafting complaints for other inmates and stated that his "abusive language and actions will no longer be tolerated."

Tyler appealed the district court's order to the Court of Appeals for the Eighth Circuit, which ruled that there was "no error of fact or law in the district court's order."

Source: *In re Billy Roy Tyler* (1988).

States' procedural rules when reviewing the claims of state prisoners in federal habeas corpus." In ruling against Herrera's argument that evidence of actual innocence entitled him to habeas review in the federal courts, Justice Rehnquist similarly referred to the deference that should be accorded to decisions of state courts and to the "enormous burden that having to retry cases based on often stale evidence would place on the States" (*Herrera v. Collins,* 1993).

These decisions notwithstanding, the number of habeas petitions filed by state prison inmates increased from 7,019 in 1980 to 10,817 in 1990 to 21,345 in 2000 (Bureau of Justice Statistics, 2002, Table 1). These increases no doubt reflect the fact that the state prison population increased by more than 400% during this time period; it went from 305,458 inmates in 1980 to 1,236,476 in 2000 (Bureau of Justice Statistics, 2002, Table 3). In fact, as shown in Figure 13.3, the rate of habeas petitions filed by state prison inmates— that is, the number of petitions filed per 1,000 inmates—declined substantially from 1980 to 1990 (from 23.0 to 15.3) but increased from 1990 to 2000 (rate of 17.3).

HOW DO APPELLATE COURTS DECIDE?

Unlike trial court judges, who typically preside alone over their courts and issue unilateral rulings, appellate court judges participate in a group decision-making process. Depending on the level of the court and the importance of the issues involved in the case, there may be three, five, seven, nine, or more judges who cast votes in the case. Moreover, "the task confronting appellate judges differs considerably from that of trial

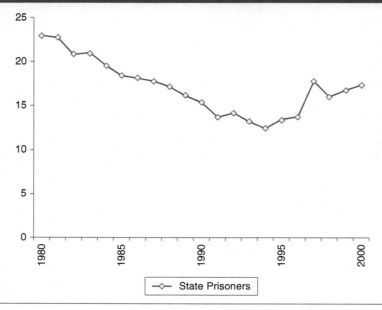

Source: Bureau of Justice Statistics (2002). Data spreadsheet available online at http://www.ojp.usdoj.gov/ bjs/ abstract/ ppfusd00.htm.

[a] Number filed per 1,000 state prison inmates.

Note: Most recent data available.

judges" (Murphy et al., 2006, p. 620). In an appellate court, there are no witnesses, no presentation of evidence, and no juries. Instead, there is the written record of events that took place at the trial and the briefs and oral arguments of the attorneys for the two sides. The task of the appellate court judge is to decide which side has presented more compelling arguments.

Although the procedures used by state and federal appellate courts vary somewhat, there is substantial similarity across courts. The process begins when the defendant files a notice of appeal with the appropriate appellate court. For defendants convicted in state courts, this would be either the intermediate appellate court or the state supreme court; for defendants convicted in federal courts, it would be the court of appeals for the circuit in which the district court is located. As we have already pointed out, the right to one appeal means that the appellate court where the first appeal is filed is required to hear the case and render a decision.

The next step is the preparation of the appellate court record, which includes the trial transcript and any documents or physical evidence introduced at the trial. Attorneys for each side then submit written statements—or briefs—that lay out each party's version of the facts in the case and interpretation of the legal issues raised in the appeal as well as any prior cases that support the attorneys' arguments. The defendant (now, the appellant) submits her brief first, and then the state (now, the respondent) submits a brief that responds to the arguments made by the appellant. The appellant identifies the legal errors that were made in the case and explains why those errors justify overturning the conviction (or sentence).

CURRENT RESEARCH

Researchers have only recently begun to ask whether judges from different backgrounds decide cases differently. This research has focused on such issues as whether former prosecutors impose more punitive sentences than former defense attorneys, whether judges' sentences become more or less severe the longer they serve, and whether Black judges or female judges dispense a different kind of justice than White judges or male judges.

In this article, Jennifer Peresie asks whether the presence of female judges on three-judge federal appellate panels affected decision making in two types of "gender-coded" cases: those alleging sexual harassment or sexual discrimination in violation of Title VII of the Civil Rights Act of 1964. There were 556 cases decided in 1999, 2000, and 2001; the decisions in these cases were made by 54 female judges and 273 male judges.

Peresie found that most decisions went against the plaintiffs in these cases but that female judges ruled for the plaintiffs more often than male judges did. She also found that judges appointed by Democratic presidents ruled more often for the plaintiffs than did judges appointed by Republican presidents.

These differences did not disappear when the author performed a multivariate analysis that simultaneously controlled for the judges' gender, race, age, ideology, and prior type of employment; whether the judge was appointed by a Democratic or a Republican president; the gender of the plaintiff; and whether the district court ruled in favor or against the plaintiff in the case. Even taking all these factors into account, female judges were significantly more likely than male judges to rule in favor of the plaintiff.

Peresie also found that the judge's gender had an indirect effect on decision making; male judges were more likely to rule in favor of the plaintiff if there was at least one female judge on the three-judge panel.

To explain these results, the author suggested that female judges affected both the nature of the decision-making process and the decisions rendered by the panels' male judges. She suggested the influence of female judges on the decisions handed down by male judges might reflect the fact that male judges "defer to female judges because male judges view them as more credible and persuasive in gender-coded cases, based on their viewpoints, past experiences, or gender alone" (p. 1783). Another possibility, according to Peresie, is that "the presence of female judges may cause male judges to moderate their anti-plaintiff preferences . . . [they] may be less willing to argue against sexual harassment or sexual discrimination claims when there is a female judge on the bench" (p. 1786).

These findings led Peresie to conclude, "Judges' gender matters, both to what the bench looks like and what it decides" (p. 1787).

Source: "Female Judges Matter: Gender and Collegial Decision Making in the Federal Appellate Courts," The Yale Law Journal, 114, 1759–1790 (2005). Jennifer L. Peresie

The respondent argues that the lower court's decision was legally correct and explains why the appellant's interpretation of the law and conclusion that the case should be overturned is wrong.

After the judges assigned to the case have received and reviewed the opposing briefs, the case is scheduled for oral argument. Each side is allowed a limited amount of time to synthesize and expand on the arguments made in writing. For example, the lawyers who appear before the Indiana Supreme Court typically have 40 minutes for oral arguments, and those appearing before the U.S. Supreme Court usually are allotted only 30 minutes each. Judges on the appellate panel often ask the opposing lawyers questions about the case. They may ask for clarification regarding the facts in the case; they also may challenge the lawyers' interpretation of the law or use of prior cases to support their arguments. (See Exhibit 13.1, "Oral Arguments Before the U.S. Supreme Court," for an example of the type of back-and-forth that takes place during oral arguments before the U.S. Supreme Court.)

After hearing the oral arguments in the case, the appellate court judges assigned to the case meet in conference to discuss and decide the case. A vote will be taken, and one of the judges in the majority will be assigned the task of writing the opinion for the court. Judges who disagree with the decision reached by the majority may write a dissenting opinion (or opinions), while those in the majority who agree with the court's decision but not its reasoning may write concurring opinions. The court's decision in the case is then announced in court and published so that it may be cited as precedent in subsequent cases.

Sometimes the appellate judges agree on the decision in a case but disagree on the rationale for the decision. For example, in the landmark case of *Furman v. Georgia* (1972), in which the Supreme Court ruled 5–4 that the death penalty, as it was being administered under then-existing statutes, was unconstitutional, the nine justices wrote nine separate opinions.

Although all five justices in the majority were concerned about the arbitrary and capricious application of the death penalty, the nature of their concerns varied. Justices Brennan and Marshall wrote that the death penalty was inherently cruel and unusual punishment. Whereas Justice Brennan argued that the death penalty violated the concept of human dignity, Justice Marshall asserted that the death penalty served no legitimate penal purpose. These justices concluded that the death penalty would violate the Constitution under any circumstances.

The other three justices in the majority concluded that capital punishment as it was then being administered in the United States was unconstitutional. These justices asserted that the death penalty violated both the Eighth Amendment's ban on cruel and unusual punishment and the Fourteenth Amendment's requirement of equal protection under the law. Justice Douglas stated that the procedures used in administering the death penalty were "pregnant with discrimination." Justice Stewart focused on the fact that the death penalty was "so wantonly and so freakishly imposed." Justice White found "no meaningful basis for distinguishing the few cases in which [the death penalty] is imposed from the many cases in which it is not."

EXHIBIT 13.1   ■   Oral Arguments Before the U.S. Supreme Court

Lawyers appearing before the U.S. Supreme Court may or may not be peppered with questions by the justices. If the attorney simply repeats the material found in the written brief, the justices may "stare impassively at the draperies, chat among themselves, write notes, read, send pages for law reports, or even occasionally nap, apparently bored by what is being said to them" (Murphy et al., 2006, p. 630).

If the case is one that raises important constitutional questions, the justices "may suddenly turn a turgid presentation into an exciting debate by posing a rapid series of piercing questions and counter questions"

(Murphy et al., 2005, p. 630). Consider the following exchange between Abe Fortas, the attorney who was representing Clarence Earl Gideon in his appeal on the basis of the trial court's refusal to provide him with an attorney to assist him in his defense, and Justice Harlan and Justice Douglas:

Mr. Fortas: Let me say this, if the Court please: If you will look at this transcript of the record, perhaps you will share my feeling, which is a feeling of despondency. This record does not indicate that Clarence Earl Gideon is a man of inferior natural talents. This record does not indicate that Clarence Earl Gideon is a moron or a person of low intelligence. This record does not indicate that the judge of the trial court in the State of Florida, or that the prosecuting attorney in the State of Florida, was derelict in his duty. On the contrary, it indicates that they tried to help Gideon. But to me, if the Court please, this record indicates the basic difficulty with Betts against Brady. And the basic difficulty with Betts against Brady is that no man, certainly no layman, can conduct a trial in his own defense so that the trial is a fair trial.

The Court: Well, Betts and Brady did not proceed on that basis; it did not deny the obvious. Obviously, a man who is not represented is not as, hasn't had as good a shake in court as the man who is represented. Betts and Brady didn't go on any such basis as that.

Mr. Fortas: Are you suggesting, Mr. Justice Harlan—which I believe to be the case—that the real basis for Betts against Brady is the following: That a man does not get a fair trial if he is not represented by a lawyer, but that the demands of federalism overweigh the absence of a fair trial?

The Court: That's what I understood the basis of Betts and Brady to be, yes.

Mr. Fortas: . . .I believe that this case dramatically illustrates the point that you cannot have a fair trial without counsel. Indeed, I believe that the right way to look at this, if I may put it that way, is that a court, a criminal court is not properly constituted—and this has been said in some of your own opinions—under our adversary system of law, unless there is a judge and unless there is a counsel for the prosecution and unless there is a counsel for the defense. Without that, how can a civilized nation pretend that it is having a fair trial, under our adversary system, which means that counsel for the State will do his best within the limits of fairness and honor and decency to present the case for the State, and counsel for the defense will do his best, similarly, to present the best case possible for the defendant, and from that clash there will emerge the truth. That is our concept, and how can we say, how can it be suggested that a court is properly constituted, that a trial is fair, unless those conditions exist.

Someone said—

The Court: Well, it isn't quite so simple as that, because there are concepts in the Federal system apart from the Sixth Amendment. We would consider that a man in a felony case hadn't had a fair shake if he wasn't tried before a jury. And I suppose the State could do away with the jury trial and you wouldn't say this trial was inherently unfair, would you?

Mr. Fortas: That's right, and that's what I want to get to, Mr. Justice.

The Court: I think you'd have to argue this on the basis of federalism.

Mr. Fortas: I appreciate that, and I am happy if we can clear the debris, if I may say so, so we can understand exactly what is at issue here. And I just want to say and to nail this, if I may, that we are not and we cannot, as I think this colloquy has disclosed, Mr. Justice Harlan, proceed on the assumption that there is any such thing as a fair criminal trial where the defendant is not represented by counsel.

(Continued)

(Continued)

And now I would like to get to the question of federalism.

The Court: Well, this federalism that Justice Harlan mentions is implicit, I gather, in all that we have written. I believe I have read all of them; have written some of them. I don't know if anyone has—any member of this Court has come out and said in so many terms it's the constitutional right of a State to provide a system whereby people get unfair trials.

Mr. Fortas: Well, Mr. Justice Douglas—

The Court: I don't believe that suggested that; I don't suppose—

The Court: I thought that's what we were talking about, isn't it.

Mr. Fortas: Well, Mr. Justice Douglas, I—

The Court: I mean, if a person can't have a fair trial without a lawyer, and this is a problem of federalism, you come down to how a State has a constitutional right to provide a system that perpetuates unfair trials.

SUMMARY

The appeals process is an essential component of the court system. State and federal appellate courts safeguard the right to due process by ensuring that the law is applied correctly during criminal trials and that fair procedures are used to secure a verdict. In the broadest sense, appellate review determines whether an offender received a fair trial. This chapter discussed the appellate process and described some of the key concepts essential to understanding its function.

It is important to remember that appellate reviews are confined to answering questions of law and do not consider findings of fact. That is to say, an individual convicted of a crime can only challenge court procedures that transpired during his or her trial. Although the Constitution does not specifically require appeals to be heard by higher courts, all states and the federal government guarantee the right to at least one appeal. This right, however, is only ensured for the defense as the prosecution is prohibited by the Double Jeopardy Clause of the Fifth Amendment from appealing a not guilty verdict.

Appeals come in various forms and arrive in appellate courts in a number of ways. Both the defense and the prosecution have limited use of interlocutory appeals, which are appeals that take place prior to the final disposition of a case. Postadjudication appeals occur after a verdict has been reached and typically involve the defense challenging procedures used or rulings made during trial. Defendants can also appeal a sentence under certain conditions. The Due Process Clause does not require that offenders be allowed to appeal their sentences, but various states stipulate situations under which individuals can do so. All death sentences, however, are required by law to undergo appellate review. Once the court of appeals hears a particular case, the judges decide to either affirm or reverse the decision of the lower court. A reversal does not mean that the release of the defendant is required but rather that, if the state decides to continue the case, a new trial must be conducted with the previous errors corrected.

The appellate process for state courts requires that a case must first go to an intermediate court of appeals (if present in the state) prior to going to the state court of last resort. A defendant must exhaust all state appeals prior to appealing to the U.S. Supreme Court. Federal cases that originate in U.S. district courts are appealed to courts of appeals for the circuit in which the district is located. After this step, a federal case can be appealed to the U.S. Supreme Court.

Until this point in the book, we have discussed the typical criminal trial process. However, in efforts to tailor decision-making procedures to specific types of offenders in diverse life situations, courts throughout the country have established a wide variety of specialized or problem-solving courts. These courts, such as drug and juvenile courts, are the topic of the next chapter.

Don't overlook the Student Study Site with its useful study aids, such as self-quizzes, eFlash-cards, and other assists, to help you get more from the course and improve your grade.

DISCUSSION QUESTIONS

1. What purpose do appeals serve in criminal cases? Why is this important?

2. What is the Double Jeopardy Clause? How does it affect the appellate process?

3. Why is the writ of habeas corpus referred to as "the Great Writ"?

4. How does habeas corpus differ from a direct appeal? Can anyone convicted of a crime petition for a writ of habeas corpus? What are the advantages/disadvantages of the use of habeas corpus?

5. Do you agree or disagree with the Supreme Court's restrictions on the use of the habeas corpus petition? Why?

6. Most criminal appeals are not heard by the U.S. Supreme Court. Why do you think that the Court agreed to accept Clarence Earl Gideon's *in forma pauperis* petition for a writ of certiorari?

7. What is the "harmless error rule," and how does it affect the appellate process? In your opinion, does the rule have a positive or negative effect on the quality of justice meted out in criminal courts?

8. Describe the processes by which a state case can make its way to the U.S. Supreme Court (see the "Key Cases: Warren McCleskey's Odyssey" box).

9. What types of cases are heard by the U.S. Supreme Court? What functions does the U.S. Supreme Court serve?

10. Why is it important for prosecutors to have the ability to file an interlocutory appeal?

11. Explain the types of appeals discussed in this chapter that are guaranteed by the Constitution. Do people convicted of crimes have the right to at least one appeal? If so, who guarantees this right?

KEY TERMS

Double Jeopardy Clause 346
Final judgment 335

Harmless error rule 336
Interlocutory appeals 335

Intermediate appellate courts 341

INTERNET SITES

Bureau of Justice Statistics: http://www.ojp.usdoj.gov/bjs

Gideon v. Wainwright Oral Arguments: http://www.oyez.org/cases/1960-1969/1962/1962_155

National Center for State Courts: http://www.ncsc.org

Sourcebook of Criminal Justice Statistics: http://www.albany.edu/sourcebook

Supreme Court of the United States: http://www.supremecourtus.gov

STUDENT STUDY SITE

Get the tools you need to sharpen your study skills. SAGE edge offers a robust online environment featuring an impressive array of free tools and resources.

Access practice quizzes, eFlashcards, video, and multimedia at **edge.sagepub.com/hemmens4e**

14

SPECIALIZED COURTS

SAGE edge™

Master the content at **edge.sagepub.com/hemmens4e**

INTRODUCTION

During the 1980s, the number of drug offenders locked up in state and federal prisons skyrocketed. In fact, the rate at which drug offenders were sent to prison went from 19 per 1,000 adult arrests for drug offenses in 1980 to 104 per 1,000 arrests in 1994 (Bureau of Justice Statistics, 1995). The staggering costs of incarcerating increasing numbers of drug offenders, coupled with mounting evidence that imprisonment was not an effective approach to dealing with drug abuse and addiction, led policy makers to search for alternative solutions that would be cost-effective, politically palatable, and successful in reducing drug abuse and drug-related crime (see "California Voters Approve Proposition 47" for one example).

This search for a more effective strategy led to the development of the drug treatment court. The movement started in 1989, when then–State Attorney General Janet Reno joined forces with Florida judges and the Dade County (Miami) public defender to establish the nation's first treatment-based drug diversion court. Unlike a traditional court, which operates according to an adversarial model and emphasizes punishment, the Miami Drug Court stressed collaboration among criminal justice officials, ongoing judicial supervision of offenders, mandatory drug treatment, and a rehabilitation program providing vocational, education, family, and medical services. The drug court movement spread rapidly. By 2015, there were more than 2,600 programs for adult and juvenile offenders operating in state and federal courts throughout the United States (Office of National Drug Control Policy, n.d.).

As evidence mounted that drug treatment courts were both more cost-effective and more successful in reducing drug use and drug-related crime, states began to experiment with other specialized courts: domestic violence courts, mental health courts, veterans'

CURRENT CONTROVERSY
CALIFORNIA VOTERS APPROVE PROPOSITION 47

In November 2014, California voters approved Proposition 47, the Reduced Penalties for Some Crimes Initiative. The initiative reclassified most nonserious and nonviolent property and drug crimes from felonies to misdemeanors and allowed offenders serving prison sentences for any of the reclassified offenses to be resentenced. The initiative also stated that offenses committed by offenders with prior convictions for serious violent crimes and certain drug offenses were ineligible for reclassification. Included among the reclassified offenses is personal use of most illegal drugs.

A report by the state's Legislative Analyst's Office estimated that the initiative would reduce both the jail and prison populations substantially and that the savings to the state would range from $100 million to $200 million per year.

courts, reentry courts, community courts, and homeless courts. These courts, which generally are referred to as "problem-solving" courts, are distinguished by several unique characteristics: a focus on solving offenders' underlying problems, a nonadversarial approach to decision making that involves social service providers as well as criminal justice officials, ongoing judicial supervision and monitoring of offenders in the program, and sanctions for noncompliance with program requirements (Farole, Puffett, Rempel, & Byrne, 2005). All of these courts, in other words, are designed to address the problems that landed the offender in court and not just respond to the offender's criminal behavior, while at the same time holding the offender accountable and protecting the safety of the community.

In this chapter, we focus on specialized courts, also referred to as problem-solving courts. We emphasize the two types of courts—drug treatment courts and domestic violence courts—that have spread most rapidly and have generated the most research. We end the chapter with a discussion of the juvenile court, a specialized court with its origins in the 19th century.

PROBLEM-SOLVING COURTS

Since 1990, specialized courts have become "an important feature of the American court landscape" (Casey & Rottman, 2005, p. 35). **Specialized courts** are limited-jurisdiction courts that focus on certain crime problems such as drugs, domestic violence, and offenders with mental health problems. These courts are similar to traffic courts in that they address a specific problem, but, as we explain, several factors set them apart. Specialized courts are also referred to as **problem-solving courts**, boutique courts, or collaborative justice courts. We use the terms *specialized courts* and *problem-solving courts* throughout the discussion that follows.

Origins of Problem-Solving Courts

Where did problem-solving courts originate? The answer lies in the problem-solving movement that has been seen elsewhere in the criminal justice system, particularly in policing. Changes in policing were sparked by influential scholarship, such as Herman Goldstein's (1979, 1990) work on problem-oriented policing and James Q. Wilson and George Kelling's (1982) "broken windows" argument. These scholars argued that targeting minor crimes, such as drug use, vandalism, and loitering, would eventually lead to reductions in more serious crimes. They also urged police departments to shift from a reactive crime control strategy to an emphasis on order maintenance and community accountability. The overarching argument was that by focusing on problems—small and large—within neighborhoods, the police would reduce urban disorder, fear of crime, and, eventually, crime itself.

Other developments in and out of the criminal justice system also encouraged the development of problem-oriented approaches, according to researchers at the Center for Court Innovation (Berman & Feinblatt, 2001, pp. 5–6). These developments included

- Breakdowns among the kinds of social and community institutions (including families and churches) that traditionally addressed problems such as addiction, mental illness, quality-of-life crime, and domestic violence

- Large increases in the nation's prison population and the resulting prison overcrowding

- Trends emphasizing the accountability of public institutions

- Advances in the availability and reliability of therapeutic interventions, which have given many within the criminal justice system greater confidence in using certain forms of treatment

- A shift in public policies and priorities—for example, the way the broken windows theory has altered perceptions of the importance of low-level crime

As the prison population doubled and then doubled again and as the need to address offender problems such as drug abuse and mental illness became increasingly obvious, jurisdictions began to search for more effective ways to meet these needs.

Not long after *problem oriented* and **broken windows** became familiar terms in criminal justice circles, Philadelphia implemented a "Protection from Abuse Court." There, a judge oversaw all of the civil protection orders in one courtroom. Next, Cook County, Illinois, established a domestic violence calendar in one of its criminal courts. These two projects were somewhat obscure, though, relative to the drug court in Dade County, Florida. It opened to much fanfare in 1989 and was the first in the United States to sentence drug offenders to judicially supervised drug treatment. Shortly thereafter, Dade County started a specialized domestic violence court, and in 1993, the first community court, the Midtown Community Court, opened in New York City's Times Square. This court was among the first to combine punishment and assistance to offenders and victims. It also focused exclusively on minor quality-of-life offenses.

The movement to establish problem-solving courts also was affected by passage of the Violent Crime Control and Law Enforcement Act of 1994. This legislation authorized the U.S. Attorney General to fund drug courts across the country. By the end of 1994, more than 40 drug courts were operating in jurisdictions throughout the United States. The Violence Against Women Act, which provided funding to states and local communities in an effort to combat domestic violence, sexual assault, and other crimes of violence targeting women, was also passed in 1994. Enactment of this law prompted a number of jurisdictions to establish domestic violence courts.

Other jurisdictions experimented with courts designed to target problems such as mental illness, homelessness, and reentry. In 1996, Marion County, Indiana, started its Psychiatric Assertive Identification Referral/Response (PAIR) program; this was the nation's first mental health court. Brooklyn, New York, then started the first domestic violence court for handling felony domestic violence cases. In 1989, San Diego implemented the first homeless court. In 1999, the Office of Justice Programs, in the U.S. Department of Justice, funded nine "reentry courts," which are specialized courts that help reintegrate parolees into the community.

TABLE 14.1 ■ Six Principles of Problem-Solving Justice	
Principle	**Description**
Enhanced information	Specialized knowledge about the problems that fuel criminal behavior (e.g., drug addiction, domestic violence, mental health problems) and about the individual circumstances of offenders themselves
Community engagement	Interaction between criminal justice officials and members of the community on issues of crime and justice
Collaboration	Collaborative efforts to improve public safety that involve criminal justice officials, social service providers, and community leaders
Individualized justice	Customized responses to offenders that seek to address each offender's underlying problems
Accountability	Monitoring offenders' compliance with program conditions and holding them accountable for noncompliance
Outcomes	A focus on outcomes for offenders and victims, rather than case processing

Source: Wolf (2007).

Distinguishing Features of Problem-Solving Courts

According to the New York–based Center for Court Innovation, problem-solving courts attempt to respond more creatively and effectively to both local crime problems (e.g., drug dealing and domestic violence) and problems of individuals (e.g., drug addiction and mental illness) that can lead to criminal behavior (Wolf, 2007). The center has identified six "principles of problem-solving justice" that make these courts different from traditional courts. These principles are summarized in Table 14.1.

The first principle of problem-solving justice focuses on the need for enhanced information—that is, specialized knowledge about the problems that fuel criminal behavior and about the background and circumstances of each individual offender. To make informed and individualized decisions, judges and other criminal justice officials need to understand the complex linkages between criminal behavior and such things as drug addiction, homelessness, and mental health problems. They also need information on the "physical and psychological health of defendants" (Wolf, 2007, p. 3). Officials working in problem-solving courts attempt to gather as much information as possible about the offender's background and criminal history before rendering a decision. To do this, they rely on assessments that identify defendants' risks and needs in a variety of areas, including substance abuse, education, employment, and mental and physical health. They use the results of these assessments to develop individualized case plans.

The second and third principles of problem-solving justice are community engagement and collaboration. Unlike judges in traditional courts, who maintain that objectivity and independence are sacrificed if community members are allowed to influence their decisions, judges in problem-solving courts believe that it is important to interact with community members and to listen to their concerns about crime and justice in the community. Related to this is the idea that public safety is improved and justice enhanced when criminal justice officials collaborate with other government agencies, social service providers, schools, and other relevant stakeholders to identify defendants' underlying problems and to develop case plans that target these problems. According to Robert V. Wolf (2007), "The point is not for courts to dictate solutions but to facilitate planning and interagency partnerships, allowing all players in the criminal justice system—along with relevant stakeholders in the community—to work together toward a common goal" (p. 6).

This leads to the fourth principle, which is individualized justice. A defendant, in other words, should be treated as an individual and not as simply another case on the court's docket. This principle is a reaction to the notion of assembly-line justice and to the assumption that punishment should fit the crime but should not be tailored to the individual. As Wolf (2007) notes, "Many court cases are not complicated in a legal sense, but they involve individuals with complicated lives. Problem-solving justice recognizes this and seeks to give judges the tools they need to respond appropriately" (p. 7). Thus, sanctions are customized to address a defendant's underlying problems and to link the defendant to needed services, with the goal of reducing recidivism and enhancing the likelihood that the defendant will become a productive member of society.

Problem-solving justice also emphasizes accountability and regular compliance monitoring. Defendants who appear in problem-solving courts are expected to comply with the requirements of the court and to complete all mandated treatment and educational programs. The courts stress that criminal behavior has consequences and that failure to comply with program requirements will be met with sanctions. Compliance is monitored through regular meetings between defendants and court personnel, and accountability is ensured by the swift and certain imposition of sanctions for noncompliance. Drug court judges, for example, closely supervise offenders who are required to participate in substance abuse treatment. The judge receives regular updates on offenders' progress, and offenders return to court frequently so that the judge can congratulate them on staying drug and crime free or admonish them for failing to follow the prescribed treatment program.

The final principle of problem-solving justice is a focus on case outcomes rather than case processing. The effectiveness of problem-solving courts is measured not by the number of cases handled per day or the average time from arrest to case disposition but by the court's graduation rate, the recidivism rates of defendants who have graduated, and improvements in defendants' educational attainment, physical and mental health, and employment prospects. One judge summarized this principle as follows: "Outcomes—not just process and precedents—matter. Protecting the rights of an addicted mother is important. So is protecting her children and getting her off drugs" (Kaye, 1999, p. 13).

As these six principles make clear, courts that engage in problem-solving justice depart in important ways from the traditional, adversarial model of the criminal court system. These courts—and the criminal justice officials and social service agency personnel who staff them—have embraced a new and, many would contend, more effective way to respond to criminal behavior and to deliver justice.

Restorative Justice and Problem-Solving Courts

Many problem-solving courts embrace, either explicitly or implicitly, the principles of **restorative justice**. Unlike other utilitarian perspectives on punishment (e.g., deterrence, incapacitation, and rehabilitation), which emphasize punishment for crime prevention and focus almost exclusively on the offender, restorative justice views punishment as a means to repair the harm and injury caused by the crime, focusing on the victim and the community as well as the offender (Braithwaite, 1989, 1999; Kurki, 1999). The goal of restorative justice "is to restore the victim and the community and to rebuild ruptured relationships in a process that allows all three parties to participate" (Kurki, 1999, p. 236).

Restorative justice is concerned with two key concepts: harm and repair. First, it is clear that crime causes several types of harm (Karp, 2001, p. 729). For example, there is the material harm, especially the damage to property and lost wages associated with crime. There is also personal and relationship harm. This can include everything from physical injury to emotional damage to victims and their families. Restorative justice also identifies public and private harms. Private harms are borne by individual victims of crime, and public harm amounts to damaged community cohesiveness.

Restorative justice is not just about harm, however. Repair is critical. That is, restorative justice emphasizes the importance of repairing the harm that crime causes and thereby restoring a sense of community. Repair can be manifested in a number of ways, such as by having the perpetrator fix damaged property. Or, as David R. Karp (2001) put it, repair "may involve restoring offenders by creating social support, integrative opportunities, and competencies" (p. 730). Repair may also "involve rebuilding communities by renewing respect for and commitment to the criminal justice system; by fostering new social ties among community members; by enriching the deliberative democratic process; and by focusing attention on community problems so that broader institutional weaknesses, such as in schools or families, can be addressed" (p. 730).

Restorative justice achieves its goals through a variety of practices. These practices include victim–offender mediation, family group conferencing, sentencing circles, and citizen supervision of probation. What typically occurs is a face-to-face meeting involving the victim, the offender, the victim's and offender's families, and other members of the community. Participants in the process discuss the effects of the crime on the victim, the offender, and the community and attempt to reach a collective agreement regarding the most appropriate sanction. Although this *process* differs significantly from the traditional criminal justice process, the *outcomes* are often similar to those imposed by judges and other criminal justice officials: apologies, restitution, fines, community service, alcohol or drug abuse treatment, anger management programs, intensive supervision probation, or short jail terms.

Restorative justice sounds good on paper, but it confronts serious obstacles depending on where it is attempted. For example, it has almost no chance of succeeding in areas where there is no defined sense of community. The whole practice is premised on the idea of community and of welcoming offenders "back into the fold." It is also unlikely that victims of serious crimes would opt for the restorative justice approach because it requires that victims and offenders work together to repair harm. Some have therefore argued that restorative justice is most likely to succeed in tight-knit rural communities or with offenders (especially young ones) who are accused of committing relatively minor offenses. (For other criticisms of restorative justice, see Levrant, Cullen, & Fulton, 1999.) Others, though, have argued that restorative justice can be effective for dealing with crimes as serious as homicide (Eschholz, Reed, & Beck, 2003; Umbreit & Vos, 2000).

In the sections that follow, we focus on two types of problem-solving courts: drug treatment courts and domestic violence courts. These two types of courts—and especially drug courts—are found in many jurisdictions throughout the United States, and there is now a substantial amount of research on their effectiveness. We then briefly discuss other types of specialized courts, including community courts, mental health courts, homeless courts, and reentry courts.

DRUG TREATMENT COURTS

Increases in the number of drug offenders appearing in state and federal courts, coupled with mounting evidence of both the linkages between drug use and crime and the efficacy of drug treatment programs, led a number of jurisdictions "to rethink their approach to handling defendants charged with drug and drug-related offenses" (Drug Court Clearinghouse and Technical Assistance Project, 1999, p. 3). Some jurisdictions, such as Cook County (Chicago), Illinois, established specialized dockets designed to manage the drug caseload more efficiently and to alleviate stress on the felony court system (Inciardi, McBride, & Rivers, 1996). Other jurisdictions, such as Dade County (Miami), Florida, created **drug treatment courts** that incorporated intensive judicial supervision of drug offenders, mandatory drug treatment, and a rehabilitation program providing vocational, education, family, and medical services.

Key Elements of Drug Courts

Although the nature and characteristics of drug courts throughout the United States vary widely, they share several "key elements" (National Association of Drug Court Professionals, 1997):

- Integration of substance abuse treatment with justice system case processing

- Use of a nonadversarial approach

VIEW FROM THE FIELD

The Role of the Drug Court Coordinator

Jacque van Wormer
Senior Regional Criminal Justice Administrator, Spokane County

Ask almost any team member involved in a drug court, and he or she will tell you that outside of the judge, one of the most pivotal roles in the drug court is that of the drug court coordinator (also referred to as a drug court administrator). Given the recent explosion of drug courts within the adult, juvenile, and dependency court systems over the past two decades, coordinators are essentially a recent phenomenon and addition to the criminal justice system. Although often defined differently by jurisdiction, this role is unique in that it requires a strong blend of administrative, practitioner, and political experience to get the job done. Duties can include providing direct case management and treatment to drug court participants, serving on the drug court team, conducting data collection, meeting with elected officials to secure funding, and presenting in front of legislative bodies. Travel across the country, and you will find that the duties and positions vary as greatly as our courts. Given that many drug courts have been able to successfully institutionalize their programs within the court structure, there is no question that the role of the drug court coordinator will continue to expand and grow within our nation's court system.

- Early identification and prompt placement of eligible participants

- Access to a continuum of treatment, rehabilitation, and related services

- Frequent testing for alcohol and illicit drugs

- A coordinated strategy among judge, prosecutor, defense, and treatment providers to govern offender compliance

- Ongoing, judicial interaction with each participant

As this list suggests, there are important differences between drug treatment courts and traditional trial courts. Drug courts are explicitly nonadversarial, the judge is an active participant in adjudication of the case and in supervision of the offender, and the focus is on treatment rather than punishment.

In the typical preadjudication drug court, drug offenders who meet the eligibility criteria for the program are given a choice between participation in the drug court and traditional adjudication. Although the eligibility criteria vary, most programs exclude offenders who have prior convictions for violent offenses or whose current offense involved violence or use of a weapon. They target offenders whose involvement with the criminal justice system is due primarily to their substance abuse. Offenders who are accepted into the program—which may last 12 months, 18 months, or longer—and who agree to abide by the requirements of the program are immediately referred to a substance abuse treatment program for counseling, therapy, and drug abuse education. They also are subject to random urinalysis and are required to appear frequently before the drug court judge. Offenders who do not show up for treatment sessions or drug court or who fail drug tests are subject to sanctions; repeated violations may result in termination from the program and adjudication and sentencing on the original charges. If the offender completes the program, the charges are dismissed.

Do Drug Courts Work?

The popularity of drug courts reflects the view that drug courts, in contrast to traditional adjudication, "work." But what does this mean? How do we measure the effectiveness of drug courts? To answer this question, we need to understand what drug courts are designed to do. Most experts would agree that these courts are designed, first and foremost, to reduce crime by preventing recidivism. There also is an expectation that drug courts will be more cost-effective than traditional adjudication. In other words, "officials want to know if drug courts reduce crime and save money doing so" (Goldkamp, White, & Robinson, 2001, p. 31). Other offender-based outcome measures would include such things as reduced drug use, enhanced education, better employment prospects, and improved mental and physical health.

The National Drug Court Institute's National Research Advisory Committee has suggested that drug courts be evaluated based on three primary performance measures:

- *Retention in the drug court treatment program*—those who complete the program or are still enrolled in the program divided by those who entered the program during a particular time period

- *Sobriety*—negative drug tests as a percentage of all tests given to drug court participants

- *Recidivism*—rate of new arrests for drug court participants, both during program participation and after program completion (Heck & Thanner, 2006)

There is mounting evidence that drug courts reduce offender recidivism and prevent drug relapse. A report by the U.S. General Accounting Office (GAO) summarized the results of 20 evaluations of 16 drug courts that had been completed by early 1997 (U.S. GAO, 1997). The GAO report indicated that these early evaluations generally concluded that drug courts were effective in reducing drug use and criminal behavior. A later review by Belenko (1998) summarized the results of 30 evaluations of 24 drug courts that had been completed by May 1998. Belenko observed that most of these evaluations concluded that criminal behavior was significantly reduced while the offender was participating in the program. For example, an evaluation of a Ventura County (California) drug court, which tracked recidivism over an 8-month time period, found that only 12% of the drug court participants were rearrested, compared to 32% of those in a comparison group. A Jackson County (Missouri) evaluation similarly revealed 6-month rearrest rates of 4% for program participants and 13% for nonparticipants.

Steven Belenko's (1998) review also included studies that assessed the impact of drug court participation on *postprogram* recidivism. Eight of the nine evaluations reported lower recidivism rates for the drug court group as compared with a comparison group of similarly situated offenders who did not participate in the drug court program. An evaluation of the Multnomah County (Oregon) drug court, for example, found statistically significant differences between drug court participants (an average of 0.59 new arrests) and drug court–eligible nonparticipants (an average of 1.53 new arrests) over a 24-month tracking period. These results led Belenko (1998) to conclude that

> although the evaluations vary considerably in scope, methodology and quality, the results are consistent in finding that . . . drug courts provide more comprehensive and closer supervision of the drug-using offender than other forms of community supervision, drug use and criminal behavior are substantially reduced while clients are participating in drug court, [and] criminal behavior is lower after program participation. (pp. 17–18)

Belenko's (1998) concerns about the studies' research designs and methodologies were echoed by another team of researchers who analyzed the results of 42 separate drug court evaluations (D. B. Wilson, Ojmarrh, & MacKenzie, 2002). Their conclusion was that "drug offenders participating in drug court are less likely to reoffend than similar offenders sentenced to traditional correctional options, such as probation" (p. 20). Their main criticism of the available literature was that many of the research designs "made no attempt to statistically control for differences between drug court and comparison participants, and a common comparison group, drug court drop-outs, has a bias favoring the drug court condition" (p. 20).

A number of drug court researchers have compared the records of those who successfully completed the drug court treatment program with those who either left voluntarily or were removed from the program because of noncompliance with program conditions. This is a methodologically questionable approach because, as one researcher has pointed out, it amounts to saying that the "successes succeed and failures fail" (Goldkamp et al., 2001, p. 32). A number of drug court evaluations avoid this problem by comparing drug court participants to those who would have been eligible for the program but did not participate (Finigan, 1998; Goldkamp & Weiland, 1993; Gottfredson, Coblentz, & Harmon, 1997; Harrell, Mitchell, Hirst, Marlowe, & Merrill, 2002; Peters & Murrin, 1998; Sechrest, Shichor, Artist, & Briceno, 1998). A common finding of these studies is that recidivism is reduced, both during program participation and following graduation from the drug court program. Other researchers have randomly assigned subjects to treatment and control conditions, finding less recidivism among drug court participants (Gottfredson & Exum, 2002; Gottfredson, Najaka, & Kearley, 2003). For example, an evaluation of the Baltimore City Drug Treatment Court (BCDTC) used an experimental research design in which offenders who were eligible for the drug court were randomly assigned to the drug court or to "treatment as usual" in a district or circuit court (Gottfredson et al., 2003). The results of the evaluation revealed that the BCDTC reduced "criminal offending in a population of drug-addicted chronic offenders" (p. 189). The rearrest rate during the 2-year follow-up period was 66.2% for drug court participants and 81.3% for offenders in the control group. Further analysis revealed that the drug court participants who received substance abuse treatment were substantially less likely to be rearrested than either the untreated drug court participants or the control subjects. This led the authors of the study to conclude that "drug treatment is an important ingredient in the success of the program, at least for the seriously addicted offenders included in this study" (p. 193).

There also is evidence that drug courts are cost-effective alternatives to traditional adjudication. For example, a report on the second decade of drug courts (U.S. Department of Justice, 2006), which acknowledged that it is difficult to determine precisely the cost savings achieved by drug courts, reported that an evaluation of the Multnomah County Drug Court in Portland, Oregon, resulted in savings to taxpayers. The savings amounted to $5,000 per participant or $1.5 million per year for the court's annual caseload of 300 participants (U.S. Department of Justice, 2006, p. 27). A study of the Superior Court Drug Intervention Program in Washington, D.C., similarly found that every dollar spent on program costs resulted in a savings of 2 dollars for crimes that were prevented (Roman & Harrell, 2001). As the authors of the U.S. Department of Justice report (2006) concluded, "Significant savings for taxpayers—primarily from reduced jail and probation time—can be achieved by using drug courts as an alternative to incarceration for drug-involved offenders" (p. 30).

The most comprehensive study of the effectiveness of drug treatment courts is a multisite analysis by the Urban Institute (Rossman, Roman, Zweig, Rempel, & Lindquist, 2011). The authors of this study measured multiple outcomes (crime, drug use, employment, family functioning, homelessness, and mental health) using data from 23 drug courts and 6 comparison sites in 8 states. They found that drug courts produced significant reductions in drug use and criminal behavior. Also, compared to drug offenders who were not adjudicated in drug courts, drug court participants were less likely to report a need for employment, educational, and financial services; they also reported less family conflict. On the other hand, there were no differences in employment rates, income, family emotional support, depression, or homelessness. The researchers also reported that although the cost of running a drug court was greater than the cost of running a traditional court, "overall, the net benefit of drug courts is an average of $5,680 to $6,208 per participant, returning $2 for every $1 of cost" (Rossman et al., 2011, p. 8).

Given the generally positive results of studies evaluating drug courts, it is not surprising that they have become the most popular type of problem-solving court in the United States. It also is not surprising that their success has prompted the development of other types of courts focusing on specific problem populations, such as defendants arrested for domestic violence.

DOMESTIC VIOLENCE COURTS

Domestic violence courts, like drug courts, developed in response to a combination of factors. One important factor was the increase in the number of domestic violence cases on state court dockets. Changes in attitudes toward domestic violence, coupled with policy changes implemented by police and prosecutors that made it more likely that perpetrators of domestic violence would be arrested and prosecuted, resulted in increases in the number of domestic violence cases that made it into the court system. At the same time, there was growing dissatisfaction with the response of the criminal justice system to crimes of domestic violence (Jordan, 2004). Critics charged that criminal justice officials did not take domestic violence cases seriously and that, as a result, "in all too many instances, either perpetrators were never brought to court or their cases were quickly dismissed" (Mazur & Aldrich, 2003, p. 5).

The movement to establish domestic violence courts also was influenced by the enactment of the 1994 Violence Against Women Act, which provided federal funding

---

VIEW FROM THE FIELD

The Need for Domestic Violence Courts

New York Judge Judith S. Kaye

One possible judicial response to the current situation is to continue to process domestic violence cases as any other kind of case, and to continue to observe systemic failures. Another response, however—the problem-solving response—is to try to design court programs that explicitly take into account the special characteristics that domestic violence cases present. If domestic violence defendants present a particular risk of future violence, then why not enhance monitoring efforts to deter such actions? If victims remain in abusive situations due to fear for their own and their children's well-being, then why not provide links to services and safety planning that may expand the choices available to them? If cases are slipping between the cracks of a fragmented criminal justice system, then why not work together to improve coordination and consistency?

Source: Cited in Mazur and Aldrich (2003, p. 6).

COMPARATIVE COURTS

As of April 2009, there were 104 specialist domestic violence courts (SDVCs) in the United Kingdom. Like domestic violence courts in the United States, these courts involve a collaborative effort by the police, prosecutors, court staff, probation officials, and social service agencies. These agencies work together to identify and track domestic violence cases, to identify the victim's level of risk for repeated victimization, to support victims of domestic violence, and to ensure that perpetrators are brought to justice.

In March 2008, the findings of an evaluation of 23 SDVCs were released by Her Majesty's Courts Service of the Home Office. The report, "Justice With Safety: Specialist Domestic Violence Courts Review 2007/08" (Home Office, 2008), assessed the performance of the courts using a variety of measures and attempted to determine whether the courts were using the best practices outlined in the SDVC national resource manual. The authors of the report found that the arrest rate for crimes of domestic violence reported to the police was high (an average of over 80%) and that about two thirds of all cases were successfully prosecuted.

The report also found, however, that there was considerable variability across courts in overall performance, with some courts having substantially higher levels of success than others in bringing offenders to justice and supporting victims. The authors of the report attributed these differences to variations in the degree to which the courts had incorporated the key principles outlined in the national resource manual. They found that the SDVCs that were more successful were those that had

- Strong multiagency partnerships

- Effective systems for identification of cases

- Independent Domestic Violence Advisor (IDVA) services with a focus on supporting victims at court

- Good training and dedicated staff

- Criminal justice perpetrator programs

- Safe court facilities

The report concluded that the "most successful courts were embedded in an approach that recognized that the SDVC was one arm of a coordinated response that addressed victim safety."

---

to the states to address domestic violence. The statute provided grants for "personnel, training, technical assistance, data collection and other equipment for the more widespread apprehension, prosecution, and adjudication of persons committing violent crimes against women" (42 USC 379[6][g]). A number of states used the funding provided by the act to set up domestic violence courts.

Like drug courts, domestic violence courts spread rapidly throughout the United States; they also are found in Canada, Australia, and the United Kingdom (Eley, 2005). According to a survey conducted by the National Center for State Courts, there were approximately 200 domestic violence courts in 1998 (Karan, Keilitz, & Denaro, 1999). More recent estimates suggest that more than 300 courts nationwide are giving specialized attention to domestic violence cases. However, not all of these are stand-alone courts that process only domestic violence cases and that coordinate with other social service agencies. Some simply reserve time on the court's calendar for specialized processing of domestic violence cases (Levey, Steketee, & Keilitz, 2001). A report by the Center for Court Innovation identified 208 *criminal domestic violence courts,* which they defined as "courts that handle domestic violence cases on a separate calendar or that assign domestic violence cases to one or more dedicated judges or judicial officers" (Labriola, Bradley, O'Sullivan, Rempel, & Moore, 2009, p. iv).

Domestic Violence Courts: Victim Safety and Offender Accountability

Unlike most other specialized courts, which focus almost exclusively on the rehabilitation of offenders, domestic violence courts also emphasize ensuring the safety of the victim. That is, these courts attempt to tailor interventions to the needs of victims (and their children), while at the same time monitoring offenders and holding them accountable for their behavior. As a focus group brought together by the Center for Court Innovation (n.d.b) put it, "Domestic violence courts do not view defendant rehabilitation as a high-priority part of the problem-solving process. This differs sharply from most problem-solving courts (with the possible exception of community courts). Rather, the mission of domestic violence courts concentrates more on the promotion of victim safety and offender accountability."

According to one survey of domestic violence courts (Labriola et al., 2009), most courts use dedicated victim advocates who accompany victims to court, explain judicial proceedings, and ensure that victims have access to needed services. A majority of the courts also issue a temporary order of protection or restraining order at first appearance and impose a final order of protection prohibiting or limiting contact with the victim at sentencing; use batterer programs in some types of cases; and typically order offenders to undergo alcohol or substance abuse treatment and/or mental health treatment. The survey also revealed a number of obstacles to effective functioning of domestic violence courts, including scarce resources, lack of training for judges and other team members, and staff turnover. Respondents further noted that the efficacy of domestic violence courts depended to some extent on the willingness of victims to cooperate in the prosecution of the case.

An example of a domestic violence court can be found in the state of Rhode Island. According to the court's website, "The mission of the Domestic Violence Court is to effectively manage a specialized domestic abuse docket within the overall framework of affording protective orders and services to victims and their families while at the same time ensuring batterer accountability and encouraging behavior changes." To accomplish its mission, the court assesses family needs and holds abusers accountable. It also has routine compliance reviews, just like drug courts. The court's goals are

- To promote the cessation of the violence

- To protect the abused party, the children of the parties, and other family members

- To protect the general public

- To hold perpetrators accountable for their violent behavior and for stopping the behavior

- To rehabilitate the perpetrator through appropriate interventions

- To convey the message that domestic violence will NOT be tolerated

Another domestic violence court is found in Lexington County, South Carolina (Gover, MacDonald, & Alpert, 2003). In that court, all nonfelony domestic violence cases are processed by a single court. This rural court collaborates with sheriff's office investigators, a victim advocate, and a full-time prosecutor. Mental health officials also work with the court to diagnose offenders' needs and assign them to the proper treatment program. The court even draws on the services of a legal advocate from a local domestic violence shelter. Most of the offenders who come before the court participate in a 26-week group-based cognitive therapy program in exchange for a suspended jail sentence. As Angela Gover and her coauthors (2003) noted, the overall goal of the Lexington County court "is to improve investigations and prosecution of domestic violence cases through increased resources, improved collaboration, and a progressive new court approach. Additionally, the goal . . . is to improve victim safety by holding defendants accountable for their actions and reducing recidivism" (p. 114).

Do Domestic Violence Courts Work?

Compared to the volume of research on the effectiveness of drug treatment courts, there is relatively little research evaluating domestic violence courts. One early evaluation compared case outcomes before and after the initiation of the Miami domestic violence court (Goldkamp, Weiland, Collins, & White, 1998). The authors of this study found that the dismissal rate for misdemeanor cases processed in the specialized court was 37% lower and that offenders who participated in an integrated batterer substance abuse treatment program were less likely than offenders in a control group to reoffend against the same victim. An analysis of the Brooklyn (New York) court also found that the number of case dismissals was reduced and that services provided to victims were expanded (Mazur & Aldrich, 2003; see also Davis, Smith, & Rabbit, 2001).

An evaluation of the Lexington County, South Carolina, domestic violence court described earlier also found positive results (Gover et al., 2003). Compared with offenders who were processed prior to the implementation of the specialized court, offenders adjudicated in the domestic violence court were less likely to be rearrested for domestic violence; they also took longer to reoffend than did the offenders in the control group. The study also revealed that the number of arrests for domestic violence increased following the implementation of the domestic violence court. The authors suggested that this resulted from a change in the response of law enforcement to reports of domestic violence; that is, law enforcement officers in the county responded by making more arrests of domestic violence abusers. According to the authors of the study, "This likely occurred because officers realized the court was taking the charges and offenders seriously" (p. 127).

There also is evidence that domestic violence victims have positive attitudes toward domestic violence courts and toward their own experiences in these courts. One study found that victims of domestic violence supported the idea of a specialized domestic violence court and reported that the existence of such a court would make them more likely to report future violence (A. Smith, 2001). Another evaluation revealed that victims whose cases were prosecuted by domestic violence courts were at least "somewhat" satisfied with the outcome and handling of their cases (Hotaling & Buzawa, 2003). A study of five domestic violence courts in England and Wales also found that victims were satisfied with both the procedures used in the courts and the outcomes of their cases (Cook, Burton, Robinson, & Vallely, 2004).

A review of the literature on the impact of domestic violence courts concluded that evidence of their effectiveness was mixed (Labriola et al., 2009). Most studies found that the domestic violence courts expedited the processing of misdemeanor cases. However, there was little evidence that the courts reduced offender recidivism: of the 10 studies reviewed, 3 reported lower recidivism rates, 5 reported no change in recidivism rates, and 2 produced mixed results. The review also noted that most studies concluded that batterer treatment programs either did not affect recidivism at all or produced very modest effects. These findings led the authors to conclude that "because the domestic violence court intervention itself varies from site to site, it is premature to focus on outcomes generically (e.g., for recidivism). Before we can ascertain which specific policies and practices produce such reductions and which do not, we need to know much more about how the courts operate and about the variations in how common policies are implemented" (Labriola et al., 2009, pp. 10–11).

OTHER PROBLEM-SOLVING COURTS

Although drug treatment courts and domestic violence courts have attracted the most attention and generated the largest body of research, they are not the only types of specialized, or problem-solving, courts. An assortment of innovative court models has been developed in an effort to address the underlying problems of defendants, victims, and communities. In fact, in 2000 and again in 2004, the Conference of Chief Justices and the Conference of State Court Administrators passed a resolution calling for "the careful study and evaluation of the principles and methods employed in problem-solving courts and their application to other significant issues facing state courts" (Casey & Rottman, 2005, p. 35).

One type of specialized court is the **community court**, which, like drug courts and domestic violence courts, focuses on partnerships with community agencies and problem solving. These courts are located in neighborhoods rather than the downtown core and emphasize finding solutions to crime problems plaguing the local community. Most of them handle only misdemeanor or low-level felony offenses and often require convicted offenders to perform community service as a condition of the sentence. As of 2012, there were community courts operating in dozens of U.S. cities; these courts also are found in South Africa, England, Canada, and Australia (Center for Court Innovation, n.d.a).

Perhaps the best-known community court is the Midtown Community Court, which opened in October 1993 in New York City's Times Square. The purpose of this neighborhood-based court is to provide "accessible justice" for quality-of-life crimes occurring in and around the entertainment district that is located in Times Square. The Midtown Community Court focuses on devising innovative responses to less serious crimes such as vandalism, shoplifting, prostitution, and minor drug offenses. Offenders convicted of these crimes are required to perform community service or make other types of restitution to the community. Social workers and other social service agency personnel work with court officials to address offenders' underlying problems, such as homelessness, unemployment, and substance abuse. The goal is to give offenders the structure and support they need to avoid reoffending.

The first **veterans treatment court** opened in Buffalo, New York, in 2008. The development of this type of problem-solving court reflects the reality that veterans have higher rates of unemployment, homelessness, substance abuse, and mental health problems than nonveterans, and that these problems often lead to involvement with the criminal justice system. One difference between veterans courts and other problem-solving courts is that the typical veterans court assigns each participant a mentor who is also a veteran of the same service. Similar to participants in other problem-solving courts, veterans court participants are required to complete relevant treatment programs; their progress is monitored by a dedicated veterans court judge and by other criminal justice and social service professionals. Although most veterans courts limit eligibility to nonviolent offenders, some critics argue that it is a mistake to do so, given that veterans who commit violent crimes may be more in need of treatment than those who engage in nonviolent crimes.

Concerns about veterans courts also have been raised by local chapters of the American Civil Liberties Union, which object to the creation of a new class of criminals based solely on their status as veterans. For example, Lee Rowland of the American Civil Liberties Union of Nevada opposed the proposed state veterans court because it provided "an automatic free pass based on military status to certain criminal defense rights that others don't have" (quoted in Lithwick, 2010). Similarly, Mark Silverstein, legal director of the Colorado ACLU, objected to the veterans court initiative there, arguing that "the legal category of 'veteran' is both too broad and too narrow, sweeping in both Vietnam and World War II veterans, who have very different experiences, while excluding nonveterans who also suffer from PTSD but aren't eligible for any special courts" (Lithwick, 2010).

These concerns notwithstanding, the number of veterans courts has grown since 2008. Inventories by the U.S. Department of Veterans Affairs (2013, 2017) found that Veteran Outreach Specialists were operating in 168 courts in 2012; by 2016 there were 461 veteran treatment courts or veterans dockets within drug, mental health, or criminal courts.

Homeless courts—such as the one found in San Diego—represent another example of specialized courts. These courts are designed to help homeless individuals resolve minor criminal matters—arrests for disturbing the peace, vagrancy, public drunkenness, or sleeping on the sidewalk or in some other public place—that may restrict their access to social services, employment, or public housing. California's Administrative Office of the Courts describes the need for homeless courts in this way:

> Resolution of outstanding warrants not only meets a fundamental need of homeless people but also eases court case-processing backlogs and reduces vagrancy. Homeless people tend to be fearful of attending court, yet their outstanding warrants limit their reintegration into society, deterring them from using social services and impeding their access to employment. They are effectively blocked from obtaining driver's licenses, job applications, and rental agreements. (California Administrative Office of the Courts, 2004)

To address these needs, homeless courts—which in San Diego and other cities hold sessions at local homeless shelters—help homeless individuals pay fines and resolve outstanding infractions and misdemeanor offenses. Defendants who are convicted in these courts typically receive an alternative sentence that involves participation in an agency program (e.g., substance abuse treatment, life skills education, computer training, job skills training) rather than a more traditional sentence of a short stay in jail and a fine.

Mental health courts are another type of problem-solving court, one developed in recognition of the fact that "jails have become the de facto mental health treatment centers" for defendants with mental health problems (Goss, 2008, p. 405). Mental health courts are important and necessary because there are many mentally ill offenders who have historically "slipped through the cracks" of the criminal court system (Watson, Luchins, Hanrahan, Heyrman, & Lurigio, 2000). By some estimates, there are more than a quarter of a million mentally ill offenders in America's prisons and jails (Ditton, 1999).

Traditionally, the criminal justice system and mental health agencies have not been close collaborators (Denckla & Berman, 2001). The purpose of mental health courts is to bring these entities together to provide needed services to mentally ill offenders. The four original mental health courts are located in Broward County, Florida; Anchorage, Alaska; King County, Washington; and San Bernardino, California. Participation in the courts is voluntary and is usually reserved for low-level offenders. In the King County Mental Health Court, a court liaison to the treatment community is present at all hearings and is responsible for linking the defendant with appropriate services. Defendants participate in court-ordered treatment programs, and their charges are often dropped after successful completion of treatment. They are also supervised by probation officers who have small caseloads and have a background in the mental health field.

Another interesting specialized court is the so-called **reentry court**. One such court, the Harlem Parole Reentry Court, began its operations in June 2001. Its purpose was to "test the feasibility and effectiveness of a collaborative, community-based approach to managing offender reentry, with the ultimate goal of reducing recidivism and prison return rates" (Farole, 2003, p. vii). The court does not adjudicate new offenses but instead provides oversight and support services to offenders reentering the community. Parolees who violate the terms of their supervision, however, are dealt with in a fairly traditional fashion.

The problem-solving courts discussed in this section are relatively recent additions to the criminal justice system. All of them developed within the past three decades. In the next section, we discuss a specialized court—the juvenile court—with a much longer history.

JUVENILE COURTS

In November 2008, an 8-year-old boy used a .22-caliber rifle to kill his father and another man who was renting a room in the family's home in St. Johns, Arizona. Initially charged with two counts of premeditated murder and facing trial in adult court, the young boy eventually pled guilty to one count of negligent manslaughter in **juvenile court**. Under the terms of the plea agreement, the third grader was to undergo a mental evaluation prior to being sentenced and follow-up evaluations at ages 12, 15, and 17.

Although this case—which involved a double murder—is not typical of the cases heard in juvenile court, it illustrates the dilemma that confronts criminal justice officials when very young children commit crimes. There is an assumption that children lack the moral and cognitive capacities to understand and appreciate the consequences of their behavior and thus are not capable of criminal intent. At the same time, there is a belief that a child who commits a crime is in need of supervision and guidance, which courts and social service agencies could provide if the child was under their jurisdiction.

The complementary beliefs that children should not be prosecuted in adult court but nonetheless require judicial supervision influenced the development of the juvenile court system. Like the other specialized or problem-solving courts discussed in this chapter, the juvenile court emphasizes treatment or rehabilitation rather than punishment, with the ultimate goal of transforming juvenile delinquents into productive citizens. The juvenile court operates under the doctrine of **parens patriae** ("parent of the country"), which gives the court authority over a child in need of protection and guidance and allows the court to act **in loco parentis** ("in place of the parents") to make decisions in the best interests of the child.

The first juvenile court was established in 1899 in Cook County (Chicago), Illinois. Prior to this time, some states passed laws requiring separate trials for juveniles and adults; others established public reformatories—sometimes called "houses of refuge"— for delinquent, vagrant, abandoned, or neglected youth. As Richard Lawrence and Craig Hemmens (2008) note, the early reform schools "were intended for education and treatment, not for punishment, but hard work, strict regimentation, and whipping were common" (p. 22). Critics also charged that the houses of refuge engaged in racial discrimination and that sexual and physical abuse were common. There also were allegations that children were being committed to reform schools for noncriminal behavior, on the premise that commitment to the juvenile institution would have beneficial effects on the child (Pisciotta, 1982).

Concerns about the ineffectiveness and abuses of reform schools spurred the development of the juvenile court system. Also influential was the so-called child-saving movement of the late 19th century, which advocated state intervention to save at-risk children who were not being adequately controlled or supervised by their parents. These reformers lobbied for legislation that would give courts jurisdiction over children who committed crimes as well as those who were incorrigible or who repeatedly ran away from home.

The traditional view of the emergence of the juvenile court characterizes the **child savers** as a group of benevolent and civic-minded individuals whose goal was to help delinquent, abused, and neglected children who were suffering due to the negative effects of rapid industrialization. However, Anthony Platt's (1977) assessment of the movement is more negative. He argued that the child-saving movement did little to humanize the justice system for children but rather "helped create a system that subjected more and more juveniles to arbitrary and degrading punishments" (p. xvii). According to Platt, the attention of the juvenile court was originally focused on a select group of at-risk youth. That is, court personnel originally focused on the children of urban, foreign-born, and poor families.

Barry Feld (1999) contends that in modern times, the juvenile court continues to intervene disproportionately in the lives of the poor. He also charges that the social welfare and social control aims of the juvenile court are irreconcilable and asserts that attempts to pursue and reconcile these two competing agendas have left the contemporary juvenile court in crisis. According to his analysis, the juvenile court is "a conceptually and administratively bankrupt institution with neither a rationale nor a justification" (pp. 3–4). He also contends that the juvenile court today offers a "second-class criminal court for young people" and does not function as a welfare agency (p. 4). Feld suggests that the distinction between adult and juvenile courts should be eliminated and that social welfare agencies should be used to address the needs of youth. His suggestion would make age a mitigating factor in our traditional, adjudicatory (adult) court system.

Jurisdiction and Operation of the Juvenile Court

The jurisdiction of the modern juvenile court is based on the age of the youth and is determined by state statutes. In a majority of states, the juvenile court has jurisdiction over all youth who were younger than 18 at the time of the offense, arrest, or referral to court (Office of Juvenile Justice and Delinquency Prevention [OJJDP], 2003b). A number of states set a different upper age limit for juvenile court jurisdiction; in 3 states, it is age 15, and in 10 states, it is age 16 (OJJDP, 2003b, p. 5). In addition, all states allow juveniles to be tried as adults in criminal court under certain circumstances (discussed later).

TABLE 14.2 ■ Delinquency Cases in Juvenile Courts, 2014*		
Most Serious Offense	**Number of Cases**	**Percent Change, 2005–2014**
Total	974,900	−42
Person Offenses	262,800	−40
Criminal homicide	900	−31
Forcible rape	8,600	−23
Robbery	20,900	−22
Aggravated assault	26,700	−46
Simple assault	173,400	−39
Other violent sex offenses	7,700	−34
Other person offenses	24,600	−51
Property Offenses	333,500	−46
Burglary	59,500	−42
Larceny-theft	166,800	−40
Motor vehicle theft	12,000	−63
Arson	4,000	−51
Vandalism	48,400	−53
Trespassing	26,500	−50
Stolen property offenses	9,700	−51
Other property offenses	6,700	−62

Drug Law Violations	128,900	−30
Public Order Offenses	249,700	−44
Obstruction of justice	128,200	−36
Disorderly conduct	65,000	−51
Weapons offenses	20,200	−52
Liquor law violations	5,900	−62
Nonviolent sex offenses	10,800	−22
Other public order offenses	19,700	−51

Source: Office of Juvenile Justice and Delinquency Prevention (2018).

*Most recent data available.

Each year, juvenile courts in the United States process approximately 1 million delinquency cases; in 2014, the number was 974,900 (OJJDP, 2018). As shown in Table 14.2, the courts disposed of 262,800 person offenses (including 900 cases of homicide and 8,600 cases of forcible rape), 333,500 property offenses, 128,900 drug law violations, and 249,700 public order offenses. The most common individual offenses were simple assault, larceny-theft, drug law violations, and obstruction of justice. The number of cases handled by juvenile courts has declined steadily since 2005, largely due to a substantial decline in the number of property offenses (down 46% from 2005 through 2014). There also was a substantial decrease in the number of homicide cases (down 31%). In fact, there was a decrease in the number of delinquency cases in juvenile court for every type of crime.

Most youth handled by the juvenile courts in 2014 were male (OJJDP, 2018). However, the proportion of cases involving females increased substantially between 1985 and 2014; females comprised 28% of the juvenile court caseload in 2014, compared with only 17% in 1985. The female caseload increased (from 1985 to 2014) 228% for person offenses, 193% for public order offenses, 136% for drug law violations, and 33% for property offenses. By contrast, the male caseload declined by 22% for property offenses; it increased by 134% for drug law violations, by 115% for public order offenses, and by 93% for person offenses. Thus, the female juvenile court caseloads increased more than the male court caseloads for each of the four major categories of offenses (OJJDP, 2018).

Although 43% of the youth adjudicated in juvenile courts in 2014 were White, Black youth were overrepresented and Hispanic and Asian youth were underrepresented. In 2014, 56% of the U.S. juvenile population was White, 15% was Black, 23% was Hispanic, 5% was Asian (including Native Hawaiian and Other Pacific Islander), and 1% was Native American. Blacks were overrepresented overall and for each of the four major categories of offenses. They comprised 36% of all cases adjudicated in juvenile court, 42% of cases involving person offenses, 36% of cases involving property offenses, 20% of cases involving drug law violations, and 37% of cases involving public order offenses. Stated another way, there were more than twice as many Blacks handled by the juvenile courts as there were Blacks in the U.S. juvenile population; for person offenses, the ratio was 2.5:1. By contrast, Hispanic youth accounted for only 18% and Asian youth accounted for only 1% of the juvenile court caseload (OJJDP, 2018).

There are important differences between the adult court system and the juvenile court system. These differences reflect the doctrines of parens patriae and in loco parentis discussed earlier; together, these doctrines ensure that the juvenile court, like other problem-solving courts, will emphasize rehabilitation, rather than punishment, of the youth. Similar to drug treatment courts, the focus of the juvenile court is on solving the underlying problems responsible for the youth's criminal behavior.

Perhaps the most important difference between the two types of court systems is that juvenile court hearings are considered quasi-civil, rather than criminal, proceedings. Whereas adults found guilty are convicted of a crime, juveniles are *adjudicated delinquent*. Juvenile court proceedings also are less formal than those found in criminal courts: The judge may or may not wear judicial robes and may or may not be seated on a raised bench, and there is more direct interaction between the judge and the juvenile. Another important difference is that juvenile court proceedings, unlike criminal court hearings, are not open to the public, and law enforcement and court personnel are prohibited from releasing the names of juveniles to the media. Finally, with very few exceptions, there is no right to a jury trial in juvenile court.

It is important to point out that in many jurisdictions, the juvenile court is not a separate court with its own judges and other court officials. Although this is the situation in a few states and in larger counties in other states, in many jurisdictions, the juvenile court is either part of a family court that handles a broad array of family matters (e.g., divorce and child custody, paternity claims, and adoption of children as well as delinquency cases) or part of the jurisdiction's trial court of limited jurisdiction. Generally, separate juvenile courts are found in jurisdictions with larger caseloads.

Transfer of Juveniles to Criminal Court

In 2014, juveniles accounted for 7% of all arrests for murder/manslaughter, 16% of all arrests for forcible rape, 21% of all arrests for robbery, and 18% of all arrests for aggravated assault (OJJDP, 2018). The number of juveniles arrested increased 100% between 1985 and 1994 but declined substantially from 1994 to 2014. Juvenile arrests for *violent* crimes increased from 66,976 in 1985 to 117,200 in 1994 (an increase of 75%) but declined to 92,300 (a decrease of 32%) in 2003 and to 42,123 (a further decline of 54%) in 2014.

The increase in juvenile crime during the 1980s and early 1990s, coupled with highly publicized cases of very young children accused of murder and other violent crimes, prompted a number of states to alter procedures for handling certain types of juvenile offenders. In 1995, for example, Illinois lowered the age of admission to prison from 13 to 10. This change was enacted after two boys, ages 10 and 11, dropped a 5-year-old boy out of a 14th-floor window of a Chicago public housing development. In 1996, a juvenile court judge ordered that both boys, who were then 12 and 13, be sent to a high-security juvenile penitentiary; her decision made the 12-year-old the nation's youngest inmate at a high-security prison ("Chicago Boy," 1996).

Other states responded to the increase in serious juvenile crime by either lowering the age when children can be transferred from juvenile court to criminal court and/or expanding the list of offenses for which juveniles can be waived to criminal court. A report by the U.S. General Accounting Office (1995) indicated that between 1978 and 1995, 44 states passed new laws regarding the **waiver of juveniles to criminal court**; in 24 of these states, the new laws increased the population of juveniles that potentially could be sent to criminal court. California, for example, changed the age at which juveniles could be waived to criminal court from 16 to 14 (for specified offenses); Missouri reduced the age at which children could be certified to stand trial as adults from 14 to 12. Currently, all but 4 states give juvenile court judges the power to waive jurisdiction over juvenile cases that meet certain criteria— generally, a minimum age, a specified type or level of offense, and/or a sufficiently serious record of prior delinquency—and 15 states have direct file waiver provisions, which allow the prosecutor to file certain types of juvenile cases directly in criminal court.

In 1966, the U.S. Supreme Court ruled in *Kent v. United States* (1966) that waiver hearings must measure up to "the essentials of due process and fair treatment." The court held that juveniles facing waiver are entitled to representation by counsel, access to social services records, and a written statement of the reasons for the waiver. In an appendix to its opinion, the court also laid out the "criteria and principles concerning waiver of jurisdiction." The criteria that courts are to use in making the decision are as follows:

- The seriousness of the alleged offense and whether protection of the community requires waiver

- Whether the alleged offense was committed in an aggressive, violent, premeditated, or willful manner

- Whether the alleged offense was against persons or against property

- Whether there is evidence on which a grand jury may be expected to return an indictment

- The desirability of trial and disposition of the entire offense in one court when the juvenile's associates are adults who will be charged with a crime in criminal court

- The sophistication and maturity of the juvenile as determined by consideration of his or her home, environmental situation, emotional attitude, and pattern of living

- The record and previous history of the juvenile

- The prospects for adequate protection of the public and the likelihood of reasonable rehabilitation of the juvenile by the use of procedures, services, and facilities currently available to the juvenile court

A recent report by the Office of Juvenile Justice and Delinquency Prevention (2014b) noted that the number of delinquency cases waived to criminal court increased by 70%

from 1985 to 1994 but declined by 61% between 1994 and 2011. (The report attributed the decline in the number of cases waived to criminal court in part to statutory changes that excluded certain cases from juvenile court or allowed prosecutors to file serious cases directly in criminal court and in part to a decline in juvenile violent crime rates.) During most of this time period, the waiver rate was highest for person offenses; however, from 1989 to 1992, the rate was higher for drug offenses than for person offenses. Not surprisingly, cases involving older youth were more likely than those involving youths 15 and younger to be waived, and cases involving males were substantially more likely than those involving females to be waived.

There also is evidence that cases involving racial minorities are more likely than those involving Whites to be transferred to criminal court. For example,

- In 2013 the percentage of delinquency cases waived to criminal court nationwide was 0.6% for White youth, 0.8% for African American youth, 0.8% for Native American youth, and 0.3% for Asian youth. Among youth charged with drug offenses, the rate was 0.6% for Whites, 0.8% for African Americans, 1.2% for Native Americans, and 0.2% for Asians (National Center for Juvenile Justice. 2015, p. 40).

- In 1996 youth of color accounted for 75% of Los Angeles County's population between the ages of 10 and 17 but 95% of the youths whose cases were waived to adult court; Asian Americans were 3 times more likely than White youth, Hispanics were 6 times more likely than White youth, and Blacks were 12 times more likely than White youth to be waived to adult court (Males & Macallair, 2000).

- Black youth comprised 60% and Hispanics made up 10% of juveniles waived to adult court in Pennsylvania in 1994; White youth made up only 28% of these cases (OJJDP, 2000).

- Blacks made up 80% of all waiver request cases in South Carolina from 1985 through 1994. Eighty-one percent of the cases involving Black youth were approved for waiver to adult court, compared to only 74% of the cases involving White youth (OJJDP, 2000).

Decisions to transfer juveniles to adult criminal courts are important because of the sentencing consequences of being convicted in criminal rather than juvenile court. Although there is some evidence that transferred youth are treated more leniently in criminal court than they would have been in juvenile court (OJJDP, 1982)—in large part because they appear in criminal court at a younger age and with shorter criminal histories than other offenders—most studies reveal just the opposite. Fagan (1991), for example, compared juvenile and criminal court outcomes for 15- and 16-year-old felony offenders in New York (where they were excluded from juvenile court) and New Jersey (where they were not). He found that youth processed in criminal courts were twice as likely as those processed in juvenile courts to be incarcerated.

Another study compared sentencing outcomes of juveniles (those under age 18) and young adults (those aged 18–24) processed in Pennsylvania's adult criminal courts from 1997 to 1999 (Kurlychek & Johnson, 2004). When they examined the raw data, Megan Kurlychek and Brian Johnson (2004) found that the mean sentence imposed on juvenile offenders was 18 months, compared with only 6 months for young adult offenders. These differences did not disappear when the authors controlled for the seriousness of the offense, the offender's criminal history, the offense type, whether the case was settled by plea or trial, and the offender's gender. Once these factors were taken into consideration, juveniles still received sentences that were 83% harsher than those imposed on young adults. Further analysis revealed that "'being juvenile' resulted in a 10% greater likelihood of incarceration and a 29% increase in sentence length" (p. 502). These findings led Kurlychek and Johnson to suggest that "the transfer decision itself is used as an indicator of incorrigibility, threat to the community, and/or lack of potential for rehabilitation, resulting in a considerable 'juvenile penalty'" (p. 505).

A more recent study (Lehmann, Chiricos, & Bales, 2017) used data on 30,913 juvenile offenders who were sentenced in Florida adult criminal courts for felony crimes to determine whether Black and Hispanic transferred youth received harsher sentences than White transferred youth. They also tested for intersections among offenders' race/ethnicity, sex, and age and examined whether the effects of race and ethnicity depend on the type of offense. The results of the study revealed that Black transferred youth pay a punishment penalty—they were more likely than White transferred youth to be sentenced to jail or prison and faced longer prison sentences than White youth. In addition, Hispanic youth are more likely than White youth to receive a jail sentence. The results also revealed that race interacted with gender; Black males were more likely than all other types of offenders to be sentenced to prison or jail.

CURRENT CONTROVERSY

In June 2001, Lionel Tate, a Black boy who was 12 years old when he killed a 6-year-old family friend while demonstrating a wrestling move he had seen on television, was sentenced to life in prison without the possibility of parole. Tate, who claimed that the death was an accident, was tried as an adult in Broward County, Florida; he was convicted of first-degree murder. One month later, Nathaniel Brazill, a 14-year-old Black boy, was sentenced by a Florida judge to 28 years in prison without the possibility of parole. Brazill was 13 years old when he shot and killed Barry Grunow, a popular 30-year-old seventh-grade teacher at a middle school in Lake Worth, Florida. Although Brazill did not deny that he fired the shot that killed his teacher, he claimed that he had only meant to scare Grunow and that the shooting was an accident. Like Tate, Brazill was tried as an adult; he was convicted of second-degree murder.

These two cases raised a storm of controversy regarding the prosecution of children as adults. Those on one side argue that children who commit adult crimes, such as murder, should be treated as adults; they should be prosecuted as adults and sentenced to adult correctional institutions. As Marc Shiner, the prosecutor in Brazill's case, put it, "This was a

(Continued)

(Continued)

heinous crime committed by a young man with a difficult personality who should be behind bars. Let us not forget a man's life has been taken away" (Randall, 2001). Those on the other side contend that prosecuting children as adults is unwarranted and misguided. They assert that children who commit crimes of violence typically suffer from severe mental and emotional problems and that locking kids up in adult jails does not deter crime or rehabilitate juvenile offenders. Although they acknowledge that juvenile offenders should be punished for their actions, they claim that incarcerating them in adult prisons for the rest of their lives is an inappropriately harsh solution. According to Vincent Schiraldi, former president of the Justice Policy Institute, "In adult prisons, Brazill will never receive the treatment he needs to reform himself. Instead, he will spend his time trying to avoid being beaten, assaulted, or raped in a world where adults prey on, rather than protect, the young" (Center for Juvenile and Criminal Justice, n.d.).

Nathaniel Brazill is still incarcerated in the Brevard Correctional Institution. He will not be released until 2028, when he will be 41 years old.

Lionel Tate's conviction, on the other hand, was overturned by a Florida appellate court in 2003. The court ruled that Tate should be retried because his competency to stand trial was not evaluated before he went to trial. The state decided not to retry Tate and instead offered him a plea agreement; Tate pled guilty to second-degree murder in exchange for a sentence to time served (which was about 3 years), plus 1 year of house arrest and 10 years of probation. He was released from prison in January 2004. In May 2005, he was back in jail in Fort Lauderdale, Florida, after he allegedly robbed a pizza delivery man at gunpoint. Because he was on probation at the time of the crime, Tate faced a potential life sentence on the robbery charge. He avoided this fate by pleading guilty; in 2006, he was sentenced to 30 years in prison.

1. What do these two cases tell us about the juvenile justice system?

2. Do you think that the outcome for Lionel Tate would have been different if his original case had been tried in a juvenile court rather than being waived to adult court?

SUMMARY

Frustration with conventional criminal courts and traditional adjudication procedures led state and local jurisdictions throughout the United States to establish problem-solving courts. These courts—drug courts, domestic violence courts, community courts, homeless courts, mental health courts, and reentry courts—take a broader and more comprehensive approach to delinquency and criminality. Rather than focusing solely on the crime for which the defendant has been arrested, problem-solving courts attempt to address the underlying social and economic factors that contributed to the defendant's involvement in crime. Specialized courts also involve collaboration among criminal justice and social service agencies and are more likely than traditional courts to incorporate the principles of restorative justice. Although most of these courts have not yet been subject to extensive evaluation, there is evidence that drug courts are effective in reducing recidivism and preventing drug relapse and that victims of domestic violence whose cases are handled in domestic violence courts generally are satisfied with the process and with case outcomes.

A specialized court with a longer history is the juvenile court, which developed in response to the child savers' concerns about the ineffectiveness and abuses of reform schools and the fate of children who were not adequately controlled or supervised by their parents. The juvenile court operates under the doctrines of parens patriae and in loco parentis, which allow the court to make decisions in the best interests of the juveniles who appear before it. These quasi-civil courts are less formal than adult courts; their hearings are not open to the public, and, generally, there is no right to trial by jury. Juvenile courts have jurisdiction over most crimes involving children under a certain age, but serious crimes involving even very young children can be transferred to the adult court system. The decision to waive the case to adult court has important consequences, as research shows that juveniles tried in criminal courts are more likely to be incarcerated and receive longer sentences than youth adjudicated in juvenile courts or young adults whose cases were originally filed in adult court.

It seems unlikely that the specialized court movement will die out any time soon. Although both problem-solving courts and juvenile courts have detractors as well as supporters, most commentators believe that the courts' focus on addressing the underlying problems of those who find themselves in the arms of the law is a more effective and less costly strategy than the traditional crime control approach.

Don't overlook the Student Study Site with its useful study aids, such as self-quizzes, eFlashcards, and other assists, to help you get more from the course and improve your grade.

DISCUSSION QUESTIONS

1. How do specialized courts, such as drug treatment courts, differ from traditional courts? What do you think is the most important difference between these types of courts?

2. What are the advantages of adjudicating cases—for example, domestic violence cases or cases involving defendants with mental health problems—in a specialized court? Are there any disadvantages to this approach?

3. How does restorative justice differ from the other utilitarian perspectives on punishment? How are the principles of restorative justice incorporated into problem-solving courts?

4. Assume that you have been asked to evaluate the effectiveness of a specialized court. How would you measure the court's success?

5. How does the focus of domestic violence courts and veterans courts differ from that of drug treatment courts and other problem-solving courts?

6. Why did arrests for domestic violence increase following the implementation of the Lexington County (South Carolina) Domestic Violence Court?

7. If you were a local elected official and could choose whether to fund a community court, a homeless court, a mental health court, veterans court, or a reentry court, which would you choose? Why?

8. How do juvenile courts differ from adult criminal courts? What accounts for these differences?

9. What are the pros and cons of prosecuting juveniles in adult criminal courts? Would

you favor or oppose a "blanket rule" that all crimes involving youth under a certain age—say 16—must be adjudicated in a juvenile court? Why?

10. What do you envision as the future of problem-solving courts? Will additional types of courts develop in the years to come? If so, what types of courts might these be?

KEY TERMS

Broken windows 362

Child savers 377

Community court 374

Domestic violence court 370

Drug treatment court 366

Homeless court 375

In loco parentis 377

Juvenile court 376

Mental health court 376

Parens patriae 377

Problem-solving courts 361

Reentry court 376

Restorative justice 364

Specialized courts 361

Veterans treatment court 375

Waiver of juveniles to criminal court 381

INTERNET SITES

Center for Court Innovation: http://www.courtinnovation.org

Center on Juvenile and Criminal Justice: http://www.cjcj.org

Drug Court Technical Assistance Project, American University: https://www.american.edu/spa/jpo/initiatives/drug-court

National Center for Juvenile Justice: http://www.ncjj.org

Office of Juvenile Justice and Delinquency Prevention: https://www.ojjdp.gov

STUDENT STUDY SITE

Get the tools you need to sharpen your study skills. SAGE edge offers a robust online environment featuring an impressive array of free tools and resources.

Access practice quizzes, eFlashcards, video, and multimedia at **edge.sagepub.com/hemmens4e**

GLOSSARY

Acquittal: occurs when a jury votes unanimously that the defendant has not been proven guilty "beyond a reasonable doubt," which is the burden of proof in a criminal case. An acquittal, or "not guilty" verdict, does not necessarily mean that the defendant did not commit the crime for which he or she was charged; it simply means that the state was unable to meet the high burden of proof necessary for conviction.

Actual cause: also called "but for" cause. If the injury would not have occurred but for the defendant's action, then there exists actual cause.

Actus reus: a guilty act, refers to the three forms of the criminal act: (1) voluntary bodily movements, (2) an omission in the face of a duty to act, and (3) possession.

Adequate provocation: a killing, which occurs after such provocation, as the law deems sufficient—that which could cause even a reasonable person to react violently.

Ad hoc assigned counsel: program under which the appointment of counsel is generally made by the court on an ad hoc basis; that is, lawyers are appointed to represent defendants on a case-by-case basis when necessary.

Ad hoc plea bargaining: term used to refer to unusual concessions defendants agree to make during the plea negotiation process.

Adjudication: one of the two key roles of the criminal courts; to process defendants who have been arrested by the police and formally charged with criminal offenses.

Administrative regulations: rules enacted by state or local agencies, such as regulations affecting food and drugs, and occupational safety requirements.

Adversarial system: Anglo-American system of criminal justice in which the prosecutor and defense attorney fight it out in a process designed to ensure

that truth will emerge. The prosecutor has the burden of proof and must demonstrate beyond a reasonable doubt that the defendant committed the crime. The defense attorney's role is to argue for his or her client's innocence and to insist that the client's rights be protected at every stage in the process. The judge serves as a neutral arbitrator, largely to ensure that proper law and procedures are followed, and a jury made of citizens determines issues of fact.

Adverse possession: doctrine that allows the user of another's land to gain title to it simply by using it for a period of 7 years without objection by the landowner. The purpose of adverse possession is to encourage people to use their property and to take steps to protect their right to the land.

Affidavit: a document stating the facts relied on to create probable cause.

Affirmative defenses: those defenses in which the defendant has the burden of production and the burden of persuasion.

Alford plea: a plea in which the defendant enters a guilty plea but denies having committed the crime to which he or she is pleading.

Alibi: when the defendant asserts he or she is not the person who committed the act charged.

Annulment: a legal determination that a valid marriage never existed between the parties.

Appellate jurisdiction: the power of a court to review a decision of a lower court.

Appellate review: process of reviewing final judgments of lower courts on questions of law, with the goal of determining whether proper procedures were followed.

Appointment: the oldest method of selecting judges by the chief executive of the jurisdiction (the president of the United States or the governor of an individual state). All 13 of the original colonies used it, and it is used today in the federal system and about 20 states.

Arraignment: the stage in the pretrial process when the defendant enters a plea.

Arrest: occurs when a reasonable person would conclude that the police in some way had restrained his or her liberty so that the person was not free to leave.

Article III courts: courts established under the authority of Article III of the Constitution.

Assault: under the common law, assault was either (a) an attempt or (b) a threat to inflict immediate harm by a person with the present means of carrying out the attempt or threat.

Assigned counsel programs: a method of providing counsel for indigent defendants. Private attorneys are appointed on a case-by-case basis.

Assistant prosecuting attorneys: work in the trenches of the criminal court system. While the chief prosecuting attorney and select supervisors set policy, it is the assistant prosecutors who appear in court, interview witnesses, oversee investigations, and negotiate with defense attorneys on a daily basis.

Attorney general: an administrator who sets prosecution priorities for deputy attorneys general.

Bailiff: usually an armed peace officer (often a sheriff's deputy) whose job is to maintain order in the courtroom and transport incarcerated defendants to and from court proceedings. At the federal level, bailiffs are U.S. Marshals.

Bailment: the temporary transfer of possession of personal property to another for a particular purpose.

Battery: under the common law, any intentional, unjustified, offensive physical contact, no matter how slight.

Behavioral accountability: involves holding individual judges answerable for their conduct on the bench. Because judges are the human element of the justice system, conduct that reflects badly on the integrity and impartiality of the justice system is likely to decrease public trust in the judiciary and should be deterred.

Bench trials: trials in which a judge, rather than a jury, renders a decision between two panels of justices, involving the same legal issue.

Bill of Rights: the first ten amendments to the U.S. Constitution, setting forth a variety of individual rights.

Bills of attainder: legislation imposing punishment without trial.

Booking: an administrative procedure involving the entry into the police blotter of the suspect's name, arrest time, offense charged, and the taking of fingerprints and photographs.

Boot camp: program that targets young, nonviolent felony offenders who do not have extensive prior criminal records. Modeled on the military boot camp, the correctional boot camp emphasizes strict discipline, military drill and ceremony, and hard labor and physical training. Most also provide substance abuse counseling and educational and vocational training. Offenders selected for these programs live in barracks-style housing, address the guards by military titles, and are required to stand at attention and obey all orders.

Broken windows: the notion that communities that allow "broken windows"—which is a metaphor for litter, decay, vandalism, graffiti, and similar types of social disorganization—to proliferate will have higher levels of crime than will communities that attend to these problems and clean up their streets and neighborhoods.

Burden of persuasion: the burden placed on the party to convince the jury with regard to a particular issue. This requires that the prosecution provide enough evidence to secure a conviction. Also called burden of proof.

Burden of production: the obligation placed on one side in a trial to produce evidence, to make a prima facie showing on a particular issue. Also called burden of going forward.

Burglary: unlawful entry accompanied by the present intent to commit another crime once inside. It may occur at all hours of the day and is not limited to dwellings but also may occur in virtually any structure.

Castle doctrine: an exception to the general rules of self-defense, stating that persons attacked in their home need not retreat from a potentially deadly invasion and/or attack.

Causation: the legal principle that the criminal act is the act that is the cause of the harm. There are two types of causation: factual and legal.

Challenge for cause: during the jury selection process, the method used by the prosecutor or the defense attorney to remove impartial prospective jurors from the jury pool. Jurors can be removed, for example, if there is evidence that they are biased against one side or the other or if they have made up their minds about the defendant's guilt or innocence prior to hearing the evidence in the case.

Change of venue: a request by the defendant to have his or her trial take place in a different location.

Charge reduction: a type of plea bargaining in which the prosecutor reduces the severity of the charge or the number of counts the defendant is facing in exchange for a guilty plea.

Charging decision: decision that the prosecuting attorney makes on whether to charge an individual who has been arrested by the police with a crime and, if so, what charges to file.

Child savers: civic-minded individuals who, during the early part of the 20th century, advocated state intervention to save at-risk children who were not being adequately controlled or supervised by their parents. Their stated goal was to help delinquent, abused, and neglected children who were suffering due to the negative effects of rapid industrialization.

Clemency: also known as a pardon. The power to grant a pardon or clemency rests with the chief executive— the president at the federal level and the governor at the state level. Pardons can be issued for all manner of crimes.

Closing argument: the statement given by a defense attorney or prosecutor at the end of a trial (after all evidence has been presented) that summarizes the case to the judge or jury and reinforces the arguments made by each side.

Code of Hammurabi: the first known written legal code. Dating back to 2076 BC in ancient Mesopotamia, the code delineated crimes and their punishments and also enumerated settlements for common disputes.

Collective incapacitation: punishment philosophy that holds that all offenders found guilty of a particular type of crime, without regard to their prior record or other personal characteristics, are dangerous and therefore should be incapacitated through a jail or prison sentence.

Common law: laws that developed through court decisions rather than statutes; judge-made law.

Common-law marriage: a legally binding marriage despite the absence of legal documents; allowed in only a handful of states today.

Community court: a specialized court, located in a neighborhood rather than in the downtown core, that handles minor offenses and emphasizes finding solutions to crime problems that are plaguing the neighborhood.

Community prosecution: involves a partnership among the prosecutor's office, law enforcement, and the community, in which the authority and power possessed by the prosecutor's office are used to identify and solve problems, enhance public safety, and improve the quality of life in the community.

Community service: a type of alternative punishment or intermediate sanction in which offenders are ordered to perform a certain number of hours of unpaid work at schools, hospitals, parks, and other public and private nonprofit agencies.

Comparative negligence: a doctrine that attempts to apportion the responsibility among each party.

Complaint: the criminal process may begin with the filing of a complaint. It may be filled out by a police officer, a prosecutor, or a private citizen. If an arrest is made first, a complaint will be sworn out afterward, usually by the arresting officer. The complaint serves as the charging document for the preliminary hearing.

Compulsory Process Clause: Sixth Amendment clause that provides, "In all criminal prosecutions, the accused shall enjoy the right . . . to have compulsory process for obtaining witnesses in his favor."

Concurrence: the union of intent and act in the criminal law.

Conflict theorists: consider society to be composed of individuals and groups with sharply different interests and to be characterized by conflict and dissention. People and groups everywhere, they maintain, seek to maximize their interests. Because resources are limited, conflict between different individuals and groups is inevitable and continuous.

Confrontation Clause: Sixth Amendment clause that provides, "In all criminal prosecutions, the accused shall enjoy the right . . . to be confronted with the witnesses against him." It guarantees the defendant's right to face and confront any witness or evidence offered by the prosecution in a criminal trial or other proceedings substantially related to his or her ability to defend against the charges faced.

Consensus theorists: emphasize how society is structured to maintain its stability and view it as an integrated network of institutions (the family, church, school, economy, government) that function to maintain social order and the system as a whole. Social stability is also achieved in this view through cooperation, shared values, and the cohesion and solidarity that people feel by being part of a shared culture.

Consent: defense raised when the victim gives consent to suffer what would otherwise be considered a legal harm.

Conspiracy: an agreement between two or more people for the purpose of committing a crime.

Constitution: a document that creates a government.

Contract attorney programs: a method of providing counsel for indigent defendants. A group of private attorneys or a law firm enters into a contract with a jurisdiction and agrees to represent indigent defendants brought before the courts in that jurisdiction.

Contributory negligence: a doctrine, once preeminent but now falling into disfavor, that holds that if an injured party was in any way partially responsible for the injuries, he or she is barred from recovering from a tortfeasor.

Coordinated assigned counsel: system under which attorneys apply to be included on a list of counsel to be appointed on an as-needed, rotational basis. As with the ad hoc appointment method, attorneys are paid on an hourly or per-case basis.

Corpus delicti: the body of the crime.

Court administrator: individual responsible for facilitating the smooth flow of cases. He or she maintains the court records, schedules cases for hearings and for trial, and manages court personnel.

Court-appointed counsel: private attorneys who are paid by the state on a case-by-case basis to represent indigent defendants.

Court clerk: someone who maintains the records of all cases, prepares the jury pool, issues summonses for jury duty, and subpoenas witnesses who will testify at trial.

Court of Appeals Act of 1891: act of Congress that created the circuit courts of appeal, a new layer of intermediate appellate courts that would hear appeals from the district courts, and gave the Supreme Court more discretion in deciding which cases to hear.

Court reporter: someone whose job it is to record all the court proceedings and to produce a transcript of the trial.

Courtroom workgroup: the officials—judge, prosecutor, defense attorney, and courtroom support staff—who work together day after day to process the criminal and civil cases that come before the court.

Crime control model: model that views the suppression of criminal conduct—that is, controlling crime—as the most important function of the criminal justice system; the primary function of the system is to control crime by apprehending, convicting, and punishing those who violate the law; emphasizes efficiency and finality, which is achieved through informal, nonadjudicatory procedures.

Cross-examination: questioning that follows the direct examination of a witness. The attorney who did not call the witness to the stand has an opportunity to question the witness about the statements made during the direct examination.

Day fine: a type of fine originating in Europe and Latin America. The fine that the offender is ordered to pay is calibrated both to the seriousness of the offense and to the offender's ability to pay.

Decisional accountability: involves holding judges answerable for judicial rulings. Were a judge to deliberately ignore the stated law and binding precedent, the judge should be held accountable.

Defendant rehabilitation policy: a charging policy based on the notion that the majority of defendants—particularly first-time offenders accused of nonviolent crimes—should not be processed through the criminal justice system; the focus of this policy is on early diversion of defendants and the use of noncriminal justice alternatives.

Defense attorneys: attorneys who represent the defendant in a case as effectively as possible while acting within the rules of the court.

Determinate sentence: sentencing system in which the legislature provides a presumptive range of confinement for each offense or class of offenses. The judge imposes a fixed term of years within this range. The offender serves this sentence, minus time off for good behavior.

Deterrence: utilitarian justification of punishment in which punishment is seen as a means of preventing the offender from reoffending or discouraging others from following his or her example. Deterrence theorists suggest that potential offenders will refrain from committing a crime if they believe that the odds of getting caught and being severely punished are high and are not outweighed by any anticipated gain from the crime.

Direct appeal: an appeal by a defendant claiming he or she did not receive a fair trial. It is allowed by every jurisdiction by statute; it is not a constitutional right.

Direct evidence: evidence, such as eyewitness testimony, that by itself proves (or disproves) a fact that is at issue in a case.

Direct examination: questioning of a witness by the attorney who called the witness to the stand.

Discovery: the process by which both parties to a case learn of the evidence the opposing side will use at trial.

Disorderly conduct: a catch-all phrase that has been held to include acts as diverse as public drunkenness, vagrancy, playing loud music, and fighting.

Diversity of citizenship: a situation where the opposing parties are from different states.

Domestic violence court: a problem-solving court with a specialized docket of domestic violence cases. A multidisciplinary team of criminal justice and social service agency officials attempt to craft interventions that will ensure both victim safety and batterer accountability.

Double jeopardy: the principle that a jurisdiction may not (a) prosecute someone again for the same crime after the person has been acquitted, (b) prosecute someone again for the same crime after the person has been convicted, and (c) punish someone twice for the same offense. This does not mean a state may not try someone again if the first trial ends in a mistrial or a hung jury.

Double Jeopardy Clause: clause in the Fifth Amendment that prevents the state or federal government from prosecuting an individual for the same crime more than once.

Downstream orientation: the notion that prosecutors' charging decisions in criminal cases reflect their predictions about the likelihood of conviction as the case moves toward trial. Prosecutors attempt to predict how the judge and jury will evaluate the defendant, the victim, and the crime.

Drug treatment court: a problem-solving court with a specialized docket of drug offenses. The court incorporates intensive judicial supervision of drug offenders, mandatory drug treatment, and a rehabilitation program providing vocational, education, family, and medical services.

Dual-sovereignty doctrine: the rule that a person may be legally tried in state and federal court for the same offense.

Due process: procedural justice that is due to all persons whenever they are threatened with the loss of life, liberty, or property at the hands of the state. Due process is essentially a set of instructions informing agents of the state how they must proceed in their investigation, arrest, questioning, prosecution, and punishment of individuals who are suspected of committing crimes. Due process rules are thus rules that attempt to ensure that people are treated justly by the state.

Due process model: model that views protecting the rights of individuals as the most important function of the criminal justice system; emphasizes reliability, which is achieved through formal, adversarial procedures.

Durham rule: a test for whether the act was caused by the defendant's mental illness. Also referred to as the *product test*.

Easement: a right to use another's real property for a limited purpose and time.

Election: the most commonly used form of judicial selection. The vast majority of state court judges are elected. Elections can be either partisan or nonpartisan.

Electronic monitoring: type of punishment that is often used in conjunction with house arrest, designed to ensure that offenders are at home when they are supposed to be. The offender is fitted with a wrist or ankle bracelet that is worn 24 hours a day. The bracelet emits a constant radio signal to a home monitoring unit, which is attached to the offender's home phone. The monitoring unit informs the monitoring center when the offender enters and leaves his or her home; it also sends a message if the offender tampers with or attempts to remove the bracelet.

En banc: appeals court justices will sit as a group, consisting of every judge on the court, to clear up any conflicting decisions.

Equity: a term derived from the Latin word for *just* and refers to remedies for wrongs that were not recognized (neither the remedies nor the wrongs) under English common law.

Excuse defense: when a defendant admits what he or she did was wrong but argues that under the circumstances, he or she is not responsible.

Expert witnesses: witnesses relied on to introduce scientific and other complicated forms of evidence.

Ex post facto laws: legislation making prior conduct criminal.

False consciousness: an ideological worldview that is contrary to people's best interests. Workers have been duped into accepting the legitimacy of the law by the ruling classes and are not aware that the law does not serve them.

Felony murder: Under the felony murder rule, an individual may be held liable for an unintended killing that occurs during the commission of a dangerous felony, such as robbery or rape. In most states, felony murder is treated as second-degree murder. There is no requirement of intent to either kill or inflict serious injury.

Final judgment: limits the timing of an appeal until after the court hands down its final judgment as to the defendant's guilt.

Fixed-fee-per-case contract: system under which the contract entered into by the attorney or law firm and the local government entity agrees to a specific number of cases to be handled for a fixed fee per case.

Fixed-price contract program: program in which a contracting lawyer or law firm agrees to accept an unknown number of cases within the contract period, normally 1 year, for a single flat fee.

Fundamental rights: those freedoms essential to the concept of ordered liberty, rights without which neither liberty nor justice would exist.

General deterrence: use of punishment to dissuade prospective offenders. Potential offenders learn of the consequences of criminal involvement (for actual offenders) and decide not to risk subjecting themselves to such punishment.

General jurisdiction: a court that has the authority to hear a variety of cases. The court is not limited to one type of case.

Geographic jurisdiction: the authority of courts to hear cases that arise within specified boundaries, such as city, county, state, or country.

Going rate: appropriate sentence for offenders with certain characteristics who are convicted of a certain type of crime. The notion that members of the courtroom workgroup generally agree on the sentences that should be imposed, based on the characteristics of offenders and their crimes.

Grand jury: a group of citizens, selected in a fashion similar to a trial jury, who listen to the case presented by a prosecutor and determine whether there is sufficient evidence to bind the defendant over for trial. The purpose of the grand jury is to ensure the government does not prosecute individuals without some proof of guilt. Thus, the grand jury is meant to serve as a check on the power of the government, serving as a barrier standing between the individual citizen and the government.

Guided discretion statutes: statutes that allow the death penalty to be imposed only if the crime involves at least one statutorily defined aggravating circumstance.

Habeas corpus: an indirect appeal that can be made by an incarcerated individual in which the authority of the state to incarcerate the individual is challenged. Habeas corpus requires the person to whom the writ is directed to either produce the person challenging his or her confinement or release that person from custody. A document challenging the legality of a person's detention.

Harm: the result of the act, the injury to another.

Harmless error rule: rule that states that an error that would not have altered the outcome of the case (i.e., a harmless error) does not require the appellate court to overrule the offender's conviction or sentence.

Hearsay: out-of-court statements made by witnesses who are not available to testify at the defendant's trial.

Hearsay evidence: evidence provided by a witness that is based on information provided to the witness by someone else. Generally inadmissible, although there are a number of exceptions.

Hierarchical jurisdiction: the division of responsibilities and functions among the various courts.

Homeless court: a specialized court that focuses on legal problems common to those who are homeless. For example, the court may help homeless individuals pay fines and resolve outstanding infractions and misdemeanor offenses.

Homicide: a broad, all-inclusive term for any killing of another human being.

Horizontal model of prosecution: model in which assistant prosecutors are assigned to units that handle specific steps or functions in the judicial process that are routine in nature and involve limited discretion.

House arrest: type of punishment in which offenders are ordered to remain at home for a designated period of time. They are allowed to leave only at specified times and for specific purposes—to obtain food or medical services, to meet with a probation officer, and, sometimes, to go to school or work.

Hung jury: occurs when the trial jury is unable to reach a unanimous verdict in a case that requires unanimity.

Not all jurisdictions require a unanimous verdict in civil or criminal cases. In those states where the verdict must be unanimous, if the jury is deadlocked and the judge believes that further deliberations would be pointless, he or she may excuse the jury and order a new trial. This is similar to a declaration of mistrial. In these situations, there has been neither an acquittal nor a conviction.

Impeachment: formal process for removing judges. At the federal level, it involves impeachment (or accusation) of a federal judge in the House of Representatives and trial in the U.S. Senate. Most states also provide for impeachment of state court judges.

Impeachment evidence: evidence that calls into question the credibility of a witness.

Incapacitation: a utilitarian justification of punishment that involves locking up—or otherwise physically disabling—dangerous or high-risk offenders to prevent them from committing crimes in the future.

Incorporation: the process by which most provisions of the Bill of Rights have been extended to the states by way of the Fourteenth Amendment.

Indeterminate sentence: sentencing system in which the legislature specifies a minimum and maximum sentence for each offense or class of offenses. The judge imposes either a minimum and a maximum term of years or the maximum term only. The parole board decides when the offender will be released from prison.

Indictment: a document formally charging the defendant with a crime handed down by a grand jury after hearing the evidence presented by the prosecutor. The requirement of an indictment before criminal prosecution is one of a handful of provisions of the Bill of Rights, which has not been incorporated into the Fourteenth Amendment and applied to the states.

Indirect appeal: an appeal that does not directly challenge the defendant's conviction; the primary one is the writ of habeas corpus, which challenges the state's right to incarcerate someone.

Indirect evidence: evidence that requires the judge or jury to make inferences about what happened at the scene of the crime or judgments about the defendant's role in the crime. Also referred to as *circumstantial evidence.*

Individual rights: those rights possessed by an individual that protect him or her from others or the government.

Information: a substitute for an indictment, filed directly with the court by the prosecutor, thus bypassing the grand jury.

Initial appearance: the first court appearance. Once a person is arrested, he or she must be brought before a magistrate "without unnecessary delay." It is here that bail is set.

In loco parentis: Latin for "in place of the parents." Philosophy that, in conjunction with parens patriae, allows the juvenile court to act in the best interests of the children who appear before it.

Inquisitorial system: system of justice found in most European countries. The parties to the case provide all the relevant evidence to the court, and the judge, not the attorneys for the state or the defense, calls and examines witnesses.

Insanity: a legal term that describes mental illness. To be found insane, the defendant must prove that he or she has a mental illness and was unaware of either the consequences of his or her actions or did not know right from wrong.

Interlocutory appeal: an appeal filed prior to adjudication of a criminal case. This type of appeal focuses on critical constitutional questions that have no bearing on the defendant's guilt (or lack of).

Intermediate appellate courts: state courts found in many states that are the first to hear appeals from lower state courts. Intermediate appellate courts must hear the appeal and render a decision before either side can appeal to the state court of last resort.

Intermediate sanction: a sanction that is more severe than probation but less severe than a prison sentence. Examples include intensive supervision probation, boot camps, house arrest and electronic monitoring, community service, and monetary fines.

Intermediate scrutiny: standard under which laws involving quasi–suspect classifications such as gender and legitimacy are reviewed. A law is upheld if it is *substantially related* to an *important* government

purpose. The burden of proof lies primarily with the state under this standard of review.

Involuntary commitment: the use of legal means to commit someone to a mental institution against his or her will.

Irresistible impulse test: test to determine whether the defendant was insane when he or she committed a criminal act.

Judges: referees, responsible for enforcing court rules, instructing the jury on the law, ruling on the admissibility of evidence, and determining the law.

Judicial accountability: involves the ability of an entity to remove or discipline judges who do not perform their jobs in an acceptable manner.

Judicial disciplinary commission: a state-level commission that is usually made up of sitting or retired judges, lawyers, and laypersons and investigates complaints filed against judges. The commission can dismiss the complaint or admonish, censure, or remove the judge.

Judicial independence: entails ensuring that judges are free to decide cases fairly and impartially based on the facts and the law without consideration of public, political, financial, or other outside pressure.

Judicial performance evaluation: based on evaluations of how well a judge demonstrates a number of qualities expected of an excellent jurist submitted by individuals who have experience appearing before the judge. Importantly, they focus exclusively on items related to the judge's behavior and not to case outcomes.

Judicial review: the power of the court to examine a law and determine whether it is constitutional. To make this determination, judges examine the law and compare it with the Constitution. This requires them to interpret the language of both the statute and the Constitution. If the judge determines the law is constitutional, he or she upholds the law; if not, he or she declares it unconstitutional and therefore void.

Judiciary Act of 1789: The Judiciary Act created a federal judicial system composed of the Supreme Court (with six justices), three circuit courts, and 13 district (or trial) courts.

Jurisdiction: the authority of a court to hear a case and render a decision.

Jury consultant: an individual hired by the defense (or, perhaps, by the state) to determine how individuals with certain background characteristics and attitudes will view the case and the parties involved in the case. These results are then used to create a profile of a juror who would be likely to acquit (or convict) the defendant. The lawyers use this profile to guide decisions during the jury selection process.

Jury instructions: prior to jury deliberation, the judge instructs jurors about the relevant law and how they are to apply the law in the particular case.

Jury nullification: a jury's decision to acquit the defendant despite overwhelming evidence that the defendant is guilty. The jury's decision is motivated either by a belief that the law under which the defendant is being prosecuted is unfair or by an objection to the application of the law in a particular case.

Jury panel: individuals selected from the jury pool for a particular case.

Jury pool: the list of names from which actual jurors will be chosen. Also known as the venire.

Jury Selection and Service Act: under this legislation, all litigants in the federal courts entitled to trial by jury have the right to juries "selected at random from a fair cross section of the community in the district or division wherein the court convenes." Importantly, the act further provides that all citizens must have the opportunity to serve on juries.

Justification defense: when the defendant admits to the offense but states that what he or she did was not criminal.

Juvenile court: a type of specialized court that handles cases involving juvenile offenders, with a focus on rehabilitation.

"Key-man" system: system under which court clerks and jury commissioners would consult with civic and political leaders (the "key men") for input on who should be placed on the master list of potential jurors. Predictably, these "blue-ribbon" juries were not representative of the community and included a disproportionately high number of middle- and upper-class middle-aged White men.

Larceny: the unlawful taking and carrying away of another's personal property with the intent to permanently deprive the rightful owner of its possession. Includes taking by stealth, by force, by fraud, and by false pretenses.

Law: a written body of rules of conduct applicable to all members of a defined community, society, or culture that emanate from a governing authority and are enforced by its agents by the imposition of penalties for their violation.

Lay witnesses: those who are called to testify at a trial about what they know of the matter at hand, and who possess no specialized knowledge.

Legal sufficiency policy: a charging policy under which prosecutors file charges in all cases in which the legal elements of the crime are present. Because prosecutors operating under this policy do not necessarily "screen out" cases where the evidence is weak, there is both a high proportion of cases that are accepted for prosecution and a large percentage of cases that are dismissed at preliminary hearings and trials.

Legislation: rules enacted by the legislature.

Liberation hypothesis: an explanation for research findings suggesting that legally irrelevant factors (e.g., the race or gender of the defendant and victim, the behavior of the victim at the time of the crime) come into play primarily in cases where the evidence is ambiguous and the outcome is therefore less predictable. The liberation hypothesis suggests that when the evidence is uncertain, jurors will be "liberated" from the constraints imposed by the law and will therefore feel free to take legally irrelevant factors into consideration during decision making.

Limited jurisdiction: the court is limited to hearing only a particular type of cases, such as traffic court, juvenile court, or probate court.

Magistrate judges: lower level judges who conduct preliminary proceedings in cases before the district court and issue warrants.

Mala in se: crimes that are universally condemned because they are inherently evil.

Mala prohibita: crimes that are defined as bad simply because they are forbidden.

Malice aforethought: an intentional, premeditated (planned) killing.

Mandatory minimum sentence: the minimum jail or prison sentence that must be imposed on an offender convicted of a particular type of crime; especially common for drug offenses and for offenses involving use of a weapon.

Manslaughter: a second category of criminal homicide that includes both voluntary and involuntary manslaughter.

Master list ("jury wheel"): the first step in the jury selection process that involves a jurisdiction establishing a list of all potential jurors within its jurisdictional boundaries who can be chosen at random to report for jury duty as needed.

Mediation: a process of settling disputes that involves bringing in a neutral third party to help the parties to the dispute resolve the matter (e.g., to work out a child custody agreement for a couple seeking a divorce). The mediator works with the parties to the dispute to reach a mutually agreeable solution but does not have any authority to render a decision.

Mens rea: "guilty mind." Liability generally does not attach based on action alone; there also must exist some sort of guilty mind.

Mental health court: a specialized court that involves collaboration between the criminal justice system and mental health agencies with the goal of providing needed services to mentally ill offenders. Defendants participate in court-ordered treatment programs and may have their charges dropped on successful completion of treatment.

Merit selection plans: when a judicial vacancy arises, a bipartisan, broad-based commission (made up of lawyers and nonlawyers) interviews and evaluates candidates for judicial positions and recommends three candidates to the governor. The governor is then required to appoint one of the people recommended by the commission.

Merit system (Missouri plan): a hybrid method of judicial selection that combines appointment and election. A judicial nominating commission, which is usually composed of laypersons, lawyers, and judges, screens potential candidates and nominates several individuals (typically three) for the vacant position. The governor then appoints one of the individuals nominated by the commission to the bench. After the initial term and at designated times thereafter, the appointee runs in a retention election in which the voters are asked whether the judge should be retained or not.

Miranda warnings: the warnings that police must provide a criminal suspect prior to questioning the suspect, if they wish to use the suspect's statements against him or her at trial.

Mixed model of prosecution: under mixed models, most cases are handled in a horizontal manner. Specific crimes, however, such as homicide and sexual assaults are handled at all steps along the process by a specialized unit.

M'Naghten rule: the most common test for insanity and is realized if a defendant did not know either what he or she was doing or know that it was wrong.

Mock jury study: a method of studying jury deliberations. Researchers use mock juries or mock trials that involve hypothetical scenarios. These may be actual mock trials, such as in a university classroom, or simple written scenarios wherein people (often college students) are asked to decide some hypothetical defendant's fate. Then the researchers compare people's demographic characteristics to the decisions they hand down.

Model Penal Code: in relation to modern criminal law, it sets forth four levels of intent: purposeful, knowing, reckless, and negligent.

Motive: the cause, or reason why an act is committed.

Murder: is a killing that occurs (1) purposefully, (2) knowingly, or (3) recklessly under circumstances exhibiting extreme indifference to human life.

Negligence: a failure to act with the appropriate level of care.

No bill: a document reflecting the decision by the grand jury not to vote for an indictment.

No contest: also referred to as *nolo contendere,* means the defendant accepts whatever punishment the court would impose on a guilty defendant but refuses to admit liability. This plea is frequently used by defendants who fear being exposed to civil liability for their criminal misdeeds.

No-fault divorce: divorce granted without assigning fault for the breakup of the marriage.

Nolo contendere: a plea in which the defendant accepts whatever punishment the court would impose on a guilty defendant but refuses to admit liability. This plea is frequently used by defendants who fear being exposed to civil liability for their criminal misdeeds. Also known as a "no contest" plea.

Nonpartisan elections: process wherein judges are selected according to their own attributes rather than on the basis of their political connections. Currently, more than a dozen states use nonpartisan elections as a means of judicial selection.

Nuisance doctrine: a doctrine that states that a property owner may not use his or her property in such a way that it has an unreasonable, adverse affect on other property owners.

Obiter dicta: Latin for "things said by the way." Supporting statements made by the courts in making their decisions. These statements are legal or nonlegal arguments used to support the *ratio decidendi* (legal principles on which the decision is based) and do not constitute precedent.

Opening statement: statement given by a defense attorney or prosecutor prior to the introduction of evidence in a trial. The opening statement usually gives an overview of the case and the evidence that will be presented from the point of view of the attorney making the statement.

Ordinary care: the level of care required to avoid committing a negligent act and being civilly liable in tort.

Original jurisdiction: the power of the court to hear the case initially and where the trial takes place.

Overbreadth doctrine: a criminal law violates the overbreadth doctrine when it fails to narrowly define the specific behavior to be restricted.

Oversight: an important function of courts, particularly appellate courts. The process of reviewing the decisions of lower courts and of criminal justice officials to ensure that proper procedures were followed and that neither laws nor constitutional provisions were violated.

Parens patriae: the original guiding principle of the juvenile justice system; literally translated as "the father of the country," the phrase refers to the government's right and obligation to act on behalf of the child—that is, to do what is in the best interest of the child.

Partisan elections: candidates are selected by and affiliated with political parties.

Penumbra: doctrine that describes the whole as greater than the sum of its parts.

Peremptory challenge: during the jury selection process, the prosecutor and the defense attorney each have a limited number of peremptory challenges, which they can use to excuse prospective jurors from the jury pool without giving reasons for removing them.

Personal jurisdiction: the authority of a court over a person.

Petty offenses: offenses that involve a potential period of imprisonment of 6 months or less.

Plaintiff: person alleging that the defendant has harmed him or her in some way and who seeks damages for the injury.

Plea bargaining: the process of negotiating a guilty plea. Typically involves either charge bargaining, where the prosecutor will offer to reduce the severity of the charges or the number of counts in exchange for a guilty plea, or sentence bargaining, where the prosecutor will agree to recommend leniency at the sentencing stage.

Precedent: decisions of another court or judge that the judge trying a case will rely on as justification in forming his or her decision.

Preliminary hearing: the stage in the pretrial process during which the judge determines if there is probable cause to believe that an offense was committed and that it was the defendant who committed it. If probable cause is established, the defendant is "bound over" for trial. The preliminary examination is a formal adversarial proceeding, conducted in open court.

Presumption of guilt: the view, prominent in the crime control model of the criminal process, which holds that defendants who are not screened out early in the process by police and prosecutors are probably guilty and therefore can be passed quickly through the remaining stages in the process. A prediction of outcome: Those not screened out early in the process are probably guilty and more than likely will plead guilty or be found guilty at trial.

Presumption of innocence: the view, prominent in the due process model of the criminal process, which holds that defendants are to be treated as though their guilt is an open question until they have been adjudicated guilty.

Privilege against self-incrimination: according to the Fifth Amendment, "no person . . . shall be compelled in any criminal case to be a witness against himself." That is, any person charged with an offense cannot be compelled to testify against himself or herself in a criminal trial.

Privileged communication: this is an exception to the general rule that all relevant evidence is admissible at trial. Certain categories of individuals generally cannot be compelled to testify in criminal cases. This includes spouses, priests, doctors, or lawyers. The things these individuals say to one another are said to be privileged communications.

Probable cause: justification for a search or seizure. Not as stringent as proof beyond a reasonable doubt but more than reasonable suspicion or a hunch.

Probation: a sanction involving community supervision of an offender by a probation officer. May also include other conditions, such as substance abuse treatment or drug testing.

Problem-solving courts: specialized courts that take a broader and more comprehensive approach to delinquency and criminality. Rather than focusing solely on the crime for which the defendant has been arrested, these courts attempt to address the underlying social and economic factors that contributed to the defendant's involvement in crime. They also involve collaboration among criminal justice and social service agencies and are more likely than traditional courts to incorporate the principles of restorative justice. Examples include drug courts, domestic violence courts, homeless courts, teen courts, and reentry courts.

Product test: a test for whether the act was caused by the defendant's mental illness. Also referred to as the *Durham rule.*

Proof beyond a reasonable doubt: this standard is used in criminal trials and means that the facts asserted are highly probable.

Proof by a preponderance of the evidence: this standard is used in civil trials and means that the facts asserted are more probably true than false. A relatively easy burden to meet.

Pro se: when defendants serve as their own lawyer and represent themselves.

Prosecutorial misconduct: occurs when a prosecutor is convinced that a person is guilty of a crime when in fact he or she did not commit the crime, giving rise to breaches of a prosecutor's ethical duties.

Prosecutors: attorneys responsible for prosecuting cases on behalf of the state.

Proximate cause: the legal principle that the criminal act is the one that is the most significant and it seems fair to hold the actor accountable for his or her actions.

Public defender program: a method of providing counsel for indigent defendants. Lawyers who are employed by the jurisdiction (typically, the county or the state) represent the indigent defendants who are charged with crimes.

Public defenders: hired by the state to work for defendants who cannot afford to hire their own lawyers.

Punitive damages: monetary awards beyond compensation that are designed to punish the defendant and to deter others.

Random cross section of the community: The Supreme Court has interpreted the Sixth Amendment's requirement that the defendant be tried by an "impartial jury" to mean that the jury pool must be a "random cross section of the community." This means that all members of the community must have an equal chance of being included in the jury pool.

Rape: carnal knowledge of a person against his or her will.

Ratio decidendi: Latin for "the reason for the decision." The legal principle or rationale used by the courts to arrive at their decisions.

Rational basis: another method of determining whether a state may abridge someone's fundamental rights. A lesser standard of proof is required, and the courts generally find in favor of the state.

Real evidence: evidence that can be admitted into trial that consists of tangible items such as weapons used in the crime, DNA or fingerprints collected at the crime scene, or other "real" objects relevant to the case.

Real property: land and items permanently attached to the land.

Reentry court: a specialized court that does not adjudicate new offenses but instead provides oversight and support services to offenders reentering the community, with the goal of reducing recidivism and prison return rates.

Rehabilitation: a utilitarian justification of punishment that involves preventing crime by reforming, or treating, offenders. The techniques used to reform or rehabilitate offenders include such things as individual or group counseling, education, job training, substance abuse treatment, and behavior modification programs.

Relevant: evidence is considered relevant if (a) it has any tendency to make a fact more or less probable than it would be without the evidence; and (b) the fact is of consequence in determining the action (Federal Rule of Evidence 401).

Res judicata: civil law analog of the prohibition against double jeopardy. Once a case has been through all possible appeals, it is decided forever.

Restorative justice: utilitarian justification of punishment that views punishment as a means to repair the harm and injury caused by the crime and focuses on the victim and the community as well as the offender. Participants in the process discuss the effects of the crime on the victim, the offender, and the community and attempt to reach a collective agreement regarding the most appropriate sanction.

Retained attorneys: attorneys selected and paid by the defendant.

Retention elections: judicial elections in which voters are asked whether the judge should be retained or not.

Retreat doctrine: a doctrine stating that a person must retreat rather than use deadly force in a situation if doing so is possible without endangering the person's life.

Retributive justifications for punishment: backward-looking justification of punishment that holds that an offender is punished because he or she has done something wrong—something blameworthy—and therefore deserves to be punished.

Right of appeal: although offenders do not have a constitutional right to appeal their convictions, every jurisdiction has created a statutory right to appeal to one higher court. The purpose of this is to ensure that proper procedures were followed by all the parties to the case, including the judge.

Right to counsel: the right to be represented by a lawyer at all the critical stages of the criminal justice process. Indigent defendants have the right to a lawyer provided by the state.

Rule of four: rule that U.S. Supreme Court justices follow in deciding whether to review a lower court decision. The case will be heard and the writ issued if four of the nine justices agree to hear the appeal.

Selective incapacitation: punishment philosophy that holds that offenders who are dangerous and likely to commit additional crimes should be incapacitated through a jail or prison sentence. Involves predicting that an individual offender, or offenders with certain characteristics, will commit additional crimes if not locked up.

Selective incorporation: certain parts of the Bill of Rights that were applied to the states. The process of how some, but not all, of the Bill of Rights were made applicable to the states through the Due Process Clause of the Fourteenth Amendment.

Self-defense: defense raised when the defendant has used force to repel an imminent, unprovoked attack that would have caused him or her serious injury. Self-defense may also apply to the defense of others or of property.

Senatorial courtesy: a process whereby the president defers to the wishes of a senator from the state where a vacancy is located in nominating a person for a district court judgeship.

Sentence agreement: agreement for sentencing leniency negotiated during the plea bargaining process. The prosecutor might agree to recommend a particular sentence, recommend that sentences be served concurrently rather than consecutively, or agree to recommend that the sentence not exceed some threshold (a "sentence lid").

Sentencing guidelines: structured sentencing system implemented by the federal government and some states. Typically, sentence ranges are determined by the intersection of a crime seriousness score and the defendant's criminal history score, and judges cannot depart from the guidelines without providing reasons for doing so.

Slow plea of guilty: a hybrid approach to case adjudication, with elements of both plea bargaining and trial. To receive concessions from the prosecutor, the defendant waives the right to a jury trial, and the case is adjudicated by a judge at a bench trial.

Solicitation: involves the intent to induce another to commit a crime.

Sovereign immunity: the doctrine that prohibits citizens from suing their government.

Specialized courts: see *Problem-solving courts.*

Specific deterrence: use of punishment to dissuade offenders from reoffending. An offender who has been legally punished ceases offending because of a fear of future punishment.

Standing mute: refusing to plead; in these instances, the court enters a "not guilty" plea for the defendant, thus preserving the defendant's constitutional right to trial.

Stare decisis: a Latin term that means "let the decision stand." It refers to the judicial practice of looking to the past for pertinent decisions (i.e., for precedent) and deferring to them. Thus, a court will not overturn a past decision on an important legal issue unless there is a good reason for doing so.

Strict liability: imposes accountability without proof of criminal intent in situations where society deems it fair to do so, such as violations of drug and alcohol sales laws.

Strict scrutiny: method of determining whether a state may abridge someone's fundamental rights. Generally found in favor of the individual.

Subject matter jurisdiction: authority conferred on a court to hear a particular type of case.

Subpoena: a court order that requires an individual to appear at a specific time and place to testify as a witness.

Substantial assistance departure: a type of downward departure authorized by the federal sentencing guidelines. The judge can impose a more lenient sentence than required by the guidelines if the defendant provides information that leads to the arrest and prosecution of another offender.

Substantial capacity test: when the defendant lacks substantial capacity to appreciate the wrongfulness of his or her conduct or know how to control it.

Substantive due process: due process rights that extend beyond procedural rights to encompass substantive rights such as free speech and privacy.

Substantive law: the law of crimes. It is defined by statute, and it prescribes (what we should do) and proscribes (what we should not do) various types of conduct. It is that code of conduct that all in a society are expected to follow, such as prohibitions on murder, assault, and robbery.

Suspect classification: classification based on race or gender.

System efficiency policy: a charging policy that emphasizes case screening as a way of decreasing office workload. This policy results in high levels of referrals to diversionary programs and in overcharging (for the purpose of enhancing the prosecutor's power in plea negotiations).

Tenancy in common: when multiple people each own an equal share of a piece of real property.

Testimonial evidence: a classification of evidence that includes the actual testimony provided by a witness during a trial. Real evidence is introduced using testimonial evidence.

Tort law: the body of civil law associated with harm caused to plaintiffs by the action or inaction of defendants.

Total incorporation: the entire Bill of Rights was applied to the states.

Total incorporation plus: applied the entire Bill of Rights, as well as other nonspecified rights, such as the right to privacy.

Transferred intent: applies to situations where a person intended to harm *A* but in error harmed *B*. To prevent the defendant from escaping liability by claiming that he or she did not intend to hurt *B* and therefore the element of intent is missing, courts developed the concept of transferred intent. The concept means that the intent to harm a person who is not actually harmed is transferred to the person who is harmed.

Trial by ordeal: under this process, the defendant would be required to perform a perilous task, such as walking across burning coals or removing a rock from boiling water. If the defendant performed these tasks and emerged without being harmed, he or she was judged innocent for surely God had intervened and provided protection. If the defendant were injured during the trial, he or she was adjudged guilty.

Trial de novo: an appeal for a new trial in the court of original jurisdiction, requested by the losing party of a case.

Trial in absentia: a trial conducted without the defendant being present.

Trial penalty/jury tax: penalty or "tax" imposed on defendants who do not plead guilty but who insist on a jury trial. Notion that defendants who go to trial will get harsher sentences than those who plead guilty.

Trial sufficiency policy: a charging policy under which prosecutors evaluate cases in terms of their likelihood of conviction at trial; they file charges only if the odds of conviction at trial are good. This policy produces both a high rate of rejection at initial screening and a high trial rate for the cases that are not screened out.

True bill: a document reflecting the grand jury's decision to indict.

Uniform Commercial Code: a code of law concerning contracts designed to standardize trade and contract practices among merchants and businesses.

United States attorney: represents the government in the federal court system. The Judiciary Act of 1789 provided that within each judicial district, an attorney shall be appointed by the president as the U.S. attorney and represent the government in federal prosecutions.

Unlawful assembly: disorderly conduct in a group setting; this includes groups assembled in public without the necessary permits, as well as riots.

Utilitarian justifications for punishment: forward-looking justifications of punishment that focus on the future criminal behavior of both the person being punished and other members of society. The goal is to prevent future crime through deterrence, incapacitation, or rehabilitation.

Venire: the list of names from which actual jurors will be chosen. Also known as the jury pool.

Venue: the same as geographic jurisdiction.

Vertical model of prosecution: model in which a case is assigned to a single prosecutor who is responsible for the case at each step in the judicial process from initial appearance through a final disposition.

Veterans treatment court: a specialized court devoted to military veterans who have run afoul of the criminal justice system.

Victim impact statement: prior to sentencing, victims are given the opportunity to address the judge, either verbally or in writing.

Void for vagueness: a statute is void for vagueness if it fails to clearly define both the act prohibited and the appropriate punishment in advance.

Voir dire: French for "to see to speak." The process of questioning a potential juror to determine whether the juror is unbiased and can decide the case fairly and impartially.

Waiver of juveniles to criminal court: the process of transferring a juvenile from juvenile court to adult court. Most states give juvenile court judges the power to waive jurisdiction over juvenile cases that meet certain criteria—generally, a minimum age, a specified type or level of offense, and/or a sufficiently serious record of prior delinquency. Some states have direct file waiver provisions, which allow the prosecutor to file certain types of juvenile cases directly in criminal court.

Writ of certiorari: an order from an appellate court, such as the U.S. Supreme Court, to a lower court requesting that the lower court send the record in the case forward for review. It means that the appellate court will review the lower court's decision for procedural mistakes or legal errors.

Writ of habeas corpus: an order requesting that a prisoner be brought before the court so that the constitutionality of his or her confinement can be reviewed. In the United States, the process begins when an individual who is incarcerated petitions a district court or the U.S. Supreme Court for a writ of habeas corpus. If the court grants the petition and issues the writ, the individual's case will be reviewed.

Writ of mandamus: a writ compelling public officials to perform their duty.

REFERENCES AND SUGGESTED READING

Abraham, H. J. (1987). *The judiciary: The Supreme Court in the governmental process* (7th ed.). Boston, MA: Allyn & Bacon.

Administrative Office of the U.S. Courts. (2015). *2014 annual report of the director.* Retrieved from http://www.uscourts.gov/statistics-reports/annual-report-2014

Administrative Office of the U.S. Courts. (2017a). *Federal judicial caseload statistics.* Retrieved from http://www.uscourts.gov/statistics-reports/federal-judicial-caseload-statistics-2017

Administrative Office of the U.S. Courts. (2017b). *Judicial business 2017.* Retrieved from http://www.uscourts.gov/statistics-reports/judicial-business-2017

Albonetti, C. (1986). Criminality, prosecutorial screening, and uncertainty: Toward a theory of discretionary decision making in felony case processing. *Criminology, 24,* 623–644.

Albonetti, C. A. (1987). Prosecutorial discretion: The effects of uncertainty. *Law & Society Review, 21,* 291–313.

Albonetti, C. A. (1997). Sentencing under the federal sentencing guidelines: Effects of defendant characteristics, guilty pleas, and departures on sentence outcomes for drug offenses, 1991–1992. *Law & Society Review, 31,* 789–822.

Alpert, L. (1981). Learning about trial judging: The socialization of state trial judges. In J. A. Cramer (Ed.), *Courts and judges* (pp. 105–147). Beverly Hills, CA: Sage.

Alschuler, A. (1968). The prosecutor's role in plea bargaining. *Chicago Law Review, 36,* 50–112.

Alschuler, A. W. (1978). Sentencing reform and prosecutorial power. *University of Pennsylvania Law Review, 126,* 550–577.

Alschuler, A. W. (1979). Plea bargaining and its history. *Law & Society Review, 13,* 211–245.

Alschuler, A. W., & Deiss, A. G. (1994). A brief history of the criminal jury in the United States. *University of Chicago Law Review, 61,* 921–928.

Alund, N. N. (2009, March 12). Judge tosses drug evidence. *Lakewood Ranch Herald.* Retrieved from http://www.bradenton.com/news/local/lakewood_ranch_herald/story/1287991.html

Amar, A. (1998). *The Bill of Rights.* New Haven, CT: Yale University Press.

American Bar Association. (1993). *ABA standards for criminal justice: Prosecution function and defense function.* Washington, DC: Author.

American Bar Association. (2000). *ABA standards for criminal justice: Special functions of the trial judge* (3rd ed.). Chicago, IL: Author.

American Bar Association. (2005). *Principles for juries & jury trials.* Chicago, IL: Author.

American Bar Association. (2006). *Standards for criminal justice: Speedy trial and timely resolution of criminal cases* (3rd ed.). Chicago, IL: Author. Retrieved from http://www.americanbar.org/publications/criminal_justice_section_archive/crimjust_standards_speedy-trial_toc.html

American Bar Association. (2009). *National database on judicial diversity in state courts.* Retrieved from http://www.abanet.org/judind/diversity

American Bar Association. (2010). *The directory of minority judges of the United States.* Chicago, IL: Author.

American Bar Association Standing Committee on Legal Aid and Indigent Defendants. (2004). *Gideon's broken promise: America's continuing quest for equal justice: A report on the American Bar Association's hearings on the right to counsel in criminal proceedings.* Chicago, IL: American Bar Association.

American Law Institute. (1962). *Model penal code.* Philadelphia, PA: Author.

American Prosecutors Research Institute. (1995). *Community prosecution implementation manual.* Alexandria, VA: Author.

Anastaplo, G. (1989). *The Constitution of 1787: A commentary.* Baltimore, MD: Johns Hopkins University Press.

Anastaplo, G. (1995). *The amendments to the Constitution: A commentary.* Baltimore, MD: Johns Hopkins University Press.

Arenella, P. (1983). Rethinking the functions of criminal procedure: The Warren and Burger Courts' competing ideologies. *Georgetown Law Journal, 72,* 185–248.

Aspin, L. T. (2007). Judicial retention election trends: 1964–2006. *Judicature, 90,* 208.

Attorney says he'll appeal conviction of nude sunbathers all the way to Supreme Court. (1985, February 2). *St. Petersburg Times,* p. 4B.

Austin, J., & Irwin, J. (2001). *It's about time: America's imprisonment binge* (3rd ed.). Belmont, CA: Wadsworth.

Baldus, D. C., Woodworth, G., & Pulaski, C. A., Jr. (1985). Monitoring and evaluating contemporary death sentencing systems: Lessons from Georgia. *U.C. Davis Law Review, 18,* 1375–1417.

Baldus, D. C., Woodworth, G. G., & Pulaski, C. A., Jr. (1990). *Equal justice and the death penalty: A legal and empirical analysis.* Boston, MA: Northeastern University Press.

Ballotpedia. (n.d.). *2015 Ballot measures.* Retrieved from https://ballotpedia.org/2015_ballot_measures

Bartlett, R. (1986). *Trial by fire and water: The medieval judicial ordeal.* Oxford, UK: Clarendon Press.

Baum, L. (1985). *The Supreme Court.* Washington, DC: Congressional Quarterly.

Bazemore, G. (1998). Restorative justice and earned redemption: Communities, victims, and offender reintegration. *American Behavioral Scientist, 41,* 768–813.

Beard, A. (2007, April 11). Prosecutors drop charges in Duke case. *Associated Press.*

Beccaria, C. (1964). On crimes and punishments (J. Grigson, Trans.). In A. Manzoni (Ed.), *The column of infamy.* UK: Oxford University Press.

Belenko, S. (1998). Research on drug courts: A critical review. *National Drug Courts Institute Review, 1,* 3–43.

Bentham, J. (1970). *Introduction to the principles of morals and legislation* (J. Burns & H. L. A. Hart, Eds.). London, UK: Athlone Press, University of London.

Berman, G., & Feinblatt, J. (2001). *Problem-solving courts: A brief primer.* New York, NY: Center for Court Innovation.

Bernstein, I. N., Kick, E., Leung, J. T., & Schultz, B. (1977). Charge reduction: An intermediary state in the process of labeling criminal defendants. *Social Forces, 56,* 362–384.

Black's law dictionary (6th ed.). (1990). Eagan, MN: West Thomson.

Blumstein, A., Cohen, J., Martin, S. E., & Tonry, M. H. (Eds.). (1983). *Research on sentencing: The search for reform* (Vol. 1). Washington, DC: National Academy Press.

Borteck, D. (2004). Pleas for DNA testing: Why lawmakers should amend state post-conviction DNA testing statutes to apply to prisoners who pled guilty. *Cardozo Law Review, 25,* 1429–1468.

Braithwaite, J. (1989). *Crime, shame, and reintegration.* Cambridge, UK: Cambridge University Press.

Braithwaite, J. (1998). Restorative justice. In M. Tonry (Ed.), *The handbook of crime and punishment* (pp. 323–344). New York, NY: Oxford University Press.

Braithwaite, J. (1999). Restorative justice: Assessing optimistic and pessimistic accounts. In M. Tonry (Ed.), *Crime and justice: Review of research* (pp. 1–27). Chicago, IL: University of Chicago Press.

Braithwaite, J., & Pettit, P. (1990). *Not just deserts: A Republican theory of criminal justice.* New York, NY: Oxford University Press.

Brigham, J. (1987). *The cult of the court.* Philadelphia, PA: Temple University Press.

Bright, S. (1994). Counsel for the poor: The death sentence not for the worst crime but for the worst lawyer. *Yale Law Journal, 103,* 1835–1883.

Bright, S. B., & Keenan, P. J. (1995). Judges and the politics of death: Deciding between the Bill of Rights and the next election in capital cases. *Boston University Law Review, 75,* 759–835.

Brody, D. C. (1995). *Sparf* and *Dougherty* revisited: Why the court should instruct the jury on its jury nullification right. *American Criminal Law Review, 33,* 88–112.

Brody, D. C. (2008). The use of judicial performance evaluation to enhance judicial accountability, judicial independence, and public trust. *Denver University Law Review, 86,* 115–155.

Brunell, T. L., Chetan, D., & Morgan, N. C. (2007, June 24). *Time to deliberate: Factors influencing the duration of jury deliberation.* Paper presented at the Second Annual Conference on Empirical Legal Studies, New York. Abstract retrieved from http://ssrn.com/abstract=996426

Bugliosi, V. (1981). Not guilty and innocent: The problem children of reasonable doubt. *Court Review, 20,* 16–25.

Bullock, C. S., MacManus, S. A., Owen, K. P., Penberthy, C. C., Reid, R. O., & McPhee, B. (2014). "Your Honor" is a female: A multistage electoral analysis of women's successes at securing state trial court judgeships. *Social Science Quarterly, 95*(5), 1322–1345.

Bureau of Justice Assistance. (1996). *National assessment of structured sentencing.* Washington, DC: U.S. Department of Justice.

Bureau of Justice Statistics. (1995). *Prisoners in 1994.* Washington, DC: U.S. Department of Justice.

Bureau of Justice Statistics. (1998). *Crime and justice in the United States and in England and Wales, 1981–1996.* Washington, DC: U.S. Department of Justice.

Bureau of Justice Statistics. (2000). *Probation and parole in the United States, 1998.* Washington, DC: U.S. Department of Justice.

Bureau of Justice Statistics. (2002). *Prisoner petitions filed in U.S. district courts, 2000, with trends 1980–2000.* Washington, DC: Author.

Bureau of Justice Statistics. (2006). *Felony defendants in large urban counties, 2002.* Washington, DC: Author.

Bureau of Justice Statistics. (2006). *State court organization, 2004.* Washington, DC: Author.

Bureau of Justice Statistics. (2009). *State court sentencing of convicted felons, 2006.* Washington, DC: U.S. Department of Justice.

Bureau of Justice Statistics. (2010). *Felony defendants in large urban counties, 2006.* Washington, DC: Author.

Bureau of Justice Statistics. (2013, December). *Felony defendants in large urban counties, 2009* (Bulletin NCJ 243777). Washington, DC: U.S. Department of Justice.

Bureau of Justice Statistics. (2014). *Capital punishment, 2013—Statistical tables.* Washington, DC: U.S. Department of Justice.

Bureau of Justice Statistics. (2018). *Prisoners in 2016.* Washington, DC: U.S. Department of Justice.

Bureau of Justice Statistics. (n.d.a). *Criminal case processing statistics.* Retrieved from http://www.ojp.usdoj.gov/bjs/cases.htm

Bureau of Justice Statistics. (n.d.b). *Federal justice statistics.* Retrieved from http://www.ojp.usdoj.gov/bjs/fed.htm#Adjudication

Bureau of Justice Statistics. (n.d.c). *Sourcebook of criminal justice statistics.* Retrieved from http://www.albany.edu/sourcebook

Butler, P. (1995). Racially based jury nullification: Black power in the criminal justice system. *Yale Law Journal, 105,* 677–725.

California Administrative Office of the Courts. (2004). *Homeless courts.* Sacramento, CA: Administrative Office of the Courts. Retrieved from http://www.courtinfo.ca.gov/programs/collab/homeless.htm

California Department of Corrections and Rehabilitation. (2013). *Realignment report.* Sacramento: Author.

Camilli, D. (2009, March 24). Lumberton man ruled incompetent to stand trial. *Burlington County Times.* Retrieved from http://www.phillyburbs.com/news/news_details/article/16/2009/march/24/lumberton-man-ruled-incompetent-to-stand-trial.html

Cardozo, B. N. (1974). The nature of the judicial process. In W. F. Murphy & C. H. Pritchett (Eds.), *Courts, judges, and politics* (2nd ed., pp. 24–27). New York, NY: Random House.

Carns, T. W., & Kruse, J. A. (1992). Alaska's ban on plea bargaining reevaluated. *Judicature, 75,* 310–317.

Casey, P. M., & Rottman, D. B. (2005). *Problem-solving courts: Models and trends.* Williamsburg, VA: National Center for State Courts.

Casper, J. D. (1971). Did you have an attorney? No, I had a public defender. *Yale Review of Law and Social Action, 1,* 4–9.

Casper, J. D. (1978). Having their day in court: Defendant evaluations of the fairness of their treatment. *Law & Society Review, 12,* 237–251.

Center for Court Innovation. (n.d.a). *Community courts.* Retrieved from http://www.courtinnovation.org/topic/community-court

Center for Court Innovation. (n.d.b). *How do domestic violence courts compare to other problem-solving courts?* New York, NY: Author. Retrieved from www.courtinnovation.org

Center for Juvenile and Criminal Justice. (n.d.). *Juvenile justice experts decry severity of life in adult prison for Nathaniel Brazill.* Retrieved from http://www.cjcj.org

Champagne, A., & Haydel, J. (1993). *Judicial reform in the states.* Lanham, MD: University Press of America.

Chicago boy, 12, will be youngest in U.S. prison. (1996, January 31). *Omaha World Herald.*

Chiricos, T. G., & Bales, W. D. (1991). Unemployment and punishment: An empirical assessment. *Criminology, 29,* 701–724.

Code of Judicial Conduct for the State of Florida, Canon 7C(1) (2014).

Cohen, T. H., & Kyckelhahn, T. (2010). *Felony defendants in large urban counties, 2006* (Bulletin NCJ 228944). Washington, DC: U.S. Department of Justice.

Colquitt, J. A. (2001). Ad hoc plea bargaining. *Tulane Law Review, 75,* 695–776.

Conrad, C. S. (1998). *Jury nullification: The evolution of a doctrine.* Durham, NC: Carolina Academic Press.

Cook, D., Burton, M., Robinson, A., & Vallely, C. (2004). *Evaluation of specialist domestic violence courts/fast track systems.* London, UK: Crown Prosecution Service.

Cooper, C. L., & Sheppard, S. R. (1995). *Mockery of justice: The true story of the Sheppard murder case.* Boston, MA: Northeastern University Press.

Crew, K. B. (1991). Sex differences in criminal sentencing: Chivalry or patriarchy? *Justice Quarterly, 8,* 59–84.

Cullen, D. P. (1992). Indigent defense comparison of ad hoc and contract defense in five semi-rural jurisdictions. *Oklahoma City University Law Review, 17,* 311–375.

Cunningham, M. D., Sorensen, J. R., & Reidy, T. J. (2009). Capital jury decision making: The limitations of predictions of future violence. *Psychology, Public Policy, and Law, 14,* 223–256.

Daly, K. (1987). Structure and practice of familial-based justice in a criminal court. *Law & Society Review, 21,* 267–290.

Daly, K. (1989). Neither conflict nor labeling nor paternalism will suffice: Intersections of race, ethnicity, gender, and family in criminal court decisions. *Crime & Delinquency, 35,* 136–168.

Daly, K., & Bordt, R. (1995). Sex effects and sentencing: A review of the statistical literature. *Justice Quarterly, 12,* 143–177.

Daly, K., & Tonry, M. (1997). Gender, race and sentencing. In M. Tonry (Ed.), *Crime and justice: A review of research* (Vol. 22, pp. 201–252). Chicago, IL: University of Chicago Press.

Davis, A. J. (2007). *Arbitrary justice: The power of the American prosecutor.* New York, NY: Oxford University Press.

Davis, K. (2007). *Defending the damned: Inside Chicago's Cook County public defender's office.* New York, NY: Atria.

Davis, R., Smith, B., & Rabbit, C. (2001). Increasing convictions in domestic violence cases: A Field test in Milwaukee. *Justice System Journal, 22,* 62.

Death Penalty Information Center. (2014). *The death penalty in 2013: Year end report.* Washington, DC: Author.

Death Penalty Information Center. (2018). *The death penalty in 2016: Year end report.* Washington, DC: Author.

DeFrances, C., & Litras, M. (2000). *Indigent defense services in large counties, 1999.* Washington, DC: U.S. Department of Justice.

Delsohn, G. (2003). *The prosecutors: A year in the life of a district attorney's office.* New York, NY: Dutton Adult/ Penguin.

Demarest, C. E. (1994, April 15). Plea bargaining can often protect the victim. *New York Times,* A30.

Denckla, D., & Berman, G. (2001). *Rethinking the revolving door: A look at mental illness in the courts.* New York, NY: Center for Court Innovation.

Devine, D. J., Clayton, L. D., Dunford, B. B., Seying, R., & Pryce, J. (2001). Jury decision making: 45 years of empirical research on deliberating groups. *Psychology, Public Policy, and the Law, 7,* 622–725.

Ditton, P. M. (1999). *Mental health and treatment of inmates and probationers.* Washington, DC: Bureau of Justice Statistics.

Dodge, M., & Harris, J. C. (2000). Calling a strike a ball: Jury nullification and "three strikes" cases. In G. L. Mays & P. R. Gregware (Eds.), *Courts & justice: A reader* (2nd ed.). Prospect Heights, IL: Waveland Press.

Domino, J. (1994). *Civil rights and liberties.* New York, NY: HarperCollins.

Douglas, W. O. (1974). Stare decisis. In W. F. Murphy & C. H. Pritchett (Eds.), *Courts, judges, and politics* (2nd ed., pp. 412–416). New York, NY: Random House.

Dressler, J. (1995). *Understanding criminal law.* New York, NY: Matthew Bender.

Drug Court Clearinghouse and Technical Assistance Project. (1999). *Looking at a decade of drug courts.* Washington, DC: U.S. Department of Justice.

Drug Court Resource Center. (1995). *Preliminary assessment of the drug court experience.* Washington, DC: U.S. Department of Justice.

Dubois, P. L. (1980). *From ballot to bench: Judicial elections and the quest for accountability.* Austin: University of Texas Press.

Duke DA answers critics: Denies unethical conduct, wants some charges dropped. (2007, February 28). *ABC News Online.* Retrieved from http: abcnews .go.com

Duke suspends lacrosse team from play amid rape allegations. (2006, March 28). *USA Today.*

Durham, A. M., III. (1994). *Crisis and reform: Current issues in American punishment.* Boston, MA: Little, Brown.

Eisenstein, J., Flemming, R. B., & Nardulli, P. F. (1988). *The contours of justice: Courts and their communities.* Boston, MA: Little, Brown.

Eisenstein, J., & Jacob, H. (1977). *Felony justice: Organizational approach to criminal courts.* Boston, MA: Little, Brown.

Eley, S. (2005). Changing practices: The specialised domestic violence court process. *Howard Journal, 44,* 113–124.

Eligon, J. (2009, January 9). 10-year sentence for "Sopranos" actor. *New York Times.* Retrieved from http://www.nytimes.com/2009/01/10/nyregion/ 10brancato. html?_r=1

Elwork, A., Alfini, J. J., & Sales, B. D. (1987). Toward understandable jury instructions. In L. S. Wrightsman, S. M. Kassin, & C. E. Willis (Eds.), *In the jury box: Controversies in the courtroom.* Newbury Park, CA: Sage.

Emmelman, D. S. (2003). *Justice for the poor: A study of criminal defense work.* Burlington, VT: Ashgate.

Englebrecht, C. (2011). The struggle for "ownership of conflict": An exploration of victim participation and voice in the criminal justice system. *Criminal Justice Review, 36,* 129–151.

Eschholz, S., Reed, M. D., & Beck, E. (2003). Offenders' family members' responses to capital crimes: The need for restorative justice initiatives. *Homicide Studies, 7,* 154–181.

Estrich, S. (1987). *Real rape.* Cambridge, MA: Harvard University Press.

Fagan, J. (1991). *The comparative impacts of juvenile and criminal court sanctions on adolescent offenders.*

Washington, DC: Office of Justice Programs, National Institute of Justice.

Farole, D. J. (2003). *The Harlem parole reentry court evaluation: Implementation and preliminary impacts.* New York, NY: Center for Court Innovation.

Farole, D. J., Puffett, N., Rempel, M., & Byrne, F. (2005). Applying problem-solving principles in mainstream courts: Lessons for state courts. *Justice System Journal, 26,* 57–75.

Federal Bureau of Investigation. (2014). *Uniform crime reports: Crime in the United States, 2012.* Washington, DC: Author.

Federal Bureau of Investigation. (2018). *Uniform crime reports: Crime in the United States, 2016.* Washington, DC: Author.

Federman, C. (2004). Who has the body? The paths to habeas corpus reform. *Prison Journal, 84,* 317–339.

Feeney, F., & Jackson, P. G. (1991). Public defenders, assigned counsel, retained counsel: Does the type of criminal defense counsel matter? *Rutgers Law Journal, 22,* 361.

Feige, D. (2006). *Indefensible: One lawyer's journey into the inferno of American justice.* New York, NY: Little, Brown.

Feld, B. C. (1999). *Bad kids: Race and the transformation of the juvenile court.* New York, NY: Oxford University Press.

Feldman, N. (2005). *Divided by God: America's church-state problem—and what she should do about it.* New York, NY: Farrar, Straus & Giroux.

Finigan, M. W. (1998). *An outcome program evaluation of the Multnomah County S.T.O.P. Drug Diversion Program.* Portland, OR: NPC Research, Inc.

Finnis, J. (1980). *Natural law and natural rights.* Oxford, UK: Clarendon Press.

Fisher, G. (2003). *Plea bargaining's triumph: A history of plea bargaining in America.* Stanford, CA: Stanford University Press.

Flango, C. R., & Rottman, D. B. (1998). *Appellate court procedures.* Williamsburg, VA: National Center for State Courts.

Flemming, R. B. (1990). The political styles and organizational strategies of American prosecutors: Examples from nine court communities. *Law & Policy, 12,* 25–50.

Fletcher, G. (1978). *Rethinking criminal law.* Boston, MA: Little, Brown.

Florida Supreme Court. (n.d.). *Standard jury instructions.* Retrieved from http://www.floridasupreme-court.org/jury_instructions/instructions.shtml

Fonda, H., & Rose, R. (Producers), & Lumet, S. (Director). (1957). *12 angry men* [Motion picture]. United States: United Artists.

Ford, D. A., & Burke, M. J. (1987). *Victim-initiated criminal complaints for wife-battery: An assessment of motives.* Paper presented at the Third Annual Conference for Family Violence, Durham, NC.

Fox, G. (2010). District Attorney Gerald Fox's statement on the U. S. Supreme Court's decision in *McDonald v. City of Chicago,* June 29, 2010. Retrieved from http://www.freerepublic.com/focus/news/2545906/posts

Frank, J. (1930). *Law and the modern mind.* Magnolia, MA: Peter Smith Publisher.

Frase, R. (2007). The *Apprendi-Blakely* cases: Sentencing reform counter-revolution? *Criminology & Public Policy, 6,* 403–432.

Frazier, P. A., & Haney, B. (1996). Sexual assault cases in the legal system: Police, prosecutor, and victim perspectives. *Law & Human Behavior, 20,* 607–628.

Frohmann, L. (1991). Discrediting victims' allegations of sexual assault: Prosecutorial accounts of case rejections. *Social Problems, 38,* 213–226.

Frohmann, L. (1997). Convictability and discordant locales: Reproducing race, class, and gender ideologies in prosecutorial decision-making. *Law & Society Review, 31,* 531–555.

Frontline. (1995). *Inside the jury room.* PBS Video.

Garrett, B. (2008). Judging innocence. *Columbia Law Review, 108*(1), 55–142.

Georgia Department of Public Welfare. (1924). *Crime and the Georgia courts.* Gainesville: Author.

Goldberg, N. A., & Hartman, M. J. (1983). The public defender in America. In W. F. McDonald (Ed.), *The defense counsel* (pp. 67–102). Beverly Hills, CA: Sage.

Goldkamp, J. S., & Weiland, D. (1993). *Assessing the impact of Dade County's felony drug court: Research in brief.* Washington, DC: U.S. Department of Justice, National Institute of Justice.

Goldkamp, J. S., Weiland, D., Collins, M., & White, M. D. (1998). The role of drug and alcohol abuse in domestic violence and its treatment: Dade County's domestic violence court experiment. In *Legal interventions in family violence: Research findings and policy implications* (National Institute of Justice Research Report). Washington, DC: Office of Justice Programs.

Goldkamp, J. S., White, M. D., & Robinson, J. B. (2001). Do drug courts work? Getting inside the drug court black box. *Journal of Drug Issues, 31,* 27–72.

Goldstein, H. (1979). Improving policing: A problem-oriented approach. *Crime & Delinquency, 25,* 236–258.

Goldstein, H. (1990). *Problem oriented policing.* New York, NY: McGraw-Hill.

Goss, S. S. (2008). Mental health court programs in rural and nonaffluent jurisdictions. *Criminal Justice Review, 33,* 405–413.

Gottfredson, D. C., Coblentz, K., & Harmon, M. A. (1997, Winter). A short-term outcome evaluation of the Baltimore City Drug Treatment Court Program. *Perspectives,* pp. 33–38.

Gottfredson, D. C., & Exum, M. L. (2002). The Baltimore City Drug Court: One-year results from a randomized study. *Journal of Research in Crime and Delinquency, 39,* 337–356.

Gottfredson, D. C., Najaka, S. S., & Kearley, B. (2003). Effectiveness of drug treatment courts: Evidence from a randomized trial. *Criminology and Public Policy, 2,* 171–196.

Gover, A., MacDonald, M. C., & Alpert, G. P. (2003). Combating domestic violence: Findings from an evaluation of a local domestic violence court. *Criminology & Public Policy, 3,* 109–132.

Graham, B. L. (1990). Judicial recruitment and racial diversity on state courts. *Judicature, 74*(1), 28–34.

Green, B. A., & Zacharias, F. C. (2004). Prosecutorial neutrality. *Wisconsin Law Review, 2004,* 837–906.

Gross, S. R., Jacoby, K., Matheson, D. J., Montgomery, N., & Patil, S. (2005). Exonerations in the United States 1989 through 2003. *Journal of Criminal Law and Criminology, 95,* 523–560.

Gross, S. R., & Mauro, R. (1989). *Death & discrimination: Racial disparities in capital sentencing.* Boston, MA: Northeastern University Press.

Guidorizzi, D. D. (1998). Should we really "ban" plea bargaining? The core concerns of plea bargaining critics. *Emory Law Journal, 47,* 753–760.

Hannaford-Agor, P. L. (2008). Judicial nullification? Judicial compliance and non-compliance with jury improvement efforts. *Northern Illinois University Law Review, 28,* 407–424.

Hanson, R., Hewitt, W. E., Ostrom, B. J., & Lomvardias, C. (1992). *Indigent defenders get the job done and done well.* Williamsburg, VA: National Center for State Courts.

Harmon, T. R. (2001). Predictors of miscarriages of justice in capital cases. *Justice Quarterly, 18,* 949–968.

Harmon, T. R. (2004). Race for your life: An analysis of the role of race in erroneous capital convictions. *Criminal Justice Review, 29*(1), 76–96.

Harmon, T. R., & Lofquist, W. S. (2005). Too late for luck: A comparison of *post-Furman* exonerations and executions of the innocent. *Crime & Delinquency, 51,* 498–520.

Harrell, A., Mitchell, O., Hirst, A., Marlowe, D., & Merrill, J. (2002). Breaking the cycle of drugs and crime: Findings from the Birmingham BTC Demonstration. *Criminology and Public Policy, 1,* 189–216.

Harris, D. A. (1992). Justice rationed in the pursuit of efficiency: De novo trials in the criminal courts. *Connecticut Law Review, 24,* 382–431.

Hart, H. M. (1958). The aims of the criminal law. *Law and Contemporary Problems, 23,* 401.

Hastie, R., Penrod, S. D., & Pennington, N. (1983). *Inside the jury.* Cambridge, MA: Harvard University Press.

Hawkins, D. (1981). Causal attribution and punishment for crime. *Deviant Behavior, 1,* 207–230.

Hayes-Smith, R. M., & Levett, L. M. (2011). Jury's still out: How television and crime show viewing influences jurors' evaluations of evidence. *Applied Psychology in Criminal Justice, 7*(1), 29–46.

Heck, C., & Thanner, M. H. (2006). Drug court performance measurement: Suggestions from the National Research Advisory Committee. *Drug Court Review, 5,* 33–50.

Hemmens, C., Scarborough, K., & del Carmen, R. (1997). Grave doubts about reasonable doubt: Confusion in state and federal courts. *Journal of Criminal Justice, 25,* 231–254.

Hepperle, W. (1985). Women victims in the criminal justice system. In I. Moyer (Ed.), *The changing role of women in the criminal justice system* (pp. 78–96). Prospect Heights, IL: Waveland Press.

Heumann, M. (1977). *Plea bargaining: The experiences of prosecutors, judges, and defense attorneys.* Chicago, IL: University of Chicago Press.

Heumann, M., & Loftin, C. (1979). Mandatory sentencing and the abolition of plea bargaining: The Michigan Felony Firearm Statute. *Law & Society Review, 13,* 393–430.

Hines, B. W. (2010). *Melendez-Diaz v. Massachusetts:* Forcing America to pay the premium price for the nation's new Confrontation Clause. *George Mason University Civil Rights Law Journal, 21,* 123–158.

Hodes, W. W. (1996). Lord Brougham, the dream team, and jury nullification of the third kind. *University of Colorado Law Review, 67,* 1075–1108.

Hogarth, J. (1971). *Sentencing as a human process.* Toronto, Canada: University of Toronto Press.

Holmes, M. D., Daudistel, H. C., & Farrell, R. A. (1987). Determinants of charge reductions and final dispositions in cases of burglary and robbery. *Journal of Research in Crime and Delinquency, 24,* 233–254.

Holmes, M. D., Daudistel, H. C., & Taggart, W. A. (1992). Plea bargaining policy and state district court caseloads: An interrupted time series analysis. *Law & Society Review, 26,* 139–159.

Holmes, M. D., Hosch, H. M., Daudistel, H. C., Perez, D. A., & Graves, J. B. (1996). Ethnicity, legal resources, and felony dispositions in two Southwestern jurisdictions. *Justice Quarterly, 13,* 11–30.

Home Office. (2008). *Justice with safety: Specialist domestic violence courts' review 2007/08.* London, UK: Home Office Criminal Justice Service. Retrieved from http://webarchive.nationalarchives.gov.uk/+/http:/www.crimereduction.homeoffice.gov.uk/dv/dv018a.pdf

Horowitz, I. A., & Forster Lee, L. (2003). The effects of jury-aid innovations on juror performance in complex civil trials. *Judicature, 86,* 184–191.

Horowitz, I. A., Kerr, N. L., & Niedermeier, K. E. (2001). Jury nullification: Legal and psychological perspectives. *Brooklyn Law Review, 66,* 1207–1249.

Horwitz, M. J. (1977). *The transformation of American law 1780–1860.* Cambridge, MA: Harvard University Press.

Hospers, J. (1977). Punishment, protection, and rehabilitation. In J. Cederblom & W. L. Blizek (Eds.), *Justice and punishment* (pp. 22–50). Cambridge, MA: Ballinger.

Hotaling, J. T., & Buzawa, E. S. (2003). *Victim satisfaction with criminal justice case processing in a model court setting.* Washington, DC: U.S. Department of Justice.

Houck, M., & Budowle, B. (2002). Correlation of microscopic and mitochondrial DNA hair comparisons. *Journal of Forensic Science, 47,* 964–967.

Huff, C. R. (2004). Wrongful convictions: The American experience. *Canadian Journal of Criminology & Criminal Justice, 46*(2), 107–120.

Hurwitz, M. S., & Lanier, D. N. (2008). Diversity in state and federal appellate courts: Change and continuity across 20 years. *Justice System Journal, 29,* 47–72.

Inciardi, J. A., McBride, D. C., & Rivers, J. E. (1996). *Drug control and the courts.* Thousand Oaks, CA: Sage.

Innocence Project. (n.d.). *Facts on post-conviction DNA exonerations.* Retrieved from http://www.innocenceproject.org/Content/Facts_on_PostConviction_DNA_Exonerations.php

Jackson, R. (1940). The federal prosecutor. *Journal of Criminal Law and Criminology 31,* 3–5.

Jacoby, J. E. (1980). *The American prosecutor: A search for identity*. Lexington, MA: Lexington Books.

Jaffe, S. R., & Lansing, S. (Producers), & Kaplan, J. (Director). (1988). *The accused* [Motion picture]. United States: Paramount.

Jefferson, T. (1789). Letter to Thomas Paine ME 7:408. *Papers, 15*, 269.

Johnson, B. D. (2003). Racial and ethnic disparities in sentencing departures across modes of conviction. *Criminology, 41*, 501–542.

Johnson, R. T. (1992, November 24). Press release, Office of the District Attorney of Bronx County, New York.

Jonakait, R. N. (2006). *The American jury*. New Haven, CT: Yale University Press.

Jordan, C. (2004). Intimate partner violence and the justice system: An examination of the interface. *Journal of Interpersonal Violence, 19*, 1412–1434.

Kadish, S. (1987). Excusing crime. *California Law Review, 75*, 257.

Kalven, H., Jr., & Zeisel, H. (1966). *The American jury*. Boston, MA: Little, Brown.

Kant, I. (1887). *The philosophy of law* (W. Hastie, Trans.). Edinburgh, UK: T. T. Clark.

Karan, A., Keilitz, S. L., & Denaro, S. (1999). Domestic violence courts: What are they and how should we manage them? *Juvenile and Family Court Journal, 50*, 75–86.

Karp, D. R. (2001). Harm and repair: Observing restorative justice in Vermont. *Justice Quarterly, 18*, 727–757.

Kassin, S., & Wrightsman, L. (1988). *The American jury on trial: Psychological perspectives*. London, UK: Taylor & Francis.

Kautt, P., & Spohn, C. (2002). *Crack*-ing down on Black drug offenders? Testing for interactions between offender race, drug type, and sentencing strategy in federal drug sentences. *Justice Quarterly, 19*, 1–35.

Kaye, J. (1999, October 11). Making the case for hands-on courts. *Newsweek*, p. 13.

Keil, T., & Vito, G. (1989). Race, homicide severity, and application of the death penalty: A consideration of the Barnett Scale. *Criminology, 27*, 511–533.

Keilitz, S. L. (2000). *Specialization of domestic violence case management in the courts: A national survey*. Williamsburg, VA: National Center for State Courts.

Kennedy, R. (1997). *Race, crime and the law*. New York, NY: Vintage Books.

Kerr, N. L. (1978). Severity of penalty and mock jurors' verdicts. *Journal of Personality and Social Psychology, 36*, 1431–1442.

Kerstetter, W. (1990). Gateway to justice: Police and prosecutorial response to sexual assaults against women. *Criminology, 81*, 267–313.

Kilpatrick, D. G., Beatty, D., & Smith Howley, S. (1998). *The rights of crime victims—Does legal protection make a difference?* Washington, DC: U.S. Department of Justice.

Kimball, J., Brown, R., Davila J., Madrid, S., and Pandya, R. (2013). *The American bench: Judges of the nation* (19th ed.). Sacramento, CA: Forster-Long.

Kingsnorth, R. F., MacIntosh, R. C., & Wentworth, J. (1999). Sexual assault: The role of prior relationship and victim characteristics in case processing. *Justice Quarterly, 16*, 275–302.

Kipnis, K. (1976). Criminal justice and the negotiated plea. *Ethics, 86*, 93–106.

Kirchmeier, J. L. (1996). Drink, drugs, and drowsiness: The constitutional right to effective assistance of counsel and the Strickland prejudice requirement. *Nebraska Law Review, 75*, 425.

Klarman, M. (2004). *From Jim Crow to civil rights: The Supreme Court and the struggle for racial equality*. New York, NY: Oxford University Press.

Koski, D. D. (2003). *The jury trial in criminal justice*. Durham, NC: Carolina Academic Press.

Kraft, I. (1982). Happy New Year—You're a juror. *Crime & Delinquency, 28*, 582–600.

Kramer, S. (Producer/Director). (1960). *Inherit the wind* [Motion picture]. United States: United Artists.

Kunen, J. S. (1983). *"How can you defend those people?" The making of a criminal lawyer.* New York, NY: Random House.

Kurki, L. (1999). Restorative and community justice in the United States. In M. Tonry (Ed.), *Crime and justice: Review of research* (pp. 235–303). Chicago, IL: University of Chicago Press.

Kurlychek, M. C., & Johnson, B. D. (2004). The juvenile penalty: A comparison of juvenile and young adult sentencing outcomes in criminal court. *Criminology, 42,* 485–515.

Kutateladze, B. L., Andiloro, N. R., & Johnson, B. D. (2014). Opening Pandora's box: How does defendant race influence plea bargaining? *Justice Quarterly.* Published online May 15, 2014. doi:10.1080/07418825. 2014.91530

Kutateladze, B., Lynn, V., & Liang, E. (2012). *Do race and ethnicity matter in prosecution? A review of empirical studies.* New York, NY: Vera Institute of Justice.

Labriola, M., Bradley, S., O'Sullivan, C. S., Rempel, M., & Moore, S. (2009). *A national portrait of domestic violence courts.* New York, NY: Center for Court Innovation.

LaFree, G. (1989). *Rape and criminal justice: The social construction of sexual assault.* Belmont, CA: Wadsworth.

Langbein, J. (1979). Understanding the short history of plea bargaining. *Law & Society Review, 13,* 261–272.

Langbein, J. H. (1999). The prosecutorial origins of defence counsel in the eighteenth century: The appearance of solicitors. *Cambridge Law Journal, 58,* 314–365.

Laster, K., & Douglas, R. (1995). Feminized justice: The impact of women decision makers in the lower courts in Australia. *Justice Quarterly, 12,* 177–205.

Launer, D., & Schiff, P. (Producers), & Lynn, J. (Director). (1992). *My cousin Vinny* [Motion picture]. United States: 20th Century Fox.

Lawrence, R., & Hemmens, C. (2008). *Juvenile justice: A text/reader.* Thousand Oaks, CA: Sage.

Leahy, P. (2016, June 16). *Statement of Senator Patrick Leahy on final passage of the Justice for All Reauthorization Act* [Press release]. Retrieved from https://www.leahy.senate.gov/press/statement-of-senator-patrick-leahy-on-final-passage-of-the-justice-for-all-reauthorization-act

Lehmann, P., Chiricos, T., & Bales, W. (2017). Sentencing transferred juveniles in the adult criminal court: The direct and interactive effects of race and ethnicity. *Youth Violence and Juvenile Justice, 15,* 172–190.

Levey, L. S., Steketee, M. W., & Keilitz, S. L. (2001). *Lessons learned in implementing an integrated domestic violence court: The District of Columbia experience.* Williamsburg, VA: National Center for State Courts.

Levin, M. A. (1977). *Urban politics and the criminal courts.* Chicago, IL: University of Chicago Press.

Levine, J. (1992). *Juries and politics.* Pacific Groves, CA: Brooks/Cole.

Levinson, S. (1989). The embarrassing Second Amendment. *Yale Law Journal, 99,* 637.

Levrant, S., Cullen, F. T., & Fulton, B. (1999). Reconsidering restorative justice: The corruption of benevolence revisited? *Crime & Delinquency, 45,* 3–27.

Lewis, A. (1964). *Gideon's trumpet.* New York, NY: Vintage Books.

Lieberman, J. L., & Sales, B. D. (1997). What social science teaches us about the jury instruction process. *Psychology, Public Policy, and Law, 3,* 589–644.

Liebman, J. S. (2002). Rates of reversible error and the risk of wrongful execution. *Judicature, 86*(2), 78–82.

Lithwick, D. (2010, February 11). A separate peace: Specialized courts for veterans work wonders. But why stop at veterans? *Slate.*

Loftus, E. F. (1979). *Eyewitness testimony.* Cambridge, MA: Harvard University Press.

Lynch, D. R. (1999). Perceived judicial hostility to criminal trials: Effects on public defenders in general and on their relationships with clients and prosecutors in particular. *Criminal Justice and Behavior, 26,* 217–234.

Lynch, G. E. (2001). Sentencing Eddie. *Journal of Criminal Law and Criminology, 91,* 547–566.

MacKenzie, D. L., & Herbert, E. E. (Eds.). (1996). *Correctional boot camps: A tough intermediate sanction.* Washington, DC: U.S. Department of Justice.

Males, M., & Macallair, D. (2000). *The color of justice: An analysis of juvenile justice adult court transfers in California.* Washington, DC: Justice Policy Institute.

Marvell, T. B. (1989). State appellate court responses to caseload growth. *Judicature, 72,* 282–291.

Massey, C. (1995). *Silent rights: The Ninth Amendment and the Constitution's unenumerated rights.* Philadelphia, PA: Temple University Press.

Mather, L. M. (1974). The outsider in the courtroom. In H. Jacob (Ed.), *The potential for reform of criminal justice* (pp. 263–290). Beverly Hills, CA: Sage.

Mather, L. M. (1979). *Plea bargaining or trial?* Lexington, MA: Heath.

Maxfield, L. D., & Kramer, J. H. (1998). *Substantial assistance: An empirical yardstick gauging equity in current federal policy and practice.* Washington, DC: U.S. Sentencing Commission.

Mazur, R., & Aldrich, L. (2003). What makes a domestic violence court work? Lessons from New York. *Judge's Journal, 42,* 5–11.

McCahill, T. W., Meyer, L. C., & Fischman, A. M. (1979). *The aftermath of rape.* Lexington, MA: Lexington Books.

McConville, M., & Mirsky, C. L. (2005). *Jury trials and plea bargaining: A true history.* Oxford, UK: Hart.

McDonald, D. C., Greene, J., & Worzella, C. (1992). *Day fines in American courts: The Staten Island and Milwaukee experiments.* Washington, DC: U.S. Department of Justice.

McDonald, W. F. (1979). *The prosecutor.* Beverly Hills, CA: Sage.

McDonald, W. F. (1983). *The defense counsel.* Beverly Hills, CA: Sage.

McDowell, G. (1982). *Equity and the constitution: The Supreme Court, equitable relief, and public policy.* Chicago, IL: University of Chicago Press.

McGuire, J., Clark, S., Blue-Howells, J., & Coe, C. (2013). *An inventory of VA involvement in veterans courts, dockets and tracks.* Washington, DC: Department of Veterans Affairs.

McIntyre, L. (1987). *Public defender: The practice of law in the shadows of repute.* Chicago, IL: University of Chicago Press.

Meissner, C. A., & Brigham, J. C. (2001). Thirty years of investigating the own-race bias in memory for faces: A meta-analytic review. *Psychology, Public Policy, and Law, 7,* 3–35.

Miller, F. W., Dawson, R. O., Dix, G. E., & Parnas, R. I. (1986). *Prosecution and adjudication* (3rd ed.). Mineola, NY: Foundation Press.

Miller, H. S., McDonald, W. F., & Cramer, J. A. (1978). *Plea bargaining in the United States.* Washington, DC: Government Printing Office.

Mirsky, C. (1994, March 4). Plea reform is no bargain. *New York Newsday,* p. 70.

Mitchell, O. (2005). A meta-analysis of race and sentencing research: Explaining the inconsistencies. *Journal of Quantitative Criminology, 21,* 439–466.

Moley, R. (1929). The vanishing jury. *Southern California Law Review, 2,* 97–107.

Moore, H. (1968). Persons and punishment. *The Monist, 52,* 476–479.

Moore, M. S. (1992). The moral worth of retribution. In A. von Hirsch & A. Ashworth (Eds.), *Principled sentencing.* Boston, MA: Northeastern University Press.

Morris, N. (1982). *Madness and the criminal law.* New York, NY: Oxford University Press.

Morris, N., & Tonry, M. (1990). *Between prison and probation: Intermediate punishments in a rational sentencing system.* New York, NY: Oxford University Press.

Munsterman, G. T., Hannaford, P. L., & Whitehead, G. M. (1997). *Jury trial innovations.* Williamsburg, VA: National Center for State Courts.

Murphy, J. G. (1979). *Retribution, justice and therapy.* Boston, MA: Reidel.

Murphy, W. F., Pritchett, C. H., Epstein, L., & Knight, J. (2006). *Courts, judges, & politics: An introduction to the judicial process.* Boston, MA: McGraw-Hill.

Mutua, A. D. (2014). Disparity in judicial misconduct cases: Color-blind diversity. *Journal of Gender, Social Policy, & the Law 23,* 23–105.

Myers, M. A. (1979). Rule departures and making law: Juries and their verdicts. *Law & Society Review, 13,* 781–797.

Myers, T. (1996). Reciprocal discovery violations: Visiting the sins of the defense lawyer on the innocent client. *American Criminal Law Review, 33,* 1277–1298.

Nardulli, P. F. (1986). "Insider" justice: Defense attorneys and the handling of felony cases. *Journal of Criminal Law and Criminology, 77,* 379–417.

Nardulli, P. F., Eisenstein, J., & Flemming, R. B. (1988). *The tenor of justice: Criminal courts and the guilty plea process.* Chicago, IL: University of Chicago Press.

National Academy of Sciences. (2009). *Strengthening forensic science in the United States: A path forward.* Washington, DC: Author.

National Association of Drug Court Professionals. (1997). *Defining drug courts: The key components.* Washington, DC: U.S. Department of Justice, Drug Courts Program Office.

National Center for Juvenile Justice. (2000). *Juvenile court statistics.* Pittsburgh, PA: Author.

National Center for Juvenile Justice. (2004). *Which states waive juveniles to criminal court?* Pittsburgh, PA: Author.

National Center for Juvenile Justice. (2015). *Juvenile court statistics, 2013.* Pittsburgh, PA: Author.

National Center for State Courts. (2002). *Are hung juries a problem?* Williamsburg, VA: Author.

National Center for State Courts. (2006). *Examining the work of state courts, 2005.* Williamsburg, VA: Author.

National Center for State Courts. (2007). *State-of-the-states survey of jury improvement effort.* Williamsburg, VA: Author.

National Center for State Courts. (n.d.). *Judicial selection in the states.* Retrieved from http://www.judicialselection.us

National Research Council. (2009). *Strengthening forensic science in the United States: A path forward.* Washington, DC: National Academies Press.

National Right to Counsel Committee. (2009). *Justice denied: America's continuing neglect of our constitutional right to counsel.* Washington, DC: Constitution Project.

Niedermeier, K. E., Horowitz, I. A., & Kerr, N. L. (1999). Informing jurors of their nullification power: A route to a just verdict or judicial chaos. *Law and Human Behavior, 23,* 331–351.

Nobiling, T., Spohn, C., & DeLone, M. (1998). A tale of two counties: Unemployment and sentence severity. *Justice Quarterly, 15,* 401–427.

Nugent, E., Fanflik, P., & Bromirski, D. (2004). *The changing nature of prosecution: Community prosecution vs. traditional prosecution approaches.* Alexandria, VA: American Prosecutors Research Institute.

Office of Juvenile Justice and Delinquency Prevention (OJJDP). (1982). *Major issues in juvenile justice information and training youth in adult courts—Between two worlds.* Washington, DC: Author.

Office of Juvenile Justice and Delinquency Prevention (OJJDP). (2000). *Juvenile transfers to criminal court in the 1990s: Lessons learned from four studies.* Washington, DC: Author.

Office of Juvenile Justice and Delinquency Prevention (OJJDP). (2003a). *Juvenile arrests.* Washington, DC: U.S. Department of Justice.

Office of Juvenile Justice and Delinquency Prevention (OJJDP). (2003b). *Juveniles in court.* Washington, DC: U.S. Department of Justice.

Office of Juvenile Justice and Delinquency Prevention (OJJDP). (2011). *Delinquency cases in juvenile courts, 2008.* Washington, DC: U.S. Department of Justice.

Office of Juvenile Justice and Delinquency Prevention (OJJDP). (2014a). *Delinquency cases in juvenile courts, 2011.* Washington, DC: U.S. Department of Justice.

Office of Juvenile Justice and Delinquency Prevention (OJJDP). (2014b). *Delinquency cases waived to criminal court, 2011.* Washington, DC: U.S. Department of Justice.

Office of Juvenile Justice and Delinquency Prevention (OJJDP). (2018). *Delinquency cases in juvenile courts, 2014.* Washington, DC: U.S. Department of Justice.

Office of National Drug Control Policy. (n.d.). *Drug courts*. Retrieved from http://www.whitehousedrugpolicy.gov/enforce/drugcourt.html

Olsen, J. (2000). *Last man standing: The tragedy and triumph of Geronimo Pratt*. New York, NY: Doubleday.

Owens, S. D., Accetta, E., Charles, J. J., & Shoemaker, S. E. (2014). *Indigent defense services in the United States, FY 2008–2012—updated*. Washington, DC: Bureau of Justice Statistics.

Packer, H. L. (1968). *The limits of the criminal sanction*. Stanford, CA: Stanford University Press.

Paternoster, R. (1984). Prosecutorial discretion in requesting the death penalty: A case of victim-based racial discrimination. *Law & Society Review, 18*, 437–478.

Paternoster, R. (1991). *Capital punishment in America*. New York, NY: Lexington Books.

Peresie, J. L. (2005). Female judges matter: Gender and collegial decision making in the federal appellate courts. *Yale Law Journal, 114*, 1759–1790.

Peters, R. H., & Murrin, M. R. (1998). *Evaluation of treatment-based drug courts in Florida's First Judicial Circuit*. Tampa: Department of Mental Health, Law and Policy, Louis de la Parte Florida Mental Health Institute, University of South Florida.

Peterson, R. R., & Dixon, J. (2005). Court oversight and conviction under mandatory and nonmandatory domestic violence case filing policies. *Criminology & Public Policy, 4*, 535–557.

Pisciotta, A. W. (1982). Saving the children: The promise and practice of parens patriae, 1838–1898. *Crime & Delinquency, 28*, 410–425.

Planning and Management Consulting Corporation. (1975). *Empirical study of frequency of occurrence, case effects, and amount of time consumed by hung juries*. Carbondale, IL: Author.

Platt, A. (1977). *The child savers: The invention of delinquency*. Chicago, IL: University of Chicago Press.

Pound, R. (1906). The causes of popular dissatisfaction with the administration of justice. *ABA Report, 29*, 395–417.

Preminger, O. (Producer/Director). (1959). *Anatomy of a murder* [Motion picture]. United States: Columbia.

President's Commission on Law Enforcement and Administration of Justice. (1967). *The challenge of crime in a free society*. Washington, DC: U.S. Government Printing Office.

Pursley, R. D. (1995). The federal habeas corpus process: Unraveling the issues. *Criminal Justice Policy Review, 7*(2), 115–141.

Pyrooz, D. C., Wolfe, S. E., & Spohn, C. (2011). Gang-related homicide charging decisions: The implementation of a specialized prosecution unit in Los Angeles. *Criminal Justice Policy Review, 22*(1), 3–26.

Radelet, M., & Pierce, G. (1985). Race and prosecutorial discretion in homicide cases. *Law & Society Review, 19*, 587–621.

Ramsey, R. J., & Frank, J. (2007). Wrongful conviction: Perceptions of criminal justice professionals regarding the frequency of wrongful conviction and the extent of system errors. *Crime & Delinquency, 53*, 436–470.

Randall, K. (2001). *Another Florida teenager receives harsh adult prison sentence*. Retrieved from http://www.wsws.org/articles/2001/aug2001

Rattner, A. (1988). Convicted but innocent: Wrongful conviction and the criminal justice system. *Law and Human Behavior, 12*, 283–293.

Reichel, P. (2005). *Comparative criminal justice systems: A topical approach* (4th ed.). Upper Saddle River, NJ: Prentice Hall.

Renzema, M. (1992). Home confinement programs: Development, implementation, and impact. In J. M. Byrne, A. J. Lurigio, & J. Petersilia (Eds.), *Smart sentencing: The emergence of intermediate sanctions* (pp. 41–53). Newbury Park, CA: Sage.

Reskin, B. F., & Visher, C. A. (1986). The impacts of evidence and extralegal factors in jurors' decisions. *Law & Society Review, 20*, 423–438.

Risinger, D. M. (2007). Innocents convicted: An empirically justified factual wrongful conviction rate. *Journal of Criminal Law and Criminology, 97*, 761–806.

Robbins, T., Kilik, J., & Simmon, R. (Producers), & Robbins, T. (Director). (1995). *Dead man walking* [Motion picture]. United States: Gramercy Pictures.

Rogers, R., Blackwood, H., Fiduccia, C., Steadham, J., Drogin, E., and Rogstad, J. 2012. Juvenile Miranda warnings: Perfunctory rituals or procedural safeguards? *Criminal Justice and Behavior, 39*(3), 229–249.

Roman, J., & Harrell, A. (2001). Assessing the costs and benefits accruing to the public from a graduated-sanctions program for drug-using defendants. *Law & Policy, 23,* 237–268.

Rosen, J. (1996, December 9). The Bloods and the Crips: O. J. Simpson, critical race theory, and the law and the triumph of color in America. *New Republic,* pp. 27–42.

Rosenhan, D. L., Eisner, S. L., & Robinson, R. J. (1994). Notetaking can aid juror recall. *Law & Human Behavior, 18,* 53–61.

Ross, D. L. (2008). *Scott v. Harris:* Seeing is believing. *Criminal Justice Review, 33*(3), 431–446.

Ross, M. (2003). *Justice of shattered dreams: Samuel Freeman Miller and the Supreme Court during the Civil War era.* Baton Rouge: University of Louisiana Press.

Rossman, S. B., Roman, J. K., Zweig, J. M., Rempel, M., & Lindquist, C. H. (2011). *The multi-site adult drug court evaluation.* Washington, DC: Urban Institute.

Rottman, D., Bromage, C., Zose, M., & Thompson, B. (2006). *Judicial Selection 101: What varies and what matters.* Williamsburg, VA: National Center for State Courts.

Rottman, D., Flango, C., Cantrell, M., Hansen, R., & LaFountain, N. (2000). *State court organization, 1998.* Washington, DC: Bureau of Justice Statistics.

Rubinstein, M. L., & White, T. J. (1979). Alaska's ban on plea bargaining. *Law & Society Review, 13,* 367–383.

Rutledge, J. R. (2001). They all look alike: The inaccuracy of cross-racial identifications. *American Journal of Criminal Law, 28,* 207–228.

Sadurski, W. (1985). *Giving desert its due.* Dordrecht, Netherlands: Reidel.

Savchak, E. C., & Barghothi. A. J. (2007). The influence of appointment and retention constituencies: Testing strategies of judicial decisionmaking. *State Politics & Policy Quarterly, 7*(4), 394–415.

Scheb, J. M., & Scheb, J. M., II. (1999). *Criminal law & procedure* (3rd ed.). Belmont, CA: Wadsworth.

Scheflin, A., & Van Dyke, J. (1980). Jury nullification: The contours of a controversy. *Law & Contemporary Problems, 43,* 51–115.

Schmidt, J., & Steury, E. (1989). Prosecutorial discretion in filing charges in domestic violence cases. *Criminology, 27,* 487–510.

Schorn, D. (2006, October 15). Duke rape suspects speak out. *60 Minutes.* Retrieved from http://www.cbsnews.com/stories/2006/10/11/60minutes/main2082140.shtml

Sechrest, D. K., Shichor, D., Artist, K., & Briceno, G. (1998). *The Riverside County drug court: Final research report for the Riverside County Probation Department.* San Bernardino: California State University, San Bernardino.

Sheldon, C., & Lovrich, N. P. (1999). Voter knowledge, behavior and attitudes in primary and general elections. *Judicature, 82,* 216.

Slotnick, E. E. (1988). Review essay on judicial recruitment and selection. *Justice System Journal, 13*(1), 109–124.

Slotnick, E. E. (2005). *Judicial politics: Readings from judicature.* Washington, DC: CQ Press.

Smith, A. (2001). Domestic violence laws: The voices of battered women. *Violence and Victims, 16,* 91–111.

Smith, C. E. (1991). *Courts and the poor.* Chicago, IL: Nelson-Hall.

Smith, C. E. (1992). From U.S. magistrates to U.S. magistrate judges: Developments affecting the federal district courts' lower tier of judicial officers. *Judicature, 75*(4), 210–215.

Sorensen, J., & Wallace, D. H. (1996). Prosecutorial discretion in seeking death: An analysis of racial disparity in the pretrial stages of case processing in a Midwestern county. *Justice Quarterly, 16,* 559–578.

Spears, J. W., & Spohn, C. (1997). The effect of evidence factors and victim characteristics on prosecutors' charging decisions in sexual assault cases. *Justice Quarterly, 14,* 501–524.

Special Commission on Evaluation of Judicial Performance. (1985). *American Bar Association guidelines for the evaluation of judicial performance.* Chicago, IL: American Bar Association.

Spohn, C. (1994). Crime and the social control of Blacks. In G. S. Bridges & M. A. Myers (Eds.), *Inequality, crime, and social control* (pp. 249–268). Boulder, CO: Westview Press.

Spohn, C. (2000). *Thirty years of sentencing reform: The quest for a racially neutral sentencing process* (NCJ 185535). Washington, DC: National Institute of Justice.

Spohn, C. (2002). *How do judges decide? The search for fairness and justice in punishment.* Thousand Oaks, CA: Sage.

Spohn, C. (2006, March 21). *The dangerous drug offender in federal court: Stereotyping Blacks and crack cocaine.* Betos Chair Lecture series. Retrieved from http://www.betochair.com/media/?mode=view&item=44

Spohn, C., Beichner, D., & Davis-Frenzel, E. (2001). Prosecutorial justifications for sexual assault case rejection: Guarding the "gateway to justice." *Social Problems, 48,* 206–235.

Spohn, C., & DeLone, M. (2000). When does race matter? An analysis of the conditions under which race affects sentence severity. *Sociology of Crime, Law, and Deviance, 2,* 3–37.

Spohn, C., Gruhl, J., & Welch, S. (1981–1982). The effect of race on sentencing: A re-examination of an unsettled question. *Law & Society Review, 16,* 71–88.

Spohn, C., Gruhl, J., & Welch, S. (1987). The impact of the ethnicity and gender of defendants on the decision to reject or dismiss felony charges. *Criminology, 25,* 175–191.

Spohn, C., & Holleran, D. (2000). The imprisonment penalty paid by young, unemployed Black and Hispanic offenders. *Criminology, 38,* 281–306.

Spohn, C., & Holleran, D. (2001). Prosecuting sexual assault: A comparison of charging decisions in sexual assault cases involving stranger, acquaintances, and intimate partners. *Justice Quarterly, 18,* 651–688.

Spohn, C., & Horney, J. (1992). *Rape law reform: A grassroots movement and its impact.* New York, NY: Springer-Verlag.

Spohn, C., Kim, B., Belenko, S., & Brennan, P. (2014). The direct and indirect effects of offender drug use on federal sentencing outcomes. *Journal of Quantitative Criminology, 30,* 549–578.

Spohn, C., & Sample, L. (2013). The dangerous drug offender in federal court: Intersections of race, ethnicity, and culpability. *Crime & Delinquency, 59*(1), 3–31. (Original work published 2008)

Spohn, C., & Spears, J. (1996). The effect of offender and victim characteristics on sexual assault case processing decisions. *Justice Quarterly, 13,* 649–679.

Spohn, C., & Tellis, K. (2014). *Policing and prosecuting sexual assault: Inside the criminal justice system.* Boulder, CO: Lynne Rienner.

Stanko, E. (1988). The impact of victim assessment on prosecutor's screening decisions: The case of the New York County District Attorney's Office. In G. Cole (Ed.), *Criminal justice: Law and politics* (pp. 227–249). Pacific Grove, CA: Brooks/Cole.

Steele, W. W., & Thornburg, E. G. (1988–1989). Jury instructions: A persistent failure to communicate. *North Carolina Law Review, 67,* 120.

Steen, S., Engen, R. L., & Gainey, R. R. (2005). Images of danger and culpability: Racial stereotyping, case processing, and criminal sentencing, *Criminology, 43,* 435–468.

Steffensmeier, D., & Hebert, C. (1999). Women and men policymakers: Does the judge's gender affect the sentencing of criminal defendants? *Social Forces, 77,* 1163–1196.

Steffensmeier, D., Kramer, J., & Streifel, C. (1993). Gender and imprisonment decisions. *Criminology, 31,* 411–446.

Steffensmeier, D., Ulmer, J., & Kramer, J. (1995). Age differences in sentencing. *Justice Quarterly, 12,* 701–719.

Steffensmeier, D., Ulmer, J., & Kramer, J. (1998). The interaction of race, gender, and age in criminal sentencing: The punishment cost of being young, Black, and male. *Criminology, 36,* 763–798.

Steinbeck, R. (2007). The fight for post-conviction DNA testing is not yet over: An analysis of the eight remaining "holdout states" and suggestions for strategies to bring vital relief to the wrongfully convicted. *Journal of Criminal Law and Criminology, 98*(1), 329–361.

Stewart, J. B. (1987). *The prosecutors: Inside the offices of the government's most powerful lawyers.* New York, NY: Touchstone/Simon & Schuster.

Strawn, D., & Buchanan, R. (1976). Jury confusion: A threat to justice. *Judicature, 59,* 478–483.

Streb, M. J. (2007). *Running for judge: The rising political, financial, and legal stakes of judicial elections.* New York, NY: New York University Press.

Strickland, S., Schauffler, R., LaFountain, R., & Holt, K. (Eds.). (2017). *State court organization.* National Center for State Courts. Retrieved from www.ncsc.org/sco

Sudnow, D. (1965). Normal crimes: Sociological features of the penal code in the public defender's office. *Social Problems, 12,* 255–277.

Suthers, J. (2008). *No higher calling, no greater responsibility: A prosecutor makes his case.* Golden, CO: Fulcrum.

Swedlow, K. (2002). Don't believe everything you read: A review of modern "post-conviction" DNA testing statutes. *California Western Law Review, 38,* 355–387.

Tanford, J. A. (1990). The law and psychology of jury instructions. *Nebraska Law Review, 69,* 71–111.

Tarr, A. (2012). *Without fear or favor in 2011: A new decade of challenges to judicial independence and accountability.* Palo Alto, CA: Stanford University Press.

Texas penal code. (2008). Retrieved from http://www.texa-spolicecentral.com/penal_code.html

Tiede, L., Carp, R., & Manning, K. (2010). Judicial attributes and sentencing-deviation cases: Do sex, race, and politics matter? *Justice System Journal, 31*(3), 249–272.

Tomkovicz, J. J. (2002). *The right to the assistance of counsel: A reference guide to the United States Constitution.* Westport, CT: Greenwood Press.

Tonry, M. (1995). *Malign neglect: Race, crime, and punishment in America.* New York, NY: Oxford University Press.

Tonry, M. (1996). *Sentencing matters.* New York, NY: Oxford University Press.

Tribe, L. (1988). *American constitutional law.* Mineola, NY: Foundation Press.

Turner, K. B., & Johnson, J. B. (2007). The relationship between type of attorney and bail amount set for Hispanic defendants. *Hispanic Journal of Behavioral Sciences, 29*(3), 384–400.

Ulmer, J. T. (1997). *Social worlds of sentencing: Court communities under sentencing guidelines.* Albany: State University of New York Press.

Umbreit, M. S., & Vos, B. (2000). Homicide survivors meet the offender prior to execution: Restorative justice through dialogue. *Homicide Studies, 4,* 63–87.

U.S. Department of Justice. (2006). *Drug courts: The second decade.* Washington, DC: Author.

U.S. Department of Justice, Bureau of Justice Statistics. (2005). *National Prosecutors Survey* [Computer file]. Ann Arbor, MI: Inter-university Consortium for Political and Social Research.

U.S. Department of Justice, Bureau of Justice Statistics. (2009, December). *Felony sentences in state courts, 2006—Statistical tables* (Bulletin NCJ 226846).

U.S. Department of Justice, Bureau of Justice Statistics. (2013, December). *Felony defendants in large urban counties, 2009.* Washington, DC: Author.

U.S. Department of Justice, Bureau of Justice Statistics. (2015). *Federal justice statistics, 2012.* Washington, DC: Author.

U.S. Department of Veterans Affairs. (2013). *Fact sheet: Veterans court inventory, 2012.* Washington, DC: Author.

U.S. Department of Veterans Affairs. (2017). *Fact sheet: Veterans court inventory, 2016.* Washington, DC: Author.

U.S. General Accounting Office (GAO). (1995). *Juvenile justice: Juveniles processed in criminal court and case dispositions.* Washington, DC: Author.

U.S. General Accounting Office (GAO). (1997). *Drug courts: Overview of growth, characteristics, and results.* Washington, DC: Author.

U.S. Sentencing Commission. (2018). *2018 sourcebook of federal sentencing statistics*. Washington, DC: Author.

Vera Institute of Justice. (1977). *Felony arrests: Their prosecution and disposition in New York City's courts*. New York, NY: Longman.

Vidmar, N., & Hans, V. P. (2007). *American juries: The verdict*. Amherst, NY: Prometheus.

Violence Against Women Act of 1994. (1994). 42 USC 379(6)(g).

von Hirsch, A. (1976). *Doing justice: The choice of punishments*. New York, NY: Hill & Wang.

von Hirsch, A., & Ashworth, A. (1992). *Principled sentencing*. Boston, MA: Northeastern University Press.

Walker, N. (1991). *Why punish?* Oxford, UK: Oxford University Press.

Walker, S., Spohn, C., & DeLone, M. (2018). *The color of justice: Race, ethnicity and crime in America* (6th ed.). Belmont, CA: Wadsworth.

Walsh, A. (1987). The sexual stratification hypothesis and sexual assault in light of the changing conceptions of race. *Criminology, 25*, 153–173.

Wasby, S. L. (1993). *The Supreme Court in the federal judicial system*. Chicago, IL: Nelson-Hall.

Watson, A., Luchins, D., Hanrahan, P., Heyrman, M. J., & Lurigio, A. (2000). Mental health court: Promises and limitations. *Journal of the American Academy of Psychiatry and the Law, 28*, 476–482.

Webster, P. (1995). Selection and retention of judges: Is there one "best" method? *Florida State University Law Review, 23*, 1–43.

Weinberg, S. (2003). *Harmful error, breaking the rules: Who suffers when a prosecutor is cited for misconduct*. Washington, DC: Center for Public Integrity.

Weitzer, R. (1996). Racial discrimination in the criminal justice system: Findings and problems in the literature. *Journal of Criminal Justice, 24*, 309–322.

Weninger, R. A. (1987). The abolition of plea bargaining: A case study of El Paso County, Texas. *UCLA Law Review, 35*, 265.

Wheeler, R. R., & Harrison, C. (2005). *Creating the federal judicial system* (4th ed.). Washington, DC: Federal Judicial Center.

Wheeler, S., Mann, K., & Sarat, A. (1988). *Sitting in judgment: The sentencing of white-collar criminals*. New Haven, CT: Yale University Press.

Wice, P. B. (1985). *Chaos in the courthouse: The inner workings of the urban municipal courts*. New York, NY: Praeger.

Wice, P. B. (2005). *Public defenders and the American justice system*. Westport, CT: Praeger.

Williams, M. R. (2017). The effect of attorney type on bail decisions. *Criminal Justice Policy Review, 28*, 3–17.

Williams, M. R., Demuth, S., & Holcomb, J. E. (2007). Understanding the influence of victim gender in death penalty cases: The importance of victim race, sex-related victimization, and jury decision making. *Criminology, 45*, 865–891.

Williams, M. S. (2006). In a different path: The process of becoming a judge for women and men. *Judicature, 90*, 104–113.

Wilson, D. B., Ojmarrh, M., & MacKenzie, D. L. (2002, November). *A systematic review of drug court effects on recidivism*. Paper presented at the annual meeting of the American Society of Criminology, Chicago.

Wilson, J. Q. (1992). Selective incapacitation. In A. von Hirsch & A. Ashworth (Eds.), *Principled sentencing*. Boston, MA: Northeastern University Press.

Wilson, J. Q., & Kelling, G. (1982, March). Broken windows: The police and neighborhood safety. *Atlantic Monthly*, pp. 29–38.

Wishman, S. (1986). *Anatomy of a jury: The system on trial*. New York, NY: Times Books.

Wolf, R. V. (2007). *Principles of problem-solving courts*. New York, NY: Center for Court Innovation.

Wolf Harlow, C. (2000). *Defense counsel in criminal cases* (Bureau of Justice Statistics Special Report). Washington, DC: U.S. Department of Justice.

Woolridge, J., & Griffin, T. (2005). Displaced discretion under Ohio sentencing guidelines. *Journal of Criminal Justice, 33*, 301–316.

Worden, A. P. (1990). Policymaking by prosecutors: The uses of discretion in regulating plea bargaining. *Judicature, 73,* 335–336.

Wright, R. F., & Levine, K. L. (2014). The cure for young prosecutors' syndrome. *Arizona Law Review, 56,* 1066–1128.

Zaillian, S. (Director). (1998). *A civil action* [Motion picture]. United States: Paramount.

Zalman, M. (2006). Criminal justice system reform and wrongful conviction. *Criminal Justice Policy Review, 17,* 468–492.

Zalman, M., Smith, B., & Kiger, A. (2008). Officials' estimates of the incidence of "actual innocence" convictions. *Justice Quarterly, 25*(1), 72–100.

Zinnemann, F. (Producer/Director). (1966). *A man for all seasons* [Motion picture]. United States: Columbia.

CASE INDEX

GENERAL INDEX

Note: Page numbers in bold indicate Glossary entries.